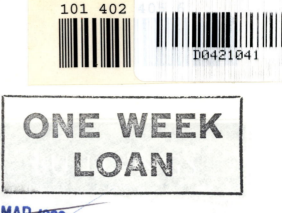

Buildings and Power shift
themes of art and techno
Buildings are primarily s
we ask about ourselves:
Everything about a buil
structure are each capabl
of new building types du
French and Industrial Re

The types are divided
directly – schools, insti
hygiene, clubs, assembly
museums, art galleries,
institutions and mechani
– mills, production utopi
is lavishly illustrated with

The aim of the book i
the modern world. It provokes questions about the ways we design, build and imagine our environment, about the ways architecture can liberate or confine our lives. *Buildings and Power* is addressed to those involved in the creation of the built environment – architects, planners and geographers and those engaged in the study of art and social history, social science and material culture – above all to anyone interested in buildings and what is written about them.

Thomas A. Markus is Emeritus Professor of Building Science at the University of Strathclyde. As an architect he has worked as a designer, teacher and consultant in Europe, North America and Asia.

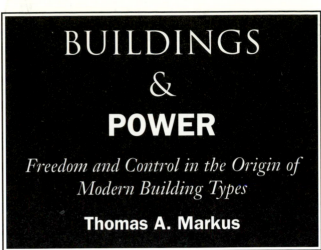

BUILDINGS & POWER

Freedom and Control in the Origin of Modern Building Types

Thomas A. Markus

LONDON AND NEW YORK

First published 1993
by Routledge
11 New Fetter Lane, London EC4P 4EE

Simultaneously published in the USA and Canada
by Routledge
29 West 35th Street, New York, NY 10001

Typeset by Solidus (Bristol) Limited
Printed in Great Britain by
Butler & Tanner Ltd, Frome and London

British Library Cataloguing in Publication Data
A catalogue record for this book is available from the British Library

Library of Congress Cataloging in Publication Data
Markus, Thomas A.
Buildings and power : freedom and control in the origin of modern building types / Thomas A. Markus.
p. cm.
Includes bibliographical references and index.
ISBN 0-415-07664-1. – ISBN 0-415-07665-X (pbk.)
1. Architecture, Modern–History. I. Title.
NA500.M37 1993
724–dc20 92-33282
CIP

ISBN 0-415-07664-1 (hbk) ISBN 0-415-07665-X (pbk)

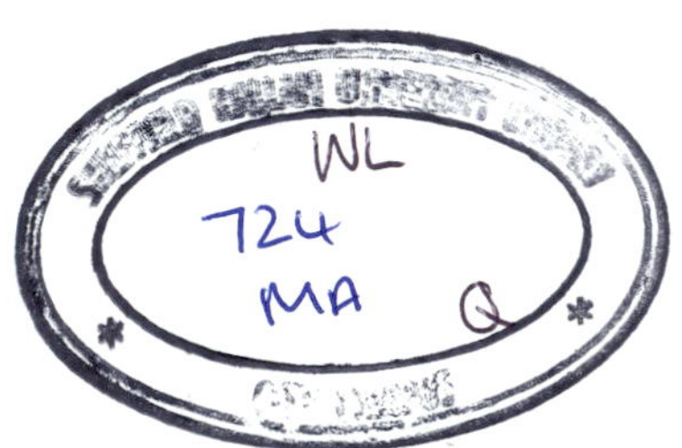

For S who emptied the night of witches and dogs
and B who filled it with glow-worms and stars.

Contents

List of figures

Acknowledgements

My interest in these ideas was sparked off by the late Professor Cordingley of Manchester University a long time ago. It has remained alive ever since. I owe a debt to those whose published work I have used, and they are referred to in the text. Because the time interval since Manchester is so long, I cannot acknowledge all those who have helped, influenced or encouraged me since then by personal contact. But to some I owe a special debt.

In recent years Peter Reed has been my constant thought-companion, not only in raising challenges to many of my arguments, but in pointing to the role of careful writing in the generation of ideas. I hope he will not feel too disappointed with the extent to which I have absorbed that message. The critical debates with Nec Teymur have been invaluable. Arie Peled's ability to integrate rational argument, intuition and artistic sensibility has served as a model. The students I have taught in my 'Spatial Order and Social Order' course at the University of Strathclyde, who refused to play the polite games of academics, have helped more than they can realise. Late in the writing of the text Lynda Schneekloth of the University of Buffalo and Karen Franck of the New Jersey Institute of Technology, have caused me to think again about function, language and type. Sophie Forgan, Bill Hillier and his colleagues, Alan Lipman and Michelle Perrot have all added insights over the years.

I have tried to respond to the incisive and helpful comments from Chris Small and Tony King on the draft manuscript. Any shortfall is not for their lack of trying.

Joen Sachs and the colleagues in his Division at the Chalmers University of Technology, Göteborg, have given me a welcome opportunity for late thought and writing.

The many librarians, archivists, academics and architects who have helped me to find illustrative material will, I hope, feel adequately acknowledged in the text relating to the figures.

Honor Mulholland has worked hard and creatively with editing, Kathryn Young with the graphics, and Alan Crumlish and Neil McLennan with photography.

I am grateful to Tristan Palmer for his faith in the project from the start, and the work of his colleagues at Routledge, especially Ricky Leaver, Sarah Lloyd, Alison Walters and Sally Close in seeing it through to publication.

Through the award of an Emeritus Fellowship, the Leverhulme Trust gave me generous support without which I could not have completed the manuscript.

Finally my family has not only put up with me during the long-drawn-out writing process, but has helped with innumerable debates, my son Gilbert especially. My wife Beryl did more than that – she also tried hard to help me convert 'Hungarlish' into English. It is not her fault if she did not always succeed.

TAM

Glasgow

Introduction

This book is about the meaning of buildings. It is addressed to those who design or study them, and to those who are frequently puzzled both by buildings and what is written about them. Whilst what a building looks like, whether the roof leaks and what it costs are matters of great concern, for most people the first question is: 'Is it good to use?' The answer to this depends on owners, designers, institutions of all kinds, and occupants, so this must be a question about society. As indeed are issues about its appearance, construction and costs whose effects reach beyond any individual.

The title implies the centrality of power to this social process. I take the stand that buildings are not primarily art, technical or investment objects, but social objects. I support this by evidence and by the ways proposed for looking beneath the surface of both buildings and what is written about them. Such analysis involves taking things apart, probing, suggesting and experimenting, and emerging with some answers.

This is not a history book but the tools are developed in the context of a critical period – the Enlightenment and the first Industrial Revolution. If they work in this familiar testbed they might serve for a better understanding of what we design, build, use, read and write today.

The period is – given some latitude at either end – the century from 1750 to 1850, the time of the Revolutions (American, French, Industrial and, at its end, 1848). Europe's and America's outer worlds were transfigured. And though Enlightenment thought was absorbed into science, religion, art and philosophy, it was not till Darwin, Freud and Marx that the inner world underwent a comparable upheaval. By then towns and buildings had undergone their revolution.

The place is – given some latitude (or perhaps it should be longitude!) of a few thousand miles west across the Atlantic or east to Russia – Britain. The Industrial Revolution is so basic to this narrative that inevitably most of the evidence is found in its cradle.

The production metropolis was mature by 1850 and had become differentiated by function and stratified by class. Steam power and the railways had liberated industry from rural, water-powered sites. At the start of the period there were a handful of building types. The most ancient, religious buildings and houses, ranging from the palace to the rural hovel, represented levels of sacred and secular power. This was extended into the public sphere in theatres and concert rooms, monasteries, colleges, schools, libraries, almshouses and guest houses. For leisure and travel there were clubs and inns. Buildings for production were modest – farms, mills, warehouses; for exchange the markets, bazaars and shops. In the guildhalls, *bourses* and exchanges are the roots of town halls. Some papal, religious, civil and military infirmaries, prisons, pest houses and institutions were of substantial size.

By 1850 there had been a typological explosion: a host of new industrial buildings, railway stations, town halls, baths and wash-houses, highly specialised urban markets; libraries, art galleries and museums; civic universities, schools and secular colleges; vastly expanded prisons and hospitals out of which grew asylums and workhouses, hotels, and offices.

Not only did buildings house new technological processes, but they were products of new technologies and they acquired commodity instead of use value. So the means – technology and investment – underwent as much transformation as the ends to serve new social purposes.

There are parallels with today, when asymmetries of power hinge not on steam power but on systems for handling information. Those who design the hardware and software stand in the position of the entrepreneurs and engineers. Mature colonialism generated a consumption of goods which matches today's consumption of services and media generated by multinational capital; it also created similar political upheavals. All these, both then and now, change patterns of relations and it is the way relations are established in and through buildings which is my concern.

The search for meaning in buildings involves many implicit ideas which make up a theoretical position. Rather than let it simply emerge, Part I sets out an explicit framework which places buildings, texts about them and the subject – the person who experiences or uses the buildings, or reads the texts – within their societies. It looks at the role of language, and especially of classification, and it proposes some analytical methods.

Analysis clarifies two kinds of relations. First those of power, based on the distribution of limited resources. Second those of bonds – which premeate and subvert all social relations.

A separate chapter discusses the idea of function and type, and leads to the themes of the following three parts.

Part II looks at the ways relations between people are shaped by buildings. It starts with places where people with little power are classified and subjected to disciplined control for the formation or re-formation of their character. The urban primary school movement took off, as did that for Sunday and industrial schools. The programme of prison, hospital and asylum building was immense, and institutions for forced labour prepared the way for the great New Poor Law workhouses after the 1834 Act.

But relations and formation of character were also structured by the élite groups for themselves in dedicated places such as coffee houses, clubs, assembly rooms and hotels.

The physical squalor in the towns and the arrival of cholera created a demand for hygienic and sanitary services which crossed boundaries of class. The places for cleansing the body and clothes – baths and wash-houses – grew into places for recreative cleansing in pools and swimming baths.

Part III is concerned with the production of knowledge; how it is stored and accessed through systems of classification in libraries, and how museums and art galleries represent in space theories about nature, industry and art. Experts were invisible and the outcome of their work was totally visible. Another type, the lecture theatre, operates in reverse with visible (and audible) experts and invisible organising principles in theories. Exhibitions, dioramas and panoramas produced knowledge for popular entertainment and as a celebration of industry.

Part IV is about things – objects which are produced and exchanged. The domestic workshop and textile mill both survive in the total production space – the industrial utopia. In the spaces for exchange – the shops, bazaars, and especially markets – is seen the genesis of today's hypermarkets and shopping centres.

The concluding remarks in Part V discuss this work in the context of current issues – specifically asking how today's discourse of architecture has been shaped by those critical hundred years. The answer to that may help us to understand both the buildings we use, and the texts we read today, and so to design, and write, better ones.

PART I

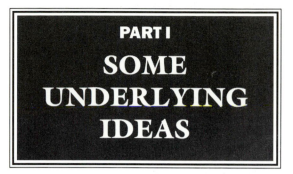

SOME UNDERLYING IDEAS

CHAPTER 1
The shape of the argument

Things and words

In the myths of Australian Aboriginals the world was created by spirits of nature – human, animal and vegetable – in the 'Dreamtime'. The intimate link between people and nature is maintained by song, poetry, stories and painting. A Dreaming site is loaded with symbolic meaning. And these rituals keep the myth alive and so give the site an invisible mental structure. That, rather than changes to its material form, make it significant. In other cultures this can easily be overlooked when space is shaped by buildings and settlements. These, by far the most important products of material cultures, are so concrete and rich, so obviously useful, that they can swamp the invisible structures which give meaning to both use and form, whether in the Australian bush or the European city.

Except for gibberish, language means something. But that buildings mean something is not a familiar idea. Of course a lot is clear. Someone has decided who can use a building. We share it with others and have little doubt whether it is a palace, a church or an electronics factory. Its form arouses feelings alongside the associations which spring from a Greek temple portico, a pointed spire, stainless steel tubes or explicit symbols such as an Imperial eagle, a Christian cross or an IBM logo. All this is part of the building's narrative. But we still find it hard to say that it means something, that there are invisible structures present.

That may be difficult with language too, but with buildings it seems much harder. The search for meaning entails a number of questions. What kinds of things do buildings mean? How do they do so? Do they have the same meanings for everyone? Do meanings change over time, even for a given person?

In language the inner and outer worlds meet. This is equally the case in buildings. This is so vital for understanding them that despite many misleading links between buildings and language which have been made, it is useful to compare our task with the work of those whose concern is language itself.

Poets, philosophers, linguists, semioticians, psychoanalysts, literary critics and workers in artificial intelligence explore meanings behind what common sense tells us. But even their most hard-fought battles, in what Eliot calls 'a raid on the inarticulate/With shabby equipment always deteriorating' (Eliot 1944: 21), rely on everyday use. Wittgenstein said that language means what its users take it to mean. So these artists and intellectuals share ordinary meanings with each other and with us. This is the secure anchor and salutory test of their work. There is no private language.

When the ordinary world is obscure and confused, digging beneath its surface is that much harder. This seems to have happened to towns and buildings as a result of an erosion which started some two hundred years ago, a period which, paradoxically, defined itself in terms of making the world clear through reason. Designers, scholars, critics and users now no longer seem to inhabit the same world. Many places no longer distinguish clearly between public and private. A shopping mall is accessible to all and hence 'public' but feels as if someone controls it, and us, through a powerful presence. Ambiguity in forms, confusion about function, or labyrinthine space deprive towns and buildings of clarity. Forms have become difficult to decode. Classical buildings are as likely to be associated with 1930s European Fascism as with republicanism or humanism; the Modern Movement with democratic freedom as with doctrinaire bureaucracy. Jameson (1990) argues that Post-Modernism has challenged the very notion of meaning with its jokes, disconnections, historical cannibalism and 'photorealism', and that its roots are in the free market of multinational capital.

Much of what is written about towns and buildings feels equally obscure, esoteric and alienating. Despite the writers sharing daily use of buildings with us, little seems to be shared in the way of responses and it is difficult to encroach into their territory. The obscurity of buildings and of the language about them are of course two sides of the same coin.

All this is sometimes defended as a mature tolerance for contradictions and layers of meaning, a view based on work such as Sennett's (1971). His defence of creative *dis*order depended, like Erikson's psychoanalytic theory of adolescence upon which it was based, on a tolerance of ambiguity and contradiction within a world which most of the time made sense. It was the hidden paradox, the unexpected conflict, the Surrealist joke which were maturing. The argument was a vindication of creative disorder, slippages of meaning which illuminate the world, but not a defence for chaos in that world itself.

Of course the media texts are more accessible. They identify visible and important issues. Some concern failures: technical ones of poor construction and shabby finishes, high energy consumption and ecological damage; or visual ones of inhuman scale, coldness, or even of disease (Prince Charles's 'carbuncle' metaphor has become a byword). In housing there is reference to vandalism, crime and lack of neighbourliness. Some concern successes: praise for key art galleries and museums; or reverence for a historic heritage which combines the sacredness of cathedrals, the splendour of country mansions, the innocence of nature in the great estates, and the inventiveness of the industrial entrepreneur. These failures and successes are real enough and the media do open them to public debate. And yet their silence over less visible failings and successes, and their blinkers, obstruct the quest for meaning. In advocating good modern design and rejecting timorous historical pastiche the distinction between the 'shock of the new' and loss of meaning is erased. And whatever the rights and wrongs of that, by squeezing out all issues other than those of form the debate is further trivialised. So it is good to stay close to language because it acts as a model for what it is like to go beneath the surface and behind silence.

Language is at the core of making, using and understanding buildings. Through it a community is able to articulate its feelings and thoughts about them, to share its experience of meaning. Much of what we think and feel is the direct outcome of descriptive texts – scholarly works, educational material, media productions, travel literature and exhibition catalogues. There is a host of prescriptive ones too such as competition conditions, briefs, legislation, building regulations, feasibility reports and design guides. These texts exist before a building is designed and yet in many ways 'design' it. Their language, like all language, cannot be innocent. The values and intentions of their authors are present in length, subdivision, tone, the degree of elaboration of parts, and the things that are not said – the silent discourse. And above all the texts use everyday speech categories. Classification puts these names for things, people, spaces and processes into an order. That buildings can be regarded as classifying devices is obvious in libraries where classification is overt and governs the location of books in space and the very structure of that space. But all buildings classify something.

The way the material world and our inner world are related through language is so problematic that only a treatise in linguistics or philosophy can unravel it. As I am neither a linguist nor a philosopher I shall not attempt that. But its essence is simple enough and in setting it out I am indebted to one of the pioneer scholars of material culture, Kouwenhoven (1982: 79–92).[1]

Every building is experienced as a concrete reality. I visit a bank. Behind its Classical entrance are glass doors, its banking hall is domed and it has an elaborate mosaic floor. Across its mahogany counter I face a familiar clerk. I see doors to other rooms and other people behind the counter, but I do not recognise these spaces nor these people. The bank has its own smell and sounds. The entire experience is unique. By calling it a 'bank' I am using what Kouwenhoven calls something 'inherently "defective" . . . a sort of generalised, averaged-out substitute for a complex reality comprising an infinite number of individual particularities' (Kouwenhoven 1982: 83). If I speak to someone whose sole experience is of the Hong Kong and Shanghai Bank's headquarters we are likely to misunderstand each other. If the hearer shares the experience of the speaker then the value of the spoken word is that it makes communication about myriads of experiences possible by means of a very limited vocabulary. But 'words do not *have* meaning; they *convey* it. But they can convey it only if the receiving consciousness can complete the current of meaning by grounding it in comparable particulars of experience' (1982: 84). Otherwise, though we exchange words we think we understand, the currents pass each other by like ships in the night. Of course the comparability might be quite remote or even only metaphorical. But, given the skills of a good novelist or poet, even such germs of shared experience are sufficient.

Kouwenhoven used this argument to justify the exhibition of artefacts as an antidote to the excessively cerebral conventions of scholarship and popular display, over-dependent on descriptive texts. The artefacts were to be used and touched, thus creating shared experience. It might be objected that this is not a problem with buildings – we fully experience them every day. But much writing is about buildings which one or both parties have been unable to experience. And 'texts' like drawings, photographs, models and computer simulations fail to reproduce their rich reality, above all the unique experience of being within space together with other people. As with the artefacts, when the particularity of experience is not shared, then what is said is not heard. When writers do not even *try* to base their abstractions on experience then, by Kouwenhoven's definition, they cannot make sense to anyone.

But he aimed not to discredit language, but to warn that its very abstraction is its weakness. Short of remaining mute nothing can be done about that; but an awareness of this fragility is a strong motivation for holding tight to experience. And in any case this shortcoming is exactly its power when it comes to analysis. We simply have no other way to deal with the invisible, mental structures.

So where are we? We are going to be concerned with buildings about which there are texts; that is, things and words (and I am adding more words). There are live debates about whether the meaning of a text (who 'writes' the text) is created by the author, or by the reader's mind. And also about the degree to which the author and the reader are socially formed. Some of these debates are profound; others, in Short's words are 'structuralist gibberish, about as digestible and intelligible as overcooked suet pudding' (Short 1991: 224). My position is unambiguous: just as meaning in language needs a speaker and a listener who are members of the same language-using community, so buildings and their texts acquire meaning when the subject (an observer, user, reader) experiences a building or a text about it; when the two worlds intersect. Subject and object are embedded in – neither free of nor determined by – their historical societies. The first world is an outer, visible one (which is, of course, the result of its author's inner world) and the second an invisible, inner world. At this intersection the Cartesian boundary between object and subject dissolves. So our study of meaning will have to embrace three domains: the building, the text and the experiencing subject, all in a language-using society. In practice I shall not be able to tackle all three in equal depth, but this map of the task suggests that power, my central theme, will permeate its every nook and cranny.

A case

If meaning springs from experience, what is it about buildings, texts and subjects that matters? The answer returns to the idea of an unfolding serial event, a building as a narrative. From the moment it is conceived, through its design, production, use, continuous reconstruction in response to changing use, until its final demolition, the building is a developing story, traces of which are always present.

In the seminal but indigestible work by Frankl (1914) which we shall consider again, he cites a part of such a narrative – the case of a medieval monastery converted to a courthouse. This troubles him, as if it were an obstacle to understanding, an unfortunate accident, rather than the inevitable stuff of history. But he does argue that if some knowledge is missing then a building makes less sense than it might.

> If we study buildings of older cultures and find one lacking in original fittings because, for example, what was once a monastery is now a courthouse, then our need to *know* something becomes still more conspicuous. The spectator who is without knowledge has even greater need for the right reference when confronted by a building designed for an obsolete purpose . . . to reconstruct the essence of the building.
>
> (Frankl 1914: 158)

Frankl contrasts this with experience in one's own time where, he says, problems can arise because whilst 'we understand without explanation the spaces created for ... common purposes' we may lack the experience to cope with a new function 'for which ... a person probably needs special instruction' (Frankl 1914: 158). Certainly for his example, a factory, this would be true for an art historian. Though the monastery-into-court is a dramatic metamorphosis of a kind for which the National Archives in Paris provide ample evidence chiefly as unexecuted, Revolutionary projects especially from the *Directoire* onwards in the 1790s[2], it is untypical, for change is normally far less abrupt.

Frankl's second example is misleading because he envisages no change in the factory. There is no *stasis* though whether change is perceptible depends on the time intervals used. History no more stops for an hour than a century. Material fabric is always different from what it was at any earlier moment. Use has also changed, minutely from day to day, dramatically over centuries. So has the experience of users and observers and hence the things said and written about the building. Transformations are partly governed by the nature of the building and those who occupy it, and partly by external events. In the monastery-into-courthouse the abrupt political upheaval is the prime cause but the possibility of change depended on material factors (space, load-bearing potential and location in the town) as well as on some kind of analogy between spaces for liturgy and for legal processes, which all inhered in the building.

Monasteries were gradually remodelled in response to changes in liturgical practice, the Rule, or the numbers of monks, expanded activities or the need for strengthening a structurally weak element (say supports for a tower) – all originating in the building or its users. Of course change can never be entirely internally generated, otherwise 'desert island history' would be possible.

The ever-changing interplay between internal and external forces should be a major task for the architectural historian but the tradition is to treat the moment of a plan or photograph, and their accompanying text, as timeless. This is a result of idealism such as Frankl's which causes him to speak of the 'essence' of a building.

But to bring the narrative to the present let us suppose that the courthouse was used until the nineteenth century when the building was restored by Viollet le Duc; that it was abandoned until it was recently converted again into a

Figure 1.1

Proposed standard layout for courts during the French revolution (n.d.)

Source: Item AE II 3076, French National Archives, Paris

chamber music concert hall. Further, that there is a good deal of historical material available: information on the first abbot and his community, their land holdings, patrons and political connections; drawings of the building as it was at the first conversion as well as of the new court arrangements; records of political debates in the two Chambers of the 1790s about the appropriation and utilisation of ecclesiastical property; an illustrated text as to model courts for the new *Tribuneaux* (Figure 1.1); a lawyer's account of its use; some scholarly articles as well as tourist literature; and the brief for the concert hall. These suppositions are not far-fetched; such a wealth of information, and more, can be recovered for thousands of buildings.

Since the only experience I can know is my own this narrative now continues as a short piece of autobiography which is fictional, but only in a trivial sense.

I am both tourist or visitor and, by profession, an architect and theoretician. I carry my history and personality, educational and professional formation, and social class. I have learnt to respond to music, architecture, people and institutions in my own *milieu* of family, friends, academic colleagues and professional bodies. I decide to listen to an evening concert and to use the occasion also to probe the meaning of the building. I want to be true to the narrative, that is to encompass its entire life from abbey church to the evening of the concert.

I see its exterior mass and detail in its setting on the edge of the *place* before it becomes dark and, in walking round it, I become familiar with the way its entrances, including the triple *portail* and its carved tympanum, are connected to and visible from the spaces outside. Inside it is now lit so that there are dramatic contrasts between the dark volumes of the vaulted mass and the strongly lit capitals, columns and sanctuary floor. I am able to wander around before the concert – from narthex into nave, to side chapels, transepts, the *chevet* and the lower crypt where the founding abbot lies buried. Both here and up above there are other tombs in the floor, walls and under canopies between columns.

My experience is of the location and general form of the building, the details of what is on its surfaces, its colour, the stories told by its carvings, the geometrical ornament. Some of the forms I can only guess at as they are in the dark. It is also of its current purpose – the musical performance which I will shortly share with the rest of the audience and the musicians. Further, I sense how its spaces are organised, even the sanctuary to which I cannot gain access, the crypt, and those outside where I have recently been. I know what is near the entrance, what lies deep in, what is next to what, how all these spaces are connected. All this makes a powerful impression.

Even before the concert I feel that I am in touch with an ordered space achieved by contrasts of dark and light, mass and detail, solid and void. It has a movement, a progression, both forwards towards the place of action, and upwards into a dimly perceived space. These arouse memories and images. The contrasts feel familiar as contradictions in my own life; the dimness as the ever-present obscurity around my understanding of the world and myself in it; the dynamics of movement as metaphors for growth; the rhythm and order as a lively but familiar security. Inevitably these are rooted in my experience from childhood, who knows in that web of events, losses, affirmations, loneliness, cherishings, sexuality, departures, violence, healing and love. The images that arise from these mingle with those awakened by the guessed purposes of others who have been or now are here; monks, judges, lawyers, witnesses, musicians, audiences. Soon, listening to the secular music played directly above the first abbot – 'founded on' him – I pick up an additional numinous sense besides its conventional meanings, one that was probably intended in deciding to play in the church. I am surrounded by tombs of its earlier inhabitants and patrons – a story evidently more ancient than the music. I connect the music, the brightly-lit performing platform and the position of the conductor with such liturgical experience as I possess. On departure I purchase a short illustrated tourist guide. The direct experience has stopped.

During the following weeks I gain access to the printed and drawn record. I connect the design with others of the same Order, in the political context of the time. I see the limitations on representation imposed by the Rule. I understand something of the wealth behind the building; the motivations of the aristocratic patrons who lie buried here; the reason why this particular master mason – recognisable from his moulding profiles – was imported. I grasp the transformation from church to court, the Republican notions of justice, and the meaning of the spatial layout and its furnishings to a working lawyer of the time. I see analogies between the position of the abbot's throne, in front of a crucifix, and the judge's chair in front of the *tricouleur*, between monks and clerical assistants, on the one hand, and lawyers and officials on the other; between lay worshippers in the nave and visitors in the public gallery of the lawcourt. Relations suggest themselves between the participants in a liturgy, and those in legal processes, validated in one case by the presence of the sacred and in the other by the State's justice. I ask in what ways the public rituals of these two hierarchical groups, deriving their authority from an invisible being at their apex, are the same and in what ways different. One aimed to create a community through shared bonds, and the other to represent the processes of power; how can the same space carry such different meanings? I begin to wonder about the tightness of fit between space and its meaning.

I learn something of the beliefs of mid-nineteenth century conservationists which enabled them to create gross distortions in the name of historical veracity. I see in the brief for the concert hall something of today's idea of culture and especially clearly, here, its association with history and the sacred. This, for me, casts light on the role of cultural buildings, including also museums and art galleries, as today's sacred places. All these 'discoveries' are welded onto my own experience on that seminal evening whose memory is alive as I write my analysis and an interpretation.

This imaginary autobiographical 'case' is a skeleton without flesh. Indeed how could it ever be complete when there are many histories, layers of meaning, relations and structures? The building, what is written about it, and what is experienced form a seamless fabric. The richness is such that there will be no opportunity to develop any single case as completely as this one potentially is. Mostly I shall deal with cases I have not even experienced. Even if I had, to follow even one through would require a monograph in its own right. But the 'case' serves its purpose.

Buildings and their texts as social practice

In the 'case' the building, the texts about it and my experience were effortlessly connected in real historical societies. To tease them out I want to represent this society-in-history as having three domains: social practices, social relations and subjects. Making buildings and writing texts about them are two particular social practices. So is the use of language, the most important practice of all. Subjects both constitute and are constituted by society. And in their social relations they discover the meanings of their practices.

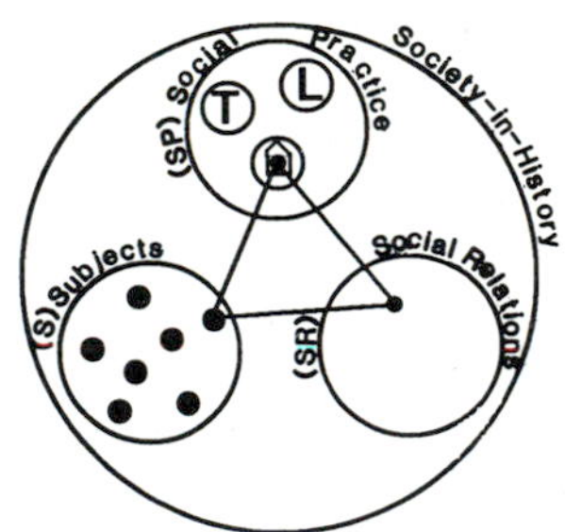

T = texts about buildings
L = language
⌂ = designing & producing buildings

The building

There were things to be seen – spaces with a geometry of size and shape, and fabric with representational and abstract ornament facing both inwards and outwards. The surfaces were articulated by openings, pilasters and ribs into subdivisions which were repeated rhythmically. Some had further applied material – carpets, wall hangings or paintings. There were symbols, emblems and written inscriptions. The column clusters and mouldings were hierachically ordered, a feature which Panofsky (1957) has related to the logical structure of Scholasticism. We saw window tracery, a heavily carved tympanum, column capitals and tomb carvings.

In a 'style' these formal elements cohere. The Classical system was eventually governed, to its last detail, by prescriptive rules – verbal and graphic – which from the fifteenth century onwards form the core of architectural texts. Stylistic prescriptions were a major export to the colonies of European empires, whether from imperial Rome to North Africa or Palladian England to South Carolina.

There were juxtapositions on or substitutions for earlier work; not only a series of medieval forms, but remnants of the neo-Classical courtroom and, now, modern plate glass, furniture and lighting. The forms tell an unbelievably rich narrative, both informative and moving. How informative and how moving depends on what intellectual and emotional equipment is brought along.

Some things we saw were more obviously to do with people. Some *were* people – playing or listening to music and selling programmes. We found or recovered evidence of earlier inhabitation and were able to imagine monks in the choir, priests at the altar (which has survived), layfolk in the nave, the judge, lawyers and witnesses in the space now occupied by the musicians, and the courtroom public in the present auditorium.

There is no limit to what is recoverable about the purpose and organising principles of the liturgy, the monastic Rule or the legal process – even down to the details of processions for particular feast days or procedures during particular trials.

For reasons adduced by Kouwenhoven, unless experience is shared the picture of function given by any text, no matter how elaborate, will remain on the surface. This becomes clear if we consider places which we use repeatedly or which, as sites of memorable events have meanings which no amount of insight by a scholar, tourist or critic can fully capture. How would such a stranger feel about, or see, our house, street or old school, the church where we were married, the office where we worked or the seaside hotel of our childhood holidays? Reconstruction will be hard work and will at best produce a passable likeness, at worst a caricature. That is to say the rich narrative about use, whether observed, remembered or recovered, is as moving and poetic as that of form, despite the dry sound of 'function'.

In the 'case' we also became aware of spatial relations. Moving in through the narthex led to a sequence of spaces each of which was visible from the one before. Sometimes there was a single route, and to return we had to retrace our steps, sometimes there was an alternative. Some spaces were shallow, near the entrance, others deep, reached after passing through many intervening spaces. Some were barred by rules signified by locked doors and signs. Each was for a recognisable purpose, and for some persons. The picture we built up was one of 'nextness' – topogical rather than geometrical – into which everything in the functional description fitted; not only who did what, when and with whom, in what form of space but where and next to whom.

So observation, experience, the texts and the drawings produced knowledge of form, function and space. In everyday life, these cohere seamlessly but for analysis of meaning it is useful to consider them as separate discourses. Of the three, form and space are permanent (unless material changes occur). Function is not – it is the social practice of use 'inscribed' into the building.

Some monastic communities had Baroque buildings. Lawcourts have been built in many styles. And both can operate in a variety of spatial structures, each of which signifies a different social relation. In other words there is no immutable relation between form, function and space despite Sullivan's famous *dictum* 'form follows function'. They are independent. And yet if it still makes sense to ask whether an entire building means something it looks as if we shall have to seek an answer in a common field which can tell us something about all its properties. That actually destroys the idea of a discourse with coherent, self-contained relations, such as 'architecture' is commonly held to be. This is a point I shall return to later. In the meantime, where shall we look?

The building came into being through the actions of owners, investors, designers, builders, craftworkers, princes of the Church and State, and legislators. To keep it in existence needs yet others such as cleaners. They, with all users, were knitted into their own historical societies. It therefore seemed natural for me to take the social relations of all these people as that common field.

Before developing that idea we need to say something about the other social practice – the writing of texts – and about the subject.

The text

Prescriptive texts are rare in the period of the monastic church, but become more frequent after the seventeenth century, starting as simple letters, becoming more elaborate Acts of the State, town council minutes, competition briefs, building legislation or design guides and finishing up as today's substantial design briefs.

The text has its own history. It appears in a place and time and in a specific form, and is produced, stored and distributed by such institutions as a monastic library, a publisher, a printer, a gallery, a university or a newspaper. It may contain numbers, tables, drawings, photographs, computer simulations and sound tracks. It adopts conventions – styles – of writing, graphics, composition and reproduction.

Subject

We know subjectivity from inside – this is familiar territory with its many-layered onion-like meanings. We know that this is a less tangible entity than the building or the text. Though I shall make no attempt to offer tools for its analysis, the subject enters the argument.

At the risk of becoming boring, it is necessary to repeat that subjects are also in society-in-history. The critic, scholar or analyst is merely another subject, despite the weight of the tomes or learnedness of the theses they produce. They are products of their personal histories, they view the evidence through their own spectacles. The 'case' was useful if for nothing else than to illustrate that there is no way of standing outside; as interpreter I was inside the narrative I was interpreting. It may be humbling but it is as well to be clear about it.

If meaning is in society-in-history we face two forms of a troublesome contradiction which has been hugely debated. One is that between the individual and society. Is the individual nothing more than the social product of genetic, environmental and economic forces? Or are there some traits which are 'essential' to being human, something we can call human 'nature' which is prior to and beyond the reach of socialisation?

The other is between material artefacts like buildings and texts, and especially works of art, and society. Are these reducable to social formation through their authors' history, or is there something 'essential', universal, which elicits the 'aha!' response?

To give an answer which feels authentic and usable for this work I want to distinguish between two kinds of human relations. The first depends on roles, structures and control of resources. These constitute an individual through social forces of power relations. For the second I have relied in part on phenomenology and on Husserl's notion of the 'lifeworld' (Husserl 1970) – a world in which I experience myself and to which I belong, through my body. I form relations, which Gorz (1989) calls 'bonds', beyond and in some way the opposites of socially constituted ones. Though developing in and through the selfsame societies, attachment to others by these bonds is not determined by social forces. Gorz uses maternal love as the outstanding example, '... by its essence a threat to any order' (Gorz 1989: 175). It is unconditional, in no way dependent on roles, contracts or justice and is not 'socialisable'. But though not socially constituted, it only grows and can only be experienced within a concrete social setting which modifies it. He could have extended his example to love in general, friendships and solidarity.

The reality of this inner world cannot be reached from outside-in. 'It is impossible to exteriorise interiority, or objectivise the subjective' (Gorz 1989: 176). But this does not require us to believe in a prior 'nature' outside history. It is in that history, and only there, that each individual's inner world is formed, by being in touch with elements of nature – seasons, weather, living plants and creatures, food, and other materials, sometimes raw, sometimes highly processed by a technological culture – and with our own and others' bodies. This is so much what being human is about, that it seems legitimate to speak of it as human 'nature'. Evolution and genetic inheritance, childhood environment and specific local culture are all formative, as they are in the ability to learn a language. But even a history that stretches back into evolutionary origins and is common to all, forms me in a unique way. I have a body, like everyone else. But the way I feel in it, the way I use it, say in a dance or in a sexual relation, is unique to me. Again, like all human beings, I have the ability to speak languages. But I use the specific language of the community to which I belong and I say things that I alone think and feel. No one else can say exactly the same things now or ever again.

It is easier to grasp the uniqueness of every person's 'lifeworld' when ancient and shared continuities are in some marked way disrupted by a moment of history. A word, smell or shape may then carry a meaning of destruction, despite it being generally a sign of healing. In architecture, after two thousand years of Classical order, Mussolini's use of Classicism may have wiped out the harmony of the Pazzi Chapel for a whole generation. Such disruptions shape both the socially constituted power relations and the bonds which spring from the inner 'lifeworld'.

And just as the individual is more than just a socially constituted creature, so society is more than a mere aggregate of its individual members.

This points to an answer to the second question. If created objects have 'essence' this originates with the 'nature' of the creator who is both constituted by and formed within society. Social analysis can explain the qualities of this object, but it will not explain it away. Here is history's dual presence again. And in so far as the object has meanings deriving from human 'nature' it will evoke an 'aha!' from others, unless a Mussolini-like event has wiped out that possibility.

The spatial setting of groups, workplaces and communities in which both kinds of relation are discovered is concrete. The buildings are more than passive containers for relations. Like all practices they are formative, as much through the things that happen in them, their functional programme, as by their spatial relations and their form. My position then is that I pay the utmost respect to material history and the social relations it creates. And in particular to bodies in building space. Without that history nothing makes sense. But even with it there remain meanings which are intractable to outside-in analysis. Here I have to rely on my own experience and hope that I share enough with others for it to be communicable in words.

Just what is the role of mind, consciousness and language in this world of bodies in space, of buildings as material containers, I have to leave to philosophers to explain.

Tools of analysis

Some of the analytical approaches are familiar and straightforward, though even they prompt questions. Others are less so and need to be described.

The building

Form

It seems hardly necessary to say that the form of the church-courthouse-concert hall produces a powerful experience. It is not only its power which makes it hardly necessary, but the tradition of historical scholarship, criticism, teaching and the media which treats form as the defining quality of architecture. Most of the analytical tools have their origins in art scholarship. They examine stylistic development, articulation, iconography and perception. This tradition is rooted in the Renaissance post-Vitruvian treatise, was elaborated in seventeenth and eighteenth century France, transformed under the influence of German idealism and archeology in the nineteenth century and flowered in the first half of the present century. Especially richly developed is the analysis of the Classical Orders. Summerson (1980) uses linguistic metaphors of vocabulary and grammar to show how their parts hang together and how the columnar system expands into larger statements in plan and elevational composition. A more analytical approach is adopted by Tzonis and Lefaivre (1986).

There is a huge body of material available for analyses of form: drawings, texts, archeological and architectural surveys, photographs and models. Little of it has been used for social interpretation and yet even historians for whom architecture has been an autonomous art form have recently acknowledged that its meaning may reside in society. Summerson (1980: 114) concludes that the language of Classicism relates to '... the whole question of architecture as a vehicle for social meaning'. Watkin (1980: 183) in his review of how architectural history is done, notes that one of its most 'striking recent characteristics is ... the increasingly determined attempt to relate buildings to the society in which they were produced', though he is pessimistic about such attempts.

For Frankl (1914) form has three components. First spatial composition – the geometry of space. The medium is the plan and his analysis of that became the inspiration for Kaufmann (1955) in his work on the 'revolutionary' architects of the late eighteenth century, and for Giedion (1944) on the Baroque. Second he analyses mass and surface by techniques based on those which Wölfflin used for the Renaissance and Baroque. He might have called this concrete material which forms space 'physiognomy' but prefers 'corporeality'. Third he considers the effects of light, colour and other optical phenomena, creating changing images with every viewpoint which coalesce in the mind into a single sensation, a view clearly derived from the then new *Gestalt* psychology.

These three combine with function to give meanings about the world. For instance the contrast between the Renaissance and the Baroque Frankl (1914) describes as 'finite' against 'infinite'; 'microcosm' against 'macrocosm'; and 'a complete, closed, self-sufficient unit' against 'a fragment that opens to the universe because it is incomplete'. These meanings were intended by the designers and are evoked for everyone who experiences the building. He sees the message as universal in two senses: it is about the universe and its meaning will persist for all time, for everyone.

Amongst the most powerful challenges to the

view of forms as metaphors are those which derive from Saussure. The idea of a sign as an arbitrary combination of a form (signifier) and an idea (signified) – the combination being created both in its generation (utterance) and in its reception (hearing/reading) through codes – has been applied to architecture. Eco (1986: 55–86) treats formal elements as parts of a sign system which becomes a code. Since one point of signs is to signify what things are for it will be better to look at Eco's ideas in the next chapter on function. But we can pick up one useful point here – the association of forms with words.

Eco (1986) distinguishes between various signs denoting construction or use. For each there is a word, such as 'dome' or 'staircase'. By extension, if a form has no constructional or functional purpose, there is no unambiguous word for it. Language cannot cope with such forms and we find it impossible to understand them. They might even be invisible. The names for the parts of the Classical system, even if the forms are rooted in primitive history, were needed not only to write the prescriptive rules, but also to see them. One of the most disorientating aspects of recent architecture is that some of its spatial and formal inventions are not nameable.

Such approaches allow new evidence about the form–function link to be used. They will make it worthwhile later to speculate of the shift from Classical to Tudor in schools, on the role of Scottish baronial in Robert Adam's Edinburgh prison and on the meaning of the Crystal Palace's 'high-technology' forms. But though semiotics may provide some insights, it fails to explain how choices are made. What is the effect of dominant groups – civil, military, ecclesiastical or, say, Freemasonic? Whose formal codes emerge? What explains exclusions – censored forms? And when forms are driven by technology, what explains technological censorship? Eventually we shall have to explain why even semiotics remained stuck in the formalist groove.

Function

The functions of monastic liturgy, Revolutionary justice, and a modern musical production speak about society. The abstract, socially-formed language oppositions 'sacred–secular', 'lawful–criminal', and 'professional–lay' became concrete in spaces and in their labels which often stand for both space and use; 'choir' and 'lawcourt' are both places and institutions.

Though the labels encapsulate all the evidence – from use, observation and texts – Frankl (1914) recognised the difficulty of reconstructing the functional narrative. Briefs, if they ever existed, have often disappeared without trace and there are few records of spoken instructions. Functional prescriptions are being continuously rewritten, and what survives may be in ephemeral texts such as account books or minutes of meetings.

Once a new function is named its ambiguity disappears. Its name affects the choice of designer, how the building is financed, its location, and the precedents used. By the late eighteenth century 'school' represented an established function. When the Sunday school emerged it was such a curious amalgam of instruction, work and worship that no one knew where to put it or how to design it. As a type of building it was equally curious – a mixture of school, mill, church, chapel and meeting room – with a life of only about twenty years. As an institution it was much more durable and operated in all kinds of buildings for over a century. Strong labels establish an identity between place and activity; this never happened for the Sunday school. Today 'supermarket' has achieved it but 'health club' has not yet done so.

The massive civic building programme of the First Empire, which Teyssot (1977: 56–65) has quantified, was partly achieved by conversion – for instance of churches into prisons, barracks and lawcourts. The extent to which a switch of label is strong enough to obliterate established meanings is discussed later. The industrial revolution created new labels such as 'cotton mill', 'railway station', 'exhibition' and 'wash-house'. More subtle than switches or the invention of new labels is re-definition; 'hospital', 'prison' and 'chapel' came to define new functions, new relations.

Once the material is assembled, its analysis starts from a set of questions. In the instance of the monastery converted to a courthouse who defined the first function? Who, and by what authority, transformed it? What physical changes were needed? Who named the functions? And what does it mean if a building designed for the first function was capable of being used for the second? This last question concerns the idea of 'type' which is considered in Chapter 2.

Space

Lefebvre's (1974) masterly analysis of space as a social production has connected abstract scien-

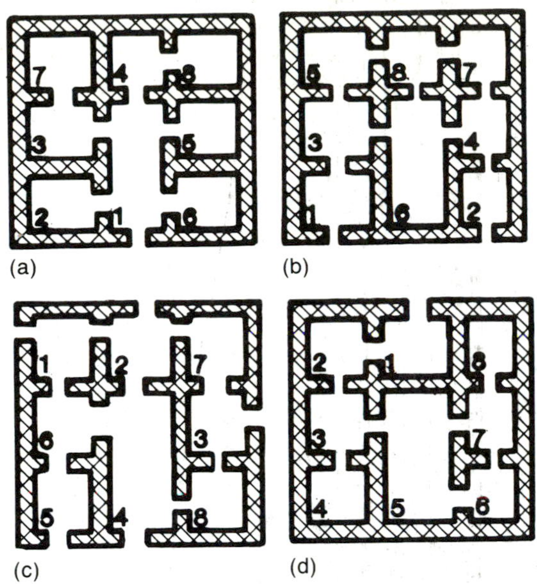

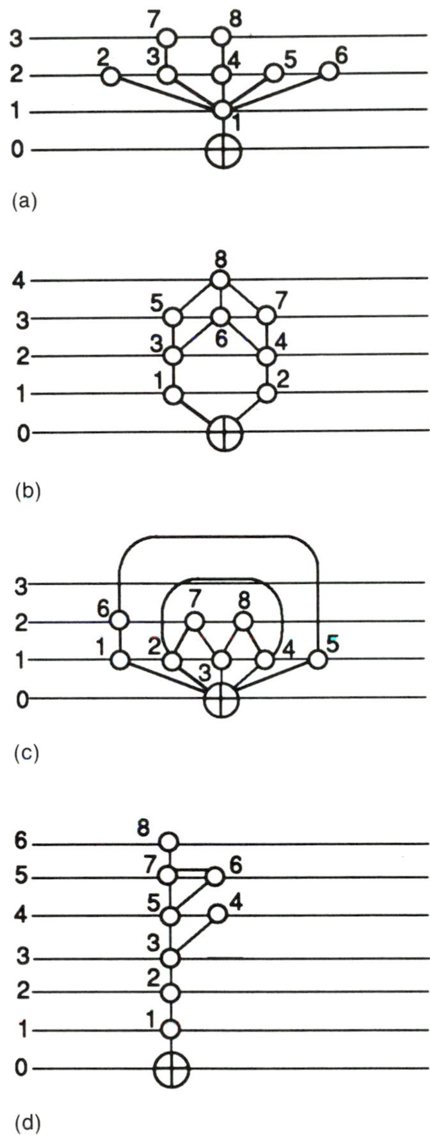

Figure 1.2

Floor plans, their spatial maps and RA values

Source: Redrawn from Hillier and Hanson (1984)

(a)	Depth	RA
⊕	0	0.321
1	1	0.071
2	2	0.321
3	2	0.250
4	2	0.250
5	2	0.321
6	2	0.321
7	3	0.500
8	3	0.500
Mean	2.125	0.317

(b)	Depth	RA
⊕	0	0.392
1	1	0.357
2	1	0.357
3	2	0.250
4	2	0.250
5	3	0.392
6	3	0.214
7	3	0.392
8	4	0.321
Mean	2.375	0.365

(c)	Depth	RA
⊕	0	0.107
1	1	0.214
2	1	0.111
3	1	0.214
4	1	0.143
5	1	0.286
6	2	0.250
7	2	0.285
8	2	0.285
Mean	1.375	0.202

(d)	Depth	RA
⊕	0	0.786
1	1	0.536
2	2	0.357
3	3	0.250
4	4	0.500
5	4	0.286
6	5	0.464
7	5	0.429
8	6	0.571
Mean	3.750	0.464

tific and social space and concrete, material space. It was not his task to push the analysis of concrete experience further. Here I will attempt that partly through the space syntax methods of Hillier and Hanson (1984) who represent spatial structures by the standard method of graphs. They have produced a rich family of measures – of which I shall use only the most elementary – all of which can be quantified, and which between them describe, and make possible the analysis of, the entire spatial configuration around and inside a building.

Underlying such techniques are a few basic assumptions. First, that the space around buildings and within them is a continuous, structured entity, which allows strangers to move around but only to admit into buildings two categories of people – 'inhabitants' and 'visitors'. The former have an investment of power and are the controll*ers*; the latter enter or stay as subjects of the system – the controll*ed* – shoppers, diners, museum visitors, inmates in hospitals or prisons (where a 'visit' may be of several years' duration), theatre audiences and church congregations. The *raison d'être* of the building is to interface the two groups and exclude strangers. Second that it is the same thing which explains both society and space – social relations. Society is organised in a way which can be described in the abstract but which, in the material world, is embedded in space. There is no a-spatial society and no a-social space. Third (in this Hillier and his colleagues follow Durkheim) that social organisation is of two kinds: organic solidarity and mechanical solidarity. The former consists of mutually interdependent relations where everyone has a role. It is often highly structured and hierarchical and usually needs to be closely related in space. Businesses and hospitals are typical. The latter is the relation between people, often equals, who share beliefs. Members of an academic community of scholars, a church or a political party have a mechanical solidarity. It often has no programmed spatial requirements – it is trans-spatial (but not a-spatial). People participate in both kinds of relation – a nurse may also belong to a church, or a factory worker to a trade union.

Figure 1.2, from Hillier and Hanson (1984), shows four formally identical plans differing only in the number of entrances and interconnections

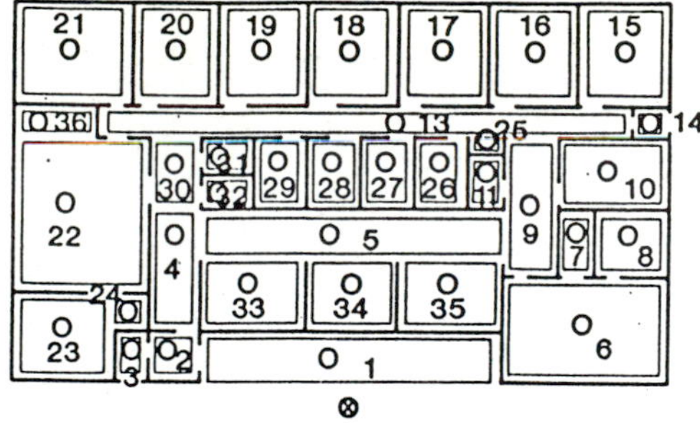

Figure 1.3a

Convex plan of a health centre

Source: Author's drawing based on Figure 1.3c

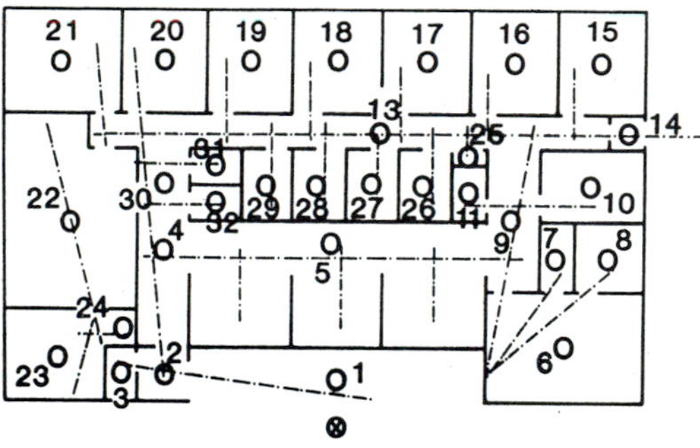

Figure 1.3b

Axial plan of a health centre

Source: Author's drawing based on Figure 1.3c

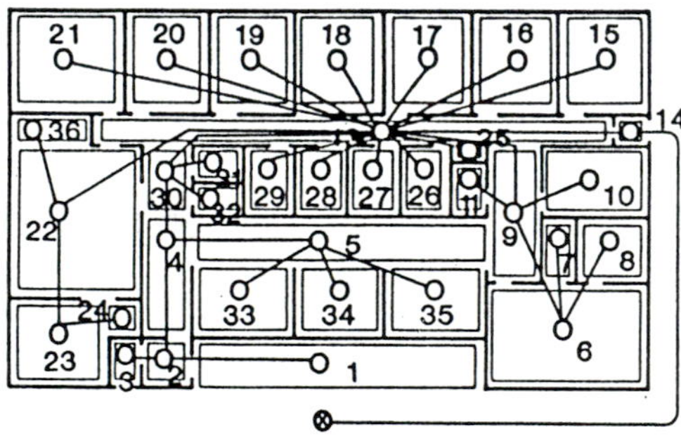

Figure 1.3c

Convex connections of a health centre

Source: Author's drawing based on an original supplied by Bill Hillier and first used in *Environment and Planning B: Planning and Design*

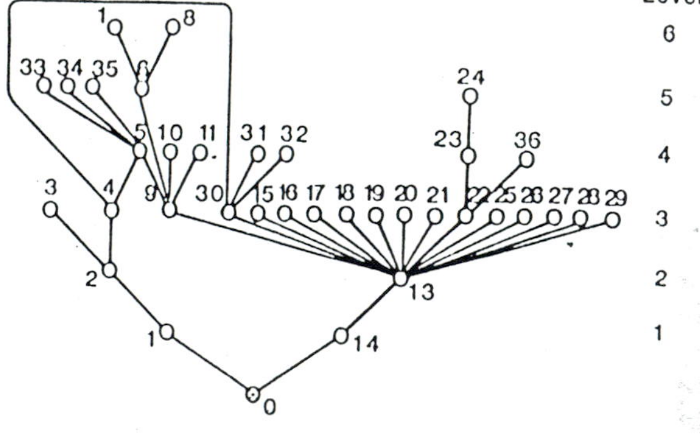

Figure 1.4

Spatial map of a health centre

Source: Author's drawing based on an original supplied by Bill Hillier and first used in *Environment and Planning B: Planning and Design*

between spaces. Each is represented by a circle (the outside by a cross in a circle) and each permeable link by a line. The resulting graphs have been 'justified' on the spatial maps by placing the spaces on a series of lines, starting with one on line 0 (in this example the outside space). Those one step from this are placed on line 1, those two steps away on line 2 and so on. The depth of all the spaces from the starting point is immediately evident; as is the presence of branching trees or looping rings. Spaces lying on the former have no alternative routes to them, whereas those lying on a ring are on at least two routes.

The spatial maps are very different. Some are shallow, some deep, some 'ringy', some tree-like. Two spaces A and B in identical relation to a third, C, are said to be 'symmetrical' with respect to C. If their spatial distances from C are different, they are 'asymmetrical'. The total amount of asymmmetry in a plan from any point relates to its mean depth from that point, measured by its 'relative assymetry' (RA), the values ranging from 0 (low) to 1 (high). Each space is a number of steps from all others; those that are, in sum, spatially closest to them all (low RA) are the most integrating. They characteristically have dense traffic through them. Those that are furthest (high RA) are the most segregated – isolated, often for privacy, or reserved for ceremonial functions. Values of RA measured from each space as well as the mean RA of each plan are given in Figure 1.2. Integration and segregation are global properties which relate a space to all the others. Measures for local properties are also available.

Most buildings are more articulated than these where each space is bounded by walls; their space is divided by re-entrant angles and projections. Figure 1.3 is of a health centre which is analysed further below. By drawing the fewest and fattest spaces that cover the entire plan, the former always prevailing over the latter, a plan of 'convex' spaces is obtained. This can be analysed in the same way (1.3a). Other elements can be chosen for subdivision – structural columns, changes in floor level or ceiling height, or articulation given by furniture, fittings or machinery – following any arbitrary but consistent rule. The ability to see from one space into adjacent spaces depends on visual axes. 'Axiality' is analysed by drawing the fewest and longest straight lines that cover the entire convex plan (1.3b). If, again, each axis is represented as a circle and each connection by a line, an axial graph can be drawn, and, as before, this can be 'justified' to show the familiar properties. Axiality has to do with the overall understanding of space especially in the urban context. The connections between the convex spaces are mapped as before (1.3c).

In public buildings there is a shallow visitor zone. Visitors interface with the inhabitants at

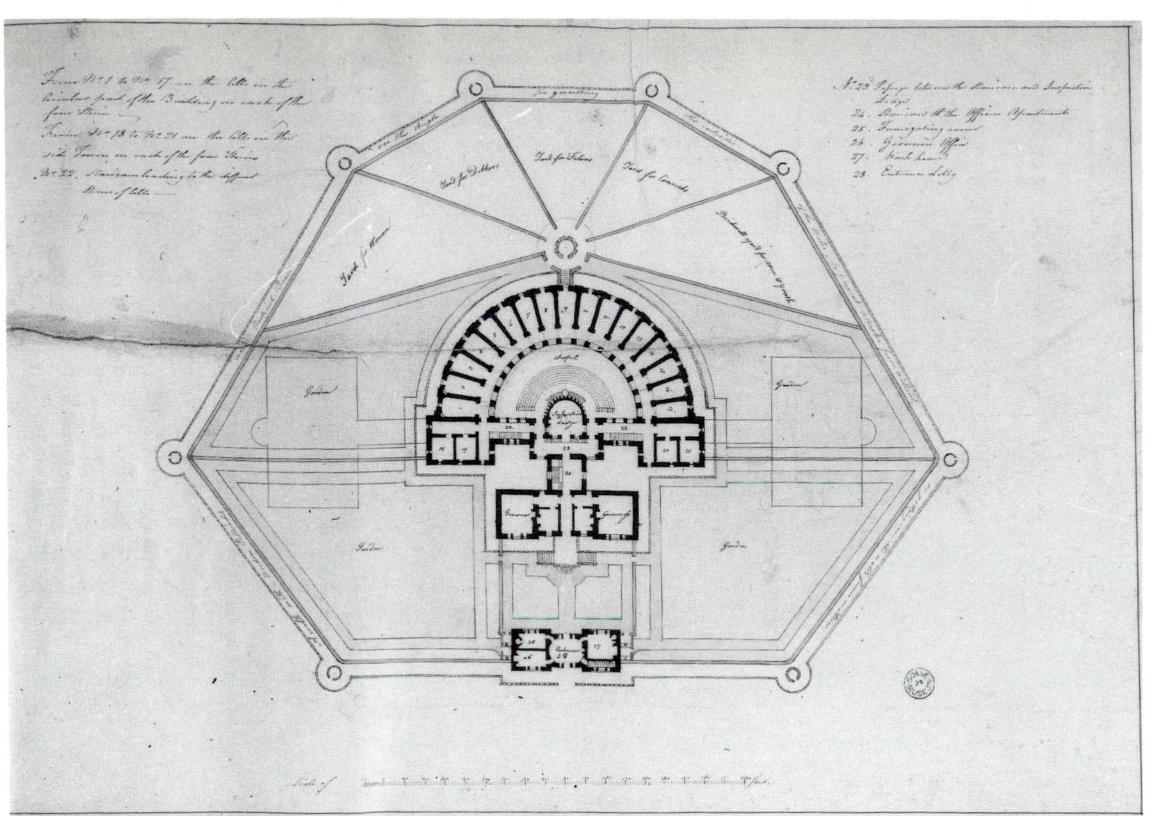

(a)

(b)

Figure 1.5

Robert Adam's fourth design for the Edinburgh Bridewell (1791), grand floor plan (a), basement plan (b), schematic plan (c), and spatial map (d)

Source: Soane Collection 32(33) and 17(33), by courtesy of the RCAHMS and the Trustees of Sir John Soane's Museum

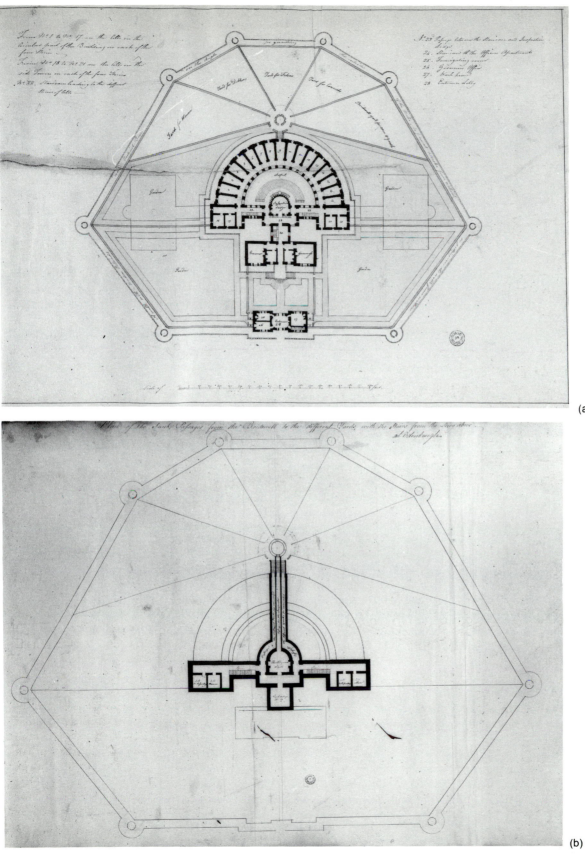

Figure 1.5 (*contd.*)

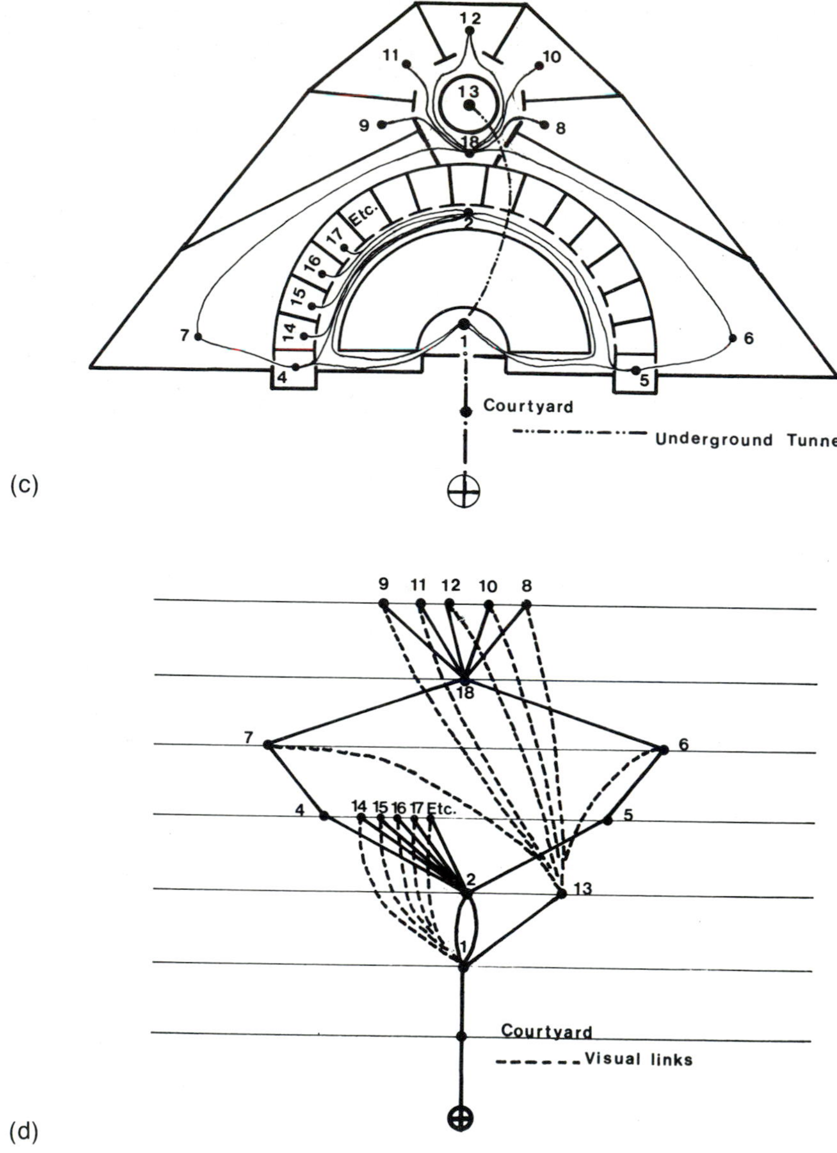

some spatial barrier which prevents deeper penetration: the counter in shops and banks, the bar in pubs, the proscenium arch in theatres, the gallery space of museums. The inhabitants occupy a zone beyond this which, to the visitors, looks deep and usually has its own access. Depth indicates power. The bank manager is deeper than the clerks, and the consultant deeper than the nurse. The person with the greatest power is at the tip of a tree, reached through corridors, stairs, outer and inner offices and waiting lobbies.

Figure 1.4 is of the same health centre as that shown in Figure 1.3. The reception area (4), lies on the two rings and on the route to every space, unless the rear (staff) entrance (14) is used. The staff and tea rooms (23 and 24), deceptively near the public entrance in formal terms, are in fact deep, on the branch of a tree. The privacy needed for these recreational areas is obtained by segregation. The consulting rooms are shallow from the staff entrance (14) but deep for the patients who have to pass through 1, 2, 4, 5, 9 and 13 to reach any of them.

The relation between spatial structure and function is loose. One model of medical practice creates deep, tree-like clinics, where patients meet doctors only in the consulting room beyond which is a deeper zone invisible to the patients, with its own entrance and circulation, designed to maintain a certain magic and to reinforce professional power. Another model results in a shallow, ringy structure with shared entrances and circulation routes, less control by reception spaces and some solidarity which spans across the doctor–patient gap.

In one kind of building, argue Hillier and Hanson (1984), the normal relationship is inverted. The visitors are deep within, increasing depth signifying decreasing power, and the inhabitants in a shallow, often ringy, zone at the surface controlling access to the deeper parts. These are institutions – the prisons, hospitals, asylums and workhouses.

I will use two examples to illustrate this. First Robert Adam's fourth design, based on Bentham's Panopticon, for the Edinburgh Bridewell (1791). Figure 1.5 shows that the prisoners, in cells at the periphery of the half drum, have access to outside exercise yards. The cells and the yards are under surveillance from two separate observation towers. The first (1) is clearly at the end of a shallow sequence of gate, entrance lobby, governor's garden, offices and house, but the second (13) appears to be deep in the plan, not where inhabitants are supposed to be. But at basement level a tunnel connects the two. The spatial map shows that this brings space 13 to the

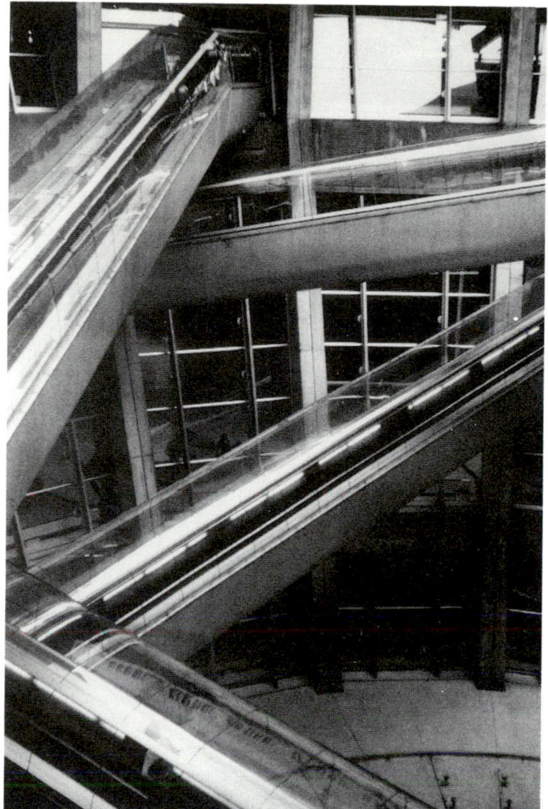

Figure 1.6

Transparent tubes at Charles de Gaulle airport, Paris

Source: Author's photograph

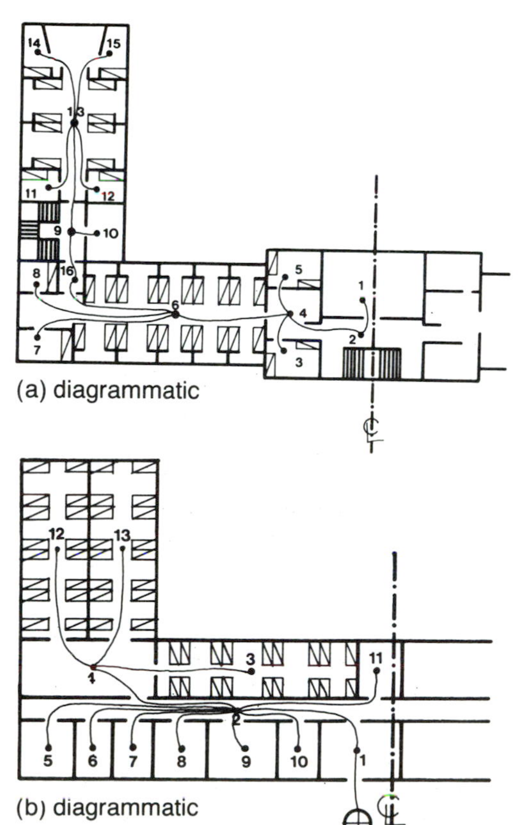

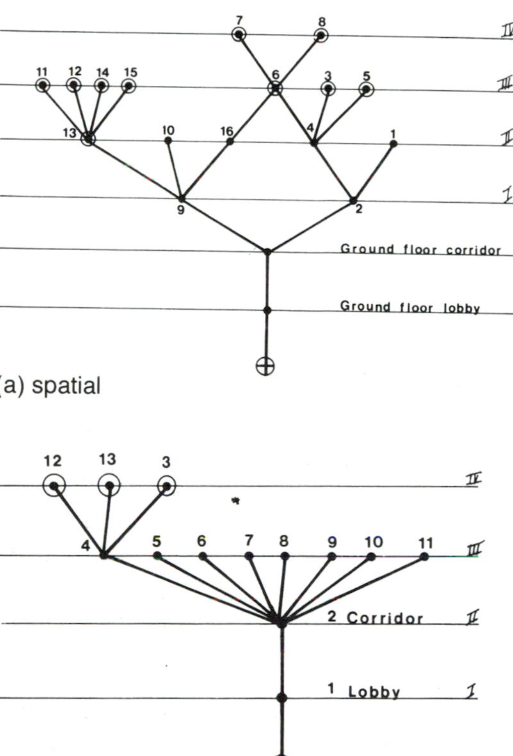

Figure 1.7

continued overleaf

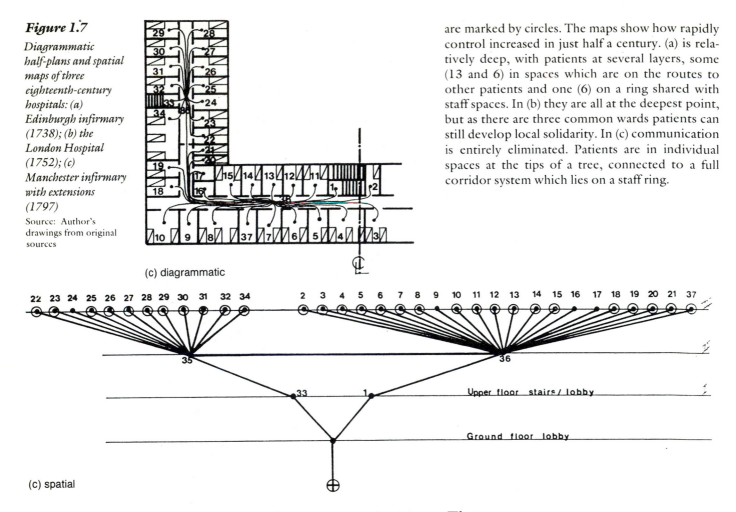

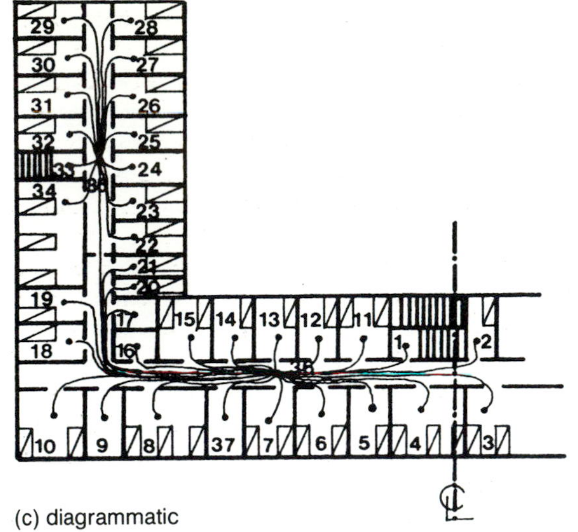

(c) diagrammatic

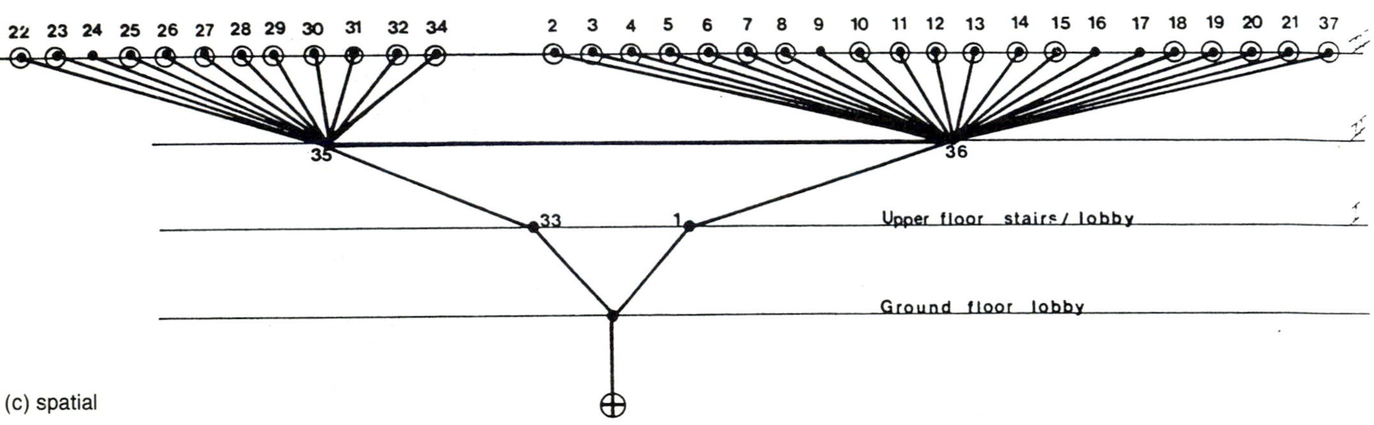

(c) spatial

Figure 1.7 *Diagrammatic half-plans and spatial maps of three eighteenth-century hospitals: (a) Edinburgh infirmary (1738); (b) the London Hospital (1752); (c) Manchester infirmary with extensions (1797)*

Source: Author's drawings from original sources

surface, only one step from space 1, so that it is located in the shallow outer zone. Also shown, by dotted lines, are visibility links. The overlaying of permeability and visibility defines surveillance.

Bridges and galleries, like the Bridewell tunnel, achieve topological adjacency which is impossible on one plane. Besides giving increased control as at Edinburgh, they can impose strict limits on the spaces used by the visitors which, formally, look misleadingly free. The tube-like cage which links prison galleries to the open hall is such a device, as are the tubes through which passengers in the Charles de Gaulle airport in Paris are moved between specific inlet and outlet points across the open central hall (Figure 1.6). The apparent freedom of the plan is negated by a transparent straightjacket. The contradiction is between an expectation aroused by form and the spatial reality.

My second example consists of three eighteenth century hospitals (Figure 1.7). In formal terms these are all 'U's. Spaces with patient beds are marked by circles. The maps show how rapidly control increased in just half a century. (a) is relatively deep, with patients at several layers, some (13 and 6) in spaces which are on the routes to other patients and one (6) on a ring shared with staff spaces. In (b) they are all at the deepest point, but as there are three common wards patients can still develop local solidarity. In (c) communication is entirely eliminated. Patients are in individual spaces at the tips of a tree, connected to a full corridor system which lies on a staff ring.

The text

The role of language in functional classification and typology has been and will be discussed. But there are more general points to be made about texts.

Although prescriptive texts were quite abbreviated up to the eighteenth century, the richness of language about space more than compensated for this. Space became a metaphor for social relations. Bender (1987) sees Defoe's description of London and especially the extraction of victims of the Great Plague from their shuttered houses into special plague houses, as part of the general move towards orderly segregation, surveillance and control which prefigured the vast penitentiary. Fielding's *Jonathan Wild* explores the power of the written record. Under the pose of public benefactor Wild earns a vast fortune as a fence of stolen property and by using his sophisticated written index collects bounties for successfully bringing criminals to book. It is just such a record of past crime that Fielding the magistrate proposed to combine with a vast classified prison to be a model city of good order, where correction of the body went hand in hand with correction of the mind. Varey's (1990) study of Defoe, Fielding and Richardson shows how space, whether of Crusoe's desert island or Clarissa's chamber, is a metaphor for changing property relations, domination by breaking down privacy (in Clarissa's case leading ultimately to her rape) and social control.

Language like this was disappearing. The loss was symmetrical. The texts about society become a-spatial and those about buildings became a-social. The Penitentiary Act of 1779 was a late survivor at a turning point, the moment when building programmes were about to become narrow technical instruments.

This Act, which became so seminal an influence on prison design, first sets out how the prisons should serve as alternatives to transportation through solitary confinement, labour and religious instruction. Others would be deterred, and the offenders would be 'reformed' and 'inured to habits of industry'. It then prescribes the site in terms of healthiness, water supply and distance from densely built-up urban areas, followed by a schedule of accommodation and requirements for exercise yards, workrooms and surveillance. All this is seamlessly interwoven with issues about finance, appointment of staff and official visitors, and the daily régime of work, worship and exercise. Building prescription and moral intention are almost one. This way of speaking came from an experience in which form and space were organic components of relations. As technical or artistic matters became separated from social issues, the very consciousness of buildings became thinner.

Prescriptions are not always written texts. Savignat's (1980) study of drawing techniques traces verbal (*parole*) and graphic representation of buildings to two different traditions. The former is that of the intellectual and scientist working with abstractions; the latter that of the practical craftsman and builder, working with concrete material. The development of drawings into elaborate artistic creations marks a loss of control by architects over the functional programme of buildings, which was taken over by scientists, politicians and intellectuals. Architects were reduced to dressing up (*habillage*) of the forms demanded by others' rational-functional briefs. The drawing became as remote from life as did the text.

But prescriptive drawings work in reverse by adding covert symbolic statements where overt verbal ones might be unacceptable. The report *Dwellings for the Working Classes* (1918) lavishly illustrated a range of plans to solve the post-war shortage, where the kitchens (a word that appears nowhere in the text) and sculleries are often adjacent to the bath, copper and wash-house. Unlike the text, the plans make explicit the role of women as manual workers in what is called the 'domestic workroom'. The more recent Scottish health centre design guide (1973) shows a wash-basin on the plan of every space where patients come into contact with staff, including the social workers' office/interview rooms. This reads as a sign for ritual purification of the pollution which occurs wherever there is contact.

Design guides prescribe not for a building but for a type. They originate in the type plans described by Alberti and the Renaissance authors, and drawn in treatises such as Blondel's *Cours* (1771–7) and Durand's *Précis* (1802–9). Durand's *Recueil* (1801) was an important contribution to the other tradition in illustrated prescription – that which uses existing specimens as exemplars. The two traditions often merged, as in the various editions of Guadet's monumental work. To decode such graphical statements requires techniques for analysing the projections used (orthographic or three-dimensional, including perspective), scale, weight and gradations of lines, use of shadows both for emphasis and for obscuring detail, representation of materials (e.g. stone joints) and the use of scales, grids and dimensions. This has not yet been attempted and I have no scope for it here.

Graphic 'texts' classify things just as do written ones and specifications, computer programs and Bills of Quantities. The principles of classification are the rules used for deciding similarity and dissimilarity.

This is a key topic in the social and natural sciences, linguistics and the history of ideas for such language classifications encapsulate power structures, ideas, practices and beliefs. It is reasonable to regard buildings as material classifying devices; they organise people, things and ideas in space so as to make conceptual systems concrete. And the classes are established in the texts.

For many tasks a durable taxonomy is a *sine qua non* because a large number of people or objects have to be arranged into classes and disposed in space in accordance with a social practice based on a theory. The division of children into classes according to age, gender, level of attainment or

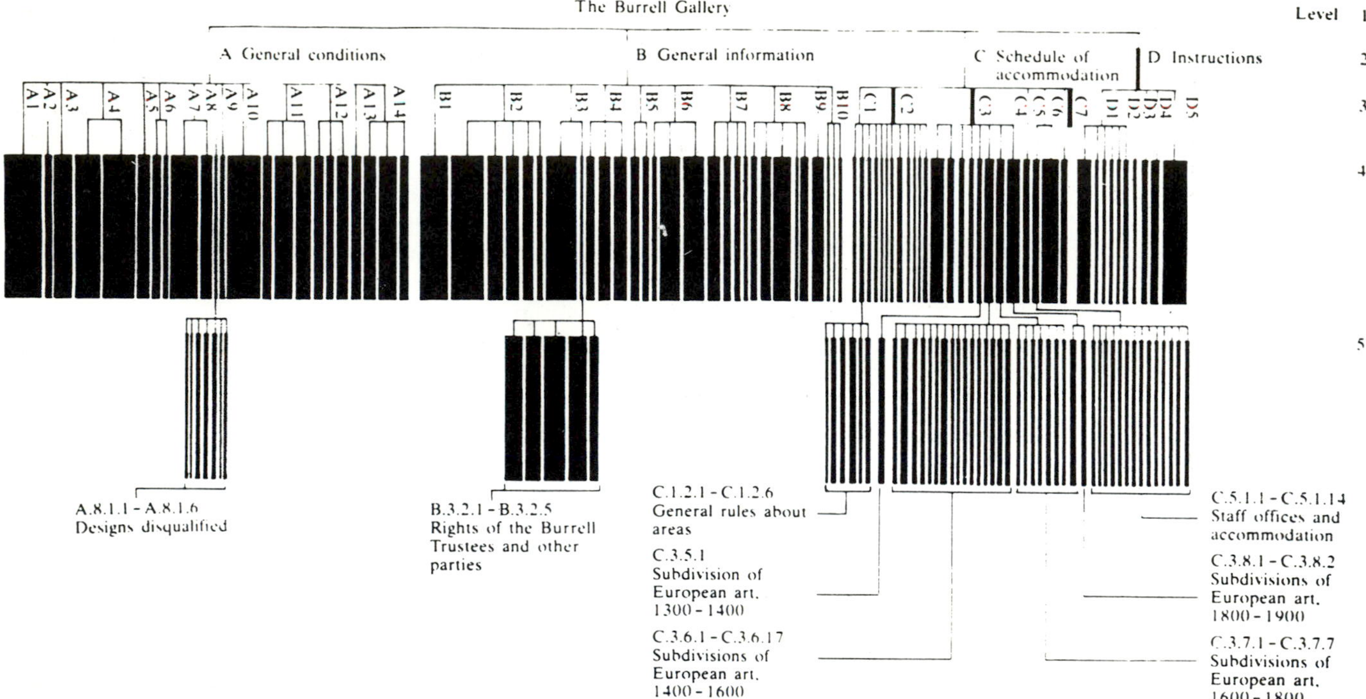

Figure 1.8

The structure of the brief for the Burrell Gallery (1970)

Source: Author's drawing based on original by Salman Othman redrawn for *Environment and Planning B: Planning and Design* (1987) 14: 474, by permission of *Environment and Planning B: Planning and Design* and of Salman Othman

subject of study, and their location in 'classrooms' according to pedagogic rules, is an overt statement of educational philosophy. The classification of patients and the relation of their spaces to those of hospital staff translates medical theory into practice; the grouping of art or museum objects is a spatial mapping of artistic or scientific theory.

Such theories are implicit in briefs. The 1970 competition brief for Glasgow's Burrell Gallery determined basic features which each of the 242 entries possessed. Figure 1.8 is a representation of the brief where each section and its subdivisions are shown at a different level according to the hierarchy of headings, sub-headings and paragraphs. At each level the volume of text is represented by the area of a block. It is clear at a glance that some sections not only penetrate deeper, but are larger than others. Length and depth of text are measures of elaboration and crude indicators of emphasis. Three sections reach to the deepest level.

A.8 sets out how designs are disqualified if they fail to meet other requirements of the brief. This is the 'gate' which operates as a meta-brief.

B.3 spells out the rights of the Trustees and other parties. The power of Burrell the collector is enshrined in legal form. It was to be made concrete by another requirement – that the main rooms of his home, Hutton Castle in Berwickshire, be reproduced. At the heart of the plan these three rooms present the essence of the founder's home, furnished as they had been in the Castle. In one powerful gesture they speak of the person, his idea of art and his wealth. Here visitors speak in awed whispers. Above all these rooms raise the history of the man, his collection and his home over the history of the objects which he collected from the immense space of the Far East, Near East and Europe over a time span which ranges from pre-history to the twentieth century. The choices were arbitrary and opportunistic. No place or time is essential. History, with the exception of the collector's own, became a pastime.

The only other part of the brief which descends to the deepest level are expansions of certain sections of European art, under C – Schedule of Accommodation. Despite the richness and splendour of the Chinese pottery and eastern carpets only the domestic product can be discriminated sufficiently to deserve this extra layer.

Text and diagram can combine into a spectacular prescription. William Stark's (1807) design for the Glasgow Lunatic Asylum was based on a brief which classified the patients by gender (men and women), economic class ('higher' and 'lower' rank – that is those who could pay and paupers) and medical condition ('Frantic', 'Incurable', 'Convalescent' and 'In an ordinary state'). These

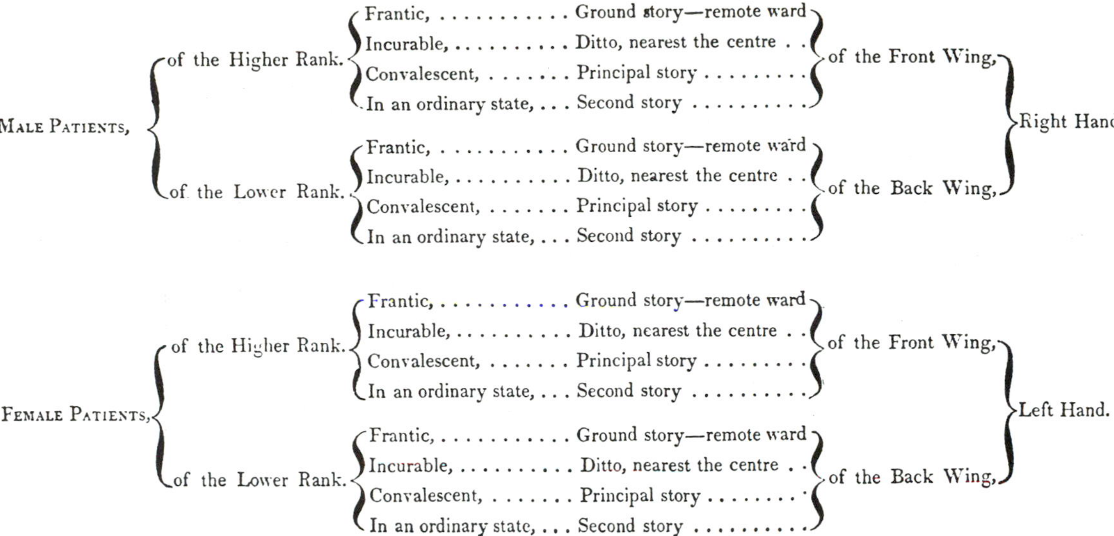

Figure 1.9

Classifications and spatial prescription for the Glasgow lunatic asylum (1807)

Source: Stark (1807), by permission of the Glasgow District Council, Mitchell Library

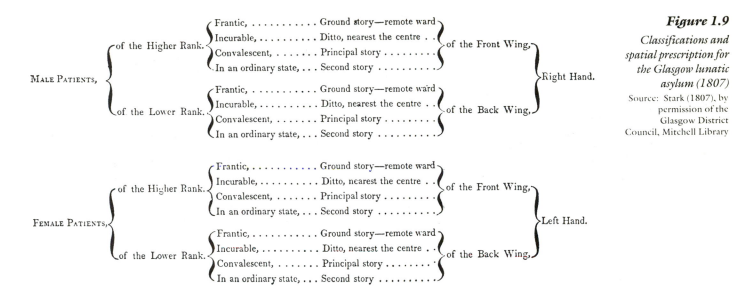

16 classes appear in the left of a diagram. The symmetrical right half locates each at a specified distance from the centre and a specified storey height (Figure 1.9). Class was directly mapped into space and form.

Peponis and Hedin's study (1982) of two galleries in London's Natural History Museum relates space to changes in theories of animal species. In that same museum some years ago a battle raged between adherents to cladistic theories of evolution and those who maintained a traditional line. The exact placing of key specimens was seen as so crucial that some curators risked their jobs by illicitly changing their location at night, in an attempt to subvert the official theoretical position.

Social relations as meanings

Some tools have been suggested for discovering the meaning, to the subject, of both text and building. If they are used, what kinds of meanings can we expect to find in the field of his or her social relations?

Buildings house bodies in space doing purposeful things; engaged in what look like material processes. We can see and touch buildings, and, above all, be in them. Taking part in a liturgical act, a legal trial or a concert is to be an actor in a material process. Whilst this is true as a basic description it would be totally inadequate to capture what is really going on were it not for the fact that 'liturgy', 'trial' and 'concert' are shorthands for events loaded with meaning. They tell us about whole sets of actors, responsibilities and power structures. They refer to religious belief and practice, abstract concepts of justice, and the skill in making, as well as the experience of listening to, music. That is they describe social relations which I have already described as being of two kinds – those of power and those of bonds. And both exist at three levels.

The first is that of the reflective individual. It may seem strange to include this in the sphere of the 'social'. It is that relationship of self-to-self which is behind Gauguin's age-old questions 'Who am I? Where am I going? Where have I come from?'. The second level of self-, or others-, to-others is the common meaning of 'social' – the entire web within which shared goals are achieved, where there is conflict for resources and power, and where institutions are created. But it is also germane to the first level for I discover myself in others. It is in speaking and listening to them that the internal dialogue is learnt.

The third level is of the self, or others, to the Other. This is not necessarily the mystical experience it was for Rat who, with his friend Mole in *Wind in the Willows* (Grahame 1950) follows the distant piping along the river. Its beauty arouses in him a 'longing … that is pain' towards his 'song-dream, the place the music played to me', a place of awe. When the dreamlike vision passes, Mole looks 'long and doubtfully at certain hoof-marks deep in the sward'. This Other is the cosmic world of natural forces and supernatural beings

Figure 1.10

Ninth-century plan of the monastery of St Gall

Source: Stiftsbibliotek St Gallen

found not only in all good children's stories but in all history. Sometimes it is like Rat's explicitly numinous experience; at others it is about the state, reason, nature, science, art or language. For Marx exploitative production methods resulted in alienation at each of these three levels – from self, from others and from nature (an 'Other' with material evidence for its existence, and hence admissible within a materialist perspective). And in buildings we constantly meet reference to such Others as divine or human order, justice, purity, fertility and death.

Our imagined 'case' hinted at each of these levels.

Power has to do ultimately with resources. Since these are finite the only freedom is to divide them in different proportions. It is the cake-slicing operation – more here is less there – so beloved of operational research scientists in their zero-sum games. Its results are seen in hierarchical structures, control, surveillance, decision processes and in differential consumption. In the design and use of buildings, power can be evenly distributed, or concentrated so as to create great asymmetries.

The monastic community had its formal structure. Inside the monastery church the roles of its members was signified by spatial location and by differences in the amount of space allocated, in the elaboration of furnishings, in seeing and being seen by others, and in entrances and circulation routes. At the apex of the pyramid was the abbot, deriving authority from external relationships of church and state and ultimately from an invisible presence who was signified by iconographic signs. The location and design of the tombs continued these relationships beyond death. Closeness to the heart of things – the altar – was one important sign for both the living and the dead.

The most controlled members of a monastic community were the sick and the young. The plan of the ninth century monastery of St Gall (Figure 1.10) fixes their lowly position. The infirmary and school are in the deepest part of the spatial structure, aligned with, and symmetrically disposed on either side of, the cosmic axis of the abbey church. Each of these two small cloisters has its own focal altar astride the same axis.

In the courthouse analogous features define the entire legal process: the judge at the apex, the state giving him authority in the name of invisible Justice which is signified in formal, functional and spatial features.

In the concert hall there is no doubt about the roles of conductor, players, organisers and audience. They are clear even to the uninitiated through the dedication of specific spaces, their sequence, imagery, lighting and furnishings. The validation and resourcing of such cultural productions is however not evident from the building; this, ultimate, source of power is revealed by printed materials (programme notes, tickets and posters) and by general knowledge about culture which is shared by performers and audience. It originates outside – as does the power of the church and the legal system – it is trans-spatial.

That source determines how the concert hall, or any building, comes into being. Someone controls the necessary resources – land, raw materials, products, tools, machines and labour, or money to purchase them. It is usually the largest investment anyone makes.

Possession of resources is power so it also purchases the freedom to appoint designers, set the terms of their employment, write the brief and select competition judges. The same groups create the rules by which the building is managed. They are formative in making building legislation, in the education of the professionals and in the provision of their institutions. The brief will be couched in their language which scholars, critics and publishers adopt. The styles of both writing and building are of those of these groups.

Because of the inevitable link between resources and power, and their highly asymmetrical distribution, to build means to create asymmetries. The moral critique of society and its buildings is justice which can measure the degree of equity in the distribution of resources and power.

But it is not as simple as that. Groups compete for power. There are counter- and sub-cultures, conflicts and shifts in its distribution. There will be 'subversive' elements in the practice of professionals and scholars. This complexity is present in buildings and their texts. A critique in terms of power has to be based on an analysis which takes this complexity on board. Some meanings are quite obvious; others, as our 'case' showed, have to be teased out.

The forms are not autonomous; tracing their origins in patronage, education, and the published texts, far from somehow explaining them away or diminishing their emotional impact, will disclose a lot that enriches experience.

Beyond what I have just said about monasteries, lawcourts and concerts there is no need to elaborate for the moment how power is visible in functions.

In space, relations of power are ever-present. Depth, asymmetries and tree-like or ringy forms control interfaces between people, and between them and objects such as museum exhibits. Haussmann's intervention in Paris involved primarily the transformation of its traditional space. Hillier and Hanson (1984: 155–63) have shown how the conversion of Victorian working class housing by today's middle class involves little change in visible forms. The estate agents' brochures will pick up double glazing and central heating but not the transformation of space by the creation of

Figure 1.11
Auschwitz, entrance gate and plan

(a)

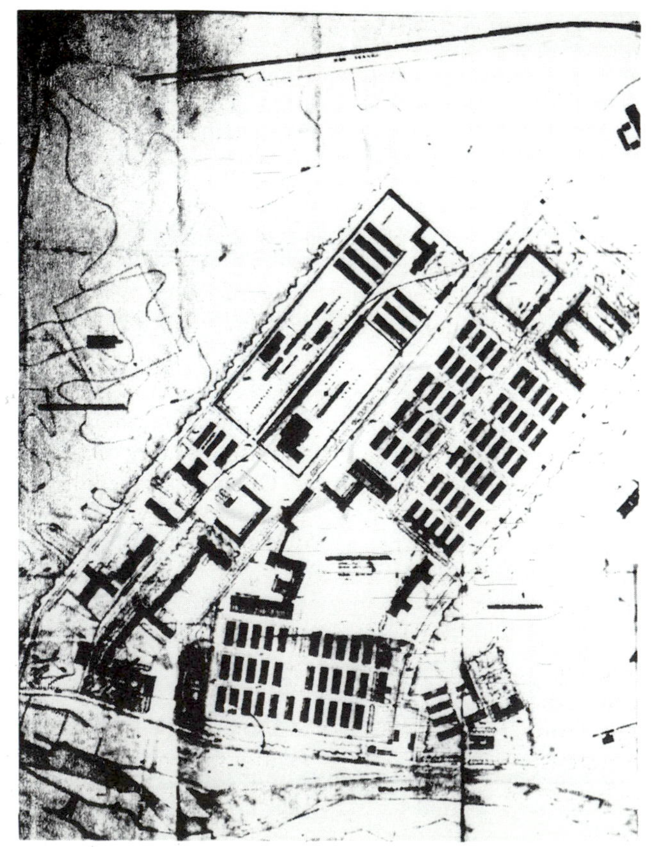

(b)

new permeabilities and elimination of old ones by opening up and blocking off doorways. If space is mentioned it is in terms of technical improvement, status or convenience. But both seller and buyer instinctively know how it creates new interfaces between the household and its visitors, and new family relations in terms of child-rearing or housework.

Though power is so clear in all these formal, functional and spatial strategies, the other kind of relation, of bonds, always accompanies it. As Gorz (1989) implies, it is its exact opposite with the strange property that instead of being about distributing finite resources – cake-slicing – the stronger the identity of the self, or the relationship between two people or within a group, the more there is to share. In personal relationships it is called love or friendship and we look to poets or theologians to speak of it. In politics it is called solidarity. It is paradoxical in another way too. For whilst it ties people by a unity of interest, it liberates. These relations survive, even flourish, in the most oppressive situations. The struggle for justice generates bonds.

Such ideas are not abstractions. They are crucial for building design. Besides materialising through the life of the body, the chief way in which power and bond relations are made concrete is through bodies in space; in the space of buildings and towns.

We have looked at those things about buildings which make power concrete. It is the same things (there *are* no others) which express, give room for, sustain, deny or produce bond relations. Images can symbolise them. Functions can be based on open-ended, easy-to-redefine briefs and rules which accommodate changing roles and activities as the spirit moves the occupants, with neither organisational nor material barriers. Spaces can be so linked that communication is free and frequent, making possible dense encounters between classes, groups and individuals. These are the basis for community, friendship and solidarity. The alternative is controlled movement, under surveillance, for narrowly defined purposes of production, or only for such basic biological needs as eating, sanitation or escaping from fire. A place can be designed for discovery of both the self and others.

So in reality buildings always have double meanings in making concrete both power and bonds. Any building which satisfied the deepest longings for both justice and the creation of bonds would be a 'heavenly mansion'. It would house the structure-less, power-less societies envisaged by both Marxists and Christians in visions so central to the Western tradition. A place for a community of love where State, class, marriage, the Church and all human institutions had withered away, to make possible totally just and unalienated relations. This vision inspired utopian writers and designers. Both strands, the just society and the loving community, are present in their work. Thomas More set the pattern for the first and William Morris's (1891) *News from Nowhere* is the most lucid expression of the second.

Primo Levi's (1962) profound observation of life in a Dystopia, Auschwitz, is evidence of how people can always form bond relations, subverting even the most oppressive institutions and their buildings. One might then be tempted to say that this project of searching for meanings, with all its attendant practical and theoreatcial difficulties, does not really matter.

Before giving way to that temptation it is worth taking a closer look. The entrance gates (Figure 1.11) announce 'Freedom through work' – a startling re-statement of the ideology of the Industrial Revolution. In reality production was not just *associated* with disease, deformity and early death; death itself was its goal. For all the world this looked like a pavilion hospital. The contradiction between the rhetoric of the gate and the hospital plan on the one hand and the reality of the process on the other has other architectural analogues. We saw one earlier – the contradiction between freedom and constraint in the tunnels penetrating into open space. Later we will meet another – Jean Genet's representation of the prison which gives its inmates the illusion of a palace. The most shattering experience is when the contradiction is between function and the agonising beauty of a city or building.

One way of reading Levi is indeed that bonds are *in*dependent of oppressive power structures. But that would be a terrible mistake. For what he describes is the incalculable price which had to be paid for the creation of bonds in a system which used buildings as a key instrument. To a lesser degree all but the most fortunate few pay a price in their daily built environment. That is the true measure of the *inter*dependence of buildings and relations, and a good reason for pursuing the search for meaning in buildings.

Types of discourse

Despite the evident social role of buildings the boundaries of architectural discourse are drawn so as to exclude it. Buildings are treated as art, technical or investment objects. Rarely as social objects. Why?

First, are there hopeful signs? Frampton, Vidler, Girouard and Fortier have all broken new ground from within achitectural scholarship; Lefebvre, King, Hillier and Hanson and Eco[3] from outside. But we are a long way yet from generally accepted social theories about buildings. Some architects have used such work in their practice when it gives intellectual spine to contentious proposals. Otherwise it has barely influenced the way architects think, speak and design or the perceptions of their public.

More connected to social history is the work which goes under the title of 'building types'. Pevsner (1979), Rosenau (1970), Seaborne (1971), Thompson and Goldin (1975), Evans (1982) and Jetter (1966–72) have given immensely detailed accounts of hospitals, markets, prisons, schools, public buildings and factories which place them in their technical, legal and political contexts. But they remain largely descriptive and types are seen as the results of these forces rather than generators of social change. King's (1980) seminal introduction to a collection of essays made the dual proposition that the study of buildings is one way to understand society and the study of society one way to understand buildings. The physical structures are translations on the ground of models in the actors' heads with all the social forces present in that model. His work is not esoteric; it is clearly written, often challenging and always insightful. Why has it not effected a bigger change?

An answer is indicated in the one type where there is a tradition of placing buildings into a social context. Housing in its settlement patterns is a central theme in anthropology, archeology and sociology. But how would one relate an anthropological study like Bourdieu's (1971) of the Berber house, Muthesius's (1982) of terrace housing, Bentmann and Müller's (1975) of patterns of domination in the Venetian villa and Ball's (1983) of economic power and housing policy? There is no framework for bringing these together. And without it the concept of society being both a producer and a product of housing remains primitive.

This is all very strange when one considers the treatment of two related kinds of objects: works of art and obviously utilitarian products.

For works of art, especially literature, film and painting, an established and growing body of work examines the role of society in their production and in the formation of the viewer or reader. Wolff's (1981) review highlights the contributions of Weber, Durkheim, Williams, Goldmann, Eagleton and Berger. Though some idealist criticism of their work has merely caricatured it to create straw men to be knocked down, there are indeed sound reasons for challenging those base (means of production) and superstructure (ideology, religion, law, education and consciousness) theories which share the determinist standpoint of one-way formative forces. The work as well as the responding subject are merely the helpless, passive end-products of social processes. Eagleton (1976) calls this 'vulgar Marxism'. Neither was given the right to a 'lifeworld' meaning, as if to grant them an active, formative role would undermine the effect of material and historical reality.

But modern theories of cultural materialism have come a long way in exploring how artists, their work and their audience form society as well as being formed by it. Certainly what is produced, what survives in the market (the galleries, the libraries, publishing houses, television studios), the dominant styles, the techniques chosen, the effects of education, the availability of resources and the role of the media are all outcomes of social forces. But these theories also recognise that artists and their audiences act upon society, and that they share non-constituted inner realities.

This kind of theory has barely affected architecture. Historians and art critics dealing with the creative arts have excluded architecture. For instance Hobsbawm (1971) in describing methods for transforming social history into the history of society, 'which is still being constructed', included literature – together with anthropology, sociology, political science and religion – as a field which would help in this transformation, but not architecture. Things have not changed in the intervening years; Timms and Collier (1988) list 'poets, painters, theorists, dramatists and film directors', but not architects, as 'not only radical artistic innovators (but the) cultural "avant-garde" helping to bring about – through the medium of art – a fundamental reorientation of society' (though one essay on *de Stijl* does touch on architecture). How is it that both the historians and the critics of art and society deny buildings the power to transform society?

The most solid architectural scholarship is produced by those who *do* view architecture as art, in a tradition stretching from Burckhardt, Wölfflin, Gombrich and Wittkower to Summerson, Rykwert and Pevsner. Scholarly and creative as this is, social forces are marginal in their analyses. In the hands of Scruton (1979) and Watkin (1980) there is even an attack on such attempts.

A surprising situation has therefore come about. Those social historians or critics – radical as they may be – who see an intimate connection between art and society, have left architecture out in the cold. Those architectural historians and critics who treat buildings *as* art objects, have left society out in the cold. What is the origin of this symmetrical silence? If these disciplines do not explain the link between buildings and society, which will do so?

Utilitarian products such as the machinery of the first Industrial Revolution, agricultural implements, weapons, computers, cars and domestic equipment have been widely studied as parts of social systems. The few architectural studies of this kind are invariably of vernacular housing. A perspective of buildings as merely utilitarian objects is as narrow as that which treats them as art. But nevertheless it is surprising that studies of material culture and anthropology have barely treated buildings, apart from houses, as parts of the social system.

Even if buildings were merely hybrids between art and utilitarian objects, why do those who study them not adopt the social analysis which is so strongly present in the parent fields? But buildings are not a hybrid; they form a unique category. There is no other class of object which through the production of material forms purposefully organises space and people in space.

The answer to my questions began to emerge at the begining of this century through an insight which came from a surprising source – mainstream German idealism whose architectural historians held that the truths embodied in a building are in its forms, and that these truths exist whether an observer is there to experience them or not. Moreover though the forms were produced at a historical moment, their meaning was, and would remain, universal and accessible for all time to intelligent and sensitive subjects. This permanently embedded 'truth' was the entire content of the form. It is Germany, and Wölfflin's name in particular, that we associate with this view. Although before Wölfflin, Semper (1860–63) had already foreshadowed the idea of material technology, functional needs and social forces as generative in architecture, we owe a radical restatement of the tradition to one of Wölfflin's most brilliant pupils.

Paul Frankl (1914) extended the theory to encompass 'purposive intention', expressed in the 'functional program' (*sic* – an American translation of the German *bauprogramme* and English *brief*). 'A history of building programs is part of cultural history'; such a 'program ... is a bridge between art and life' (Frankl 1914: 160). The meaning of a building cannot be unravelled without analysis of the 'program' which arises from 'purpose'. 'Insofar as purpose is the essence of architecture, architecture is its (i.e the purpose's) manifestation'. A spectator confronted by a (functionally) obsolete building, 'without historical knowledge' sees 'in its great display of artistic forms ... mere ornament' (1914: 158). Frankl defines a building as a 'theatre of human activity' which, when empty, becomes a 'mummy' for 'people *are part of architecture*' (1914: 159: my emphasis).

Frankl's message is revolutionary in placing function centrally into an analysis of meaning together with spatial composition, the treatment of mass and surface, and the use of light, colour and optical effects. These last three put him in advance of the conventions. But eventually Frankl fails to pursue the full consequences of his insight. He recognises that people's activity in a building, prescribed by a brief and recovered through historical analysis of this 'program', is something specific to its place and time – that is, its history. It involves studying 'change in social expression' (1914: 160). But, since, in secular buildings at least, 'individual purposes are created by the needs of everyday life, it is obvious that they have their undisturbed continuity' (1914: 191). This can be understood in one of two ways.

Either these functional needs of everyday life have a 'continuity' unchanged by history except in their accidents. In that case the idealist argument has been transferred from form to function; functions have become universal, a-historical phenomena which are permanent and unalterable. As we know them in daily life they are shadowy versions of some pure archetypes and they are embedded once and for all in a building; given adequate evidence all observers, for all time, will recognise and respond to them.

Or, according to the alternative implication, these functions, or 'purposes' become transformed into architecture only because of intention (a key concept which Frankl acknowledges as originating with Burckhardt and Wölfflin). 'It is the practical and material certainty of purpose that determines the building program and hence the spatial form, but only intention gives purpose to its artistic character' (Fankl 1914: 161). Without intention, there is no artistic form, and without artistic form there is no architecture. And artistic form has already been defined in idealist terms. So the link between function and form is internal to the work of architecture and is also immutable; it hinges on the intention of the creator (or producer). But since this can never be known, Frankl one way or the other finally betrays his insight into the formative role of function. But his view is nevertheless of great significance and prepares the way for another analysis.

If Frankl looks 'out there', beyond history, for the source of meaning in both forms and functions, the consequence, which he recognises, is that the relation between them is also 'out there', and history is relegated to an unavoidable enabling process in which immutable truths materialise. But if we give history a formative role, we will then find 'in here' the source of the relation between form and function. A given form can be used for any function and, *vice versa*, a given function can take on any form. The relation is not contingent or immutable but the outcome of the specific historical narrative in which we, when we arrive, have a place too. Without rigorous analysis, several generations have discovered this and intuitively rejected Louis Sullivan's version of Frankl's theory. The surprise is that Frankl, so imaginative and daring in other ways, ever propounded it. One of my tasks is to carry on where he left off.

CHAPTER 2

Why can we use buildings?

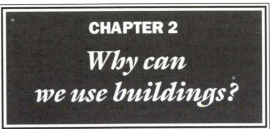

Dream places and real places

In a recent newspaper article on good eating (Flynn 1989: 22) the food correspondent described a newly re-opened Edinburgh restaurant housed in a re-furbished '... large white roadhouse glowing with neon like a glitzy ocean liner that has slipped its moorings in Miami's *Art Déco* district and sailed into the wrong port ... (sitting) incongruously alongside the suburban semis and (a) car-choked roundabout'. Its interior is '... a breathtaking example of Thirties Americana gone stunningly mad – miles of chrome, leaping statuettes, scooped lights, sunburst motifs galore.' The piece was striking in three ways.

First, in the full article the discussion of the building comes before that of the food. Secondly comments on the building, apart from noting the incongruity of its location, refer entirely to its *Art Déco* style. And thirdly there is no comment on the even more bizarre incongruity mentioned in passing, that besides the restaurant and bars, the building houses a ballroom, a cinema and a chapel. What do we call it? How do we know what to do when we get there? (The architects for the original 1930s scheme were apparently thrown out of their professional body for taking part in property development [*Architects' Journal* 1989: 6]; if only it had been for creating an incomprehensible building.)

Like the 'case' of our church-turned-courthouse which was originally part of the monastic complex, the Renaissance town palace – of which Frankl cites the Palazzo Medici in Florence as an example – was a functionally integrated whole with '... private living rooms, rooms in which the patron conducts his business, guest rooms, housekeeping rooms, stables, store rooms, chambers for the servants, and a private chapel' (Frankl 1914: 165). It caters for a multitude of uses but:

> not one of these is predominant. All the individual purposes appear to be equal aspects of the main purpose. The building is intended to absorb evenly the life of the patron in all its complexitiy ... (with) a coordination of purposes .... The purposes of individual rooms should correspond to the actual activities of the inhabitant; the reality of life
>
> (Frankl 1914)

by which he means the social reality of Renaissance Florence. Functions of individual spaces could be understood because the relations between them were meaningful. Why is the twentieth century complex of restaurant, bar, ballroom, cinema and chapel not like the monastery or palace?

In the Aboriginal Dreaming place the mental pictures made sense of the material reality. As in the monastery and the Florentine palace, but not the Edinburgh roadhouse, invisible structures gave meaning to what was visible. Of course it is easy to grasp at a glance the basic material process of, say, eating. But this individual biological need can equally well be satisfied in a dining room, college hall, station snack bar, pub, canteen, restaurant, night club or at a beach picnic. In each of these not only is there is a different relation between the eaters, but between them as consumers and the providers of food. These differences are not trivial – they explain who eats there, with whom, what is the nature of the contract between the producers and consumers, how the food is acquired, stored, cooked and served, and how the shared eating, as a sign, forms part of wider relations of family, study, military service, entertainment or travel. This is even more evident in meals devoid of biological purpose – whose *raison d'être* is to work as signs within religious rites.

We distinguished the social reality behind each of these eating places by using appropriate labels which could have been further elaborated; 'military mess' or 'student cafeteria' are both forms of 'canteen'. Such words place the activity into its social context; they form parts of ordinary function-language. And they signify both a kind of place and a kind of use, often so much so that the same word, 'choir' and 'court of law' (already mentioned), or 'chapel' and 'school', refer to both institutions and buildings.

It is possible to tear the actual activity and its space out of context, but one cannot do this with the words. They resist, and remain firmly context-bound. Con-text precisely describes this – the word within the text created by a language-using community. It is not hard to imagine what goes on in a school classroom. The identical space in a railway station or an art gallery would leave us at a loss to know either what the space or the entire complex is about. As long as there is no word for it, that is as long as function-language cannot cope, we cannot feel at home.

'Material process' is not only one in which some material substance is transformed. Ritual enactment of a liturgy in a church or dramatic enactment of a system of justice in a lawcourt are as 'material' as the cooking, serving and eating of food, in that these too occur in space defined by material boundaries, containing material objects, and, above all, containing bodies. The eating places, like 'church' or 'lawcourt', acquire meaning only through the relations they represent. Of course the practical requirements of any material process have to be satisfied, otherwise we are not dealing with a building at all, though it might still qualify as a piece of sculpture.

So what is this experience of use? The most direct is when we are actors. Less directly, we may have to read intentions into the actions of others whom we merely observe. That needs knowledge of things beyond what is evident, since intentions are invisible. It is easy to make mistakes about the meaning of what goes on in a strange culture or new situation.

If even observation is impossible the task becomes one of deduction from material evidence such as furniture, equipment and objects like books, machines or computers, and labels on rooms. In archeology such artefacts as tools, hearths or clay tablets – functional evidence *per se* – are used for decoding the social relations of use. But there are two other pieces of information essential for archeological reconstruction: the forms of the building and the organisation of its space. The shape and size of rooms, the way axes link them, the materials used, the decorative treatment of walls and floors, and any carvings or paintings (the iconographic programme) are all strong formal clues. And the way the building is entered, the permeability of one space to another, the way indoor and outdoor spaces are linked are all strong spatial clues. Given enough evidence of form, found artefacts and space, the use, that is the meaning, of the entire complex and all its individual spaces is discovered.

In Chapter 1 I adopted form, function and space as the basis for analysis. It now turns out that archeologists do just that. It is true that we may have other evidence such as texts, drawings and photographs which they lack. But it does suggest that decoding a building is unconscious archeology.

A discussion of use, and the function-language which describes it, now needs to be set into the theoretical framework outlined in the previous chapter. Three domains of society-in-history were identified: social practices, social relations and the subject. I suggested that people ('subjects') discover and create meanings in social relations, and that these form and are formed by their social practices – the things they do together. Designing and producing buildings are social practices. So is the writing of texts about them. The most universal social practice, characteristic of human beings everywhere, is the creation and use of language, involved in all other practices and hence in the establishment of all relations. It lies at the heart of meaning, and is therefore central to the question of what buildings mean.

A building's form, function and space each has meanings in the field of social relations, each is capable of signifying who we are, to ourselves, in society and in the cosmic scheme of things. And each speaks of both power and bond relations. This is readily seen in function and space, but less so in form. The meanings of forms are carried in two ways. First, beyond the obvious cases of Imperial eagles, Christian crosses, or IBM logos, we associate certain architectural forms with certain functions as a result of long experience.

How such association works is discussed below. But secondly forms carry meanings directly, they work as metaphors for relations. This enables all art, in Eliot's words, to be 'a raid on the inarticulate', to speak of things beyond the reach of everyday spoken language.

If a building in its totality carries a meaning it does so because the meanings of its individual discourses converge to a point in the domain of social relations. This point is located by everyday use and by everyday function-language created and shared by a using and speaking community. That such a point is unique to an individual is the result of their inner 'lifeworld'. But that it shares a common zone with others – so we can speak of a 'cloud' of points in this domain – is the result of belonging to a community.

Fu = function
Fo = form
Sp = space

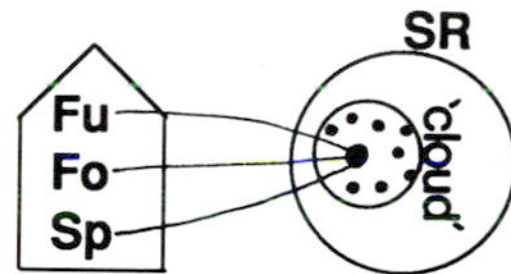

Up to about the middle of the eighteenth century the meanings of form, function and space converged in a regular and predictable way, without ambiguity. A town palace of the kind described by Frankl, a church, or a market had forms and spatial structures which were understood and accepted as appropriate for each of these uses. Enlightenment reason, the political upheavals of the American and French Revolutions, and the technical and social one of the Industrial Revolution fractured this stable world. Clients ceased to be a homogenous class. Architects came from different social backgrounds, and no longer necessarily shared language or class with clients. A whole range of formal solutions became possible: various versions of the Classical, Gothic, eclectic forms drawn from all kinds of sources, and even the high-tech 'non-style' of glass and iron. The traditional spatial structures were no longer reproduced without question. Above all the new social relations demanded all kinds of new types – created by aggregations of earlier ones, or disaggregation and specialisation.

In the former category some must have seemed as strange, in their day, as the Edinburgh roadhouse is today. The Theatre Royal in Plymouth (1811–19) was part of a complex which comprised a hotel, a ballroom, a club and an assembly room. The attached Athenaeum housed the Literary and Philosophical Society. What did its élite users make of it, what did they call it?

Equally puzzling were the novel types of the latter category – created by the opposite process of disaggregation and specialisation – as in the branching of the prison, hospital, school, asylum and workhouse from the pre-1834 poorhouse trunk. Whether puzzling or not, the ebb and flow of functional grouping lies at the core of architectural history. And all the time words evolve to describe new functions. Their study might be as germane as Darwin's taxonomies were to biology.

The new freedom which the fracture made possible worked in several ways, which are usefully considered through six historical cases which show how meaning changes – that is how it moves around in the domain of social relations.

The first case is the dramatic narrative of the church-courthouse-concert hall. Form and space, material properties, remained virtually unchanged. The shift of function to a new use, representing new social relations with new meanings, 'drags' form and space with it to a newly convergent point. The fact that the church may continue to carry echoes of the worshipping, liturgical community might serve a useful ideological purposes for the new State. But it is seen as a new place. The meaning of its forms and spaces is transformed and the word 'courthouse' adequately defines it.

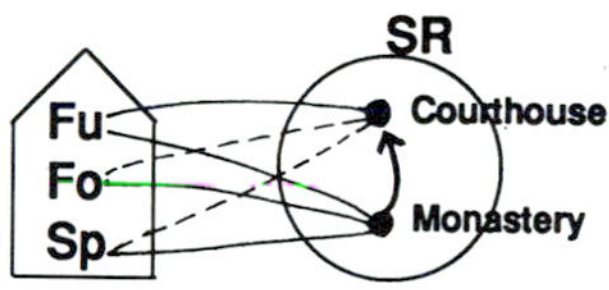

Prior to the eighteenth century the long tradition of Classical forms had made it adaptable to many places and for many uses. Soon this freedom became a feature of other formal languages. Existing medieval forms were not only adapted to a range of new uses, but inspired new, equally adaptable, versions (Gothic Revival). And as new formal languages developed, right up to twentieth century Modernism, they were seen as usable universally, for any function.

The freedom to design for a given use in many ways creates another 'cloud' in the domain of meanings. Just as a community of individuals can share meanings in a 'cloud', a given individual may assign a whole range of different buildings the same meaning, inside a 'cloud'. For instance we can read all kinds of buildings as a library.

The second case is that of another change of use in our period – this time accompanied by material changes too – the conversion of the ancient abbey of Fontevraud to a prison. When such a splendid building is used for a squalid or oppressive purpose, the meaning of its function may refuse to converge with that of its form and space. That is another way of saying we find it difficult or impossible to accept that this is a prison. There is a contradiction, which is measurable by the distance between two points in the domain of social relations. Things are not what they seem or feel to be. In extreme cases such a gap is sensed as bizarre or meaningless; in less extreme ones as simply puzzling and destroying the sense of feeling at home.

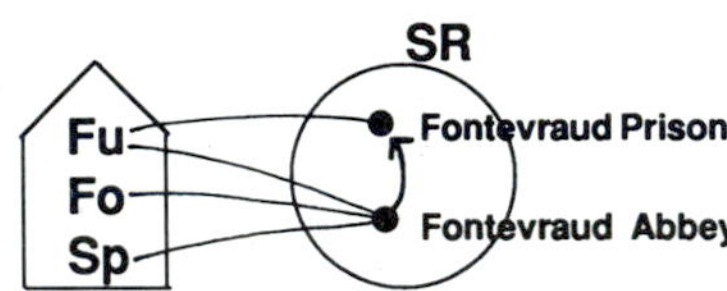

When someone's words, facial expression and gestures are contradictory we respond in much the same way. Modern drama has exploited such contradictions on stage, not as a model of what relations should be off-stage but as a way of probing what they are like in everyday life. There is certainly a need for such creative experiments in architecture; but once they are transported into the street – once the stage and the street become indistinguishable – everyday urban experience becomes alienating and bizarre, and the experiments cease to be of any significance.

In the third case, the power of form and space is used to redefine completely the meaning of a traditional function. The use of forms derived from the high-tech imagery of industrial buildings and machines, and spatial structures derived from the supermarket in the Sainsbury building at the University of East Anglia, makes it possible to redefine art objects as commodities in an industrial-market economy. In another case, the placing of a community of university scholars into a building with the deep, tree-like spatial structure of an institution, makes it possible, despite the rhetoric of creative intellectual freedom, to undermine the community's traditional function by introducing features associated with surveillance, control and absence of communication.

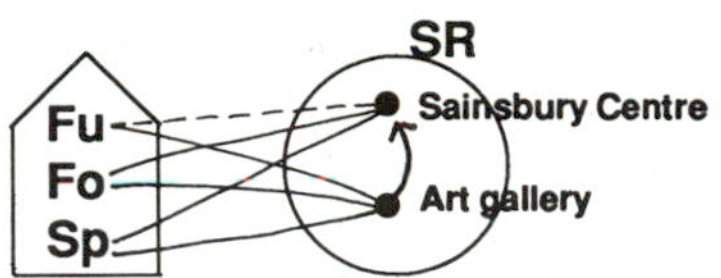

The danger of the new freedom is seen in this third case; it is precisely that such innovatory and often highly exhilirating designs do not *seem* to be contradictory; the buildings redefine social practices by assigning them new (and seemingly coherent) meanings which are hard to reject without analysis. Not surprisingly their sponsors work hard to block analysis. Of course the contradictions, whilst intentional, are not calculated. And neither are the three blocking strategies each, in a different way, focusing on the formal discourse.

One strategy, while rightly stressing the independence of the discourses, also insists on their autonomy. Venturi's (1966) 'complexities and contradictions' and Derrida's and Tschumi's 'deconstructions' (Derrida 1986: 65–75) are two recent attempts to make this theoretically respectable. The unease, the contradiction, dislocation and historical cannibalism are not seen as defects but as the authentic experience of post-industrial society. Form is autonomous, free of functional connotations. Function is trivialised to a technical-utilitarian definition which, since it is self-evident, can be contained within the boundary of 'architecture'. Neither needs analysis in social relations. But function-labels are still used.

Another insists that the form-function link still has the same strength, internal to architecture, as it possessed in the old tradition. Function is treated in the same way as in the first strategy and since this offers little scope for criticism of any depth – it is its concomitant, form, which absorbs critical energy.

The last strategy is to define architecture by the single, dominant and autonomous discourse of form. In architecture-as-art function effectively disappears.

In none of these strategies does space (in its structural sense) appear.

It is language that saves the day and prevents these three strategies from succeeding. In the first two, since the functional labels they still use are based on everyday speech and are parts of everyday language, they cannot fail to point to our social and 'lifeworld' relations. This undermines the trivial definitions of function as well as their autonomy. But the relations between the three discourses may appear so random that we may give up the struggle and simply learn to live with multiple, even contradictory meanings. Or we may cling, despite constant disappointments – despite things not being what they seem to be – to the promise which the second version holds out that the stable form–function link is still in place. The third version – that buildings are simply art objects – despite Prince Charles and the massive efforts of the profession, does not seem to carry conviction yet. Few people, if asked where they had been, would answer 'I was in a swirling Baroque space' or '… in a high-tech red cube' (shades of *Parc de la Villette*).

But to return to the cases, the fourth shows how meanings may become contradictory unintentionally. The destruction of the harmony of the Pazzi Chapel, which I have mentioned, for those who had lived through Mussolini's régime and his use of Classicism, may also have created for them a contradiction which simply cannot be eradicated. For that generation, the forms carry meanings which will never again converge with the meaning of a civilised use such as a school or a theatre.

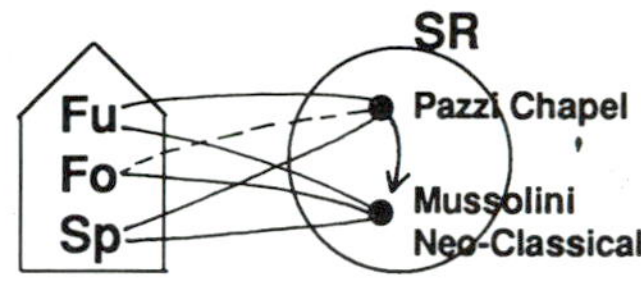

In the fifth case, a radically new function generates an equally new formal language and spatial structure. The meanings, astonishing as they are, converge, but in a new place in the domain of social relations. Something quite new is being said. We will see how the Crystal Palace did this for machinery, nature, art and labour relations.

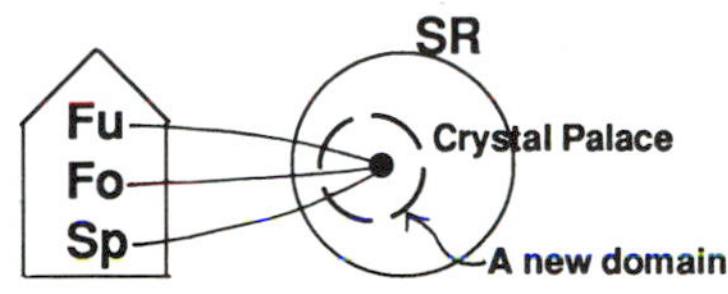

The new juxtaposition of two previously clear and unambiguous types represents the sixth, and final, case. The Classical or Gothic facade building hiding the engineering shed behind, which reached its epitome in St Pancras Station with Scott's French *chateau* hotel and station offices in front of Barlow's great shed, is an example. At first the combination was contradictory, non-convergent. But it came to be accepted as the very essence of the type 'railway station'; so much so that when, in the same year as the Crystal Palace was built, a rare case occurred where the shed was exposed at the front – Cubitt's King's Cross – *this* came to be seen as *a*typical. An accepted and comforting screen was stripped away. The contradiction here was not between two discourses, or two different types, but between one and an absence, a void.

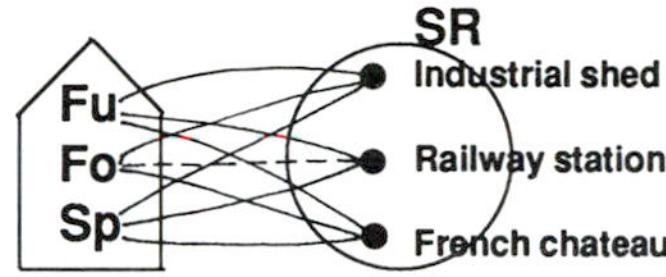

It should be clear that coherent meaning in a building is no guarantee that this will be a cause for rejoicing. We are as likely to discover oppressive or asymmetrical relations as ones which give us a dignified place in a just process, enlarge our 'lifeworld' or support the formation of bonds. All we have avoided is 'gibberish'; as with spoken language, there is no reason why the truth should be palatable.

Even if buildings have clear meanings, we need to be able to place each unique experience into some kind of framework, a structure which makes sense at a more general level. This is what 'type' does. Before finishing this chapter with a discussion of type, I want to look more closely at the particularly strong link between form and function before it broke up in the mid-eighteenth century.

Form and function

The form–function relation was taken for granted in the Renaissance. The range of functional types was small and patronage stable. Purpose was defined in unambiguous, elementary and unchanging terms. What happened in a lawcourt, theatre or market were a-historical 'givens' of justice, drama or exchange, formed in ancient times. 'Type' meant 'origin', archetype.

Theoretical works merely expanded on some linguistic aspects of function. For Alberti (1485, 1980) society was stratified and classified. Each class of people '... should have designated (for it) a different type of building', some suitable for 'society as a whole', others only for its 'foremost citizens' and yet others only for 'common people'. Buildings for each *stratum* were named. His tripartite stratification uncannily resembles Le Corbusier's (1925) division of the City for Three Million People: first, '... princes of affairs, captains of industry and finance, political leaders, great scientists ... ' and so on, who were to occupy the centre, '... the seat of power'; second, those whom David Hume would have called 'of the middling rank', who occupy intermediate zones, '... the workers whose lives are passed half in the centre and half in the (peripheral) garden cities'; and third '... the great masses of workers who spend their lives between suburban factories and garden cities' (Le Corbusier 1925: 100). But, unlike Alberti, Le Corbusier had to invent new urban forms for these classes.

When he came to expand this principle into detailed planning, Alberti (1980) elaborates on the country or town palace for his second class and discusses a few public buildings for the first. One is the basilica with its variety of forms. Its 'original role' is a 'covered assembly room where princes met to pronounce justice', with an apse, or 'tribunal' and porticos added to 'give it greater dignity'. So ancient use, linguistic labels and spatial articulation are linked in an archetype. Another is the theatre where Alberti distinguishes entertainment, artistic and sporting functions, each of which '... requires a different building ... each with a different *name* (my emphasis) such as 'theatre', 'circus' or 'amphitheatre'. Each has its characteristic plan form and appropriate vocabulary of the Orders.

In the mid-eighteenth century the plan was still of marginal interest. Diderot's *L'Encylopédie* article on 'Architecture' has plans for an abbey with its church, several town mansions and planning details for *salons* and their staircases. Under 'public buildings' he laments the lack of suitable examples of town halls, exchanges, libraries, markets, and hospitals. Extant ones are either in buildings designed for another purpose, or so old that they 'cannot serve either as exemplars or as authority'. Only a few fountains and triumphal arches live up to his expectations. He does pick one example, Carpentier's design for Rouen town hall, but illustrates it only with an elevation. Of the 24 plates added in 1776–7, three are devoted to Choquet de Lindu's *bagne* (discussed in Chapter 4) – a huge land-based prison with an integrated arsenal which originated in France's traditional galleys or hulks in the major ports, Brest in this case. It was probably its scale and novelty which caused him to include it as the sole example of non-sacred public planning.

Blondel made a last-ditch attempt (1771–7) to hold function and form in a fixed relation. Using a biological analogy, he spoke of *genres* of buildings, each with an appropriate *charactère*, such as 'male', 'frivolous', 'rustic', 'light', 'naive', 'terrible', 'uncertain', 'vague', 'masculine' or 'cold', achieved by expressive forms. The *genres* included factories, colleges, military buildings, hospitals, mints, baths, vauxhalls and fountains. Each achieved its 'own manner of being, suitable for it alone, or those of its kind' by pairwise matchings of a *genre* and a *charactère*. A few hundred words for each *genre* describe its major spaces and its outline form. But the six volumes of plates contain only plans for town and country mansions, churches and gardens. In contrast, suitable Orders for each *genre* are lavishly discussed and profusely illustrated.

The neo-Classical architects extended this concept to an *architecture parlante*, speaking through allegorical and metaphorical forms. A familiar example is Boullée's Palace of Justice sitting on top of the prisons (c. 1781–97).

> It seemed to me that in presenting this august palace raised on the shadowy lair of Crime, I should not only show to advantage the nobility of the architecture on account of the resulting contrasts, but I should also have an impressive metaphorical image of Vice overwhelmed by the weight of Justice.
>
> (Rosenau 1976: 98–9)

Ledoux echoes this: 'The temple illuminated by justice forms a salutory opposition to the dark places devoted to crime (1804: 3).

Quatremère de Quincy (1832) developed a theory of character which encompassed the form of the plan, ornamentation, massing, and construction. The inclusion of both utility and technology associated 'type' as intimately with use as the fit with the human body ('the needs of nature') did for furniture and clothes. The link is still between function, or *programme*, and form; either directly or through the formal consequences of selecting the appropriate technology.

Quatremère drew together two strands: those of Blondel and his neo-Classical pupils such as Boullée, and of Durand at the École Polytechnique who had divested the Orders of all metaphorical meaning. To him they were merely an assembly of standard elements, to be composed hierarchically into arcades, colonnades and walls (Durand 1802–9). The column capital as a simple trapezium-shaped block, irrespective of its Order, was a scandalous proposition. The elements, with the addition of roofs or vaulting, could be assembled into rooms and ultimately complete buildings on the gridded graph paper he supplied to his students.

In the *Receuil* (1801) Durand drew to a uniform scale examples of every functional type from all periods and places, using a standard technique for both plan and elevation. Despite the rigorous graphics, the organisation of the book displays a confusion and deep anxiety about 'type'. He tried the following possibilities, in separate Plates, without arriving at a consistent solution which satisfied either logic or instinct.

1 Function without history: barracks, arsenals and prisons; triumphal arches and gates.
2 Function linked to place: Persian, Chinese, Turkish and Moorish houses; Italian houses and gardens.
3 Function with loosely specified history: ancient theatres; modern theatres; Gothic houses.
4 Function spanning history: Gothic and modern churches.
5 Function linked to both place and named architect: Italian houses by Scamozzi.
6 General types as drawn by an artist: various public buildings on the *Champs de Mars* drawn by Piranesi.
7 Form with function: domed churches.

Durand believed that the morphological system of the *Leçons* coupled to the precedents in the *Receuil* would enable his students to solve any *programme* no matter how innovatory the social needs which gave rise to it.

For the theory that character inheres in forms which can be tailored to any function to be plausible, a building had to be conceived as empty of people or things, and outside history. But a rational age which saw the birth of sociology could not exclude function, so it was idealised. Any change of use ruled out discussion of character and type.

The transfer of such theories to the Gothic system of the nineteenth century was painless. Pugin (1843: 9) pours scorn on 'pagan' (i.e. Classical) forms for their 'inconsistency … In no one instance has the purpose or destination of the building formed the ground-work of the composition'. Had it done so, this purpose would have led, unfalteringly, to a 'pointed' (i.e. Gothic) solution. The bond between form and function is not in question – only the gross lapse of taste in its interpretation.

In semiotics the form–function link survived into modern theory though, as Lefebvre (1974) has pointed out, its architectural version is not all that new for Vitruvius had already arrived there by developing a full lexicon of elements, a syntax for their combination and a style manual based on the Orders.

> In all matters, but particularly in architecture, there are these two points: the thing signified and that which gives its significance. That which is signified is the subject of which we may be speaking; and that which gives significance is a demonstration on scientific principles.
>
> (quoted by Lefebvre 1974: 270)

Semiotics is not about obvious and trivial symbols such as the imperial Hapsburg eagle. It concerns the omnipresent architectural elements of all buildings. Eco (1969, reprinted 1986) speaks, first, of primary architectural signs – whose forms denote utilitarian functions. He cites the window opening (for light and air) and stairs or ramps (for ascending). He proceeds to secondary signs which are about what he calls 'social utility'. A throne is not merely a sitting place – it also signifies 'regalness', a symbolic function 'of real social utility'. The sign works by connotation and is secondary only in the sense that such functions presuppose the primary ones. He uses the Gothic ogival vault pierced by great windows to develop the relation between primary (in this case constructional and lighting) and secondary (symbolic) functions. The latter, following Abbot Suger and Eco's own analysis of Neoplatonic ideas, are symbols for 'the effusiveness of divine created energy' and 'participation in the divine essence'.

Eco identifies three codes which give signs meaning: technical, based on engineering technology; syntactical, based on plan forms such as circular or greek-cross, or massing such as high-rise; and semantic, which includes the system of primary and secondary signs he has already established. He adds two further categories. The first comprises 'ideologies of inhabitation', functions which are defined by such labels as common room, dining room or parlour. The second, a larger scale 'sociological' typology with such labels as hospital, villa, school, palace or railway station, appears merely to distinguish space complexes from single spaces. Why the former is not 'sociological' is not clear.

He maintains that whilst spoken language can carry any ideological content, leaving the speaker free 'to improvise novel messages' (although the 'very way it is articulated obliges one speaking it to see the world in a certain way', which gives the language an 'ideological connotation') the three architectural codes cannot be used in this free way. Whatever innovation they are capable of is strictly limited by custom and precedent. The codes of real potency on which architecture is based are external to it – and he calls them 'anthropological' by which he means 'social exigencies'. It is there that genuine innovation can occur, 'in systems over which (the architect) has no power' despite the possibilities of 'poetic function'.

Because the three codes all point to meanings derived from outside the field of architecture, there is no possibility of autonomous forms – a system of 'pure "arrangement"' such as is said to exist in poetry, painting or music. This is asserted, not explained. Why can architectural forms not elicit responses, carry meanings, similar to those elicited and carried by poetry, painting or music which are seen as having an autonomy? Because, for Eco, it is precisely the transformation which takes place when forms act as social signs which distinguishes architecture from art.

His analysis admits only a narrow range of building properties. All are material elements of the building: technical forms – of structure or elementary environmental control; specific and narrowly utilitarian forms such as roof, door or stair (an echo of Durand here); and stylistic forms such as ogival vaulting or neo-Gothic arches. In the light of his insistence that meaning cannot be found within the discourse of architecture, that all forms have to be referred to an external discourse ('anthropology'), the exclusions are surprising. They include the organisation of the plan, the way functions are described or prescribed in speech and texts or labelled on buildings and drawings, the actual pattern of activities which can be observed or inferred, and the morphology of space.

So while Eco's approach deepens the explanation of forms by moving away from the methods of art history, two defects remain. First the kinds of things he admits into the analysis is surprisingly limited. Secondly there is no supporting argument for differentiating between architectural forms, for which he denies autonomy, and those of poetry, painting and music, for which he grants it. From these two defects flow important practical and theoretical consequences. The first limits the questions to be asked and therefore the kind of evidence to be gathered for analysis. It would have us exclude much of the richest material by preserving the idea that architecture is a formal discourse.

The second creates a chasm between architectural forms and those of other arts. It interprets the non-autonomy of the former only in terms of their outside-in, social constitution leaving out of account their meaning in terms of the inside-out, 'lifeworld'. It makes non-autonomy total. Conversely it grants art forms an autonomy which is total, denying that besides their 'lifeworld' meaning, which his 'pure "arrangement"' seems to be, they too need to be analysed in terms of meanings in social relations. An opportunity for a comprehensive and balanced theory, where architectural forms could at long last share a home with art forms, has been missed.

Sad as this is, the small examples which follow show that the semiotic analysis nevertheless does illuminate the form–function relation.

In Chapter 11 the evolution of civic buildings is traced to their origin in markets which were located in central places. There their trade was highly visible and their spaces made as permeable as possible to the surrounding urban fabric to maximise the probability of chance encounters which might lead to transactions. The result was the typical open arcaded or colonnaded space with a vaulted or timber roof. In time the producers or merchants who controlled the market for, say wool or dairy products, built their own chamber above the open market, a space which acquired, as Tittler (1991) has shown, corporate, legal and guild functions which eventually grew into civic government. When the fully fledged modern town hall emerged in the nineteenth century to house all the bureaucratic activities of local government, the ground floor sometimes included a flattened *loggia*, as in Jones' Gothic version at Bishop Auckland or Hare's Renaissance version at Taunton. In its most abstract form the arcade or colonnade became a low relief *appliqué* as in Godwin's Northampton town hall (Figure 2.1). The primitive function in its three-dimensional open trading space is commemorated here by a compressed pattern, a sign for the origins of the type. To regard it merely as a way of articulating the base or of creating a rhythm – not something Eco would do – is to impoverish it.

The power of forms as ideological signs sometimes causes sponsors to prescribe a style. In 1835 the Houses of Parliament competition demanded a Gothic or Elizabethan solution. Ruskin's intervention (in which he spoke of a temple to the 'Goddess of getting on') focused a fierce debate about style and politics onto Mawson and Lockwood's Gothic adopted for the Bradford Wool Exchange in 1864 (Hardman 1986 and Webb 1976). In Chapter 3 we shall see that when a new teacher training college ('Normal Seminary') was required in Glasgow in 1845 following the Disruption of 1843, the choice of Tudor was as unquestioned as had been David Hamilton's shorn-down Classical for its predecessor, a few years earlier.

Though architectural rhetoric re-affirmed the form–function link periodically in the nineteenth century, in reality its fracture is evident in the frequency with which the link is redefined. The break from Doric Euston to French Gothic St Pancras represents much more than a change in taste. It was not limited to termini – it occurred equally in small provincial stations. There was a tangible shift of feeling. The first enthusiasm was marked by an idealisation of world-wide travel, associated with older patterns of learning and static 'culture' for which the huge Doric gateway was appropriate. Soon the sentiment changed to a dynamic, romantic vision, with strong national, or at least North European connotations. In details, too, these shifting relations are specific and far from arbitrary as for example in the adoption first of Classical and then of Gothic forms for the revolutionary technology of structural cast iron.

VIEW OF THE TOWN HALL, NORTHAMPTON.—MR. EDWARD W. GODWIN, ARCHITECT.

Figure 2.1

Northampton town hall (1861)

Source: *Building News* (1861) VII, 8 November, opp. p. 892

What is a type?

The form–function link was one way of defining type. Functional labels were satisfactory for they had predictable formal consequences. Prescriptions, teaching texts and classification systems carried in the head and used for communicating experience could all use these labels for they were a shorthand for an immensely rich social description. For a long time they also defined conventional spatial structures. These labels are still useful for narrower, more pragmatic purposes where form (or space) is of no interest. Schneekloth and Bruce (undated) describe their use in urban zoning, building regulations for fire resistance or thermal insulation, teaching, some kinds of research and in institutions. But, for the reasons I have discussed, they are no longer adequate as a way of organising experience into a stable structure which we carry in our heads. They do not provide the elements of a classification which helps to construe the world in a way that makes it easy to find meanings.

If we reject the mess of multiple typologies, each just applicable to one discourse, what is there which might correspond to what Eco calls the external field of 'social exigencies' and which I have called social relations? Clearly that domain is multi-dimensional; a point represents a unique combination of many qualities, and yet it will represent a typical conjuction which we can recognise and recall.

For buildings, what might the dimensions of that domain be? What, beneath the experience described by such labels as 'museum' or 'office', do we really sense? Why is a co-operative workshop sensed more like a community broadcasting station than a 'factory' despite the fact that its machinery and processes resemble the latter much more than the former? And why is a 'factory' sensed more like a barracks than a hostel, despite the fact that the sleeping accommodation of barracks and hostels is so similar?

Some of the dimensions we are dealing with seem to be: power–bonds; closed–open; constrained–free; hierarchical pyramids–non-hierarchical nets; centripetal–centrifugal; co-operative–competitive; conforming–subversive; traditional–innovative; tightly defined–loosely articulated; productive–existential; local (and spatial)–global (and trans-spatial); institutional–negotiated. But there are no common words about building use which capture such dimensions.

A typology based on relations – not only of people but between them and knowledge and things – is not yet within reach. Ordinary language and daily experience are not yet tuned to it. Much work needs to be done and perhaps this book will be useful as a marker. Clearly language will remain as crucial as it was in the safe, old system and as it remains in the partial, fragmented typologies which will have to serve in the meantime. It will be the sure anchor which enables us to make a satisfactory response to authentic design innovations whilst protecting us against those which threaten the self and society with disintegration.

PART II
BUILDINGS AND PEOPLE

Introduction

If meaning in buildings is about relations one should expect to find it in three kinds – between people, between people and knowledge, and between people and things. Ultimately all are social for all are about people, but the focus shifts. Some types work directly – they organise, classify and control people. Of course knowledge and things are also involved – for instance the curriculum in a school or the products made in a workhouse. Conversely, in the types which work indirectly through knowledge or things – for instance museums or markets – there are always actors present to make direct relations such as those between curators and the public, or between stallholders and customers.

This Part is about people – the places where social character is produced in two different ways. Either a régime is imposed by those with power to form the social character of those without or élite groups freely choose, for themselves, processes for doing this. I have called the first formation, or re*formation*, and the second creation or re*creation*.

The formative institutions are for children – the urban infant, primary and Sunday schools, industrial and agricultural schools, and the teacher training colleges of Chapter 3 where modern ways of forming character were invented.

Character deformed through the pathologies of physical or mental disease, the moral disease of crime, or unproductive habits, could be *re*formed in entirely new institutions. The care of the poor, old and orphans, though still founded on religious and philanthropic traditions, took on new legislative and coercive dimensions. The great building programme of hospitals, asylums, prisons, workhouses and various kinds of almshouse is the subject of Chapter 4.

Those who controlled all this continuously redefined their own character and reaffirmed the power of their own privileged classes by an internally-driven, non-coercive process. Its freedom makes it more appropriate to speak of the re*creation* of character, the title given to Chapter 6. The coffee houses, clubs, assembly rooms and hotels were the sites of leisure, courtly ceremony and ostentatious consumption of both things and time.

One might imagine that the needs of the body and the dangers to which it was exposed through cholera and urban squalor would cross boundaries of class. Yet the baths, wash-houses and swimming pools of Chapter 5 – the places for cleansing the body and clothes, and for physical exercise – have the same reformation–recreation dimension.

CHAPTER 3
Formation

'An incomparable machine – a vast moral steam engine'

The Age of Reason had given predictable order an immense status before mechanisation took command. Once that occurred mechanical metaphors percolated deeper than merely into science and philosophy. The machine appeared in the re-definitions of class, childhood, family, gender, nature, hygiene, discipline and religion and so exerted influence on the people-centred types, above all in the new schools where all these are at work. This seems a good place to start.

This was an innovatory type far removed from the great military academies and colleges for the élite and the endowed schools for the poor. As these new schools were a response to the growth of the urban proletariat they first appeared in Britain. But their intellectual and political roots were in French Encyclopaedism, Rousseau, the reforming spirit of Absolutist régimes of Continental Europe and the ideology of the American and French Revolutions. So these modest institutions became the battleground for some of the fiercest ideological struggles of the early nineteenth century. Every shade of politics and religion was involved. Parliament took an active part. Ireland and, to a lesser extent Scotland, were used as colonial testing grounds. The methods were exported from Britain to Europe, the colonies and America where, despite their completely different political contexts, the buildings remained remarkably similar. This suggests a deeper ideological unity founded on a similar model of relations.

Order, harmony and virtue were at the core of that model. Nothing new in that – a long tradition of imagined ideal societies shared these same goals. Davis (1981) distinguishes between two forms. One was total but also realistic in its grasp of human nature (it idealises society, not human nature), and its goal was order rather than happiness. The other was the bucolic Land of Cockaygne, idealisations of nature in Arcadia, and the perfect moral commonwealth, which depended on the moral reform of individuals and looked to the millenial restoration of Paradise. The machine gave both a new direction which we shall see in the production Utopias of Chapter 10; what is relevant here is the centrality of education.

Production and education were linked in the earliest visions. The model plan for New Brunswick and New Harlem, Yarranton's (1677) rural settlement for the poor (Figure 3.1), contained spinning schools conducted in a large work-room with a central 'little Box like a Pulpit'. Around the edges were benches, 'as they are in our Playhouses' – that is tiered – on which about two hundred children are seated, spinning. On a Box in middle of room – 'sits the Grand Mistress with a long white wand in her hand'. In silence, she taps any idle child. If this is not enough, she rings a little bell fixed to the Box out of which comes a woman who takes the child away to be chastised in 'another room'. Next to the spinning school were three others. In the first girls made lace, in the second boys made toys in a process of subdivided labour as clear as any Adam Smith might have desired – some making heads, some bodies and some legs, and in the third boys painted the toys and made 'slit pictures'.

Yarranton's scheme foreshadows the key elements of the industrial revolution school:

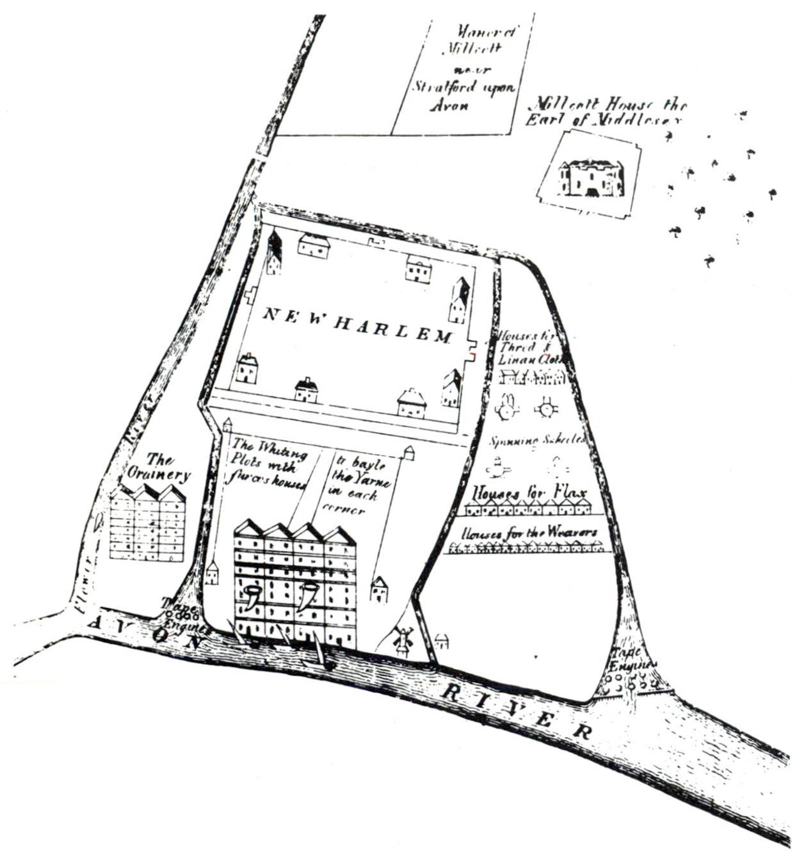

Figure 3.1

Yarranton's New Harlem (1677)

Source: Yarranton (1677), reprinted in West (1830)

1 The inverted theatre – perfect visibility for surveillance, the stage now being the domain of the observer, the auditorium of the observed
2 Discipline – its source and its place of execution being hidden
3 Silence
4 Productive work
5 Hierarchy – mistress, punitive woman, children
6 Religious symbolism – the pulpit

Coleridge's (1817) machine metaphor in the title of this section was the highest accolade to a new system of education in its most innovatory form – the monitorial school.

Without state support, and with only tiny parental contributions, these schools had to rely on philanthropic charity, and so efficiency was vital. The untrained teachers' moral virtue was the only guarantee of performance. The children would soon labour in the mills driven by water or steam (ideally constant power sources, but in reality subject to fluctations and frequent breakdown) so they needed to learn strict time-keeping, discipline and compliant behaviour. Their bodies were capable of clockwork regulation and their minds, in Locke's words, were like 'an empty cabinet ... a white paper void of all character' and 'without any ideas' (1689–90). The whole person could be transformed by a system with the regulatory power of a machine.

Undoubtedly a new type was emerging, but its meaning has not been properly analysed; it is the familiar symmetrical silence. On the one hand in otherwise excellent educational histories the buildings are marginalised – as in the case of the schools at Spitalfields (McCann 1977) and Kennington (Silver and Silver 1974). On the other hand architectural scholars have also ignored it. Pevsner's (1979) otherwise comprehensive catalogue excludes schools entirely. To her credit monitorial schools are at least mentioned by Rosenau (1970) alongside more traditional institutions. Seaborne (1971) devotes some space to them, and I examined their Scottish history (Markus 1982: 201–61). Nevertheless so far the picture is far too sketchy.

If order and work were so central to the new relations it is useful to glance at precursors from the perspective of orderly workplaces. Though the link between education and poor relief or incarceration is organic here the educational spaces have been teased out; the entire institutions are examined in Chapter 4. But we shall also look at those punitive institutions which were child-centred – reformatories, industrial and agricultural schools and the model workhouse schools created by the New Poor Law in 1834.

Precursors

Schools – of a kind

Though it was in the eigteenth century workhouse that the seeds of many educational practices are found, radical ideas were around a century earlier. Thomas Firmin's huge Quaker establishment of 1676 in Little Britain, where children were taught reading and spinning, is called by the Webbs (1963: 106–7) a 'school, factory, wholesale warehouse and retail shop'. Quakers were also behind Bellers' 'Colledge of Industry' (1696). In Chapter 10 we will see Robert Owen using it as a model. Poor children were to be taught reading, writing, arithmetic and manual trade skills without punishment and a library, herb garden and 'Laboratory for preparing Medicines', were amongst its innovations. Contemporary with John Carey's 1696 Bristol House of Industry which became a famous model, a group of local Quakers built a workhouse with a factory, orphanage, almshouse and school. In 1686 a 'Colledge of Infants', or 'General Nursery' or 'Infantory' was set up in the disused Clerkenwell Workhouse in what the Webbs regard as a unique experiment. In 1702, using Bellers as a model, it was re-used by the Quakers for a school, almshouse and orphanage. Another Quaker school, Ackworth, was established at Pontefract in Yorkshire in what had been the northern branch of the London Foundling Hospital.

Workhouse children were taught basic reading, writing and, more rarely, arithmetic coupled to religious instruction and training in manual work. A 1786 review of workhouses defines them as 'Nurseries of Religion, Virtue and Industry'. Children feature amongst the inmates of all the workhouses listed, commonly with their own workspace. In Bishopsgate Street there were 129 children (increased to 400 by the early nineteenth century (Wilkinson 1819) in two 150-foot long workshops. The boys' lodgings were located above these workrooms, the girls' over the chapel which separated the workhouse from the prison. Boys had reading and wrting lessons; for the girls sewing and knitting replaced writing. The children worked eighty spinning wheels. In other houses they often shared in the adults' oakum picking, weaving or shoemaking. In St Marylebone an ex-schoolmaster was appointed as first Master. When it moved to a new workhouse the 1774 enabling Act specified that it was to admit the poor, both healthy and sick, diseased and infirm; the profligate and idle who were to be corrected; and infant poor, to be educated 'in habits of industry, religion and honesty', the profits from their labour to be used for their own upkeep as well as for the Parish.

The provision for children gradually became separated out into a school for education, or an industrial school for work as Locke, Commissioner of the Board of Trade, had proposed as far back as 1697 in his Parish 'working schools'.

A miniature factory

Education and work were integral parts of penal institutions such as the San Michele complex in Rome (Chapter 4). In Britain the industrial school had its origins as much in education as in carceral and Poor Law institutions.

The fifteenth century reading and writing schools, responding to pressures placed on apprentices by the guilds, were additions to a system which included Parish schools and endowed grammar schools which taught grammar and singing to entrants to university, the church and the professions. During the Reformation some of these disappeared and others became independent. The gentry fell over backwards to endow new grammar and petty schools for the poor.

By the late seventeenth century subscription Charity schools were absorbing a greater proportion of benefactions than the grammar schools. Their prototype was at Westminster (1688). To the core curriculum of religion, reading, writing, arithmetic and manual work, subjects such as navigation were sometimes added. The Society for the Propagation of Christian Knowledge (SPCK), founded in 1699, began to claim these schools as its own creation but recent scholarship (Simon 1988: 113–29) has cast doubt on the claim. It is also clear that the SPCK's original policy of a balance between education and work quickly shifted in favour of the latter, so that by the 1720s it was effectively sponsoring workhouses and industrial schools characterised by coercion and harsh discipline.

Seaborne (1971) describes the Charity schools as having, characterstically, a boys' and a girls' schoolroom, a master's and a matron's lodging and, in the larger urban schools, a great hall or chapel used for prayers and bible reading. The division between the sexes was either lateral on plan, or by storey height as in Thomas Bowdler's Shrewsbury Charity school.

In Scotland the 1560 *Book of Discipline* envisaged a nationwide network of Parish schools. There were perennial difficulties with resources, and a series of seventeenth century Acts were designed to make the notional system real. The last in 1696 established a minimun stipend and a house for the schoolmaster in every rural Parish. Despite financial and organisational difficulties, Scotland now had a national, graded system of Parish, Burgh Grammar and high schools, colleges and universities unmatched anywhere in Europe.

The Scottish Society (SSPCK), with Presbyterian in place of Anglican backing, was set up in

1709 to sponsor Charity schools on the English model but soon developed a programme of spinnning or industrial schools which were given strong impetus after 1745 as projects on the forfeited estates. By 1758 there were 167 industrial schools, training boys in blacksmithy, shoemaking, and agriculture, and girls in spinning, knitting and sewing (Scotland 1969: 99–100).

Industrial schools were sometimes very large; at Bath there were 180 children (Cruttwell 1789: 25). The 'class' began to develop here. In London's Golden Square industrial school the Rules (Spark 1792) demand that the school master 'shall *class* the Boys that can read, and the School Mistress the Girls, according to the Progress they have made, Nine in a *Class*' (my emphases).

They were favourite projects of evangelicals. Sarah Trimmer of Old Brentford spent much of her later life and fortune in promoting them. She linked the Parish Charity, Sunday and industrial schools and even imported a circular spinning machine for twelve girls.

Thomas Bernard (1809) describes some of the industrial schools sponsored by the Society of Bettering the Condition of the Poor. Kendal's 1799 school for 112 children used the new monitorial system and took special pride in the boys' shoemaking. A cost exercise shows its profitability '... standing proof that the productive powers of children may be advantageously exercised, at an early age ...' (*State of the Schools of Industry* 1801).

The girls' school at Bamburgh (Bernard 1809: 193–4) had a work room 40 feet long by 20 wide occupied by jersey spinning machines on the floor whilst the (hand) flax spinners were on a lateral gallery 'erected ... so that the mistress has a full view of the whole number at once'. In an adjacent small room 'classes' of ten girls received one hour's instruction a day in religion, psalmody, reading, writing and arithmetic. A smaller upper floor room was for girls' knitting and sewing. This disciplined production vividly recalls Yarranton's (1677) silent and punitive supervising mistress.

Paradoxically, with increasing industrialisation, the industrial school gradually disappeared. What had never been probable became obviously impossible – to make it, if not profitable, at least self-supporting. The New Poor Law of 1834 allowed the Commissioners to replace it with huge workhouse schools and, with legislation in 1857 and 1866, by *reformatory* industrial schools for young offenders. By 1865 only 30 of the old-style schools survived in England and 19 in Scotland (Watson 1869). In continental Europe the same metamorphosis created such spectacular projects as the French young offenders' institution at Mettray.

Innocent and destitute

The orphan institution *par excellence* was London's Foundling Hospital, founded by Thomas Coram in 1742 (McClure 1981) and completed to designs by Theodore Jacobsen, in 1745. In studying European precedents Jacobsen included the Paris *Hôpital des Enfants Trouvés* (a daughter institution of the catch-all *Hôpital Général*) formally set up in 1670 and soon to become a model for the provinces; the *House of Wheels* in Lisbon – named after a device similar to the French *tours* in which abandoned infants could be left in one half of a rotating cylinder and admitted without anyone even catching a glimpse of the depositor; and the Almoners' Orphanage in Amsterdam.

The plan was the familiar U, the square chapel at its centre and the two great three-storey boys' and girls' wings embracing a green on the entrance side. The ground floor housed the dining rooms and kitchens, offices and the General Court Room. To be interviewed there the mothers who sought admission for their babies entered by a side entrance, thus making the space shallow with respect to the deep residential accommodation on the upper floors. Boys and girls entered upper level galleries separately at either end of the chapel, whilst the public occupied the ground floor.

Jonas Hanway, an early Governor who also became Treasurer, had a less well known proposal – the 1783 naval school for poor boys to be built on waste land (Figure 3.2) designed to ensure an adequate flow of qualified seamen into the Navy. He had already founded the Marine Society for this purpose in 1756 and proposed to establish free county schools to teach agricultural and manufacturing skills alongside seamanship. The first floor has a combined school room and working deck – the naval equivalent of the work room – where spinning, knitting and weaving were taught alongside seamen's skills. The ends were allocated to officers – the captain, boatswain, steward and 'pupils' (a naval equivalent of the usher or assistant teacher).

There were great schemes besides those

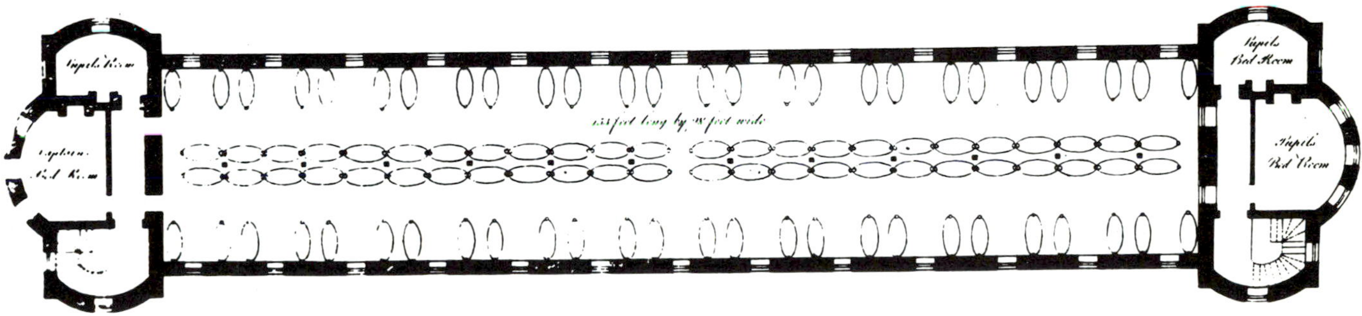

Figure 3.2
Jonas Hanway's naval school (1783), exterior view and upper floor plan
Source: Hanway (1783)

Jacobsen had visited. The Prussian Elector Frederick III had an organised poor relief system in the 1690s, of which one component was the huge Frederick Hospital in Berlin where orphans were accommodated alongside the old, the sick and the deranged. He was also behind a venture in Saxony where the Pietists were exerting an important influence. Deeply influenced by Comenius and the Moravian tradition, Franck, their leader, placed Latin and science at the centre of the curriculum. For pedagogic method he relied on a type of 'associationist' psychology in which impressions derived from objects, pictures or activity were coupled to abstract ideas. There was a 'citizens'' and a 'poor' school. The former prepared boys for studies to enter the professions or the church, the latter was for both sexes. Each had a master and was subdivided by age, between boarders and those living with families, and the latter by sex. One 'poor' class was taught language

Figure 3.3
Orphan house at Glaucha (1698–1701)
Source: Franck (1705)

and science and was combined with a 'citizens'' class in 1699. There was also an apothecary's shop and, established as a Royal privelege, a printing press and bookseller's stall.

His orphan house at Glaucha near Halle (1698–1701) had, according to John Wesley's notes of 1738 (Curnock 1909: II 17), a U-shaped plan, with two rearward projecting wings. The enraving of the front elevation, together with Wesley's and Franck's descriptions (Franck 1705), in the absence of plans is the basis of conjecture on the spatial organisation.

My guess is that the central upper entrance was for the 'citizen' children, staff and the public – the controllers and those visitors who were social equals. There are three ground level entrances: one central – which probably led to the rear court – and two lateral for the two sexes of the 'poor' school. The shared language and science classroom established a ring across two deep trees at the tips of which were the sleeping quarters for the boys and girls in the upper storeys of the wings.

The division of the elevation into three, paired, floors, suggests teaching, eating and work spaces on the lower two floors; staff residence and offices in the middle, and servants' and ushers' spaces in the dormered roof.

By 1704 Glaucha had a 'normal' school for teacher training. Franck's pupil Hecker went on to establish normal schools in Pomerania (1735) and in Berlin (1742) from which, by Imperial ordinance, country teachers were to be supplied.

Throughout German States other grand solutions were being tried. I shall refer again to Count Rumford's Bavarian experiments especially his great Military Workhouse in Munich – effectively a manufactory administered by the army to produce goods for military use (Rumford 1797: 3–112). Here the poor worked at textile operations – spinning, weaving and making finished articles – in cotton, wool, flax and hemp. There were special chilren's workrooms; those too young to work were paid simply to attend and observe from seats around the edge until, according to Rumford, they begged to be allowed to join their older mates. They also had daily classes. Rumford exploited the military connection, for the paper the children used for writing was later turned into cartridge cases. But it was the social grouping that was really innovatory.

The entire workhouse far from being structured around 'vertical' production, was spatially divided, according to workers' skill, into what Rumford calls 'classes'. The children soon abandoned their dedicated space to join their families, so that 'the spinning halls were filled with the most interesting little groups of industrious families ... busy ... cheerful ... pleasing object(s)' (Rumford 1797: 89). This reproduced under ideal conditions the domestic production of the poor Munich families. It also worked in reverse, for the adults were apparently persuaded to join the children's classes.

The pastoral colony

Work was not necessarily in a pre-industrial factory. The most obvious production, agricultural, was linked to education well into the industrial revolution in institutions designed to turn morally disordered urban children into 'sturdy peasants' in the innocent pastoral environment. As the children lived at home, their houses and productive space widely dispersed, the system had few buildings to show. It is more evident in the texts of poor law administration and philanthropy.

Hanway again features; he wanted children to be raised under the supervision of the Foundling Hospital in 'the sweet air of a well-situated country village, where good milk and good bread is to be had' (Taylor 1979: 301). Older children should be apprenticed to rural husbandmen, who had 'more natural good sense, & a stronger bias to virtue' than mechanics, manufacturers or even farmers. Such deep suspicion of the town, urban labour and wealth was to grow into a palpable force.

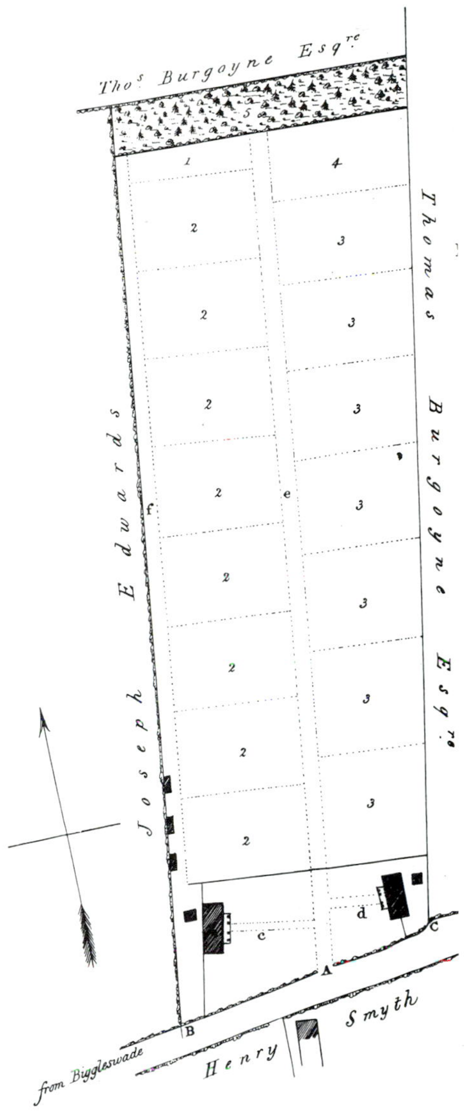

Figure 3.4
Montagu Burgoyne's rural settlement (1829)
Source: Burgoyne (1829), by permission of the Librarian, Glasgow University Library

Soon the idea of settlements for the poor on rural wastes became irresistably attractive. The rhetoric of gardens, agriculture and nature pervaded educational literature. Pastoral innocence is contrasted with urban depravity. Remote wilderness, awaiting military subjugation and cultivation, is seen as a colony. Later all this is incorporated into the grand visionary projects of Chapter 10.

Montagu Burgoyne (1829) proposed a settlement for forty boys and forty girls aged 8 to 14 years old at Potton in Bedfordshire. Each had a school of industry where the curriculum included shoemaking, mending clothes, sewing and agricultural work. The central visitors' entrance is flanked by two separate ones for the boys' and girls' schools (Figure 3.4). The boys had small plots for experiments on manures, seeds, new crops and tree grafting. They were also to dig, plough, hedge and ditch, whilst the girls learnt dairying and needlework, washing, ironing, mending clothes and housewifery 'for service'. Burgoyne was taken with the new infant school at Brighton and also knew the model school at Baldwin's Gardens so it was natural to include a monitorial infant school. He saw this as a 'colony at home' which used waste land and dealt with poverty and education on the model of Colonel Bosch's Drenthe settlements (Kloosterhuis 1981) and William Allan's set up in 1825 at Lindfield near Brighton. Allan provided schoolrooms, a library and reading room, and workshops where before moving on to shoemaking, weaving, printing and farming, the children plaited straw – an occupation widely recommended by reformers and utopians alike for its simplicity, cheapness of raw materials and pastoral innocence.

'Rural colonies' aimed to isolate the poor or criminals in remote communities – the more distant the better. Coram himself had been involved in the scheme for debtors' and poor persons' colonies on the River Savannah in Georgia.

At first these rural projects were for the moral and physical wellbeing of children. But soon it was the pupil teachers' turn to be isolated from urban corruption. The 1819 Prussian laws for normal schools required that they were to be located in moderate sized towns to preserve the pupils from 'dissipation, allurements and habits of a kind of life' (such as exist in large towns) 'which does not accord with their future condition' (Cousin 1833).

Religious groups were specially influenced by the ideology of nature in the selection of sites. At the 1748 Kingswood School near Bristol John Wesley wanted a site near enough to the city for parents to visit, 'not yet too near, and much less in it; which would have been attended by greater evils' (Ives 1970: 8). The rural setting gave scope for such 'recreations' as chopping wood and digging, since all play was un-Christian. Thompson (1968: 416) sees here the 'pitiless ideology of work', which though softened in other communities, still justifies Lecky's 'religious terrorism' as a description of what was done in the name of 'moral rescue'. Ives has shown the influence on Wesley of Comenius and the Moravians whose motherhouse at Herrnhut he had visited; it was not only a model for Moravian communities such as Fulneck in Yorkshire, but probably even for the layout of such factory villages as David Dale's Catrine in Ayrshire.

Lancaster, as a sideline from urban monitorial schools, experimented with a rural version with a 'house, college and garden' on the Duke of Somerset's estates at Maiden Bradley, mixing religious utopianism with his mechanistic ideas (Dickson 1986: 66). 'I may found there an Economy nearly similar to those established by the Moravians, but with more emulation interwoven in its system'. This was to be a 'colony of industry' similar to Lindfield. Horticulture, says Lancaster, not only qualifies youth for gardening and labour but '... prepares the mind of youth of both sexes, to love rural, domestic life; (and) affords agreeable and profitable employment to the peasant during his leisure hours that would otherwise be spent in idleness' (1805: 121).

The sabbatarian fortress of virtue

A completely new movement, the Sunday school, appeared. Its influence was to be deep. There may be dispute as to Robert Raikes's role in its invention in Gloucester in 1781 (Laqueur 1979) but there is none that, as its chief propagandist in the 1780s, he was largely responsible for its early phenomenal growth.

For Thompson (1968) religious ideology in the Sunday schools was a focus in the conflict between working and middle classes. The teaching inculcated virtues of discipline and order and by pointing to happiness hereafter, deflected critique from current social evils. It created an *inner* coercive moral force which ensured submissiveness. Although individual Methodists became radical working class leaders he chose Methodism to demonstrate a process which worked for both masters and workers, having '... this dual role as the religion of both the exploiters and the exploited' (Thompson, 1968: 412). A balance was achieved between indoctrination, the building up of a sense of community and 'the psychic consequences of the counter-revolution' expressed in 'conversion' and other religious phenomena. He is uncompromising in his judgement of the narrow, bigoted and morally crippling nature of these schools.

Laqueur has put a telling counter-proposition. Though he set out to validate Thompson's thesis he concludes that despite the difficulty of precisely defininining 'class' (one that Thompson himself recognised) Sunday schools managers, teachers and children were working class and the system served their evangelical and educational aims. The division was not between classes but between those who worked –whether artisans or managers – and those who did not. The Sunday school transmitted the values of work and discipline 'as against overt social and political values' (Laquer 1979: 239).

Cliff (1986) accuses Thompson of producing evidence on religion rather than on Sunday schools and even that over-weighted to Methodism. He notes the arrival of the 'genteel' teachers, and, with them, middle class methods of management and teaching material written by philanthropic, conservative and evangelical authors such as Sarah Trimmer. Turner (1988) argues that the movement provided 'invisible religion', a working class means for self improvement dominated by 'labour aristocrats' rather than mill owners and that it was subject to occasional 'gusts of radicalism and revivalism'.

In Scotland and Ireland, though so different in their social and religious environments, Sunday schools also became favourite evangelical projects. By 1793 Glasgow had eleven and this was matched in other towns and in rural areas where the SSPCK played a part. Thomas Chalmers established some and it was in the Sabbath Schools that his protégé David Stow started his work in 1816 before moving on to the famous infant and junior day schools discussed later.

In Ireland the Sunday schools had to cope both with pre-industrial urban poverty and deep religious division. It is all the more remarkable that it was Dublin which generated the special building type for inter-denominational Sunday schools which in the next decade briefly flourished in England.

Of the three Sunday schools established in Dublin by 1786, the one in St Catherine's Parish grew so rapidly that by 1798 it needed the substantial three-storey building for the Dublin Free (Weekly) School erected in School Street with contributions from Catholic, Church of Ireland and Quaker sponsors. This seems to be the first purpose-built Sunday school in the world and both the institution and its building came to play an important part in Irish education.

The sponsor was the Committee for Educating Children of the Poor. Soon it opened its doors to weekday pupils, changing its name in 1808 to the

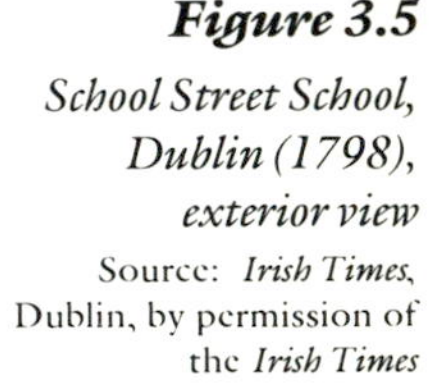

Figure 3.5
School Street School, Dublin (1798), exterior view
Source: *Irish Times*, Dublin, by permission of the *Irish Times*

Dublin Weekly and Daily Schools. When in 1811 the Society for Promoting the Education of the Poor in Ireland was founded it made the school its head-quarters for promoting the Irish monitorial system until it moved to Kildare Place in 1814, thence to be known as the Kildare Place Society. That story is told later.

There are contemporary descriptions but the earliest drawings and photographs date from the 1920s to the 1960s.[2] Figure 3.5 shows it shortly before demolition; the plans in Figure 3.6 are reconstructions. The two schoolrooms – one each for the boys and girls – were on the first floor, accessed directly from outside by flights of steps (unequal in length because the site slopes). Each had a fireplace on the front wall, and each was also entered from the central stair hall, as were the top floor spaces. The ground floor had at least two, possibly three, street entrances; the central one leading to the stair hall and domestic rooms for teachers and visitors, and one or two smaller ones into store rooms and soup kitchens. The presence

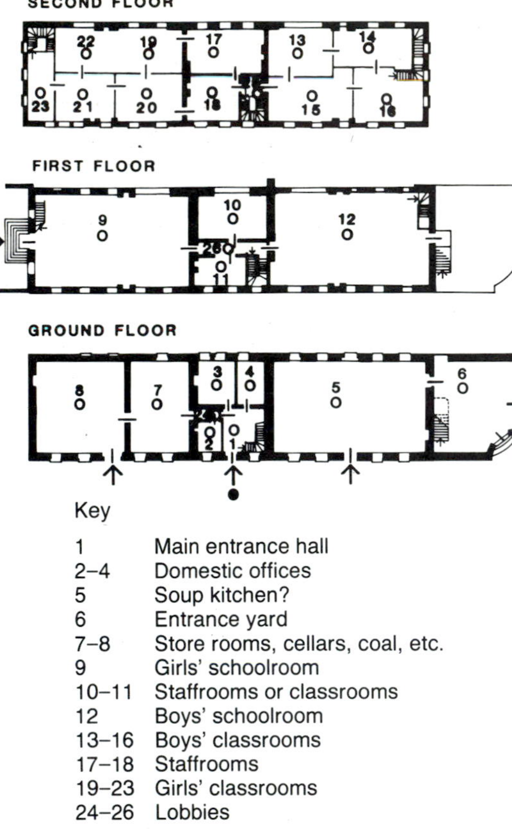

Figure 3.6

School Street School, Dublin (1798), plans

Source: Author's drawings based on drawings in the Department of Education, Dublin

of a single fireplace in each schoolroom suggests that they were not subdivided. The first and second floor centre sections had smaller spaces, probably teachers' rooms and classrooms.

Little is known of the original régime. One anonymous author (Church of Ireland Training College, undated: 15) suggests that even before 1811 both the monitorial system *and* classroom teaching were used. Rumford's hand is palpable in the 1799 conversion of the ground floor, already used as a temporary soup house, into a model Permanent Public Kitchen and a distribution centre for food to the poor. Later a bakehouse was added.

Figure 3.7 is the probable spatial structure. The two schoolrooms are shallow – entered by the children directly off courtyards entered from the street – and on rings, since the teachers enter them from the central hall. This plan controlled the interface so that the children would only become aware of the teachers when the latter emerged into the schoolrooms from their own quarters.

By now hundreds of English Sunday schools were operating in barns, converted houses, mills and chapels. The first to be purpose-built, in 1802, was in London at Friars' Mount, Bethnal Green[3], to rehouse the Hoxton Methodist Sunday School founded in 1798, only second in London to the contemporary Methodist Sunday school in Golden Lane. Although no plan exists an 1809 map[4] shows its outline – 66 feet long and 37 wide. Its two storeys accommodated 1000 children. The whole space could be thrown open into the 'large room' for singing and prayer, and then subdivided by movable tri-partite wooden partitions into 'distinct apartments for teaching'; eight on the first and seven on the ground floor – the staircase occupying the eighth. This arrangement is said to be conducive to order and silence and to save time 'in the Children's taking their seats'. In other words the chilren's seats in the large room are so pre-arranged that when it is subdivided they are already in their class positions.

The 'large room', which was to become a marked feature of the early buildings, had an older history. At Golden Lane there were, from the start, removable partitions on the second floor used to form 'something like an assembly room' (Grosvenor 1856: 38). By 1801 the Minutes refer to 200 children in the 'large room'. The term was a language strategem to avoid anything like 'chapel', 'church' or even 'meeting room' – all with connotations of conventional religious space which, to the ministers of the denominational services, would have suggested competition.

The boys and girls were separated by floor since they should 'invariably be kept quite distinct, and if possible, in separate rooms'. If, in a single school room, this is not possible they should be 'kept apart at the extreme ends of the room'. There is repeated reference to *classes* and a description of a 6-class system, starting with the alphabet, through spelling and reading words with increasing numbers of syllables, and finishing with Bible reading and spelling. 'Place-capturing' is used, apparently adopted from the fledgling monitorial system; children stand in rows for spelling and as they rise and fall in their relative performance, answer-by-answer, they take each other's places as a way 'of engaging their attention and stirring up a proper degree of emulation'. A child had to satisfy its own teacher and that of the higher class if it wanted to move up. Spatial location within a room and in the whole building became both a sign and an instrument of ceaseless competition.

During a teacher shortage 'scholars themselves' can be used – again, shades of the monitorial system which was soon consciously adapted to Sunday schools, despite a dilemma. In the true monitorial system economics and discipline led to a single open schoolroom with (child) monitors teaching reading, writing and arithmetic to small groups ('drafts') under the constant eye of the master or mistress. The drafts either stood in semi-circles against the walls or sat on their forms for writing. The Sunday schools from the start adopted policies which militated against this arrangement.

First they were committed to 'teachers', adolescent or adult laypeople, each provided with a separate classroom. Secondly the Bible was the basic text and reading a means to enable children to read it. There was a prohibition against teaching other subjects, especially writing – a vital part of the monitorial system – which was seen as the thin end of a secular wedge. It might turn children into active, potentially creative subjects, instead of passive vessels of instruction. Apart from widespread nervousness about over-education of the working class, even whole-hearted supporters of secular weekday education opposed its spread into the Sunday school on Sabbatarian grounds. The prohibition was eroded, especially by the Methodists who from the beginning at Golden Lane taught writing – first on weekday evenings and soon early on Sunday mornings.

But Lancaster adapted to these limitations. In his address to Sunday school superintendents (1809b) he argues that the absence of groups seated on forms and writing on slates undermines the pattern of simultaneous spelling and reading in the semicircles, and he opposes the assembly of children 'in different rooms under one roof'; they should all be assembled 'in the same room, properly fitted up, however large their number'. But aware that this is unacceptable to Sunday school managers he recommends 'an entirely new' adaptation (that is compromise). The seats are to be arranged so that groups of 6 to 8 boys can see one 'lesson' – printed cards of enlarged letters, words or texts. Since there is no writing all the children will be seated continuously and taught by monitors with these cards, though he admits that the forest of cards on stands will greatly hinder effective surveillance. Moreover there will be a loss of economy on books and cards. But he still prefers it to putting, say 400, children into separate spaces with, say, 70 teachers. He also praises the Stockport Sunday School.

Lancaster's message was taken to heart by the Friars' Mount managers. By 1813 (Wentworth 1813) they have adopted two tiers of monitors, under a Superintending Monitor, who accompany children between the 'assembling room' and the 'classrooms' and supervise the removal of the partitions. It is unclear whether there are now classrooms *additional* to these partitioned-off spaces.

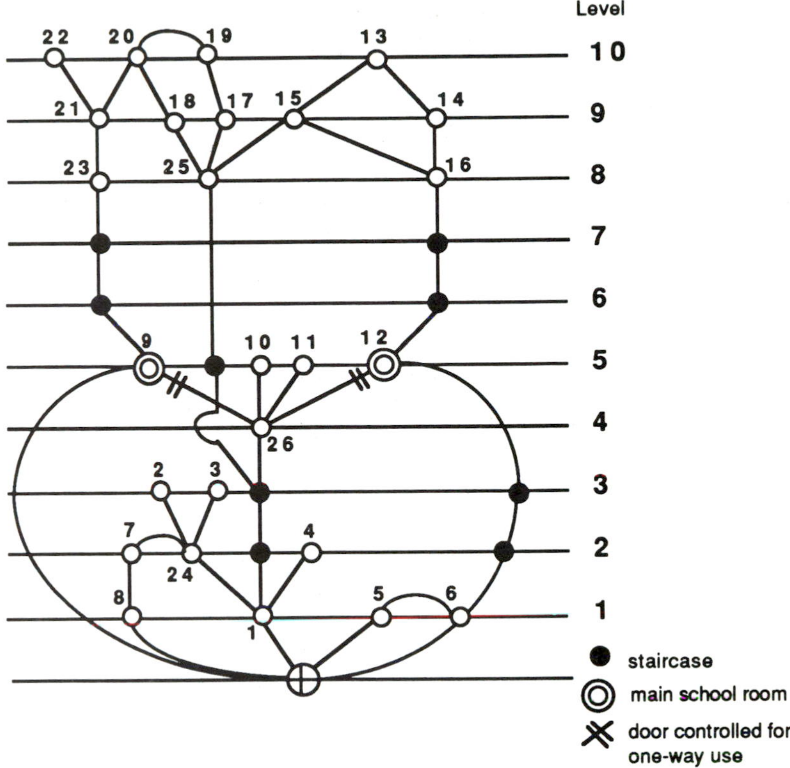

Figure 3.7

School Street School, Dublin (1798), spatial map

Source: Author's drawing

Soon the Sunday School Union has fully incorporated Lancaster's rules and, influenced by Friars' Mount, recommends a complex five-level hierarchy of monitors, the lowest grade working *with* the teachers in their separate spaces (1816). Here they are told 'to take their seats in their respective classes, at the opposite end to which the teacher sits' (Lancaster 1809b). And Lancaster accepts the use of individual books.

The second English Sunday school of this type was erected in Stockport where in 1784 there were already six schools, including a small purpose-built one. From the start whilst supported by the Established church and Unitarians, Wesleyans were to forefront. In 1794 they became 'Methodist' Sunday schools, a reflection of the principal source of support – but remained non-denominational. By 1797 proposals were afoot for building a chapel, Sunday school, preachers' houses and five 'large schools' at a cost of £7,000 (Stockport 1797). The 1796

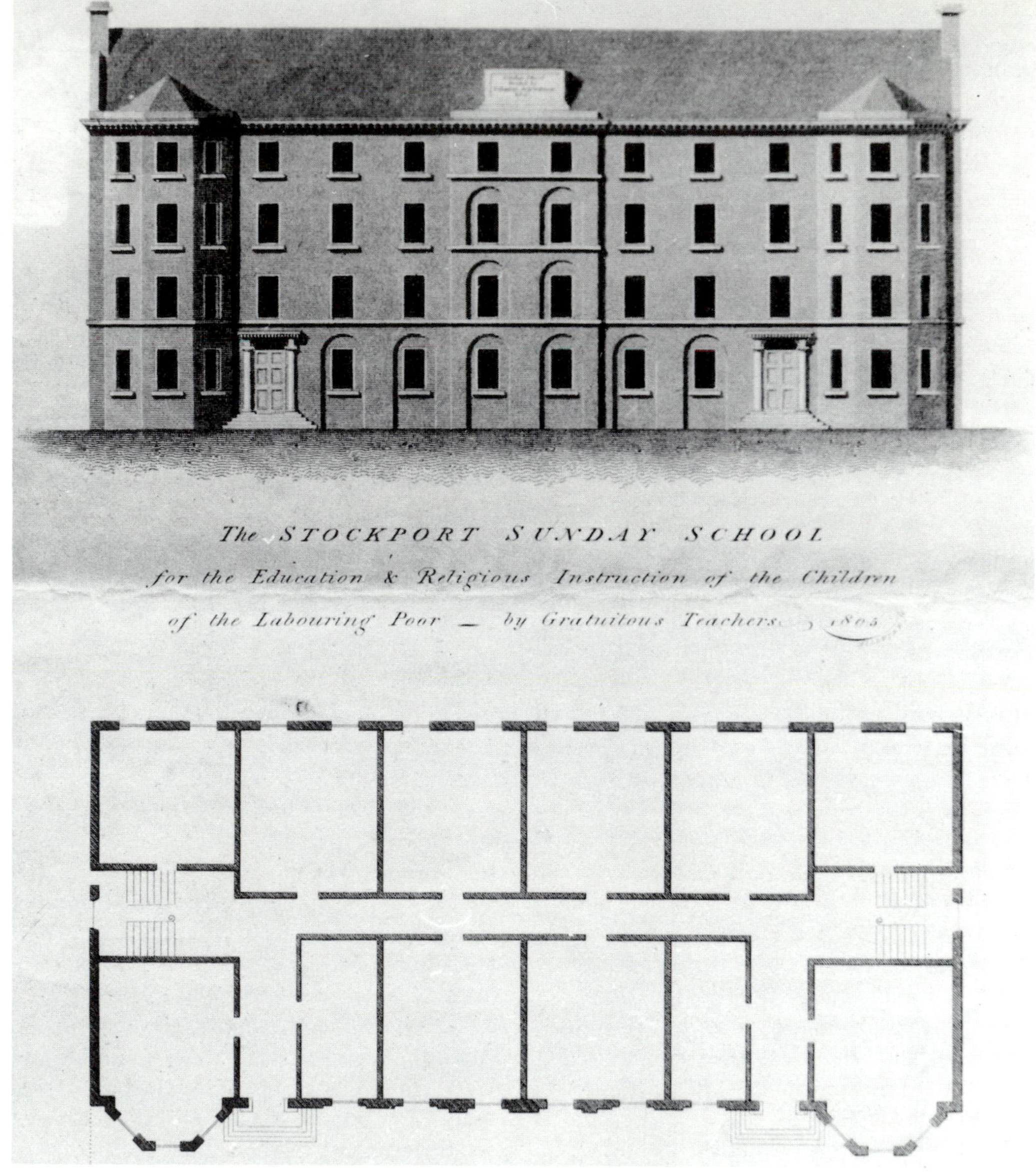
The STOCKPORT SUNDAY SCHOOL
for the Education & Religious Instruction of the Children
of the Labouring Poor — by Gratuitous Teachers, 1805

Figure 3.8
Stockport Sunday school (1805), exterior view and plan (the attic skylights do not yet appear)
Source: Stockport public library

Committee Minutes first mention a 'large room' in which apparently writing was taught, despite the general proscription (Stockport 1796: 7).

Hadfield and Gosling (1984) quote 1802 Minutes in which the newly appointed Inspector, Joseph Mayer, called for 'an amazingly large School' which, after a vigorous subscription campaign, was started in 1805. With 3000 children and, after extension in 1835, 5000 it became the world's largest Sunday school. Boys and girls had separate entrances and staircases at the two ends (Figure 3.8). Outside it appeared to have four storeys. The ground and first floor did indeed have classrooms and offices, one floor for each sex, but the upper two were combined into a single height 'large room' which could seat all the children and teachers (Figure 3.9). There was a table, pulpit and organ at one end; level seats in the centre and under the side galleries and raked seats at the other end and on the galleries. There was a marked chapel image, but it was far grander in scale, ornament and finishes than any Dissenter would have seen. Although a contemporary publication[5] anticipates the teaching of writing in the 'large room', the controversy between the Methodist Mayer and the Church of England was only resolved in 1815, when twenty-four writing rooms were constructed in the roof void, lit by small, flush sloping skylights.

The simple brick exterior with the two shorn-down classical entrances would have signified to contemporary observers both an institution and a mill. Methodist and other chapels at this time often had side elevations (Dolbey 1964) which gave the appearance of a two storey building, the double row of windows made necessary by raked side galleries which impeded double height windows. Nevertheless here something more was involved, for the two rows of windows for the 'large room' were undifferentiated from those below, thus adding architectural to linguistic camouflage.

The committee was inspired to devise a metaphor of peace and strength during the upheavals of 1832 when, '... at a time of political excitement ... it is hardly possible to approach the town ... without encountering one or more of these quiet fortresses, which a wise benevolence has erected against the encroachments of vice and ignorance' (Thompson 1968: 397).

Macclesfield followed Stockport in 1813 with a new building for its Sunday schools founded in 1796. It still stands, now used as a heritage centre (Figure 3.10) and the contemporary model made by the builder survives. The building so resembles Stockport's that it is either the work of the same designer or the result of careful plagiarism. There are two entrances and a contemporary view of children processing out of the building shows the same differentiation by gender. The ground and first floors, one for boys and one for girls, each had ten rooms – for classes, teachers and the superintendent – whilst the upper two floors were combined into the galleried 'large room'. As at Stockport, the exterior gives no hint of this huge upper space which could accommodate over 2000 children and 200 teachers.

Writing was taught in the 'large room' from the start. The first year's accounts have an item for ink and quills and the holes for inkwells and grooves for quills are still evident in the original desks. Non-sectarianism was even more marked than at Stockport – for in addition to Established and Dissenting groups, the Masons took a prominent part. Moreover there appeared to be no fear of undue competition for the 'large room' was used for 'public worship ... sermons and lectures' (Corry 1817).

Probably the last building of this *genre* was in Bennett Street, Manchester (1818) originally for St Clement's Parish but transferred to St Paul's in 1824. It was again a four-storey building (Figure 3.11) with end staircases. It is not known whether there was a 'large room' but the 1918 Centenary celebration programme speaks of a 'lecture' room. It was as late as 1860 before a writing school was established (Milner 1880: xx).

Figure 3.9

Stockport Sunday school (1805), interior of the 'large room'

Source: Wild (1891)

Miserable as the pedagogic content of the curriculum was, the Sunday schools were the sole provision for thousands of children, even after the monitorial day schools took root in the 1820s and 1830s. And as Wadsworth (1951: 119) points out what had started as 'a form of police action from above (was) transformed by the genius of ordinary people into a vital part of democratic society'. The change is evident in the later generation of buildings. Small classrooms have gone; the mill image is replaced with that of the church, both Gothic and Classical. The plans become that of an open hall or nave and as church day schools – often for infants – also used the space, teaching galleries appear.[6]

Setting the machine into motion

Everything was now set for Coleridge's 'great moral steam engine' to get moving. There was some political activity: in 1802 work and education were legally linked in Peel's Health and Morals of Apprentices – really the first Factory – Act. It limited to twelve the working hours of children farmed out to the mills by workhouses, and made education in the three 'Rs' during the working day and in religion on Sundays compulsory but was rendered nugatory by the combination of parents, employers and workhouse

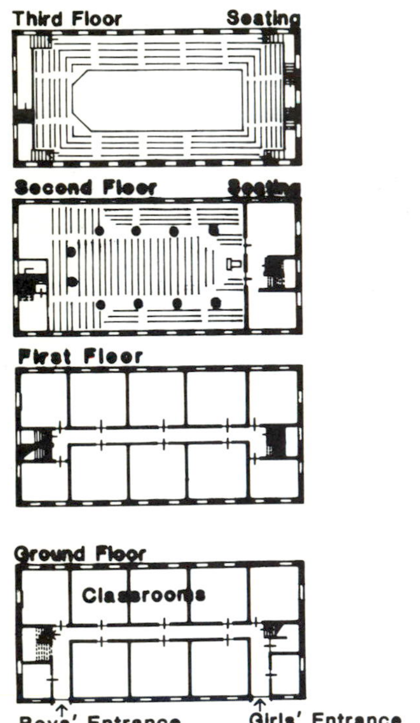

Figure 3.10

Macclesfield Sunday school (1813), plans, exterior view and interior of 'large room' from a contemporary builder's model and plans

Source: Macclesfield Museums Trust (exterior and large room); author's drawing (plans)

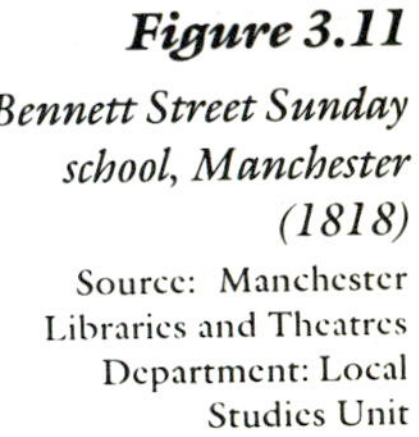

Figure 3.11

Bennett Street Sunday school, Manchester (1818)

Source: Manchester Libraries and Theatres Department: Local Studies Unit

masters. The efforts of the Whigs Whitbread and Brougham and the Radicals Mill, Place and Bentham bore fruit with the setting up of the Select Committee on the Education of the Lower Orders in the Metropolis in 1816; it had been preceded by enquiries into Irish education. But Government moved only slowly towards its first intervention in 1833. Long before then two forces converged to create a new urban school system: philanthropy, recognising the desperate plight of poor children, and fear, for property and of public disorder. Besides, the mills needed a disciplined workforce. It was the moment for Andrew Bell's and Joseph Lancaster's crucial intervention with their competitive monitorial (or 'mutual') systems.

Had Enlightenment ideas taken a stronger hold Bell and Lancaster would have had an easier time. Adam Smith had warned that with the division of labour the worker would become 'as stupid and ignorant as it is possible for a human creature to become ... his dexterity in his own particular trade, seems, in this manner, to be acquired at the expense of his intellectual, social and martial virtues'. He needed education to understand the interest of the country, defend it at times of need, and make him 'less liable ... to the delusions of enthusiasm, and superstition, which, among ignorant nations, frequently occasion the most dreadful disorders' (Smith 1776: 177–81).

But an educated workforce did not appeal to English Tories some forty years later. Patrick Colquhoun, magistrate and author of *A Treatise on the Police of the Metropolis* (1806) disliked the monitorial system even in its more conservative, Bell version. Smith's educated labourer could get out of hand. A minimalist economic solution would keep intact pre-industrial social relations whilst smoothing the development of industry. Only so could one avoid elevating

> their minds above the rank they are destined to fill in society, or ... an expense ... beyond the lowest rate ever paid for instruction. Utopian schemes for an extensive diffusion of knowledge would be injurious and absurd. A right bias to their minds, and a sufficient education to enable them to preserve, and to estimate properly, the religious and moral instruction they receive, is all that is, or ought ever to be, in contemplation. To go beyond this point would be to confound the ranks of society upon which the general happiness of the lower orders, no less than those that are more elevated, depends; since by indiscriminate education those destined for laborious occupations would become discontented and unhappy in an inferior situation of life, which, however, when fortified by virtue, and stimulated by industry, is not less happy than what is

> experienced by those who move in a higher sphere, of whose cares they are ignorant, and with many of whose anxieties and distresses they are never assailed.
>
> (Colquhoun 1806: 12–13)

Throughout Europe a dimension from education as a dangerous but necessary evil to an instrument for radical change was emerging. Along it lay any number of religious, political and philosophic positions which shaped not only rhetoric but every material detail down to the design of classroom furniture.

Economy in the cost of teachers was crucial. And what could be more economic than the machine? Coleridge's imagery was more than poetic rhetoric – a practical principle of order and discipline, and for maximising the use of time, space and teaching material. Lancaster claimed to be teaching 1000 children with one master by using child-monitors (1805: 23) and soon increased his claim to 10,000 (1806) as did Bell (1808a). A master who was

> able and diligent, could, without difficulty, conduct ten contiguous schools, each consisting of a thousand scholars ... Like the steam engine, or spinning machinery, it diminishes labour and multiplies work, but in the degree which does not admit of the same limits. For unlike the mechanical powers, this intellectual and moral engine, the more work it has to perform, the greater is the degree of perfection to which it is carried.
>
> (Bell 1808a)

Bernard waxes lyrical:

> The man who first made practical use of the *division of labour* gave a new power to the application of corporal strength, and simplified and facilitated the most irksome and laborious operations. To him we are indebted for "the greatest improvement in the productive powers of labour, and for the greater part of the skill, dexterity, and judgement which with which it is anywhere directed or applied" (quoting from Adam Smith) ... But that man, whatever was his merit, did no more essential service to *mechanical*, than Dr. Bell has done to *intellectual* operations. It is the division of labour in his schools, that leaves the master the easy task of directing the movements of the whole machine instead of toiling ineffectually at a single part. The principle in manufactories, and in schools is the same.
>
> (Bernard 1809: 35–6).

Although initially acknowledging each other's work, Bell and Lancaster soon competed for recognition as the inventors, accusing each other of plagiarism. Failing that, they claimed that earlier systems had anticipated their competitor.[7] But these were no more than the old system of ushers and boy assistants which existed even in Elizabethan grammar schools in what Curtis (1967: 96) calls 'a kind of monitorial system'. After 1805, stemming from Sarah Trimmer's initial attack on Lancaster, accusations and counter-accusations were flung about in profusion. To this day no definitive answer has emerged.

Bell certainly established publication priority with the 1797 description of his experience at Fort St George in Madras; hence the 'Madras system' label. He used boys of 11 to 14 as 'teachers' and those of 7 to 11 as 'assistant teachers' to teach 'classes' of 9 to 34 boys in a school of 200. Pairs of boys, one in the role of teacher the other of scholar, were supervised by the assistant teachers; they, in turn, by the teachers under the surveillance of three schoolmasters. 'After this manner the school teaches itself'(Bell 1797). The whole is finally under the superintendent 'whose scrutinising eye must pervade the whole system, whose active mind must give it energy, and whose unbiassed judgement must maintain the general order and harmony'. Although monitors are not named, here is the prototypical text; its underlying themes are mechanical efficiency, economy, military-style order, and an all-seeing, all-knowing, just controller.

In 1797 Bell tried to persuade David Dale to adopt his system at New Lanark. Soon he was experimenting in St Botolph's, Aldgate and in Swanage and, as we have seen, it was adopted in the Kendal industrial school in 1799.

Lancaster's first experiments were in a Sunday school he started on New Year's Day of 1798 in a room of his father's Southwark house. He then moved into a workshop, also his father's, and soon hired two workshops in Borough Road. In the autumn this became a day school and by 1799 he had 130 pupils at their lessons for 6 to 8 hours a day and was using monitors. In 1801 he erected his first schoolroom enlarged in 1803 from its original size of 35 feet by 33 to a length of 75 feet to accommodate 700 children. In the same year he published the first account, far more detailed than Bell's, of his full-blown monitorial system. In the following year he built a new room for 1000

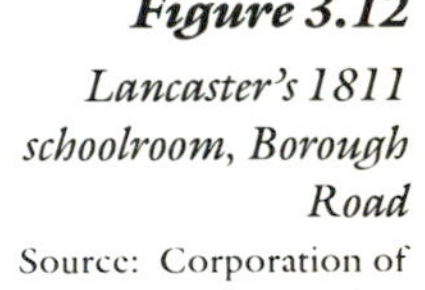

Figure 3.12
Lancaster's 1811 schoolroom, Borough Road
Source: Corporation of London: Greater London Record Office (Maps and Prints) (No. 4673)

boys in Belvedere Place, Borough Road, enlarged to 1200 capacity in 1811 to remain his model school till 1817. It also trained teachers of girls. In Figure 3.12 the older boys are seen writing on slates (occasionally they used paper and a quill pen) whilst the youngest write on sand trays on Bell's method. The spelling cards are on posts amongst the seats; one monitor is carrying a pile of cards with letters or numbers on them which will be hung on nails around the edge of the room. Here 12 to 20 boys will stand in semi-circular 'drafts' with their monitor. Hanging from the roof are kites, hoops and racquets – prizes Lancaster awarded when boys accumulated sufficient award tickets. Others were medals, money, books and pictures.

Whilst academic excellence was rewarded, punishments were never for poor performance but for talking, disorderly behaviour, bad language, disobedience and arriving dirty. They ranged from wearing admonitory labels or a wooden log around the neck, to wooden shackles tying the legs or both elbows behind the back. The most severe offenders were put in a sack or basket and raised to the ceiling by a rope, or shackled together round the neck by a wooden yoke and made to walk backwards. Conventional corporal punishment was not used; and these, even more barbarous forms had virtually disappeared by the 1820s.

The essence of 'mutual' teaching was the individual and successive instruction of each child by a monitor – island pairs of pedagogy – a caricature of the ancient master–pupil relationship. Both Bell and Lancaster placed a head monitor in overall charge under the master. In Bell's model school the boys were divided into three aisles, each under a monitor; within each, groups of up to 36 children were formed into 'classes' of equivalent proficiency, taught by a monitor and asssistant. Sometimes they were further subdivided. In Lancaster's version although a 'class' also meant all the children in the school of a given level of proficiency, the pedogogic group was a 'draft' of 12 to 20, each under a monitor. Other monitors looked after slates, clothes or registers for the entire school.

Two principles are already developed: 'emulation' and 'place-capturing'. The first pitted children against each other in pairs. The second gave competition *spatial* outcomes. When a child performs better than one above it, they swop places, as do entire classes – a method of marking rank in space which we have seen in the Sunday schools.

Although Lancaster was originally supported by the aristocracy, philanthropists, MPs and even Royalty, soon the Establishment and Evangelicals in the Church of England took fright at the success of a system run by a Dissenter and transferred their support to Bell, forming, in 1811, the National Society for Promoting the Education of the Poor in the Principles of the Established Church. Within a year work began on its model school in Baldwin's Gardens, Holborn, with S. P. Cockerell as the architect (Figure 3.13). There was a 60 foot square boys' schoolroom, and one for girls 60 feet by 40. The former had fixed benches and desks

Figure 3.13

Plan and interior of schoolroom of Bell's 'national' school at Baldwin's Gardens, Holborn (1811–13)

Source: Hamel (1818), British and Foreign School Society Archives

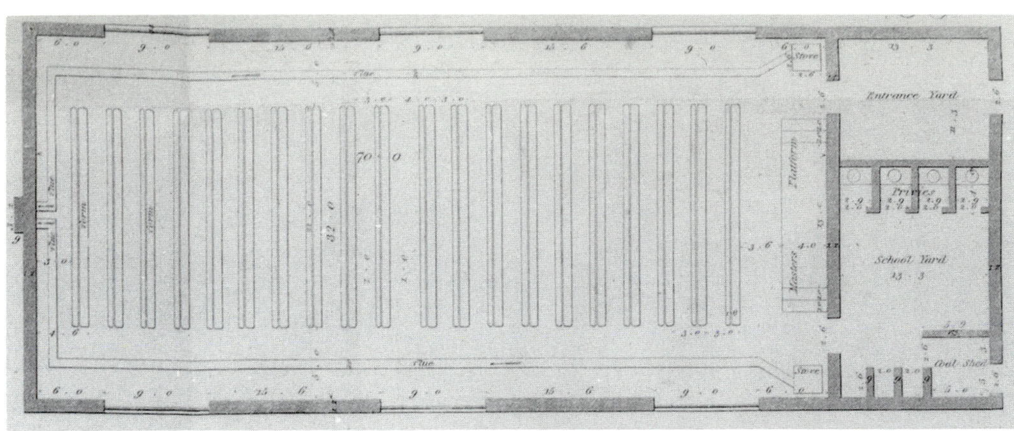

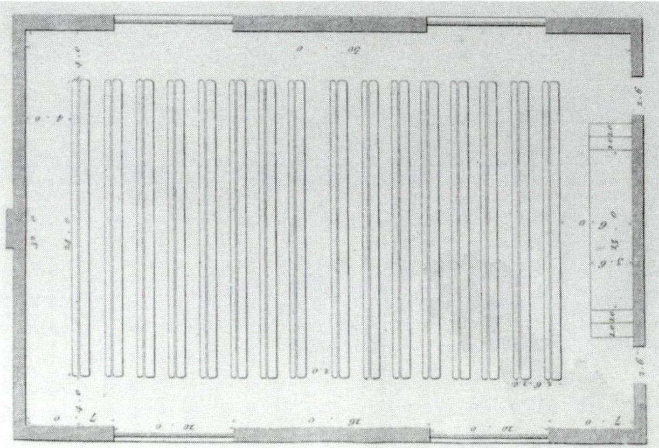

Figure 3.14

Lancaster's schoolrooms for 320 and 280 boys (1809)

Source: Lancaster (1809), plates from 1811 edition, Brynmor Jones Library, University of Hull

along the outer walls, as well as a line of sand trays and benches, for writing, and loose benches which allowed the boys to be formed into U-shaped hollow squares in the three aisles in classes of 36 for instruction in reading and arithmetic, the monitors central on the fourth (open) side. Alternatively children would stand in semicircles for these activities. The girls' room originally also had loose benches and two large work tables for sewing (National Society 1814: 194). The plan shows it with fixed wall writing benches and densely spaced loose benches in parallel rows for a sewing lesson, with a monitor's stool for each class.

Bell, like Lancaster, ranked children by performance; the genius and the dunderhead are paired in equivalent and opposite locations in the teaching 'U's and the pairing continues for those with intermediate abilities. 'First and last should be opposite one another, the rest at equal distances and the opposite sides equal; and the teacher to stand where he can see and have command of the whole class' (Bell 1827: 20).

After 1804 substantial National schools were built at home and abroad. Manchester had one for 1000 children in 1809 and the system was adopted in both British and Russian army barracks. In 1814 the original Abbey Orchard Street building in Westminster was replaced by one for 1000 children designed by William Inwood and in 1817 the Society received its Royal Charter.

As Lancaster spent much time travelling and creating propaganda, including his first Irish trip in 1806, and also because he was quite hopeless at managing finances, a group of friends formed a committee of Trustees in 1808 to pay off debts and improve management. They were led by another Quaker, William Allan who was well-connected – amongst others with Wilberforce, James Mill and two Royal Dukes – and had been involved with Robert Owen at New Lanark.

In 1810 the Committee of the Royal Lancasterian Institution for the Education of the Poor of Every Religious Persuasion was formed. Lancaster continued to cause financial and organisational problems. Following the adoption of a formal constitution in 1813 the Society adopted its final

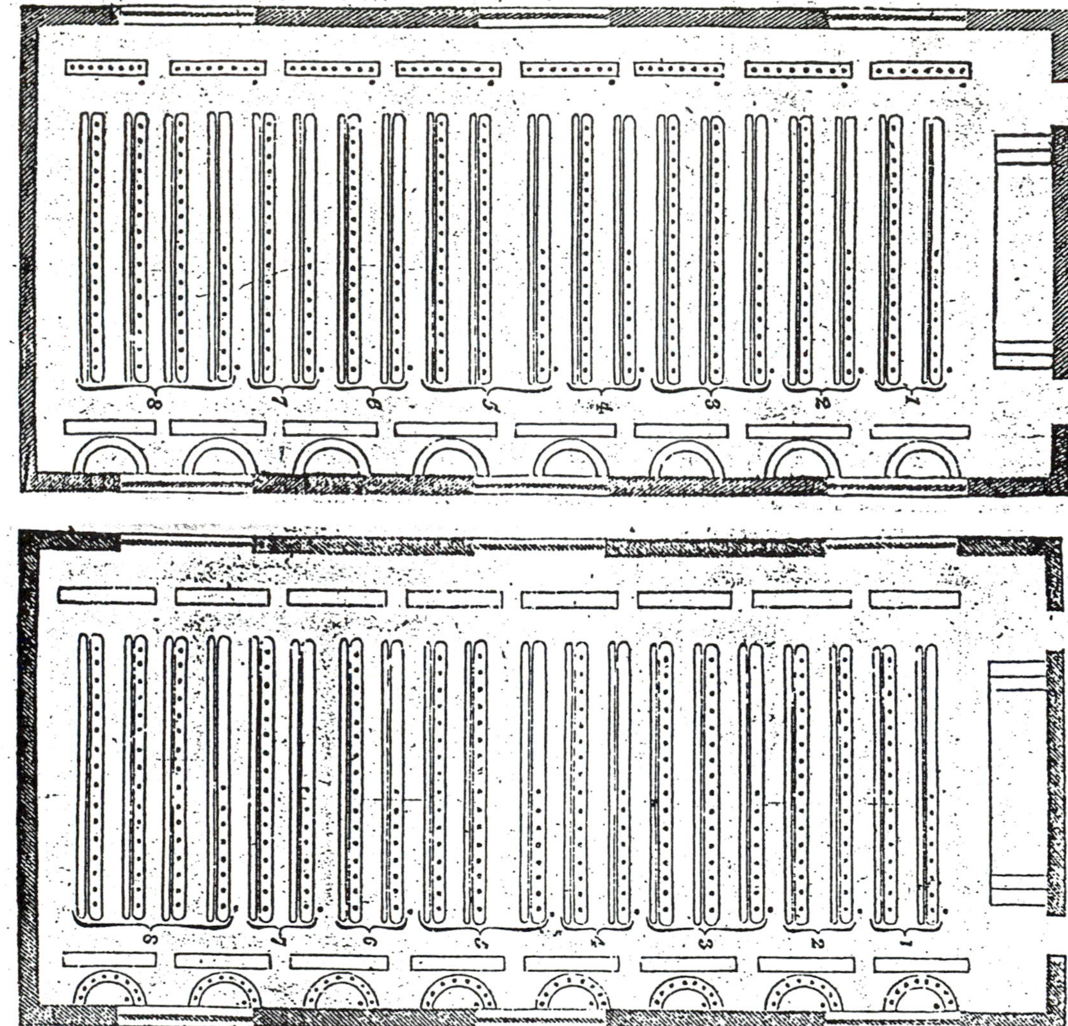

Figure 3.15

Dynamic reproduction of boys' movements on two Lancasterian schoolroom plans (1810)

Source: Lancaster (1810) plates 1 and 2, courtesy of the Friends Historical Library of Swarthmore College, Swarthmore, Pennsylvania

title, the British and Foreign School Society, in 1814. After more scandals, debts and accusations Lancaster resigned as superintendent of Borough Road in that year but continued to travel, publish, engage in often doomed experiments, found schools at home and abroad and to make increasingly sweeping claims for his system until his death in America in 1838.

The handbooks published between 1809 and the 1820s elaborated the teaching methods and illustrated details of schoolrooms, furniture and equipment. They deserve a closer look before returning to the new model ('normal') schools opened in Borough Road in 1817.

Two plates (Lancaster 1809c) show schoolrooms for 320 or 280 *boys* 'on a compressed plan', with desks holding 16 to 18, all facing towards the master (Figure 3.14). Back-to-back desks or those facing the wall are condemned as 'a cause of serious inconvenience, and the cause of much disorder, as the consciousness of being under the master's eye, has a tendency to prevent half the common school offences'. Buttresses, projecting fireplaces or other protrusions give opportunities for 'being out of their master's sight'.

The floor is flat for 15 feet in front of the master's desk; then it slopes up at 1:15 for ease of surveillance. Sections show stoves, with floor warm-air ducts and high level windows. Details appear of entrances, yards and privies – the latter at the deepest part of the simple tree-like spatial structure.

By 1810 a dynamic representation is used. The boys are represented by dots – some in seats, writing, others along one side of the room in lines of eight with their monitors, ready to move to the reading stations; then the dots are shown at their reading semi-circles on the other side of the room having moved at the sound of a bell (Figure 3.15). On the frontispiece a group of seated boys hold up their slates on the monitor's command 'Show slates!'. Written on them is a sentence which, Lancaster says, 'every Briton will wish to be engraven, not only in memory, but on the hearts of the rising generation – Long live the King!'. Such images, and constant dedications to Royalty and Dukes, was a permanent feature of Lancaster's name-dropping and fawning. An

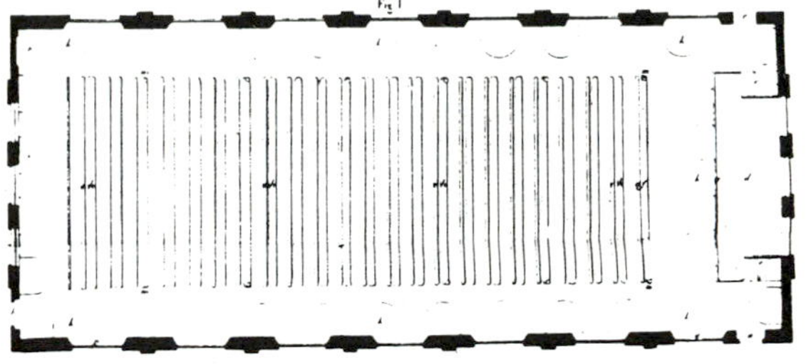

Figure 3.16

Plan of Lancaster's Borough Road schoolroom (1816–17)

Source: Hamel (1818), British and Foreign School Society Archives

Figure 3.17

Interior of Borough Road schoolroom

Source: Hamel (1818), British and Foreign School Society Archives

Figure 3.18

Borough Road school, front elevation (1817)

Source: Guildhall Library

Figure 3.19

Children's body postures and groupings in Lancasterian schools (1818)

Source: Hamel (1818), British and Foreign School Society Archives

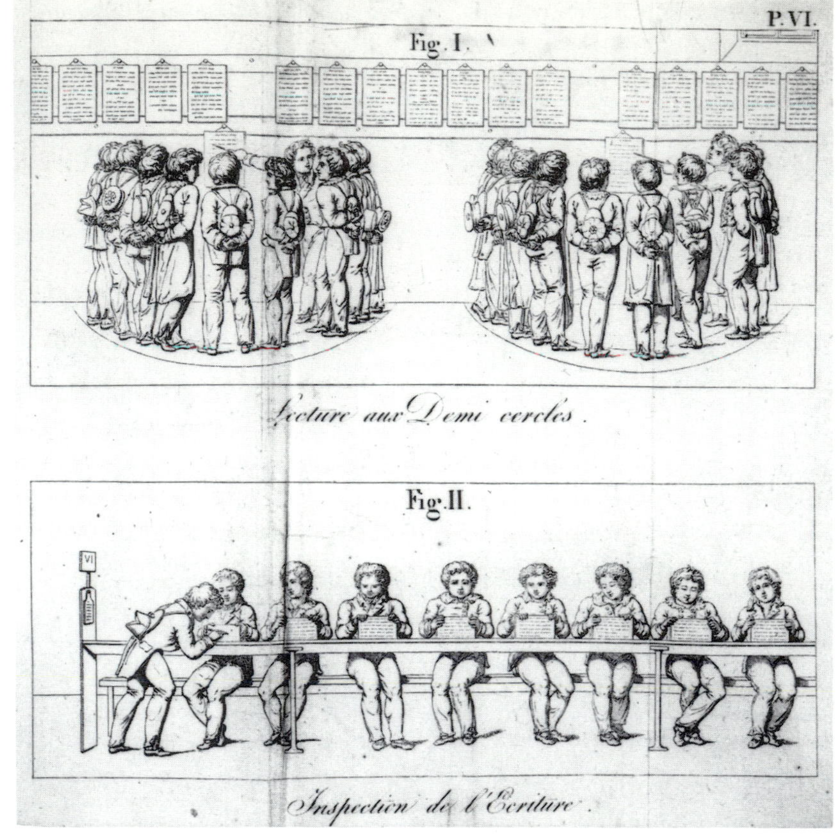

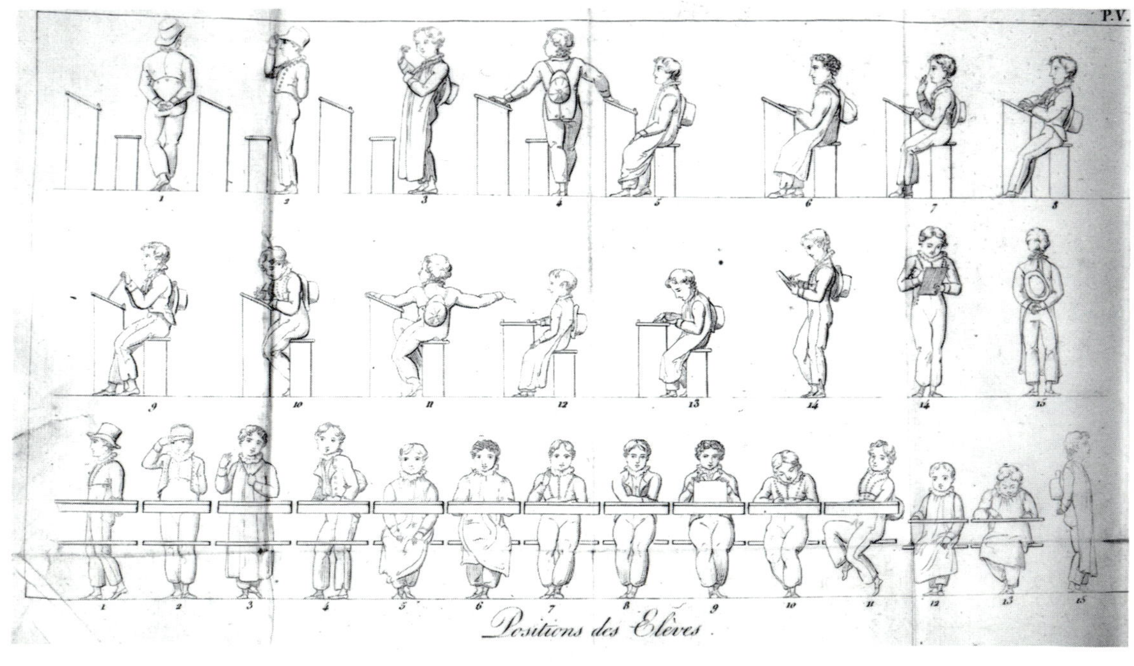

Figure 3.20

Monitor's seat, movable lesson stand, alphabet wheel and bench with holes for hats for American Lancasterian schools (1820)

Source: 1820 N.Y. Manual, courtesy of the Friends Historical Library of Swarthmore College, Swarthmore, Pennsylvania

Monitor's Seat and Desk.

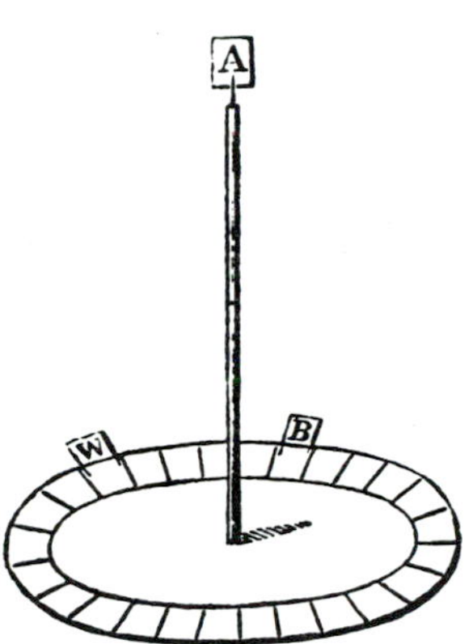

Moveable Stand.

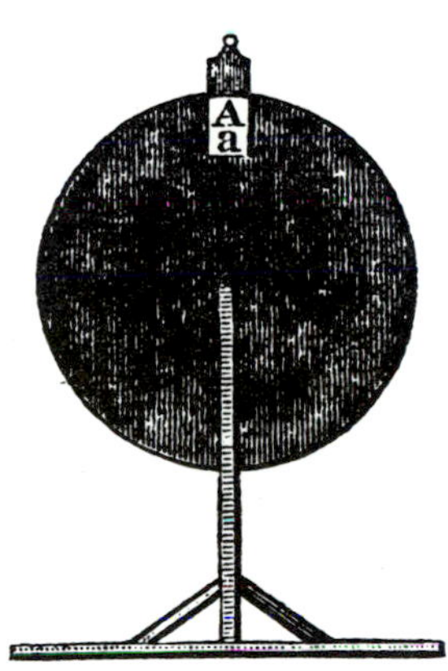

Alphabet-Wheel.

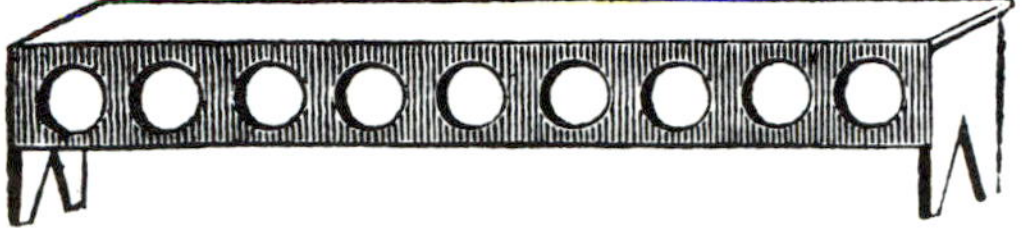

Bench with holes for Hats.

Figure 3.21

French monitorial school in the rue de Port-Mahon, Paris (1818)

Source: Musée Nationa de l'Education, Paris

identical American edition of 1812 has one alteration – the frontispiece shows the letter D (for 'democracy'?) on the slates!

In 1816 much of the earlier material re-appears but the model plan is almost that of the boys' room at Borough Road now under construction with a double entrance from the street next to the master's platform so that 'visitors on entering the school may have a commanding view of all the children at once' (Figure 3.16). At the other end is a door to the playground and privies. There are 19 rows of parallel desks, each for 16 children. Around three sides and also against the platform are 31 teaching semi-circles. The interior view (Figure 3.17) shows the master, the superintending monitor on a stool, the monitors at the ends of the desks where their drafts are seated, and a group of visitors.

In 1817 Borough Road opened its splendid buildings designed by Samuel Robinson (Figure 3.18). It served as a worlwide exemplar for more than a quarter of a century. The central block housed the Society's offices, men's and women's training institutions, a book repository and residential accommodation for pupil teachers; the two symmetrical wings the boys' and girls' model schoolrooms.

Illustrations henceforth show in minute detail the schoolroom and its equipment as well as body postures, gestures and location of slates, hats and other paraphernalia (Figure 3.19).

The American Free-School Society produced an 1820 edition of the Manual. A school had been set up in 1806; following Lancaster's second visit in 1818 the New York model school was established. Its plan is standard, but furniture is becoming more elaborate; Figure 3.20 shows the movable lesson stand, the alphabet wheel and the

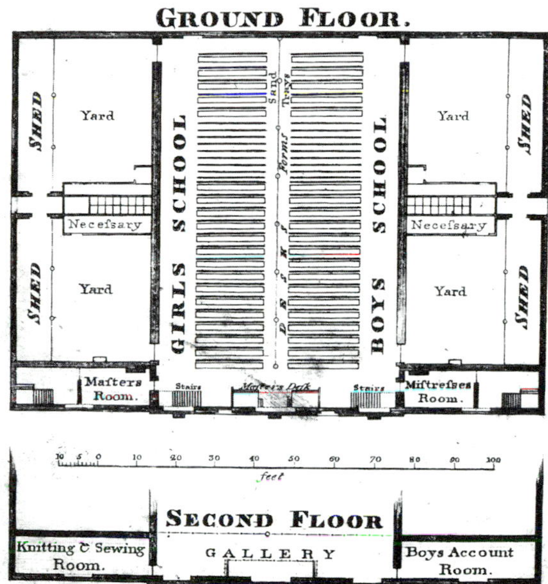

Figure 3.22

Manchester and Salford national school (plan, 1812) and Duke Street national school, Macclesfield (1813)

Source: Manchester Reference Library and Macclesfield Museums Trust bench with holes for hats. Moreover the monitor now has his own seat and sloping desk. A special supplement on a girls' school goes into immense detail on how monitors can supervise sewing and knitting. Wood (1839), during an 1838 visit, notes that the schools have one schoolroom over the other, with a 'primary' (infant) school frequently in the basement. He reports many schools in church basements.

By 1821 Lancaster had settled in Baltimore and in a new edition describes how he rejected the possibilities of studying for the ministry and was drawn to the Society of Friends by his conscience which he calls 'the monitor of his own heart'. So the system now is responsible both for an external order and the most secret inner movement.

From 1831 the Society was publishing comprehensive Manuals (British and Foreign Schools Society 1831) with plans for schools of various sizes which were now widespread across Europe. Sweden had them after 1810 (Ohlander 1923), as did Russia, and in France it was clearly the chief system both in the capital and the provinces (Tronchet 1972? and Ponteil 1966). A specialised Parisian school for geometrical drawing used the Lancasterian methods in the 1820s (Francoeur 1824, 1827). Prototype plans for urban and village schools appeared in a French 1819 handbook (*Guide de l'enseignement* 1819). During the First Empire existing buildings were converted to 'mutual' schools. In a classical building; under the ormolu clock and the watchful eye of the Emperor, a writing lesson is taking place in the rue de Port-Mahon school. The room is full of visitors and the ditty at the foot of the engraving describes the progression from sand to polished slate and finally to paper (Figure 3.21).

The system was even harnessed to the education of American Indians, a project that Lancaster actively espoused on his 1818 visit (Rayman 1981: 395–409).

In the meantime the message of Baldwin's Gardens was diffusing through trained teachers and model designs. Either boys and girls were separated by a central aisle as at the 1812 Manchester and Salford National Schools or by floor as in the grander 1813 Macclesfield school (Figure 3.22). In the former the single row of peripheral writing desks was replaced by fifteen facing the master, behind them nine rows of forms, and at the very back five of sand trays.

Baldwin's Gardens itself had to move into the Westminster Free School on expiry of its lease in 1832.

National, like British, shools, spread worldwide: Nova Scotia, Cape Town, Russia, and Barbados. But, unlike Lancaster, Bell continued the manual work traditions of Sarah Trimmer and the Charity and industrial schools: 'Every institution for training up of the poor, I regard as imperfect if it does not embrace industry – their appropriate virtue, to which they cannot be too early trained and habituated' (Bell 1808b). Early reports abound with references to shoe-making, spinning, knitting, agricultural and horticultural work and straw plaiting (though Lancaster too had his favourite rural scheme for making straw hats).

Monitors had to keep pupils ceaselessly under surveillance and be, in turn, under the master's eye. In 1848 (Harris and Tearle 1848) the Society produced a detailed guide to schoolrooms and 'class' arrangements: 'all the parts of the scholastic machine must be properly adjusted, every wheel must perform its appointed work ... the whole machine of the school-room is set in motion' (1848: 57) so that the ensuing 'perfect discipline' will produce an atmosphere like that in a church (1848: 67). The U-shapes are designed to achieve elaborate visual control. Monitors were to be seen by the master, and see the faces of their class and of adjacent classes, and also each other's so that they can 'indicate, by a look or a motion, what is wrong' (1848: 15) without the need to speak and thus distract the children; children were not to see the faces of those in other classes. A change already prefigured at Manchester and Salford was the abandonment of the wall writing desks and their replacement by double or triple rows in blocks (Figure 3.23). Government recommended this arrangement from the start of its intervention and by 1844 offered to pay two thirds of the cost of converting old-style Bell writing desks (Council on Education Minutes 1845: 113).

The 'Madras' system inspired new geometries of competition. John Stoat (1826), master of Islington Parochial Schools, disliked place-capturing; instead he wanted children to move around in a ring (Figure 3.24) clockwise or anti-clockwise in 'perpetual motion' according to performance. Each time a child passed the umpire – whose job was only to keep records of movement – he gained or lost a medal according to the *direction* of rotation. Children were not relocated by performance and they taught each other in pairs, always the superior child teaching the inferior.

Jeremy Bentham absorbed monitorial develop-

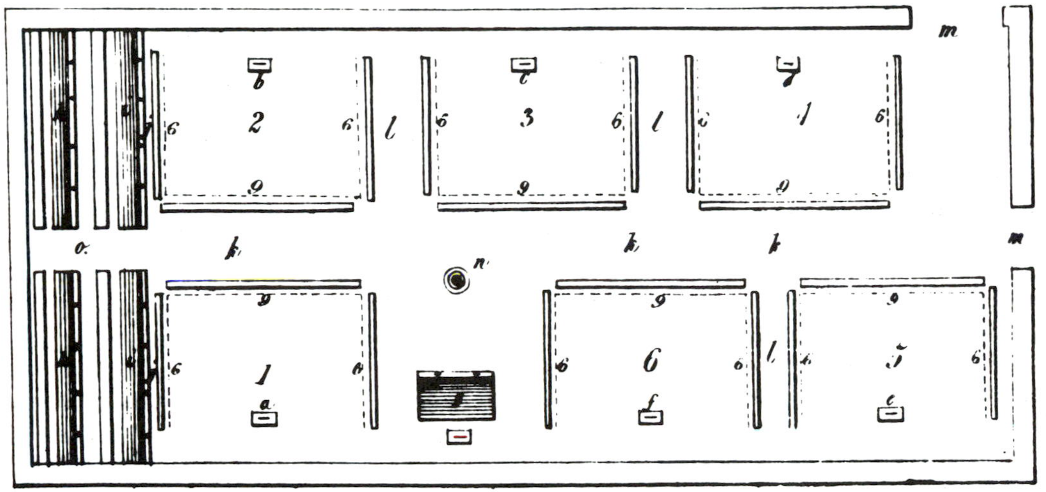

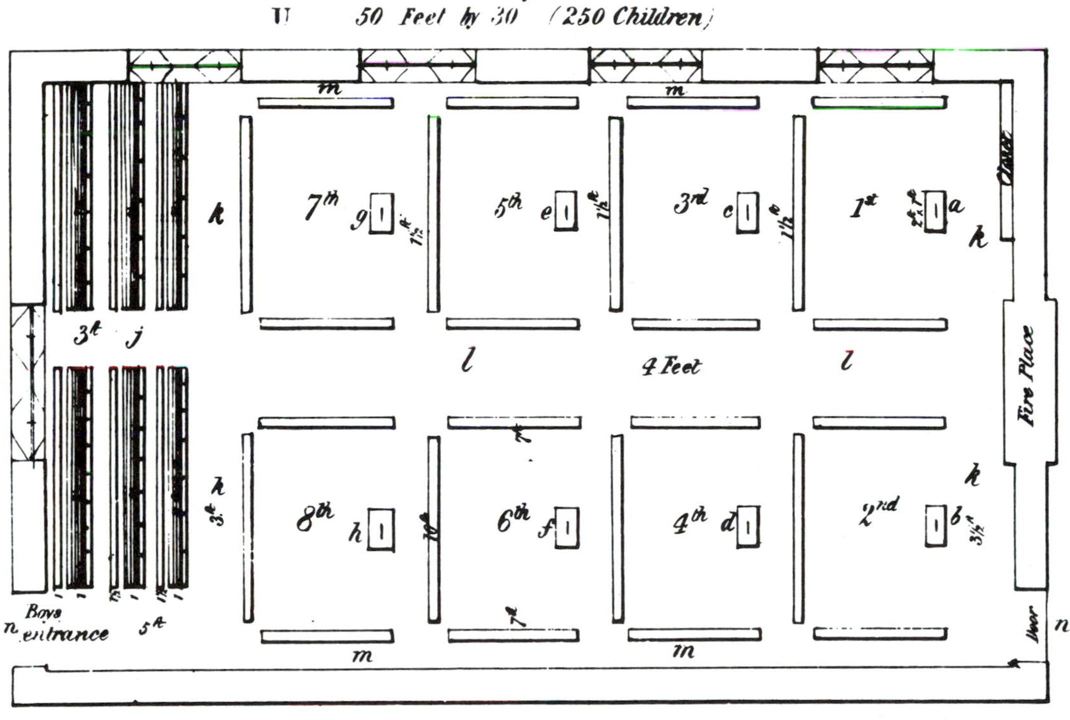

Figure 3.23
'National' (Bell) recommended schoolroom layouts with 'U's designed to prevent children in one 'class' making eye contact with those from another; writing desks in double and triple rows (1848)
Source: Harris (1848), The National Society

ments for his own purposes. He moved in the circles of Brougham, Place, Mill and Allan, and was acquainted with Owen's New Lanark. When in 1815 Place could find no school for his nine children Bentham immediately set about designing one (for his own garden) with the help of James Bevans, whose prison and asylum designs appear later. The system was to be 'Chrestomathic' – for use 'in the middling and higher ranks of life' – where a grand 'encyclopaedic table' of knowledge determined the sequence in which subjects were taught. They were to be practical and intellectual, with emphasis on science, history and geography. Classics were eschewed, unless needed for one of the learned professions. Stress was placed on

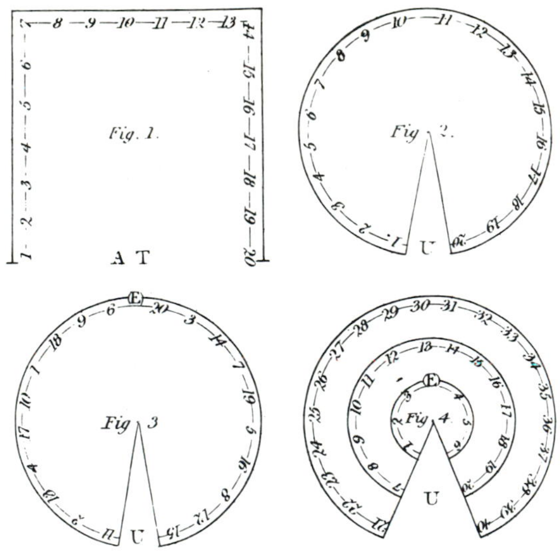
Fig. 1.
A T
Fig. 2.
U
Fig. 3
U
Fig. 4
U
(E)
The Numbers described on the above Figures are intended to represent the children of the classes, & their individual relative proficiency.
Fig. 1. A class of children arranged in the order of proficiency as evinced by competition for places, according to the Madras system of Education. No. 1. the Superior No. 20. the inferior Child, &c.
Fig. 2. The Circular Class. U. The station of the Umpire.
Fig. 3. The Numbers here shew the mixed state of the superior & inferior Children, and the advantageous position of the superior part of the Class for instructing the inferior Children, which is produced by the method of working circulating classes. (E) The place of the Medal stand or point of reckoning.
Fig. 4. The compound circulating class. (E) The point of reckoning &c. as described in the Treatise.

What is God?
A Spirit
How should we worship him?
In Spirit and in Truth

Figure 3.24

Stoat's 'circulating' class (1826)

Source: Stoat (1826), by permission of the Librarian, Glasgow University Library

system, logic, the use of pictures, models, experiments, machinery and continuous assessment.

Bentham had proposed circular Nursery Panopticons in 1794, next to a Panopticon prison, situated at the centre of a semi-circle of cottages for fallen women. This was probably his 'Northotropium' for 'The innocent offspring of clandestine love' (Evans 1971: 34). His twelve-sided Chrestomathic school (Figure 3.25) had seats for 900 boys taught by a single master in the centre surrounded by six monitors in a ring. Although using Bell's more mechanical system, in general he favoured Lancaster whose teaching semi-circles appear around the walls. The floor sloped up to these. The spirit of the 1791 Panopticon design was alive in:

> the sentiment of an invisible omniscience … The principle of central and complete inspection, which a simple architectural contrivance affords, has been proved so wonderfully to augment the powers of superintendence, that it cannot fail materially to improve the influence of the teacher in a seminary of instruction.
>
> (Bentham 1816)

While Bentham's mind ranged over the whole range of educational schemes – for the poor as for the middle classes, from nurseries, through infant, primary and secondary schools to university, and from buildings to curricula – those who struggled with practical projects could not afford the luxury of such breadth. Amongst them were the founders of infant education.

The formation of the infant character

Robert Owen's visions of an orderly industrial community are discussed in Chapter 10. In 1799 he found at New Lanark Dale's school for children under six (the age at which they started work in the mills) taught by full-time dominies, with evening instruction for the older ones. Owen raised the minimum age for work to ten, and set out to change infant education in his New Institution for the Formation of Character. Children from the age of two to ten, occasionally twelve, were to have 'all their habits, bodily and mental, formed to carry them to a high state of perfection; … for to these people are entrusted the care and use of nice and valuable machinery' (Owen 1812: 20). Ultimately the labouring class will 'become so well instructed, as to (be able to) distinguish clearly between its true and apparent interests' (1812: 21). 'The child will be removed, so far as is at present practicable, from the erroneous treatment of the yet untrained and untaught parents' (1813: 135). These ideas flowed naturally from Locke's belief in the malleability of the human mind, Hartley's associanist theories and Rousseau's assertion of innate freedom. But Owen insisted that his applied to all classes. 'Children are, without exception, passive and wonderfully contrived compounds; … (they) may be formed collectively to have any human character' (1813: 110). This gives an opportunity not only to change the individual but to re-shape social structure. By judicious training 'the infants of any one class in the world may be readily formed into men of any other class' (1813: 174).

According to his son Robert Dale Owen (1874: 101) the start of the building in 1809 became the focus for the conflict between Owen and his partners concerning expenditure on visionary socialism. Though completed in 1813 Owen could not afford to fit it out till 1816. At first he envisaged saving the youngest children from 'material injury in the formation of their characters (from) the primary evils' of undiscipline, unreason and moral confusion, by simply providing a supervised playground; each child:

> on his entrance into the play-ground, is to be told in language which he can understand, that 'he is never to injure his playfellows, but on the contrary he is to contribute all in his power to make them happy'.
>
> (Owen 1813: 134)

The children were getting basic education on the ground floor. The over-fives moved up one level to the organised schoolrooms into a full system of infant education.

The building (Figure 3.26) had a basement store room, a ground floor with three rooms, including an infants' classroom (Robert Dale claims there were two), a dining room and kitchen, and an open 140 by 40 foot first floor, intended as a schoolroom for the older children, a lecture room and a church. Soon it was divided into two; the larger part for its original purposes, the smaller for use as lecture or ball-room, for teaching dancing and singing, and occasionally as a reading class room. It appears in the famous print which also shows the visitors' gallery on slender iron columns at one end (Figure 3.27). According to Robert Dale the larger room, laid

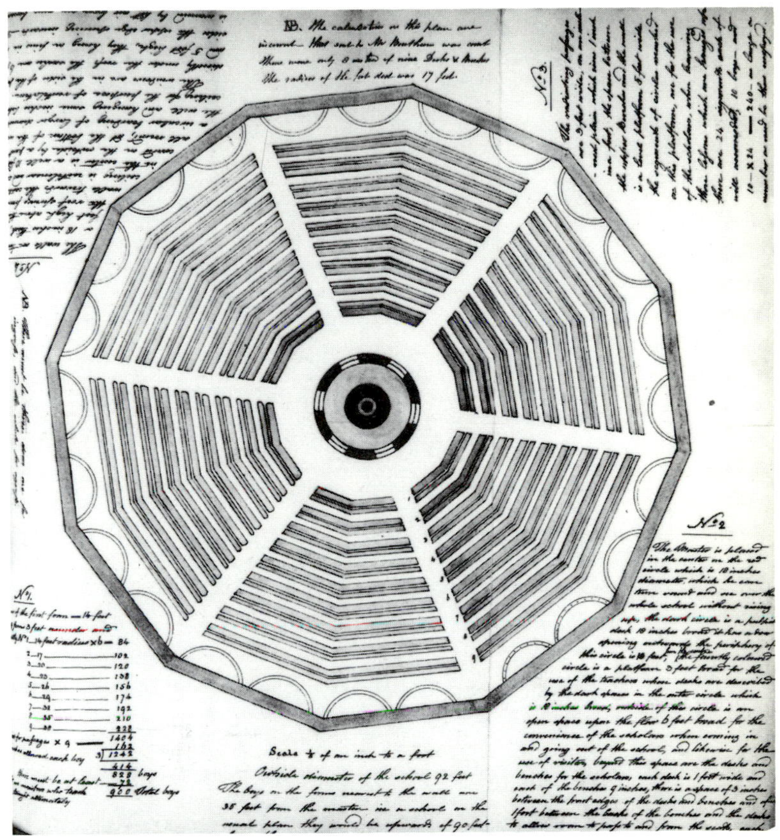

Figure 3.25

Jeremy Bentham's twelve-sided 'Chrestomathic' monitorial school (1815)

Source: British Library 'Place Papers' 60

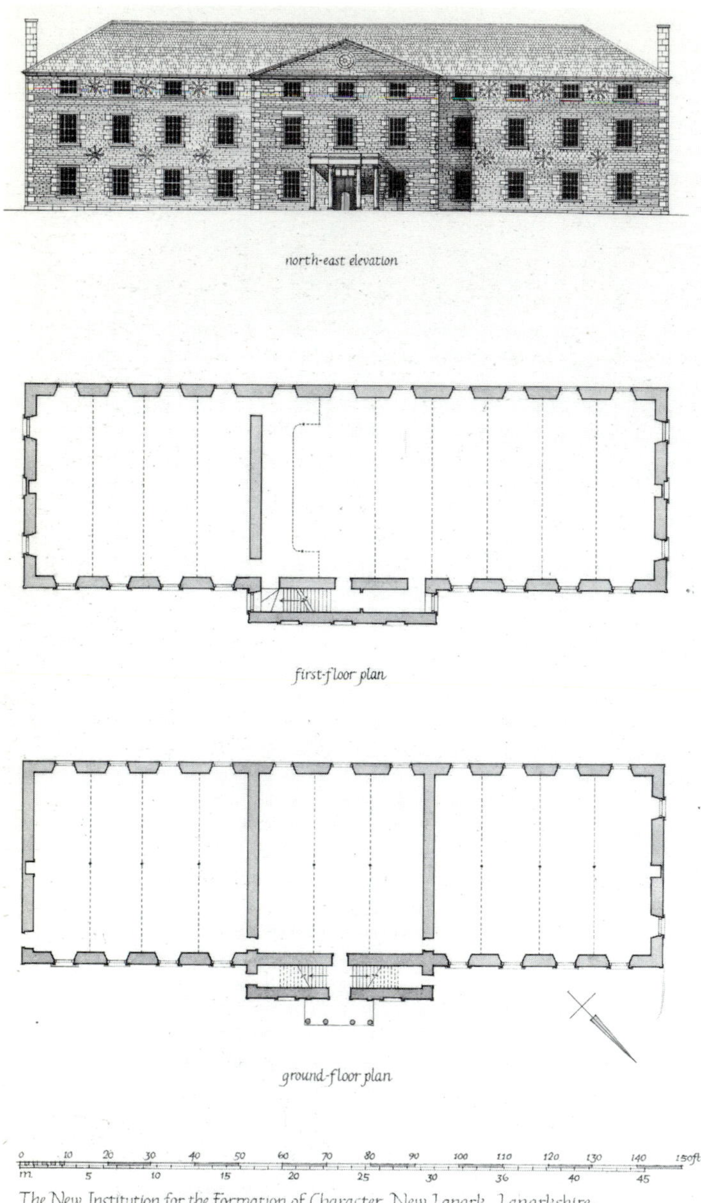

Figure 3.26

The New Institution for the Formation of Character, New Lanark (1809–13), elevation and plans

Source: RCAHMS Edinburgh (LAD/22/28), © Royal Commission on the Ancient and Historical Monuments of Scotland

out on Lancasterian lines, had 'galleries' round three sides; these were either tiered steps or a single platform (1824).

The latest heating system was used – warm air, the hollow cast iron structural columns acting as vertical ducts – whose origin is traced in Chapter Ten to William Strutt's cast iron framed Derby mill.

A second school was built in 1817.

Owen was ambivalent about monitors. At a dinner for Lancaster held in Glasgow Owen supported him strongly, reckoning that both Lancaster and Bell would 'for ever be ranked among the most important benefactors of the human race' (1813: 105). But soon he distinguished between the 'manner' of their system – which he continued to support – and its 'matter' which he said lacked content and was merely mechanical. For whilst the 'children may be taught, by either Dr. Bell's or Mr. Lancaster's system, to read, write, account, and sew, (they) yet acquire the worst habits, and have their minds rendered irrational for life (by) this mockery of learning' (178–9). For room layout Lancaster was his guide, though certain of Bell's details 'are very deserving of adoption'. Owen employed an infant master, a mistress and about ten assistants, probably teenagers, as monitors.

The master was James Buchanan; though devoted to and expert with the infants, he left in 1818 to set up the first English infant school at Brewer's Green in Westminster – according to Owen at Brougham's request. More likely Buchanan left of his own volition after a quarrel, and probably Owen's later derogatory remarks sprang from resentment at the attribution to Buchanan of the *invention* of infant education. The evidence suggests that it was indeed Buchanan's natural inventive genius and simple kindness which inaugurated a system for which Owen had merely supplied a bare room and a playground, and certain abstract ideas with little pedagogic content.

There was emphasis on objects and pictures, walking, dancing, singing, and rhythmical recitation. The alphabet and numbers were introduced through play. A toga-like dress became the school uniform and quietness, order and discipline were underlying themes. Boys over five were drilled in military exercises in the playground, including how to handle guns – initially wooden ones with the intention of graduating to real ones later – so as to provide a local force to replace the militia and thus 'to render the most effectual defence of their country'. Of course that was written during the final stages of the Napoleonic Wars when Owen found his reputation as a dangerous rationalist, Deist-agnostic and internationalist to be a real hindrance.

McCann and Young (1982) give the best account of Buchanan's role. A year after opening Brewer's Green in 1819 he became a Swedenborgian in the same congregation as Samuel Wilderspin who became involved with its Sunday school in 1816 and in 1821 with a day school. In 1819 Wilderspin moved to Spitalfields and by

Figure 3.27
The New Institution for the Formation of Character, New Lanark (1809–13), interior
Source: New Lanark Conservation Trust

1820 was being given instruction by Buchanan at Westminster. At the same time Joseph Wilson, a Spitalfields silk merchant and Evangelical committee member for Buchanan's school, wanted to open a similar one in his home Parish – one of great poverty – where two National and two Lancasterian Schools were already operational. Buchanan recommended Wilderspin and in 1820 the Infant School in Quaker Street was set up, opposite the 1819 National School. Wilderspin as master and his wife as mistress took up residence in the schoolhouse.

Whilst the system owed much to Buchanan, there was close contact with Owen who claimed greater affinity with Wilderspin than with Buchanan. Its ideological basis was a mixture of undogmatic religion (arising from Wilderspin's Swedenborgianism), Owenite rationalism, Enlightenment ideals, Evangelical philanthropy and production-oriented ideas of discipline. After 1825 he added the ideas of Pestalozzi developed at Yverdun.

Little is known about these converted premises in Quaker Street except that they had his first innovation, a key feature of later infant schools: an enclosed brick-paved playground with vines, trees, a flower border and flower pots in the centre. The first edition of Wilderspin's seminal book on infant education (1823) under various titles went through seven British and foreign editions by the 1850s and was a powerful influence. It described the Quaker Street curriculum, though the building has to be imagined from his prescriptive model.

He recommends a schoolroom measuring 50 feet square for 300 infants, with posts for suspending alphabet cards, and an adjacent 'classroom', measuring 15 feet square – his second innovation. Here the master or mistress taught reading or arithmetic to a 'class' of children of the same age or having the same ability, in circles or squares, sometimes around a table with wooden teaching blocks or other aids. The room was also used for examination of individual children and for training monitors.

The benches around the walls of the schoolroom seat 175, the remaining 125 being accommodated on four 'forms' at one end of the room, which can be raised on pulleys to the ceiling (recalling Owen's use of pulleys at New Lanark to raise the canteen tables for dances). There is a central stove and a master's desk at one end – where all can see him and from which 'they may be governed by a motion of the hand'. The forms are the progenitors of Wilderspin's third design innovation – the raked teaching 'gallery' whose

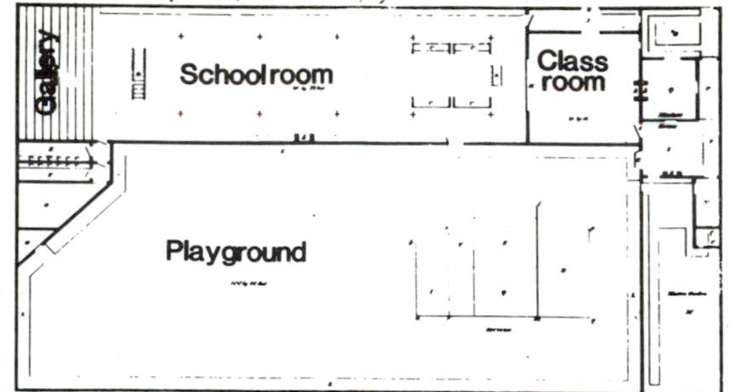

Figure 3.28

First published plan of Wilderspin's infant school (1825)

Source: Wilderspin (1825)

invention he ascribed, later, to the need to teach all the children *together*, as they were in the classroom, in what soon became known as the 'simultaneous' method. 'I then made various experiments with seats, but did not succeed, until, at length, the construction of a gallery, or succession of steps, the youngest occupying the lower and the eldest the higher, answered the desired end' (Wilderspin 1832: 5–6). It is not until the 1825 edition that it took this developed form.

In 1824 (171) the playground as both *simulacrum* and laboratory is developed: 'The playground may be compared to the world, where the little children are left to themselves, there it may be seen what effects their education has produced'.

By 1825[8] a plan and section appear for the first time (Figure 3.28). The teaching gallery is fully-fledged. The classroom is 80 feet by 20 with four pews for visitors in front of the master's desk, a rostrum for the monitor when he teaches in the gallery and teaching posts; the playground has flower borders and the kitchen of the attached master's house projects into the playground so that he can see the children whilst at dinner. The peripheral seats are divided at 15 foot intervals by vertical partitions to separate the classes; each space has the children's and their two monitors' names over it.

In 1824 the short-lived Infant School Society was founded; subject to increasing attacks by Established churchmen for 'liberal' and 'scientific' tendencies it was wound up in 1828 after which Wilderspin continued independently. In the following year he began to distance himself from both Owen and Buchanan, calling their schools 'asylums' to keep children out of mischief, rather than places 'of moral and intellectual cultivation' which was his 'original and untried' task. His claims as originator of infant education become increasingly extravagant.

Both pedagogic and material recommendations become more detailed. Children were to be

Figure 3.29

City of London infant school, Bishopsgate (1828)

Source: Corporation of London: Greater London Record Office, Third Report of the London Infant School Society (1828)

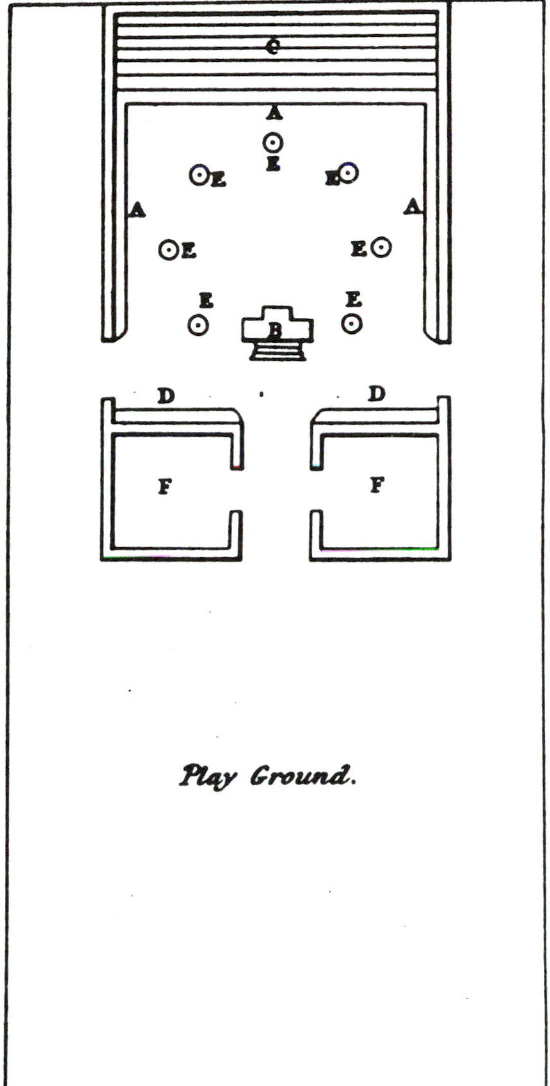

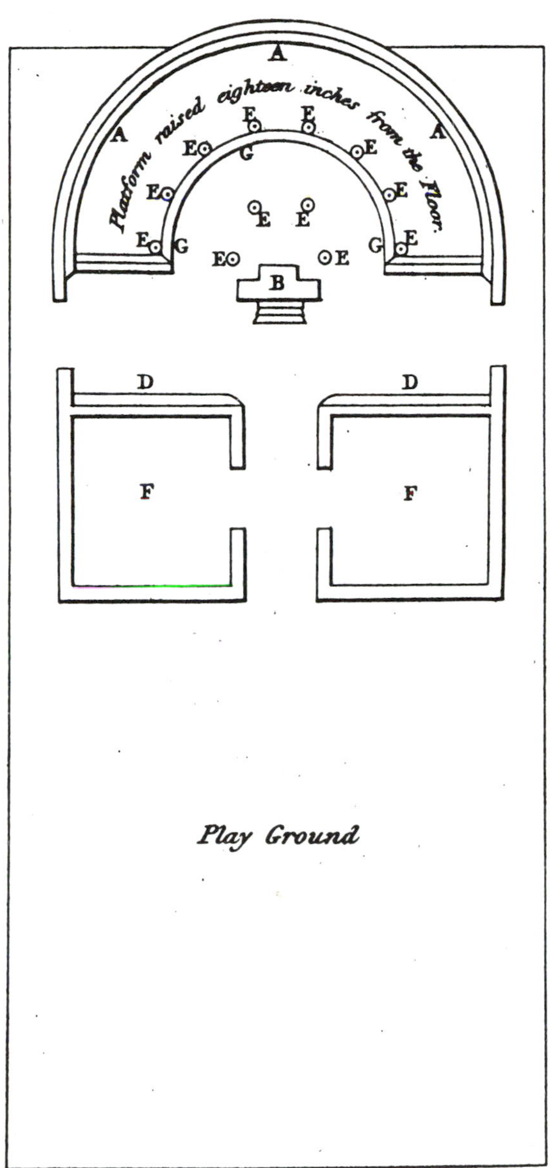

Figure 3.30
Wilson infant school plans (1825)
Source: Wilson (1825), British Library

'classed' by both 'capacity' and age and were to move as they showed changes in ability so that classes would remain homogeneous. The width of the schoolroom is increased from 22 feet to 30 and the master's desk gets a rostrum.

The critics founded the competitive Committee of the City of London Infant Schools in 1825 which by 1828 had its own model school in Liverpool Buildings, Bishopsgate, differing from Wilderspin's in that children sit in three concentric semicircles and teaching posts have gone (Figure 3.29).

By now others were taking a lead, amongst them David Goyder, also a member of Buchanan's and Wilderspin's Swedenborgian congregation, who set up his school at Bristol in 1821 on established lines: playground with flowers and trees, a classroom, schoolroom with teaching circles, several ranks of monitors, use of pictures and objects and indoor swings. The floor was marked out for rhythmical figure marching and his illustrations show children in geometrical groupings. The:

> mechanical parts of the System, particularly the marching, which has delighted every visitor who has attended the School, will be found perhaps one of the most efficient ways to promote subordination which has yet been adopted ... coincident with principles of the truly benevolent Robert Owen Esq.
>
> (Goyder 1825: v–vi)

'Order is heaven's first law' (1824: 18) and punishments for its breaches are more severe than Wilderspin's; they included wooden handcuffs for fighting and wooden stocks on the legs for running away.

Another Wilderspin disciple, William Wilson, brother of Joseph and Vicar of Walthamstow, founded a celebrated school there in 1824. He was the author of a Manual in 1825 that ran into several editions. Naturally he saw the infant school as a Parish institution, one of whose objects was to eliminate troublesome children ('removing many a noxious weed') before proceeding to the National school. The children's attention had to be held with 'the smallest possible bodily exertion'. The teacher should appear to be the same distance from each child. Wilson expands on the faculties to be formed for discipline in later life: the mind – memory, judgement, conscience and heart, and the body – health and cleanliness. The 'morning purification' was to be accompanied by choral washing songs. For older infants, besides reading, arithmetic and religion, there was writing for the boys and sewing for the girls. There is division into classes, and monitors are used (girls are unsuitable). Boys and girls are to be separated immediately after morning assembly to opposite sides of the room; this 'will encourage a delicacy of mind and propriety of manners'.

Wilson presents two layouts (Figure 3.30). In one the gallery extends in two wings to embrace a circle of teaching posts alongside which two monitors stand or sit on stools. At the head of the circle is a double platform rostrum for the monitor to stand in front of the superintendent. Two additional rows of seats for older children (possibly monitors?) are *behind* the rostrum as they do not require continuous supervision. The route to the playground is between two classrooms. In the classroom children of the higher classes receive personal instruction and are also individually examined. In the other the gallery is replaced by a double row of apsidal seats, at the back of a wide platform which has the teaching posts at its edge. The timetable is a hybrid with categories of space, curricular content and teacher. It defines four teaching modes: 'rostrum, gallery, classes and class-room'. The first takes place in the gallery, led by a monitor. The second is also in the gallery, but superintendent-led, and confined to religion (hymn singing and 'moral lessons') and the one arithmetical theme too difficult for monitors to tackle – division. 'Class' teaching is by monitors in the main room whilst 'class-*room*' teaching is by the superintendent.

By 1829 the 'large room' contains an oval 'fold' for the smallest children who will not stay still. There are two sets of privies entered from the playground. The girls are admitted as monitors for their own sex and as supervisors of the fold, whilst the boy monitors also supply a 'monitor of the (whole) school', to teach from the rostrum. The classroom also has a primitive gallery – two rows of seats on two levels – and a lesson suspended on the 'silent teacher' (teaching post). The timetable contains a fifth category – the 'circular class' in which the tiny infants are taught rudimentary religion and morals, natural history, spelling and mental arithmetic. Class teaching for boys includes writing. A powerful new metaphor appears – the husband and wife head a 'family' and a 'brotherhood'; the children are in 'subjection and obedience to their instructors in place of parents' (Wilson 1829: 25).

A stern Evangelical critic of Wilderspin's was Thomas Bilby, master of the Chelsea Infant school under the auspices of the London Society. Amongst the three model plans he published with Ridgeway in 1834 (Figure 3.31) one projects the gallery in the apsidal form already seen in Wilson's proposals. The privies are removed from the schoolroom but the master's and mistress's house is arranged so that they can directly observe the schoolroom, the playground and the privies. In a diagram Bilby explains how sensation combines experience of space and time. Hence the spatial properties of the school are as crucial as the imparting of a sense of past, present and future.

In an 1840 edition Wilderspin innovates with a scheme for an integrated two-storey junior school with separate infant accommodation. He shows two uses of the gallery: in the first a master teaches with a monitor, and in the second all the children are distributed on two sides of the room (boys on one, girls on the other) and the rear row of the gallery, so that monitors can gain access to them

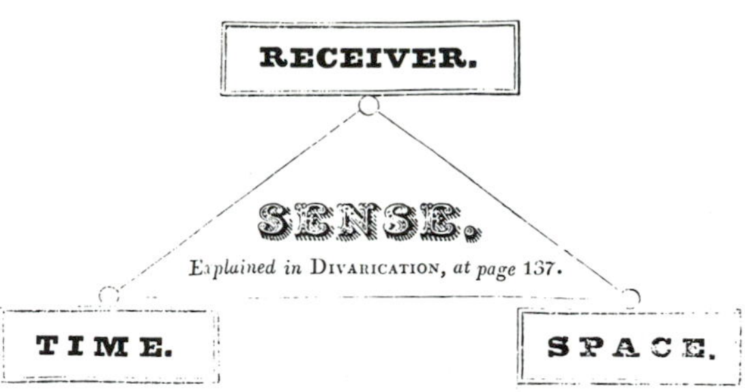

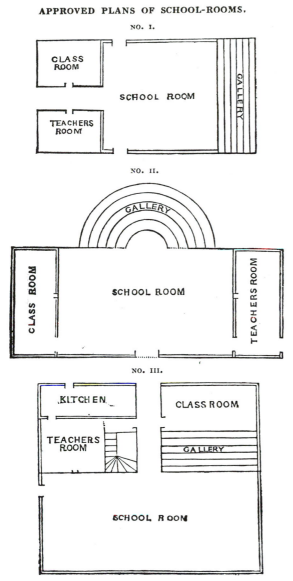

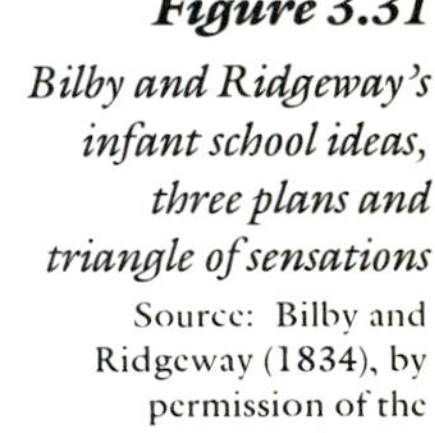
Figure 3.31
Bilby and Ridgeway's infant school ideas, three plans and triangle of sensations
Source: Bilby and Ridgeway (1834), by permission of the Librarian, Glasgow University Library

for class teaching (Figure 3.32).

In 1836 the Home and Colonial Infant School Society began to organise schools on the Evangelical lines of Bilby and Ridgeway, whilst Wilderspin continued his own work which was adopted in Europe. Cochin (1845) records the setting up of the first infant school in Paris in 1828 in an extensive hybrid plan with Lancasterian boys' and girls' schools. A screen in the girls' opens on Sundays to reveal a sanctuary and altar aligned on the axis of the mistress's platform. The infant room has a gallery and longitudinal rows of seats facing the teaching posts and teaching semicircles.

Italy's first infant school was set up in Cremona in 1829 (Catarsi and Genovesi 1985).

In formal terms the infant schools were catholic in style and scale. At Dublin it was heavily Classical; at Cheltenham Gothic; in Liverpool two identical Corporation schools were 'municipal' Tuscan. In Southwark the 1814 Kent Road Wesleyan Sunday Schools, which became an infant school in 1826 was a smaller, single storey version of the Liverpool buildings.

The infant school was an amalgam of scientific rationalism, Dissenting, Evangelical and Established religion, and Radical philosophy. On top of Wilderspin's overt, but not-much-publicised Swedenborgianism, was his covert adherence to phrenology where he found just those links between body, brain, intellect and emotions which he could project into a total pedagogic system where space became crucial.

Experiments in remote places

The semi-colonial status of Scotland and Ireland invited daring innovation. Lancaster perhaps sensed on his first visit in 1806 that the British government was about to use Ireland as a laboratory for State intervention and that this might be his route to official backing. Ireland had its own Charity and Protestant Charter schools. But for the vast majority there was no provision in 1787 when Thomas Orde introduced his comprehensive plan into the Irish Parliament. Though rejected, it aroused sufficient interest for a Commission of Enquiry to be set up which reported in 1791. Amongst its startling proposals was the building of 700 new schoolhouses. In 1799 Edgeworth was instrumental in setting up the next Parliamentary enquiry; he also proposed building schoolhouses. This too failed to clear the legislative hurdles but a National Board of Education was set up in 1806 and published fourteen reports by 1812. The last recommended a central Board of Education to administer

Figure 3.32

Two uses of Wilderspin's gallery (1840)

Source: Wilderspin (1840), British Library

government grants for new schools, control of textbooks and establishment of training institutions. This was two decades in advance of mainland Britain. The Report enabled the government to aid the Kildare Place Society from 1815.

The Society set up in 1811 at School Street has been mentioned. From the start it was non-sectarian and Lancaster was invited to its first meeting. Two years later he sent his trainee John Veevers to start teacher training by 'exhibition'. After the move to Kildare Place in 1814 and the award of an earmarked grant the following year it adopted the new name.

By 1813 the Society published its *Hints and Directions for the Building, Fitting-Up, and Arranging of School-Rooms* (Society for Promoting the Education of the Poor of Ireland 1813) mostly culled from Lancaster's 1811 publication of the same title. The model plans show a 5-foot aisle on one side, for the lessons and a 3-foot one on the other for ciculation, without teaching semi-circles. For country schools a playground is recommended, and for the girls' room a clear space for needlework.

Number 4 Kildare Place was converted by William Farrell into offices and on the adjacent oblong plot a new pair of model schoolrooms were put up in a two-storey block.

Apparently there was a reaction, for in 1825 the Society felt obliged to argue the case again for giving education to the poor, and included the usual calculus of education *versus* the cost of crime. Besides 'neatness and cleanliness', the goal was the ordering of space and time: 'where so much depends on regular distribution of time' there should be a conspicuous clock and a large notice hung up 'Let there be a place for everything, and let every thing be in its place'. After the National Schools were set up in 1831 these 'two great rules of order' were rewritten as 'A time for every thing, and every thing in its place' (Hyland and Milne 1987: 117).

The Society's non-sectarianism was under attack from Catholics, and the Irish Education Enquiry set up in 1825 published nine strongly critical reports two years later. In 1831 an Act was passed for a national system under a Board. Government support for the Society ceased but it continued its activities in Established church schools; in 1839 the Church Education Society was founded and eventually took over the lease of Kildare Place though it was not until 1878 that the Society formally ceased to exist.

Some of its schools were transferred to the Board which also constructed new ones of all sizes, types and styles, retaining various forms of the monitorial system except in the smallest rural schools. Boys and girls had separate yards – with privies – entrances and schoolrooms. By the late 1830s teaching galleries appear. The durability of the system is evident in the Board's 1858 model design for 120 children (Design No. 4) and for 100 in 1863 (Design No. 3) which still retain the double schoolroom under a single teacher and even in end-of-the-century plans (Design Nos. 1, 3, 5A and 10B 1890) retain the semi-circles.

The Commissioners' Second (1835) Report proposed thirty-two model schools, one for each County. By 1844 the only one built was the Central Model School in Marlborough Street, Dublin. Designed by Jacob Owen in 1837 and opened in 1838, its infant school was to Wilderspins's specifications and he took charge of it (McCann and Young 1982: 237–53). Its 64 by 31 foot schoolroom had three classrooms opening off it, and playgrounds. Higgins (1826) as far back as 1826 had advocated infant schools in Dublin based on a mixture of Pestalozzi and Bell.

In 1846 the Commissioners drew up design rules for the Model schools, of which seven opened in 1848, some designed by Owen, architect to the Board of Works. They had infant, male and female junior schools each for 100 children; infants in the middle, boys and girls in lateral wings. In smaller towns infants could be replaced by a model agricultural school (British Parliamentary Papers 1870). The system was Lancasterian, with the addition of classrooms including some for teaching art and elementary science. In 1848 the old School Street School was transformed into the West Dublin Model School.

The largest Model school was Frederick Darley's two-storey building in Belfast opened in 1857. The schoolrooms have Lancaster semi-circles even in the centre aisle of the boys' preparatory and the adults' rooms. The infants have a gallery as well as forms and teaching semi-circles, whilst for the juniors, galleries are limited to classrooms for 'simultaneous' teaching, though even here teaching semi-circles are crammed in. The girls' school room has two-person work-tables instead of benches.

It is no surprise that education in which utility, rationalism, scientific experiment, Evangelical religion and phrenology were combined should have flourished in Scotland. I have already explored that history elsewhere (Markus 1982: 201–61) but some of it is relevant here.

Though Bell was a Scot, he had less influence than Lancaster whose more flexible religion accounts for his good relations with Owen. By 1810 there were three Lancasterian schools in Glasgow; Edinburgh had a Society in 1815 and a school on Calton Hill and other towns followed. *The Edinburgh Review* (1808: 61–73) maintained Scotland's interest in Lancaster commending specially its cheapness and its military discipline which 'renders them (the poor) more tractable and less ferocious'.

Following violent riots in Edinburgh on New Year's Day 1812 it was decided to open Sabbath (Sunday) schools throughout the city. But Bible study was hampered by the children's inability to read, so in 1813 a Kirk Sessional school was set up, first in Leith Wynd and a year later in Market Street, under Sheriff John Wood's direction. Each Parish was entitled to send a few infants. The monitorial régime was in a 90 by 30 foot school-

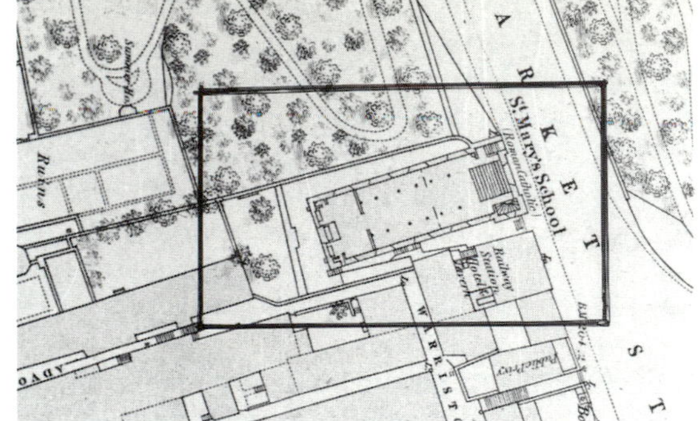

Figure 3.33

Edinburgh's Sessional school (1814), Market Street, plan

Source: Edinburgh O.S. map 1852–4, by courtesy of Edinburgh City Libraries

room. By the time of the 1852–4 Ordnance Survey map (Figure 3.33) it had become St Mary's school and a teaching gallery and playground are shown which suggests imports from Wilderspin, either directly or *via* David Stow in Glasgow; if the latter it must have been after 1836 when Stow was still regretting their absence (1836: 7). Seating was of the Bell type – writing desks against the walls and a clear central space where classes of thirty children are formed into circles with their monitor and assistant monitor in the centre. The Gothic-Baronial exterior shows a large window over the gallery. There was also a basement 'box class' where the tiniest children place 'boxes' with letters painted on them in a frame (Town Council of Dundee 1827). In 1850 there were 104 Sessional schools in Scotland; Market Street was in use for teacher training by 1826.

But real innovation was in infant education. David Stow, a Glasgow businessman, set up a system of Sabbath schools in 1816. But as 'training of one day in seven, as an antidote to the contaminating influence of the rest of the week' was inadequate he proposed to 'look abroad for some more efficient moral engine' (1836: 57). This was to be an infant school conducted on Bible principles. The Glasgow Infant School Society was born in 1827 and in 1828 its first school 'For training infants and practising Normal students' was set up in Drygate. The 'normal' (model) indicated its teacher training function, soon extended from one month to six or more.

The single storey converted house (Figure 3.34) already featured all the essential Stow features. Wilderspin, whom Stow visited in 1820, was a strong influence and trained the first Master and Mistress, the Caughies, to teach in the open schoolroom and to use the playground – 'the uncovered schoolroom ... a little world of real life' where mental, moral and phyical character is best developed and 'consequently where moral habits can best be formed' (Stow 1836: 135). The playground is a Garden of Eden – children would respect fruit trees and plants and by not touching these desirable things they would show 'that moral teaching in schools would be the cheapest police'. Play on the circular swing was accompanied by counting 'to a lively tune or sing(ing) a

Figure 3.34

Stow's first model infant school, Drygate, Glasgow (1828)

Source: Stow (1860), Jordanhill College of Education, Glasgow moral song or rhyme' (1836: 136) under surveillance by the master during his lunch in the classroom which reminded them that 'Thou God seest me'. The artist's drawing emphasises the Cathedral, perhaps as a sign of Stow's loyalty to the Church of Scotland, whilst John Knox, on his Doric column in the adjacent Necropolis, towers over the roof.

Stow was aware of experiments in Prussia and France and those by Pestalozzi at Yverdun. Soon his 'Training System' was formally articulated and the work of Owen, Wood and Wilderspin acknowledged. The monitorial system – 'mutual instruction by monitors ... is equally valuable to the scholar and to the master ... (and) forms a very important feature of the Infant School' (Stow 1836: 2). Later he adopted it in his Junior school also. It was not till 1839 that, like others before him, he reacted: 'No monitors. Monitors can only teach facts – they cannot develop or train' (1839: 22).

Of Owen, Stow is openly critical. His system is:

> chiefly gymnastics and other physical exercises, accompanied by a certain amount of intellectual instruction by means of pictures ... nearly destitute of any cultivation of one of the most important parts of our moral nature, viz. the religious affections and habits.
>
> (Stow 1836: 6)

His judgement of Wilderspin is more measured: physical training is 'complete' and whilst the intellectual method is open to further advance it is 'a great improvement on the old system he had to contend with at the commencement'. But 'in the Religious department the instruction given ... is very incomplete' with its emphasis on Scripture history and the attempt to teach an undogmatic Christianity (1836: 5).

Physical, intellectual and moral formation had to be balanced. Since Thomas Chalmers, Minister of St John's Parish in Glasgow when Stow started his Sabbath schools, leader of the Evangelical wing of the Church and later engineer of the Free Church Disruption in 1843, remained Stow's mentor, Evangelical religion was seen as the basis of both intellect and morality.

Order, discipline and habit formation were essential hence the emphasis on 'training' – a fusion of Locke's *tabula rasa* with the Book of Proverb's 'Train a child in the way he should go and when he is old he will not depart from it' which became Stow's working programme as the bulwark against the 'contaminating influence of evil example' by which he felt surrounded in Glasgow (1834: 35).

Stow uses the popular calculus – education *versus* the cost of crime. It is from the ranks of infants of the '... third or lowest moral class ... breathing such a pestilential atmosphere (that) at a future period, our bridewells, jails, and convict-ships will be replenished' (1834: 35). Unwittingly Stow echoes Owen who in his 1821 plan for the County of Lanark responded to the opinion that his Utopian settlement might avoid the need for further prisons by doubting the wisdom of admitting criminals but foreseeing that it would accommodate not only the 'industrious' but also the 'middling and higher classes of society'. This is the tripartite division which Stow is too coy to spell out.

His two pedagogic inventions were 'sympathy of numbers' and 'picturing-out'. The former is the mutually beneficial effect of putting large numbers together. This 'social sympathy may prove the very means of moral improvement', a mirror image of the 'concentrated masses of human beings (in) large cities and factories ... (which) afford peculiar facilities and encouragement to vice'. The city and the mill are scenes of vice, confusion and violence; through the 'sympathy of numbers' they can be turned 'morally and consequently *politically* into great national blessings' (Stow 1836: 61, my emphasis).

The negative urban sentiments are opposed by an idealised pastoral vision: the parochial schools of Scotland had '... rendered her peasantry at once intelligent and moral' (Stow 1839: 61). The cloister-like enclosure of the playground with its flower beds and shrubs, becomes a metaphor for an island of innocence in a sea of vice.

'Picturing-out' includes the use of analogy, ellipsis, question-and-answer and pictorial representation. In practice Stow's system borrowed freely from all the available methods – monitors (initially), galleries, supervised playground, the classroom (eventually containing its own small gallery), swings, teaching posts, 'lessons' on cards and writing desks against the wall.

Everything is designed for surveillance. The schoolroom, classroom and playground are so connected that children proceed from the first (under monitors) to the second (under the master), to the third (under the master's remote surveillance) and then return to the schoolroom; 'this rotary movement continues until the prescribed time allotted to that part of the system is exhausted' (Stow 1836: 122). As with Bell, for

Figure 3.35

Stow's ideal plan (1834–6) and interior of infant and juvenile galleries (1836)

Source: Stow (1836), Glasgow District Council Libraries, Mitchell Library

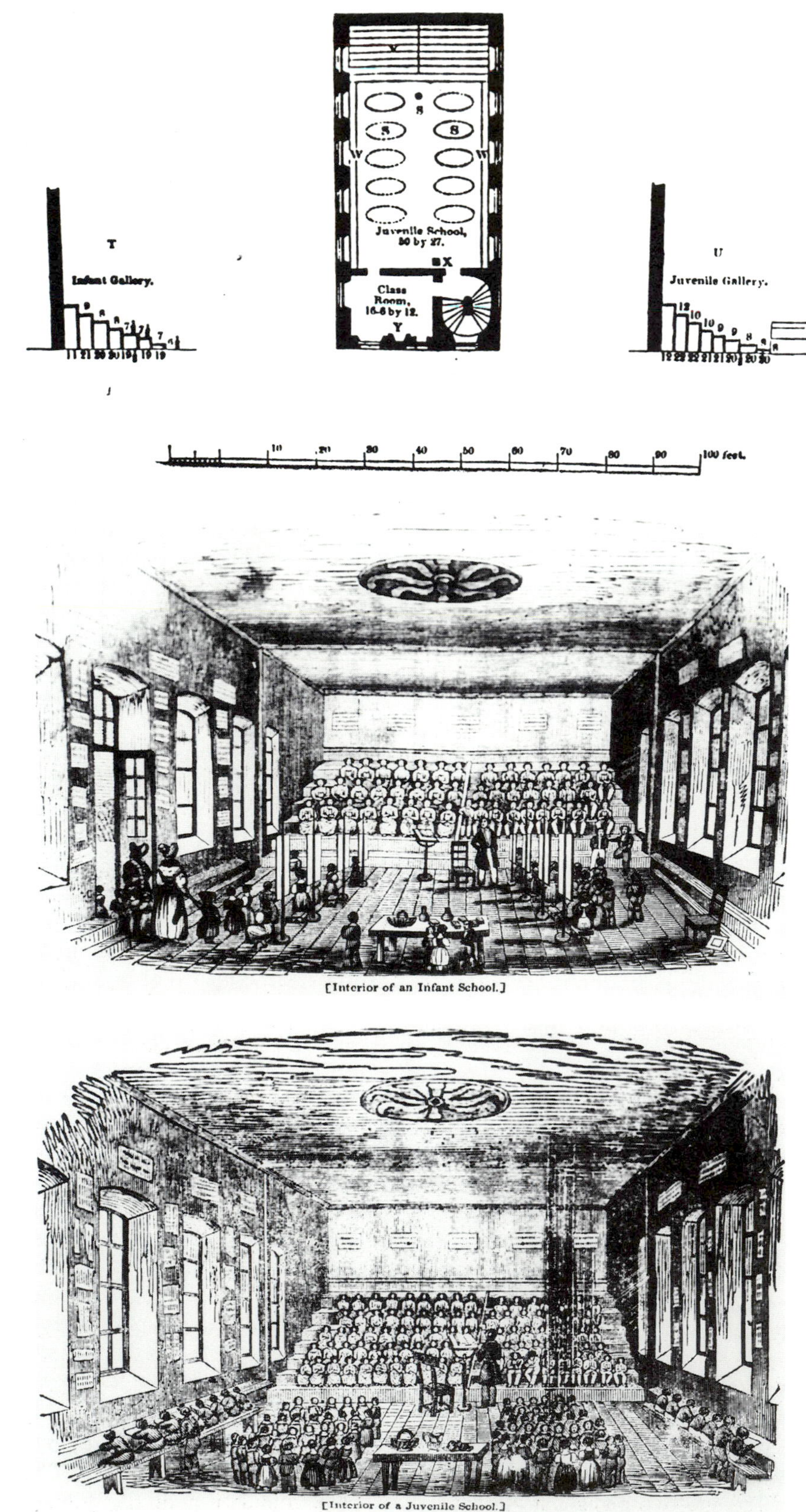

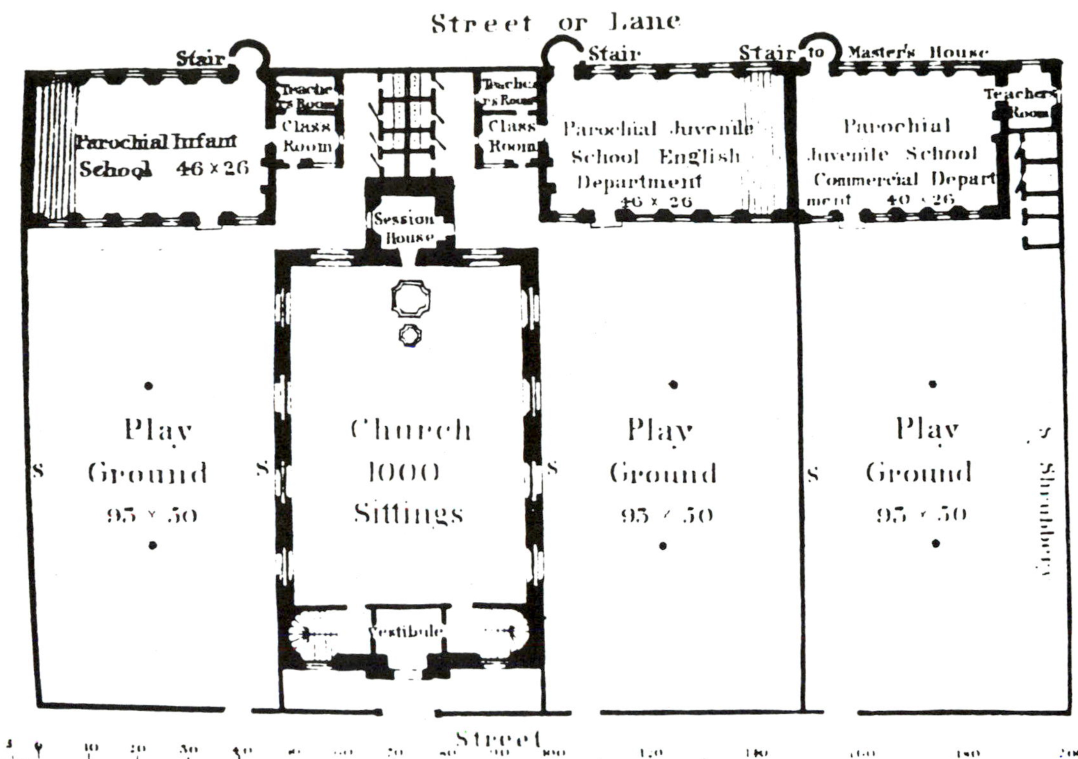

Figure 3.36
Stow's Parochial Institution (1834)
Source: Stow (1834), Glasgow District Council Libraries, Mitchell Library

writing the children sat at peripheral desks facing the wall. The gallery had to be large enough for the entire school as this

> enables the children to fix their eye more easily upon the master and enables the master to observe and direct more perfectly every movement of the children. The social principle is concentrated in the gallery, and greatly more influential than when children are seated around the schoolroom, at desks, or on scattered forms; the attention of all is secured; all receive one lesson, and all learn.
>
> (Stow 1836)

The teacher also needed aural control: 'every word spoken by the master or scholars is more easily heard by all when thus seated' (69). Here is the 'simultaneous' system which was to become the major pedagogic tool for over a century. Here is too is a thinly-veiled critique of monitors.

Stow's programme of building and writing quickly got under way. In 1829 two schools were under construction, both in St John's Parish; Marlborough Street and Chalmers Street (Infant School Establishment and Female Sewing School). His first major publication (1834) describes the former and illustrates the latter. Both had schoolrooms 46 feet by 26 and two playgrounds – with flower borders, swing posts and privies – classrooms and galleries. The second is a two-storey structure with a juvenile school, for 6 to 12- or 14-year olds, on the upper floor.

In 1832 St David's Parish infant school opened in John Street as did Steel Street in the Saltmarket which became the model school to which the Caughies, master and mistress from Drygate, moved. In 1834 another opened in Cowcaddens Barony Parish. By 1833 the experimental extension to juveniles at Chalmers Street had become policy and the first separate juvenile school was built, also in St John's Parish, in Annfield Street. Its 'English' and 'Commercial' streams – that is academic and practical – created a division which was to survive in British education well into the twentieth century. In 1834 Stow described, and in 1836 illustrated the fully developed ideal plan (Figure 3.35). This is simply one wing of the Normal Seminary shortly to be built. For the first time interior views of the teaching galleries in the infant and juvenile schools appear.

In 1834 a unique 'Parochial Institution' appears (Figure 3.36) with a church at the centre and three schoolrooms in the arms of a 'T', surpisingly the only time Stow created a material sign for the integration of religion with education.

The foundation of the Glasgow Educational

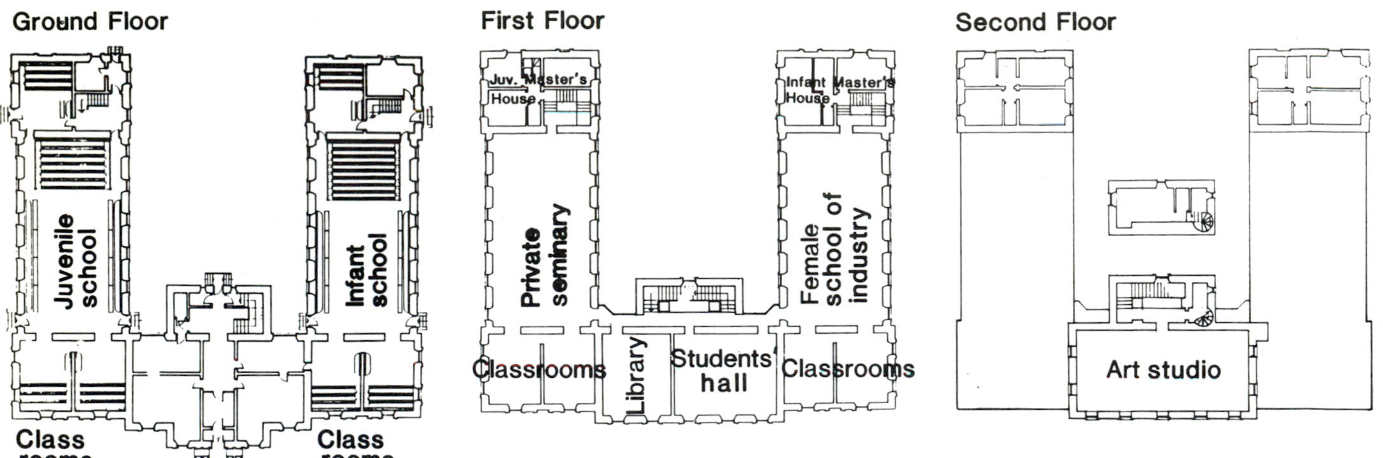

Figure 3.37

Glasgow Normal Seminary (1836–7), plans of three floors, contemporary view and today

Source: Drawn by the author and Robert Craig (plans); *Granny and Leezy* (1860) in Jordanhill College Library (drawing); author's photograph

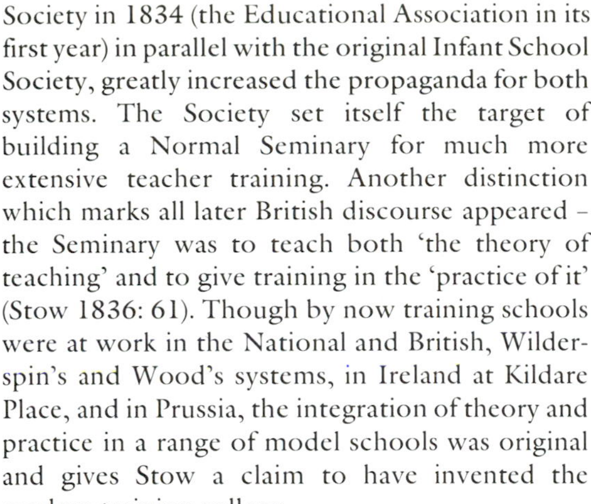

Society in 1834 (the Educational Association in its first year) in parallel with the original Infant School Society, greatly increased the propaganda for both systems. The Society set itself the target of building a Normal Seminary for much more extensive teacher training. Another distinction which marks all later British discourse appeared – the Seminary was to teach both 'the theory of teaching' and to give training in the 'practice of it' (Stow 1836: 61). Though by now training schools were at work in the National and British, Wilderspin's and Wood's systems, in Ireland at Kildare Place, and in Prussia, the integration of theory and practice in a range of model schools was original and gives Stow a claim to have invented the modern training college.

David Hamilton, Scotland's leading Classical architect of the day designed the shorn-down Classical Normal Seminary in 1836. Building started in that year and was part-complete in 1837. No records of a brief, fee or plans have survived. As the building is extant Figure 3.37 is based on measured drawings and a reconstruction of the internal arrangements. There were four model schools, two in each of the symmetrically located two-storey wings on either side of the central courtyard; an infants', a juvenile, a

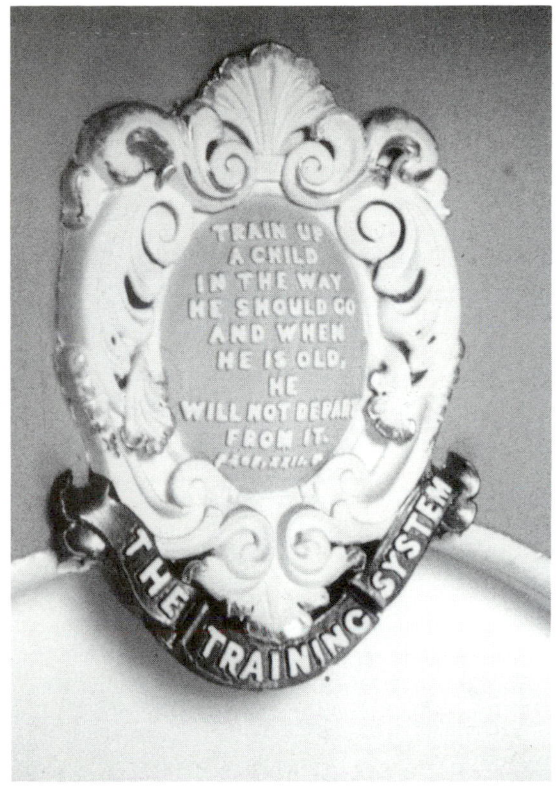

Figure 3.38

The Book of Proverbs basis for the 'moral training system' at Glasgow's Normal Seminary

Source: Author's photograph

Figure 3.39

Second building of Glasgow Normal Seminary (1845)

Source: Stow (1850), in author's possession

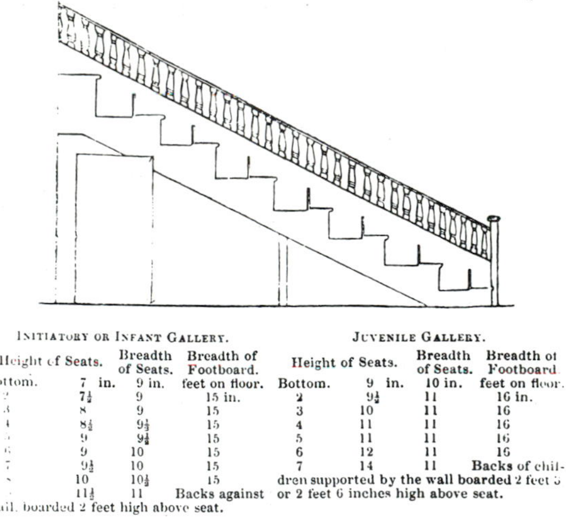

INITIATORY OR INFANT GALLERY.

Height of Seats.		Breadth of Seats.	Breadth of Footboard.
Bottom.	7 in.	9 in.	feet on floor.
2	7½	9	15 in.
3	8	9	15
4	8½	9½	15
5	9	9½	15
6	9	10	15
7	9½	10	15
8	10	10½	15
	11½	11	Backs against

wall, boarded 2 feet high above seat.

JUVENILE GALLERY.

Height of Seats.		Breadth of Seats.	Breadth of Footboard.
Bottom.	9 in.	10 in.	feet on floor.
2	9½	11	16 in.
3	10	11	16
4	11	11	16
5	11	11	16
6	12	11	16
7	14	11	Backs of chil-

dren supported by the wall boarded 2 feet 3 or 2 feet 6 inches high above seat.

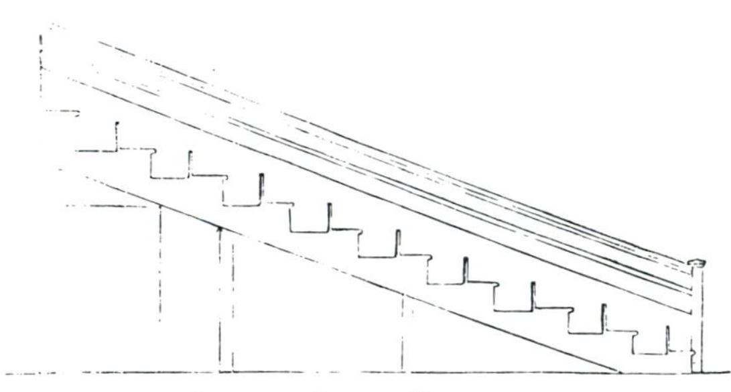

GALLERY.—JUVENILE DEPARTMENT.

Figure 3.40

Details of galleries for infants and juveniles and for the female school of industry in Stow's schools

Source: Stow (1850), in author's possession

('private', that is fee-paying) commercial school for boys and a female school of industry. The Caughies took charge of the infants, and the Aulds, from Steel Street, of the juveniles, all under a Rector. In the same year the first edition of Stow's *Training System* appeared and ran to ten editions by 1854.

The central tower housed the janitor's house and director's office on the ground floor, library and a student's room on the first and an art studio on the top floor. Somewhere there was also a museum of 'natural and artificial objects, articles of manufacture and commerce, and a few models of machinery'. The first floor has an ingenious cantilevered wooden 'by-pass' corridor which makes the two upper schoolrooms spatially shallower than if they had been accessed *en suite* as would often have been the case in these corridor-less days. A shield in the entrance hall (Figure 3.38) carries the Old Testament maxim upon which Stow founded the Training System.

With the 1843 Disruption (the foundation of the Free Church) Stow and his staff were ejected from what was Church of Scotland property and the New Free Seminary was built to Thomas Burns' design a short distance away and opened in 1845 (Figure 3.39). The change from Classical to Baronial-Tudor represents a shift in Evangelical consciousness; education and learning now adopt a modern, popular and national model rather than that of remote Classical culture.

Stow produced a wealth of designs over the next twenty years, Classical and Gothic, rural and urban. Where site constraints made a ground-level playground impossible it was located on the roof. In successive editions details of gallery and furniture designs become elaborated (Figure 3.40). Every seat and coathook plays a part.

The paradox of the industrial town remained; on the one hand a theatre of vice, disorder and moral decay, on the other, through early education, a potentially creative, moral and productive force. It could not only share in, but surpass the dream of rural innocence: 'However highly in the moral scale, therefore, agriculturalists may be elevated, the inhabitants of a large town may be raised higher still' (Stow 1834: 286). Here is the reformative power of the moral engine. Education is a production process like that into which the children will be released – '(it) is pursued with more efficiency when there is a proper subdivison of labour, on the part of the teachers, and of classification in regard to the ages of the scholars'. The correct curriculum:

> ought to have a useful solid tendency, such as will fit them (the children) to become good servants – good tradesmen – good fathers – good mothers, and respectable citizens. The intellectually cultivated christian mechanic is the best safeguard of our nation, and his moral worth is the very salt and leaven of civil society,
>
> (Stow 1834)

whilst his female counterpart is prepared for the role of 'frugal housewife, attentive sister or help to an aged parent' (1836: 173–6). Out of this limited Scottish, in fact Glasgow, experience, sprang an ideology that was to have far-reaching consequences for educational practice.

The construction of poverty and childhood by law

At the start of this narrative, poverty, work and education were intertwined; at its end state intervention made them even more so.

With the Irish experiment in state funding underway, Parliament at last tackled the domestic situation by making an annual grant of £20,000 in 1833 disbursed through the British and National Societies to meet half the costs of schoolhouses. The air was thick with religious controversy, between Establishment and Dissent, and belief and agnosticism. The state intervened decisively in 1839 when the Committee of (Privy) Council on Education was set up and the grant became £30,000. The virulent controversy now focused on the powers to inspect the National Schools. The Church of England's objections were overcome by a concordat in 1840. The new Committee appointed James Kay (later Kay-Shuttleworth), a doctor, as its secretary. His book on the condition of Manchester's working classes, published as cholera first hit that city, corroborates Engels' later work. But Engels could not have supported Kay's justification for workers' education as a means of weakening the power of unions whose members have 'least knowledge and virtue' and nevertheless influence the:

> more deserving and intelligent portions of the labouring class ... The radical remedy for ... treating (workers) as a mere animal power necessary to the mechancial processes of manufacture ... is such an education as shall teach the people in what consists their true happiness, and how their interests may be best promoted.
>
> (Kay 1832: 111)

A year after the enactment of the 1834 New Poor Law, Kay became an Assistant Commissioner to find, in his first posting to East Anglia, a 13-year old boy in charge of a workhouse school during the master's absence through sickness. Kay now became convinced of the need for pupil-teachers – not merely substitutes for monitors – but young teachers apprenticed to an experienced master or mistress, followed by a period of formal preparation in a training college. He absorbed Continental ideas from Fellenberg and Pestalozzi and a belief in the gallery and simultaneous teaching from Wood and Stow in Scotland. On arrival in London in 1838 he put these to the test in the Norwood model workhouse school of 1100 children for which he imported a Wood-trained teacher. Its fame made Kay a natural choice as Secretary for the new Committee and so education and poor relief were intertwined as soon as the state intervened in both. Here was the origin of many key design innovations which Seaborne and others fail to locate.

At Norwood, struggling against huge bureaucratic odds, he converted a long room which also doubled as chapel into a schoolroom with a gallery at one end and six classes for simultaneous teaching (Figure 3.41). As a result of his work several training colleges were set up, mostly under the auspices of the Church of England. By 1845 it had twenty-two, with galleried schoolrooms, 'U's and classrooms.

After 1834 industrial schools were built within the workhouse programme. Kay promoted his designs both through the Commissioners' *Reports* and the Council's *Minutes.* In the fourth *Report* (1838) the Commissioners' architect Kempthorne had a design (Figure 3.42) for 450 children with four classrooms and a dual-rake gallery for infants and juveniles. The fifth (1839) had a similar project, but Kay proposed a separate juveniles' gallery; also a museum for mechanical and other models, clearly envisaging modern teacher training methods. Kempthorne's even grander project in 1840 (Figure 3.43) provides for 450 orphans, teacher training and model schools – all inspired by Stow's Glasgow venture. There are seven classrooms with stepped floors around a central, galleried infant school, dormitories, a horse-shoe form central lecture theatre, a chapel, extensive residential accommodation for both single and married pupil teachers, and craft workshops. This complex type reached its apogee in the palatial establishments at Liverpool and Manchester enthusiastically greeted by the Committee's first Inspector Seymour Tremenheere in its fourth (1842–3) *Minutes*.

For ordinary schools the funds were much more modest. Nevertheless the Committee immediately embarked on an innovative programme of model plans. Through Kay many of its ideas parallelled the Commissioners'. But school architecture had to embody fine differences demanded by ideological and political

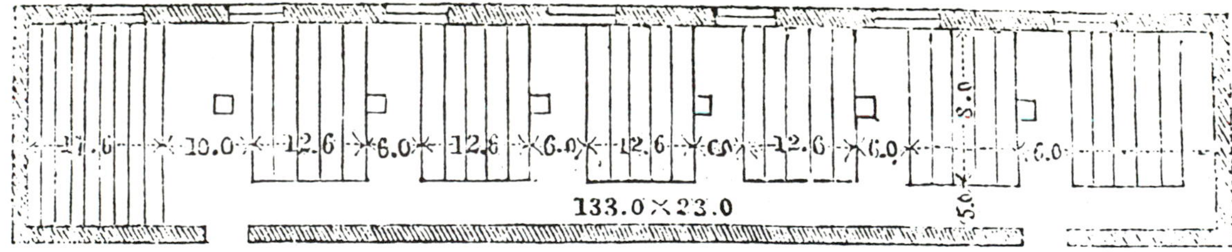

Figure 3.41

James Kay's model workhouse school at Norwood (1838)

Source: Minutes of the Committee of Council (1839–40)

conflict. Kay's commitment to a régime of master and mistress with pupil teachers, and one qualified assistant teaching each class by the simultaneous method, was total. Though reluctantly accepted for mechanical tasks and limited instruction of the youngest children, the model plans had to recognise that the Societies, through whom the grant was disbursed, were unwavering in their commitment to monitors.

So in its first models, also designed by Kempthorne, the Committee was forced to dilute its 'simultaneous' ideal with 'mutual' instruction into something called the 'mixed' method. To understand the plans these terms have to be analysed.

The mutual or monitorial system has been described. The child-instructors teach their fellows individually and successively in small groups in desks, Bell 'U's or Lancaster semicircles. The schoolrooms had fixed peripheral writing desks, or fixed rows of desks in the middle on a gently sloping floor.

The Committee drew on the simultaneous system used by Stow for both infants and juveniles. The master taught the entire school in the gallery, and smaller classes, based on age or attainment, in the classroom (where examination was individual). The classes were also taught simultaneously in the gallery either by separation in *time* – taking their turn – or in *space* – between the front and back, by rows, or by segments divided by gaps or curtains at right angles to the seats.

With only a few classes the master could teach them all, either in rotation or by combining them into one. As the school grew the number of classes increased beyond his capacity and the Committee proposed the use of pupil or assistant

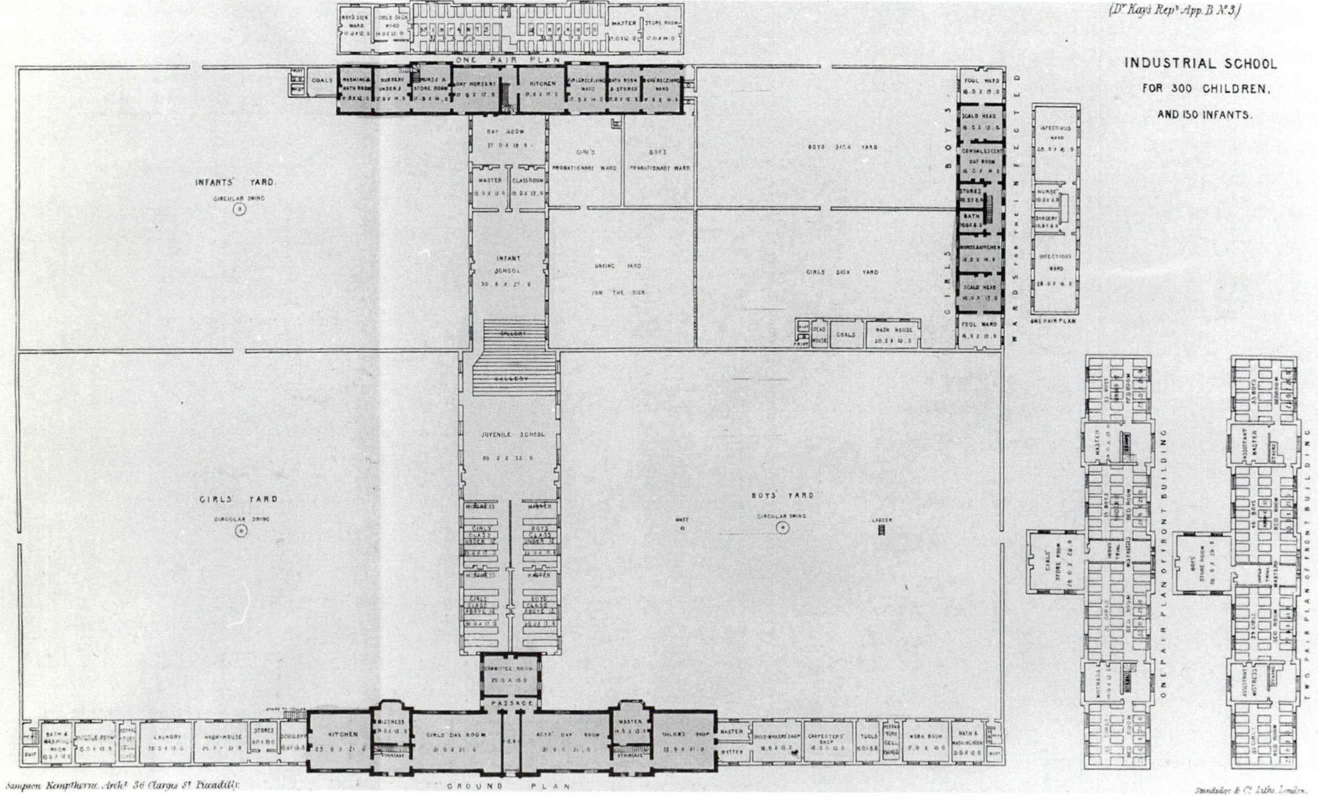

Figure 3.42

Kempthorne's design for an industrial school for 450 children for the Poor Law Commissioners (1838)

Source: Fourth Annual Report of the Poor Law Commissioners, Jordanhill College Library, Glasgow

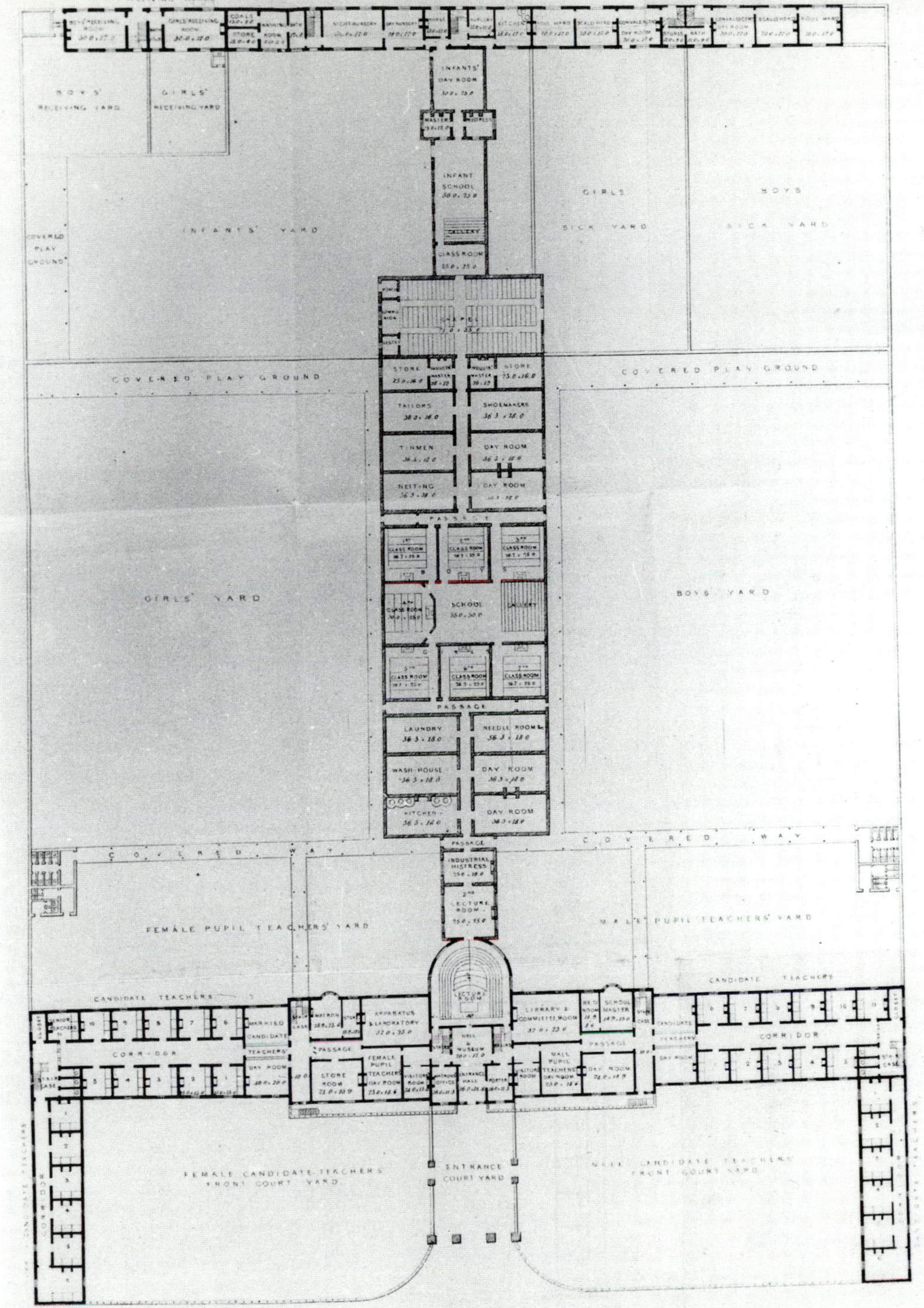

Figure 3.43

Kempthorne's design for an orphan house and normal school for 450 children (1840)

Source: Minutes of the Committee of Council (1839–40)

teachers under his surveillance. Only when funds were short were monitors admitted, but even then only exceptionally for mutual instruction. This 'mixed' system combined simultaneous with mutual teaching to the extent that the school was broken up and direct supervision of its parts delegated from the master to subordinates.

The models assume the spatial division of children according to attainment, and sometimes sex, into classes. They are seated in desks fixed on steps which form a shallow and space-consuming tier. There are two or more schoolrooms of such desks, usually separated by low partitions; the sexes and classes are further divided either by

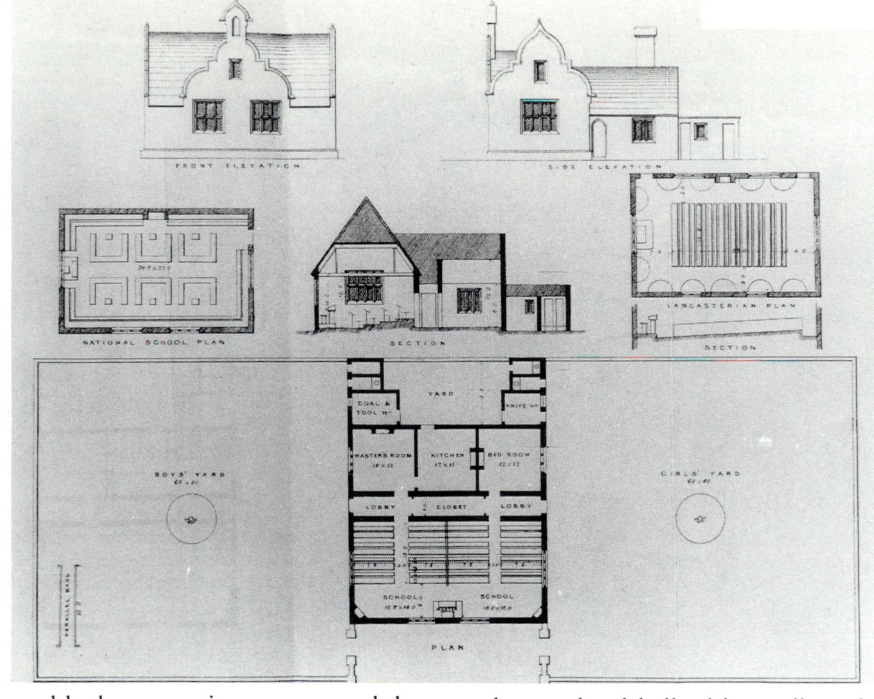

Figure 3.44

Committee of Council model plan for 80 children (1839–40)

Source: Minutes of the Committee of Council (1839–40)

rows, or into blocks, sometimes separated by curtains or mobile partitions. In the smaller schools a single master's desk controls two schoolrooms. In the larger ones each has a desk, which is occupied by the master and pupil or assistant teacher in turn. The largest models have separate *class*rooms.

Infants, with their own master or mistress, have a large school hall with a gallery that accommodates them all. Sometimes they have also small classrooms, on the Wilderspin-Stow model. When the infants are out at play the entire junior school can be taught in the gallery – say singing or religion – and the hall and its gallery are also used for the school's morning and evening religious assembly.

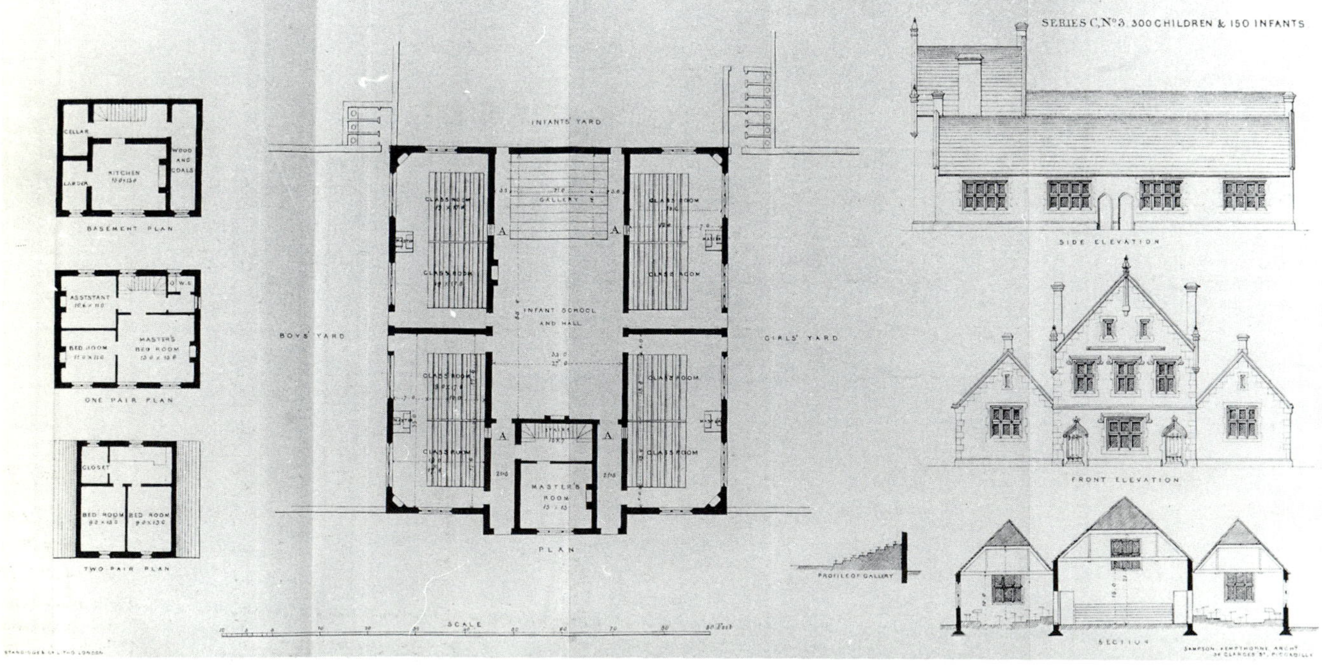

Figure 3.45

Committee of Council model plan for 450 children (1839–40)

Source: Minutes of the Committee of Council (1839–40)

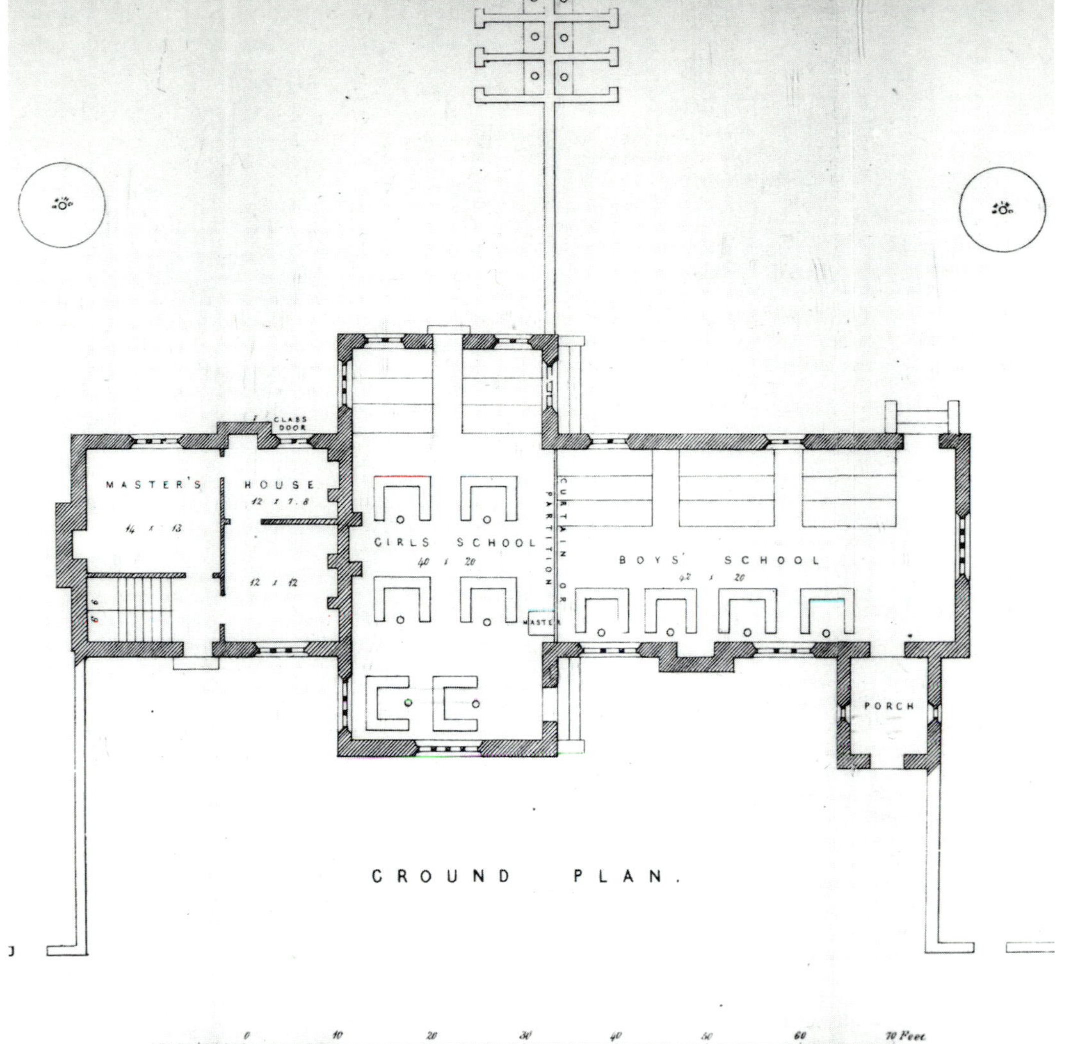

Figure 3.46

Committee of Council model plan for 273 children (1844–5)

Source: Minutes of the Committee of Council (1844–5), British Library

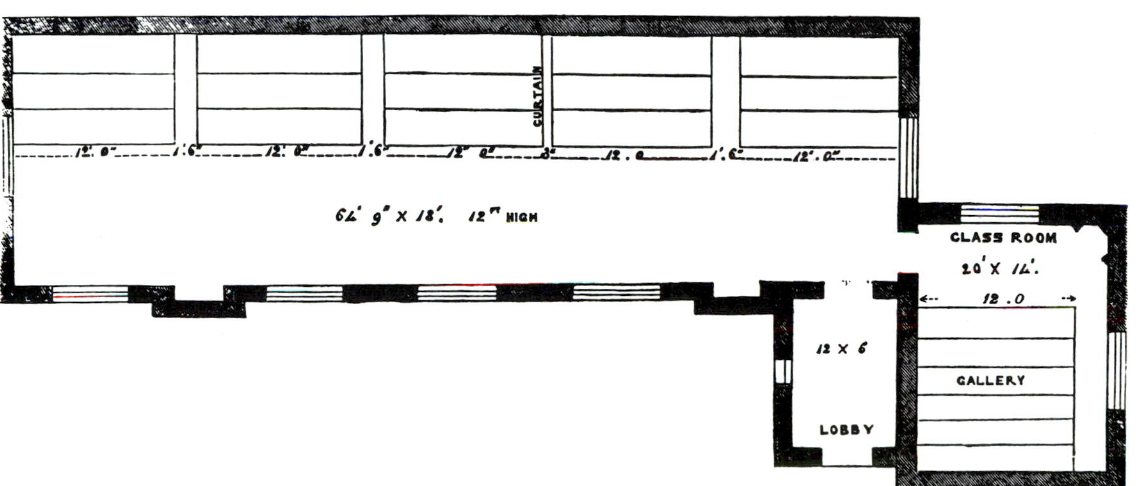

Figure 3.47

Committee of Council model plan for 120 children (1851)

Source: Minutes of the Committee of Council (1851), British Library

Figure 3.48

Plans of Robson's New North Street (board) school (c. 1874)

Source: Robson (1874), redrawn by author

SECOND FLOOR

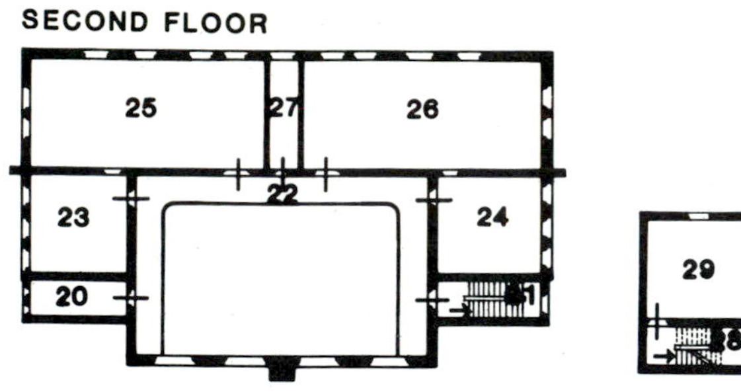

FIRST FLOOR

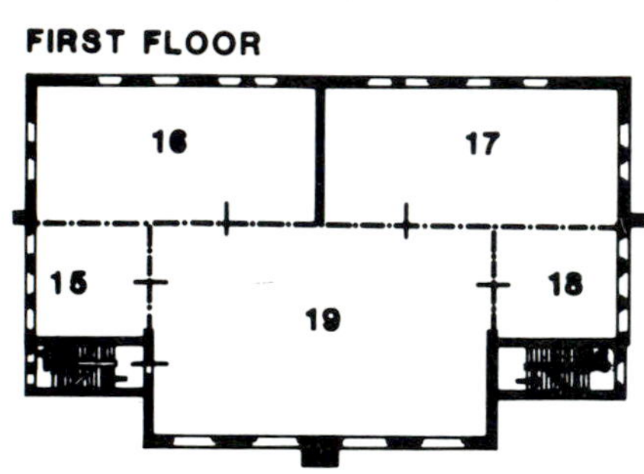

GROUND FLOOR

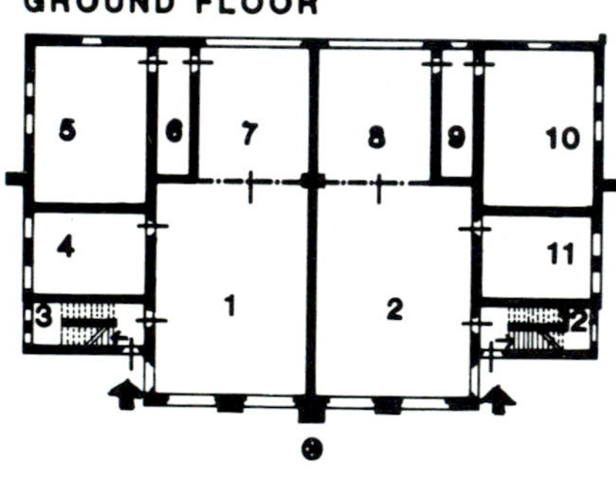

Key

1 Boys' schoolroom
2 Girls' schoolroom
3 Stairs
4 Boys' classroom
5 Babies
6 Toilets
7 Boys' gallery
8 Babies
9 Toilets
10 Babies
11 Girls' classroom
12 Stairs
13 Stairs
14 Stairs
15 Classroom
16 Boys' schoolroom
17 Boys' schoolroom
18 Classroom
19 Hall
20 Stairs
21 Stairs
22 Corridor/balcony
23 Classroom
24 Classroom
25 Girls' schoolroom
26 Girls' schoolroom
27 Toilets
28 Stairs
29 Girls' classroom (third floor)

The Societies' entrenchment forced the Committee to publish alongside each plan a Bell and a Lancaster 'mutual' alternative (to a smaller scale and more lightly engraved). So the paradox arose that it was the most disadvantaged Poor Law children who first benefited from the most advanced teaching and training methods.

The first *Minutes* (1838/40) had four groups of plans, the first for small schools, several including infants. The second is for larger schools, with Bell and Lancaster alternatives (Figure 3.44). The third has an important innovation: a large central 'hall', which serves as the infant school with a full-size gallery, and classrooms instead of schoolrooms. Figure 3.45 is for 300 chidren and 150 infants. The fourth group has a three-storey version for cramped urban sites, which shows a single teaching semi-circle in front of the master's desk.

The acute shortage of trainee teachers forced the Committee to revert to a partial mutual system and, since about four-fifths of its grants had been taken up by National schools, it abandoned attempts to placate both Societies. Designs by its new architect Westmacott in the 1844 *Minutes* have schoolrooms with Madras teaching 'U's, combined with blocks of fixed seats (Figure 3.46).

In 1851 the oscillating models finally came to rest with tiered blocks of partitionable desks in a hall, no 'U's or semi-circles, and a galleried infant schoolroom (Figure 3.47). This type of plan survived even after the 1870 Education Act when the London School Board's architect Robson, created a hybrid in the New North Street School in Shoreditch, with a central hall, most of the classes grouped in threes in large schoolrooms, the rest in separate classrooms (Figure 3.48). The boys' and girls' entrances are widely separated, leading by playgrounds into infant schools, each with a small and a large gallery and seats, and then to the junior classrooms.

The spatial structure (Figure 3.49) shows the depth and articulation achieved after a half century. Categories are structured by trees. The first branching, in the street, is the gender division. Within each the two staircases are roots for the next two sub-trees – infants and juniors. The deepest spaces in the former are for 'babies' (5 and 10) and in the latter for the girls' classrooms (23, 25, 26, 24 and 29). The youngest and females at these tips signifies their definition as the weakest groups. Had the boys' staircase continued beyond the first floor, instead of finishing at the mezzanine lavatory, the ring shown by the dotted line would have linked the two gender trees. The integrating function of the second floor corridor (22) is also evident.

Though Robson (1874) published examples with short corridors or corridor-galleries, it was well into the twentieth century before the fully corridored primary school appears, only to disappear again after World War II.

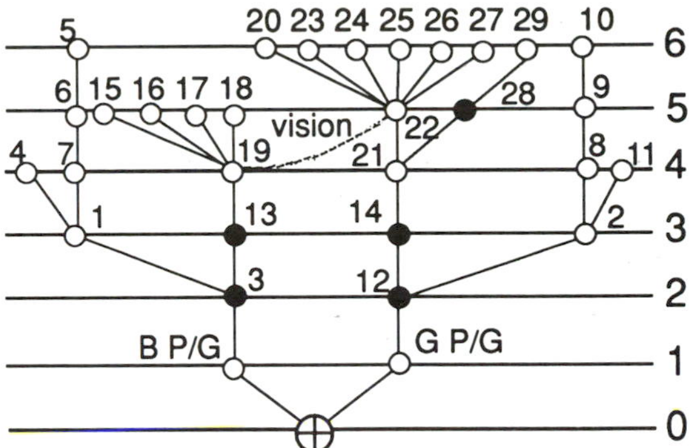

Figure 3.49

New North Street (board) school spatial maps

Source: Author's drawing

Republican virtue

In America greater recognition was given to individuals and small groups. An 1831 plan by Alcott (1832) already has individual desks for simultaneous teaching (Figure 3.50). Another has monitorial semi-circles with a master's and a monitor's desk on the platform, separate boys' and girls' entrances and blocks of desks in rows of five. Barnard's plans of 1848 cater for varieties of simultaneous teaching with desks for two pupils. Although a Lancasterian plan is shown, 'there is hardly a school in the whole country now conducted on the pure Lancasterian system' (1848: 201).

Barnard's 1850 edition illustrates New York adaptations of Lancaster models. The infant school has a gallery for 200, inward facing rows of desks in four blocks, and no teaching semi-circles. The two upper floors house the primary boys' and girls' schoolrooms, with forward-facing rows of desks, eight in each with a monitor's station at the end and a classroom ('recitation' room). In another plan desks for 18 chilren face inwards, with teaching ovals round lesson posts down the centre of the room. New York also promoted new, ergonomically designed cast iron revolving chairs – Mott's patent – shaped to prevent curvature of the spine and drooping shoulders (Figure 3.51). The gender bias of the medical reports, that this affects only girls' posture, anticipates the narrative of the typist's office chair.

Innocent nature and disciplined bodies

Posture is but part of the powerful set of ideas around issues of sex, hygiene and the body. We have seen nature – simple, pure, virtuous and creative – as the inverse of the city's chaos, dirt, immorality and decay. There are elaborate rules for washing, and punishments for arriving with dirty hands, face or clothes. The sexes are segregated in entrances, playgrounds, privies and teaching spaces. Schoolroom ventilation, heating and fresh air are carefully controlled, partly by specifying a minimum volume of space per child. Health, like education, is a profitable investment:

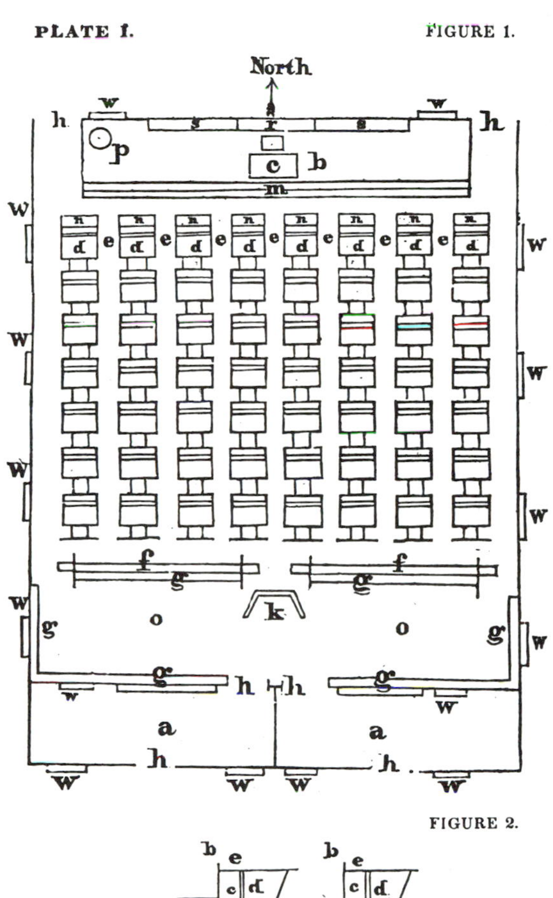

Figure 3.50

Alcott's schoolroom with individual desks (1832)

Source: Alcott (1832), British Library

Figure 3.51
Mott's patent revolving cast iron chair (1850)
Source: Bernard (1850), British Library

> Health, as well as time, is money; and it is a most mistaken economy which confines a child to those arrangements and to that atmospheric impurity, which render him unfit for vigorous effort and thus slowly, though safely, impair his constitution.
>
> (Alcott 1832: 7)

In Germany this control is transferred from air to light.

But there is more than cleanliness. The body itself needed discipline if the mind and character were to become tractable. McIntosh *et al.* (1957) and Smith (1974) have explored the influence of Continental, especially German, precedents, and of the English public schools on the body régimes called 'physical education'. The connection between gymnastics and militarism is strong. In the monitorial schools the prescriptions for individual posture, gesture and eye contact were as detailed as those for groups of bodies controlled by painted lines or brass strips on the floor and monitors' rules. The face, and especially the eyes, signified character and willingess to learn. The sloping floor, the raised master's platform, the raked gallery and the tiered desks were direct instruments for visual surveillance. For phrenologists even the shape of the skull was germane to pedagogy.

Owen's, Wilderspin's and others' systems of dancing, marching and rhythmical movement to music were extensions of static body discipline into time. There is a telling analogy. The machine and the mill demanded a fixed adjacency for the worker's dwelling; shifts, chimes and clocks extended this relation from space to time.

The calculus of morality

Everywhere resources were crucial – for buildings and land, teachers and their training, and books, paper, pens and play equipment. Pallister (1973: 147–58) quantifies mid-century capital investment. Seaborne (1971: 140–2) shows that for National Schools the initial average cost of about £2/place had decreased by 20 per cent by the 1820s and 1830s.

One way of reducing land and building costs was to use the foundations, walls and roof of another building – exactly what was done in 1838 in the Catholic Parish of St Patrick in Livesey Street, north Manchester by putting the boys' school above a row of terraced houses, with the open schoolroom entered from a stairway at one end.[9] This spatial structure reproduces that of the open loomshop above workers' terrace housing examined in Chapter 10.

The first shed-like structures had little ornament and only minimum expenditure on finishes. Once schools became fit projects for architectural practice the costs shot up. For instance in the hands of Kendall, author of a standard early work on school design in 1847, the costs are increased by fifty per cent. Clarke, five years later, pushed them up by a factor of three in comparison to forty years earlier, only a little of which was due to inflation.[10] This comes about less from an increase in space standards, though the 1851 Committee *Minutes* did augment them, nor from improved quality of finishes, but because the building became 'architecture' – that is formally elaborated.

Slightly beyond the crude utilitarian shed was shorn-down Classicism. In the 1830s Tudor became the favoured style, domestic in contrast to the foreigness of Classical and its association with monumental buildings such as Smirke's British Museum. The supplanting of Tudor by Gothic, once schools appear in the architects' portfolio, was not only a result of the dominance of Pugin's Gothic Revival, but of ideology. It was consciously chosen for economy and its Christian connotations in contrast to the pagan Classical; Kendall argued that the school building ought to 'partake of a semi-religious and semi-ecclesiastical character' (Seaborne 1971: 212). He also saw the expansion of education as 'a noble opportunity for the exhibition of national architecture'. Gothic had *rural* or small-town character which matched the educational reformers' suspicion of the city. Rationalist or Non-conformist sponsors were slower to embrace something so strongly associated with Establishment but even Wesleyans gradually abandoned the Classical (Jobson 1850). In Scotland the appeal of Gothic was weaker; Stow's designs were a-stylar or vaguely Classical and even as late as 1850 only one Gothic scheme is shown. In Rebublican America the Classical tradition was more robust. In the 1848 edition of Barnard's standard work all the schools are severely Classical with the exception of the huge Gothic New York City Free Academy, whose architect James Renwick argues that its great hall could be 'in no other order' and hence the exterior had to comply, apart from being far cheaper than 'Grecian, Roman or modern Italian' (Barnard 1848: 183–4).

Capital and running costs were on one side of the equation; on the other was crime prevention, with its estimated reductions in property loss and cost of police and prisons. This calculus is universal amongst the educational pioneers, irrespective of religious or political affiliation. It is used by Raikes, Owen, Bell, Lancaster, Wilderspin and Stow. Kay reckons that even if only one tenth of workhouse children, as a result of inadequate education, ultimately become a public charge through felony or pauperism, the cost of maintaining them and their families for half of each year would far exceed the cost of a fully developed educational system (Kay 1839: 12).

Invisible engines

The Industrial Revolution school is commonly read as a social laboratory and instrument for shaping society. Without evidence about how its relations were materialised, this remains unconvincing. And that evidence is precisely what is needed for a typological explanation of the buildings.

At the heart of the changing relations is the emergence of class. The great Enlightenment project of classification had eroded the continuous order of Pope's 'Great Chain of Being' to replace it with elaborate taxonomies, whether in botany or in society.

Hamilton (1980) reminds us that though Adam Smith employed class *concepts* he did not use the word and later writers appear to have borrowed it from education; in a reference to study at the University of Paris it appears as early as 1517. Specially significant were Smith's concepts of 'sympathy' – universal shared interests, moral equality – and 'emulation', whereby differentiation results from self-improvement. We have seen both terms used in education. But for Smith they were united, whereas in education 'emulation' (competition) became the opposite of 'sympathy' (sharing and co-operation).

The pre-monitorial school created a direct interface between teacher and pupil. Pupils were neither a cohesive group nor in competition. The monitorial system, whilst preserving a pairwise interaction, changed relations by introducing competition, initially between individuals through continuously changing rank orders, and later between classes defined by such abilities as being able to read words of different number of syllables. Within classes or 'drafts' there was no solidarity as there were was no common teaching. The class boundaries, as in society, remained relatively fixed but within them individuals were competitively mobile. Boundaries could be crossed but with great effort; those based on age not at all.

Space became a sign for two kinds of structure: competitive, resulting from place-capturing within classes or drafts, and from separation of classes based on achievement into rows, blocks or rooms, and organisational as in Bell's 'aisles' and in the grouping of Lancaster's 'drafts' in semi-circles and in desks with a monitor's stool at the end of each. In both power flowed along the deep, tree-like hierarchy: master, head monitor, monitors, assistant monitors and children.

With Wilderspin came the first significant shift in relations. Groups are now taught in common. They shared their interaction with the teacher and this experience formed the basis of solidarity. This was especially the case when the entire school was in the gallery, where solidarity *without* class division was a perfect representation of Smith's 'sympathy', but classes taught simultaneously in the classroom would also develop solidarity, alongside inter-class competition as they were achievement-based. Also, since examination remained individual, the solidarity of simultaneous teaching was always weakened by individual competition.

Wilderspin's playground was designed to

develop character and moral behaviour through co-operation and shared play. Whereas the school- and class-rooms fostered solidarity and competition under central control, the playground appears to be the analogue of the free market with potential for untrammelled competition, only restrained by the rhetoric of morality which proposes co-operation as a strategy for survival. This was a real attempt to overcome the aspects of human nature which create social conflict. But, unlike the unrestrained market, it recognised the possibility for destruction from the darker side of human nature. The real guarantor of peace was discreet surveillance, which can be read as an analogue of the state as a guarantor for justice.

The final step came with the separation of the entire school into classes, simultaneously taught. The separate blocks of tiered seats, either in an open schoolroom or hall, or in individual classrooms, is the final spatial corroboration of the new society's mixture of individual identity, class solidarity and class confict.

Hamilton (1983) sees another source for the class system – Robert Owen's method of teaching older children by 'familiar lectures' in 'classes of from 40 to 50' and the not unconnected contemporary system of class teaching in Glasgow University.

The separate classroom was, from its inception, associated with high status. For qualifed teachers this increasingly became their goal, giving independence and freedom from surveillance. A corrollary was the corridor where encounters between children, teachers and relatives were unprogrammed and where discipline was more difficult to enforce. So as the teachers gained freedom in the classroom, the children gained it in the corridor.

The emergence of class is also evident in labels. Stow distinguished between 'English', 'commercial' and 'industrial' schools – approximating to bourgeois, artisan and unskilled classes. This was built into the model schools of his Normal Seminary. It is not a big step to the industrial, technical and grammar schools replaced in Britain by the comprehensive school. The analysis of the early schools helps to explain the emergence, today, of a newly divided system under market conditions.

All the innovators invested great resources in explaining and propagating their theories and practices. The manuals and handbooks were widely diffused. Though at first they focused on curriculum, model lessons and pedagogy, in every instance architectural guidance quickly followed. And it was given by educators. First, because the building type did not yet form part of the architect's portfolio – any more than did the textile mill in its innovatory phase. Secondly because to educational innovators the building, down to its last coathook, was as powerful as model lessons, timetables or systems of rewards and punishments. It could not be safely entrusted to anyone else. The Committee of Council merely continued the tradition, and the marriage of pedagogy and design was never severed. It survived the 1870 Act, the 1906 Code and re-appeared more strongly than ever after World War II in the Building Bulletins of the Ministry of Education which established new spatial patterns for new teaching methods.

Amongst them was the 'open plan': loosely structured class and activity spaces, articulated but undivided from each other, intended to give flexibility in teaching, activities and timetabling. Without concrete spatial boundaries, surveillance by head teachers over their colleagues, and by the latter over children, became much easier. The corridor, considered a waste – in fact the freest and most unprogrammed space – disappeared in a return to the monitorial schools where furniture and subtle floor markings were used for structuring space without hindering visibility.

If the Sunday, infant and monitorial schools were models of the hierarchical production relations of the mill, the open-plan school is a model of the electronic office, where material articulation of power has become more subtle and despite the egalitarian rhetoric of flexibility, privacy and space for relative automony have disappeared. At the same time, in both school and office, surveillance is increased and accompanied by greatly increased invisible controls, in schools by written records, reporting and assessment procedures on children, and performance appraisal of staff, and in offices by the recording and monitoring that is built into information networks. Planning and forecasting extend control from the past and present into the future. Where space and its hardware had been instruments for the visible exercise of power in the 'engine', they now become a setting for invisible controls.

CHAPTER 4

Re-formation

The great confinement

Foucault (1977) used this phrase for a 'phenomenon of European dimensions' which was born with the 1656 decree setting up the landmark *Hôpital Général* in Paris. A system was invented for collecting and confining those who in one way or another could introduce chaos into the social order. After confinement, a whole range of régimes could be imposed to heal, reform or punish these individuals, and to make them work. There was an extensive list of categories: the physically or mentally ill, those suffering from the moral disease of crime or unable to work as a result of old age or infirmity, the poor, the physically and mentally handicapped, the homeless and vagrant, orphans and deviants of all kinds. For the next two centuries this programme consumed by far the greatest slice of public building resources in the construction of poorhouses, workhouses, orphanages, almshouses, prisons, hospitals and asylums. Since their history has been much more fully researched than that of the schools, the task is to select from this narrative just those key features which illustrate how the architecture of confinement works.

The previous chapter looked at the places designed to form children's character by stamping it with innocence and fitness. If that failed, a programme of *re*-formation was needed for those who had become deformed by various pathologies. This too was an exercise of power. In the period which is Foucault's starting point it was external, power over others. The Enlightenment's faith in reason added its inverse – internal, rational power over the self.

Now there was a paradox: internal power became subject to the same social structures as external since with the power to coerce went the power to turn the subjects of the confining régimes into agents of their own reformation. And the institutional buildings were designed to achieve this dual outcome.

At the same time the élite groups invested authentically free energy in the re-creation of their own character, to ratify their status both as individuals and as members of their class. For this they created buildings, the subject of Chapter 6, which adopted the iconography and formal devices of their own dwellings. Hence they are rich in allusions to palaces, *chateaux*, country houses, town mansions, castles and military fortifications.

It is no surprise then that the institution has been seen as an analogue of the palace both by its innovators and by modern authors. W.A.F. Browne, appointed as the first superintendent of the Crichton Royal Asylum in Dumfries in 1834, sees the asylum as a lunatics' palace, standing in a domain which they cultivate themselves. They are both lord and labourer:

> Conceive a spacious building resembling the palace of a Peere, airy and elevated, and elegant, surrrounded by extensive and swelling grounds and gardens. The interior is fitted up with galleries and workshops and music rooms. The sun and the air are allowed to enter every window, the view of the shrubberies and fields and groups of labourers is unobstructed by shutters or bars; all is clean and attractive … The inmates all seem to be actuated by the common impulse of enjoyment, all are busy, and delighted by being so. The house and all

> round appears a hive of industry. All are anxious to be engaged, to toil incessantly, and in general without any recompense than being kept from disagreeable thoughts and pains of illness. They literally work in order to please themselves ... There is in this community no compulsion, no chains, no whips, no corporal punishment, simply because these are proved to be less effectual means of carrying any point than persuasion, emulation and the desire for gratification.
>
> (Browne 1837: 229–30)

The 'moral' régime coupled external controls (though without the use of physical force) to internal reformation, both imposed by coercion.

Jean Genet (1967) in *The Thief's Journal* even more clearly identifies the control system of a total institution – in this case a prison – with the rules of the palace. But he goes further – he even identifies the prisoner (visitor) with the palace guest:

> Prison offers the same sense of security to the convict as does a Royal Palace to a King's guest. They are the two buildings constructed with the most faith, those which give the greatest certainty of being what they are – which are what they meant to be, and which remain. The masonry, the materials, the proportions and the architecture are in harmony with a moral unity which makes these dwellings indestructible so long as the social form of which they are the symbol endures. The prison surrounds me with a perfect guarantee. I am sure that it was constructed for me – along with the Law Court, its annex, its monumental vestibule. Everything therein was designed for me in a spirit of the utmost seriousness. The rigour of the rules, their strictness, their precision, are in essence the same as the etiquette of a royal court, as the exquisite and tyrannical politeness of which a guest at that court is the object. The foundations of the palace, like those of the prison, inhere in the fine quality of the stone, in marble stairways, in real gold, in carvings, the rarest in the realm, in the absolute power of their hosts; but they are also similar in that these two stuctures are one the root and the other the crest of a living system circulating between these two poles which contain it, compress it and which are sheer force.
>
> (Genet 1967: 71–2)

The 'sheer force' is that of the inhabitants' 'power' – in one case of the institution's controllers in the other of royalty. The visitor – court guest or prisoner – is equally powerless.

If palaces so resemble asylums and prisons that even their forms are hard to distinguish, as both Browne and Genet suggest, additional information is needed about function, spatial structure and the rules which govern daily life. All these represent the distribution of power between categories of participants. Goffman (1970) has analysed the total institution at a sociological level and Foucault as a power system which forms a chapter in the history of ideas. But analysis of its buildings is still problematic.

In Chapter 1 I have already referred to Hillier and Hanson's (1984: 183 *et seq.*) discussion of 'reversed' types, which is their term for institutional buildings. Their function is not the concretisation of the everyday 'taken-for-granted' social relations but their 'restoration (and) purification' – the processes I have described as formation and reformation.

If the target in the school is potential pathology, then in the hospital or prison it is actual. Within this latter group they identify two sub-types. In one the pathology of *individuals* needs the direct interface between them and those with specialised knowledge – for instance doctors or nurses – to effect a cure. Control through space and by rules is a means for the protection of this interface. In the other such control directly addresses the pathology of *society*. It segregates inmates as a class, places them under surveillance and returns them to society. The direct interface between individual visitors and specialist inhabitants is secondary. The prison is the example *par excellence* of this sub-type, though they first illustrate it with a famous eighteenth century lunatic asylum in Vienna. They argue that the two sub-types have significant spatial differences.

One particular pathology was itself spatial – vagrancy broke the spatial boundaries on which the pre-industrial economy depended at every level from the nation to the Parish. Restoring vagrants to their 'origin' was legally enforced from the late middle ages. For those who could not or would not be restored specialised institutional space was created.

In all these places order is based on stable categories of people, objects and activities, together with a set of rules – much stronger and more explicit than in other buildings – which govern their interactions. They establish diurnal, weekly and seasonal timetables and shifts; and they specify the duration and repetition of events. The rules are, equally strongly, built into space and its management. They define the location of persons and things, they control the paths of movement and the degree of choice as well as the visual paths, they define programmed encounters and place limits on those occurring by chance. Time and space are joined in rules which govern the opening times of specific spaces. In short the building and its management determine who does what, where, with whom, when and observed by whom.

Development is from mixed, non-specific to specialised and segregated types. But despite such outstanding cases as the catch-all *Hôpital Général*, there were some earlier specialisations in pest-houses and orphanages. And, equally, there were some late non-specialist survivors in the Old Poor Law catch-all workhouse. In its New Poor Law successor the two strands eventually converge; it houses as wide a range of inmates as the *Hôpital Général*, but its parts reproduce the highly specialised features of hospitals, prisons, asylums, schools and factories. It is a good place at which to conclude this narrative; a good place to start is one of the oldest types – the almshouse for the old and infirm.

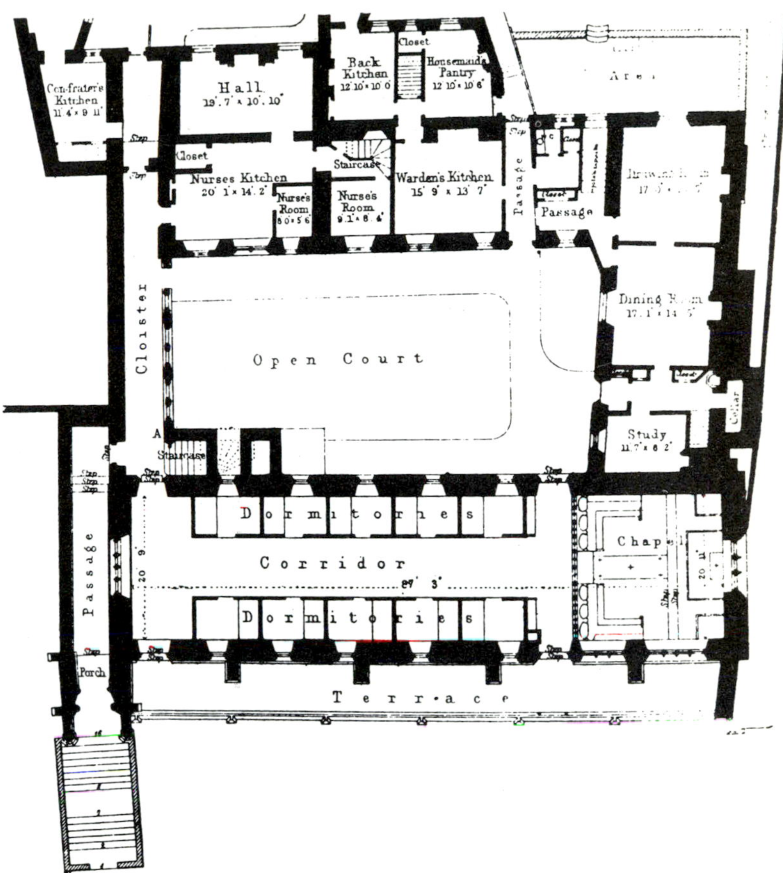

Figure 4.1

Browne's hospital, Stamford (1493), ground floor plan

Source: Godfrey (1955), Faber & Faber

Age as pathology

Heath (1910) makes an important distinction between the almshouse and the so-called 'hospital' of the Middle Ages, a different kind of house for the same kind of inmate. This is really a distinction in the way space was organised. In the latter, he says, there is a communal gate and one or more communal space, whilst in the former the residential accommodation is in the form of 'tenements' – that is independent units, each with its own entrance either direct from the street or off a shared courtyard. Both had chapels, but the relation of these to the residential accommodation was also different. In the 'hospital' it is at one end of a long dormitory hall, centrally aligned on its axis. The late fifteenth century Browne's Hospital at Stamford (Figure 4.1) is like this with partitioned dormitory rooms on both sides of an open central hall and a double height chapel at one end. It has the features of a medieval hospital proper; these and the possible origins of the form in the shrine are discussed below. Access to the hall from the outside is by a porch and long corridor as well as from a central open courtyard. On the floor above an 'audit' room (council chamber) sits over the hall in the same relation to the chapel; in other words the chapel, deep in space, serves as a symbolic space which integrates secular with sacred power.

A familiar example of Heath's 'tenemental' form is Wren's 1685 Morden College, Blackheath (Figure 4.2) where the entrance is on the axis of the chapel and the chaplain and treasurer inhabit two projecting wings on the main front. In another Wren design, the Wardenry at Farley, Wiltshire groups of houses symmetrically flank the central warden's house, and the entrances of both warden and inmates are directly off the street (perhaps they should be called 'outmates').

An extraordinary mixture of the two is the little almshouse founded in 1593 at Beamsley in Yorkshire for thirteen women; six in small two storey houses in a plain rectangular block and seven in a circular structure, the rooms radiating around a central chapel, five opening from it and two from the entrance passage (Figure 4.3). These two rooms are the shallowest spaces, the chapel is at mid-depth and the other five rooms are the deepest.

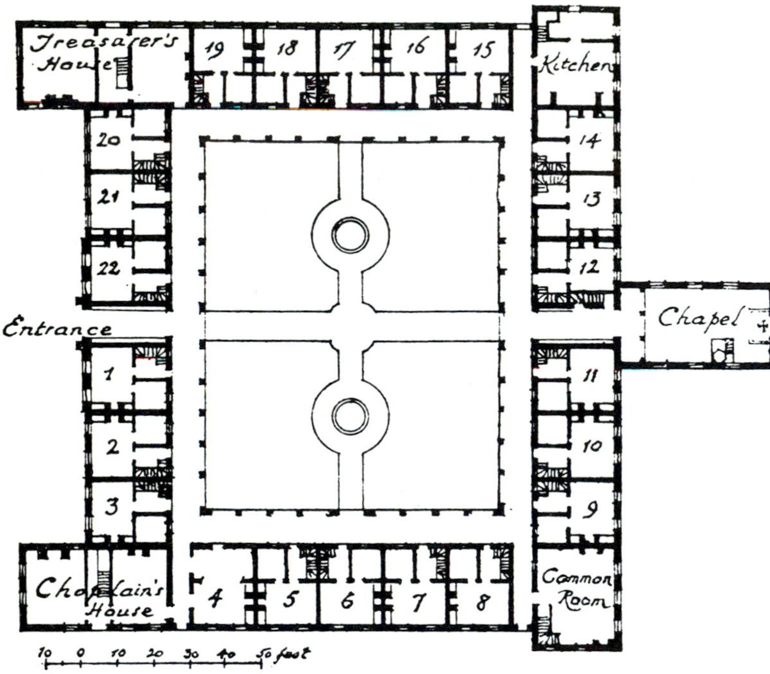

Figure 4.2

Morden College, Blackheath (1685), ground floor plan

Source: Godfrey (1955), Faber & Faber

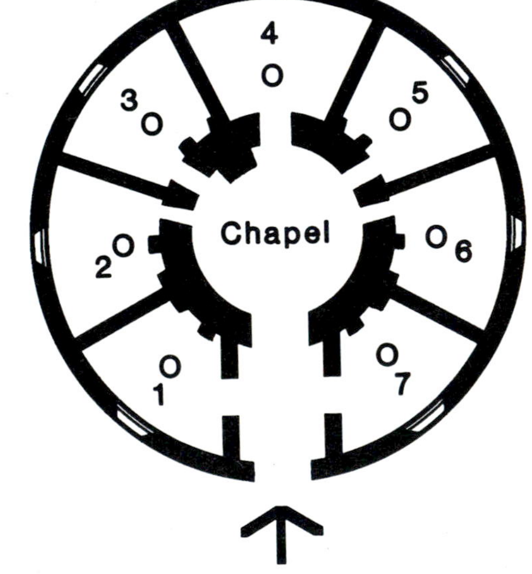

Figure 4.3

Beamsley hospital, Yorkshire (1593), plan

Source: Redrawn from Clapham and Godfrey (1955)

The unproductive poor

The trust deeds for almshouses and 'hospitals' ensured that their occupants were genteel. They may have been in straitened circumstances (for instance clergymen's widows) but they were never coerced into work as were the unemployed or vagrant poor in the institutions set up after late sixteenth century legislation.

To the traditionally destitute poor, infirm, widowed and orphaned were added, during trade depressions and rural unemployment caused by population growth and the change to pasture, the new urban poor. In France the *ancien régime* institutions, until the Revolution (Williams 1979 and Forrest 1981), coped with these. In Britain the first break came in 1539 when the pre-Reformation monastic, manorial, religious and Royal institutions were replaced with a series of experiments culminating in Elizabeth's Acts of 1597 and 1601. The Old Poor Law was designed to cope with those who were unproductive and a threat to property and stable order who had become an excessive burden on Parishes. For the post-feudal, guild-centred mercantile society they were disruptive in two ways. First, they tended to move about – they lacked roots in space. Hence the attempts at limiting mobility, such as Henry VIII's Acts which licensed beggars to beg only in defined districts. The legislation culminated in the seventeenth century Acts to remove vagrants to their 'home' Parishes through powers of settlement. Secondly, they were unproductive, without a master. Traditionally domestic production had been enforced. Now institutions were designed to give them an institutional master and thus make them stable and productive under one roof.

An early plan was Rowland Vaughan's in 1610 (Kirkman Gray 1905: 55–8) for a mill with looms for wool and silk, employing in all 2000 people. The model was collegiate: in the vast paupers' dining room there was to be high table for 'knights and gentlemen'.

By 1630 a number of Parish workhouses had been established (Oxley 1974: 80). Provision for the poor under the Puritan régime may not have represented real progress because demographic and employment changes themselves decreased the problem (Kirkman Gray 1905: 80). Parliament created the London Corporation of the Poor in 1647, which could set up workhouses and houses of correction. Two were erected – the London Workhouse off Bishopsgate Street, and another in the Minories (Kirkman Gray 1905: 73). The former originally had two parts – one for children, the other for petty criminals – joined by a shared chapel. The prison fell into disuse and was demolished. The theoretical distinction between punishment (as in the Bridewell and houses of correction) and employment continued to be carefully made but the only two Corporation workhouses combined them. In practice here, as all over Europe, they were beginning to merge.

But Statutes continued to separate the 'impotent poor' from 'idle, sturdy and disorderly beggars' (8 and 9 William III. c 30). The deep moral imperatives behind the legal distinction have persisted from the Old Poor Law to modern social service legislation. Ambiguity has nevertheless always existed as much in the buildings as in the régimes. By the end of the seventeenth century the workhouse had become a penal institution.

The 1696 Bristol Corporation of the Poor is regarded as the precursor of numerous later Corporations (Webb and Webb 1963: 101–48) and its workhouse as the precursor of a system that was to last well into the nineteenth century. Anne Digby's (1978) meticulous study of the Poor Law in Norfolk shows that in fact the Old and the New were more continuous than is often assumed. And this continuity applies as much to the design of the workhouses as to the legislation. She lists twelve houses of industry in Norfolk alone, several dating from the eighteenth century, which were merely adapted after 1834 to the requirements of the new Act with regard to classification and segregation. Several Parish Unions did not replace these adapted buildings till the 1850s.

Other towns soon followed Bristol and an Act of 1722 legalised what had been long become *de facto* practice. Apart from the so-called Gilbert's Act of 1782, which gave a firmer basis to workhouse projects of Parishes and Parish Unions, there was no significant legislation till 1834. By that time there were hundreds of these institutions, either incorporations or Gilbert Unions. To Crabbe, who grew up in Suffolk and must have experienced these in East Anglia, they were 'Pauper Palaces',

> That giant-building, that high-bounding wall,
> Those bare-worn walks, that lofty thund'ring
> hall!
> That large loud clock, which tolls each dreaded
> hour,
> Those gates and locks and all those signs of
> power;
> It is a prison with a milder name,
> Which few inhabit without dread or shame.
>
> (Crabbe 1810: 287)

In fact there is evidence that the carceral conditions were more a feature of the New than of the Old Poor Law workhouse which offered a good measure of comfort, tolerant rules, and often civilised working conditions. It was precisely this which made them, according to the Commissioners of 1832, far too desirable, with the consequence of a huge public burden. The new Act had as its primary goal the creation of a life so uncomfortable that no one would wish to enter or remain in a workhouse except as a last resort. A new Assistant Commissioner defined this as making the existing institutions 'wholesomely repulsive'. He claimed to have seen three generations continuing to live in one workhouse and inmates boarding up or locking their empty rooms whilst they went on holiday, and noted a substantial diet of meat, fish and fresh vegetables, good winter heating and, by the standards of the day, adequate medical care (Longmate 1974: 82–3).

The buildings varied in size and type and the scarcity of plans hinders analysis. Baker's study of the Potteries (undated) covers both small domestic workhouses and the huge complex at Stoke-on-Trent, whose first building was erected in 1832 but most of which is subsequent to the New Poor Law of 1834. As with almshouses, there were workhouses which correspond to Heath's 'tenements', with direct street entrance to separate units, and others which were fully institutional and controlled. Their multiplicity is well illustrated by Derby, a small provincial town in 1791 with only five Parishes four of which had their own workhouse which a contemporary observer condemns as places of idleness and corruption which should, but do not, contain a 'manufactory' (Hutton 1791: 60–3).

Strong rules and categories are often clear in texts which approximate to briefs. The new House of Correction to be erected in Parkhurst Forest under an Act of 1771 was intended to have

> . . . a convenient building, or part of a building, to serve as an hospital for the reception of such aged, sick, or infirm persons, and young children, as are not able to work; one other building or part of a building, to serve for the reception, maintenance and employment of such poor persons as are able to work; and one other separate building, or part of a building, to serve as a house of correction for the punishment and keeping to hard labour such idle and disorderly persons, who, being able, shall refuse to work or otherwise misbehave themselves.
>
> (Geo III, XI c43: 6–7)

The categories were not only by age, degree of infirmity and gender (though this last was taken as so obvious that it is not stated) but also by interior disposition with regard to work.

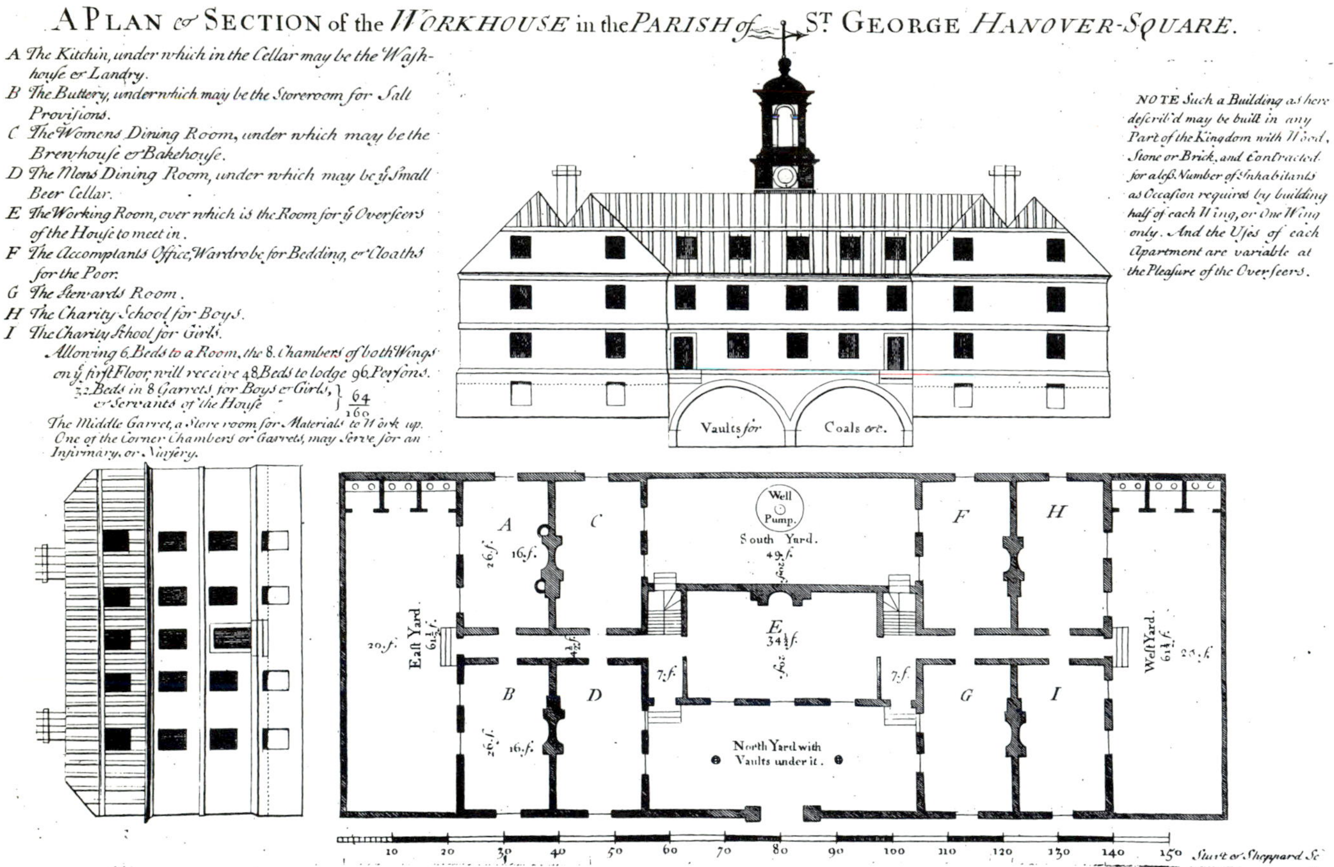
A PLAN & SECTION of the WORKHOUSE in the PARISH of St GEORGE HANOVER-SQUARE.
A The Kitchin, under which in the Cellar may be the Wash-house & Landry.
B The Buttery, under which may be the Storeroom for Salt Provisions.
C The Womens Dining Room, under which may be the Brewhouse & Bakehouse.
D The Mens Dining Room, under which may be ye Small Beer Cellar.
E The Working Room, over which is the Room for ye Overseers of the House to meet in.
F The Accomptants Office, Wardrobe for Bedding, & Cloaths for the Poor.
G The Stewards Room.
H The Charity School for Boys.
I The Charity School for Girls.
Allowing 6 Beds to a Room, the 8 Chambers of both Wings on ye first Floor, will receive 48 Beds to lodge 96 Persons.
32 Beds in 8 Garrets for Boys & Girls, & Servants of the House 64
160
The Middle Garret, a Store room for Materials to Work up.
One of the Corner Chambers or Garrets, may Serve for an Infirmary, or Nursery.
NOTE Such a Building as here describ'd may be built in any Part of the Kingdom with Wood, Stone or Brick, and Contracted for a less Number of Inhabitants as Occasion requires by building half of each Wing, or One Wing only. And the Uses of each Apartment are variable at the Pleasure of the Overseers.
Vaults for
Coals &c.
Well
Pump.
South Yard.
North Yard with Vaults under it.
East Yard.
West Yard.
10 20 30 40 50 60 70 80 90 100 110 120 130 140 150

Figure 4.4

Parish workhouse, St George's Hanover Square, London (1725)

Source: British Museum Department of Prints and Drawings

Three years after the 1722 Act a workhouse was started in Mount Street, London, for the parish of St George. Its designers, Benjamin Trimbrell and Thomas Phillips, had in mind a model for 'any part of the Kingdom', not only capable of being built in 'wood stone or brick' but of almost infinite flexibility. If need be only one wing or one floor could be used, and 'the uses of each apartment are variable at the pleasure of the Overseers'! This suggests that despite novel labels they saw the design as a stable 'type'.

Above cellars, food stores, brew and bakehouses, the ground floor (Figure 4.4) has a central, mixed-sex workroom, with men's and women's dining rooms to one side and boys' and girls' charity schools to the other. Beyond these, symmetrically on either side, are the men's and women's work yards. There is a central front entrance yard and a central rear ablution yard. All is enclosed by a high wall. Over the workroom the Overseers' room separates the first floor men's and women's dormitories. The attic floor has rooms for servants, and for the boys and girls separated by a central materials store.

On the spatial map (Figure 4.5) only the central spaces – the workroom and the front and rear yards – lie on rings, as no doubt were the first floor Overseers' and the top floor store rooms. These are all the genderless spaces. The mixed-gender workroom on a ring makes its function supervisory, almost ceremonial, in comparison to the segregated work yards which, with their sets of privies, and the rear court are the deepest ground floor spaces. Hygiene and work are the most controll*ed* and administration is the most controll*ing*. Sleeping spaces, on the upper floors, are deeper, and those of children and servants, the weakest members of the institution, are deepest. Access through the single gate is under surveillance by the steward through his window – a step towards the fully inverted outer inhabitant space.

As they increased in size, workhouses grew side pavilions creating 'U's with work and sleeping space remaining deep. The shift to incarceration demanded tighter control so that open courts were enclosed and multiple entries eliminated.

The industrial towns spawned particularly formidable workhouses: Birmingham (1770s), Manchester's new workhouse (1791–2), and

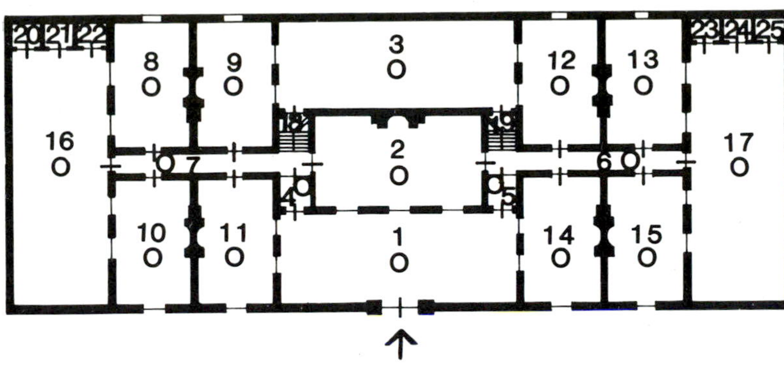

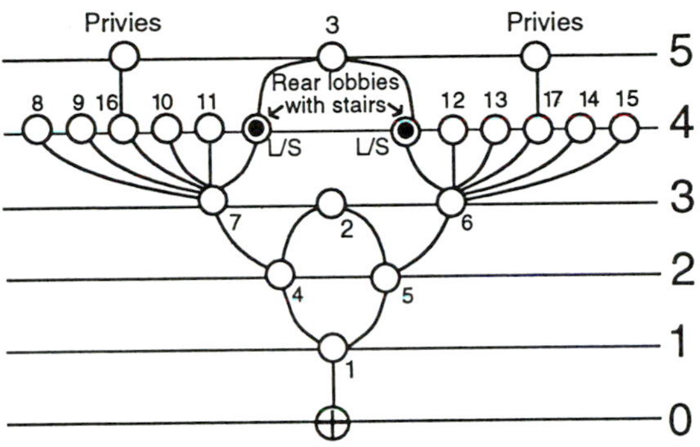

Key

1 Entrance hall
2 Workroom
3 Washyard
4 Lobby
5 Lobby
6 Corridor
7 Corridor
8 Kitchen
9 Women's dining room
10 Buttery
11 Men's dining room
12 Office and store
13 Boys' charity school
14 Steward's room
15 Girls' charity school
16 Men's work yard
17 Women's work yard

Figure 4.5
Parish workhouse, schematic plan and spatial map
Source: Author's drawings

Liverpool's house of correction and poorhouse (1770–1) which had a huge first floor dining hall seating 500, and spinning and other work rooms above it, and two detached blocks of 42 houses, with 126 'apartments' of the older type. In Leeds (1726–1800) attempts to make the wool and flax spinning profitable or even self-financing were unsuccessful (Anderson 1980: 75–113). As 'factories', in the midst of real new industry, these places were notable failures.

The removal of the children in 1776 into a separate block from the Edinburgh charity workhouse was not just expansion; the old moral imperative still demanded separation of the innocent and the culpable poor. Later an observer expressed pleasure at the prospect of a Bridewell 'for sturdy beggars, vagrants and pilferers' whose labour would pay for it. This would 'put the Poorhouse under better order and subjection' leaving it only for the 'sober and indigent' (Tod 1783: 35–6). The same imperative caused moral distinctions to be marked in another material form – through clothing. Belfast's Charitable Society poorhouse (1771) housed children, sick (of various categories), insane, prostitutes as well as 'sturdy beggars' – inmates rounded up as vagrants by the Society's 'Bangbeggar' and carried to the Black Hole of the poorhouse in his Black Cart. But beggars judged to be genuine were marked by a badge.

The 'U', 'E' and 'H' became the dominant eighteenth century British institutional plans. These forms are significant. Fleming (1962: 62) looks for their origins in the Ordnance Board's barracks. But the obvious precedent is in country houses, castles and chateaux whether on the grand scale of François Mansard's Château de Maisons (1642–50) or the more modest Aston Hall (1618–35) which share certain features: symmetry on the entrance axis, central block, projecting side wings and a forecourt enclosed by the wings. Perhaps the barracks were its earliest *adaptation.*

It was a natural choice for institutions which were located on cheap peripheral open land for reasons of segregation, fresh air, aquatic hygiene and, in the case of hospitals, to prevent contagion or infection. If one compares plans of Manchester in 1794 and 1831 (Figure 4.6) large bubbles of space are seen to survive around the New Bailey prison, the workhouse and the infirmary even after they had become embedded in the growing city. On such sites a narrow urban plan, or the French 'hôtel' plan with its court fronting the set back mansion, make little sense. The 'U' and its

1794 | 1831

Figure 4.6

Space bubble around urban institutions, Manchester's prison (a), workhouse (b), and infirmary (c), in 1794 and 1831

Source: Green's 1794 map and Thornton's 1831 map

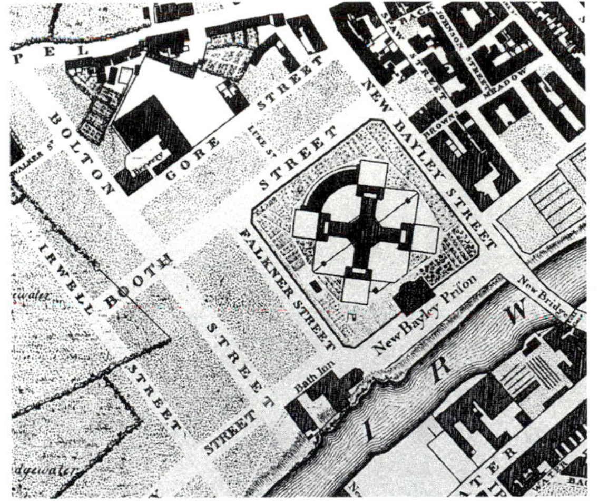

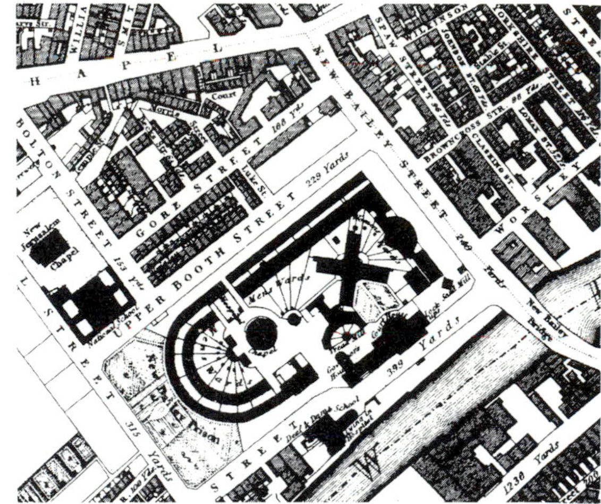

(a) Prison

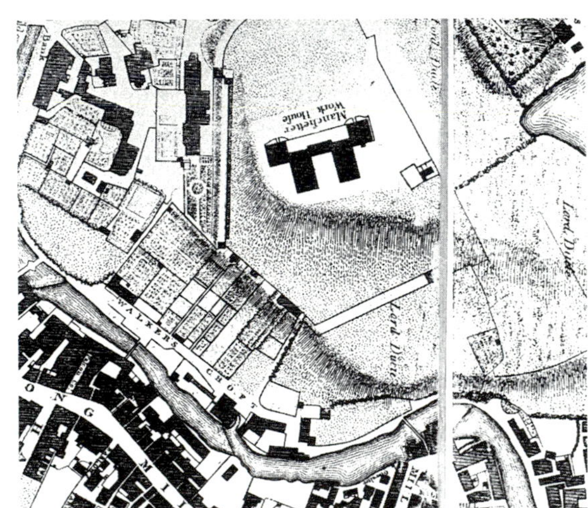

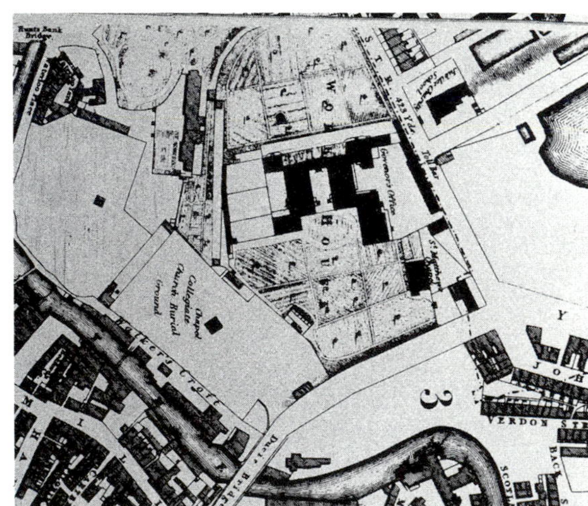

(b) Workhouse

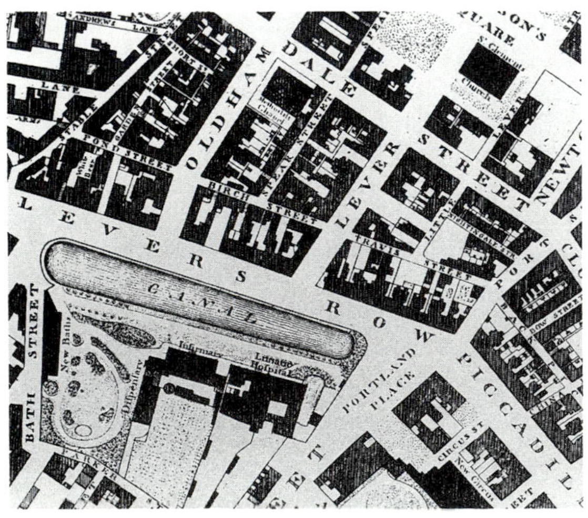

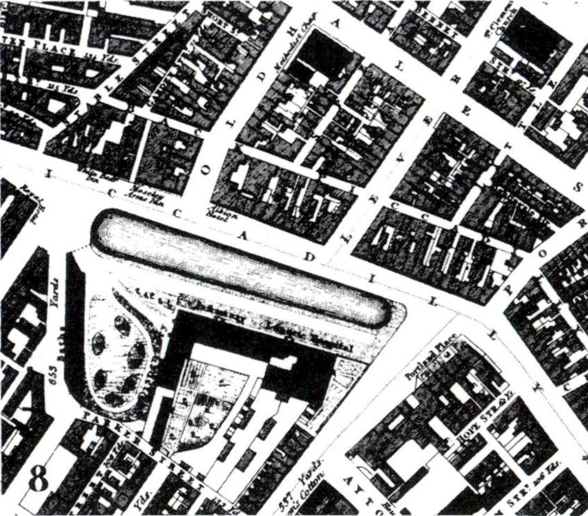

(c) Infirmary

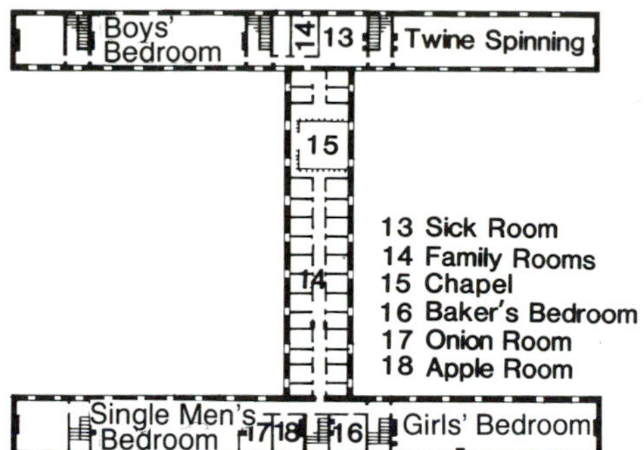

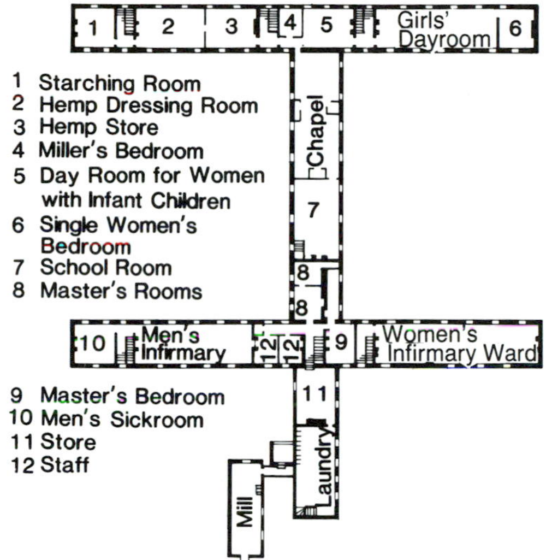

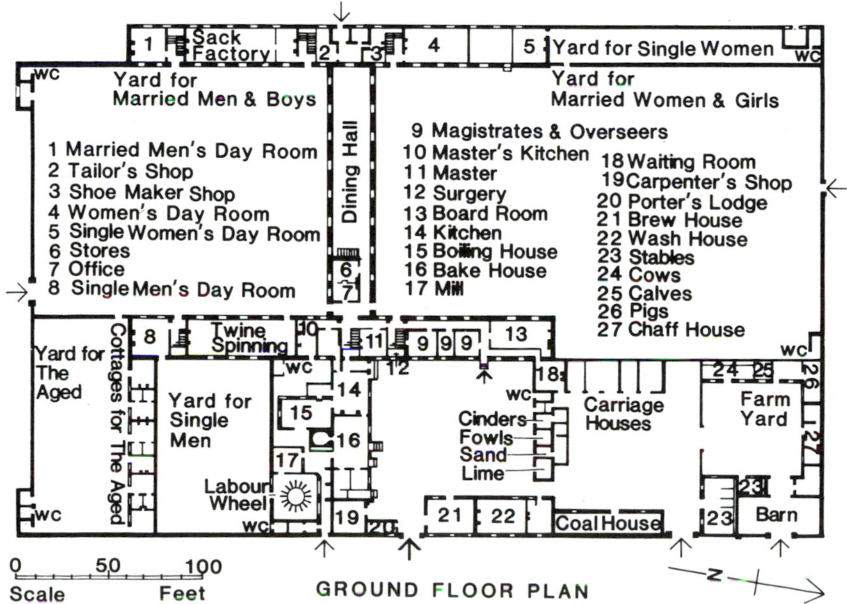

Figure 4.7

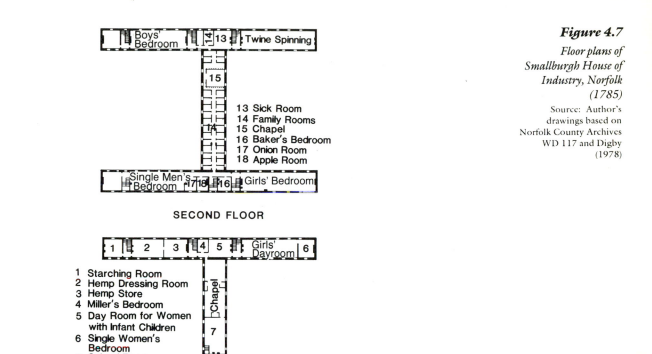

Floor plans of Smallburgh House of Industry, Norfolk (1785)

Source: Author's drawings based on Norfolk County Archives WD 117 and Digby (1978) derivatives were both practical, reasonably compact, and a reproduction of the familiar power seen in the country mansions.

Despite the longevity of the block plan, the space within the envelope responded to changes in régimes and legislation, that is, to changes in power relations. This has already been shown in Chapter 1 in analysing the space of three eighteenth century U-form hospitals. The same happens in the workhouse. Even before the New Poor Law, post-1834 workhouse, the old forms grew more complex. Anne Digby's (1978) review of the eighteenth century Norfolk workhouses includes the Smallburgh House of Industry; it is a transitional type of the most advanced kind which accommodated an increased number of residents and great organisational complexity. It prepared the ground for the 1834 changes so well that it was easily adapted by simply re-labelling spaces.

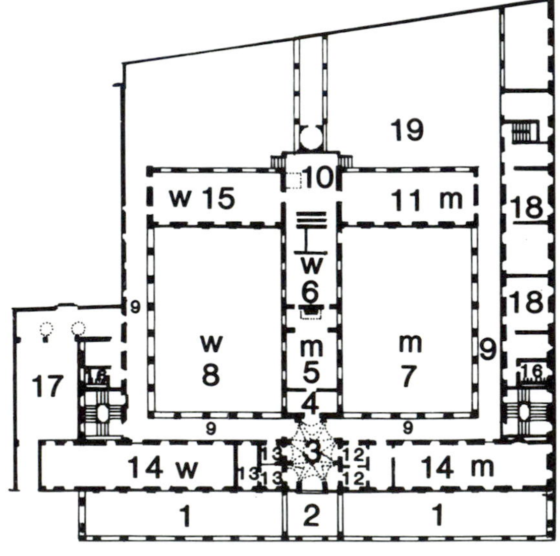

Key

1 Grand porch
2 Principal entrance
3 Hall
4 Public chapel
5 Men's chapel
6 Women's chapel
7 Men's courtyard
8 Women's courtyard
9 Cloister
10 Kitchen
11 Men's dining room
12 Chambers
13 Parlours and chambers
14 Men's and women's workshops
15 Women's dining room
16 Privies
17 Washplaces
18 Offices
19 Service court

Figure 4.8

Workhouse at Casale Monferrato designed by Vittone (1740s), ground floor plan

Source: Author's drawings based on '*Un Edificio di Publica Utilita etc.*'. Edizioni dell'Orso, Piacenza, 1982

Though available plans (Figure 4.7) date from 1834, they do present a clear picture of the earlier, three storey 'H' form. On the ground floor additional forward projecting blocks and a peripheral wall create six exercise and service yards. The entrance, through one of these, is between the magistrates' and Overseers' rooms, and the boardroom. The central spine has a huge dining hall. A row of old people's cottages is entered from a dedicated yard. The first floor has infirmaries, day spaces and workrooms; the central spine has a chapel and adjacent school room over the dining room. The top floor has a double banked row of family cubicles in the spine, with their own chapel at the head on the pattern of the medieval infirmary hall. For exercise the married couples are separated by sex into separate yards. The top floor also houses boys', girls' and single men's dormitories and more workspaces.

The work régime was intended to be self-sufficient and even profitable. It included wool and hemp spinning and agriculture on the compact farm incorporated into the plan. Corn grinding on the labour wheel was a productive not punitive process. Beer and bread were produced in the house. Later when it became apparent that even self-sufficiency, never mind profit, was unattainable, work was re-oriented towards acquiring industrious habits through sack and net production.

Smallburgh was integrated, classified, segregated for most purposes, and its spatial structure foreshadowed the nineteenth century institution: outer, shallow locations for valuable goods and products, and for the master's, magistrates' and Overseers' spaces, the deeper space shared between residential and production units.

In Continental Europe cruciform, quadrangular and radial plans had been around since medieval times to allow open wards to have sight of a central altar, but their spatial organisation was more primitive than Smallburgh's. In Vittone's grandiose 1740 scheme for the workhouse at Casale Monferrato (Figure 4.8) the chapel formed a spine – with separate spaces for men and women residents, and the public – which symmetrically divided the men's and women's courts. The entrance and the shared kitchen serving the two dining rooms are on the same axis. The two huge workrooms and the upper floor dormitories, accessed by the two grand staircases, are at the deepest levels; the chapel is intermediate, and the offices are shallow when viewed from the side entrance but deep from the main entrance. The

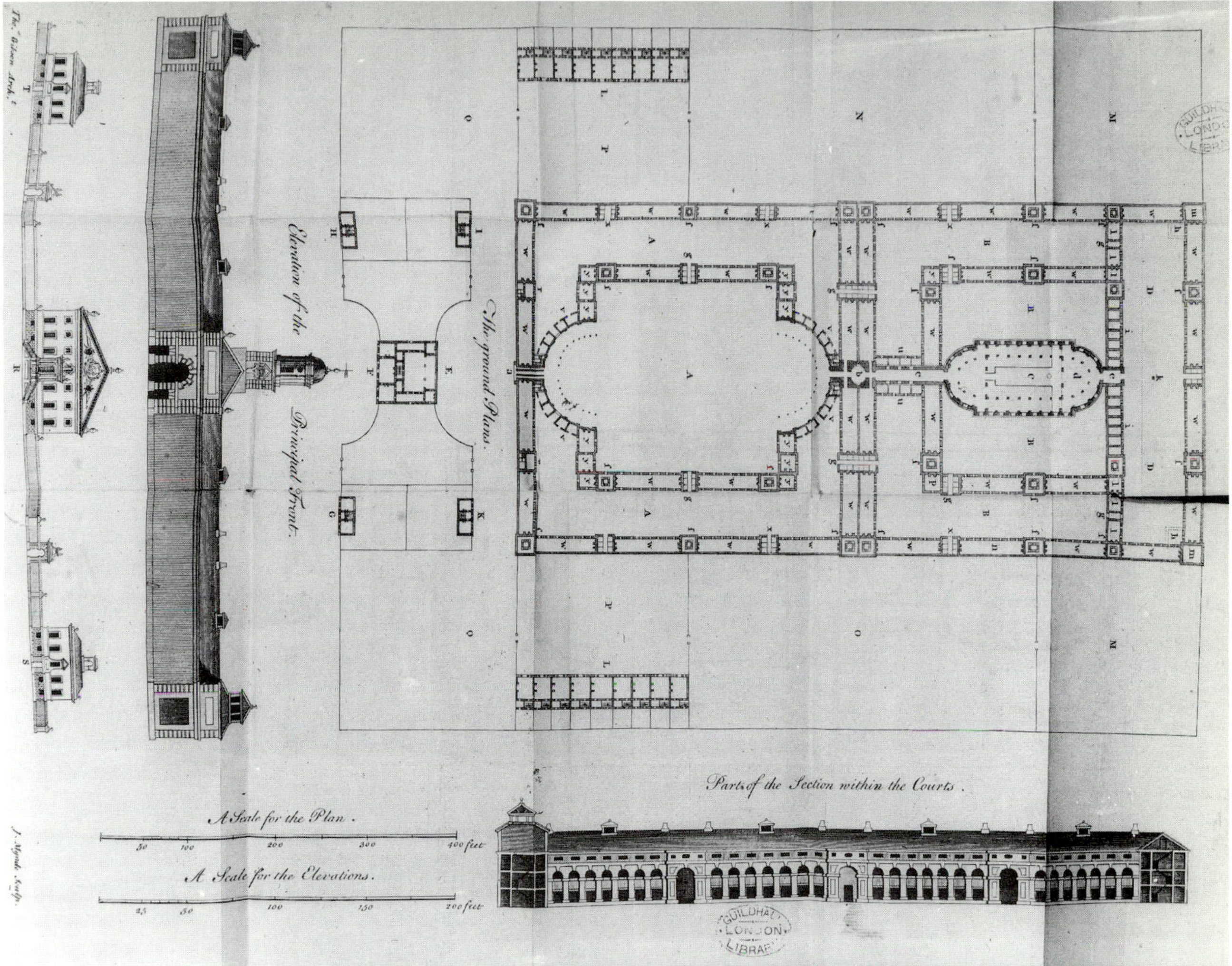

Key

A Men's courts, containing 3000 persons
B Women's courts, containing 2000 persons
C Chapel
D Prison court, containing 1000 persons
E Justice hall
F Governor's house
G Deputy governor's house
H Chaplain's house
I Treasurer's house
K Receiver's house
L Sutleries
M Burying-grounds
N Women's airing-ground
O Men's airing-ground
P Sutlery-grounds
Q Front gardens
R Elevation of the Governor's house
S Front of the Deputy-governor's house
T Ditto of the chaplain's house
a Principal gate
b Place of the steeple
c Men's way to the chapel
d Prisoners' chapel
e Prisoners' way to their chapel
g Gates
h Prisons, or fasting-rooms
i Cells
k Whipping post
l Keepers' houses
m Lodges for the assistants
n Women's infirmary
p Matron's house
r Officers' houses
s Stairs
t Men's infirmary
u, v Privies
w Workrooms, above which are the lodging-wards, 160 in number
x Lodges for the watchmen and assistants
y Storehouses

Figure 4.9

Fielding's Middlesex County House (1753)

Source: Guildhall Library

reversal is, as yet, incomplete; inhabitants do not unambiguously occupy the shallowest levels, nor is access to visitors only through inhabitants' domain.

Though uncommon in Britain, the spectacular 1753 scheme for combining punishment, poor relief and education in Thomas Gibson's design for Fielding's Middlesex 'County House', used a powerful configuration of this kind (Figure 4.9). Entrance is through two gates which flank the central governor's house and 'justice hall'. The first court, for men, has workrooms on the ground floor and lodgings above, and, at both ends, great apsidal ranges of privies. There is a central processional way to the chapel. The two courts are connected by guarded gates. Deeper still is the house of correction, where the inmates have their own entrance into a secure part of the chapel. There were to be 5000 men and women in the 'county (work) house' and 600 men in the house of correction.

Fielding had '... the idea of a body of men united under one government in a large city'. Evans (1982) sees it as a bridge between the old house of correction and the penitentiary which was shortly to arrive, with its emphasis on institutional structure and a specialised architecture. We have seen how Bender relates it to Fielding's fictional output.

Chapter 3 looked at the children in Rumford's grandiose Bavarian 'Military Workhouse'. Under pain of severe punishment for evasion, beggars were rounded up by military police and forced to work in what was really a large textile concern for the army. The four-storey building was a converted mill. A single entrance led into a courtyard off which opened workshops in 'large halls', a long drying room with tenters for stretching the cloth, a fulling mill and the wash-house and privies. Rumford emphasises the 'elegance' of the building, whose *leitmotif* was 'order, peace and health'.

Its catering gave full rein to his lifelong obsession with food economy, healthy diet, fuel efficiency, feeding régimes for the poor and kitchen design which he also exercised at the London Foundling Hospital, the Misericordia hospital in Verona, the Dublin house of industry, the model kitchen in the Dublin Linen Hall, and the experimental kitchens in the new Royal Institution in London in 1801. Possibly his Irish connections account for the design of the Stove Tenter House in Dublin (1814) – an industrial building where wool weavers thrown out of work in winter when outdoor cloth drying was impossible were provided with a three-storey fireproof building with cast iron columns, stoves and fireproof floors to afford 'a perpetual summer to the industrious' – a motto cast into an iron plate (*Gentleman's Magazine* 1818: 113–16).

Later I shall discuss Jeremy Bentham's Panopticon, the circular 'inspection house'. From 1795 he had been in close contact with Rumford and the Münich scheme's provisions for an economic and rational diet greatly impressed him. Perhaps equally influential were Rumford's draconian measures for dealing with unemployment. From the start pauper poorhouses were prime Panopticon candidates alongside penitentiaries, schools and hospitals. After some ten years of unsuccessfully propagating it, Bentham persuaded Arthur Young to feature a polygonal version, entirely built in cast iron, in his 1797 *Annals of Agriculture*. A network of them was to be created by the National Charity Company to house not only paupers but also prisoners discharged from Panopticon penitentiaries on the assumption that after completing prison labour at a profit to the prison contractor, they would be unemployed and a charge on the poor rates. They would now be rounded up and re-employed under central surveillance in these 'subsidiary' institutions, at a rate below that of the market, and hence with substantial profit to the contractor. As Bahmueller (1981) remarks, 'the difference between prison and workhouse might be lost on them (the discharged prisoners)' – all the more so in near-identical buildings.

I finish this chapter with the New Poor Law workhouse – the final 'flower' of institutions, standing in sharp contrast to these less formalised, aggregative, weak-rule-governed workhouses. But strong rules are in evidence elsewhere.

The sad

One place to find strong rules is in the hospital. They are intended to achieve an order which is made concrete in a whole variety of ways. The use of axes and lines of vision in various converging patterns is amongst the most powerful for it brings into play the most direct sense experience – what we see. It is all the more puzzling why, from the beginning, such axes are also used in plans where in reality they could not be experienced. The model monastic plan for St Gall has the sick and novice monks at the rear, their cloisters and altars aligned on the axis of the major basilica. But there was no way in which this cosmic alignment could be sensed; it was a paper (or parchment) device of the designer.

The long medieval infirmary hall opened onto and was aligned with a chapel. It was the ubiquitous model for European hospitals, poorhouses, orphanages and lazarettos and grew into more complex versions in 'L's, crosses and spoked wheels. Hillier and Hanson (1984) see it as an evolution of the shrine. Their example is the late thirteenth century hospital at Tonnerre (Figure 4.10). According to Viollet le Duc it had an upper level gallery for nurses' circulation above the cubicles for the sick aligned on either side of the central hall. Its central altar at one end is separated from the hall by the tomb of the foundress, Queen Marguerite of Burgundy, who had had direct access to the gallery by an upper level bridge from her palace. There was also access at ground level from the conventual buildings next to her palace. The hall was also entered directly from the street through a porch opposite the altar.

Hillier and Hanson (1984) read this as their first sub-type, designed for dealing with individual pathology. Medical staff move freely down the centre of the hall, a 'distributed' space (that is on a ring, permeable to more than one other space) which brings them into direct contact with the patients. But there is a piece of explanation missing: the hall is shallow with regard to the outside if approached directly from the street, and deep if approached through the spaces of the palace or the convent. In the former case it is non-institutional, visitors interfacing with inhabitants – who emerge from their deep space with its own entrances – in shallow, distributed space. Entering directly into the hall is like entering a public building. This is the consequence of a particular historical stage in medical culture when direct access to patients by relatives and friends (another, more literal category of 'visitor') was still considered an essential part of practical care. Equally importantly the sick, many of whom were on the threshold of death, were seen as suffering pilgrims clearly *en route* for heaven. To join them on their final journey in sight of the altar was not only a meritorious act of compassion but of public worship. As medical régimes changed, the hospital, whilst still providing each patient with a direct interface with staff, began to resemble the second sub-type where bedspaces (like prison cells) are not in shallow, distributed space, but

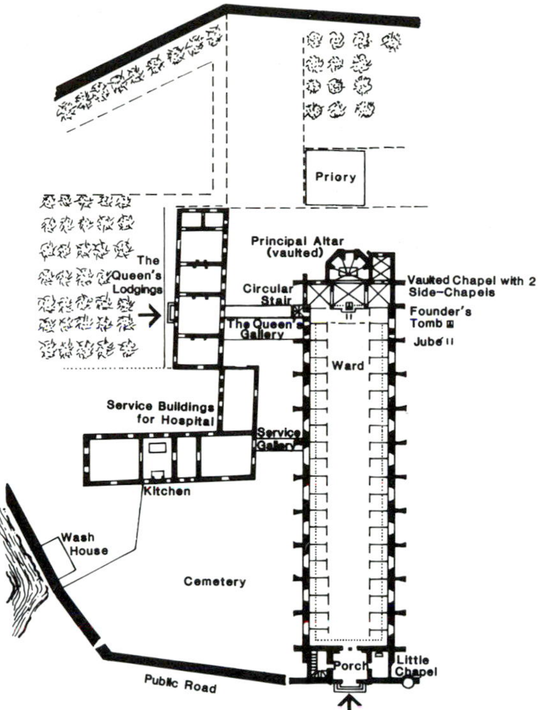

Figure 4.10

Tonnerre hospital (1293)

Source: Author's drawing based on Viollet le Duc

deep within the structure at the tips of branches of trees. That is the alternative structure of Tonnerre, if access to the patients is considered through the palace or convent.

In the contemporary Hospital of the Holy Ghost in Lübeck the infirmary hall was entered from outside by two doorways between three altars which faced into a combined vestibule and public chapel. The chapel has the reverse role to that at Tonnerre – it is a threshold, not a sanctuary. The great hall is axially aligned on the central altar but is entirely blocked from the patients' view. As at St Gall, it is an axis without experiential basis. Even where altars were on the hall side immense distances and intermediate blockages of beds and curtains made it impossible for all but those nearest to see and hear what went on.

Thompson and Goldin (1975) trace the axial hall and focal altar to the fifth century. From the Middle Ages till the nineteenth century cruciform and radial versions flourish. Howard (1791: 58) describes this durable and robust form as 'Roman Catholic'. Its best known Renaissance version was Filarete's fifteenth century double cross hospital (Figure 4.11) for his ideal town Sforzinda.

The only English example, the Savoy Hospital in London built in the form of a Latin cross by Henry VII (1508–19) was directly inspired by the

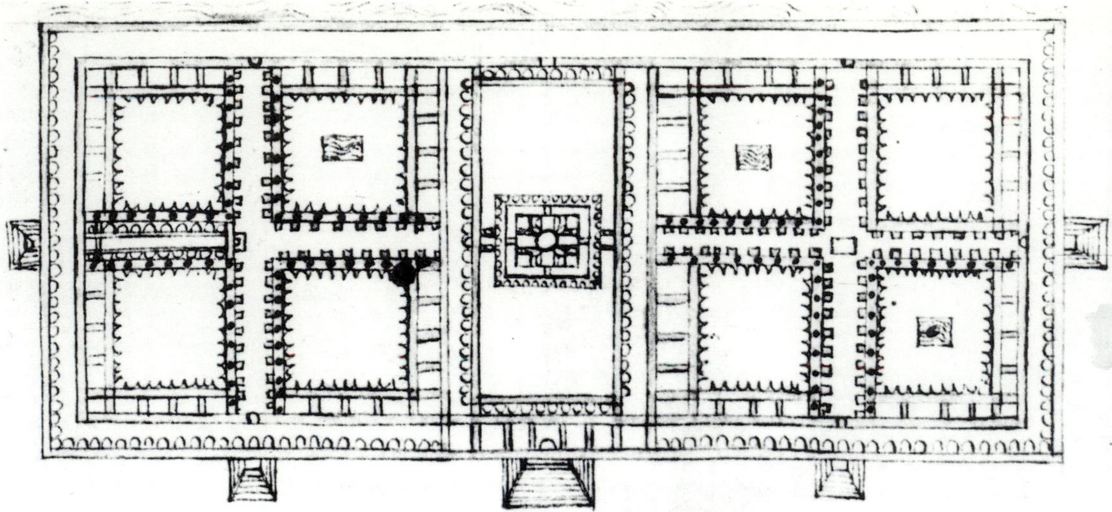

Figure 4.11

Filarete's ideal hospital (c. 1465)

Source: *Filarete's 'Treatise on Architecture'*, Yale University Press, author's copy

Florentine Santa Maria Nuova, but evidence for an altar at the crossing is lacking (Colvin *et al.* 1975: 196–206).

Contrary to Howard's view, the form emerges even in Presbyterian, Enlightenment Scotland in the hands of the great 'improver' Sir John Sinclair whose hospital for the new town of Thurso (1801) is four-armed.

It was not only for ever-increasing numbers that the cross was transformed into the spoked wheel – but to embody the disease classification which Enlightenment clinical theory demanded. And architects responded on a grand scale which verged on urban planning. Desgodets in 1779 tried an eight-armed version (Rosenau 1970: 61), as did Laugier. Sturm's 720-bed hospital of 1720 prefigures the great experiments of the 1770s and 1780s for replacing the Paris Hôtel Dieu destroyed by fire in 1772. In Petit's six-spoked four-storey plan the central altar was surmounted by a massive ventilation cone (Petit 1774). It says something about architectural history that Kaufmann's influential work on neo-Classicism (1955: Plate 143) illustrates the huge scheme by Poyet for 5200 beds in sixteen 84-bed wards with only an elevation.

Gazing at the centre in a radial hospital assured patients that Providence was present. It also made them aware of the presence of others gazing at the same point from wards which they could not see. The central altar gradually became more accessible, ceasing to perform as a shrine in deep sacred space. Finally it was replaced altogether by a point of surveillance and became, by the use of various devices, part of the controllers' shallow space. The direction of the gaze was inverted; instead of all seeing a common point, all were seen from it. The centre ceased to be unifying, offering supernatural validation and affirming a shared existence, and now isolated, divided and over-powered.

The transformation was the result of rational science which also created a new form of its own – pavilions around courts or in parallel echelons on either side of a single or dual spine. These too were capable of organisation into grand compositions. But alongside them the palatial tradition of enclosed courts, 'U's, 'H's or 'E's already encountered in workhouses, was equally alive. It made growth by accretion easier, especially when older buildings were being converted, and was adaptable to any size or site, whereas the radial or pavilion plans were virtually fixed.

One version of this tradition was used in the largest schemes in what might be called the 'metropolitan' model. Each case carried the imprint of a unique history of monastic charity, Enlightenment philanthropy and science, Absolutist order-making or plague control. Its multiple courts, wings, arcades and spurs, the result of periodic demolitions, additions and conversions, makes it difficult to see that they all use classification by gender, economic status and disease category. Churches, boardrooms and financial offices dominate by formal means of domes, height and location on main axes. Gradually the tight control of the interface with the public which characterised the early plague houses, became more general. At the same time – by the end of the eighteenth century – the spatial 'inversion' is complete.

The Hôpital St Louis (1607–12), a contagious disease outpost of the Hôtel Dieu was based on elaborate segregation strategies. At the front only the church and the kitchen penetrate the wall that separates the huge central court surrounded by the plague wards from the outer world. At the rear the priests and nursing sisters have lodgings which also open both to the plague court and to the back street. From the patients and the public in the church they are deep; from the street they are shallow.

The twelfth century St Thomas's in London became one of Edward VI's Royal hospitals in 1553. When rebuilt (1693–1709) it acquired its final form of three great courtyards: the outer for women, the middle for administration and the chapel, and the inner for men. Whereas in Filarete's plan the sexes were symmetrical in relation to the outside world and the church, here they were asymmetrical. This created a number of ambiguities: not only are patients in both the deepest and the shallowest spaces, with the staff at an intermediate depth, but the space occupied by the women would, in institutional buildings, signify greater power than that occupied by the men. In non-institutional buildings the reverse would be the case. This unlikely outcome suggests that, besides the ambiguous location of the staff zone, the two models had been compressed into one building.

Guy's, across the road, was designed for the incurables and lunatics with which St Thomas's could not cope. The original plan was a double arcaded courtyard, with a central dividing block of wards raised on an open arcade across the main, entrance axis. By 1780 two forward projecting lateral wings enclosed an outer courtyard fenced and gated from the street and gave it its final form. In the centre of one new wing was the chapel; on the same axis facing it in the other, the treasurer's house and governors' court room. These three spaces on the lateral axis signify controlling powers – religion, resources and the law. The building had now acquired the hallmarks of the reversed type: shallow inhabitant domain, and deep visitor domain.

Joseph II gathered the almshouses, orphanages, civil, military, maternity, venereal and trade brotherhood hospitals, and lunatic asylums spread all over Vienna into one huge complex – the *Allgemeines Krankenhaus*. The only way of breaking it down into manageable parts was to categorise its patients by ability to pay, gender and medical condition, a classification that shaped it.

In the reversed institution power decreases with increasing depth. If the inmates' space can be entered from two directions, as at Tonnerre or St Louis, there may be ambiguity. But not necessarily. In Copenhagen's Frederiks hospital (1752–57) the single storey wards round the enclosed quadrangle the sexes were divided not laterally, but front to back by a wall which continued across the courtyard and sliced the whole plan into two. The hospital could be entered from two opposite ends; in one case through shallow staff and kitchen space, in the other through the spaces of the nobility (who provided the money) and their servants. Increased depth from either end represents decreased power. The nobility's space signifies their curious dual role both as patients and as controllers.

The simpler 'pragmatic-palace' is associated with provincial hospitals, but this too had its origins in the metropolis where hospitals converted from grand houses were inevitably of the palace form. St George's broke away from the Westminster and started life in a 1719 London mansion – Lanesborough House near Hyde Park – converted into the hospital (1733–39) by the addition of two wings to make a Palladian 'H'. What was originally a modest mansion was turned into an institution by the addition of elements precisely appropriate to a palace. This was natural enough. But it is more surprising that it became the model for a generation of hospitals designed as such *ab initio*. Two in London were the newly

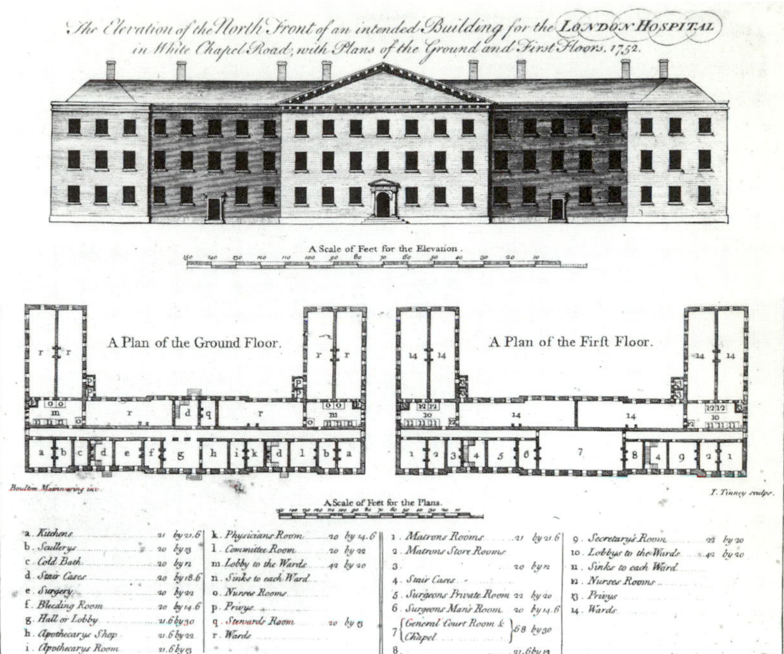

Figure 4.12
Mainwaring's London Hospital (1752)
Source: The Royal London Hospital

planned London (1751–2) designed by Boulton Mainwaring (Figure 4.12) and James Paine's (1755) Middlesex. The model crossed the Atlantic. The great Pennsylvania Hospital (1770s) designed by the Scottish architect Robert Smith was a conventional 'H'. But the same form in New York (1773–75) anticipates the extended Manchester Infirmary discussed in Chapter One with its central corridor between the wards.

Hundreds of small urban hospitals of Europe and America were modelled on these great schemes and consistently reproduce certain of their key features; not only those already described for the 'metropolitan' cases, but large open wards often also used for circulation, privies, baths and other sanitary spaces concentrated in blocks at ward ends or in open yards, top floor central operating theatres and elaborate means for ventilation control.

Amongst *new* smaller urban infirmaries in Britain probably the first was Winchester's in 1736, built whilst St George's was already under reconstruction. At least twenty were added by the end of the century.[1] Two are sampled here. Liverpool Infirmary (1749) has the entrance hall, chapel and Governors' Courtroom (A) on the central axis as its shallowest space (Figure 4.13). Both the physician's and surgeon's rooms (B and C) lie on shallow rings, permeable to the hall and to the inner corridors (G). The matron's and apothecary's quarters fill the remaining ground floor space. The first floor has two 18-bed wards, in each wing, for the two sexes. Above are two 11-bed wards, and a central, sky-lit, operating theatre. Each of the three floors has a compact sanitary block at its extremity, and there is a basement kitchen.

Gloucester (c. 1760) is more elaborate (Figure 4.14). The central chapel (H/19) on the ground floor has the committee room (34) above it on the first floor and the operating room (44) on the second. The lateral 18-bed wards (K/1, D/17, 30 and 39) have privies at their deepest point (E). The central corridor with the staircases constitutes the only ring. These communicating routes control and integrate the entire space and are, of course, the inhabitant domain.

The great courtyard plan was teased out into

Figure 4.13

Liverpool infirmary (1749)

Source: ***Rules and Order of the Public Infirmary at Liverpool***, Liverpool 1749, Liverpool Record Office, Liverpool Libraries and Arts

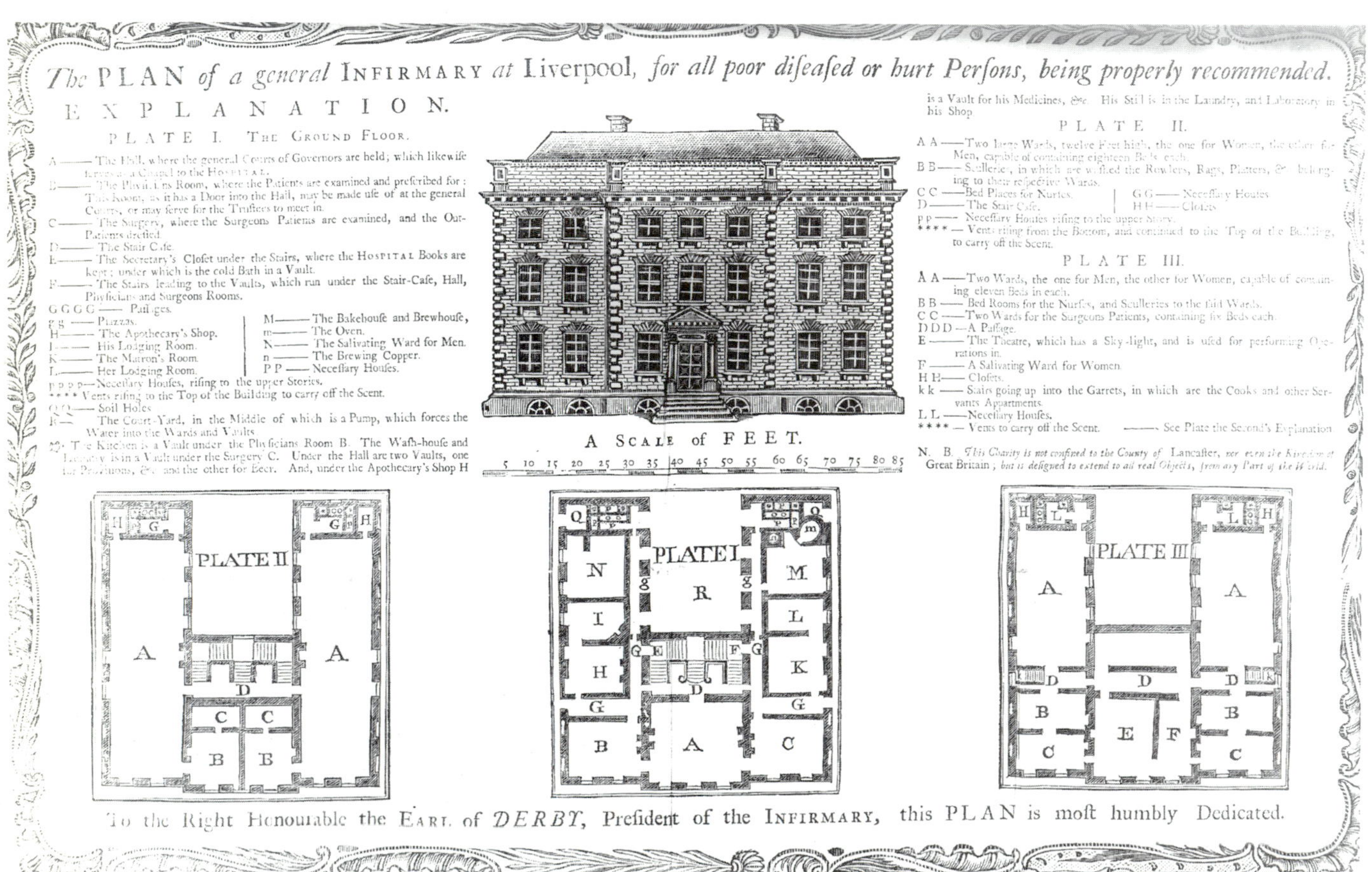

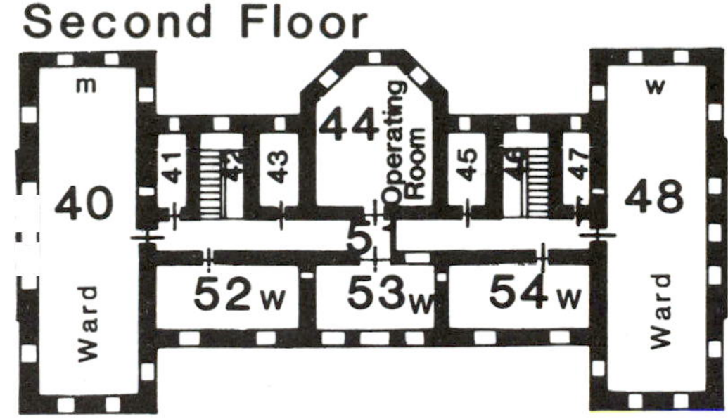

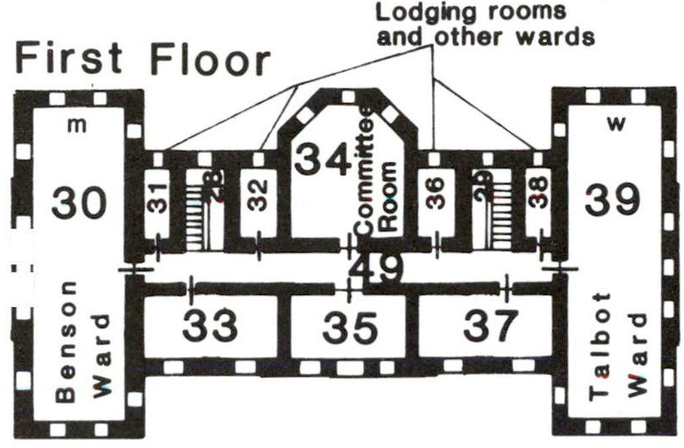

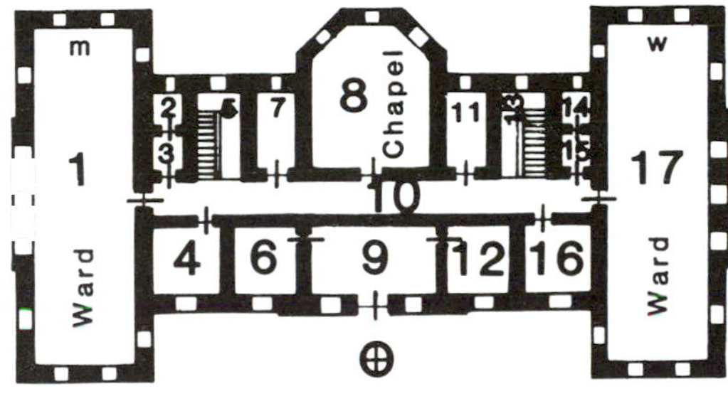

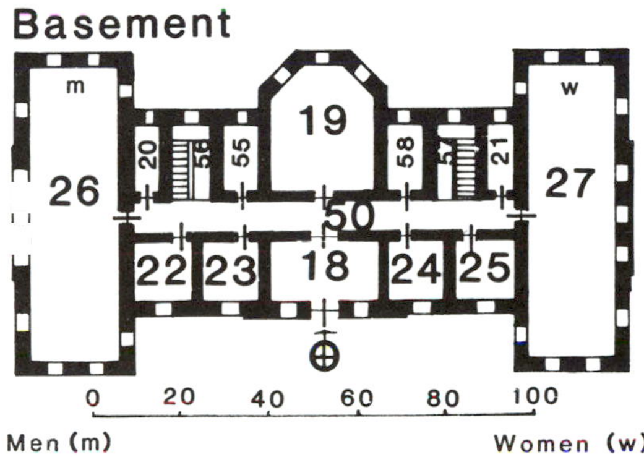

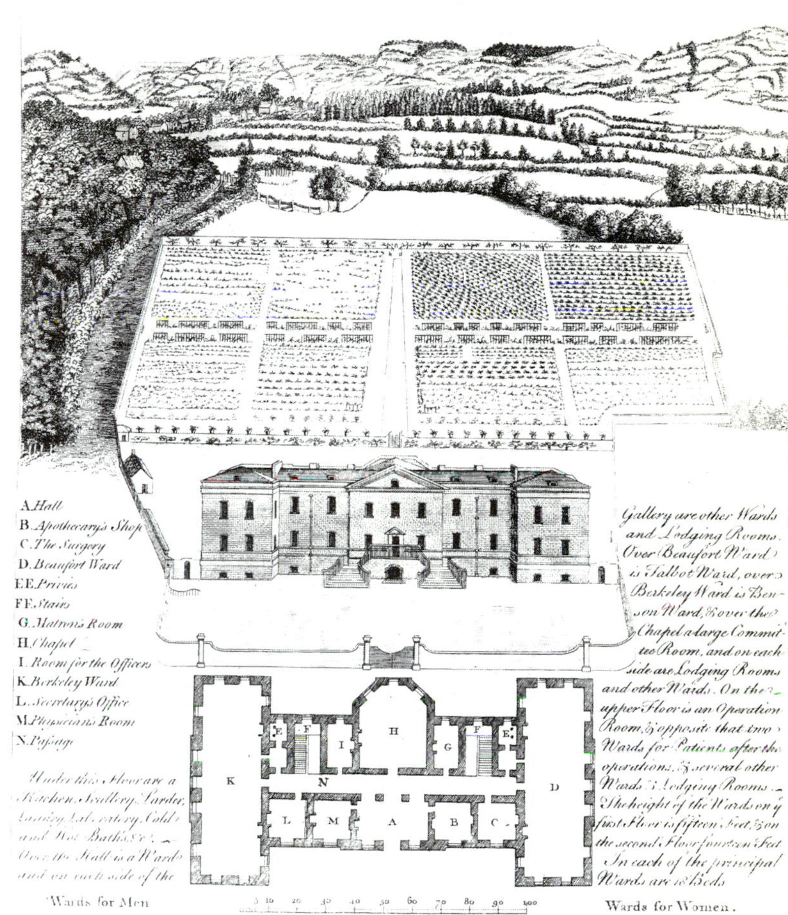

Figure 4.14

Gloucester infirmary (c. 1760), plan and elevation, schematic plans and spatial map

Source: *The State of the Gloucester infirmary for the year 1764*, in Gloucestershire County Library (plan and elevation); author's drawing (schematic plans and spatial map)

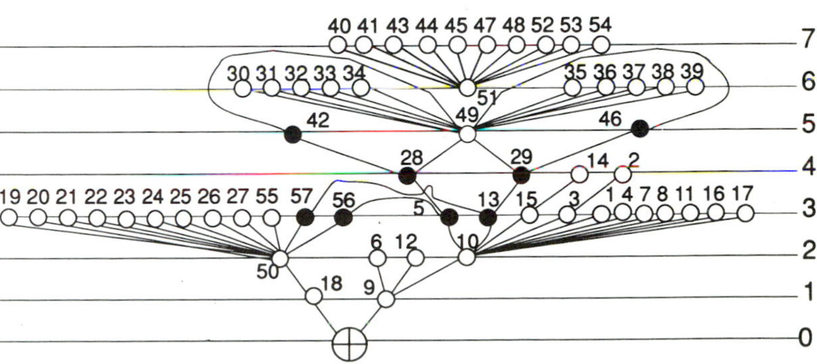

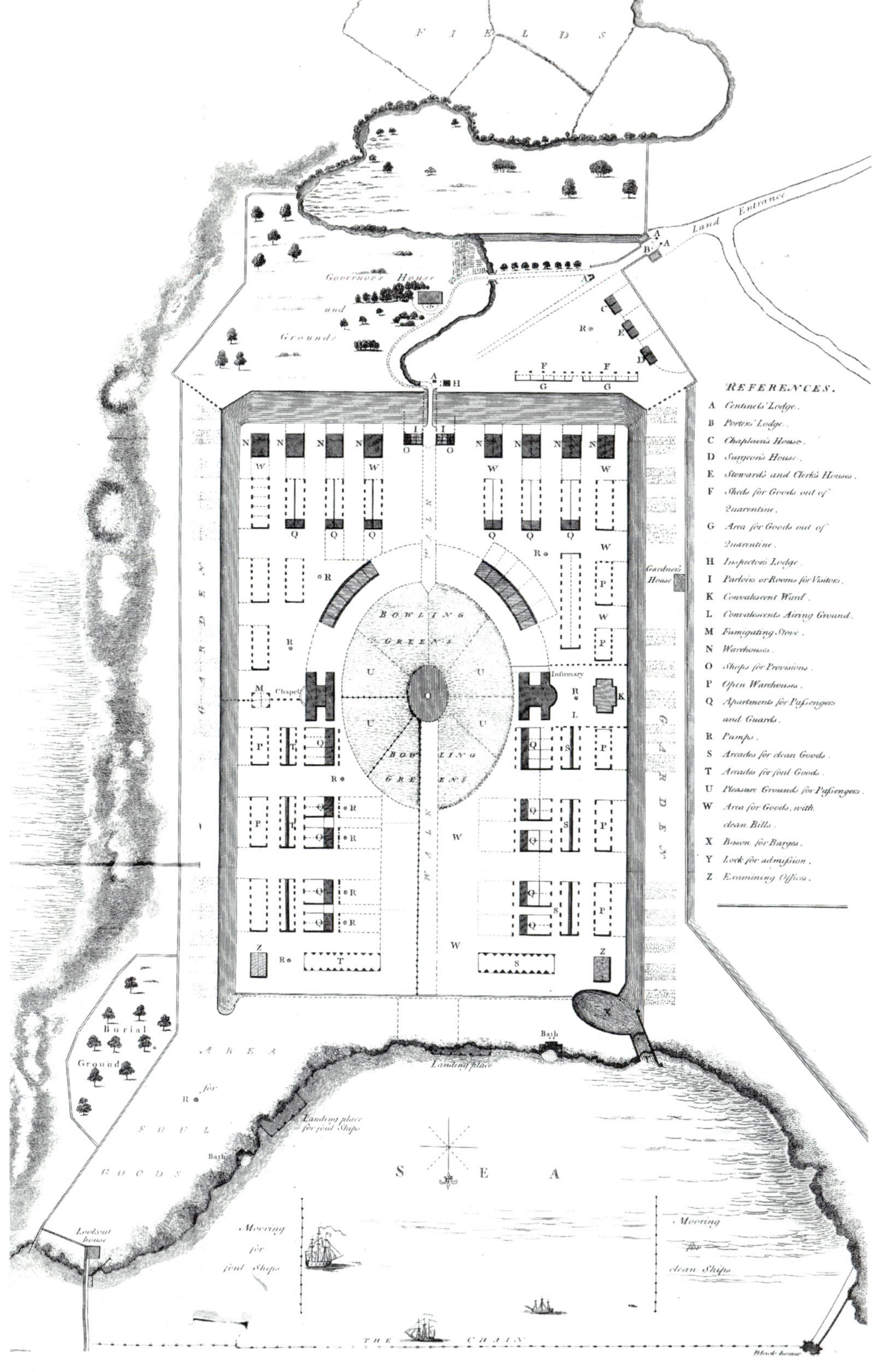
FIELDS
Land Entrance
Governors House
and
Grounds
BOWLING GREENS
Chapel
Infirmary
Gardners House
Burial Ground
AREA
for
FOUL
GOODS
Landing place
Landing place for foul Ships
Bath
SEA
Mooring for foul Ships
Mooring for clean Ships
Lookout house
THE CHAIN
REFERENCES.
A Centinels' Lodge.
B Porters' Lodge.
C Chaplain's House.
D Surgeon's House.
E Stewards' and Clerk's Houses.
F Sheds for Goods out of Quarentine.
G Area for Goods out of Quarentine.
H Inspector's Lodge.
I Parlors or Rooms for Visitors.
K Convalescent Ward.
L Convalescents Airing Ground.
M Fumigating Stove.
N Warehouses.
O Shops for Provisions.
P Open Warehouses.
Q Apartments for Paſsengers and Guards.
R Pumps.
S Arcades for clean Goods.
T Arcades for foul Goods.
U Pleasure Grounds for Paſsengers.
W Area for Goods, with clean Bills.
X Bason for Barges.
Y Lock for admiſsion.
Z Examining Offices.

Figure 4.15

Howard's ideal lazaretto (1789)

Source: Howard (1789), British Architecture Library

CHOLERA IN THE ASYLUM.

REPORTS

ON

THE ORIGIN AND PROGRESS

OF

PESTILENTIAL CHOLERA,

In the West-Yorkshire Lunatic Asylum,

DURING THE AUTUMN OF 1849,

AND ON

THE PREVIOUS STATE OF THE INSTITUTION.

A CONTRIBUTION TO THE STATISTICS OF INSANITY AND OF CHOLERA.

BY

THOMAS GIORDANI WRIGHT, M.D.,

VISITING PHYSICIAN TO THE ASYLUM;
MEDICAL VISITOR OF LICENSED HOUSES FOR THE INSANE IN THE WEST-RIDING;
PHYSICIAN TO THE WAKEFIELD HOUSE OF RECOVERY, &c.

LONDON:
LONGMAN, BROWN, GREEN, AND LONGMANS;
AND
ILLINGWORTH AND HICKS, WAKEFIELD

MDCCCL.

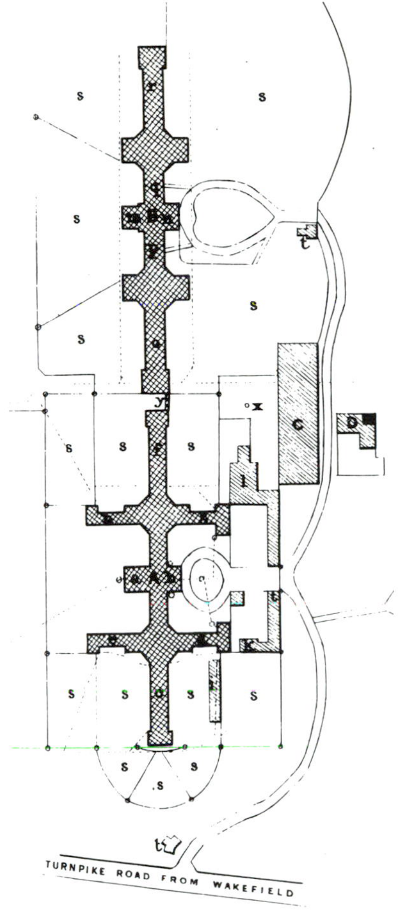

Figure 4.16

Title page and plan from the study of cholera in the West Yorkshire asylum (1850)

Source: Wright (1850), British Library

detached pavilions in James Gibbs' St Bartholomew's (1729). The motivation was fresh air to combat the spread of infection and contagion. By the end of the century pneumatic hygiene was an obsession. Thompson and Goldin (1975) suggest that Gibbs might well have been inspired by the 1719 outbreak of plague in Marseille.

The mysterious role of air, clean and foul, now occupied the leading scientists, naval doctors and inventors. Foremost was Stephen Hales (1743) whose wind-mill ventilator was designed for ships, mines, prisons, hospitals and workhouses. It was tried out with some success on Newgate prison. On ships, however, where scurvy was the chief problem, neither his nor that of the Swedish military architect Triewald proved effective. Sutton, a layman, devised another method which he specifically recommends for hospital ships, prisons and slave ships ('the Guinea trade for Negroes').[2] In the French navy enormous strides in ventilation experiments were taking place[3].

As long as infection routes were poorly understood the natural response was to use distance. Creating a space between ward blocks was the equivalent, at the level of the individual building, to the ancient town planning practice of placing plague and pest houses at or outside the city walls, often with a body of separating water. When plague struck, a sanitary cordon was created by guards at gates and those affected were concentrated in hospitals within the walls or, if possible, outside. Sealing all houses where a stricken householder had been identified was the alternative used in London in 1665. It was that mixed up, unsegregated policy which Fielding later so fiercely attacked (Bender 1987).

Foucault (1982: 195–228) sees the discipline of anti-plague measures – isolation, segregation, classification, continuous surveillance, recording, control of every detail (for instance burning of clothing and minute examination and disinfection of mail) – as a model for the power exercised in

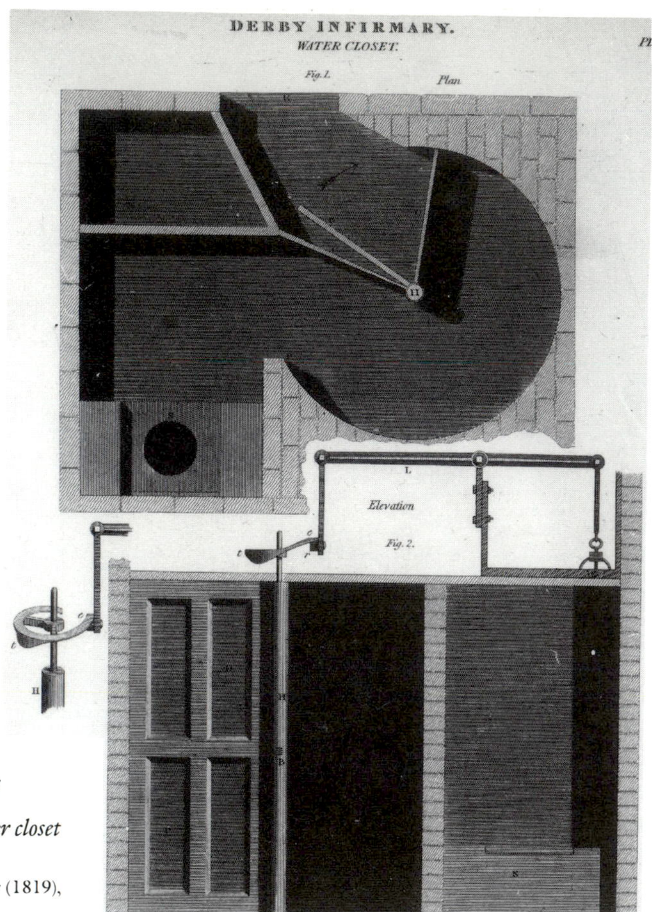

Figure 4.17

Sylvester's water closet (1819)

Source: Sylvester (1819), British Library

penal régimes. Venice built its great island lazaretto in 1403 in response to a quarter century of plague outbreaks. Howard (1789) describes its régime: a 'prior' is in absolute charge of security, quarantine and, aided by physicians, medical matters. Seventeenth century lazaretto designs had individual cells surrounding an open court, with a central chapel open to all sides. Around the periphery was a bridged moat: Jetter (1966) describes Furttenbach's of 1628 and two by Geiger in 1634. Marseille's was admired by Howard and inspired him to publish his own ideal plan (Figure 4.15) in 1789.

The risk was greatest at ports exposed to sudden infection from personnel, freight or clothes carried by ship. Elaborate régimes for isolation, quarantine and distancing were undertaken (Bergdoll 1987, Hildesheimer 1981). These ports were not only centres of trade but seats of navies and therefore the potential for rapid transmission in ships, barracks, hospitals, hulks, galleys and arsenals was immense. Not surprisingly these naval bases became experimental models for public health and hygiene since a body of powerless individuals – whether military or sick – were ideal subjects of study. The tradition lasted; as late as 1850 a study was published on the spread of cholera in the West Yorkshire asylum at Wakefield (Wright 1850). The movement of goods and people, and the first appearance of the disease at various spots, were meticulously recorded, and surveys made of the sewers and drains (Figure 4.16). There was speculation that disease was spread by 'effluvium from the excretions of patients' and infected water as a prime cause is dismisssed.

One would imagine that hospitals would be the pioneers in sanitary services. But in fact the first innovations were in mills, where the consequences of sickness spelled financial ruin. In Chapter 10 we will see the transfer of combined heating and ventilation technology from the Strutt cotton mills to Derby Infirmary. Sylvester (1819), a Strutt protégé, published its details and also of the ingenious water closets (Figure 4.17), steam kitchen equipment and laundry. The one horse power basement steam engine raised water to a roof tank and by means of a horizontal shaft drove a washing machine. The basement baths were to be open to the public as a means of raising revenue. Sylvester's plans must constitute one of the earliest service drawings; indeed he recommends that 'All apparatus and machinery for warming and ventilating apartments, for washing and drying linen, and for culinary purposes, should be represented in the original drawings of the buildings ...'. He went on to install such systems for lunatic asylums in Wakefield and Nottingham, the new jail at Maidstone and the North Staffordshire infirmary.

In naval and military hospitals strict hygiene was easily translated into space. It was a small step from the age-old spatial discipline of camps and the battlefield to repetitive échelons of identical blocks. Samuel Wyatt designed a prefabricated pavilion 'moveable hospital' in the 1780s (Robinson 1979: 36–9) intended as a sample block of a row. In France before and during the Revolutionary times the focus on ventilation in military and naval hospitals created the pavilion layout. Rochefort naval hospital (1782) had eight pavilions connected by a central block, surrounded by an enormous open and planted space. Cherbourg's (1787) was on a more modest scale, with three huge detached wards in a 'U', joined by an open arcade, with a central chapel facing the court at the base of the 'U' (Voldman

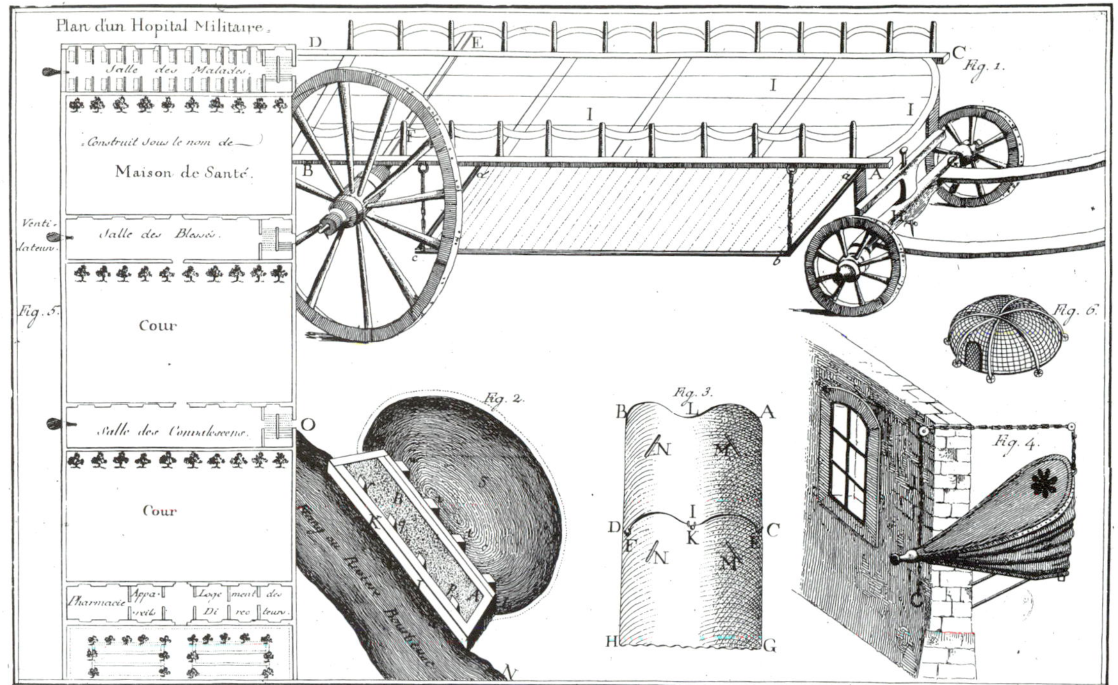

Figure 4.18

Lecointe's (1793) military hospital ('Fig. 5') and its bellows-operated ventilation system ('Fig. 4')

Source: Lecointe (1793), Bibliothèque Nationale, Paris, item Tc34, 3A

1981: 25–33). A model military hospital (Lecointe 1790) shows a division into four parallel pavilions – for the sick, the wounded, the convalescent and the administrative services (Figure 4.18) with bellows-type ventilators inserted at the ends of the wards. An *ancien* Paris Hôtel Dieu doctor recommended trumpet-shaped 'aspirateurs' for ventilation, as in the military hospital at Nancy (Gastellier 1791: 8 and figure opposite 33). According to a decree of the National Assembly for the *Conseil de Santé* (Audin-Rouvière 1793: 20) civilian hospitals were to be ventilated on the principles established by the army.

The military tradition was durable; Brunel used it in his prefabricated army hospital erected at Renkioi in the Crimea in 1855.[4] Florence Nightingale (1859) cites Brunel's as a near-ideal solution. She failed to stop the construction of the hopelessly outdated hospital at Netley. It was not till the Herbert hospital was erected at Woolwich (1858–64) that Britain had a fully-fledged pavilion military hospital, with a single spine corridor. France was half a century ahead both in its military and its civil projects.

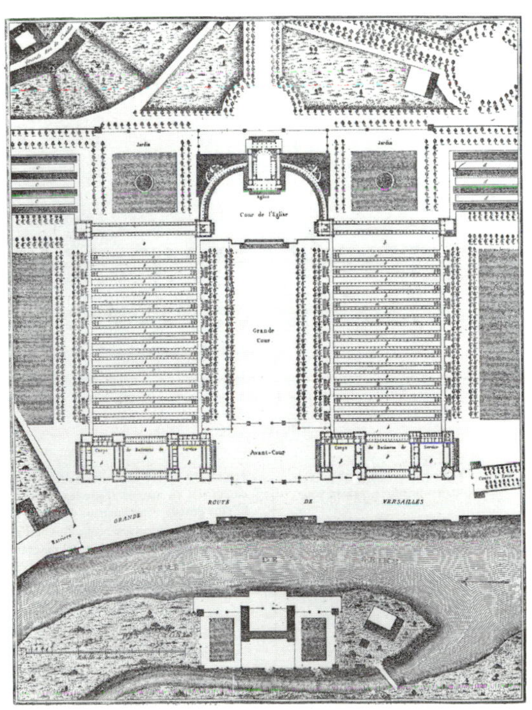

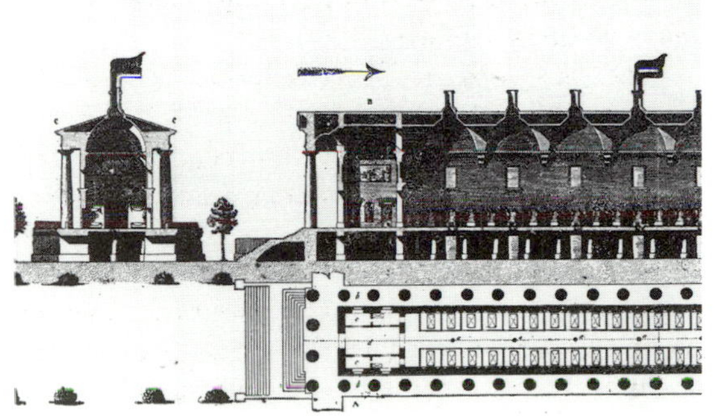

Figure 4.19

Le Roy's Hôtel Dieu (1773–89), plan and detail of ward block

Source: C. Tollet (1892) *Les Edifices Hospitaliers depuis leur Origine jusqu'à nos Jours*, Paris, Bibliothèque National, Paris

Figure 4.20

Stonehouse naval hospital (1756–64)

Source: Howard (1784), author's copy

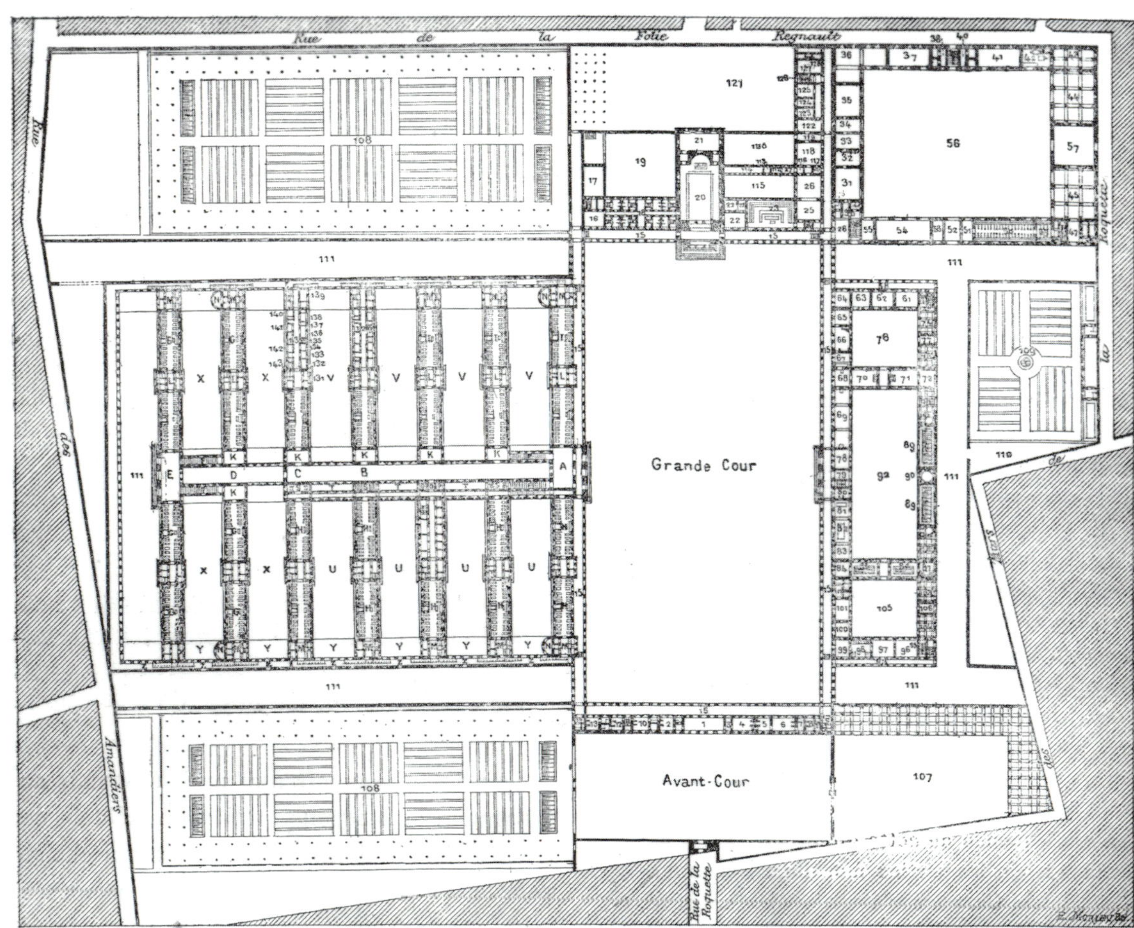

Figure 4.21

Tenon's and Poyet's 1787 hospital

Source: C. Tollet (1892) *Les Edifices Hospitaliers depuis leur Origine jusqu'a nos Jours*, Paris, Bibliothèque National, Paris

When fire destroyed the infamous Paris Hôtel Dieu in 1772 and scientist and doctor members of the French Academy of Sciences addressed themselves to its replacement they used the lazarettos as evidence. They initiated a spate of ideas. First was the 1773 design of le Roy, a physicist *Membre*. It was four years before the architect Viel presented it to the Academy. The Academicians did not recommend it until 1786 and even so only published it in 1789 (Greenbaum 1974: 122–40). Le Roy arranged eleven elongated pavilions, each like a pedimented temple with its peristyle of columns and Doric-columned porticos at the ends, on either side of a great central courtyard, one side for men the other for women (Figure 4.19). They were linked by a corridor. At one end were service buildings, at the other a central chapel. The wards were raised for ventilation through the floor and apertures in domes above.

Figure 4.22

Bamberg witch-house (1627)

Source: City of Bamberg Archives

Did Le Roy have non-military precedents? Wren's unexecuted and little-known design for Greeenwich hospital (1696–1702) had six partitioned pavilions on either side of a colonnaded court with Inigo Jones' Queen's House at the head. A small prototype which certainly favourably impressed the Academicians Tenon and Coulomb on their visit to English hospitals in 1787 was Stonehouse naval hospital (1756–64) at Plymouth (Figure 4.20) designed by Rowehead. Ten three-storey ward blocks, and intervening smaller service blocks, were connected by a colonnade which forms a ring and joins the axially-placed church at the deepest point. It was illustrated by Howard (1789) and also in Durand's *Parallèle* (1801).

In the second Report (1787) Tenon and Poyet produced a pavilion plan (Figure 4.21). Finally, in the 1788 *Mémoire* to the Academy the Commission produced its own version, drawn by Poyet and based on Tenon's design.[5] Other versions abounded in the next half century – but it was not until 1846 that Paris had a hospital based on these principles – the Lariboisière.

The pavilion remained a model for military style penal institutions, such as the depot at Norman Cross, Huntingdonshire (1786–1816) for French prisoners, or the penal 'colonies' with military régimes for its young inmates such as the famous agricultural colony at Mettray in France, designed in 1839 by Abel Blouet and much influenced by de Tocqueville, one of the founders. It was only towards the end of the nineteenth century that the pavilion finds wider penal applications but it is outside my scope to analyse its carceral use.

What are we to make of the uncanny similarity between places of healing and places of torture and murder? That is not a hypothetical question. Between 1623 and 1633, by conservative estimates 600 male and female 'witches' were killed in Bamberg as part of a particularly intense outbreak of persecution during the Thirty Years' War (Russell 1980, Lincoln 1896, Zink 1982). Though this was happening all over Europe as far as I know Bamberg was unique in having a special building in which suspects were detained, examined – usually under torture – and finally sent to death by burning. This was the 'Malesitzhaus' or 'Drudenhaus' (witch-house) erected in 1627 by Bishop Johann Georg II and demolished in 1655 (Figure 4.22). The two floors have single cells and examination rooms on either side of an open central space at the end of which, on both floors, is an apsidal chapel. The torture rooms were in an adjacent building, connected by a door to one side of the chapel. The form and spatial structure is basically that of Tonnerre and innumerable late medieval almshouses and infirmaries. Its exterior is barely distinguishable from the exactly contemporary Augsburg Holy Spirit hospital.

For an explanation one has to look to the judicial processes of witch trials. On arrest an individual was isolated and closely observed during examination in a cell which was the deepest space, whilst guards, inquisitors and torturers were in the shallow, central space. The Church controlled the process and religious ideology validated it. The axial symmetry with the chapel at its head represents the same distribution of power that we found in the hospitals. The tortured victims were suffering from individual pathologies and needed the same direct attention as the patients. But the witch-house created a paradox. By replacing the open ward with separate cells it both created privacy for each inmate and removed solidarity between them. The isolated individuals lost all power and could now be bracketed into a class (of possessed heretics) since the space of a witnessing community whose solidarity strengthens each individual had been obliterated. The enclosed prison cell does exactly this – its isolated occupant is a member of a pathological class.

The bad

The literature on prisons is enormous, even richer than that on hospitals.[6] A small sample of this familiar material is enough to look for meanings.

We have seen how difficult it is to distinguish carceral institutions up to the mid-eighteenth century. Even those that are recognisable had, with a few exceptions, a mixture of inmates – debtors, felons (awaiting trial or execution) and petty criminals. Many were in adapted houses and warehouses, or fitted into town gates. Newgate was one of three London gates which served as prisons. Different categories of prisoner were clustered vertically around each staircase. Undistinguished in its exterior, only its location at the city wall identifies it. Strangers under arrest were confined to the city boundary; there was less danger of their becoming invisibly diffused into the city crowd. And the strength of this metaphor has been mentioned earlier: an aperture in the city's 'body' needed a purifying filter.

Bender (1987) says such prisons were 'liminal'; neophytes were admitted into a society of chaos, paradox, squalor and disease by rites of passage on crossing the threshold of an enclosure within which there was 'classless liberty'. Gay's *The*

Beggar's Opera uses these contradictions as its central theme. Prisoners' accommodation depended on the fee they could pay and other prisoners extorted 'garnish'. Moreover it was highly permeable; goods, persons and information passed freely in and out, controlled by the keeper for his profit and barely discouraged. Prisons had taprooms, stalls, shops and barbers, and the keeper ran the female section as a brothel. Apart from the main gate with its dense traffic, there were grated begging windows where prisoners and the public communicated freely.

Beccaria (1764) brought Enlightenment ideas to this chaos. An essential component of the contractual proportionality between a crime and its punishment was discipline and punitive *labour*. On the frontispiece of the third edition (1765) Justice, in the guise of Minerva, makes a dual gesture: on the one hand of horror at an executioner who presents her with the heads of executed criminals, on the other, one of approval at some instruments of work – hoes, hammers and saws.

Beccaria's aims to bring to an end idle chaos and unmeasured punishment would have been impossible to realise had it not been for two pressing problems.

The first was the scourge of gaol fever which took a heavy toll of prisoners and all in contact with them. The disease was equally widespread in ships, hospitals and barracks. Pringle showed in 1750 that a single malady was responsible. For the rest of the century its assocation with dirt, overcrowding and inadequate ventilation directed the search for the cause towards 'putrid' or vitiated air rather than the louse, the actual transmitting agent of typhus. Hence enormous effort went into ventilation by raising the building on legs and teasing out its elements, as well as by mechanical devices. Other strategies were to place sites on 'airy' high land; to increase the number of washing places, latrines and laundries and

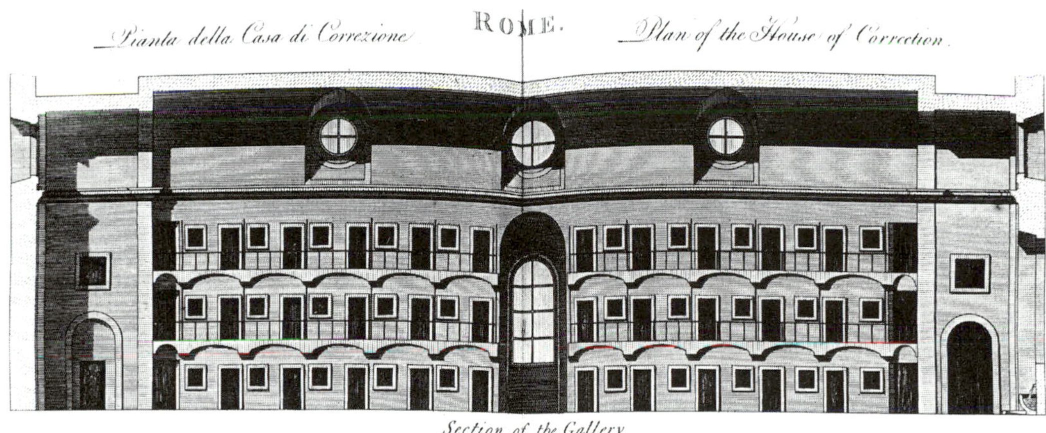

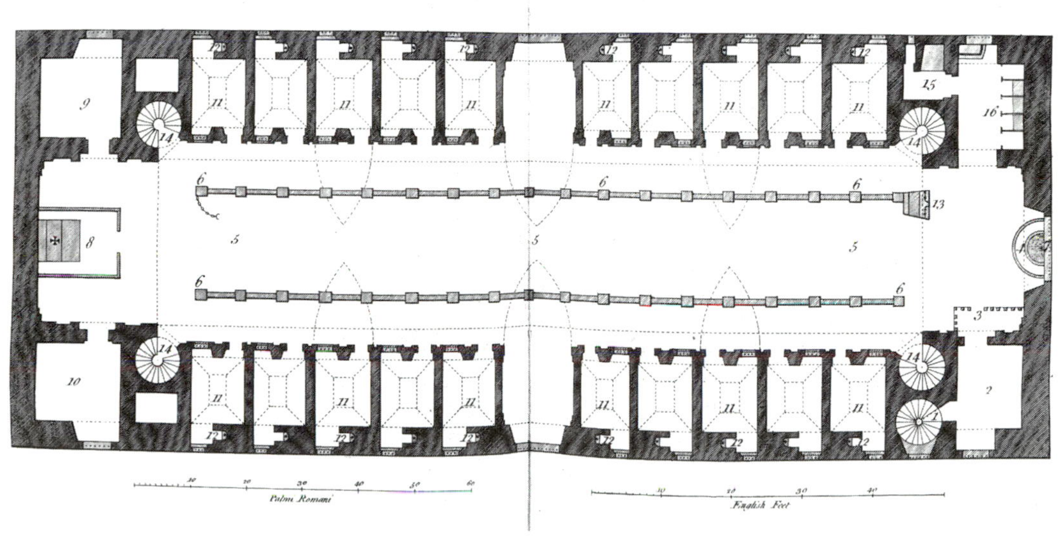

Figure 4.23

Young men's prison, San Michele, Rome (1701–4)

Source: Howard (1784)

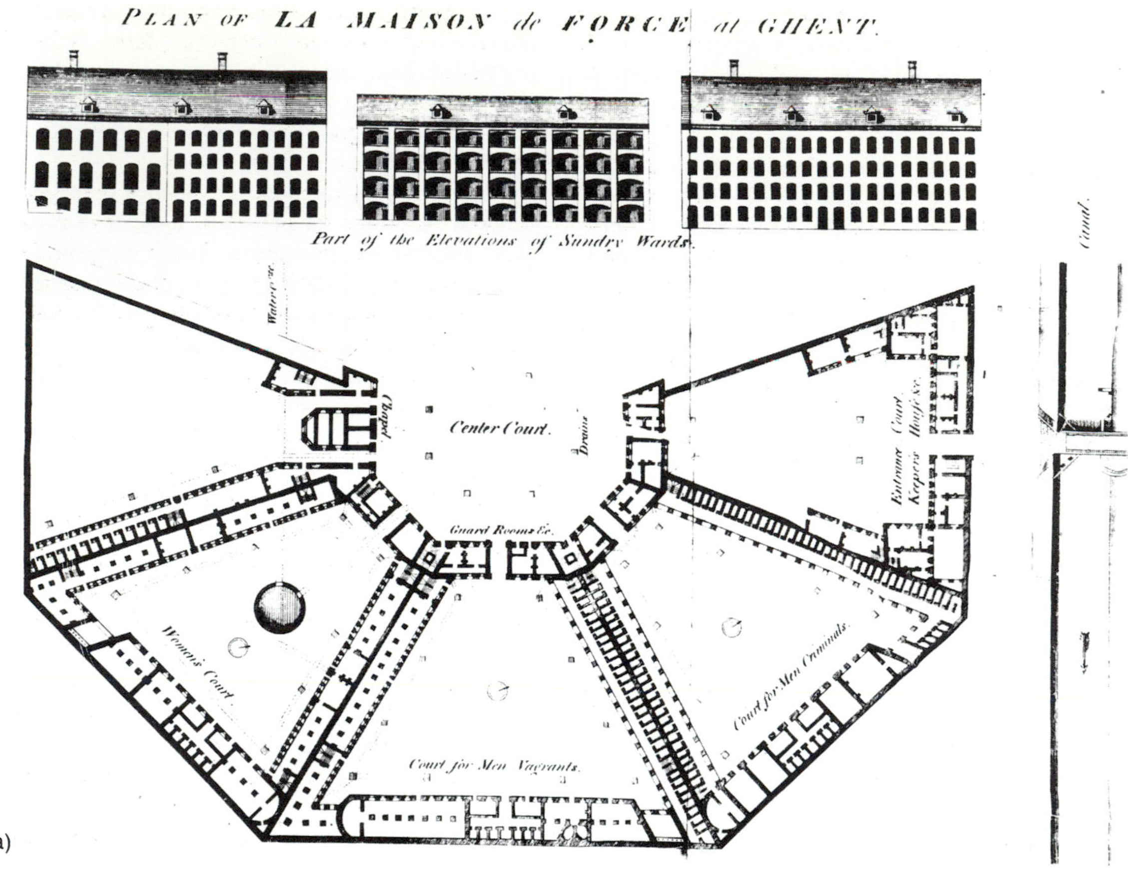

(a)

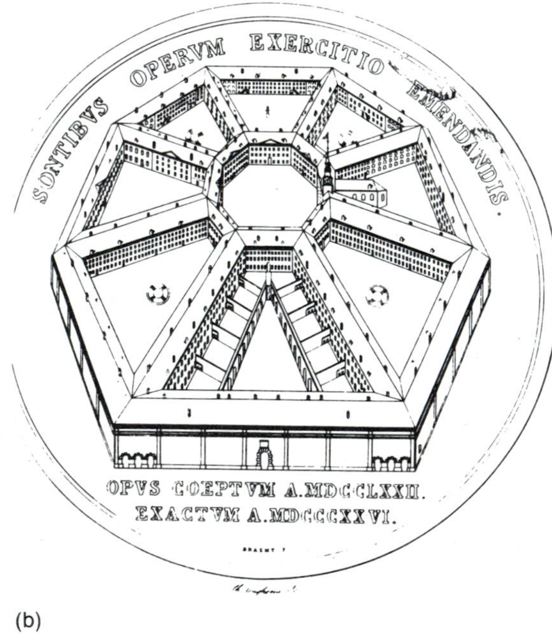

(b)

Figure 4.24

Maison de force, Ghent (1722), part-plan, sections and elevations (a), and aerial view (b)

Source: Howard (1784), author's copy (a), and Vilain XIIII (Jean Jaques Philippe), *Procédé d'un Premier Memoire etc.*, Ghent, British Library (b)

concentrate them in remote sanitary blocks; and to provide fresh running water.

The second problem was related – moral contagion. If vice could spread like disease, the sanitary precautions could be extended by classifying and segregating prisoners. This became the dominant theme in Howard's sustained critique. At its most elementary it involved segregation of the sexes – far from common in his time. Young inmates were not to be corrupted by the older *habitués* and there was to be separation between types of offenders – vagrants, petty thieves, prostitutes, felons and debtors. The market had already achieved segregation by economic class – those who could pay bought superior accommodation, with space for their servants, better food and drink, and greater freedom of access by relatives.

Though Filarete's 1460s *Treatise* had sanitary and segregative provisions the most influential prison to show their effects was San Michele in Rome. But it was innovatory in more ways than these.

In a sweeping gesture which recalls the *Hôpital Général* and anticipates the *Allgemeines Kranken-*

haus Pope Innocent XI set up the *Ospizio Generale* in 1686 to collect and make visible all Rome's poor.[7] His successor Innocent XII continued the work. There was an orphanage, women's shelter, almshouse, workshops and training facilities. It was to this that Clement XI added the young men's prison of San Michele (1701–4) as strictly segregated from the earlier categories of inmates as those already were from each other. Clement XII completed the project by the addition of a women's prison (1734–5).

Continuous galleries gave access to three tiers of individual cells and there was an open central hall (Figure 4.23). Each cell had its individual latrine. The basement had weaving shops, whilst in the ground floor hall wool spinning was carried out in complete silence – hence the *Silentium* inscribed on a large sign. At one end of the central axis was an altar. In earlier designs Fontana placed this in the centre, and his drawings show radiating lines to prove that it was visible from each cell. At the other end was a large fountain. Clement XI was not the first Pope to have proposed disciplined work in an enclosed and observed space. Part of Sixtus V's grandiose plans for the social and physical re-shaping of Rome was to collect the unemployed poor, house them in dwellings constructed in the upper floors of the Colosseum, and convert its ground floor into a huge wool spinning manufactory (Giedion 1952: 226).

The *Silentium* prophetically foreshadowed what was coming: discipline, segregation, surveillance, attention to fresh air and sanitation, silence, work and penance. Its three-storey galleried hall was a prototype that survived into the late nineteenth century.

Its modernity was lost on the English establishment when it sought ideas for rebuilding Newgate in the 1750s. Eventually George Dance the Younger's 1768 design was adopted – composed of segregated courts enclosed by common 'wards'. On the central axis was the keeper's house and behind it the chapel raised on vaults. A pair of turnkeys' lodges gave access by a labyrinth of passages to the courts and wards as well as taprooms. Although each ward had a semicircular privy tower, based on earlier designs by William Jones, Newgate convinced Howard and the reformers that prison design would have to be fundamentally rethought.

They already had a model, widely publicised in Howard's work, in the octagonal segregated *Maison de Force* at Ghent designed for Count Vilain XIIII (sic) by Montfeson in 1772 (Figure 4.24). Five of the eight courts and their surrounding four storeys of cells were completed, with the entrance and chapel on the central axis. The internal octagon was a workspace surrounded by the guards' quarters none of which would have given surveillance of more than *one* court but all of which gave total surveillance of the workspace.

When Howard (1777) produced his ideal County gaol he incorporated central surveillance but without the full rigours of the radial model which he regarded as 'Catholic' or Absolutist. Each prisoner was to have a separate cell whose 'solitude and silence are favourable to reflection; and may possibly lead them to repentance' (1777: 22). Each class had its own block 'raised on arcades' and exercise yard. The chapel and the gaoler's house were central – the latter overlooking the single entry gate, to each side of which a turnstile controlled entry into the prison.

The ending of penal transportation during the War of Independence precipitated a crisis. Some substitution was possible by using hulks. Howard strongly condemned these and despite some improvements he still considered them 'utterly destructive of morals' due to lack of segregation (Howard 1784: 466). It was not till 1787 that the first convicts were transported to Botany Bay. In the meantime it became clear that prisons would have to be built for long term confinement and labour. We have already looked at the 1779 Penitentiary Act designed to achieve this. A competition for the male and female penitentiaries elicited 63 entries, amongst them two monumental schemes by Soane. The premiated design (1782) for the male penitentiary was by William Blackburn and that for females by Thomas Hardwick.

Though Blackburn's design has disappeared and the national penitentiaries were never built, he became recognised for the remainder of his short life as Britain's leading prison architect and Howard's most faithful interpreter. After various experiments with plans offering some kind of surveillance in 1786 he produced his first radial scheme in which the wings were connected to the centre, for Ipswich. The prison with central surveillance had arrived and was to last over a century. He followed the plan with others, including Liverpool (1795) where six free standing blocks radiated from a point in the gaoler's house, making possible surveillance of the exercise yards and the exteriors of the blocks, but not of the double-banked cells inside (I have detailed elsewhere a similar project by Wardrop

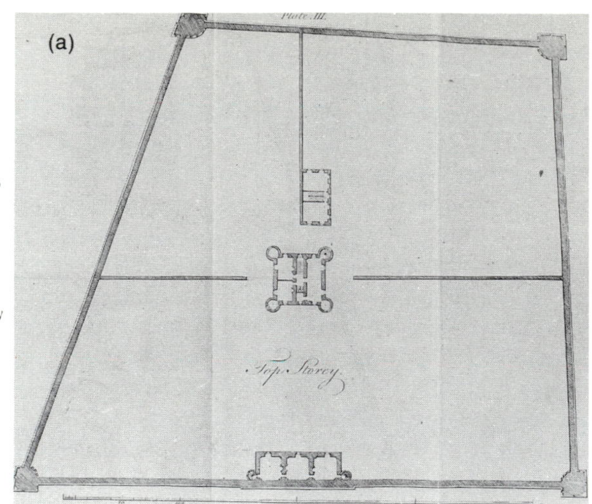

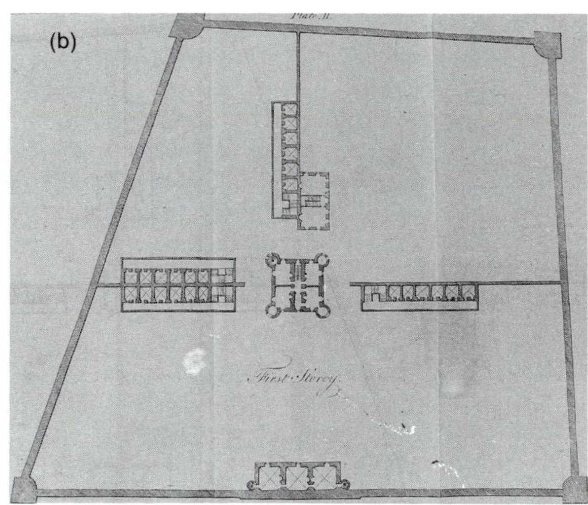

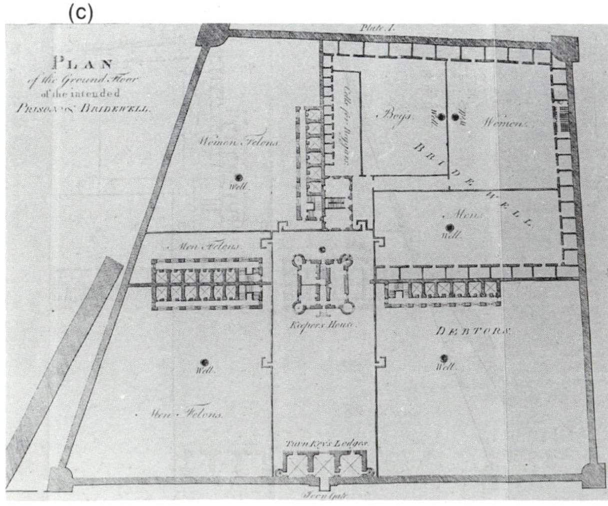

Figure 4.25
Cockburn and Steuart's 1782 proposal for an Edinburgh Bridewell plans, second floor (a), first floor (b), ground floor (c)
Source: Cockburn and Steuart (1782), Edinburgh Public Library

for the Edinburgh Bridewell in 1791 (Markus 1982: 66–9)).

There must be doubt however about the usual claim made for Blackburn's originality in inventing the inspection principle (Evans 1982: 211). In the year of the penitentiary premium awards, Lord Provost David Steuart of Edinburgh and a Sheriff Depute of the County, Archibald Cockburn, published a Bridewell design whose history I have detailed elsewhere (Markus 1982: 65–8). In essence it was a three-storey, three-armed radial plan, with a central keeper's house, detached from but with sight of the three cell blocks. One of these had back-to-back cells whilst two were single-banked (Figure 4.25). Its classes and sexes were fully segregated – felons, debtors, young offenders and a Bridewell. A surgeon and a chaplain to preach every Sunday were provided. They had original ideas about separate airing yards, construction, drainage, ventilation and security. Swivel guns on the outer turrets could shoot either inwards or outwards in case of riots, devices which, in their opinion, would have prevented the burning of Newgate during the Gordon Riots two years earlier (Steuart and Cockburn 1782).

But their most startling insight was into central surveillance: 'The centrical situation of the Governors's house, and the precautions already described, for strength and security, will render the number of inferior officers and servants much smaller than would otherwise have been necessary' (Steuart and Cockburn 1782: 12). This is not only in advance of Blackburn, but uncannily anticipates Bentham's ideas on central surveillance and economy of staff by nine years.

Inevitably the older tradition of cruciform blocks and courts survived and even Howard's ideal penitentiary (1789) returned to it. And despite the new use of axes for surveillance, they continued as traditional and symbolic signs. In Robert Reid's second project (1807) for Glasgow's Justiciary buildings (Markus 1982) the central axis aligns the following sequence of elements: main entrance, main lawcourts on two floors, felons' and debtors' courtyards bisected by the axis, keeper's apartments with a view into each of four yards, and the chapel above it, and finally execution platform at the rear. The axis creates a unified map of an inevitable chronology and cosmology.

So at the end of the century three types co-exist: small haphazardly planned prisons, sometimes combined with other institutions, in converted or aggregative buildings; the old formal, axial designs, with régimes hardly touched by reforms, and few classification or preventative sanitary measures; and Howard's, the Scots' and Blackburn's innovative forms which took on board the moral effects of solitary confinement and silence, organised work and attempts at central surveillance. Into this varied scene burst Jeremy Bentham with his Panopticon 'inspection house', first imagined during a visit to his naval engineer brother Samuel in Russia in 1786, as a response to the proposals arising from the 1779 Act. It was published in two versions in 1791 (1791a, 1791b).

What struck me when I first published his proposals was the inversion I have already described for hospitals, from looking *towards* the central altar to being observed *from* the centre (Markus 1954). Though the Panopticon has since undergone repeated interpretations (for instance Evans 1982, Foucault 1977, Himmelfarb 1968) which have added many new insights, I have not changed my view that this was its real power.

Samuel Bentham had difficulty in finding skilled workmen to supervise his factory. Jeremy proposed to place a supervisor in the centre of a circular 'inspection house' to watch the unskilled workers. And this simple idea became Jeremy's lifelong obsession. He outlined its 157 advantages in a table at the front of the publication. His belief in architecture was absolute – 'Morals reformed – health preserved – industry invigorated – instruction diffused – public burthen lightened – Economy seated as it were upon a rock – the Gordian knot of the Poor Laws not cut but untied – all by a simple idea in Architecture!' This now famous act of faith lays out the complete functional programme which included workhouses, schools, prisons, hospitals, asylums and mills. William Reveley, an architect, translated it into a built form (Figure 4.26).

The governor was in a tower at the centre of a cylinder of cells – revised from four to six floors within the year of publication – invisible to the prisoners and to the turnkeys who patrolled an intermediate annular passage, whilst the prisoners, lit from behind, were continuously visible. Everything was worked out in painstaking detail: iron construction, controlled lighting to give one way vision (originally listening tubes were proposed for one way hearing as well), individual cell sanitation, ducted warmed and cooled air, remote control sun blinds over the annular well, fire extinguishing system and fireproof floor construction. Some of these innovations originated with Samuel and in mill design; others Jeremy invented.

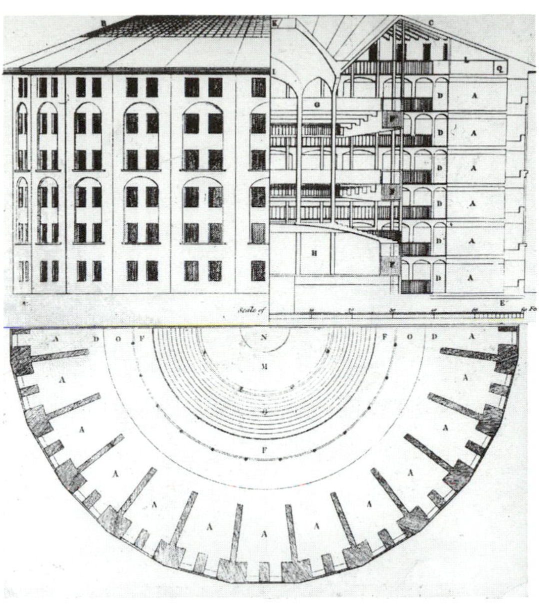

Figure 4.26
Second version of Jeremy Bentham's panopticon (1791)
Source: Bentham (1791)

Utilitarian philosophy could not have materialised in anything as fitting as the Panopticon. Central surveillance achieved total and continuous control. The benefits of productive labour would accrue to the keeper who was contracted to run the prison. Classification was by productive capacity rather than type of crime. The building, its controllers and its inmates would work together in clockwork regularity of space and time.

The ideas became deeply influential. Though many centric prisons were built, some claiming to be Panopticons, with one exception none were. They lacked that total asymmetry of power which was an essential feature. Inmates could see and hear each other, or they could see their keepers, or there were periods when they escaped surveillance.

The exception was Edinburgh's Bridewell (1791). I have described elsewhere (Markus 1982) Robert Adam's three grand traditional designs produced in competition with other architects, his meeting with Bentham within weeks of the publication of the *Postscript*, and the series of Panopticons he then produced. They differed from Bentham's only in being *half* cylinders. But in the final, executed version (Figure 4.27) much to Bentham's disgust, a major defect was introduced – the day workrooms were placed opposite the cells, thus making night-time surveillance

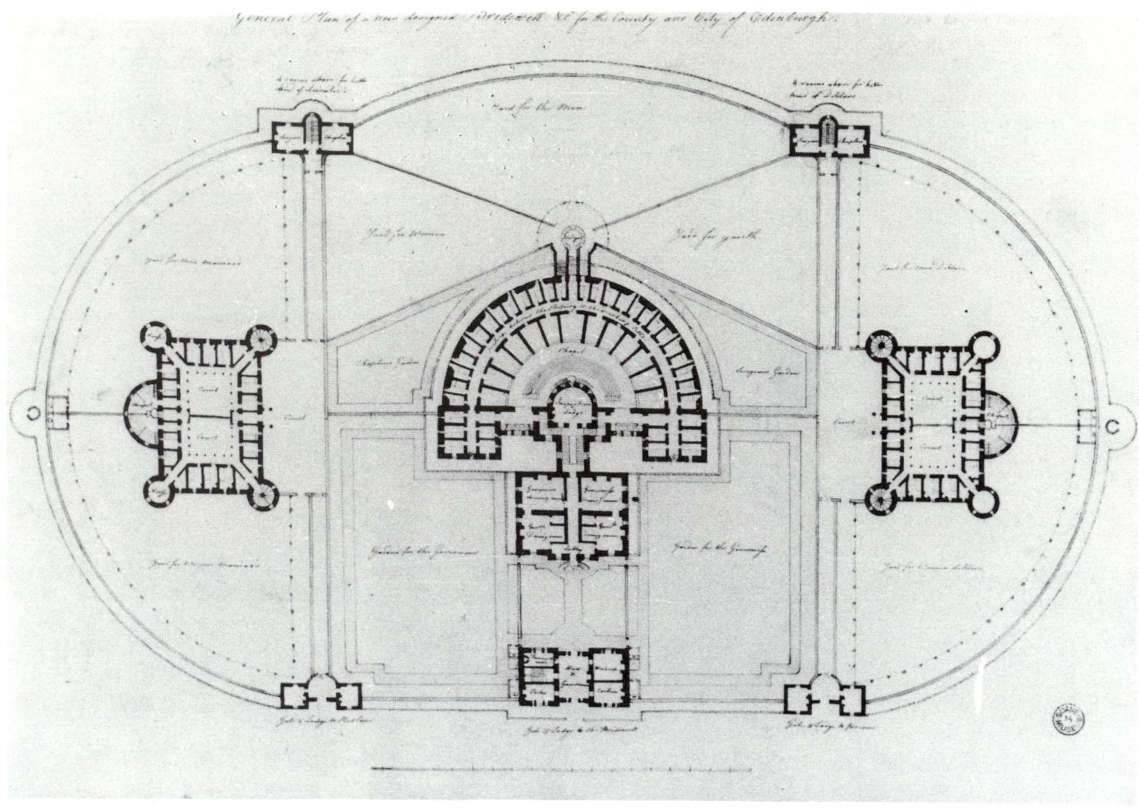

Figure 4.27

Robert Adam's fifth and final design for the Edinburgh Bridewell, plan (only the centre portion was built) and exterior

Source: RCAHMS – Soane Collection 33(34), by courtesy of the RCAHMS and the Trustees of Sir John Soane's Museum (plan); Thomas H. Shepherd (1831) *Modern Athens etc.*, London

Figure 4.28
The so-called 'round building' at Belper (1803–13)
Source: Mrs E. Robson, Belper

impossible. This, in Bentham's eyes, deeply flawed the entire project. Nevertheless it is significant that despite worldwide propaganda over twenty years and huge political agitation, only in Scotland's capital (where the 'inspection' principle appears to have been invented) was it received with sufficient alacrity and enthusiasm for it to be built. The fertile ground on which the seed had fallen was the curious duality of late-Enlightenment utilitarian invention with reactionary, anti-radical political sentiment.

In Chapter 1 I chose Adam's fourth Edinburgh design – his second Panopticon – to analyse the spatial structure of this extraordinary object. The result showed two fundamental features. First, that the lines of visual surveillance from the inner control tower to the cells and from the outer one to the exercise yards gave a shallower structure than permeabilities based on movement. Second that an apparently deep space, the outdoor inspection tower, was brought to the shallow surface by the basement tunnel, thus preserving the purity of the 'reversal'. Bentham was just the person to exploit the contradiction between space and form – between real control and apparent freedom.

One other building can lay claim to the Panopticon title. Indeed it was a solution to Samuel's original problem. Strutt's mill complex at Belper in Derbyshire (discussed in Chapter 10) included a so-called 'round building' (1803–16), a three-storey circular mill divided by fire walls into eight segments, any of which could be sealed (Figure 4.28). It was for high-fire-risk scutching, so surveillance was doubly needed. The central helical staircase had viewing slits into each segment. On the top floor a cylindrical chamber with an inspection aperture slowly revolved, driven by a roof vane when there was sufficient wind, otherwise cranked by hand.[8] It is likely that the Benthams' idea arrived at this rural textile settlement by the route of the Lunar Society, of which Arkwright, a partner of Strutt's, was a member or through direct contact which went back as far as 1793 or 1794 (Fitton and Wadsworth 1958: 181–2 and Schofield 1963: 349–51).

All Bentham's efforts failed to realise a national

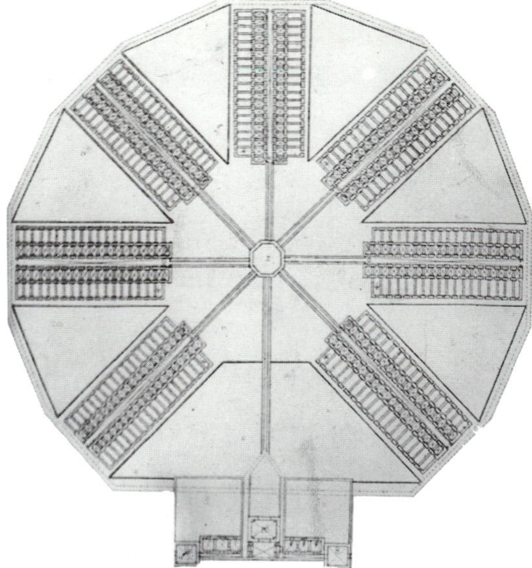

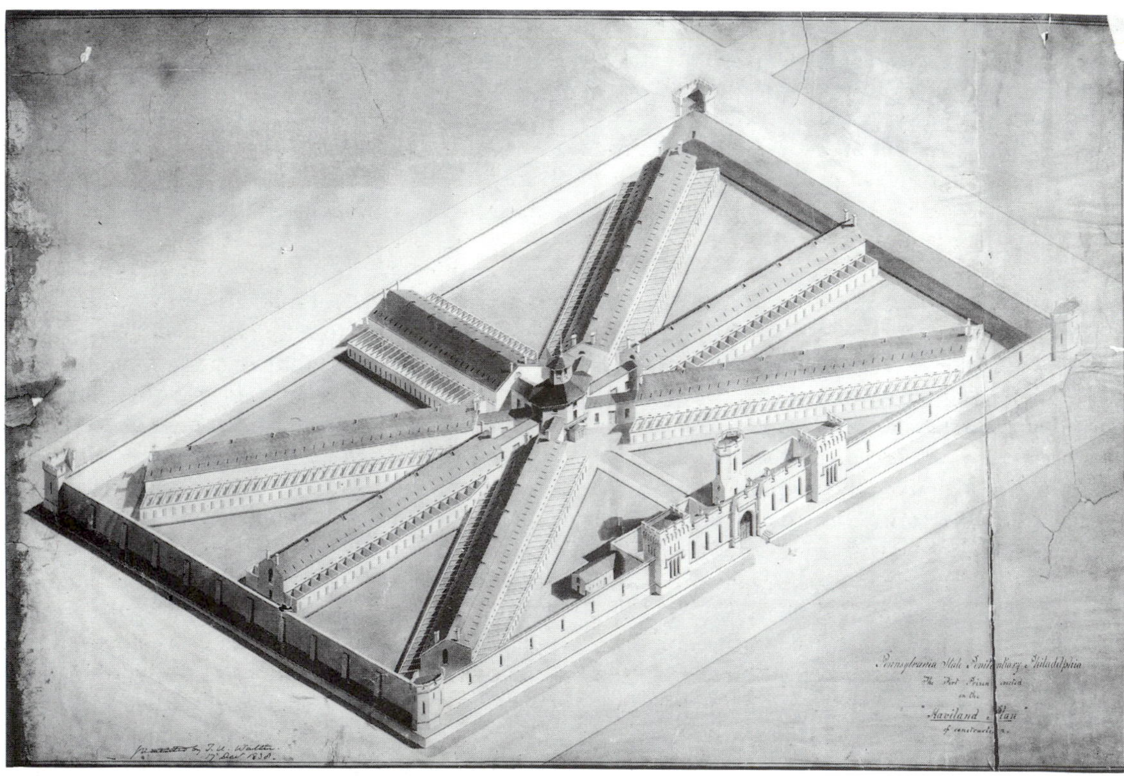

Figure 4.29

Eastern State Penitentiary, Philadelphia (1821–9), plan and aerial view

Source: M. Demetz and G. A. Blouet (1837) *Rapports etc. sur les Pénitenciers des Etats Unis*, Paris (plan); BAL, RIBA Drawings Collection W/14/7 (aerial view)

Panopticon prison. Eventually the Government compensated him and built, on one of the chosen sites, the Millbank Penitentiary – a vast complex in which six pentagons surrounded a hexagon with a central chapel. Though each pentagon had central inspection nothing less Panoptical could be imagined. The prison was expensive to construct, inefficient in staff and maintenance, and unproductive. It became a national scandal.

The 'haunted house', Gertrude Himmelfarb's apt name for it (1968), left three lasting legacies: central inspection, an emphasis on individual segregation; and the dream of profit from carceral labour.

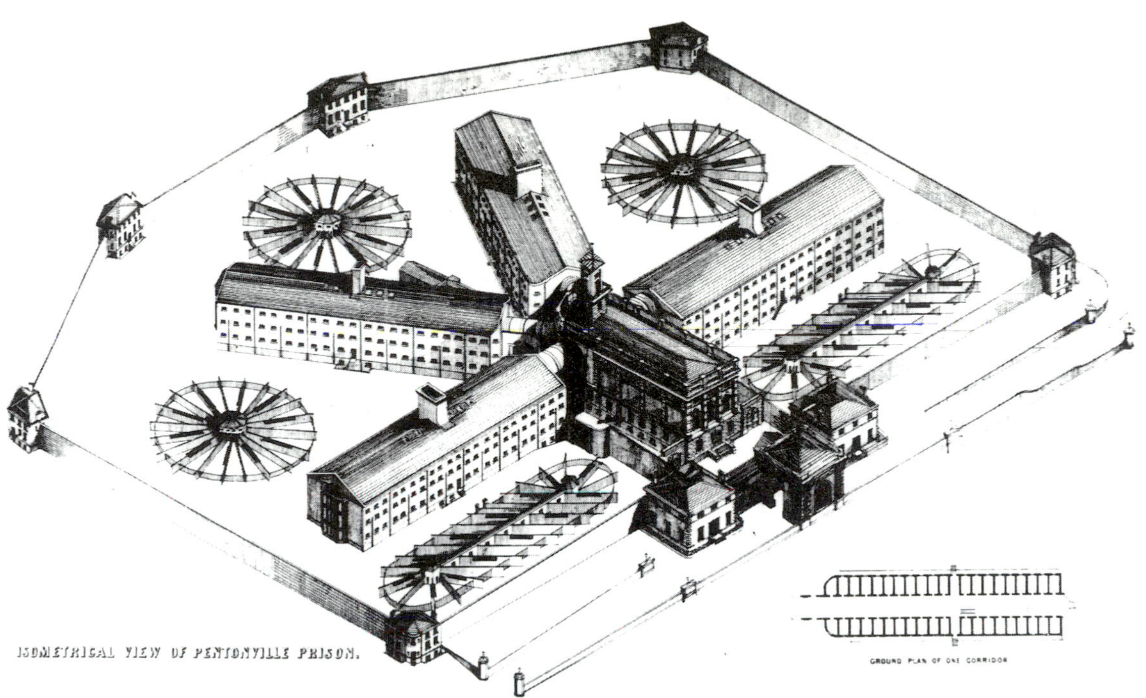

Figure 4.30

Pentonville prison (1840–2), aerial view

Source: Joshua Jebb (1844) *Report on the Construction, Ventilation and Details of Pentonville Prison*, London

Bentham had foreseen that cellular solitude was crucial to prevent prisoner solidarity. Also that successful central surveillance required the guards themselves to be under surveillance in hierarchically ascending layers in which the Governor was finally subject to Boards, Visitors, Commissioners and Overseers.

These ideas became concrete in radial forms which were given a great impetus by the model plans of the Society for the Improvement of Prison Discipline published in the 1820s just when the Philadelphia Eastern Penitentiary at Cherry Hill (1821–9) was under construction. Its designer was James Haviland, an English pupil of Elmes who had himself had a go at grandiose plans in 1817 (Markus 1954). Seven arms radiated from a central observatory (Figure 4.29). Each of its 250 prisoners had a small garden adjacent to his cell. Eventually the purity of the intention was diluted with the addition of a second, garden-less storey to increase the capacity to 400. The perpetual cell-bound solitude brought it strikingly close to a Carthusian monastery. Some saw in this 'separate' system a humane, morally efficacious order; others a pathological one, leading to insanity and incurable zombie-like states.

In the alternative 'silent' or 'Auburn' system (named after the New York prison) separate cells went alongside shared daytime workrooms in which total silence was enforced through an army of rules and guards. Controversy raged between upholders of the two systems. On the whole America went 'silent', with its punitive rather than reformatory ideology, whilst Britain and Continental Europe favoured the 'separate' system with its strong faith in 'contemplative' self-reform. Before its full horrors discredited it in the latter half of the century, great multi-storey radial 'separate' prisons, with wings uncannily like Rome's *Silentium*, had become the European norm. Pentonville (1840–2) designed by Joshua Jebb was the model (Figure 4.30). Four three-storey cell blocks radiate from a point on the axis of the chapel. Tiny wedges of circular exercise yards keep prisoners rigidly segregated. Each cell is self-contained in its work, sanitary, heating and ventilation provisions. Solitary, silent confinement was initally intended as an eighteen-month stepping stone to transportation. By 1847 there were 51 prisons in Britain alone built or under construction on the Pentonville prototype.

Bentham's third legacy was productive labour. The keeper's contract was explicit and Bentham saw it as a way for making a fortune. The contract between him and prisoners was implicit but made visible in the disciplined régime and its building. Of course the earlier houses of correction and Bridewells had a tradition of penal work – often in textiles. It was Cubitt's invention of the improved treadwheel in 1819, however, which promised

Figure 4.31

Adjustable sails on top of a treadwheel

Source: H. Mayhew and J. Binny (1862) *Criminal Prisons of London*

Figure 4.32

Hand-turned crank in a 'separate' cell

Source: H. Mayhew and J. Binny (1862) *Criminal Prisons of London*, author's own copy of reprint

Figure 4.33

Male and female hooded convicts

Source: H. Mayhew and J. Binny (1862) *Criminal Prisons of London*

large productive capacity, mainly in grinding corn. Melossi and Pavarini (1981) see the same labour relations in the penitentiary as in the contemporary mill. The parallel increasingly strains the imagination as production first becomes secondary and then vanishes. The punitive severity of the treadwheel was adjustable by angling the sails on a vertical shaft to offer more or less resistance (Figure 4.31). A totally unproductive device introduced into the cells of the 'separate' system was the hand-turned crank (Figure 4.32) attached to a counting device (and mounted on a Doric column).

Communication by word or expression was forbidden in the 'silent' system. In the 'separate' system the rare group activities – for exercise and attending chapel – were carried out under the anonymity of hoods (Figure 4.33) and even inside the chapel, which the hooded figures entered through labyrinthine passages, individual boxes screened prisoners from each other so that they could see only the preacher (Figure 4.34). Here was the final break with the Tonerre tradition. The worshipping *corpus* of individuals united into a community by contact, joint singing and processions is replaced by a set of silent, immobile and isolated individuals. Re-entry into society was to be achieved by fracturing all social bonds.

Figure 4.34

Interior of Pentonville prison chapel

Source: H. Mayhew and J. Binny (1862) *Criminal Prisons of London*

The ideology of holy penance and pastoral virtue is still alive in today's reforms. The new prisons proposed in the British Home Office Design Guide (1989, 1991) have been likened to 'monasteries' whose isolated two-storey blocks, with spatial segregation of hardened offenders from others, is a 'village' (*Building Design* 1989: 60). Paradoxically, in the light of my use of the word, what is located at the centre is not a church but 'recreation'.

In fact what is put at the centre – in the text, in form and in space – is a reliable clue to meanings.

If we turn to an institution which, unlike hospitals and prisons, is the invention of the Enlightenment and the Industrial Revolution – the asylum – this becomes clear.

The mad

The last two decades have witnessed a break with the descriptive history of insanity presented as a felicitous stream of medical and social progress. The newer analyses by Rothman (1971), Foucault (1967), Szasz (1971), Scull (1982) and Donnelly (1983) are at once illuminating and contradictory. Rothman's puts the rise of the American asylum into the context of segregation, social control of the poor and deviant, and the exercise of economic power. He has been subjected to a strong critique by Scull for falling prey to 'cultural chauvinism' (Scull 1981: 144) by locating the birth of the asylum in America and ignoring the earlier European experience, for mounting a 'polemical assault', and for 'cultural idealism' in his creation of a negative, a-historical and malign repressive force (Scull 1982: 256). Foucault's theory of 'the great confinement ... a gigantic moral imprisonment' of the eighteenth century brackets asylums with prisons and hospitals into a realisation in the classical age of that 'great moral city of which the bourgeois conscience began to dream in the seventeenth century (where) the laws of the State and the laws of the heart (are) at last identical' (1967: 60–1). For Szasz the 'manufacture of madness' is a socio-medical-legal conspiracy both to empower professionals and to control the poor and the deviant. Scull acknowledges the force of these contributions but emphasises the need for careful historical analysis. Only thus can one avoid both blinkered optimism and reductionism, and the sweeping rhetorical history whose power resided, and perhaps still does so, in its appeal to the anti-institutional and anti-expert movements. Scull's analysis is the more powerful for being rooted in material reality. Donnelly, like him, according to one reviewer (Just 1983: 21) has abandoned '... a Whiggish sociology of unbroken human progress (and) ... passed through the fires of Marxist and sociological revisionism' to emerge with something between 'liberal and materialist postures'. What distinguishes Scull and Donnelly is their close attention to detailed empirical data. As a result asylum buildings feature more prominently, but even they cannot see them as formative objects; they are merely outcomes.

Even when extracted from a jumble of institutions the specialised places for confining the insane still remain ambiguous. In one context the penal model dominated; the insane had responsibility, and even criminal motives were imputed to their bizarre, unruly and destructive behaviour. The régimes and the buildings resembled prisons. In another context the model of malady has the upper hand; there was moral innocence, genuine sickness capable of diagnosis, subject to clinical experiment and curable in a kind of hospital. The first model assumed the pathology of a class, the second of individuals. Both developed from a third which, whilst it had ancient roots, became focused during the Enlightenment. These were not people at all; since they had lost the use of reason and therefore the ability to hold rational discourse, the very characteristics which for the Age of Reason defined human nature, they could quite properly be treated as animals. Neither punishment nor cure were relevant. There was no hint of cruelty in the unquestioning acceptance of chains, manacles, kennels, cages, filthy straw bedding, and physical coercion. It was but a small step to exhibit the insane for amusement.

Institutional care went back to ancient and medieval Europe. Its nature depended on which model was used. Confinement was coupled to exclusion in cells, walls and gatehouses – such as those in medieval Lübeck. Foucault recalls how madmen were collected on the *Narrenschiff* (Ship of Fools), confined and sent on journeys to distant lands. By the end of the fifteenth century madness had replaced death as the root of a cosmic fear. The madman as showing the '*déjà-là*' of death replaces the leper who 'as a living man (was) the very presence of death' (Foucault1967: 16 and 291). But in the next hundred years the other model emerged, with insane cells in hospitals and new specialised caring institutions.

There is far less material on these buildings than on prisons and hospitals. Jetter's (1971) study of French and German asylums from 1780 to 1840 is, after twenty years, still one of the most complete. For England Forsyth's (1969) unpublished dissertation is a parallel and equally thorough source. I have worked on the Scottish material (Markus 1982).

So the asylum occupies an unstable space between prison and hospital. From the former it takes individual, solitary cells, from the latter the ward that it transforms into a unique space which is locally free but securely bounded – the 'gallery'.

The duality causes the 'centre' to oscillate between altar or church – or at least a feature such as a domed space which recalls the sacred space – and inspection. In general asylums are 'reversed', with shallow inhabitant and deep visitor space. But the gallery, which after the invention of 'moral' treatment becomes a social space shared by patients and staff, appears near the surface and makes the entire structure more shallow.

The type becomes recognisable through the consistent use of passages, tunnels, segregated stairs and inspection holes (which combine secrecy with security), walled gardens and courts, classification by space, and labyrinthine plans. Inmates were cut off from outside and from each other in categories of gender, behavioural symptoms and economic class. And market forces created private, profit-making 'madhouses' for both paupers and bourgeois paying patients (Parry-Jones 1972).

Economic class was also linked to etiology. One school ascribed the higher-than-average rate of lunacy amongst the wealthy to the enfeebling effects of over-refined 'civilisation'. But gradually certain forms of mental disease, especially 'moral insanity' (today's psychopathy) came to be associated with the dissolute lifestyles of the poor – an association with an old history, on which the treatment of the insane on the prison model in the *Hôpital Général* in Paris was based. Hence, too the Bethlehem (Bedlam) in London, a thirteenth century foundation with special provision for lunatics by 1377, was attached to the Bridewell (for criminals) in 1557; special lunatic cells appear in the seventeenth century. Cells, lining the two sides of its huge wards, survived the palatial rebuilding of Bedlam by Robert Hooke (1676).

But the cells opened onto a wide day 'gallery' which became a unique feature of asylums as a socialising space for patients where mixing could be allowed without losing control over segregation between men and women and security. It appeared in George Dance's St Luke's (1751) and survived in James Lewis's design for the third Bethlehem hospital (1811).

The gallery was almost exclusive to English-speaking countries. Jetter's (1971) German examples show a variety of cells on long corridors. The prison at Celle (1710) had an asylum added to it (1731). Both were winged, symmetrical buildings, men on one side, women on the other, enclosing courtyards. The prisoners' windows faced the outer world, with an inward-facing control corridor, those of the insane faced an inner world of exercise yards, with an outer corridor. The difference embodies two different theories of reform. Criminals are face to face with innocent nature which will move their conscience. Lunatics will be cured by contemplating each other in a purified and orderly sociability.

Even in the most advanced régime of the late eighteenth century – Joseph II's *Narrenturm* in the *Allgemeines Krankenhaus* in Vienna – the insane were housed in a five-storey round tower with vaulted cells around its periphery, an internal corridor, and a transverse interior block for the guards.

Both the Bicêtre and the Salpetrière in Paris had insane accommodation from the start. Conditions were horrific – inmates were shackled in damp, cramped and insanitary cells. The idea of isolation and secure open surrounding space was re-interpreted by the architect Viel at Salpetrière (1786–9). Small pavilions of back-to-back cells (*loges*) faced gardens, tree-lined avenues and courts separated by iron grilles to keep intact the classification – 'senile, curable agitated cases, incurable ones, idiots, escapees, sowers of discord and the melancholy'. There were to be 600 *loges* in addition to accommodation for 200 epileptics and 150 deformed, with elaborate fresh air systems, but the Revolution interrupted the work. At Bicêtre the principle of *loges* was developed further in 1822. They were now single banked, opening to an arcade and courtyard on the ground floor and a wide corridor above. That this module, Esquirol's *carrés isolés*, was capable of infinite multiplication is evident in the great asylum at Charenton (1838) with sixteen units symmetrically disposed around a central church and administrative block.

Loge had an earlier equivalent in English. Jonathan Swift left the bulk of his estate for building a lunatic asylum in Dublin. He was no stranger to the subject as a Governor of London's Bethlehem from about 1722. He was also a Governor of Dr. Steevens' nearby hospital where a fellow Governor, William Fownes, suggested an asylum as a sister institution. Swift requested the Mayor and Corporation to grant him a plot of land, and eventually a charter for erecting St Patrick's was obtained in 1746 and the designs by George Semple accepted in 1749. They were based on a sketch by two Trustees which, in turn, was strongly influenced by a letter written to Swift in 1733 by Fownes in which he describes '*lodges*' and 'galleries'. Semple formed these into a 'U', with three-storey men's and women's wings

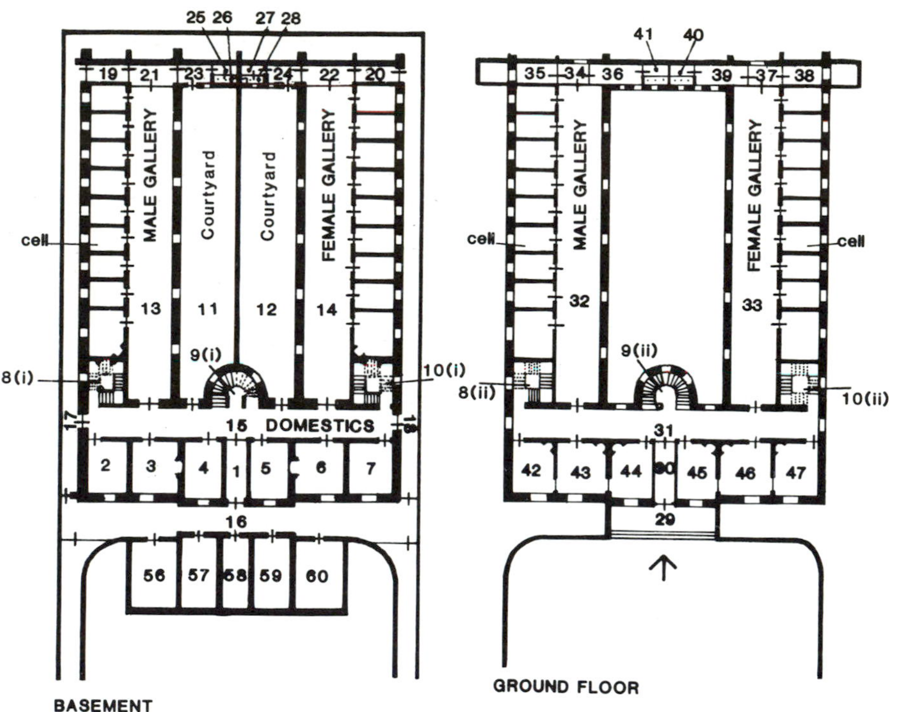

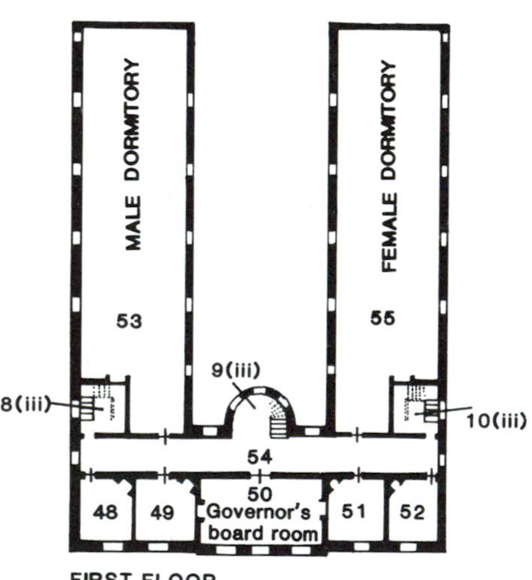

Figure 4.35

Semple's plans for St Patrick's hospital, Dublin (1749)

Source: Author's drawing from Semple's original drawings in the hospital archives

(Figure 4.35). The ground and first floors have wide galleries with lateral cells and the second (top) floor has open wards to be used at the Governors' discretion for idiots, convalescent patients or 'quieter' lunatics.

The front looks like a two-storey building as the ground floor kitchens and domestic offices are entered under the entrance steps, accessed by a sunken curved double carriageway. Two rear exercise yards are separated by a storeyheight wall. There is a ceremonial semi-circular central stairway, and two lateral service stairs leading to lobbies which give access to the patients' quarters on the three floors through gates locked by the staff. The spatial structure (Figure 4.36) shows that the split-level entrance results in all cells appearing at the same level, whilst the top floor open wards are much deeper. Though there are numerous rings, the locked gates and doors which make all access routes to patients permeable in

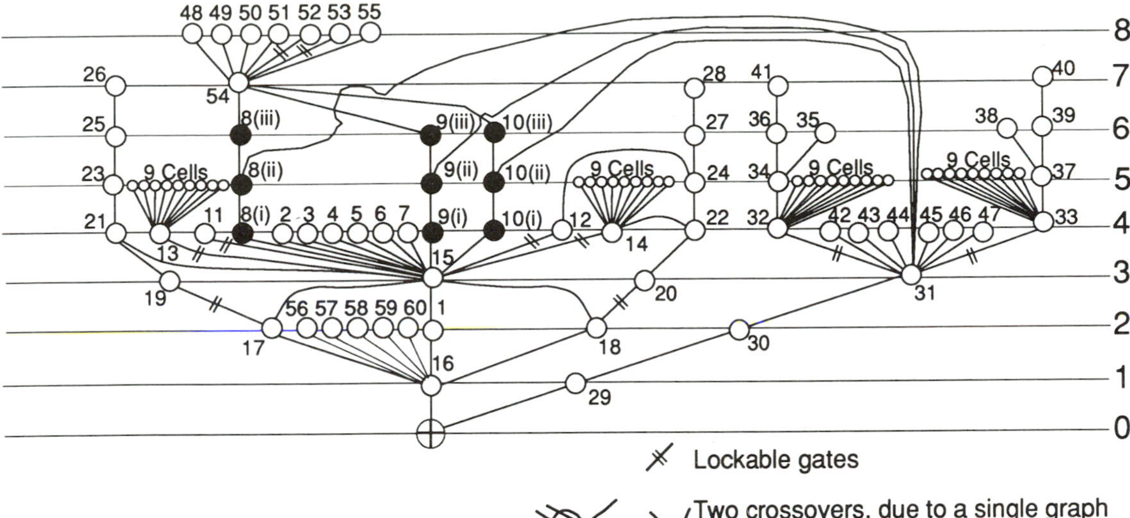
Lockable gates
Two crossovers, due to a single graph representing three floor levels.

Figure 4.36
Spatial map of St Patrick's hospital
Source: Author's drawing

one direction only (marked on the drawing by a double bar), limit these to staff whilst the patients are on trees. The inversion is still incomplete: on the one hand a number of domestic offices are shallow, entered from the ground floor hall, but on the other the Governors' Board room and other administrative offices are on the third floor at the deepest point.

Swift's enlightened views and such works as the *Treatise on Madness* by Battie (1758), first physician of St Luke's, in which he advised against bleeding, emetics, blisters and cathartics, signalled a wind of change which was about to blow through the asylum world. 'Moral treatment' arrived. For physical constraint and isolation it substituted social pressure resulting from interactions between patients, and between them and staff, self-esteem, distracting amusements, orderly work, sound diet, limited freedom, a salutory feeling of fear, gentle persuasion and, in some varieties, religious emotions. The metaphor of the family became the guiding image for its social organisation. Dark, cold, damp, overcrowded and insanitary cells were totally rejected and buildings were regarded as integral to the régime. Pinel (1800: 179) for instance, recommends architects and doctors to form an alliance (*se concerter*) so that each class of patient should not only be segregated and under surveillance, but in a specifically tailored environment. Thus melancholics need access to cultivated gardens, maniacs need silent and shady places, as peripheral as possible, and both need to be shielded from the degrading spectacle of idiotism and senility. He recommends continuous surveillance by the *police intérieur* so that a doctor can 'observe and describe' all symptoms (1800: 177).

Pastoral settings and graceful buildings provided the promotional images to attract the wealthy patients from their country estates. And, as in the schools, they were antidotes to urban chaos. For those who now took a psychological view of insanity this environment was therapeutic and replaced the harsh phyical remedies used by the doctors who clung to somatic theories. The new régimes did not require doctors as directors though house physicians were included in subservient roles. From the long battle the doctors emerged victorious but only at the cost of a fundamental change once the failure of their régimes became overwhelmingly obvious.

The victory achieved by combining the psychological and somatic models first transformed the mad-doctor into alienist and eventually into psychiatrist. A vital connecting link in the early decades of the nineteenth century was phrenology (Cooter 1984). Spurzheim's anatomy enabled emotional and behavioural disorders to be mapped into zones of the brain, the seat of the mind, whose diseased organs could be identified and treated like any other. Cranioscopy – the study of the skull for underlying deformations – took a strong hold, and *post mortem* dissections led eminent surgeons and alienists to claim discovery of brain lesions. Phrenology deeply influenced such key figures as John Connolly at Hanwell asylum. It expired but left the field permanently changed. There was less emotional involvement

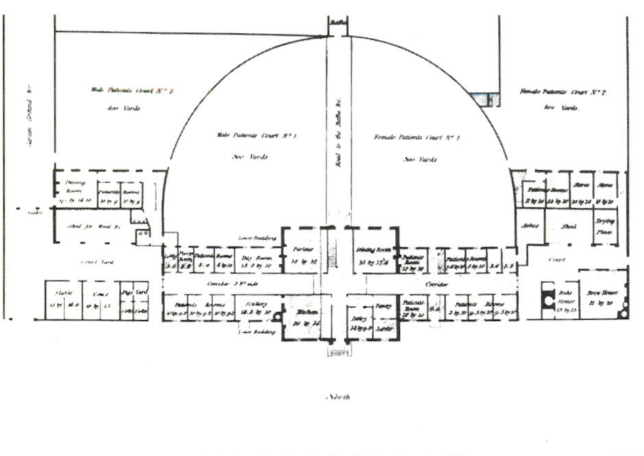

Figure 4.37

The Retreat, York (1794–6), ground floor plan and exterior

Source: Tuke (1813)

with the patient (not merely because the huge new pauper asylums made this unfeasible) and the attempt to relate function to structure shifted the direction of clinical research. Phrenologists worked in education, imprisonment and production. Later we will come across the Fourierists' belief that built forms need to harmonise with brain structure. Future studies of phrenology as a material culture may reveal the extent to which the design of hospitals, asylums, prisons, schools or factories was affected.

'Moral treatment' was based on the belief that lunatics had reason, even though damaged, and conscience – inner raw material which made them responsible for their *own* cure. It was inevitable that the changed economic conditions of the competitive free market should emphasise responsibility for choice (Scull 1981). Internal self-discipline could be expected of the insane, the prisoner, the schoolchild or the workman as much as of the consumer.

Two people are usually credited with the independent invention of 'moral treatment': William Tuke in York and Philippe Pinel in Paris. But it was in the air: John Ferriar at Manchester and Edward Fox in Brislington House near Bristol (1804–6) were applying parallel methods, as had Vincenzo Chiarugi at Florence and Joseph Daquin of Chambery, whose published descriptions appeared in the early 1790s. Tuke's grandson Samuel did not publish the first account of The Retreat, written under his grandfather's supervision, until 1813 whilst Pinel's *Traité* had appeared in 1800.

In a dramatic gesture which has become deeply engraved in the history of psychiatry Pinel struck off the lunatics' shackles at the Bicêtre when he took charge in 1793. Two years later he took charge of Salpetrière also. Whether his being a doctor was cause or effect, the French model became medical, committed to scientific observation and experiment. Tuke on the other hand was a practical Quaker businessman with humane and religious motivations. Despite these differences their régimes were similar. But the latent medical–lay divergence present in 'moral treatment' at its inception erupted into the open conflict already referred to.

Tuke founded The Retreat in 1792. The buildings (1794–6) were designed by another Quaker, John Bevans (whom we have already encountered in connection with Bentham's Chrestomathic school). In keeping with Quaker emphasis on moral discipline, simplicity, decent, homely comfort, nature, and the family as a model community, the building (Figure 4.37) aimed for rural domesticity (though Samuel denies the 'rural farm' description of the Genevan doctor Delarive). Patients were classified by sex and severity of disturbed behaviour. Anne Digby (1985) has shown some differentiation by ability to pay (and patients sponsored by Quakers paid less), but on the whole diagnosis prevailed; for instance one day room is for patients of 'the superior class, with regard to behaviour and to capacity for rational enjoyment'. But there *are* hints of classification by social class; patients of 'a superior class, both in respect of *terms* and disorder' are referred to and though large rooms in the central block are described as suitable for 'a person in any rank of life' their 'distinct attendant' makes this a disingenuous claim.

The gardens and fields are therapeutic tools, and the rabbits, sea-gulls, hawks and poultry in the walled exercise yards were intended to awaken 'social and benevolent feelings'. All rooms opened off wide galleries in the tradition of St Luke's, with day rooms, controlled fresh air and a modern heating system. Care was taken to avoid all penal features. There were no window bars and even iron sash bars were covered in wood. There was no central surveillance nor even committee or Board rooms. The superintendent's dining room and parlour are shared on occasion with quieter patients. Everywhere the 'family' is emphasised (Tuke 1813: 103).

The Retreat had wide influence in Britain and continental Europe, but was most faithfully reproduced in America. In Scotland after the opening of the first purpose-built asylum at Montrose (1781) and the second in Aberdeen (1800), the movement made rapid progress, influenced by both Paris and York. This should be no surprise; Scotland led Europe in medical education, inherited late Enlightenment rationality and George Combe made Edinburgh pivotal in phrenology. When Pinel and his pupil Esquirol established the first systematic clinical lecture course on psychiatry in Paris a number of Scots attended: Andrew Combe – George's doctor brother, Alexander Morison who first visited Paris in 1818 and became an influential writer and teacher on mental disease, and Robert Christison who became Professor of Medical Jurisprudence at Edinburgh University.

An outstanding Scottish disciple of Pinel's was Andrew Duncan. As early as 1792 he proposed an asylum for Edinburgh, but it was 1807 before a start on the Morningside designs could be made by Robert Reid. The building, which I have described elsewhere (Markus 1982), was quadrangular with a keeper's apartment central on each side. As at The Retreat, the front keeper's dining room was shared with the patients and placed next to their day room, on the principle of a 'family' house. The corner pavilions and four detached blocks at the front had large rooms for paying patients; the paupers were in double banked small cells. Four sunken passages led from each keeper's apartment to meet at a central inspection room in the quadrangle – a topological device which recalls the tunnel in Adam's nearby Bridewell.

In 1807 William Stark published a startlingly different design for Glasgow (it was actually ready in 1806, and possibly in its formative stages in 1804). Critical of inadequate classification and surveillance in England and at Edinburgh, Stark's sole goal was to overcome these deficiencies. I have already described how the 16 classes of patients called for by the brief and shown in Figure 1.9 were located in space. The problem was to reconcile the freedom of patients to move about 'without any interference or controul' (sic) with the 'classing of patients … which the more minutely it is pursued, the more it increases the difficulty of preserving the individuals from that degree of confinement which is both irksome and injurious' (Stark 1807: 16).

The inevitable outcome of the brief was an equal-armed greek cross plan with a central staff staircase surrounded by keepers' and patients' day rooms (Figure 4.38). The eight exercise court-

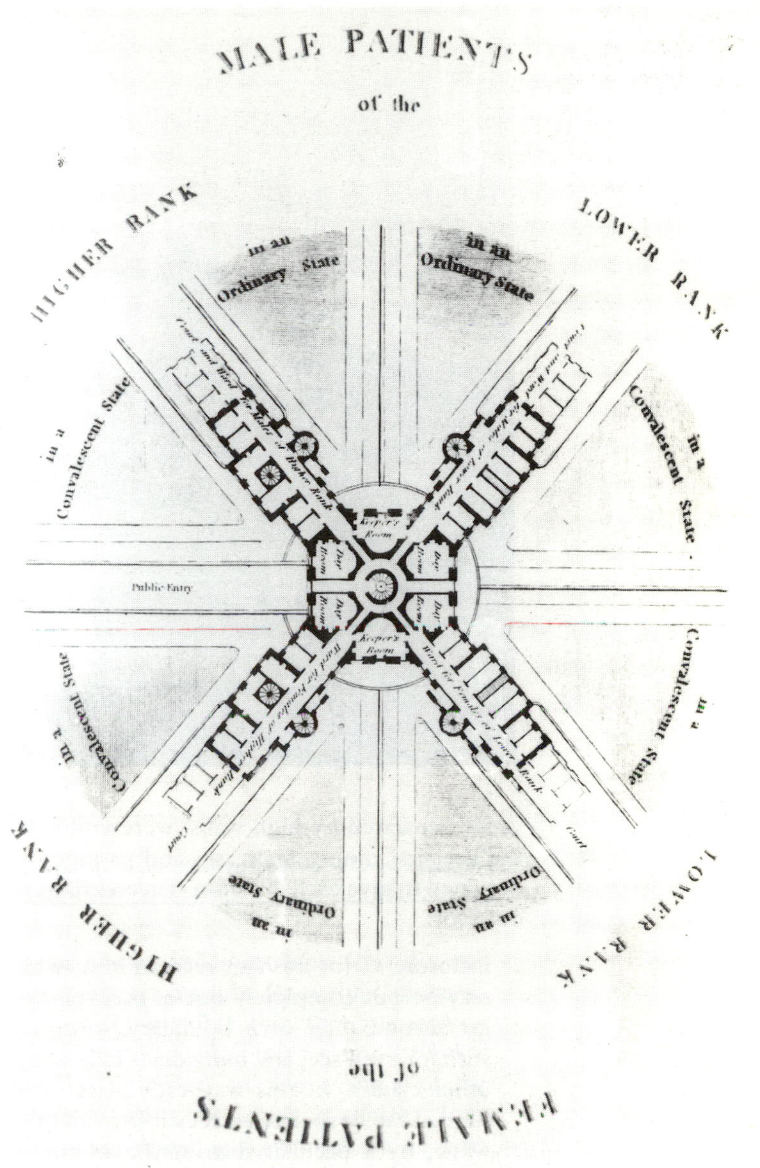

Figure 4.38

Glasgow lunatic asylum (1807), plan

Source: Stark (1807), by permission of the Glasgow District Council, Mitchell Library

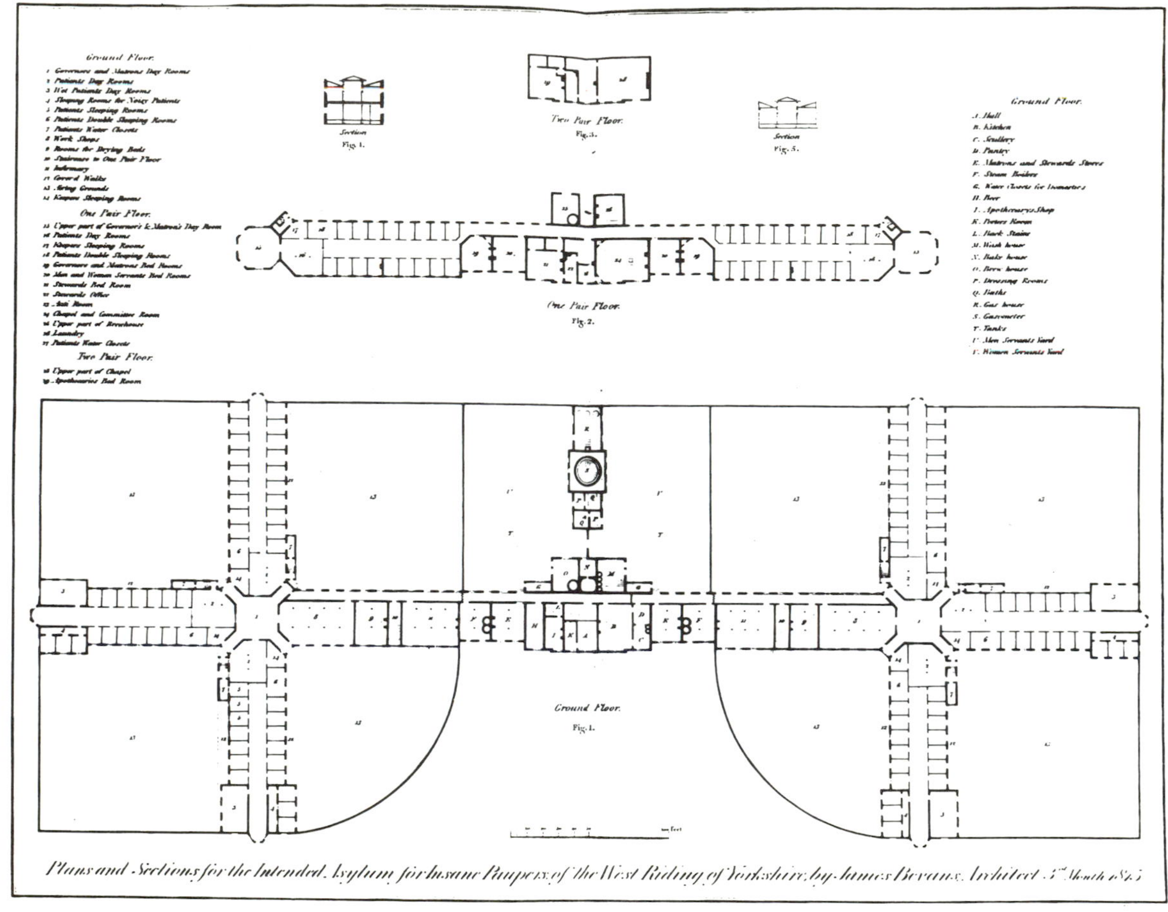

Figure 4.41

Bevans' entry for Wakefield asylum competition (1815), plan

Source: Committee on the State of Madhouses (1819), British Architecture Library

Gloucester project started by Nash (continued after Stark's death by Wheeler and completed by Collingwood in 1823). Patients were in three blocks according to economic status: first class in the double banked cells of the elegant front crescent, second class in two great courts at the rear and the third, pauper, class in cells – every bit as cramped and unventilated as the Paris *loges* – which backed onto a central spine wall.

When he died suddenly in 1813 Stark had just started on his last asylum – for Dundee – where he adopted an 'H' plan with single banked, originally single storey, classified cell wings facing planted gardens. Contemporary critics claimed that it was intended to convey the image of a rural farm. It is certain that he had come a long way from the centralising rigours of Glasgow, possibly having heeded Tuke's warnings and after visits to Montrose, York and Bristol. But his freer planning and greater use of landscape may have been but one sign of a more comprehensive internal revolution of which his report on the landscaping of part of Edinburgh New Town (Reed 1982: 115–53) was another.

The four Reports in 1819 of a Parliamentary Commission set up in 1815 show how regressive thinking had become. Bevans proposes a seven-armed radial asylum (Figure 4.40) with full central surveillance from an annular 'inspection gallery'. His submission for the 1815 Wakefield competition (Figure 4.41) had two great greek cross patient blocks linked by central service and administrative rooms and a chapel with completely separate access for men and women, submitted under protest to accord with the 'printed particulars' which set out Tuke's anti-panoptical advice. 'It is a great deal more expensive than I have any idea is necessary'. A simpler version for 70 pauper lunatics was also printed. His preferred solution is radial not unlike his model prison submitted to the Select Committee on Gaols in 1819 (Figure 4.42). Bevans, despite his Quaker background, was a utopian utilitarian in the purest Bentham mould, dreaming of

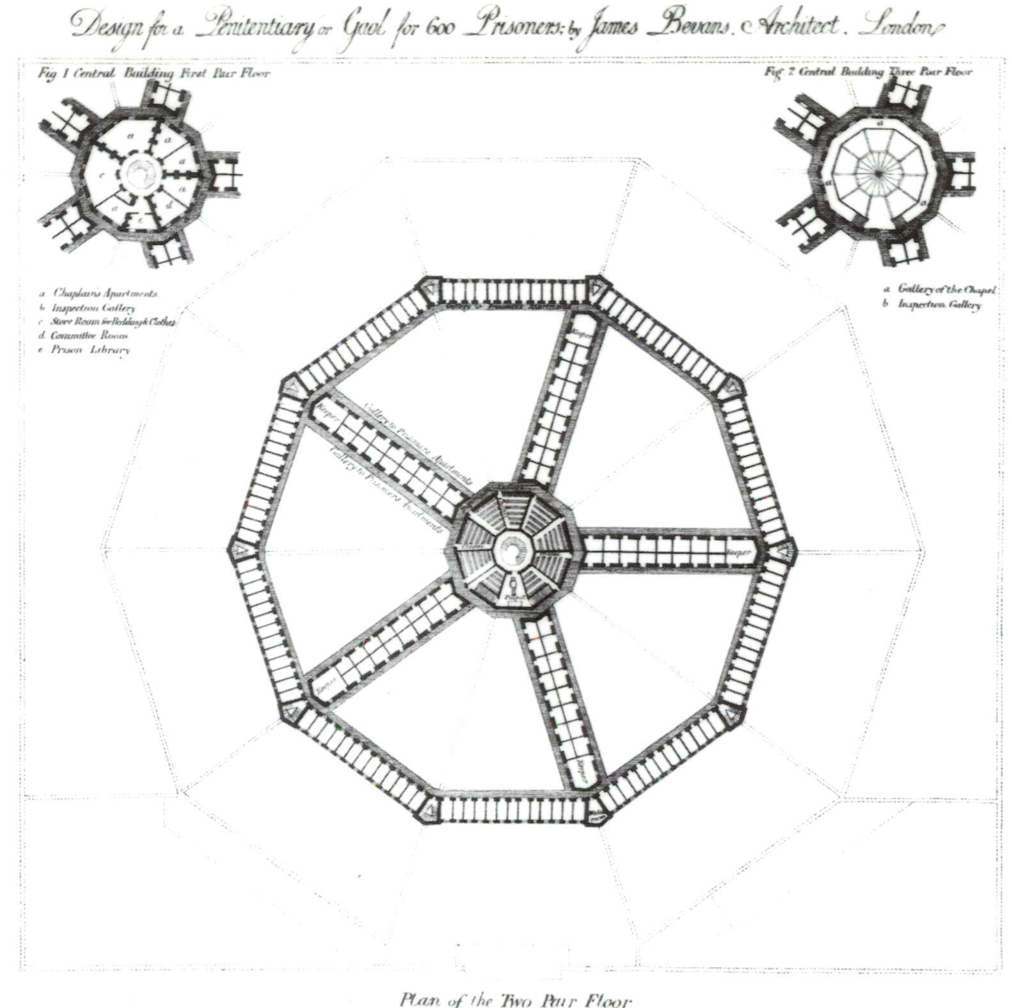

Figure 4.42

Bevans' model radial prison (1819), plan

Source: Select Committee on Gaols (1819), British Library

total projects on a grand scale.

William Watson and James Pritchett were chosen from forty entrants for the Wakefield competition whose brief was written by Samuel Tuke. Though it called for accommodation for 150 paupers, the design appears to undershoot this significantly. Like Bevans', it has two cruciform blocks – one for each sex – connected by central medical, domestic and administrative spaces. The men's 'governor' and the women's 'matron' have two-storey maisonettes in the centre of the two crosses. A wedge shaped space, with lockable doors, allows private communication between their two levels as well as continuity with the central staircases which rise from ground level. This one-way permeable device ensures that the 'inhabitant' space is brought spatially onto a surface ring, as indeed does another configuration in the connecting block which brings the first floor committee room to the surface (Figure 4.43). Wakefield became influential as a prototype; similar solutions lasted well into the century. Outstanding amongst these was the Crichton Royal Asylum at Dumfries whose architect, William Burn, had already tried out his skills in completing Stark's Dundee design.

Though a further Parliamentary enquiry in 1827 focused specifically on Middlesex, the resulting 1828 Act introduced national provisions. It created the Hanwell Asylum (1831, extended in 1838) – designed by another Quaker under Tuke's influence, William Alderson. Three hundred and thirty patients were accommodated symmetricallly in single and double-banked wings

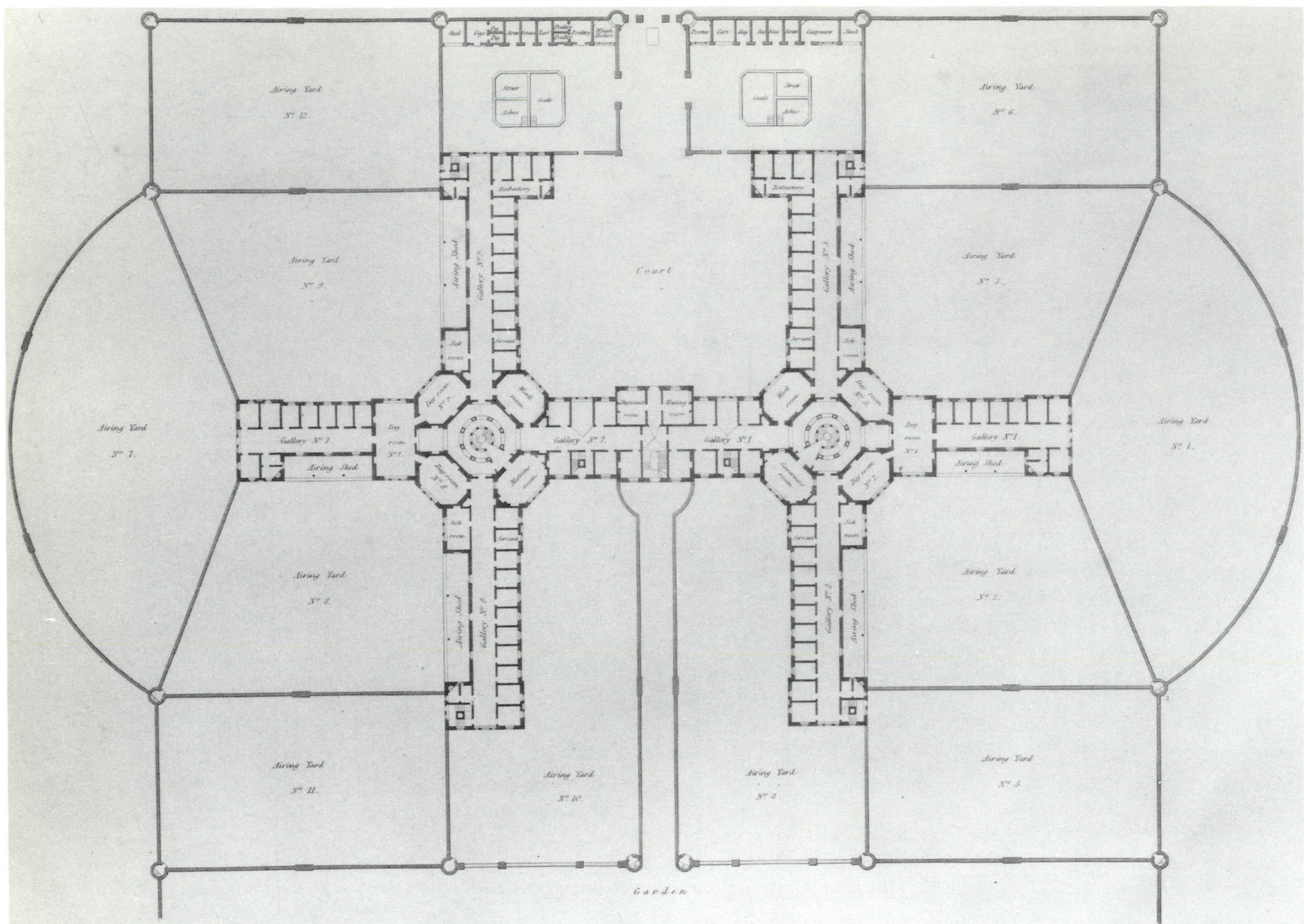

Figure 4.43

Watson and Pritchett's Wakefield asylum (1815)

Source: Watson and Pritchett (1815), British Architecture Library

for men and women, the superintendent's and other staff quarters in the centre with direct access from the entrance. The first superintendent and matron were Dr Ellis and his wife who had been in charge at Wakefield. Their departure was used to formalise the medical–lay divergence by splitting the clinical responsibility in 1839, under John Connolly, from the administrative. Connolly's régime of 'non-restraint' – a development of 'moral treatment' – became a milestone in psychiatric history and also aroused a good deal of opposition from both conservative doctors and the established church (Connolly 1847).

Between 1812 and 1844 thirteen large county asylums opened in England. Some, like Cornwall (1820) and Chester (1829) were radial; others immense 'U' or 'H' linear blocks. Cells opening off wide galleries were standard, as were classified day rooms. A few made half-hearted provision for workspaces. The growth in patient numbers, scarcity of resources and the increasing control by the medical profession resulted in significant changes. Hanwell grew from 300 to 1000 patients at a rate of 18 per cent a year. Even small rural asylums doubled or tripled their capacity. Under such pressures the early hopes for a curative, domestic, 'family' scale institution evaporated. Staff to patient ratios decreased, régimes became more custodial despite the gradual acceptance of doctors as directors, and buildings became surveillance-oriented, larger, more crowded and spartan – in fact carceral.

The Lunatic Asylums Act of 1842 provided for the Metropolitan Commissioners in Lunacy to report on all the English asylums. Their 1844 Report led directly to the Lunatic Act and the Lunatic Asylums and Pauper Lunatics Act of 1845. What had been permissive under the 1808 Act now became compulsory every County had to build. The number of vast, overcrowded asylums rapidly grew. Even Middlesex, with by far the largest institution at Hanwell, decided to build a second asylum at Colney Hatch in 1851.

The carceral trend was worldwide. In America the South Carolina asylum at Columbia (1822) was designed as a nine-sided semi-polygon (though it was never completed). Joseph Frank, doctor son of the director of the Vienna General Hospital, proposed a four-armed windmill plan in 1818 whose single-banked corridors met at a point (Figure 4.44). This plan materialised in 1834–46 in the Erlangen asylum (Jetter 1966).

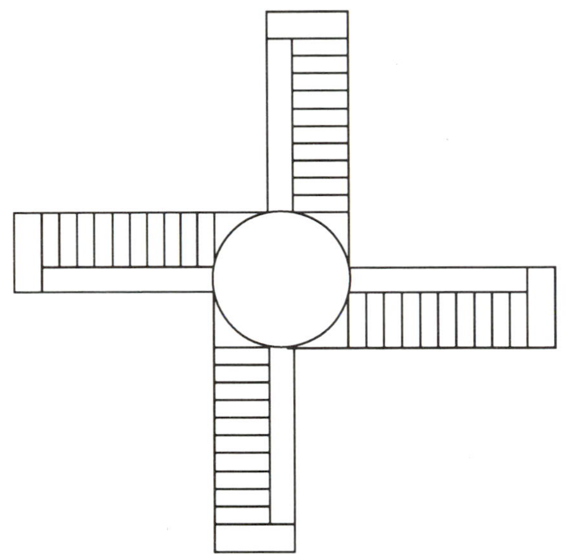

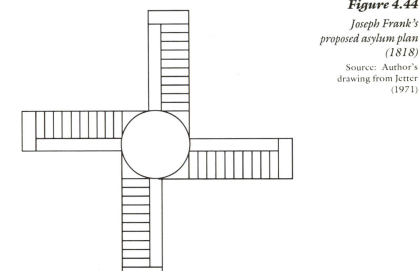

Figure 4.44
Joseph Frank's proposed asylum plan (1818)
Source: Author's drawing from Jetter (1971)

The new workhouse

Although pauper lunatics were the target of the asylum programme, they were still to be found in workhouses. The 1832 Royal Commission on the Poor Law had Edwin Chadwick for its Secretary. He had been Jeremy Bentham's private secretary till the latter's death in 1833. Little wonder that he brought a clear, utilitarian logic to the task. The 1834 Report recommended sweeping change and the legislation was passed in the same year. Though Chadwick had expected to be appointed as one of the three Commissioners, he in fact continued as Secretary. Architecture was top priority as an instrument for achieving the aims of 'indoor' (i.e. in workhouse) relief. Just as the Committee of the Council on Education four years later was to give detailed guidance on school buildings in its very first Report, so the new Commissioners published three model plans in their first Annual Report (Parliamentary Sessional Papers 1835) and one more in the second. The young architect Sampson Kempthorne worked for both bodies and had he not emigrated to New Zealand in 1840, where he died shortly afterwards, his work would have covered Britain. We have already seen Kay-Shuttleworth's linking role. It is an amazing aspect of British institutional reform that a handful of men were responsible for forming, implementing or challenging the new policies: John Stuart Mill and his son James, Bentham, Chadwick, Kay-Shuttleworth, Kempthorne and Owen.

Initially the general mixed workhouse under one roof was never intended. The Report suggested four separate buildings – for the aged, children, able-bodied men, and women. The Commissioners were sometimes confused, proposing to use an existing workhouse for one function and new ones for the three others. But under severe constraints of capital and staffing they soon veered towards the single, large institution, powerfully advocated by Sir Francis Head, one of the Assistant Commissioners. His vision of an all-encompassing pastoral, 'low, cheap, homely building' was the basis for one of the models in the First Report. Five hundred inmates in over fify single room 'cottage' dormitories were arranged on two floors around a rectangular court (Figure 4.45). Head insisted that the 'height of rooms, the thickness of walls, etc. etc., shall not exceed the dimensions of the cottage of the honest, hard-working, independent labourer'. This was his interpretation of the Commissioners' 'less eligibility'. The committee room, Board room and guardian's house are clustered by the entrance. A bay window on the upper floor of the last 'commands (a) view over (the) whole establishment'.

But he, like others then and since, misunderstood the principle. It did not mean that the workhouse should provide lower material standards of food, hygiene or buildings than the lowest outside. The discipline of work, a rigid timetable, separation of the sexes (including married couples other than the aged), sometimes even separation of young children from their mothers, and abstinence from tobacco and alcohol, would be so undesirable that any life outside, except in extreme circumstances, would be preferable (more 'eligible').

Since Chadwick increasingly disagreed with the Commissioners it has often been assumed that

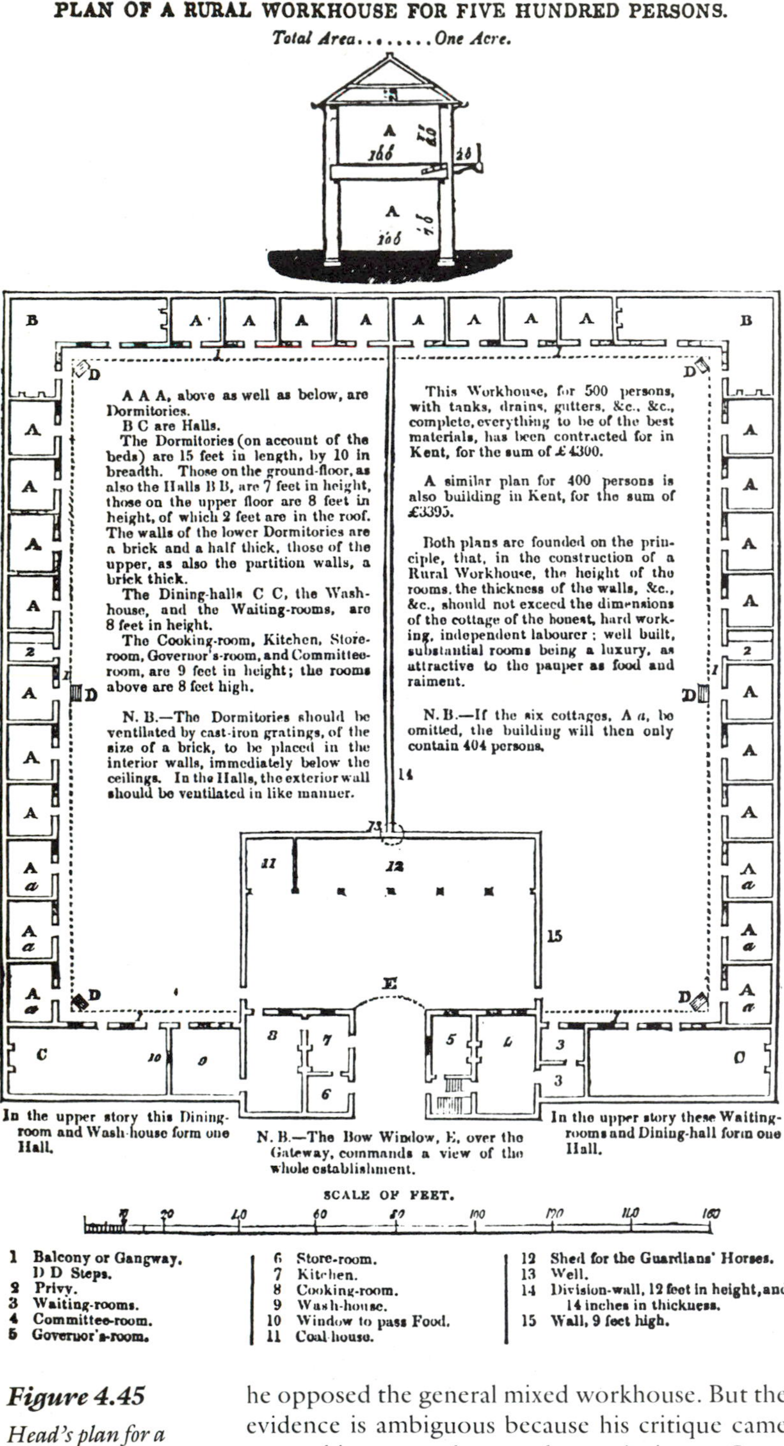
PLAN OF A RURAL WORKHOUSE FOR FIVE HUNDRED PERSONS.
Total Area........One Acre.
A A A, above as well as below, are Dormitories.
B C are Halls.
The Dormitories (on account of the beds) are 15 feet in length, by 10 in breadth. Those on the ground-floor, as also the Halls B B, are 7 feet in height, those on the upper floor are 8 feet in height, of which 2 feet are in the roof. The walls of the lower Dormitories are a brick and a half thick, those of the upper, as also the partition walls, a brick thick.
The Dining-halls C C, the Wash-house, and the Waiting-rooms, are 8 feet in height.
The Cooking-room, Kitchen, Store-room, Governor's-room, and Committee-room, are 9 feet in height; the rooms above are 8 feet high.
N. B.—The Dormitories should be ventilated by cast-iron gratings, of the size of a brick, to be placed in the interior walls, immediately below the ceilings. In the Halls, the exterior wall should be ventilated in like manner.
This Workhouse, for 500 persons, with tanks, drains, gutters, &c., &c., complete, everything to be of the best materials, has been contracted for in Kent, for the sum of £4300.
A similar plan for 400 persons is also building in Kent, for the sum of £3395.
Both plans are founded on the principle, that, in the construction of a Rural Workhouse, the height of the rooms, the thickness of the walls, &c., &c., should not exceed the dimensions of the cottage of the honest, hard working, independent labourer; well built, substantial rooms being a luxury, as attractive to the pauper as food and raiment.
N. B.—If the six cottages, A a, be omitted, the building will then only contain 404 persons.
In the upper story this Dining-room and Wash-house form one Hall.
N. B.—The Bow Window, E, over the Gateway, commands a view of the whole establishment.
In the upper story these Waiting-rooms and Dining-hall form one Hall.
SCALE OF FEET.
1 Balcony or Gangway.
D D Steps.
2 Privy.
3 Waiting-rooms.
4 Committee-room.
5 Governor's-room.
6 Store-room.
7 Kitchen.
8 Cooking-room.
9 Wash-house.
10 Window to pass Food.
11 Coal-house.
12 Shed for the Guardians' Horses.
13 Well.
14 Division-wall, 12 feet in height, and 14 inches in thickness.
15 Wall, 9 feet high.

Figure 4.45

Head's plan for a model workhouse for 500 (1835)

Source: British Parliamentary Papers (1835)

he opposed the general mixed workhouse. But the evidence is ambiguous because his critique came some thirty years later and two Assistant Commissioners who were his strong supporters – Tufnell and Kay-Shuttleworth – were its advocates though, as we have seen, the latter wanted to separate the school.

There were two models by Kempthorne in the First Report for 300 paupers; one Y-shaped within a hexagonal boundary of workshops and service buildings (Figure 4.46) the other cruciform within a square boundary (Figure 4.47). Though the Act specified seven classes, his plans only classified by sex and between adults and children, with an additional '1st' and '2nd class' division. The central master's quarters opened into the day rooms and wards and had windows into each court. An indication of strict economy was the telescoping of the schoolroom with the children's dining room and the huge adult dining room with the chapel.

In the Second Report Kempthorne had a smaller workhouse for 200.

The rate of building was phenomenal. In 1835–6 the Commissioners approved 127 workhouses, the largest with up to 500 beds, and alterations and enlargements to 78 existing Gilbert union buildings. By 1839 about 350 had been built. Many architects followed Kempthorne's cruciform models. He himself designed several before he emigrated, of which Abingdon (1836) was the first. Initially these designs were well received by the professional press as '... excellently arranged (for) separation and classification', even though Loudon's *Architectural Magazine* (1835) compared them to 'the panopticon principle, the master's house being in the centre, or in the focus of whatever may be the form of the plan' (511–12). But soon Cobbett called them *Bastilles*.

Walls, partitions, iron grilles and gates soon sliced up the wings and courts as the sevenfold classification was enforced with ever-increasing precision: aged or infirm men, able-bodied males over thirteen years old (increased to 15 in 1842), boys between seven and thirteen, aged or infirm women, able-bodied women and girls over thirteen (increased to 16 in 1842), girls from seven to thirteen, and all children under seven. There were also separate 'refractory' (punishment) and lunatic cells.

These designs were not only expensive – between £20 and £40 per place between 1840 and 1858 (British Parliamentary Papers 1857–8: 379) – but the need to provide each class with separate day, night and outdoor space gave rise to immense planning problems. Soon easier plans emerged, with a large central and a number of smaller, sometimes detached, blocks. As early as 1849 the City of London workhouse adopted a more dispersed model (Figure 4.48). It also introduced even further refinements into classification by dividing 'able' men and women into first and second class, and inventing a new 'unruly' categ-

WORKHOUSE FOR 300 PAUPERS,—GROUND PLAN, No. 1. (E.)

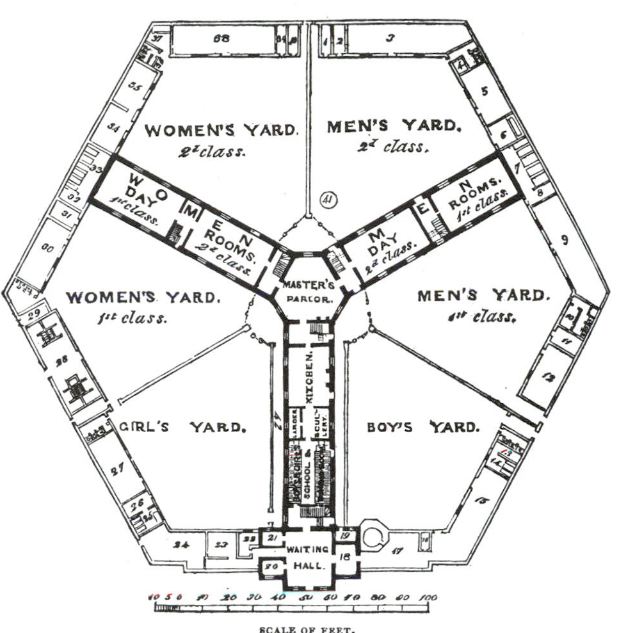

1 Dead House.
2 Refractory Ward.
3 Work Room.
4 Dust.
5 Work Room.
6 Washing Room.
7 Receiving Ward, 6 beds.
8 Bath.
9 Work Room.
10 Dust.
11 Washing Room.
12 Flour and Mill Room.
13 Washing Room.
14 Receiving Ward, 3 beds.
15 Work Room.
16 Coals.
17 Bakehouse.
18 Bread Room.
19 Delivery Room.
20 Porter's Room.
21 Searching Room.
22 Store.
23 Potatoes.
24 Coals.
25 Receiving Ward, 4 beds.
26 Washing Room.
27 Work Room.
28 Piggery.
29 Slaughter House.
30 Work Room.
31 Washing Room.
32 Bath.
33 Receiving Ward, 6 beds.
34 Wash-house.
35 Laundry.
36 Dust.
37 Washing Room.
38 Work Room.
39 Refractory Ward.
40 Dead House.
41 Well.
42 Passage.

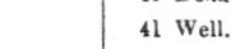

WORKHOUSE FOR 300 PAUPERS,—ONE PAIR PLAN, No. 2. (E.)

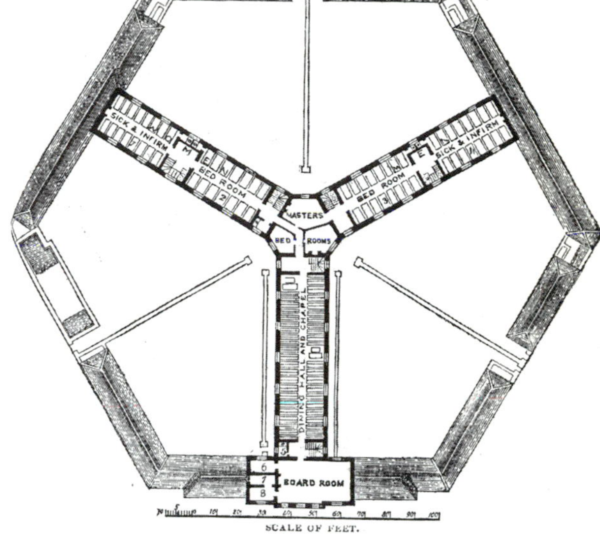

1 Sixteen in single beds.
2 Twenty-seven in double beds.
3 Thirty-two in single beds in two tiers.
4 Sixteen in single beds.
5 Water Closet.
6 Clerk.
7 Strong Room.
8 Ante Room.

PERSPECTIVE VIEW OF A WORKHOUSE FOR 300 PAUPERS. (E.)

SAMPSON KEMPTHORNE, Architect,
CARLTON CHAMBERS, 12, REGENT STREET.

Figure 4.46
Kempthorne's design for a model workhouse for 300 (1835), ground floor plan, first floor plan, and aerial perspective
Source: British Parliamentary Papers (1835)

WORKHOUSE FOR 300 PAUPERS,—GROUND PLAN, No. 1. (F.)

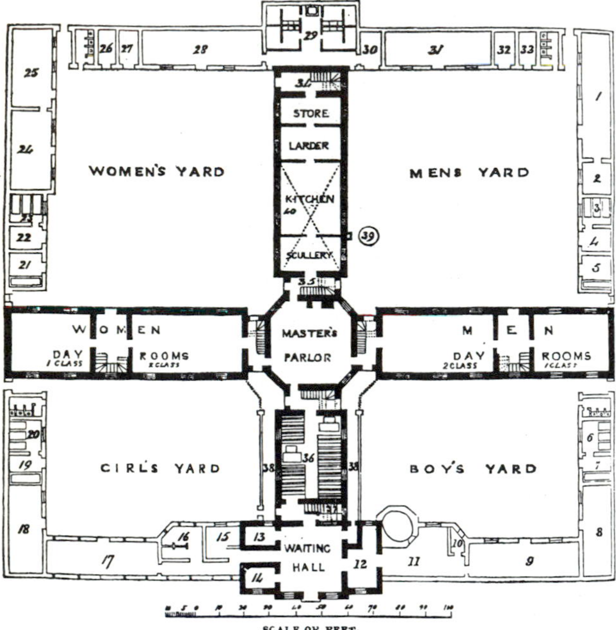

1 Work Room.
2 Store.
3 Receiving Wards, 3 beds.
4 Bath.
5 Washing Room.
6 Receiving Ward, 3 beds.
7 Washing Room.
8 Work Room.
9 Flour and Mill Room.
10 Coals.
11 Bakehouse.
12 Bread Room.
13 Searching Room.
14 Porter's Room.
15 Store.
16 Potatoes.
17 Coals.
18 Work Room.
19 Washing Room.
20 Receiving Ward, 3 beds.
21 Washing Room.
22 Bath.
23 Receiving Ward, 3 beds.
24 Laundry.
25 Wash-house.
26 Dead House.
27 Refractory Ward.
28 Work Room.
29 Piggery.
30 Slaughter House.
31 Work Room.
32 Refractory Ward.
33 Dead House.
34 Women's Stairs to Dining Hall.
35 Men's Stairs to ditto.
36 Boys' and Girls' School and Dining Room.
37 Delivery.
38 Passage.
39 Well.
40 Cellar under ground.

WORKHOUSE FOR 300 PAUPERS, ONE PAIR PLAN, No 2. (F.)

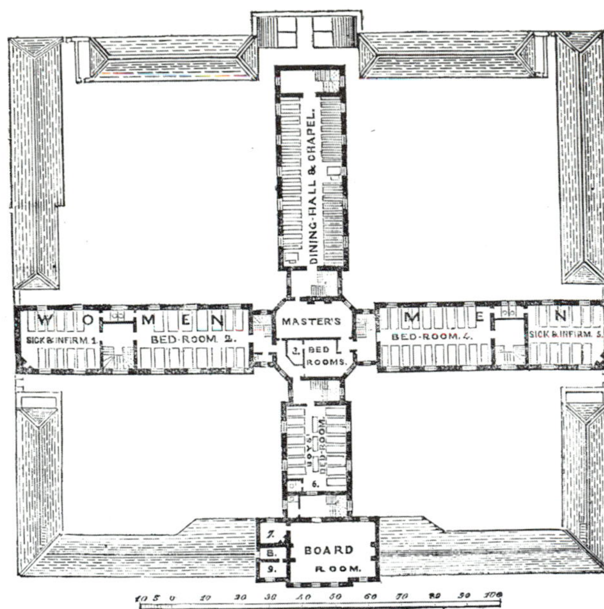

SCALE OF FEET.

1 Twelve single Beds.
2 First class, 30 in double Beds.
3 Closet.
4 First class, 38 in single Beds, in two tiers.
5 Twelve single Beds.
6 Thirty-six in single Beds, in two tiers.
7 Clerk.
8 Strong Room.
9 Anti-Room.

Figure 4.47

Kempthorne's design for a model workhouse for 300 (1835), ground floor plan, first floor plan, aerial perspective

Source: British Parliamentary Papers (1835)

PERSPECTIVE VIEW OF A WORKHOUSE FOR 300 PAUPERS. (F.)

SAMPSON KEMPTHORNE, Architect,
CARLTON CHAMBERS, 12, REGENT STREET.

ory. In a later version – the West London workhouse of 1864 – the 'unruly' have become 'incorrigible'. In 1868 the Commissioners ratified this trend in a *Memorandum* which recommended separate buildings on one site. By the end of the century the last vestiges of the great 'pauper palace', whose heyday lasted less than thirty years, disappeared: the Commissioners recommend separate sites.

The unitary workhouse – school, orphanage, bridewell, prison, hospital, almshouse, asylum and factory under one roof – was a complete departure from the undifferentiated institution of the eighteenth century. Each element had its precise history, each unambiguosuly identifiable and at its most advanced point of technical development. This apotheosis of institutions was raw material for the most creative artists, from Dickens to Pugin. And its immensity dominated the landscape.

For Head it was an overwhelming sign of power, inspiring to its staff and Guardians and awesome to the poor – one false step and they would cross the boundary between poverty and pauperism:

> The very sight of a well-built efficient establishment would give confidence to the Board of Governors; the sight and weekly assemblage of all the servants of their Union would make them proud of their office ... while the pauper would feel it was utterly impossible to contend against it.
>
> (quoted by Longmate 1974: 87)

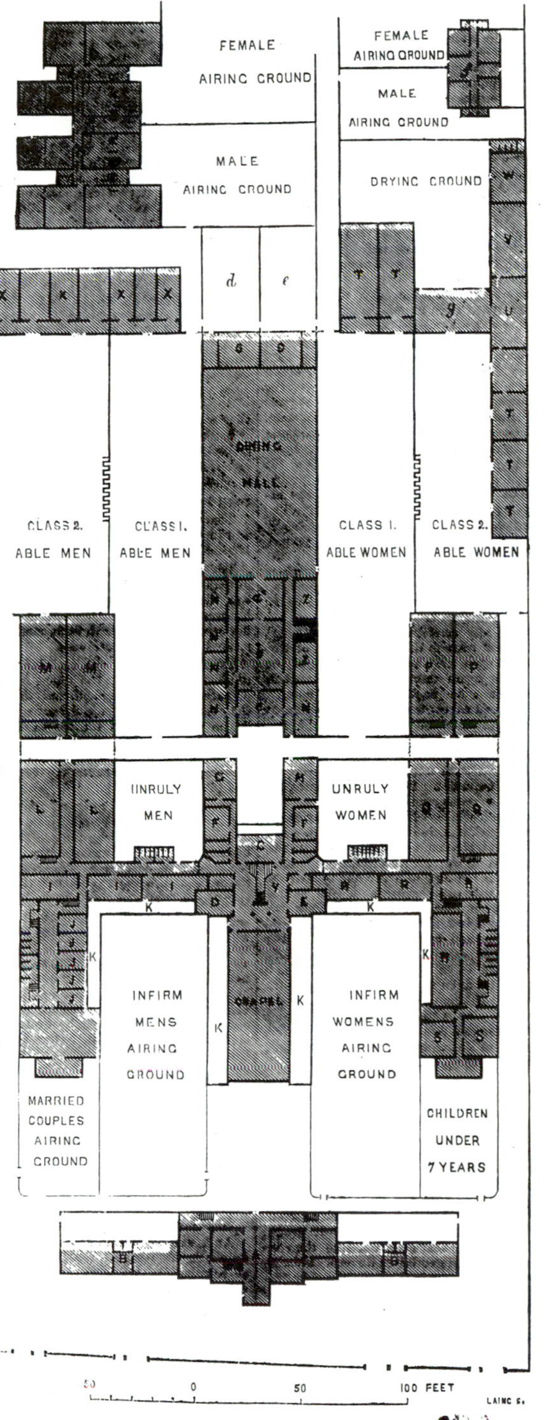

Figure 4.48
City of London workhouse (1849), plan
Source: *The Builder* (1849) VII(342): 400, 25 August

CHAPTER 5

Cleanliness is next to godliness

The discipline of the workhouse, as of the prison and asylum, was achieved by external control over the body and internal moral reform by a coerced conscience. One instrument – cleanliness – was targeted on both body and soul through elaborate systems of water supply, elimination and drainage, the obsession with fresh air, therapeutic use of nature and, above all, the washing of bodies and clothes. The tie between cleanliness and morality made hygiene the natural focus of reforming régimes. Inside institutions it could be enforced but outside it had to be done by persuasion, so public facilities for the poor to wash their bodies and clothes became a major project.

Since the human body and the elements of nature – trees, grass, flowers, water, sky – are universal 'givens', innocent of class boundaries, one might expect their role in the environment also to cross social divisions. In rare, negative, cases it does; the devastation of the 1830s cholera epidemics though not classless, easily crossed such frontiers. But in general the same rules are at work in buildings as elsewhere so it is no surprise that in the types dedicated to the use of water, the body and nature have one meaning in reformation and another in recreation. The apparently universal images of water on which Illich (1986) meditates – based on drinking, washing of bodies and clothes, germination, sport and health – become instruments for control in the baths, wash-houses and laundries for the poor, the focus of this chapter, but metaphors for regeneration and visible ratification of superior status in the spas dedicated to the drinking of and bathing in mineral waters, and in other élite baths.

The thermal baths of Classical Europe and North Africa were the exclusive preserve of the wealthy, for the luxurious buildings were expensive and, in the absence of hot springs, so was the fuel for heating the water. The Roman tradition of hot air sweating baths survived in the Near East, Russia and Finland and returned to Europe in the sixteenth century as the Turkish bath whose eighteenth century successor – the *stove bath* or *bagnio* – had to overcome a reputation which combined exclusiveness with licentious practices before the new bourgeoisie and then the poor would take to bathing.

The water of mineral springs was also taken internally so the curative purpose of spas was clearer and they developed a different élite tradition (though some medieval baths, notably at Bath and based on earlier Roman establishments, did cater for the poor). Harrogate, Buxton, Scarborough and Tunbridge Wells, Bath, and great centres in continental Europe such as Ulm and Baden, were well established by the seventeenth century. The medicinal properties of the waters had been the subject of numerous treatises and pamphlets from as early as 1562 (Turner 1562). An entire life of masques, balls, races, eating, drinking, music and gambling revolved round these waters, which needed special spa buildings: bath houses, hotels, assembly rooms, pump rooms, specialised shops, gaming and other clubs, concert rooms, covered arcades and promenades.

The spa was challenged by the sea and fresh cold water. Sir John Floyer's *An Enquiry into the Right Use and Abuse of the Hot, Cold and Temperate Baths in England* (1697) set a pattern of serious medical treatises, often separated from quackery by a thin line. Doctors began to send patients to specially constructed cold baths; in Edinburgh the College of Surgeons and Barbers erected a bath-

Figure 5.1

Margate sea bathing infirmary (1791), John Pridden's sketch plan, and elevation

Source: Kent County Council, Margate Library (plan); *Gentleman's Magazine* (1797) LXVIII: Plate opposite p.841, October, British Library (elevation)

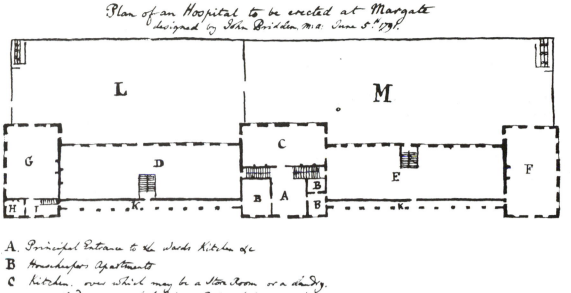

Plan of an Hospital to be erected at Margate designed by John Pridden, M.A: June 5th 1791.

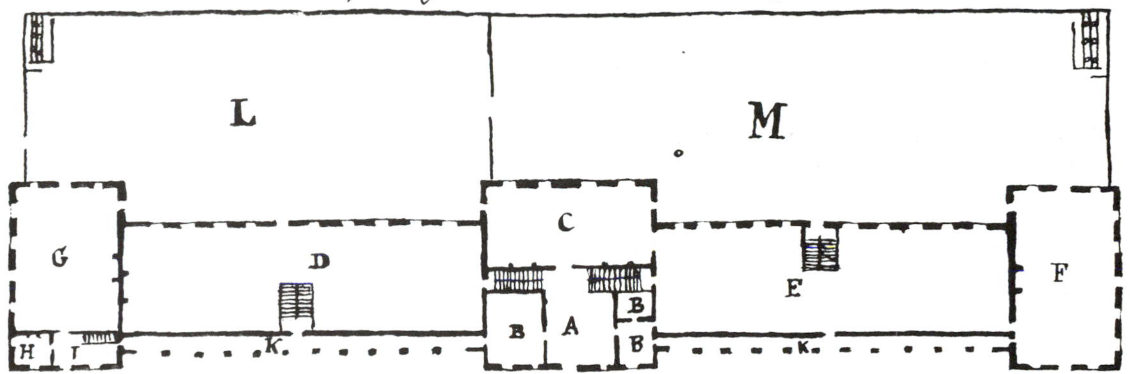

A. Principal Entrance to the Wards Kitchen &c
B Housekeepers Apartments
C Kitchen. over which may be a Store Room or a Laundry.
D mens Ward capable of holding 22 Beds & the Room over will hold 24 Beds } Total Number of Beds 92.
E Womens Ward Do — — — — — — Do — — — — — — }
F Dining Room over which may be apartments for the female Servants.
G Committee or Meeting Room }
H Medicinal Room — — } over which may be apartments for the apothecary
I Ante Room — — — — }
K Piazza.
L }
M } yards in which may be erected any necessary extra building as a Wash-house Scullery &c &c.

(a)

Key

A Entrance
B Housekeeper
C Kitchen
D Men's ward
E Women's ward
F Dining room
G Committee room
H Medicinal room
I Ante room
K 'Piazzas'
L Men's yard
M Women's yard

GENERAL SEA-BATHING INFIRMARY, MARGATE.

(b)

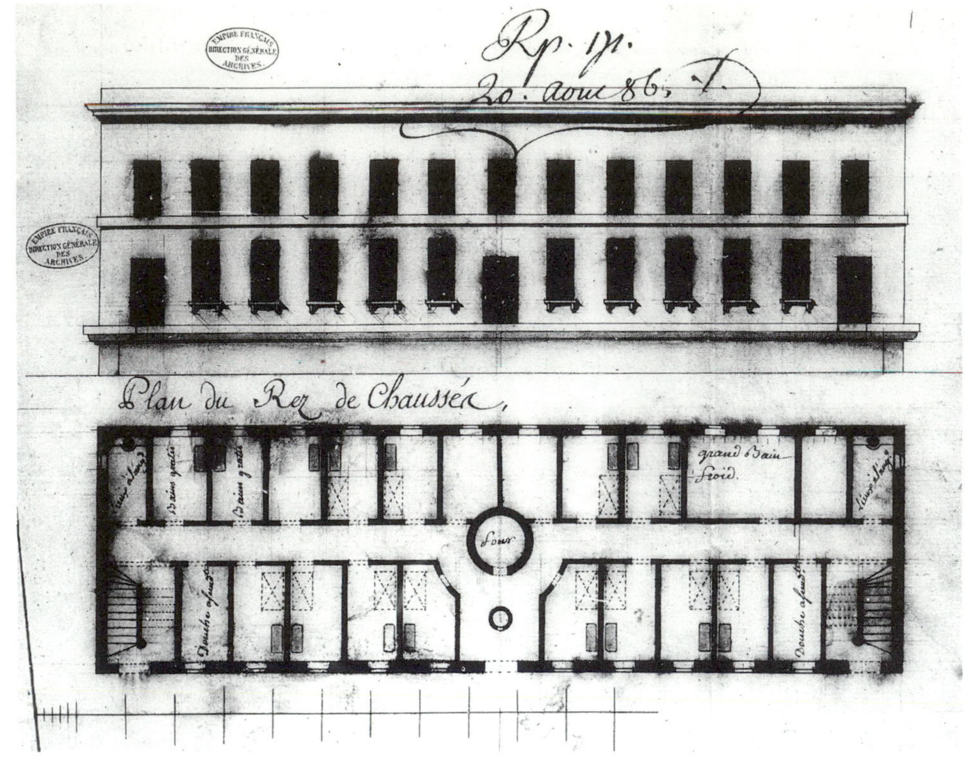

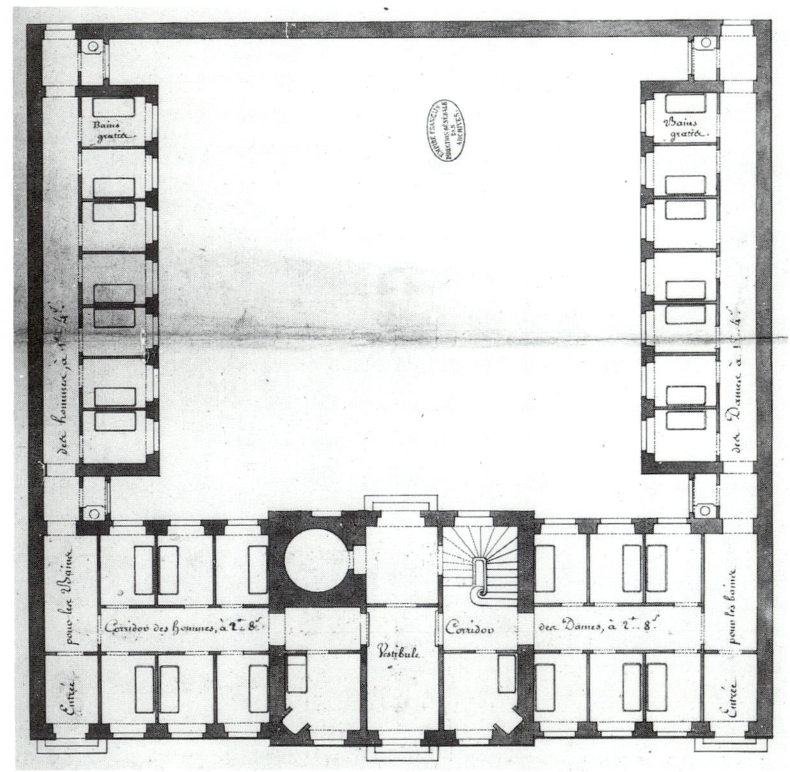

Figure 5.2

Albers' designs for baths in Versailles (1787)

Source: French National Archives, O1 1863 and O1 1838

house in 1697 and the College of Physicians followed suite in 1712 (Boog Watson 1979). Private establishments benefited from the medical publicity, authentic or not. In 1722 together with Baynard, Floyer published a work which ran into many editions showing that cold baths were already established and giving medical respectability to the claimed health-giving properties of salt water. Some sea-water bathing was grafted onto existing spas. At Scarborough by 1720 both men and women took therapeutic dips; the former rowed themselves out to sea to bathe in the nude, whilst the latter stayed near the beach, draped. Soon bathing machines replaced this arrangement.

Some early public bathing establishments were extensions of hospitals, and though conceived as sanitary measures, were not used by patients but generated a fee income. Edinburgh Infirmary incorporated them in 1738 and Manchester Infirmary in 1779. It was some time before poor patients gained access.

The drift from inland spas to Brighton began in the 1730s, and was given a boost by aristocratic patronage. Three baths captured the sea at high tide for continuous bathing and, by means of false bottoms which could be raised and lowered, offered any preferred depth. There was an 'observation chamber' from which spectators could watch the bathers. When the Prince of Wales began curative sea-bathing in 1783, Brighton's privileged position was sealed. The town began to reproduce the leisurely, 'recreative' architecture of the capital. Granville notes that if you do not glance at the sea, and close your ears to its murmur, 'you will be inclined to believe that you are walking in one of the leading streets of the metropolis. Brighton is a portion of the "west end" of London *maritimized*' (1841: 565).

Sea bathing also caught the philanthropic imagination. The General Margate Sea Bathing Infirmary (today with its 'Royal' prefix), brainchild of the London physician Dr John Lettsom, was designed to provide fresh air, sun and a sea-water régime for the Metropolitan poor. Since amongst the sketch plans produced in 1791 by the Reverend John Pridden, the local promoter, one was his own (Figure 5.1) he has been credited with the final design (Colvin 1954: 475–6) which was in fact by a Canterbury surveyor called Mathews (Royal Sea Bathing Infirmary 1791–3). He followed Pridden, with a central, two-storey entrance block, two lateral ward wings for men and women, fronted by 'piazzas' (arcades) and a pair of wings at right angles containing committee rooms, dining room and offices.

Baths on the Seine were gradually elaborated into floating Classical buildings; entrance was by fee under medical supervision, though a few free places were provided. The best-kown was Poitevin's (1762) with twinned tubs on either side of partitions.[1] These twinned tubs in cubicles were the model for the building permit requested by a M. Albers in Versailles (1787) for use by members of the Court. It had showers (sideways, vertical and horizontal), hot and vapour baths, a communal cold bath, and a central heating stove. In an even grander proposal the men's and women's entrances are at two extremities with a central staff entrance (Figure 5.2).

Paying establishments for the middle classes rapidly spread in Europe. Swimming was added to the floating tub-baths on the Seine (*Deux Siècles . . . Paris* 1984). In Glasgow, there were separate fresh-water swimming and 'stretching' baths for men, women, boys and girls in 1800 (Cleland 1816: 405–6). Vienna had its Diana open air pool by 1804. Often newspaper reading rooms or libraries are incorporated. The sketch books of Glasgow's leading late eighteenth century architect David Hamilton have one scheme with a refreshment room, a conversation room and a room for the reception of drowned persons (not, presumably, extracted from the baths). Another has both hot and cold baths and a central, domed, music and conversation room. The accompanying sketches of Roman baths tell a story: lurking not far beneath the surface is a nostalgia for an innocent arcadia where cleansing, social intercourse, the arts and leisure are combined into a single Classical idyll. This vision was soon shattered by the realities of urban squalor.

Before the really poor were washed, for a short period provision for artisans was added to the middle class establishment, with careful spatial segregations into two or three classes achieved by differential fees. Alongside the warm, cold and vapour baths, and showers in individual rooms, 'plunge baths' surrounded by individual or group dressing rooms appear in the first decades of the nineteenth century. These were large pools, often edged by colonnades on the Roman model, with steps into the water. 'Plunging' was one step from 'stretching' and one towards 'swimming'. There was a strange ambiguity: the intention was cleansing but swimming could not be prevented though it could be discouraged by limiting size and depth.

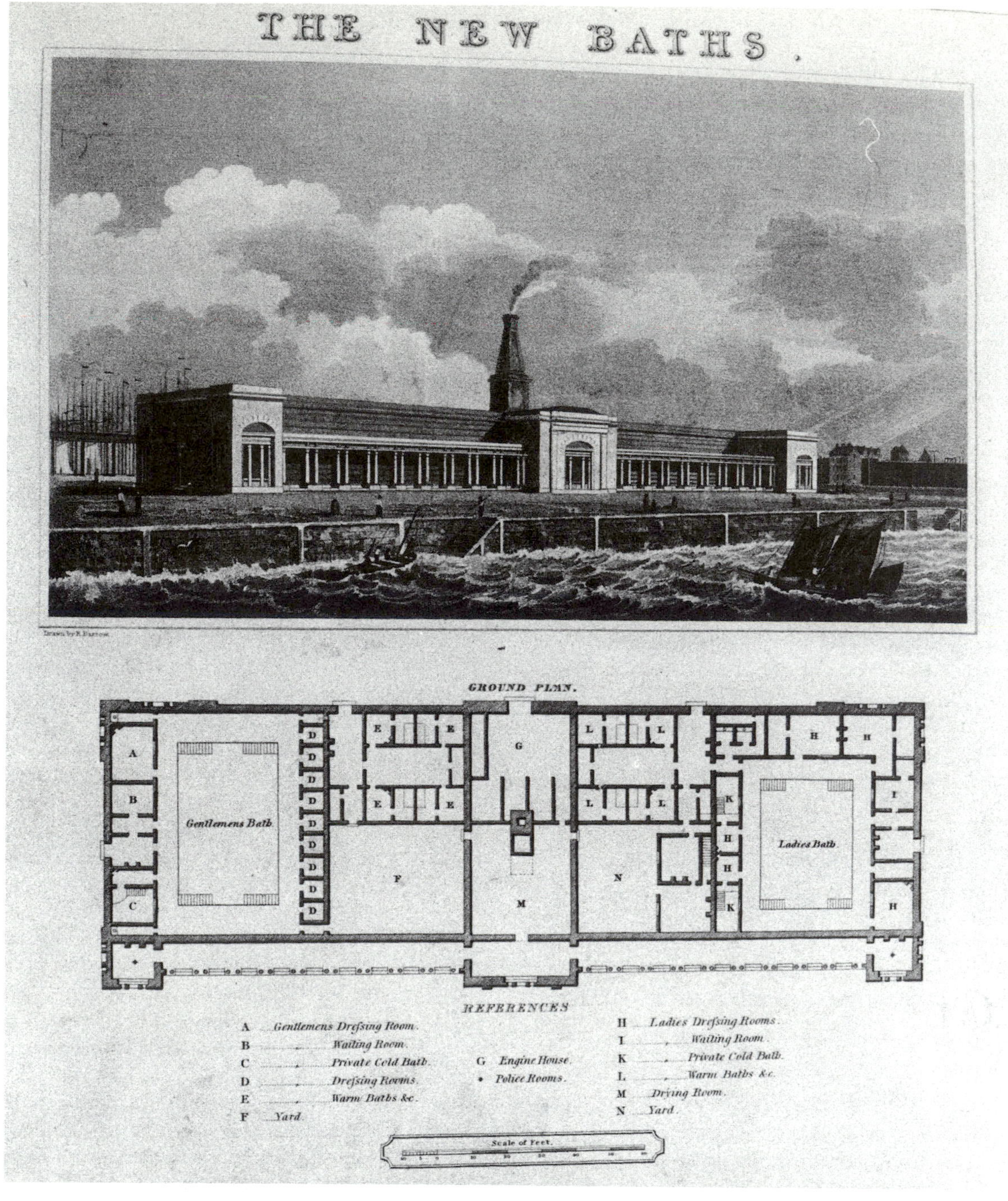

Figure 5.3

Pier Head Baths, George's Dock, Liverpool (1826–9)

Source: Plate published by Gore and Son, Castle Street, Liverpool (n.d.), possibly from *Gore's General Advertiser*, Brown, Picton and Hornby Libraries, Liverpool Record Office, Liverpool Libraries and Arts

Separate entrances and planning devices were used to graft economic onto gender segregation. Plunge baths were either for men only, or, if for both sexes, the men's was significantly larger. A London Turkish bath with a simple classical elevation had a central entrance for men, and two lateral ones, smaller and angled, one for women and the other for horses (Goodman 1982: 12–14).

Once the artisans were provided for, on the assumption that they would not have servants, clothes washing was added. Wash-houses, tubs and ironing rooms appeared. The first British town to make provision for two-class bathing and limited clothes-washing was Liverpool. The Pier Head Baths in George's Dock (1826–9) was a truly radical project (Figure 5.3) designed by John

Foster junior, surveyor to the Corporation. There was much ambiguity in the plan. The river (rear) side had a central entrance which led, by a shallow portico, to a drying room also accessible from the engine room and service entrance on the opposite side. By 1856 the portico had become a committee room, and the drying room a laundry as was probably the orignal intention. The service and public entrances were at the (landward) front, from an enclosed yard whose entrance was large enough for a horse and cart to deliver fuel and collect ashes. The lateral men's and women's entrances led to suites of warm baths around a saloon, and to the plunge baths with dressing rooms, private cold baths and waiting rooms. The men's plunge bath was larger, and both were originally open to the sky. On the men's side a large 'gentlemen's' dressing room, with its own fireplace is distinguished from nine small 'dressing' rooms. The women had three large dressing rooms, each with a fireplace, and two private cold baths.

Other towns kept in step. By 1830 Birmingham had a complex of ten baths, for both sexes' 'immersion and amusement' at Lady-Well.[2] Besides hot, cold and sweat baths, it had a very early open air recreational rather than medicinal swimming pool in a garden.

Liverpool's baths were finished three years before cholera arrived. Within months of appearing in Sunderland in 1831, it reached Liverpool and much of Lancashire and Yorkshire in 1832. In a population of 230,000 Liverpool had about 5000 cases and 1500 deaths, apart from those which broke out on board ships which had set out from its port. Intense and horrifying as cholera was, there had already been earlier outbreaks of typhus ('the fever'). That and tuberculosis were the most durable diseases of the century. Perhaps because they were so 'normal', it needed the sudden appearance of the new disease to jolt government into action with the setting up of a sanitary enquiry in 1839, under Chadwick when he was still Secretary to the Poor Law Commission. His classic report (1842) had immense influence. The statistical survey on housing, public health, disease, poverty and urban sanitation was thorough and devastating. It led to the 1848 Public Health Act and further legislation and enquiry. Of course there had been earlier legislative attempts. From the late eighteenth century Local Boards of Health sprang into action during particularly severe outbreaks of disease – such as the 1795–6 typhus epidemic in Manchester, and the first cholera outbreaks in 1831–2. Pre-Chadwick legislation was through local Police, Paving, or Lighting Acts. Building Acts were also used for housing and sanitary control. London's 1774 Act was followed by many others; Liverpool's in 1825, 1839 and 1842 and finally 1846, which authorised the Corporation to appoint Britain's first Medical Officer of Health.

Baths and wash-houses became a public health issue once cholera appeared. Silk's 1835 Bill to establish them for the poor and destitute fell by the wayside. The movement was revived by the Committee for Promoting the Establishment of Baths and Wash-Houses for the Labouring Classes (1844) which built an experimental bath-house and laundry in Glasshouse Street, East Smithfield in 1845. 35,000 used it for baths and 49,000 for washing and ironing in its first year. The Bill promoted by the Committee resulted in the 1846 Public Baths and Wash-Houses Act. Even before that was enacted it built a second experimental establishment in Euston Square, London. Both were modest, containing small bath cubicles, with spaces and equipment for washing and drying clothes.

But Liverpool had anticipated the Committee. The baths and wash-houses for the poor built in Frederick Street (1842) were not only the first in the city, but in Britain (Report ... Wash-house 1925). The plan (Figure 5.4) is of an embryonic new type. The principal entrance leads to a staircase, a waiting room, parlour, two private (higher class) baths and presumably – since there is no extant first floor plan – to the keeper's flat. The parlour, with its two internal doors as well as door and window into the yard, doubled as the pay office. The waiting room opens both towards the two private baths and to the yard. A more modest entrance leads into a yard from which eight (lower class) bath cubicles open. A staircase leads to a first floor bathroom – either containing an identical set of eight cubicles or further private cubicles – and a reading room. Opening off the yard are privies, the boiler house, ash pit and coal house, a staircase leading to the basement wash-house and drying room (with hot air pipes) below the bathroom, and a wash-house 'for infected cloths' (sic). How the first floor accommodation interconnects must remain a matter for conjecture but probably the reading room was accessible from both staircases.

The shortcomings of the plan were already evident to a Sub-committee of the Corporation's

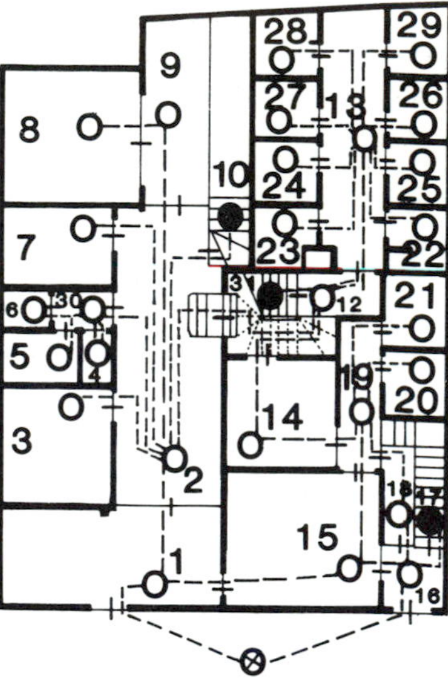

Key

1 Yard
2 Yard
3 Wash house
4 Privy
5 Ash pit
6 Privy
7 Coals
8 Boiler house
9 Yard
10 Stairs to basement wash house
12 Landing and stairs to bath and reading rooms above
13 Bathroom
14 Waiting room
15 Parlour
16 Principal entrance
17 Stairs to upper floor
18 Passage
19 Passage
20 Private bath
21 Private bath
22 Bath cubicle
23 Bath cubicle
24 Bath cubicle
25 Bath cubicle
26 Bath cubicle
27 Bath cubicle
28 Bath cubicle
29 Bath cubicle
30 Lobby
31 Landing and stairs to bath and reading rooms above

Figure 5.4
Frederick Street baths and wash-house, Liverpool (1842), ground floor plan and schematic plan showing connectivity
Source: *Report . . . Wash-house* (1925), and author's drawing

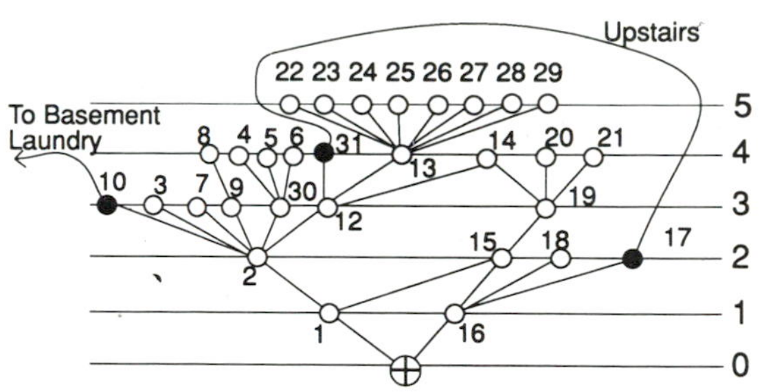

Figure 5.5

Frederick Street baths and wash-house, Liverpool (1842), spatial map

Source: Author's drawing

Health Committee only five months after the opening (Report … Wash-house 1925: 4). The building is too small; the bathroom should have had windows on both sides for light and air; the laundry should not have been in the basement but should have opened into a spacious yard to give sun and air for clothes drying. Most significant is the comment that in future the bathrooms should be on the ground floor, divided 'down the middle (so) that both sexes may bathe at any hour of the day'. In other words in this first bath both private (higher) and lower class cubicles were unisex, separation being by division of time rather than of space.

From the street the spatial structure (Figure 5.5) bifurcates – one side the keeper's quarters, private (i.e. upper class) baths and, probably reading room, the other lower class baths, services, clothes washing and drying, privies and, possibly, also the reading room. The privies are shared by, and accessible to both classes. This split separates things perceived as soiled – dirty clothes, infected clothes, privies and dirty bodies (lower class baths) – from things perceived as clean – keeper, clean bodies (upper class baths) and, probably, reading. The two trees are joined into rings by spaces 14 and 15 – the waiting room and parlour – spaces forming part of both the keeper's and and the visitors' domains. The deep spaces on remote branches of trees are those where technical apparatus cleans bodies and clothes – baths, privies, laundry and wash-house for infected clothes.

The polarities men/women, upper/lower class and clean/dirty became a lasting feature after the 1846 Act. In 1847 the first parish baths built under the Act were opened in Orange Street, St-Martin-in-the-Fields. Within five years London had seven establishments; these have either disappeared or been substantially rebuilt. Weinreb and Hibbert (1983: 624–5) give a useful list of survivors. By 1851 there was one or more in some 25 towns (*Builder* 1851: 834) and the Committee opened its own grand model in Goulston Square, Whitechapel (Figure 5.6) designed by P.P. Baly in 1847, the first under the Act. The four entrances embody both gender and class distinctions. The pair in the centre are for men – first and second class entering into a shared lobby and then dividing. The lateral ones are for women. Another pairing is left, second, and right, first class. The plunge bath, for men only, has a separate entrance at the front and the wash-house is at the rear.

The meaning of the entrance locations is analysed on Figure 5.8 in terms of locational 'dominance' (front/side/rear; centre/edge). The classification distinguishes by gender (men/women), by economic class (first/second), and by function (body- cleansing/body-exercise-with-leisure/clothes cleansing). It is evident that body cleansing for both first and second class men is more dominant than the women's equivalent; that the (classless) men's plunge bath shares a position with women's first and second class body cleansing; and that clothes cleansing (in the women's domain) has the lowest position.

The Act laid down maximum charges for a full range of bathing and washing facilities, including open air bathing but, oddly, not for plunge baths. It prescribed twice the number of baths for the labouring classes as that of 'any higher class' and an Amending Act of 1847 applied the same ratio to washing places.

In Liverpool, as in all large cities, the demand far outgrew the provision and a second bathhouse in Cornwallis Street opened in 1851. By 1854 the Frederick Street establishment was rebuilt and dedicated entirely to laundry use.

The pattern is familiar: immediately following legislation a few architects not only collar the commissions but produce the standard textbooks. In this case Ashpitel and Whichcord (1851) were first, and Baly (1852) followed quickly with model plans. That for large towns (Figure 5.7) has first and second class division for everything – men's and women's baths, men's plunge baths, and laundry. Only the second class laundry has drying cabinets and an ironing room; the more luxurious first class was for those women, or their servants, who had sufficient drying and ironing facilities at home. Men enter at the front, women at the side, as before, in accordance with a morphology of classes where gender takes priority over economic class.

Ashpitel and Whichcord's Bilston baths and wash-house (*Builder* 1852: 597) has a *'swimming'* bath, much larger than the typical plunge bath and for men only. In their textbook (1853) this

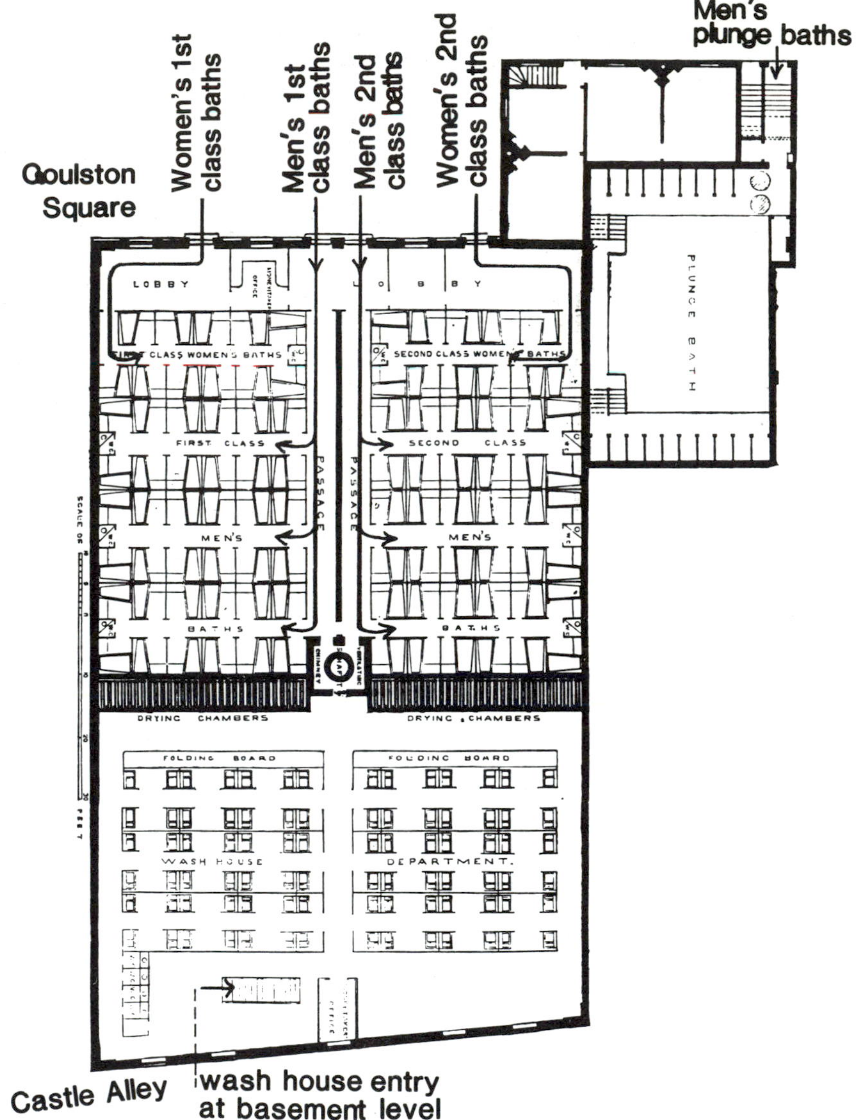

Figure 5.6

Baly's model baths, Goulston Square, Whitechapel (1847), plan

Source: Baly (1852), British Architecture Library

significant label change continues. In one huge scheme there is a large swimming pool for each of the first and second class men, but none for women. But both sexes have small plunge baths. In another men are divided into *three* classes ('gentlemen', 'first' and 'second') but share a swimming bath, in the spirit of Republican Rome, whilst women have neither sub-division into class nor a swimming bath; their wash-house has a side entrance.

In a plate recalling Hamilton's sketch books, two model baths are grouped with those of Diocletian and Pompeii. The larger has two huge *swimming* baths for men, and a tiny *plunge* bath for first class women.

The spatial structure, the entrance locations (Figure 5.8) and the formal imagery carry a number of meanings. First, gender definition has primacy over economic class and function. Secondly, as the body gradually becomes released from hygiene, to stretching or plunging and finally to the full freedom of swimming, provision for men always has priority, both chronologically and in space. Thirdly female distinctions in economic class and function are less articulated than male ones; women represent a *general* category less capable of internal discrimination.

Baly's image of 'women at work' (Figure 5.9), with four round-shouldered, almost hunchbacked figures enclosed in highly mechanised washing

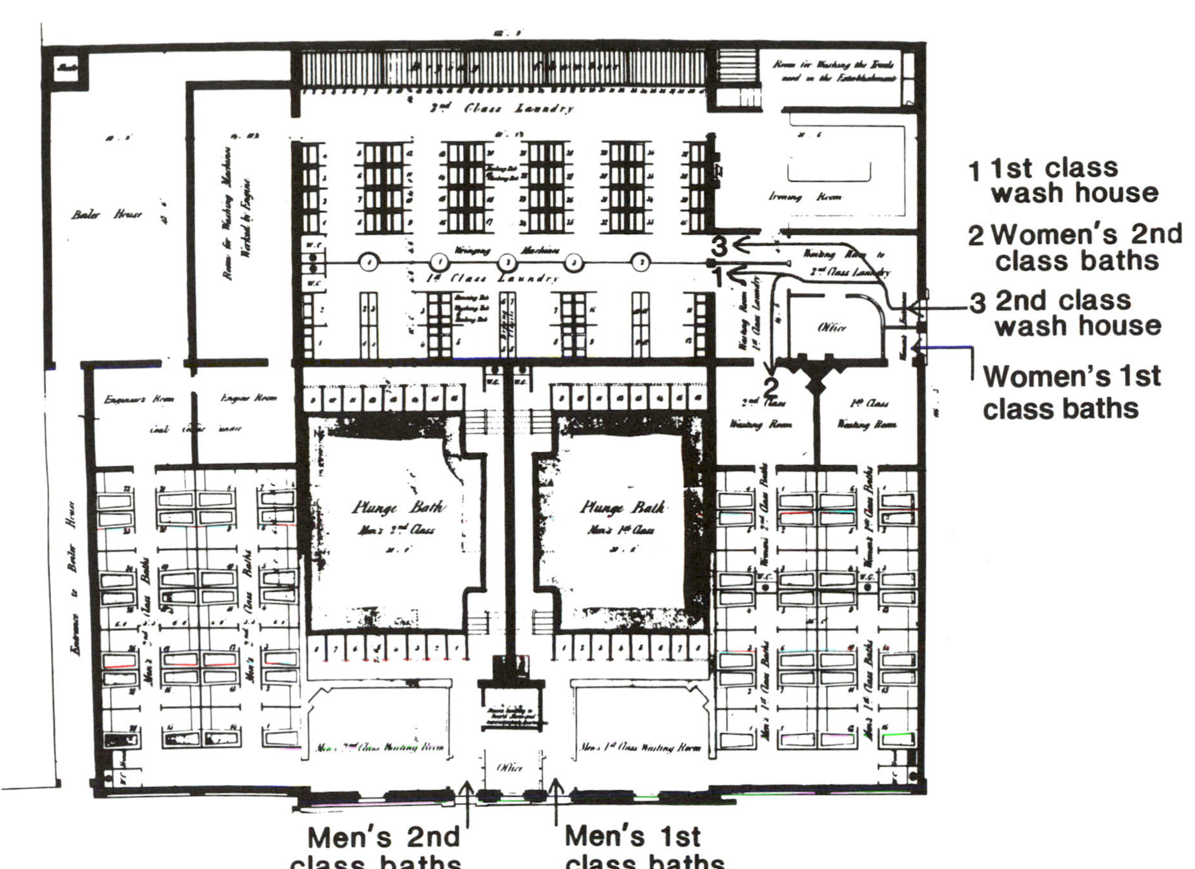

Figure 5.7

Baly's model baths and wash-house 'for large towns' (1852), plan

Source: Baly (1852), British Architecture Library

Figure 5.8

Map of dominance in baths and wash-houses, Goulston Square (a), and Baly's 'large town' model (b)

Source: Author's drawings

Key

M = Men
W = Women
1 = First class
2 = Second class
B. Cl = Body cleansing
B. Ex/L = Body exercise/leisure
C. Cl = Clothes cleansing (washing, drying, ironing)
—·—· Adjacency in space

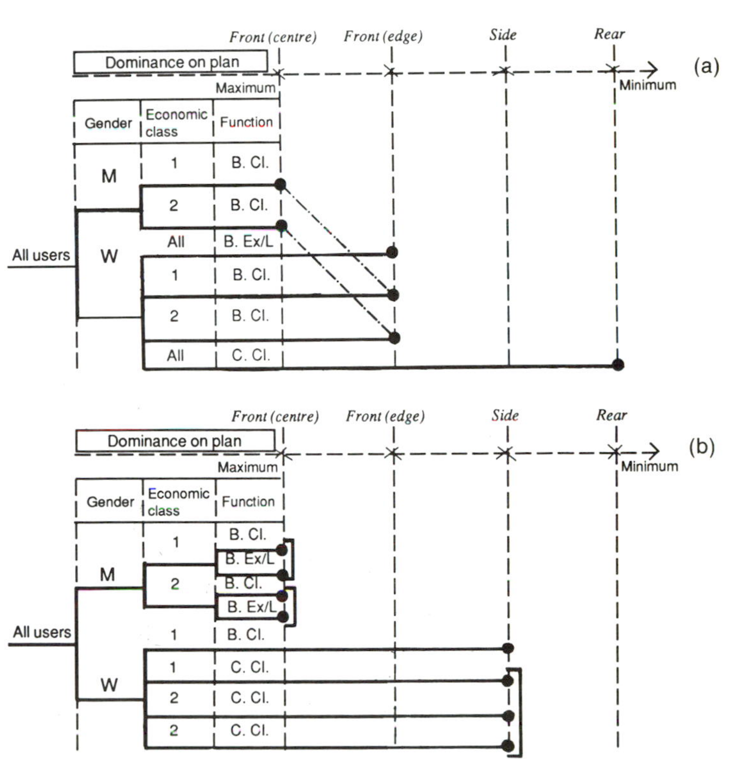

and drying compartments, is in striking contrast with his allegorical frontispiece (Figure 5.10) where serene young women crowd around a fountain, to give drink to a poor man, fill jugs, and wash children. Not an item of laundry or an unwashed adult – the sole targets of baths and wash-houses – sullies the scene. The labouring women are isolated and contained; the water nymphs are in a free social group.

The building is itself a metaphor. Since dirt was equated with crime, a place which cleanses is a place of morality and decency. Division is the rule: entrances separate by class and gender and lead to isolated cubicles and partitioned wash rooms. A fear expressed in Parliament was that wash-houses would:

Drawing shewing the Arrangement of a Washing and Drying Compartment with Women at work.

1. *Woman Washing.*
2. *Woman hanging up her Linen.*
3. *Wash and Boiling Tub.*
4. } *Drying Chamber heated by Hot Water.*
4a. } *Drying Chamber heated by Gas.*
5. *Slide Door to enclose the Chamber.*
6. *Balance Weights for Slide Doors.*
7. *Hollow Bricks to confine the heat in the Chamber.*

Scale of ... *Feet*

Figure 5.9

Women at work in washing and drying compartments

Source: Baly (1852), British Architecture Library

Figure 5.10

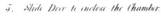

Baly's metaphor of cleanliness

Source: Baly (1852), frontispiece, British Architecture Library

> take women from their homes, to the neglect of their children and domestic duties; that it would cause them to congregate in great number, the good and the bad together; and if it did no worse, would lead to gossiping and tattling.
>
> (quoted by Goodman 1982)

The home was the model: in the clothes-washing cubicles 'every woman was entirely separated from her neighbour and did her work as privately as if in her own washouse' (quoted by Goodman 1982: 13). Cheap drying horses in long ranges might become places of gossip and were replaced by expensive individual cubicles. Ironing needed large open space for a communal activity but, since here working women might establish solidarity, the rhetoric of 'decent privacy' was soon mobilised to suppress it.

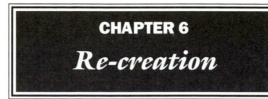

CHAPTER 6
Re-creation

Cleanliness is a thread common to both reform and recreation, each of which generated its characteristic building types. Those for the latter, the subject of this chapter, had to be places where a self-selected group could unite to share leisure and pleasure. The activity had to be visibly, even ostentatiously, the group's, not the private ostentation of, say, a dandy in a street or even of a landed family in its country seat. It could be eating and drinking; playing games; gambling for large sums; sports and collaborative pastimes; washing and bathing; dancing; taking part in musical and dramatic performances; or taking holidays. Sometimes it needed a temporary luxurious residence.

These places are not like sports stadia, race courses, and inns – excluded here – which either span social classes or are specifically for those with little power. Popular recreation may have an element of voluntary choice, but it cannot be a re-assertion of a non-existent power. Rather it is an escape from the reality of powerlessness, or an assertion of the alternative power of the crowd. It shares more with fairs or bear-baiting and especially with carnivals which license a temporary inversion of power. Only a thin line divides it from demonstrations, marches or ultimately riots. Often it uses temporarily appropriated or interstitial urban space. The public provision of major buildings or parks for popular recreation is itself a political act; the municipal swimming pool and the spa are as different as chalk and cheese since the resources for the first are conditional on the acceptance of tight spatial and managerial conditions, often built into legislation.

There is one other exclusion – the theatre, where scholarly work is vast. The way its distinct entrances and auditorium zones articulate social class, using the mechanism of price, influenced the lecture theatres considered later.

These new types were the *habitats* of controllers rather than controlled. What can be predicted about them? If status is to be visible then the audience has to be large. Moreover the process is mutual – participants are both actors and audience. This needs large, unobstructed space for chance encounters with a choice of routes, that is rings. The group is exclusive but, once admitted, unconstrained. That implies that the encounter space is shallow and access to it is by one or a few tightly controlled 'gates' in a firm boundary. The exterior would declare something of the opulence within; the interior would reproduce the familiar features of élite residences.

One prototype, the coffee house – not the contemporary French café, an all purpose drinking and eating place for both sexes and for all classes – has only hints of these features. It was a seventeenth century invention in Oxford (Ellis 1956) soon copied in large numbers in London, many destroyed in and rebuilt after the Fire. By the end of the century there were over two thousand, concentrated where commercial and social power was exercised – the banks, exchanges and major trading houses, universities, lawcourts, élite scientific and medical societies, and theatres. Each had its specialised clientele. By the mid-eighteenth century the City of London is thick with coffee houses, some on substantial sites. They had a single space, with fireplace, tables, benches and chairs, and adjacent service apartments, often on the first floor above a shop or office. Plans of run-of-the-mill coffee houses are scarce. Better known are grander examples such as Robert Adam's New British Coffee House (1770)

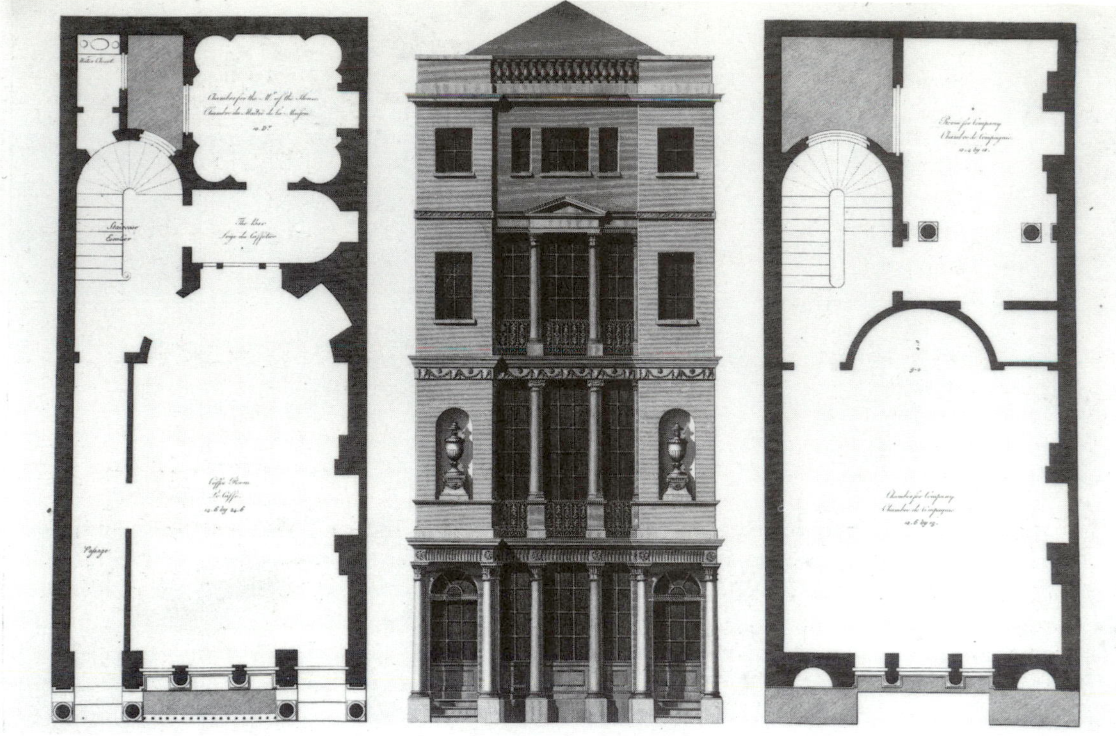

Figure 6.1

Robert Adam's design for the New British Coffee House, Cockspur Street, London (1770)

Source: *The Works in Architecture of Robert and James Adam* vol. 2 (1779 and 1786), facsimile V, plate iv, British Architecture Library

– the haunt of London's Scots in Cockspur Street (Figure 6.1). The large ground floor coffee room has two axes of symmetry; on the shorter lies the main entrance opposite the fireplace. The master is located behind the bar. The staircase leads to two 'company' rooms on the first floor and the master's residence above.

As *habitués* formed more tight-knit groups, disseminating priveleged information by word of mouth, printed handbills, newspapers and pamphlets, they created partitioned boxes to mark their identity. Increased entrance charges gave greater selectivity until finally some groups clubbed together and bought up entire coffee houses for their exclusive use. This was the birth of the club as well as of famous business houses such as Lloyds and the Stock Exchange. The close association with the professions, the military, politics and business inevitably made coffee houses a male preserve, a tradition carried through into clubs.

The first London clubs such as Boodle's were formalisations of the coffee house in the guise of an elegant house. The owners were individuals not corporate bodies. In some, such as Brooks' designed by Henry Holland (1774), the major space was the 'subscription' (gambling) room. When White's was remodelled by Robert Adam (1787-8) the tri-partite, bi-axial coffee room was its dominant space.

But the new early nineteenth century club, whilst remaining élite and male, was corporate. Its new management and rules needed a new type of building. To understand it requires analysis of plans, which speak of function and spatial ordering. But compared to arcane speculations about style these are scarce in the literature.

The United Service Club, founded in 1815 as a post-Waterloo celebration of military solidarity, occupied rooms in Albermarle Street before moving to Robert Smirke's club-house (1817–19) in Charles Street (Figure 6.2) where its largest spaces were the ground floor coffee room, tri-partite as the New British and White's had been, and a saloon above it. There were also a dining room, library, four parlours, and basement kitchen and staff quarters. The plan became a standard model, but as yet there are few significant rings.

By 1827 the building was too small and John Nash designed the new house in Pall Mall. In his original scheme (Figure 6.3) the long coffee room was at the rear of the ground floor, again with a tri-partite articulation. The library above was of the same size.

With William Wilkins's University Club (1822–6)

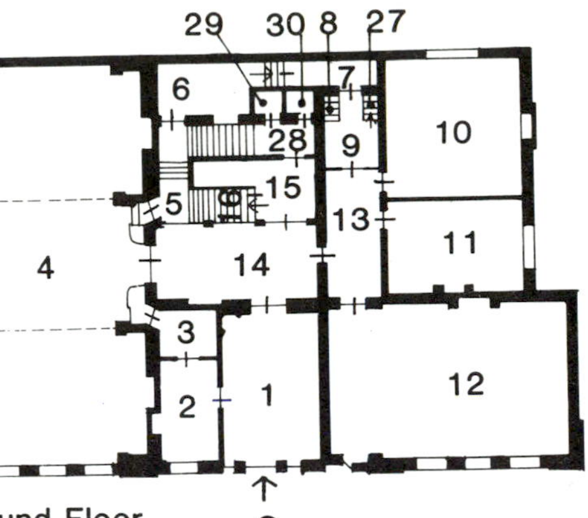

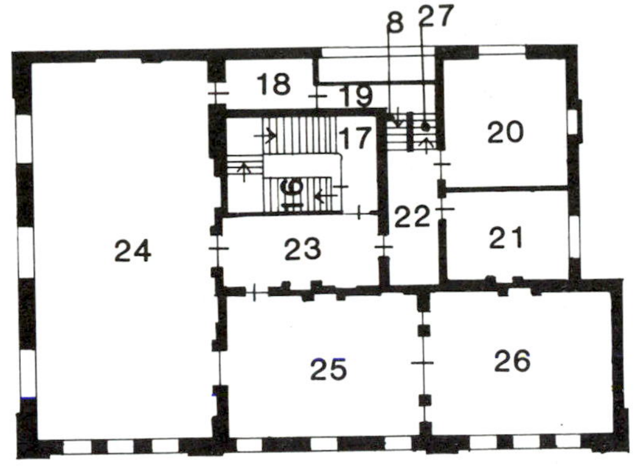

Key

1	Entrance hall	16	Stairs
2	Steward's room	17	Landing
3	Lobby	18	Waiting room
4	Coffee room	19	Landing
5	Landing	20	Parlour
6	Service space	21	Parlour
7	Service space	22	Passage
8	Stairs	23	Ante room
9	Lobby	24	Saloon
10	Parlour	25	Library
11	Parlour	26	Library
12	Dining room	27	Stairs
13	(Use not known)	28	Landing
14	Stairhall	29	Service cupboard
15	Landing	30	Service cupboard

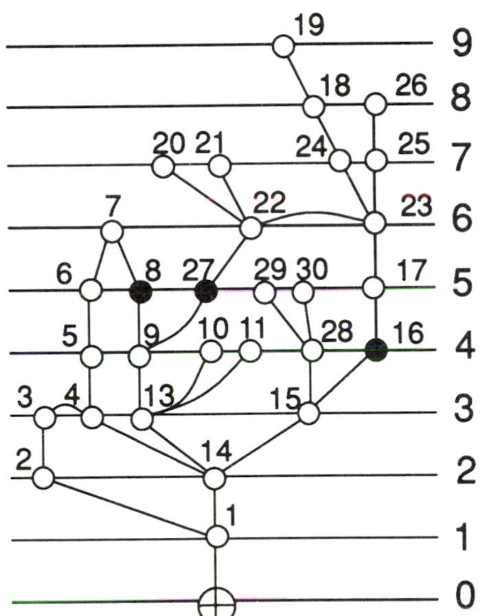

Figure 6.2

United Service Club (1817–19), plan and spatial map

Source: Author's drawing

also in Pall Mall (Figure 6.4) the plan reached maturity: central entrance into a grand stair hall, standard coffee room occupying the full depth of the building, and dining and committee rooms on the ground floor. On the first floor there was a lofty saloon over the coffee room, two library/reading rooms and five members' dressing rooms. Two more floors, not in evidence on the elevation, contain seventeen servants' bedrooms. The kitchen and related services are in the basement.

Smirke, by combining the College of Physicians and the Union Club (1824) on one site in Trafalgar Square (though with separate entrances), made the link between club and profession unusually explicit. The boom was now on; the building of Crockford's and the Oriental overlapped Decimus Burton's Athenaeum (1827–30), where the ground floor coffee room is full depth and the morning and writing rooms form a small ring. The upper floor had a 100 foot long tripartite drawing room stretching over the entire width of the building, library and committee room.

In Charles Barry's Travellers' Club (1829) in Pall Mall, reputedly based on the style of Raphael's Palazzo Pandolfino in Florence, the narrowness of the site pushed the entrance into one corner, leading to an open internal court and a principal staircase well in the depth of the building (Figure 6.5). The coffee room – in its conventional form – stretched the full width across the rear (as did the library above it); nevertheless spatially it is shallow, being linked to the entrance by a short passage through the stair hall. The morning room across the front leads to the dining room which is also accessible from the stair

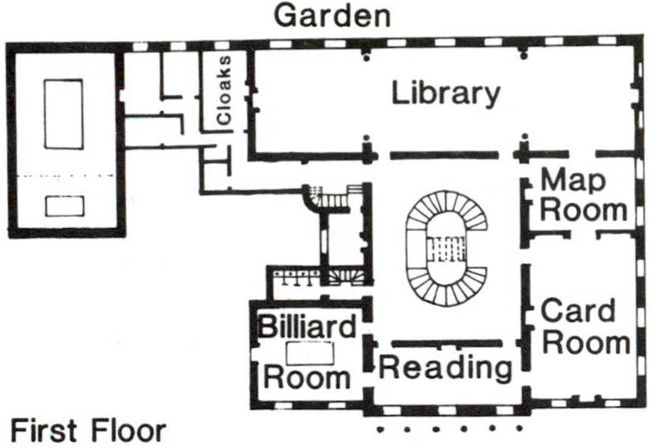

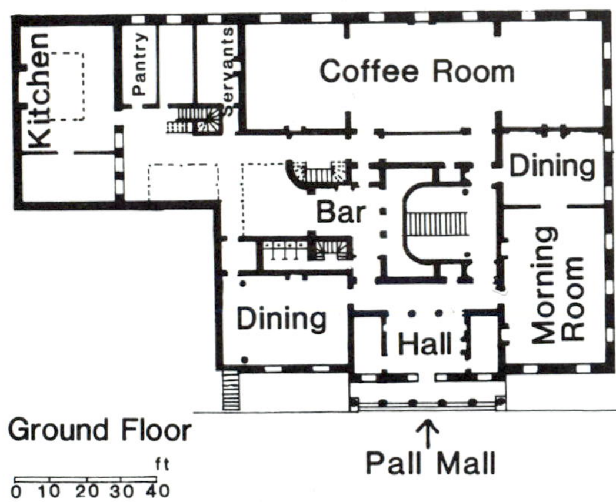

Figure 6.3
United Service Club (1827), plan
Source: Author's drawing

hall and is therefore on a shallow ring. The upper floor has the card and drawing rooms across the front. The steward's and card accountant's bedrooms are in a block entered from the service stair but since the latter is also permeable to the card room, where the servants and members interface, this whole suite lies on a ring from the ground floor.

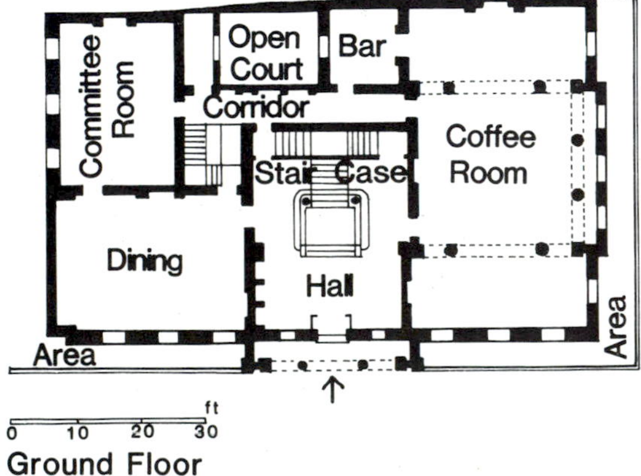

Figure 6.4
University Club (1822–6), plan
Source: Author's drawing

Barry's most important contribution in the *palazzo* style – perhaps inspired by the Farnese – was the Reform Club (1837–41). Its 'reforming' members were behind the 1832 Reform Act, just as those of the adjacent and contemporary Carlton were its opponents. Its real significance resides however not in its style but in the way the plan was organised for the complex brief (Figure 6.6). At its centre was an atrium, initially open to the sky and glazed around its sides, finally covered and roof-lit and open around the sides, surrounded by galleries from which the main apartments open. The coffee room occupied the entire rear, south wing, again elaborately divided into three by two entrances and pilastered spurs. On either side of the entrance were the lower library or morning room, and the dining or strangers' room. On the first floor, and matching the coffee room below, was the drawing room, the upper library above the lower, a smaller private drawing room and the committee room. There were also billiard and card rooms. The entire basement was occupied by a huge and elaborate kitchen and other service accommodation.

Servants were in the attic accessed by a sealed internal staircase. Members' bedrooms on the floor below and on the mezzanine had a staircase from an independent street entrance. Other stairs gave even greater segregation: one for maidservants from the basement to the members' bedrooms; one for members from the ground floor to the mezzanine baths; and a separate one to the billiard room.

Most innovatory was the service system: banks of WCs, two lifts, forced warm air heating combined with ventilation, and a steam engine under the pavement in Pall Mall which heated air in a steam-air heat exchanger to be distributed under pressure from a fan driven by the engine. The engine also raised coal hoists, pumped domestic water to storage tanks and heated hot water. The building was gas-lit, and some burners were ventilated so as to extract their own combustion products and also to ventilate the entire room. The location of service spaces, ducts, shafts and hoists was an important organising principle. The more perceptive critics recognised this as a truly modern building.

Foremost was César Daly (1857). The club is:

> not an inert mass of stone, brick and cast iron, but almost a living body with its own systems of blood circulation and nerves. In its walls, so

> fixed in their appearance, there actually circulate gas, steam, fluids, liquids; in carefully examining it one discovers flues, conduits, wires – the arteries, veins and nerves of this new organised being – by means of which heat is conducted in winter, cool air in summer, and throughout the year light, hot water, cold water, nourishment for the body and all those accessories which speak of a high civilisation.
> (Daly 1857: 346–7)

Service orders are transmitted silently through 'secret passages' avoiding the usual tangle of metal wires, bells and noise. 'In this building, modern science is our servant: it is prompt, obedient, clean . . .'. Modern critics might learn from Daly's recognition that its modernity lies not 'in the architectural style of its facade, which is of the Italian school, nor in the organisation of the plan, intelligent as that is, but in something more intimate, invisible to the eye, not immediately obvious, but nevertheless palpable everywhere and in everything': comfort.

The combinatiom of communal and residential space makes it a precursor of the urban hotel. But the hotel's residential accommodation was open to all; access to specific hotels or different parts of a given hotel was governed by price which replaced membership as the instrument of exclusion. Moreover its public spaces, also open to non-residents for a range of social, entertainment and commercial functions, still incorporated elements from the coffee house and club. But the grand space of another tradition – that of the assembly rooms – was also grafted on.

I have already mentioned them as elements of the spa. But they were more ubiquitous. Their origin was dancing and entertainment in aristocratic mansions. Balls accompanied by card games and refreshments were celebrations of the opening or closing of the hunt, marriage marts, or social exchanges. When the space in the houses was not grand enough (despite, in a number of cases, the addition of ballrooms) or lacked a sufficiently prestigious location, existing urban spaces such as shire halls or grammar schools were temporarily appropriated (Girouard 1986: 542).

From the 1720s specialised assembly rooms appeared, sometimes as components of town or Shire halls (Girouard 1986: 542–4). At Warwick the Court House was too limited for the larger race week assemblies. In the new Shire Hall (1754–8) designed by Sanderson Miller the enormous entrance area became a ballroom and the lawcourts then formed card rooms. In Belfast a 'very spacious and elegant' upper floor assembly hall was added (1769) to the modest single storey market hall (1766). In Birmingham and Truro assembly spaces were added to theatres. The truly independent building is a clearer case of the type, and was often intended to unite previously separated assemblies of different social class – for instance those in and out of trade.

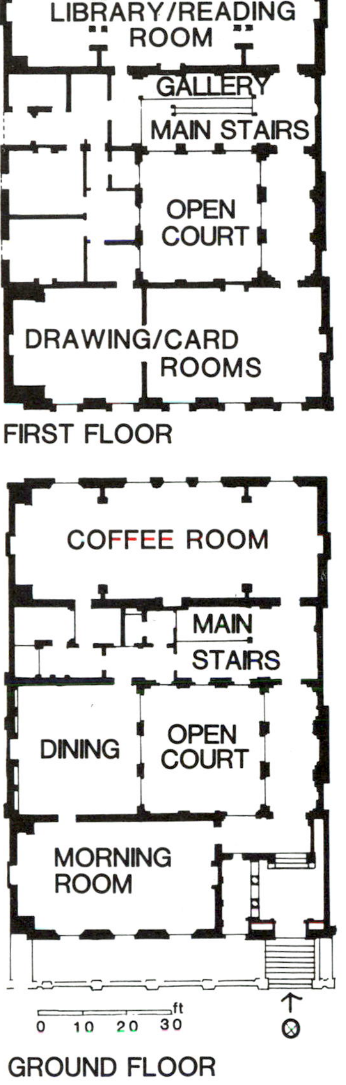

Figure 6.5 *Travellers' Club (1829), plan*
Source: Author's drawing

The early, and still surviving, modest room at Stamford in Lincolnshire (c. 1726) was eclipsed by Lord Burlington's York Assembly Rooms (1730–2). William Newton's Old Assembly Rooms at Newcastle-upon-Tyne (1774–6) has the same organisation: a formal entrance lobby leading

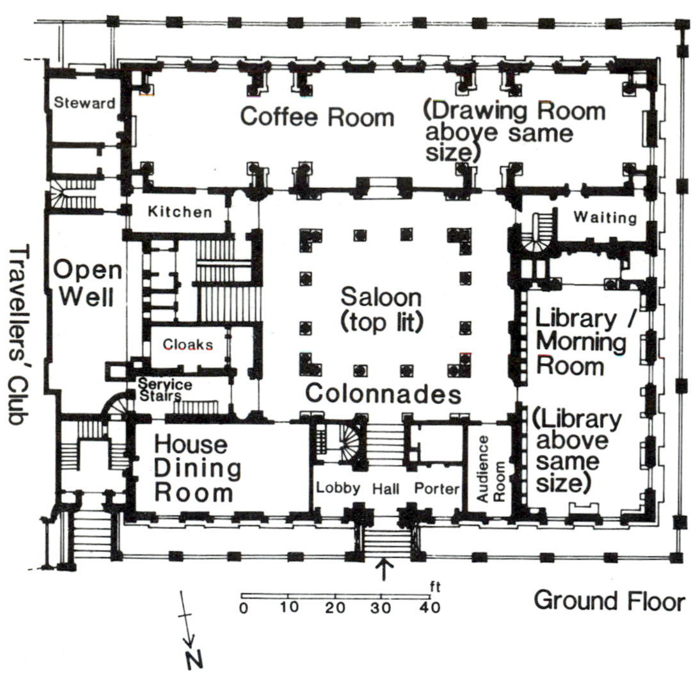

Figure 6.6

Reform Club (1837–41), plan

Source: Author's drawing

straight to the large supper room with the ballroom above; a smaller assembly room over a subscription library and coffee room; and connected card rooms, sitting rooms and bars, all lying on shallow spatial rings (Figure 6.7).

Girouard reckons that in England and Wales at least seventy assembly rooms were built in the century from 1720 – possibly two or three times this number (1986: 766). Neale's (1981) seminal discussion of the most prestigious one, in Bath, contrasts with descriptions of architectural gems or anecdotes of *milieux* of elaborate social rituals. He adopts Castells' definition of space as a social product in opposition to:

> histories of building and architecture in eighteenth-century Bath (where) it has sometimes been the practice to raise questions about the social significance or meaning of Bath. This has usually arisen from the belief that architecture, including the architecture of eighteenth-century Bath, is art. For then it becomes proper to ask questions about architecture similar to those asked about other forms of art. And, as art, Bath may be thought of as a kaleidoscope of individual and sometimes collective acts of creativity, rather like the Book of Kells or St Peter's in Rome. It may also be thought of as embedded within an artistic tradition; it could not have been built had not Brunelleschi created the Pazzi Chapel in Florence and Palladio written his *Quattro Libri dell'Architettura*. And so one may ask questions about the meaning of Bath.
>
> (Neale 1981: 172–3)

Neale says these questions are usually answered in one of three ways. First, 'objectively' – concerned with appearance. Buildings are described in their form and visible functions. Second, 'expressively' – an attempt to understand inner intentions such as John Wood's ideas about Classical towns and the unity of man and nature. Third, in a 'documentary' way – 'Bath as some kind of collective thing symptomatic of ideas and concepts outside or beyond the city itself. It is said ...' (referring to Summerson, Ison, Pevsner and others) 'that the city reflects the Spirit of the Age, Whiggism, or the Age of Reason' (Neale 1981: 173).

Neale's analysis uses the material evidence to disentangle the web of social processes – conflict, solidarities, economic forces and concludes that:

> the Rooms, once its proprietors had successfully eliminated their competitors, carried out the same social task. For a price it provided a social forum for the preservation and promotion of order, decorum, and regularity in society; at least at the upper levels. It was, therefore, not only an expression of competition but also a secular symbol of the moral order felt necessary for the efficient functioning of a market society. Without such a moral order, the market economy of civil society is ever in danger of degeneration, of collapsing into licence, even within the ranks of the propertied – absolute property breeds absolute self interest.
>
> (Neale 1981:225)

John Wood the Younger's New Rooms (1769–71) became, with York, the spatial model (Figure 6.8). It had been preceded by two in Terrace Walk – Harrison's 'Lower' Rooms (1708) with a large ballroom added in 1720 and further enlarged in 1749, and Lindsey's (later Wiltshire's) Rooms, built to designs by John Wood the Elder (1728–30) where 'Beau' (Richard) Nash, Bath's Master of Ceremonies from 1708 to 1761 devised his social régimes which, with those of Captain William Wade, his successor in the New Rooms, became the model of etiquette.

The west entrance for sedan chairs led into a portico and vestibule to which those arriving by carriage walked along glazed-in arcades from the two corner pavilions. A central corridor leads to an octagonal, top-lit antechamber which gives access to the three main spaces: ballroom to the north, tea room to the south and, straight ahead to the east, the octagonal card room which also connects the two other spaces. Beyond the tea-room serving bar was the ladies' drawing room and water closets. Two symmetrical staircases lead to three musicians' galleries, that for the card room having an organ. The spatial structure consists of two shallow surface rings constituted by the entrances, a central tree, two inner rings of the three main spaces and then a deeper tree, at the tip of which is the ladies' drawing room (Figure 6.9). The meaning is clear: free and open mingling at the surface interfaces with the three streets; controlled access to all public spaces; freedom for a variety of encounters within them; and then a highly segregated and deep space for those who, in their quintessential 'gentleness', are perceived as weak – the women.

Almost contemporary was Ensor's round assembly room (1764–7) added to Dublin's Lying-in-Hospital (1751–4), henceforth known as The Rotunda. From the start the founder, Dr Mosse, on the Peter and Paul principle raised money for the hospital by developing houses and pleasure gardens for the wealthy on surrounding land (Browne 1947). With two further assembly rooms added in 1784 the complex became an architectural metaphor for philanthropy – élite wealth maintaining the most deprived – as in London's Foundling Hospital and Bath's General Hospital. But here, by attaching the most potent sign of conspicuous wealth, assembly rooms, to a women's charity hospital, the interdependence of capital and poverty was marvellously displayed both by buildings and by the continuous juxtaposition of the two groups of people. Adam Smith's 'invisible hand', which creates social benefit as the unintended consequence of even naked greed, was made concrete.

Music was always a component, as it was in the popular public gardens and halls like Vauxhall and Ranelagh. But this was also the time of specialised concert rooms sponsored by music societies so they and, as we have seen, assembly rooms, were added to old inns when public recreational or spa space was in short supply. Pevsner (1979: 170–2) places the transition from inn to hotel at the moment when, instead of being grafted on, such space becomes integrated. But the new prototype was also a response to the demand for temporary

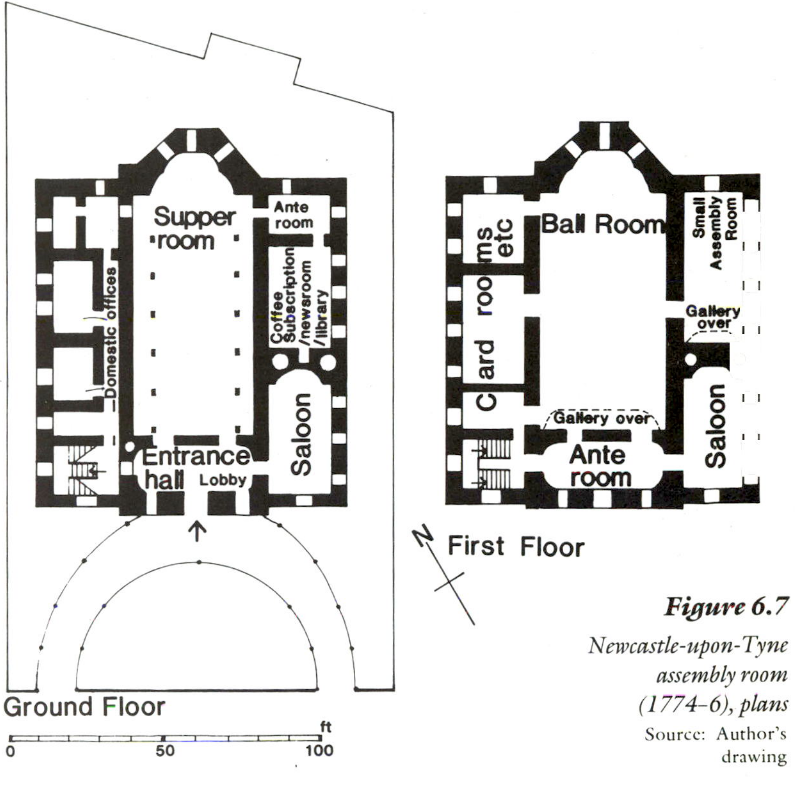

Figure 6.7

Newcastle-upon-Tyne assembly room (1774–6), plans

Source: Author's drawing

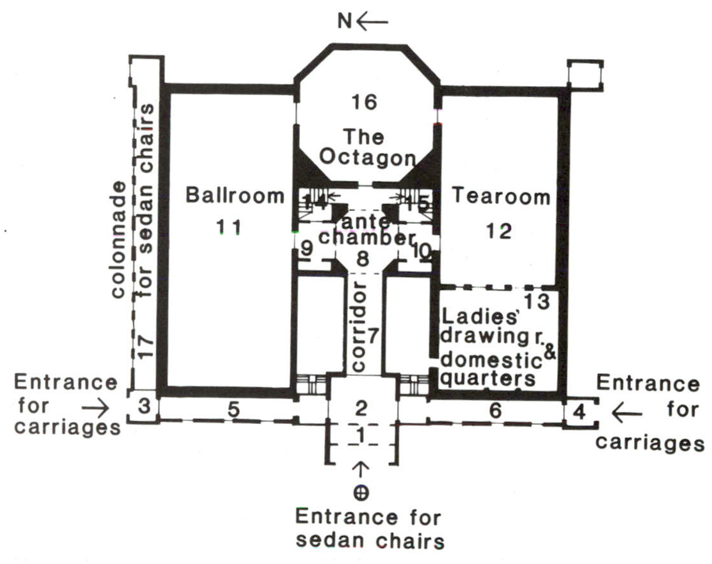

Figure 6.8

Bath's New or Upper assembly room (1769–71), plan

Source: Author's drawing

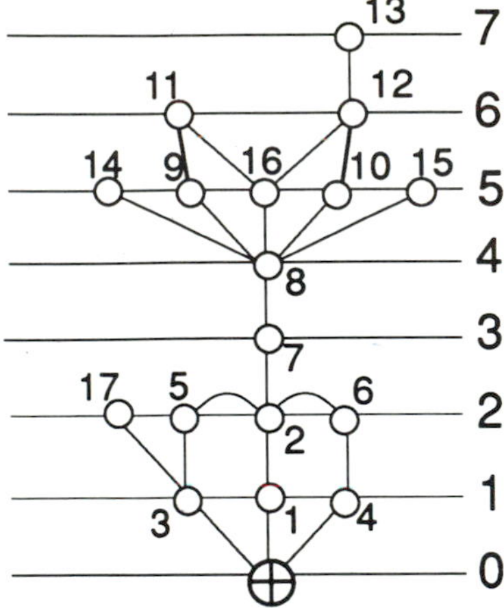

Figure 6.9
Bath's New or Upper assembly room, spatial map
Source: Author's drawing

urban accommodation created by the entrepreneurs and commercial travellers of the early Industrial Revolution and, once the railway network was developed, by a vast travelling public.

Naturally the new hotel drew on and transformed the older spatial and functional elements: the inn, with courtyards, guest rooms, dining rooms and stabling; the coffee house; the club with coffee, morning and 'company' rooms and libraries; the assembly, concert and ballrooms; the watering and bathing place with cubicled baths, pools and pump rooms; and, on occasion, more surprising admixtures of a learned society with its lecture room, the theatre or the shop.

Pevsner's (1979: 172) prototypical case of the *Badischer Hof* at Baden-Baden (1807–9) was matched by a British hotel equally eccentric in its combination of funtions – Foulston's Royal Hotel (1811–19) at Plymouth (Figure 6.10). Attached, and creating the symmetry of the main elevation, was a theatre. Also, but with a separate entrance, the Athenaeum – the local Literary and Philosophical Society. The hotel entrance was adjacent to the two theatre entrances, with two more at the side. There was a billiard room, card rooms, a vast dining room also used as an assembly tea room; a modest coffee room and a first floor ball room. The ground floor had a row of private dining rooms; on the first and second rows of completely interconnected rooms were usable at choice as bedrooms, dining rooms or sitting rooms, so that various sized suites could match demand. There was also a 'commercial' room for meetings and travelling exhibitions of samples. The complex was planned around a great courtyard with stables, hay lofts and other service spaces, whilst the basement had servants' rooms.

In America the main innovation was size. The City Hotel in New York (1794–6) had 73 rooms; Asher Benjamin's Boston Exchange Coffee House (1806–9) 200, with a subscription library, a dining room for 300, a Masonic hall and a central five-storey domed atrium on the floor of which was a merchants' exchange. By the 1820s and 1830s the establishments were vast – Baltimore's City Hotel (1825–6) had over 200 bedrooms, Boston's Tremont (1827–30) 170, Astor House in New York (1832–6) 309 and the St Charles in New Orleans (1837) 600. Sanitation had to become more sophisticated as it moved to upper floors. Whereas the Tremont's eight ground floor privies were on the remote side of the courtyard, and its eight bathrooms in the basement, Astor House had 17 bathrooms and upper floor privies.

The railways generated the multi-class hotel: the first the Prince of Wales in two converted houses for the first Paddington Station (1838). The Bridge House Hotel at London Bridge Station (1838) was the first to be purpose-built. At Euston Philip Hardwick designed a 'hotel' (the Adelaide) and a 'dormitory' (1839); the latter had bedrooms, with some small attached sitting or drawing rooms, and a coffee room for breakfast, whilst the former was on more conventional, lavish lines with suites of rooms and full dining facilities. The class division of the trains enabled first class passengers to drive their carriages alongside the railway and have them lifted and fastened onto flatcars, either to travel in them or in luxurious railway 'carriages'. The same class division which shaped the station's space, was now extended to the hotel.

The final step was the combination of hotel and station at the head or side of the train shed. This created a complex planning problem. The ground floor waiting rooms and ticket offices were classified by economic class and the former also by gender. They had to allow permeability from the street to the shed. Passengers had to be separated from hotel guests – travellers, non-travellers and non-residents – who expected entry from both the station and the street. G.T. Andrews' York station and hotel (1840–1) was one of the earliest. Despite the plan's complexity, certain prototypical features survive intact – notably the coffee room and ball or assembly room. Their durability is remarkable; Henry Curry's London Bridge Station Hotel (1861) has a coffee room, ladies' coffee room and a library – elements of a spatial tradition over a century old – and 150 bedrooms above (Figure 6.11).

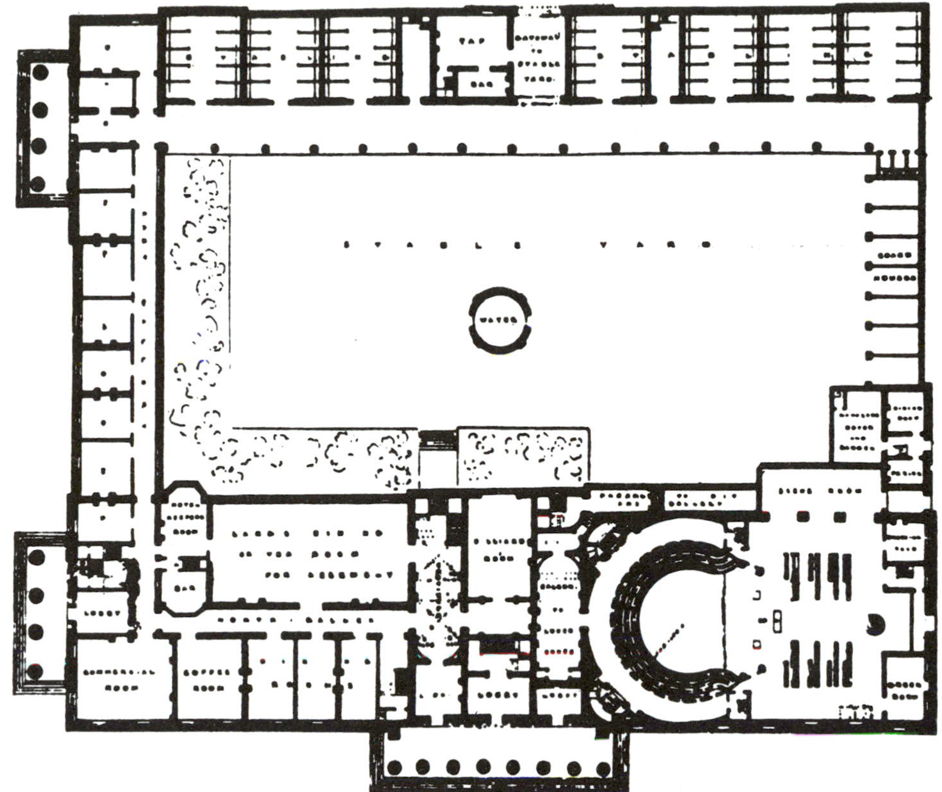

Figure 6.10
Foulston's Royal Hotel, Plymouth (1811–19), ground floor plan and exterior view
Source: Foulston (1838), British Library

The huge multi-storey railway and independent urban hotels could only be realised by stretching the technologies of structures, construction, services and lifts to their limits. These are examined in Chapter 10. The hydraulic lift became standard from the 1850s and the penetration of all the floors by vertical tubes of space was an entirely new planning concept. Westminster Palace Hotel (1858) designed by W. and A. Moseley, although only five floors high, had one (Figure 6.12). In the 1860s the 300-bedroom Grosvenor Hotel was more famous for its lifts than its palatial accommodation. Initially they were used for luggage, but passengers soon trusted them. The servants' and cheapest rooms in attics and upper floors (or basements), remote from street noise and fumes, suddenly became the most desirable and expensive.

Developments in waterclosets, water supply and drainage caused equally radical planning changes. Until these became feasible at all floor levels with constancy, adequate pressure and without noxious smells, César Daly's vision of the truly 'organic' building remained a dream. Once this occurred, guests ('visitors') could be shot smoothly and at speed into deep (that is, high) private and clean apartments. The public space, still visibly like that of the mansion, palace and club, was shallow. The two zones, one for ostentatious social interactions the other for private hygienic retreat, together constituted the setting for re-creation.

A paradoxical spatial structure develops. The owners – the railway companies or commercial

Figure 6.11

London Bridge Station Hotel (1861), first floor plan and exterior view

Source: Unknown (possibly an 1860s edition of *The Builder*)

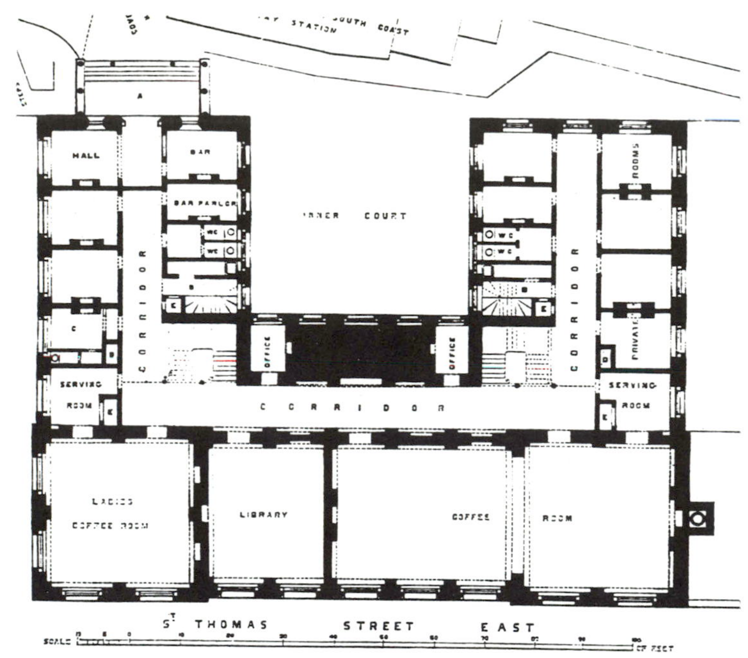

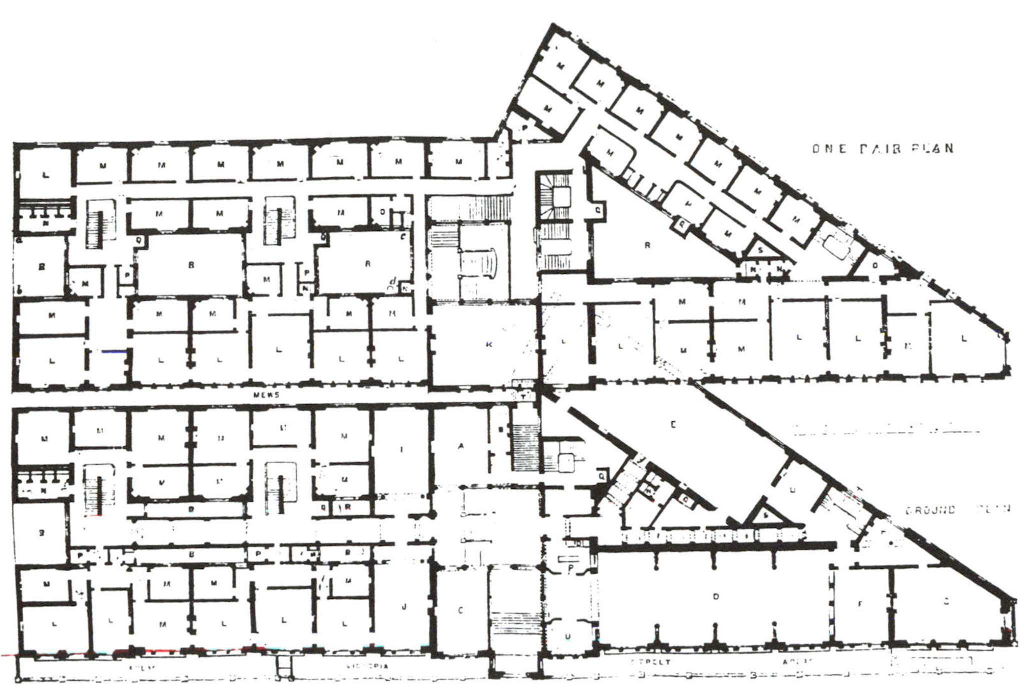

Figure 6.12

Westminster Palace Hotel (1858), plans and front elevation

Source: *The Builder* (1858) April 10

developers – are the 'inhabitants' and should be deep in spatial trees. The 'visitors' should be in outer, shallow rings. But in fact they are in both. The operation of the market has given them the power to turn the owners into their agents, or servants, and buy their way into deep, inhabitant space, without the connotations of the powerless 'visitor' space of institutions. This is not the reversed building. The 'inhabitants', too, are forced to become bi-zonal, operating at the surface as porters and waiters, in deep managerial, financial and personnel offices, and in both zones as servants.

Genet's comparison of the prison with the palace under modern market forces takes on a new meaning. Those with economic power are able to inhabit all space – near (shallow) or remote (deep) – in an analogue of the colonial system. The urban hotels, latter-day palaces, resemble prisons in their spatial structures and sometimes, as a result of the cosmetic and camouflage impulses of reforming prison designers, even in their forms. Only functional labelling, derived from abstract systems of law or rules of management, differentiate them.

PART III

BUILDINGS AND KNOWLEDGE

Introduction

The types in Part II produced social relations. This part is about buildings which produce knowledge. They can do that in several ways. One is to collect and store objects and display them in museums and galleries or make them available for use in libraries. These emerged during our period from restricted, élite domains into the public sphere. Collections of living specimens in zoos and botanic gardens also made the passage from science and medicine to popular instruction. It could also be done by the unique mixture of instruction with entertainment offered by panoramas and dioramas; or by celebrating production and trade in exhibitions. Many of these buildings were ephemeral.

The usual way of producing knowledge is to teach. The characteristic teaching space is the lecture theatre which often reflects the common origins of social relations and knowledge; for instance the first plan for London's Royal Institution had separately entered sections of the theatre for artisans and 'polite' audiences.

Since knowledge is power one should not be surprised by the huge investment in these buildings and their contents by the state, city authorities, Royalty and aristocracy, learned societies, and churches – even in conditions of cultural poverty such as those following the Restoration. And once the working class organised to obtain power it, too, invested capital in knowledge.

Museums, galleries and libraries became subjects for architectural competitions and teaching in the French academies before the Revolution. After a long run of sacred and princely subjects the *Grands Prix* had ten library, museum, exhibition, zoo and botanic gardens subjects in the century from 1744 to 1846 after which they occurred with increasing frequency. Like Ledoux's, Boullée's and Durand's domed pantheons, greek cross galleries and huge axial courtyards, the entries were formal rather than functional explorations.

A familiar pattern recurs. First, all-purpose conglomerates divide into specialised types. At some point these coalesce into a new supertype but maintain their individual specialisation. The early libraries had collections of pictures, sculptures, natural history curiosities and treasures, and anatomy theatres had anatomy museums. After these components developed into distinctive types they again converge – either in single buildings like the British Museum or grouped on one site like South Kensington. Even such modest institutions as Athenaeums and mechanics' institutes with lecture rooms alongside libraries and museums were supertypes.

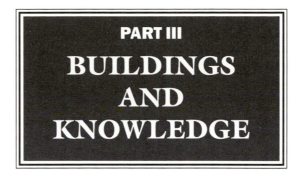

I have already considered how grouping and sequencing depend on a theory of some part of knowledge – in the case of the library on a theory of *all* knowledge. From such theories spring the classifications represented in space. The experts and their theory are hidden; the outcome of the theory is visible in its totality.

In the buildings for teaching, the theory – say of anatomy – is presented through speech, specimens and experiments. Its totality can only be grasped through a course – a series of lectures backed by curricula, programmes and timetables – or through texts. As in the museum, the theory remains hidden, but here the expert, disclosing a small part at a time, is visible.

Because a museum is a classifying device, by continuously moving through its space the visitor recovers the entire system. In the auditorium the visitor is stationary and recovers a fragment of the system.

There was a practical issue. Art objects, museum collections and books have to be seen; lecturers have to be both seen and heard. Seeing and hearing were so central that they became key issues and in the case of dioramas and panoramas encouraged inventions bordering on the fantastic. Traditionally it had been the theatre which taxed designers' acoustic and lighting ingenuity; now, with the aid of new sciences, it was harnessed to the production of knowledge.

CHAPTER 7

Visible knowledge

Objects in space

Buildings for collections are based on programmes of use and circulation which fit the classification. I have already described how a theory of art is embodied in Glasgow's Burrell Gallery and Peponis and Hedin's evidence about theories of evolution in the Natural History Museum.

Forms also contribute, in at least three ways. First iconographically; Duncan and Wallach (1980) show how images, ornament, scale and formal elaboration were exploited to signify the power of the Republican state as guardian of national heritage after the French Revolution. Masson (1981) has examined how mural decorations and sculpture allegorically and symbolically represent the contents of libraries. In the Merton College tomb of Sir Thomas Bodley, founder of Oxford's Bodleian, the allegorical figures of Liberal Arts, Grammar, Dialectic, Rhetoric, Music, Arithmetic, Geometry and Astronomy which decorate it are a 'pictorial catalogue' and heaps of books replace the columns and pilasters of the Orders.

Second, forms work through plans and volumes; Forgan (1986, 1989) shows how changing scientific and teaching paradigms shaped the auditoria of lecture theatres.

But, third, beyond being paradigmatic or didactic tools, forms work *per se*. Sometimes they unify the container and the contained. Exhibits placed in fixed locations – niches, rooms or shrine-like terminals of axes – become actually or metaphorically part of the stonework. When works of art are integrated into a palace or garden the formal language is enriched and the owner's status enhanced.

The rational grid of the Enlightenment and the technology of the Industrial Revolution generated an alternative – a safe, well-lit warehouse. Despite faint memories of the palace, many of the vast nineteenth century galleries were neutral spaces dissociated from their contents and usable for any type of object in any sequence. Today another strategy is available: to make the building itself into a piece of sculpture independent of its contents.

The choice of form is especially agonising when the container is itself a historical munument. Scarpa's conversion of Verona's *Castelvecchio* uses a meticulous archeological approach. The excavation guided his uncompromisingly modern additions and the placing of exhibits. In the same spirit Gasson fixed specific exhibits into the fabric of Glasgow's Burrell Gallery. On the other hand Foster's Sainsbury Centre is in the 'warehouse' tradition; though the technology of the building creates a new metaphorical language this does not fossilise the exhibits. In his Stuttgart *Staatsgalerie* Stirling combines the neutral 'warehouse' for the paintings with monumental circulation space conceived as sculpture. Venturi and Scott, by placing key Renaissance paintings on critical visual axes, adopt the palace spatial tradition for their extension to London's National Gallery.

Texts besides the brief and textbooks are also formative in the organistion of space: the inventories, lists, guides, indices and catalogues which are part of every collection. By summarising the material they stand outside it. They are located in a dedicated space which is not always accessible to the visitor.

In one kind of collection such texts are ambiguous for they are identical to the objects to which they refer; and they have to be accessible to the visitor. This is the library. The literature guides, indices, handbooks, bibliographies (including bibliographies of bibliographies) and, above all, the catalogues stand outside the collection. Yet they are also texts, so the catalogue of a particular collection may contain an entry to itself. The logical effect of this is as disturbing as the visual one of the Klein bottle or the doughnut whose continuous surface makes its hole at once inside and outside. To avoid such ambiguity, the catalogue is given a privileged position, not shelved 'inside' under the appropriate class. (Though the catalogues of *other* libraries are dealt with precisely in that way.) The books it refers to cover the totality of knowledge. So the catalogue, in a compressed way, is equally total. Whether in the form of bound volumes, card indices or a computer database, the catalogue is 'outside'. Its creation and control defines the power of the professional librarian. It is central intellectually, formally and spatially.

The storehouse of knowledge

Its antiquity and epistemological totality makes the library an *arche*type. And since from the beginning other objects of knowledge were stored with the books it is also a *proto*type of the later museum and art gallery. A good place to start.

Literacy is both a tool for the extension of knowledge and for domination. Anthropologists have noted how writing and reading are ways for alienating land from non-writers through lawcourts and bureaucracies. Wills, testimonies, written law and property deeds create assymetries of power and the spaces for producing, storing and using them become privileged. A conflict arose when general literacy demanded cheap texts in space accesible to all. Control could no longer focus on the materiality of books and buildings but had to focus on the content of books and their organisation. The duality of restriction and diffusion present at its birth is ever-present in the history of literacy, and shapes its space.

The act of reading depends on bringing people together with two material entities – books and space. Roche puts it like this:

> The relationship between the presence of books and the space in which they are put to their diverse uses casts light upon the manner in which social, political and educational organisations exist as invisible and abstract entities, and structure the practices of the educated and of the mass of the people.
>
> (Roche 1979: 141)

He identifies the spaces of production and sale, those of private and semi-private reading, and the 'place which is proper to the book, the privileged space of conservation and circulation, the library'.

Private 'privileged' spaces had restricted access. Such libraries had a simple functional programme: a secure boundary, safe storage for the manuscripts or books, the possibility of checking them against an inventory, the ability to find them quickly with the aid of a catalogue which is related to their spatial organisation, and a comfortable space for reading.

In medieval monastic and collegiate libraries parallel rows of shelves, at right angles to the walls, alternated with aisles where readers could sit or stand. These coincided with the windows. O'Gorman (1972) contrasts this narrow, north European *studium* space with the broader tripartite, vaulted Italian 'basilica' library of the late middle ages, in which columns created a nave with two aisles. Clark's (1901) classification of library furniture, though subject to controversy on dates, is widely accepted in principle (Morrish 1973–5: 87–107). He identifies first the 'lectern' system where the books rested on single or double sloping surfaces, and the reader stood or sat facing this slope. The books were usually chained, and sometimes also stored on shelves under the lectern. The model was liturgical. Seats could be single or double, movable or fixed. The 1610 print of the University of Leyden library, where readers stand using a footrest (Figure 7.1), shows the upwards growth of the lectern. For Clark this is a transition to his second system – shelved partitions which separate the single-sided or back-to-back seats of the seventeenth century Oxford and Cambridge college libraries by 'stalls'. One of the earliest (1598–1602) was built by Thomas James, the librarian for the collection gifted by Thomas Bodley to Oxford University.

The invention of printing and the consequent explosion in book production and use required more reading and shelf space. The centre was left open for reading tables and the side and end walls also had to be shelved – Clark's third, 'wall',

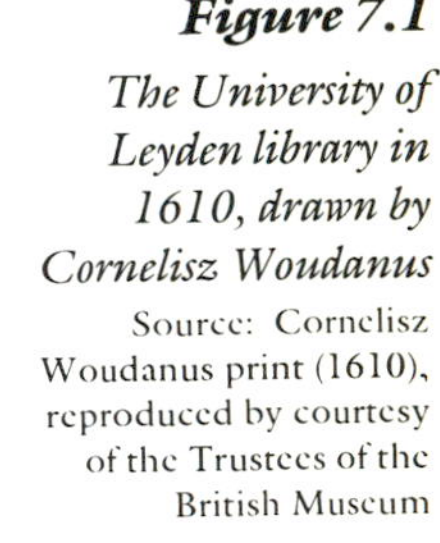

Figure 7.1

The University of Leyden library in 1610, drawn by Cornelisz Woudanus

Source: Cornelisz Woudanus print (1610), reproduced by courtesy of the Trustees of the British Museum

system (Figure 7.2). Further growth required galleries as at Cardinal Borromeo's Ambrosian Library in Milan (1603–9). In Wren's combined stall-with-wall system at Trinity College Cambridge (1676) the bays between the stalls became miniature reading rooms. The wall system dominated the nineteenth century and is indeed still in common use.

James marked the ends of each Bodleian stall by a list of its shelf-by-shelf contents. These formed the basis of his first printed catalogue (1605), one page for each stall, giving the space and its furniture the same structure as that of the catalogue. In the Leyden print the artist has placed such inscriptions boldly on the stalls to show the classes and sequence of the catalogue. The number of bays for a subject is determined by the number and size of its volumes; the number of pages in the catalogue only by the former.

As subject classes became increasingly subdivided they needed an alphabetical author index. Aspects of a given subject which appeared under various classes were collated into an alphabetical subject index. Both represent struggles with the multi-dimensional nature of knowledge. When a philosopher is also a librarian the correspondence between epistemology, book classification and spatial organisation becomes most illuminating. In the attempts from Bacon to Kant to unify scientific knowledge within consistent *schemata*, Leibniz is a key figure. He dreamt of a 'demonstrative encyclopaedia' to avoid the disaster of scholarly chaos threatened by the explosion of knowledge. The fear of 'that horrible mass of books which keeps growing' (quoted by McRae 1961: 70) was concrete in his imagination. Publications at cross purposes to each other would fragment knowledge and bring scholarship into disrepute.

Leibniz came into the service of the Dukes of Brunswick in 1676 as councillor and librarian to John Frederick in Hanover. On appointment in 1690 to look after the huge and celebrated library founded by Augustus the younger at Wolfenbüttel, but now neglected by his sons, he was able to create, though not fully put into practice, a

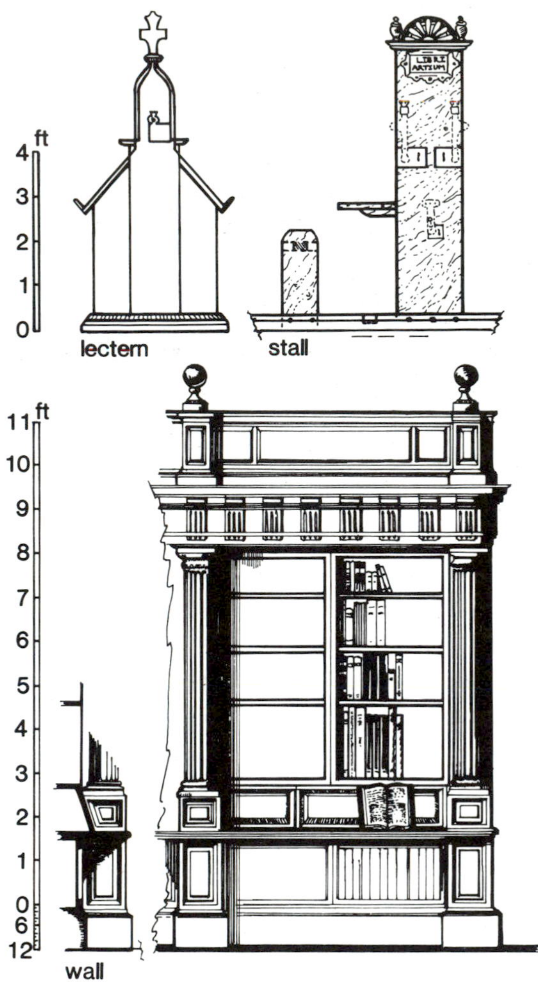

Figure 7.2

'Lectern', 'stall' and 'wall' library systems

Source: Author's drawings based on Clarke (1901)

classification system based on this philosophical quest. Moreover he superintended the erection of Europe's first purpose-built secular library.

He was familiar with European systems (Newman 1966), in particular Naudé's work of 1627, with its insistence on both a subject and an author catalogue. Leibniz was only twenty-two when he started to develop his idea of a universal encyclopaedia in which all knowledge would be arranged in an alphabetically classified subject order. The elementary concepts in the works indexed would be represented by symbols which, in combination, formed complex ideas (Couturat 1901). Eventually the encyclopaedia would obviate the need for books altogether!

His appointment expressly forbade alteration to administration or organisation so he was unable to compile a classified subject catalogue. Instead he published his ideas in two versions (a longer and a shorter one) and carried out the mammoth task of completing the early author catalogue. For the actual arrangement of the books he was stuck with Augustus's original 23 classes, based on Conrad Gesner's 1548–9 system, with four omissions and three subsitutions. Within each class the books were subdivided by format and numbered according to fixed shelf locations. A shelf-list catalogue had been maintained from the start (Newman 1966: 30 and Schulte-Albert 1971: 140).

Leibniz regarded the library as a storehouse of knowledge ('*magasin de science*') whose printed equivalent would be his encyclopaedia. No matter how sophisticated the catalogues and indices, the spatiality of real books arranged linearly on shelves was a limitation which was contrary to logic:

> It is usually found that one and the same truth may be put in different places according to the terms it contains, and also according to the mediate terms or causes upon which it depends, and according to the inferences and results it may have. A simple categoric proposition has only two terms; but a hypothetic proposition may have four, not to speak of complex statements.
>
> (Leibniz 1896: 623)

It is precisely to overcome linearity, which ignores the multi-dimensional relations amongst books, and forces a librarian to choose one amongst many possible relations, that made the classified, alphabetic subject index so essential. In it the user could 'find together all the propositions into which the term enters in a sufficiently remarkable manner . . . The index may and should indicate the places where the important propositions which concern one and the same subject' are found (1896: 625). Were it the librarian rather than the philosopher speaking, and we substitute 'books' for 'propositions', we have in a nutshell the perennial problem with which all systems before and after Leibniz have struggled: where, in space, to locate all the books dealing with a single subject or by a single author. Despite the development of sophisticated systems with facets, secondary and tertiary classes (as in Dewey and UDC), and multi-dimensional computer databases, as long as books are on shelves the issue remains.

Each book is at the tip of a branch growing out of an evolutionary trunk. Richardson (1935: 3–5) says that starting at the tips of the branches and travelling back, into increasingly higher level cate-

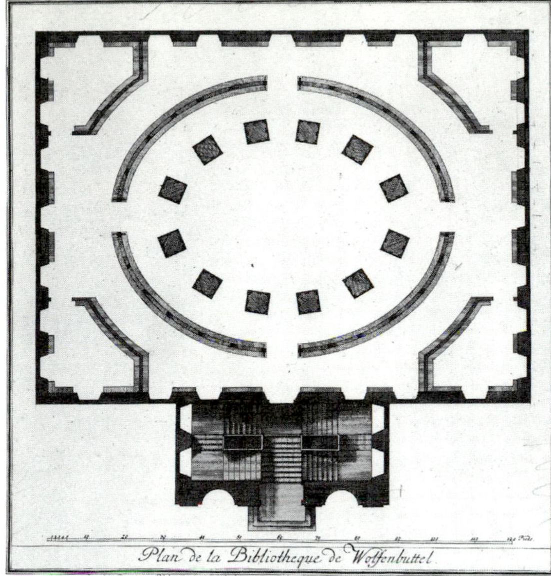

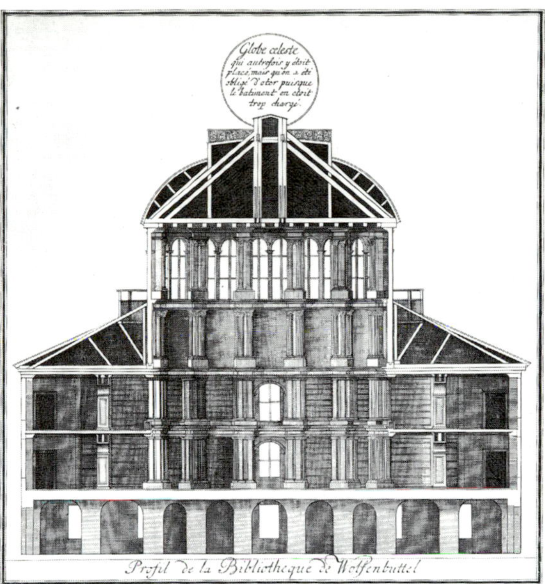

Figure 7.3 *Herman Korb's design for the Wolfenbüttel library (1766–9), plan, section and elevation*
Source: From three engravings by A. A. Beck, Department of Manuscripts and Special Collections, Wolfenbüttel Library

gories, is to travel along the tree towards its roots. Classification is the inverse of evolution, starting with the complex and finishing with the simple.

Relating classes of knowledge, even individual books, to space is closely linked to the techniques for memorising. Frances Yates's (1984) marvellous account of the 'Art of Memory' describes the techniques of memorising which associated facts or ideas with specific places in a building. They culminated in Camillo's famous sixteenth century memory theatre in which the whole world, natural and supernatural, is represented in a seven-tiered semi-circular building, to be viewed from the normal stage position. At every position on each level images represent a part of knowledge. Under the tiered steps are drawers containing masses of manuscripts. Yates, though she admits that this begins to 'look like a highly ornamental filing cabinet', argues that its grandeur is in 'the Idea of memory organically geared to the universe'. All this has its roots in medieval and renaissance mysteries – cabalism, neoplatonism, hermeticism, astrology and the occult – a tradition which Yates traces from Aristotle to Ramon Lull in the thirteenth century, through Giordano Bruno, John Dee, Robert Fludd and the Rosicrucians to Leibniz. She links the Lullian use of symbols to the invention of symbolic logic and specifically to that of calculus. Leibniz's universal encyclopaedia and its symbolic language is the organic outcome of memory arts. Her work enables one to see the systematic arrangement of books on library shelves as both memory and encyclopaedia. All the hermetic thinkers collected immense libraries and, as French's (1972: 40–61) study of Dee shows, the arrangement and cataloguing of texts was a first priority. Leibniz worked in that tradition.

Herman Korb's new library (1706–19), a four storey rectangular structure of wood, without either lighting or heating, had a central oval dome on twelve square pillars (Figure 7.3). It was intended to be topped by a huge globe but this was abandoned on account of its weight. The books were on two floors in the oval ambulatory, and against the pillars and the outer walls. The four corner rooms housed catalogues, Bibles and incunabula. Manuscripts and duplicates were kept in the gallery of the dome.

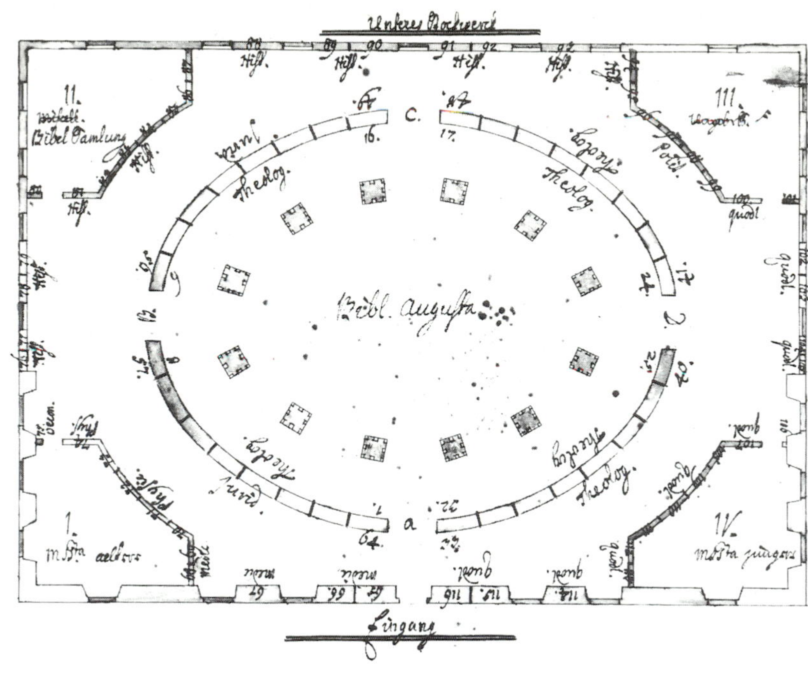

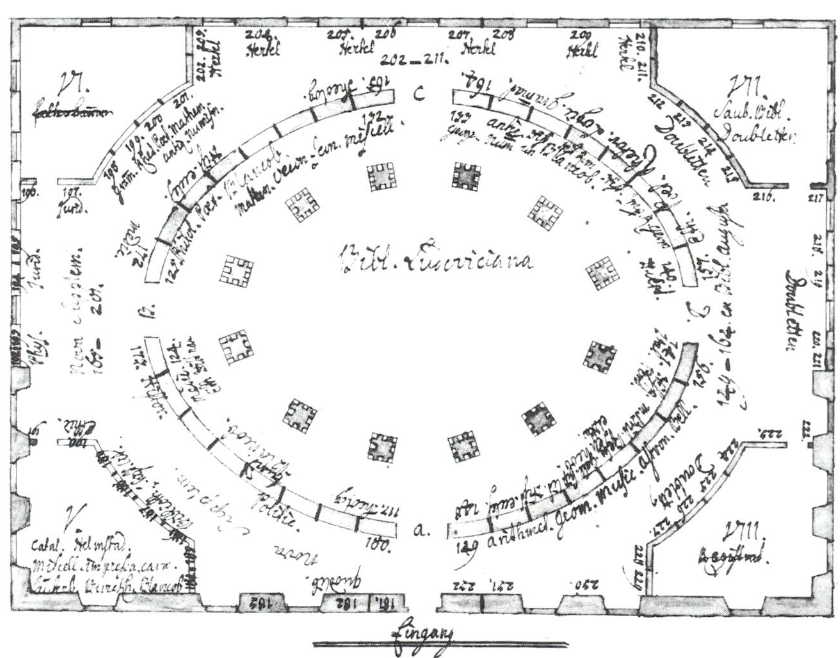

Figure 7.4

Eighteenth-century ground and first floor plans of the Wolfenbüttel library, showing book arrangement

Source: Drawing by unknown hand (c. 1767–70), Lower Saxony State Archives, Wolfenbüttel

A later drawing of the book layout (Figure 7.4) shows some new collections (acquired after 1705) on the upper level but the lower preserves the original classes with theology and jurisprudence in the main ambulatory. Since domes have a cosmic meaning which can be traced back to Rome's Pantheon it is apt that works representing divine order and human justice should be here. The library also had a collection of maps, globes, town plans, genealogical trees, portraits, mathematical instruments, and objects which had belonged to Luther.

Figure 7.5

Interior of Boullée's design for the Royal Library (1784)

Source: Boullée's *Mémoire*, Bibliothèque National, Paris

The integration of the bookcases with the curved surfaces can be interpreted simply as the application of Baroque to yet another building type. But the books seem to have a more generative role signifying that knowledge is the origin for form. Had Leibniz been free to choose a system of images to act as a metaphor for his encyclopaedic vision he would, I think, have chosen Baroque. Certainly Wölfenbüttel became a model for centric libraries: amongst the best known were Vienna, by Fischer von Erlach, Mannheim and Stuttgart. And this was the natural language also for the monastery library (Achilles 1976) where books, walls, ceilings, furniture, paintings and sculpture were fused into one sumptuous and dynamic surface. Some were galleried, either on columns or cantilevered, others 'basilical'; outstanding examples were Melk, St Gall, Altenburg and Admont.

Not only Baroque designers used books as an element in the formal language. In Boullée's 1784 Royal Library an immense four-storey wall system, stepped to give galleries without cantilevers – 'a vast amphitheatre of books' – became a substitute for rustication (Figure 7.5). This base is 'crowned with an order of architecture so conceived that far from distracting attention from the spectacle of the books, it would offer only that decoration necessary to give yet more brilliance and nobility to this beautiful place' (Boullée c. 1781–97: 105).

This, the more modest of two schemes, was intended to fill in the courtyard of the library which had been adapted from the *Palais Mazarin* in 1724. The other had an immense cruciform plan, a central domed rotunda, reading rooms in the four arms and books in the peripheral blocks as recommended in Blondel's *Cours* and by Durand. In the latter case the space under the central dome is for 'surveillance' of the spokes which are filled with wall shelves. But the reality of systematic shelving, catalogues, secure storage, expansion, reading space and surveillance proved these grandiose visions to be unworkable. The centuries-old direct link between shelves, books, staff and readers, as in Wolfenbüttel, was fractured. Sweeping consequences followed from the acceptance that books would have to be stored in stacks, that readers needed reading rooms, and staff their own space.

Libraries could now have spatial structures which accommodated a hierarchical bureaucracy. Book storage space could grow with the collection and be located in deep space barred to the public. Surveillance could concentrate on the readers and the books they were using rather than on the stored items. Catalogues and indices, whose preparation became a specialised task

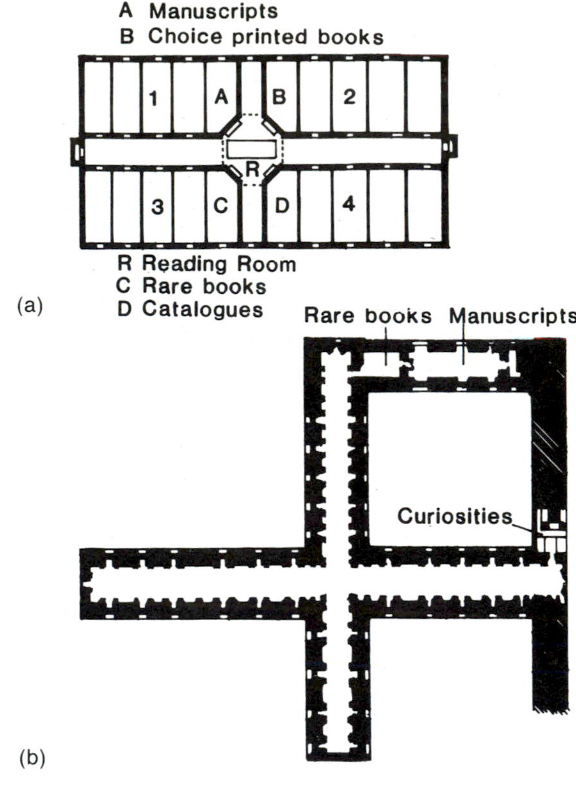

Figure 7.6
Plans of the mid-eighteenth-century Ducal library at Karlsruhe (a), and the old St Geneviève library, Paris (seventeenth century) (b)
Source: Author's drawings from several sources

carried out behind closed doors, became focal elements.

Commonly quoted as precursors of the new type are Franck's Pietist institution at Halle, already discussed, and the mid-eighteenth century Ducal library at Karlsruhe with a small central octagonal reading room at the crossing of four passages which quartered the library into four stacks. The seventeenth century (old) St Geneviève in Paris with stall type stacks in four cruciform arms and a reading room at the crossing is a seminal example (Figure 7.6).

These transitional plans put readers at the geometrical centre and at depth. The real break came with the publication of Leopoldo della Santa's (1816) work on a 'universal public library'. The plan (probably because it was drawn by a librarian and not an architect) conflates two levels (Figure 7.7) so that the entrance leads by a grand staircase to an upper lobby and thence to the reading room, but also to the rectangular corridor which in turn leads, without change of level, to the same reading room. That has no books, only tables, statues and platforms in the four corners for assistants with a dual function – surveillance and bringing the books requested by the readers at the cataloguer's window. The catalogue, located behind his office, is reached through a series of corridors and finally a private office. The spatial map (Figure 7.8), on account of della Santa's topological error, assumes that the corridor, reading room, offices, stacks, workshops, washrooms/toilets and stores are on one plane. (This leaves the four corner stairs – for 'ascending to the upper level' – as ambivalent puzzles.) The cataloguer's office is the deepest space but the visual link through its window, shown by the dotted line, brings it forward to the control zone. Readers can get no further than the reading room; the two doors into the corridor and then to the book stacks and offices are only for staff. The two rings in the depth of the building control all book and office space as well as the reading room, which lies on both. With the disappearance of the traditional shallow space shared by prince, librarian and scholarly reader in a familiar solidarity, there is now a remote professional librarian hidden deep in space but able to exercise surveillance.

Domed centric spaces are important metaphors for universal knowledge and not only in Continental Europe. James Gibbs's Radcliffe Camera in Oxford – and Hawksmoor's alternatives (Bodleian Library 1982), Wren's design for a circular library at Trinity College Cambridge, and Chambers' library at Buckingham House for George III were in this tradition.

It was alive and well in Benjamin Delessert's 1830s circular Royal Library schemes for Paris which coincided with the first moves to fill the hollow square of the British Museum courtyard with a reading room. A circular version first appeared in 1848. Della Santa's ideas were influential in the succession of proposals. Panizzi the librarian eventually had his circular concept accepted by the Trustees and Sidney, Robert Smirke's younger brother, gave it architectural flesh in 1852 (Figure 7.9). Work started in 1854.

Though most readers would use stack material, the Reading Room wall was still lined with 20,000 classified reference works arranged on three tiers with two galleries. This surface is a cylindrical map of knowledge – the wall system *par excellence.* At the centre, from which radiate the readers' tables, sat the Superintendent surrounded by concentric rings of the catalogue. The enclosed space of the Superintendent and his (or, today, her) staff is elongated, but, to preserve the unimpeded movement of the public, cut short before

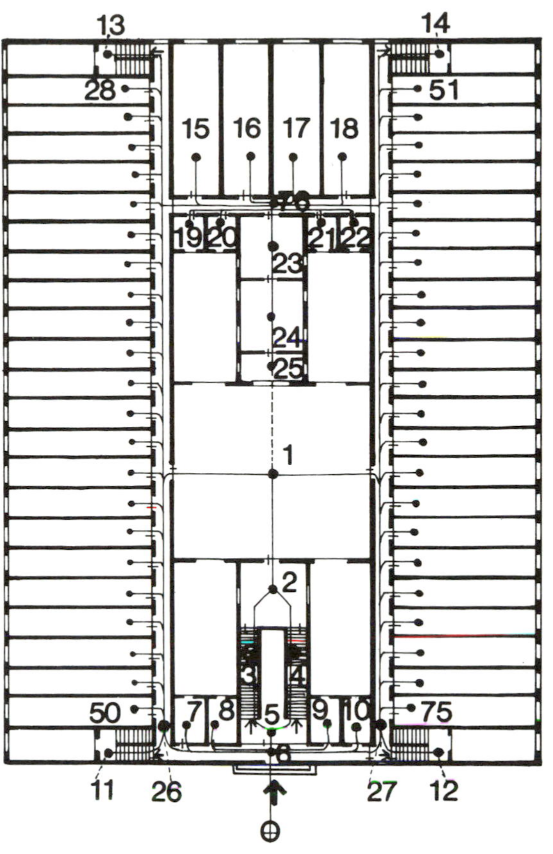

Figure 7.7 *della Santa's ideal public library plan and connectivity (1816)*

Source: Author's drawing based on della Santa (1816)

Key

1	Public reading room
2	Vestibule
3–4	Double staircase to reading room
5	Entrance hall
6	Corridor
7–10	Storerooms, workshops and toilets
11–14	Staircases
15–18	Special collections
19–22	Librarian's and assistants' offices
23	Private reading room
24	Catalogue room
25	Cataloguer's room
26–27	Corridor
28–75	Bookstacks
76	Corridor

reaching a peripheral door from which a passage leads both to the North Library – used by readers – and to restricted stacks and deep staff spaces. At this point a topological ambiguity breaks down the distinction between 'inhabitants' and 'visitors'.

The dome with its central oculus was modelled on the Pantheon and had a diameter only two feet less. It has cosmic meanings as elemental as those of the original. The physiognomy of the cylinder is constituted by the books, a mere sample of the knowledge hidden in stacks and accessible through the catalogue and staff intervention. The centre, under the eye of the dome, represents power both in the total surveillance it exercises and in being enclosed by the ring of catalogues into which all knowledge is compressed.

The British Museum (which was also an art gallery) and its library brought together elements which were already highly developed as separate types. As it was one of the last attempts to create a unified metaphor for national culture, it is a good point to move from the grand book collection to the endowed, subscription or public libraries, and those of the learned societies and mechanics' institutes. Their aims were more modest: élite social intercourse, amateur scholarship, institutional learning, workers' education and popular entertainment or instruction.

The growth of public libraries in the three centuries from the invention of printing was both a cause and a consequence of the changed reading habits. Post-Reformation ecclesiastical libraries became accessible to secular users through endowment, though often under Parish or grammar school control. Bray's 1697 scheme in English Parishes, with SPCK support from 1699, resulted in fifty-six libraries by 1730. Thomas Kirkwood's similar 1699 plan for Scotland, with Church of Scotland support, resulted in seventy libraries being set up in the Highlands and Islands in the five years from 1704 with schoolmasters as librarians. New secular town libraries were also set up; Ipswich and Norwich had the first two, entirely municipally controlled early in the seventeenth century. In Scotland municipal control was even earlier (Kelly 1966). Roche (1979: 141) notes the relationship between educational change and urban reading habits in France.

Few of these had purpose-built space. Robert Redwood's 1615 endowed public library in Bristol is typical both in its sequence of ownerships and buildings. Initially it was put into a disused medieval building in King Street (Ison 1952: 92–4 and Tovey 1859). A splendid 1740 Palladian rebuilding provided a 38 by 25 feet space over a new librarian's house. In 1786 a wing at right angles was added. In 1772 its use had become restricted to members of a 'subscription' library with shareholders. It did not revert to free public access again till 1853 after substantial remodelling under the 1850 legislation.

Other flourishing eighteenth century libraries and newsrooms were in coffee houses and clubs,

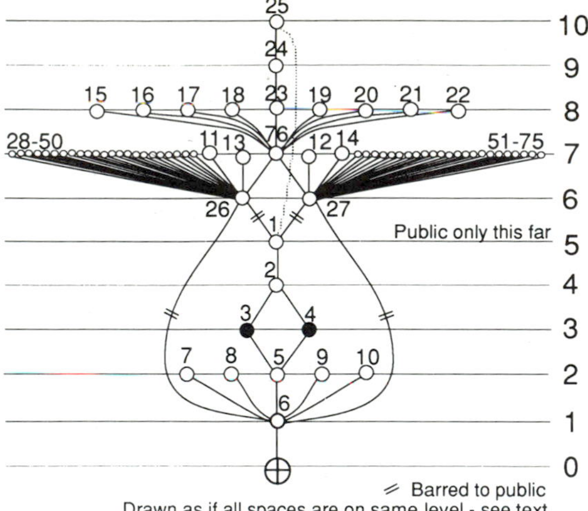

Figure 7.8

Spatial map of della Santa's library

Source: Author's drawing

and in spa and seaside resorts. In London's largest business office, the East India Company's Leadenhall Street complex built in 1726 and continuously extended for over a century, the 60 foot long first floor library housed not merely a commercial collection but some 1600 volumes of oriental manuscripts.

The 'polite' recreational libraries were on the 'circulating' principle run by booksellers for profit, the first in Edinburgh (1725). Often they were in or above a book and stationery shop (combining two of Roche's three spaces for the production of literacy), sometimes in exchanges or assembly rooms. In Cheltenham Short's advertised 10,000 religious works 'suitable for the cottage or the palace' (Rowe 1845: xlviii). The Royal Lee Library sold books, prints and music, had a circulating library and a large reading room. Bath had ten bookshops with circulating libraries by the end of the eighteenth century, one with more than 500 monthly subscribers. Neale (1981) notes that Ricardo first became interested in political economy when he lighted on Adam Smith's *Wealth of Nations* in one of these. It is a sobering thought that:

> the mind from which sprang, on the one hand, modern positivist economics and, on the other, one strand in Marxist socialism, received its original stimulus to take up the study of political economy through Mrs Ricardo's belief in the magical power of Bath's hot springs and in her husband's frequenting a bookshop.
>
> (Neale 1981: 35)

The reading habits of the rich leisured classes, a part of their social life, were vitally linked to the country's economic development since the core of the stock, apart from theology, was historical and political. One reason for the rapid growth of subscription libraries was the arrival of the romantic novel marketed to women, who were excluded from debate in the core areas and hence had been virtually excluded from the libraries.

In contrast to the theological bias of the bourgeois circulating library Scottish lead miners at Leadhills in Lanarkshire set up a fully-fledged subscription library in 1741 with a wide spread of secular works. Their example was followed in the adjacent village of Wanlochhead in 1756. At first the miners kept the books in the school, moved them in 1788 to a converted house and in 1850 built a special library. It was on a smaller scale than other Scottish workers' libraries; one of the most extensive was founded in 1791 for the antimony miners at Westerkirk, Dumfries-shire. The first English workers' subscription library (the 'Economical Library') was set up at Kendal in 1797 and was eventually incorporated in the Mechanics' Institute. In Birmingham a similar assocation was formed in 1799 based on a collection originally set up for a Sunday school two years earlier.

The bourgeois and workers' subscription initiatives branched out in different directions. The former came to maturity in Lyceums, Athenaeums and Literary and Philosophical Societies for which the burgeoning mercantilism of Lancashire and Yorkshire was fertile ground. The Liverpool Library, originally of the gentlemen's subscription type, was set up in 1757 by the amalgamation of three reading societies which had met in houses and clubs. In 1800–02 Thomas Harrison built the splendid Lyceum in Bold Street (Figure 7.10) on one main floor with a basement and mezzanine. It was circular with a shallow dome and a first floor gallery which also gave access to the librarian's room. Its entrance was separate from that of the club whose main space was a newsroom where shipowners and captains could also observe wind direction by means of a dial operated by a vane on the roof. In 1798 a parallel institution – the Athenaeum – with (non-ciculating) library and newsroom – was built in Church Street. The Royal Institution was opened in 1817 as a complete adult education centre (in a converted 1799 house) to house the Literary and Philosophical Society, the Academy of Arts with its exhibition space, teaching spaces for art, design, music,

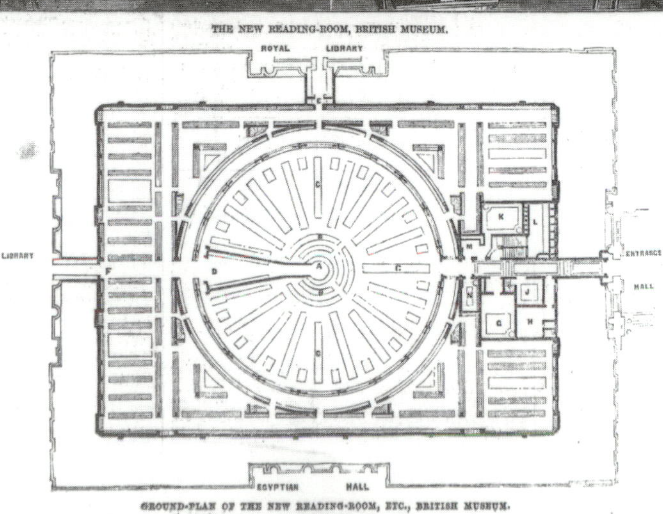

Figure 7.9

Smirke's design for the British Museum Reading Room (1852), interior view and plan

Source: *Illustrated London News* (1857) 9 May, British Library

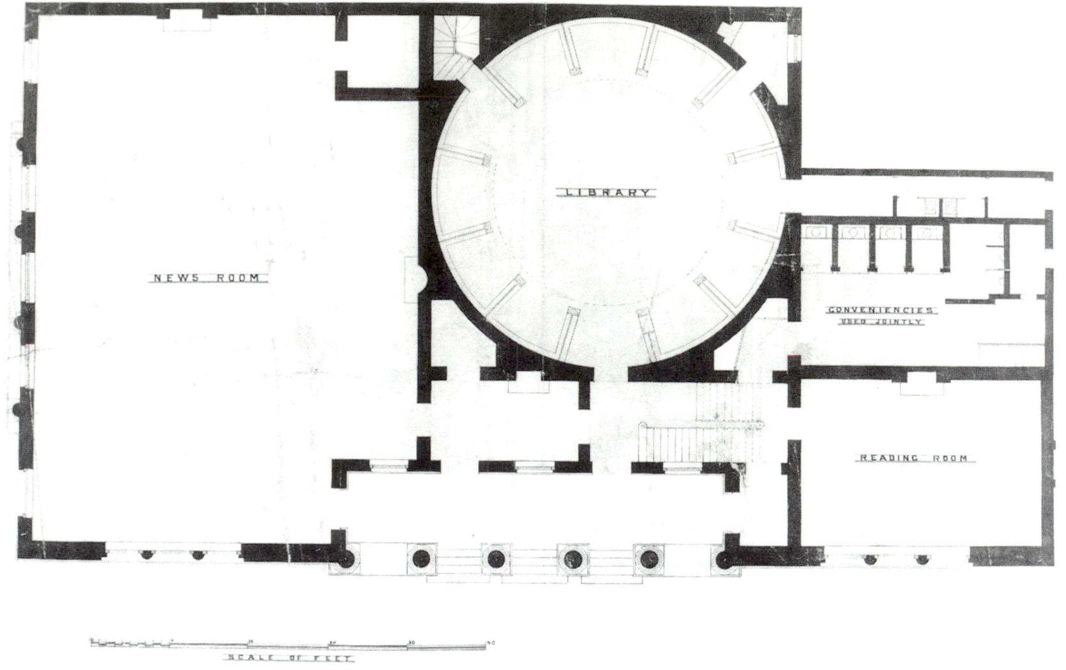

Figure 7.10

Harrison's Lyceum, Liverpool (1800–2), plan and exterior

Source: Liverpool Records Office (plan); and Austin *et al.* (1839) *Lancashire Illustrated* (exterior) classics, literature, mathematics and science, and a laboratory and observatory. It had a periodicals room, library, art gallery and museum – all of its collections forming nuclei for later municipal projects (Ormerod 1953).

Equally diverse was library provision in Manchester. Its 1781 Literary and Philosophical Society had its own buildings by 1804 in George Street, with a library. The most interesting building was Thomas Harrison's Portico Library (Figure 7.11) in Moseley Street (1802–6). In 1836 Barry added the Athenaeum to his earlier Royal Institution – its chief elements being a library and newsroom.

In response to cheap books, the popularisation of science and the investment of surplus resources in buying reading time, there was a massive growth in demand for these libraries. They acquired prestigious, purpose-built buildings in central civic locations.

Of course there was no alternative to Classical. The Society for the Promotion of Knowledge and Virtue by Free Conversation set up in Rhode Island in 1730 acquired Abraham Redwood's library in 1747 and a year later built a Roman Doric temple to Peter Harrison's design to house it (Figure 7.12).

A real rise in artisan literacy from about 1800 (West 1981) and the working class initiatives generated a variety of libraries, lecture classes, societies and clubs. In the 1820s they came to fruition in the Mechanics' Institutes. They all had libraries, but these were little more than large rooms. Their most innovatory spaces were lecture rooms and laboratories discussed later. It was disagreements concerning the mechanics' library and their teaching apparatus that caused the Glasgow Mechanics' Institution to separate from John Anderson's Institution in 1823. Three of the four projects Brougham (1825) recommends for mechanics are book-based: a library; discussion groups based on book clubs; the production of cheap and practical textbooks; and instruction by means of lectures.

By 1850 the 700 institutions housed a huge stock of almost 700,000 volumes (Hammond and Hammond 1947: 162). There was a substantial bourgeois Whig input into the foundation of the Institutes. But despite that, as Russell (1983) shows, there is little evidence to suggest that they were instruments of repression. The control of reading, which must have gone against the grain with radical and scientific free-thinking founders, is about the most tangible. Controversial religious material and anything which might be construed

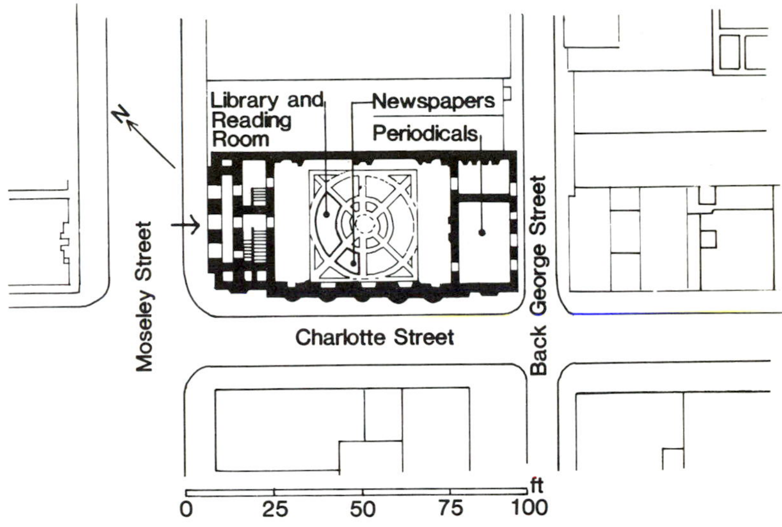

Figure 7.11
Harrison's portico library, Manchester (1802–6)
Source: Author's drawing (from O.S. map)

as politially radical were excluded. There was no perceived threat in emphasising the crucial role of the libraries. Easy access was considered vital and, as the Manchester and Liverpool plans given later show, was ensured by placing them one step from the entrance hall. Moreover reading newspapers for most working men was only possible in public houses 'where he must drink as well as read' (Chambers 1850). Since there were marked moral, and specifically teetotal, intentions in most of these foundations, and since reading, unlike the timetabled classes, was a spontaneous activity, everything was done to make the step from the street to the reading room feel like the step into the pub.

French artisans' education – and reading – was much more centralised through the *Conservatoire des Arts et Métiers* set up by Decree in 1794 in the Priory of St Nicholas, a complex that had grown from the eleventh to the seventeenth centuries. It now housed a museum of industrial models, laboratories, classrooms and a library (in the refectory). Classes modelled on those in the *Conservatoire* spread rapidly into the provinces (Artz 1946) and had their own specialised libraries.

The State's acquisition of the great collections was politically less important than its legislation for universal access. The building type which emerged – the publicly owned library – fused a number of strands, and broke down boundaries. The collection was catholic enough to appeal to both the educated and the barely literate reader. It contained books, periodicals and journals. There was less control in the book-buying policies. The

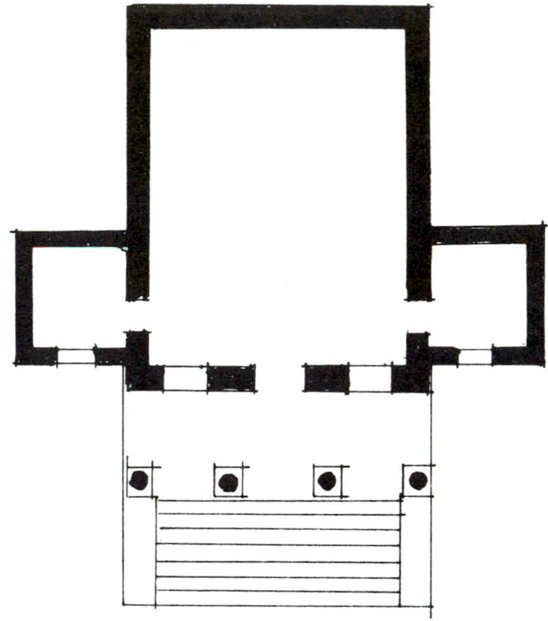

Figure 7.12
Redwood library, Newport, Rhode Island (1748), plan and exterior view
Source: Redwood Library and Athenaeum

Museums Act of 1845 had already permitted libraries – and three were founded before 1850 by municipalising private ventures: Canterbury, Warrington and Salford. Following the 1849 Select Commmittee Report the Libraries Act was passed in 1850 (1853 for Scotland). It repealed the Museums Act and enabled local authorities to raise a half penny rate provided this was approved in a referendum and it also covered museums and picture galleries.

Progress was quick; Winchester (1851) was first, then the industrial Midlands and North where Mechanics' Institutes and adult education were well advanced: Manchester (1852) in the former Owenite Hall of Science in Campfield, Liverpool (1852) with a new building with stacks for 100,000 volumes, a reading room for 450 readers, a students' room, several classrooms and a lecture theatre for 400 in 1860, and Sheffield (1856) starting in the Mechanics' Institute Hall, and absorbing the Lyceum Club's newsroom and library. Everywhere artisan and bourgeois literacy intermeshed.

There was the usual sequence: legislation, resources, specialist architects and design guides – in this case John and Wyatt Papworth's (1853), based on a clear ideology. Recommending Brunet's recent classification (1842) they warn

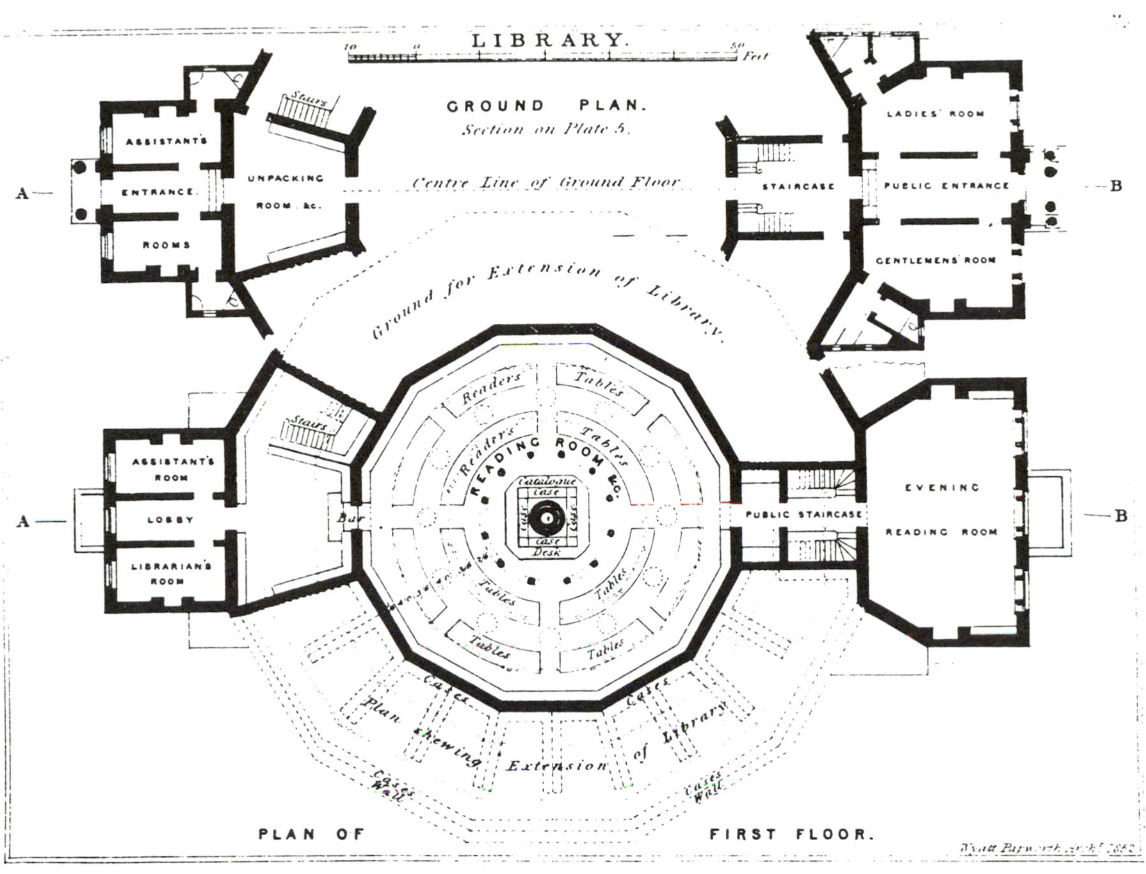

Figure 7.13

Plan of Papworth and Papworth's model library (1853)

Source: Papworth and Papworth (1853)

'...to be well supported by the lower classes, the library must contain books that a narrow-minded librarian might consider only amusing' and he must have the power to deny certain books to 'youths and ladies'. Woodthorpe's Dover library (1850), over a colonnaded covered market, is the stylistic examplar because its 'pure Italian' style (is) so completely identified with the growth of intellect'. One model is a miniature British Museum – twelve-sided, with central surveillance from a point enclosed by catalogues and concentric rings of readers' tables (Figure 7.13). An upper evening reading room is for workers who cannot come during the day.

The cabinet of curiosities

Leibniz's was one way to produce knowledge, by conserving texts. Another is to collect concrete samples of the universe. I have linked the Memory Theatre and the library. Damisch (1982: 9) does that for the museum; to take a walk through it is like taking one through the memories stored in the mind, or through the texts and images arranged in the Theatre. But the Renaissance scientists soon parted company with the Art of Memory.

The Muses, children born of Zeus and Mnemosyne, goddess of memory, sing of the origins of the world and celebrate great moments of history. Each specialised in a form of language or knowledge – epic, lyrical and erotic poetry, tragedy and comedy, sacred hymns, choral song and dance, history, astronomy and, later, pastoral poetry. A *museion* was an association of scholars dedicated to the Muses and working in a research institute, sometimes, as at Alexander's, associated with a library. When the Romans attached collections of art treasures the word began to have modern connotations of wealth, victory, ancestry, status and worship. Treasures are either valuable *per se*, perhaps of precious metal, or with an implied value – for instance curios, or rare specimens acquired through costly expeditions to distant lands or by purchase. Either way they signify wealth. A reliquary, coronation stone or ancestor shrine is sacred because of its association with martyrdom, sacred ritual or venerable ancestry.

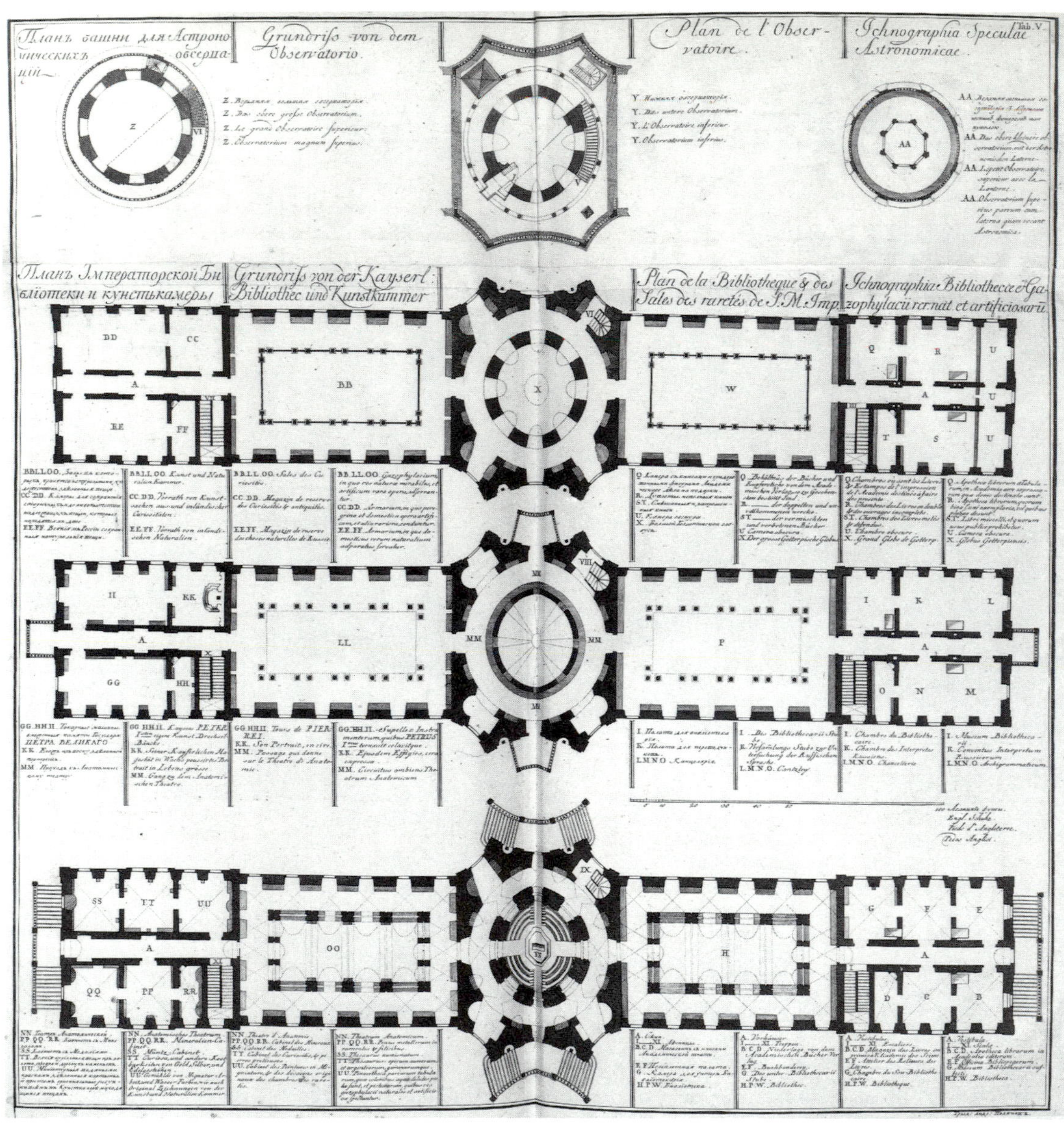
Tab. V
Grundriß von dem Observatorio
Plan de l'Observatoire
Ichnographia Speculae Astronomicae
Grundriß von der Kayserl: Bibliothec und Kunstkammer
Plan de la Bibliotheque & des Sales des raretés de S.M. Imp.
Ichnographia Bibliothecae & Gazophylacii rer. nat. et artificiosarū

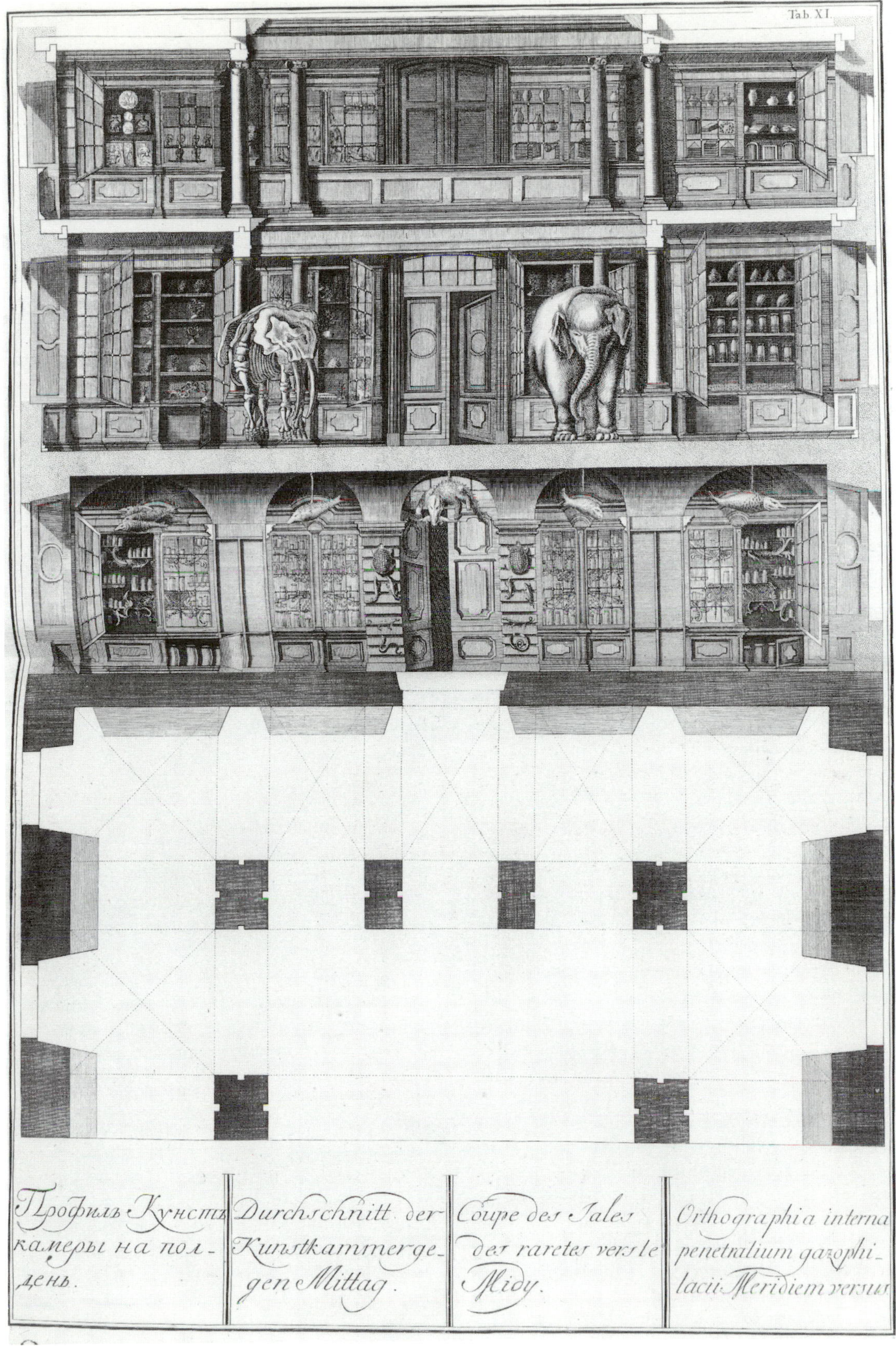

Figure 7.14
continued overleaf

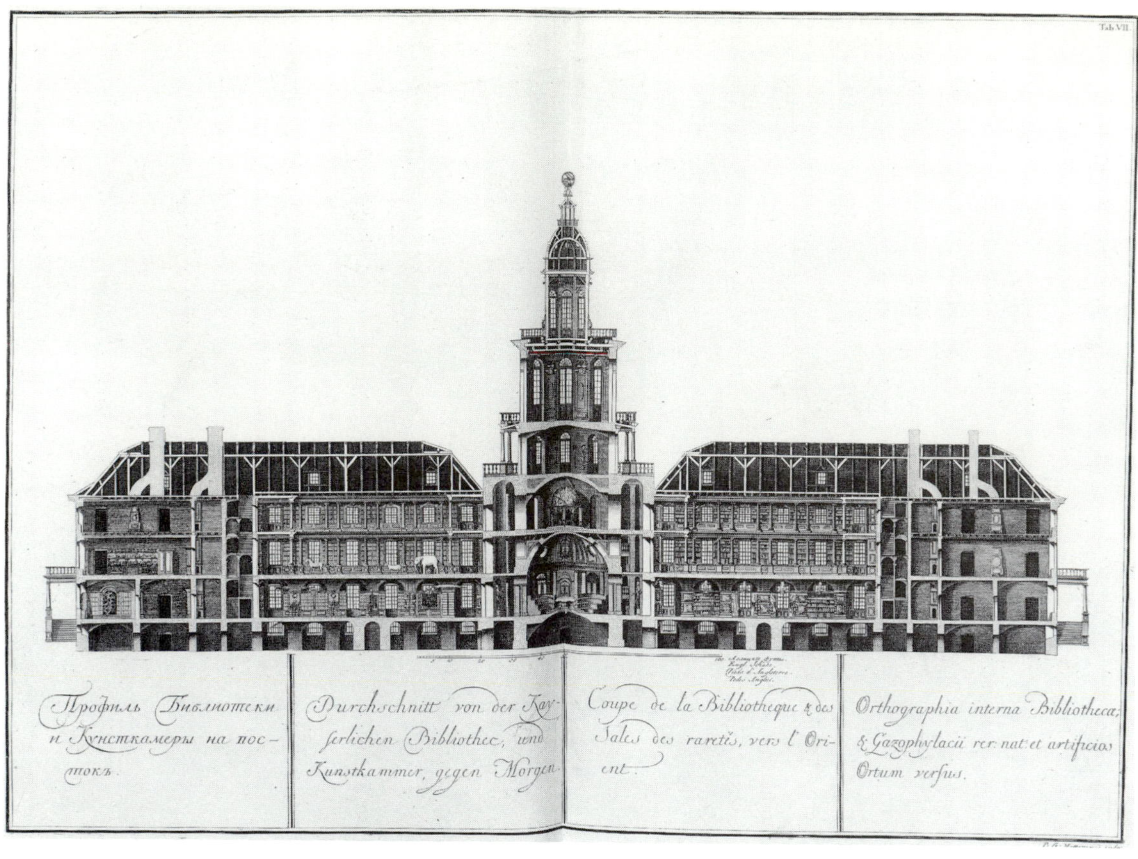

Figure 7.14

Peter the Great's Kunstkammer, *St Petersburg (1718–34)*

Source: as detailed in Note 1 (1741), copied through the kind cooperation of Roger Gaskell, Cambridgeshire

To Gombrich (1977) a visit to a famous painting is still like a pilgrimage to a shrine. Though the ideas of treasure house and shrine have survived till today, in the Renaissance they were transformed by reference to distance, either in time – antiquity – or space – the remote land. These defined two types: antiquarium and cabinet of curiosities.

Royal and aristocratic collectors created or expanded collections. Elizabeth I's palaces were crammed with paintings, tapestries, globes and busts with little semblance of organisation – at London's Tower there was a heterogenous menagerie, an exhibit of coins at the Mint and weapons at the Armoury. Nor did James I introduce much more order; but families such as the Lumleys and the Howards started rudimentary museums. At Arundel House splendid painting and sculpture galleries were added by Inigo Jones; they were catalogued and illustrated by Europe's best engravers and William Harvey guided Arundel's scientific collecting.

Robert Cotton created a garden of antiquities at Conington Castle and in his London home an unrivalled collection of coins, manuscripts and books, later to form founding elements of the British Museum. In Versailles, German ducal palaces and, of course, Papal and other palaces in Rome, collections of antique sculpture were being amassed.

A high point in Royal collections was Peter the Great's *kunstkammer* and library at St Petersburg and the adjacent Academy of Sciences (1718–34). After the death of the first architect Matarnovy in 1719 Gerbel, Quarengi, Zemstov and others took over.[1] Fortunately its original state is known from the splendid set of 1741 plates (Figure 7.14) despite alterations made after a fire in 1747 and even more radical ones in the next century.

The three floor library and the museum are on either side of the elliptical anatomy theatre, with viewing galleries on the floor above, which is entered directly. The tower houses a huge globe and no less than three observatories. Vertical communication, apart from that within the tower, was by two lateral stairs so that access to the centre is always through library or museum spaces which form rings. Both had galleries. The museum was divided between 'natural' and 'art' (i.e. 'artificial') objects. The former included anatomy, zoology, botany and geology; the latter scientific

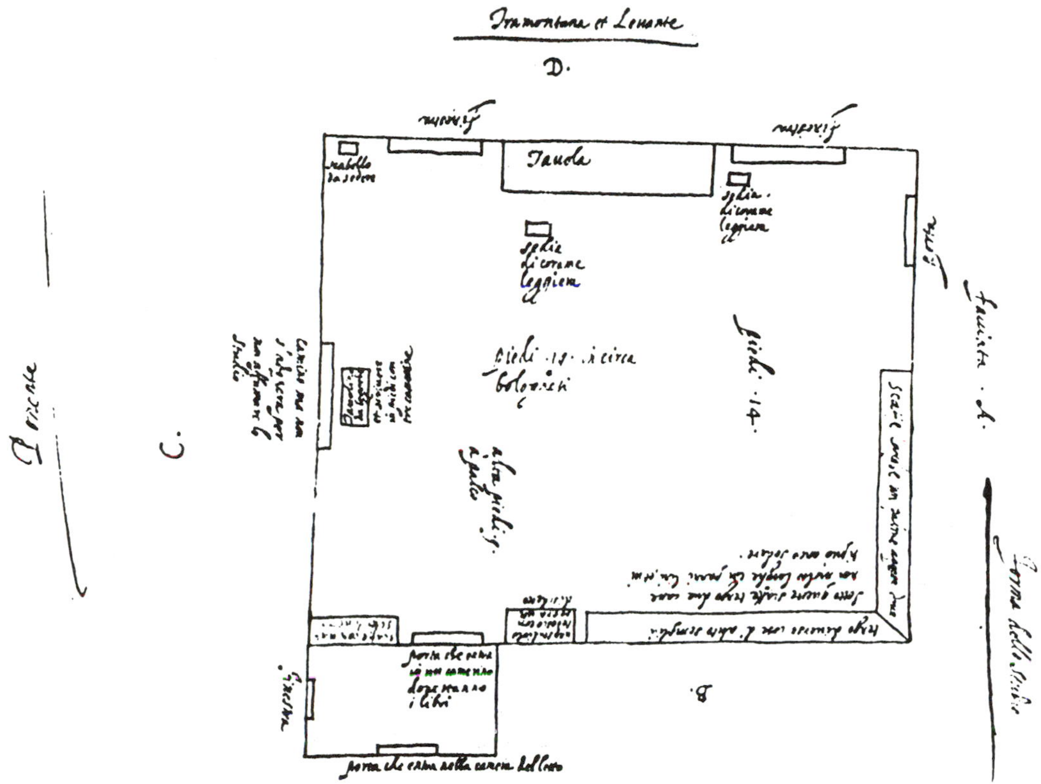

5

Figure 7.15

Plan and interior elevation of Giganti's sixteenth-century museum at Bologna

Source: Original in the Ambrosian Library, Milan, MS 85 sup.234r and 235r; this copy reproduced by kind permission of Professor Laurencich-Minelli (1984) instruments, sculpture, wax figures, an ethnograpic collection of clothes, paintings, jewellery, medals and coins.

The Academy was entered through its own library. Despite its title, Peter had always envisaged that painting, sculpture and architecture schools would be added to the physics laboratories, instrument and printing workshops, and lecture theatres, though this only happened after his death in 1725.

He drew on a long tradition of art and curio cabinets (*kunst-* and *wunderschranken* or *kammern*) whose story has been traced by von Schlosser (1978) and Impey and MacGregor (1985). Though more modest in scale these were intellectually in advance of Peter's splendid collection. They were created by travellers, scientists and learned societies as one part of Bacon's four-part prescription for a repository of knowledge: a library, a zoological and botanical garden, an experimental laboratory, and a:

> goodly, huge cabinet, wherein whatsoever the hand of man by exquisite art or engine has made rare in stuff, form or motion; whatsoever singularity, chance, and the shuffle of things hath produced; whatsoever Nature has wrought in things that want life and may be kept; shall be sorted and included.
>
> (Bacon 1594)

Progress from hermetic collections such as Borghini's for Francesco I de' Medici (Bolzoni 1980: 255–99), to the sixteenth century museum of Aldrovandi, Professor of Natural Philosophy at Bologna, is clear. Aldrovandi classified specimens in 4554 little drawers in two cupboards – a precursor to the card index which transforms each of these into a small text. It is in Bologna, centre of the new humanist sciences, that one would expect to find a rejection of artificial structures such as the Art of Memory. Laurencich-Minelli (1985: 17–23) comments that the substitution of the Italian 'studio', 'studiolo', 'guardroba' and 'museo' – all applied to the Bolognese collections – for the German 'wunderkammer', accurately represented the move from the occult to science.

Classification would now be logical, based on scientific observation and experiment. The system acquired two key characteristics of language syntax – concordance and order. The first clusters together items which are alike, the second locates them in a correct sequence. Any object could be unambiguously placed by answering two questions: 'With what other objects should it be grouped?' and 'Where should its group be located with respect to all others?'

Amongst the methods used was colour coding of each cupboard according to the material of its contents in systems going back to Pliny who categorised works of art according to their raw material. There was sufficient syntactic accuracy that in the absence of a written record the spatial order allows categories to be recovered as Laurencich-Minelli (1985) has done from the plan, elevation and inventory of Giganti's sixteenth century museum (Figure 7.15).

Engravings, jewellery, coins and medals, shells, stones, two-headed pickled embryos, ostrich eggs, giant spiders and ethnographic curios were brought into a unified space. The cabinets were beautifully crafted, uniting storage and exhibition on shelves with cupboards below, and grouped in special rooms which effectively became larger cabinets. Larger pieces of sculpture were on pedestals or in niches, and the walls were hung with pictures. The superficial chaos, not unlike that of small town museum of today, belies the immense effort made at combining all this into a unified intellectual system.

One influential attempt was Samuel Quiccheberg's (1565) *theatre* of knowledge:

> The headings (inscriptions of the classes) in this most extensive theatre incorporate each and every substance in the universe, and outstanding statues, so that this same theatre can also rightly be called the elegant storehouse of artistic and wonderful objects, and of every rare treasure and precious case, statues and pictures, which are to be sought and consulted here in the theatre, so that by regular inspection and handling of them a unique knowledge of the objects and remarkable wisdom can be quickly, easily and safely obtained.
>
> (Quiccheberg 1565)

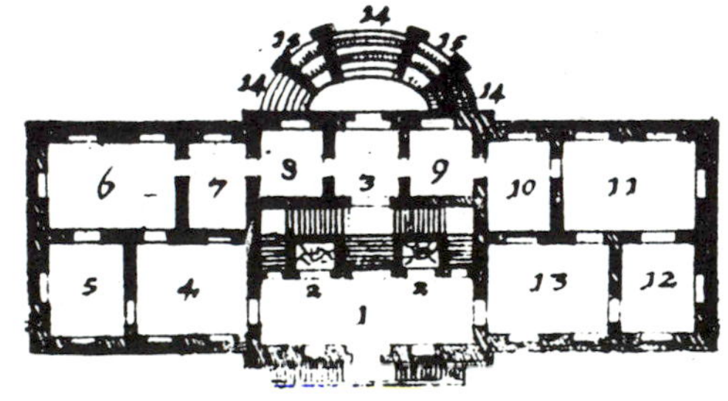

Figure 7.16

Sturm's 'house of curiosities' (1707), plan

Source: Anonymous (1707) *Des Geöffneten Ritter-Platzes Dritter Theil etc.*, Schillern, Hamburg, courtesy of the Newberry Library, Chicago

The 'cases' are cabinets. Significantly, the collection is not only to be seen but *felt* through handling. This is still close to Camillo's Memory Theatre which was little more than thirty years old. Quiccheberg's five classes, each further subdivided hierarchically, are:

1 Religious and historical paintings
2 Sculpture, archeology and numismatics
3 Natural history
4 Science and mechanics represented by tools and instruments; material related to games, sports, and pastimes; arms and armour; costume
5 Painting and engraving; genealogy; portraits; heraldry; textiles; fittings and furnishings

The cabinets first moved to a special chamber and soon to dedicated buildings on which treatises began to appear. Sturm's 1707 'house of curiosities' has three floors (Figure 7.16) and a botanic garden with a conservatory, a small menagerie and an aviary outside. Each of its few paintings were to be hung at high level, representing those subjects exhibited immediately below. The collections were too large to be seen simultaneously so they had to be seen in their correct sequence and since the plan had many rings (that is optional routes) the only way to avoid intellectual chaos was for the Treasurer to guide each visitor room by room, floor by floor.

Neickelio (1727) adds anatomy and a library to four categories – Treasures, Art, Natural History and Curiosities. The solitary user (Figure 7.17), reading between a classified library and specimens from a collection, unites invisible and visible knowledge in a sanctuary-like space with steps, altar rails and curtains drawn back in a chancel arch.

Such collections abounded in England and Scotland. James and Andrew Balfour's was combined with Robert Sibbald's and presented to the Edinburgh College of Physicians. Edinburgh University received it and, as late as 1765, turned its library into a 'museum for natural curiosities'.

One of the largest early buildings is the Oxford Ashmolean Museum designed by Thomas Wood, a master-mason (1679–83). The collections have been traced by Ovenell (1986) to John Tradescant the elder, a gardener. His museum and garden in Lambeth were inherited by his son John the younger in 1638. The public had access to this 'closett of rarities' whose 1656 catalogue records the usual strange mix. Elias Ashmole acquired it and, adding his manuscripts, donated the whole to Oxford University in 1678.

Figure 7.17
Nickelio's museum and library (1727)
Source: Nickelio (1727), British Library

The new building was on three levels (Figure 7.18). The ground floor school of natural history was a splendid lecture theatre, entered on ceremonial occasions from the east, and otherwise from Broad Street in the north. The main staircase linked it to the first floor museum whose specimens were used for lectures. The Keeper's quarters, in an attached two-storey wing with its own internal staircase, had access to both floors. The first Keeper and Professor of Chemistry, Robert Plot, was not only an eminent Fellow of the Royal Society but also, as recent research has confirmed, involved in hermetic mysteries and alchemy. So had Ashmole been, despite being a founder member of that Society, whose activities 'would soon give the *coup de grace* to the concepts of the neoplatonic cosmos in which astrology, alchemy and magic were legitimate subjects of learning' (Josten 1985: 5), the very subjects which link Ashmole, Plot and the museum to the Memory Theatre. The basement chemistry laboratory was entered from a dual staircase on the north and had originally no internal connection with the building for reasons of safety and salubrity; the danger of fire and explosion was countered by the solid vaulted ceiling and smells were unable to percolate upstairs. There were also social reasons – chemistry teaching was to a lower class of student and was carried out by Plot's assistant, Christopher White.

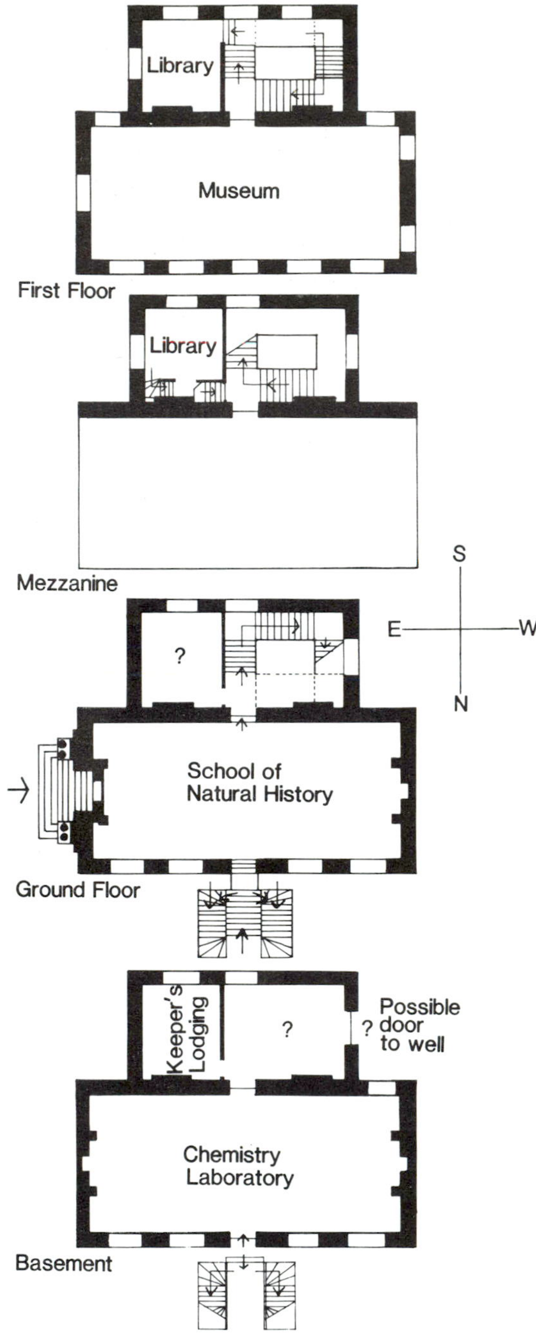

Figure 7.18

Ashmolean Museum, Oxford (1679–83), reconstructed floor plans and view of east front

Source: Reconstructed by author from plans, views and advice from the Bodleian Library, Oxford, A.V. Simcock of the Oxford Museum of the History of Science, and R.F. Ovenell (plans); Coney's 1816 print, Oxford Museum of the History of Science (view)

Ashmole had insisted on the transfer of Oxford's existing collection from the anatomy school, other than specimens needed for teaching. The teaching itself eventually followed though even from the beginning Plot gave anatomy classes in one of the small rooms, possibly at the oblong demonstration table surrounded by three tiers of seating which Thomas Bugge, a Danish traveller, sketched in 1777 (Figure 7.19). By this time the school had a large collection of instruments in cabinets.

The laboratory and the lecture theatre reproduce the Royal Society's at Gresham College and as Nehemiah Grew's catalogue (1694) shows, the Society's collection was similarly classified in a mixture of science, the occult and curiosity which is difficult to grasp today. For instance the human anatomy section had not only Egyptian mummies, but the 'entire skin of a Moor'. The skulls purported to demonstrate that the male's was larger than the female's, thus able to accommodate a more substantial brain 'although a little house may be well furnished and look better than a great one that stands empty'! There was intense interest in calculi – stones formed in the gall bladder or kidney, and fossils – whose origins were mysterious, even to the great Scottish surgeon and 'man-midwife' William Hunter.

I have described (Markus 1985: 158–77) how Hunter agitated for Government money to set up an anatomy school. Amongst other benefits would be a place to train artists. His ideal plan (Figure 7.20) shows a 47 foot diameter circular theatre, a long library and museum, and a square house. The diagram shows no spatial connections; but it seems clear that the library and museum connected the house with the theatre which would have its own, side, entrance for students. After the rejection of his pleas in 1765 he bought a house in Great Windmill Street which Robert

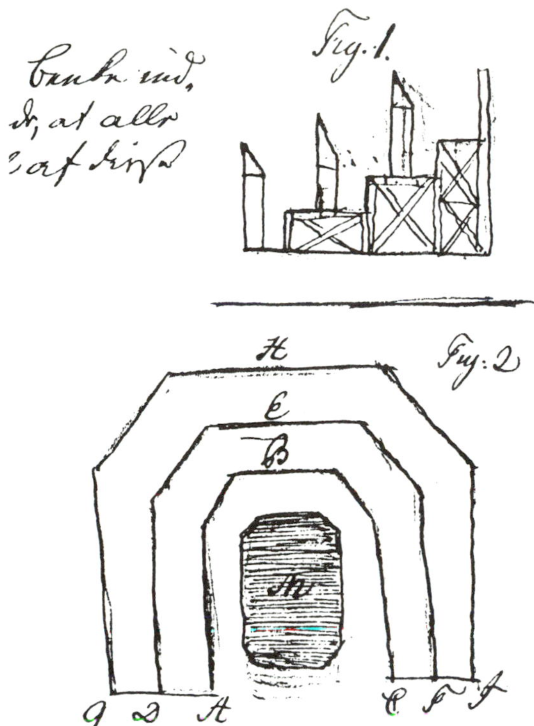

Figure 7.19

Thomas Bugge's sketch of seating layout in Ashmolean museum's experimental philosophy lecture room (1777)

Source: Department of Manuscripts, Royal Library, Copenhagen

Mylne converted and expanded by adding a library with museum, a picture gallery and, further back, an upper level anatomy theatre over preparation rooms and living quarters for a lecturer (Figure 7.21). It opened in 1768.

Its spatial map (with an upper level conjecture based on Mylne's plan) shows that the three main units – theatre, gallery, and library with museum – are each three steps deep from outside. The last was on a ring linking the house to the teaching block (Figure 7.22). Beyond providing Hunter with a sheltered route this makes spatially concrete the dependence of the surgeon and man of learning on both his collections – anatomy, curiosities, medals, coins, books and pictures – and his clinical experience, in part obtained in his house where he treated patients.

There was another unity – within the collections. A contemporary description speaks of each being, in Hunter's presence, 'a centre of instruction and illumination. Now (after his death) the chain of all these truths is broken; all is mute in this vast building' (Vicq d'Azyr 1805: 387). The chain refers, as Rolfe (1985) has shown, to Pope's 'Great Chain of Being' to which Hunter subscribed. Essentially it was a form of syntactic order based on a theological and poetic, rather than a scientific, system. It was continuous and graduated, extending from stones, through plants and zoophytes, to mammals, man, angels and, finally, God. It was based on three principles – Aristotle's continuity and gradation, and Plato's plenitude – that is, that all possible kinds of things exist. The discovery of extinct species, such as the Irish Elk, became the focus of heated debate for it seriously threatened the Chain. Objects such as calculi – the stony growths of the body – were regarded as specially important boundary cases because they grew, unlike stones, but were neither flesh nor plant.

Hunter's clinical lectures locate the mind in the brain the 'place of (its) immediate residence; which shall have all the requisites for the union of spirit and body'. The nervous system allows the brain to move the *mind* from place to place by issuing instructions to the skeleton and muscles of the limbs. The ability to procreate gives this 'animal machine', quite unlike artificial machines, 'characteristics of the divine architect' (Hunter

Figure 7.20

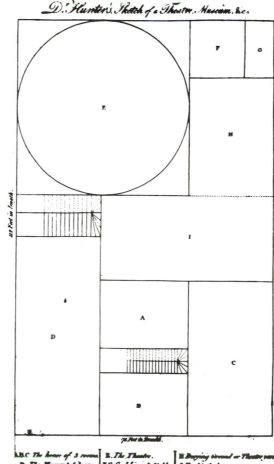

William Hunter's ideal school of anatomy, library, museum and house

Source: Hunter (1784), British Library

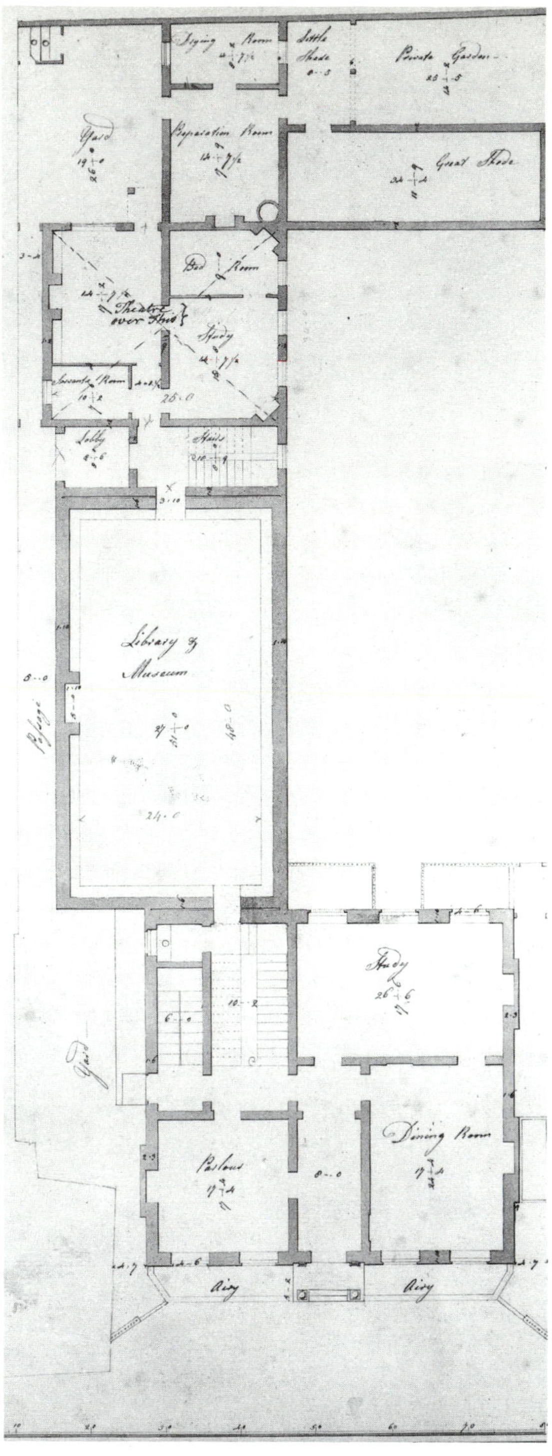

Figure 7.21
William Hunter's Great Windmill Street school of anatomy, library, museum and house (1766–8)
Source: Original drawing by Robert Mylne, by permission of the Librarian, Glasgow University Library

1784: 92). This unity of the structures and functions of the human organism was further evidence for the seamless unity of the Chain. As in Sturm's museum it needed a cicerone to guide one through the collection and thus maintain a sequence which space could not do unambiguously. No wonder that without Hunter the collection became 'mute'.

When Hunter died in 1783 he left much of his collection, and a sum of money for housing it, to Glasgow University. Mylne prepared an early design (Figure 7.23). Although it was so different in form, the London spatial structure survives in the depth of the three main elements and their linkage (Figure 7.24).

Several architects prepared proposals, the most profilic of them David Hamilton who combined the museum with surprising elements such as a chapel. The University abandoned the idea of attaching the anatomy theatre, partly in case of a repetition of the riots against dissection which had recently occurred when anatomists were suspected of body-snatching. The commission went to William Stark in 1803 for a three-floor, domed solution. The basement, apart from service quarters, had the antiquities; the ground floor natural history and anatomy; the first floor the library, pictures and coins (Figure 7.25).

One reading of the division between levels is that the foundations are ancient history; the natural world is the present; and the abstract world of knowledge, art and artefacts is built on historical and empirical reality. The spatial map (Figure 7.26) shows an extension of this metaphor. Under the dome, on both the ground and first floors, is the root of a triple fork. The root and the two side prongs are spaces for the visible – natural history in one case and pictures in the other. One step from the root and embraced by the outer prongs, is a space for something invisible – anatomical structures in one case and book knowledge in the other. This progress from surface to depth later became a feature of much museum layout.

On becoming the first Professor of Anatomy to the Royal Academy within a week of its foundation (1769) Hunter was able to make explicit his conviction that artists needed a deep understanding of the human body in order to paint its surface forms expressively. His lectures demonstrated the organic link between outward form, function (physiology) and locational structure (anatomy). The questions to his audience, 'what does it look like?, what does it do? and where is it?', are analogous to our search for meaning in buildings through form, function and space.

All museums have political meaning, and this is clearest in national collections. The British

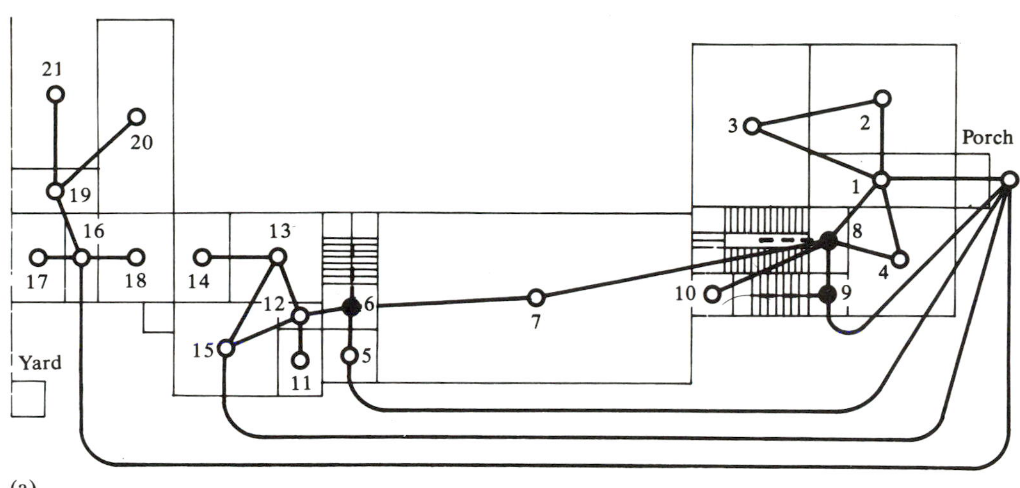

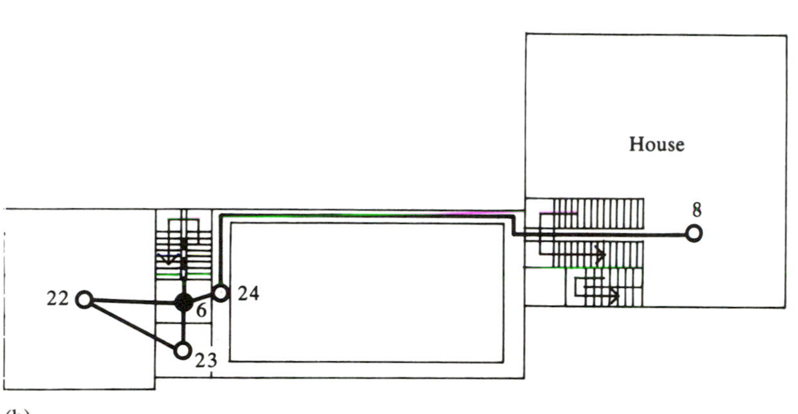

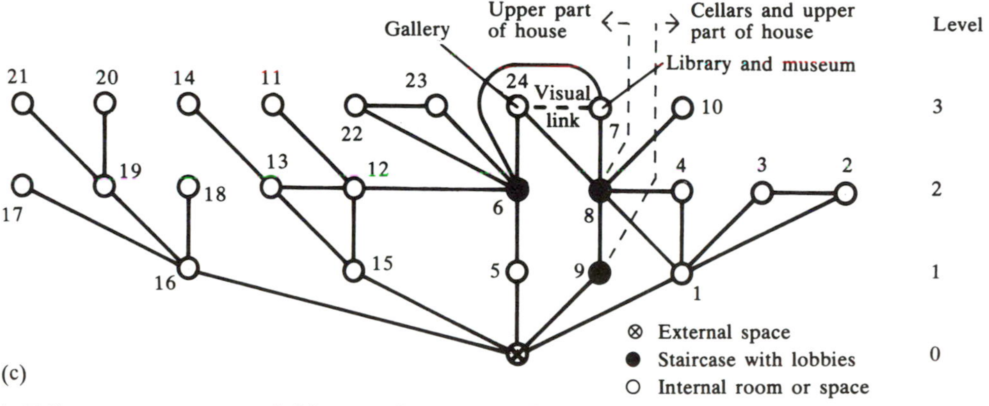

1 Hall
2 Dining room
3 Study
4 Parlour
5 Lobby
6 Stair to anatomy theatre
7 Library and museum
8 Main stair
9 Rear porch
10 Service stair
11 Servant's room
12 Dissecting room
13 Study
14 Bedroom
15 Living room?
16 Passage
17 Drying room
18 Preparation room
19 Little shed
20 Great shed
21 Private garden
22 Anatomy theatre
23 Lecturer's room
24 Gallery

Figure 7.22

Schematic plans, ground floor (a), first floor (b), and spatial map (c), of William Hunter's Great Windmill Street building

Source: Author's drawing, redrawn by *Environment and Planning B: Planning and Design* (1987) vol. 14, Pion, London

Museum was founded by Act of Parliament in 1753 to house the collections of natural history, coins and books gifted to the nation by the Trustees of Sir Hans Sloane as well as the Cotton library which had been left in 1700. In 1757 the Royal Library was added by George II. By this time a building had been found: Montagu House in Bloomsbury, built in 1675 for the Duke of Montagu to designs by Robert Hooke the mathematician, destroyed by fire in 1686 and rebuilt in the form of a French town *hôtel*, possibly to designs by Pierre Puget. The Museum opened in 1759. It was the treasury-cabinet tradition carried to a vast conclusion; printed books on the ground floor, manuscripts, coins, medals, ethnographic collections, pictures, prints, drawings, antique sculpture and remains, natural history specimens, anatomy collections, stones, minerals and fossils on the first. The garden was redesigned to be both ornamental and medicinal. The rooms of the house were corridor-less, creating *en filade* plan sequences. In practice due to the mismatch between the size of objects and spaces the syntax frequently broke down (Figure 7.27).

It is impossible here to trace the growth of the collections, the various building additions, or the start of Robert Smirke's new design in the 1820s. Mordaunt Crook (1972) has done this as a narrative of 'architectural politics'. Smirke's final plan (Figure 7.28) continued the *en filade* convention,

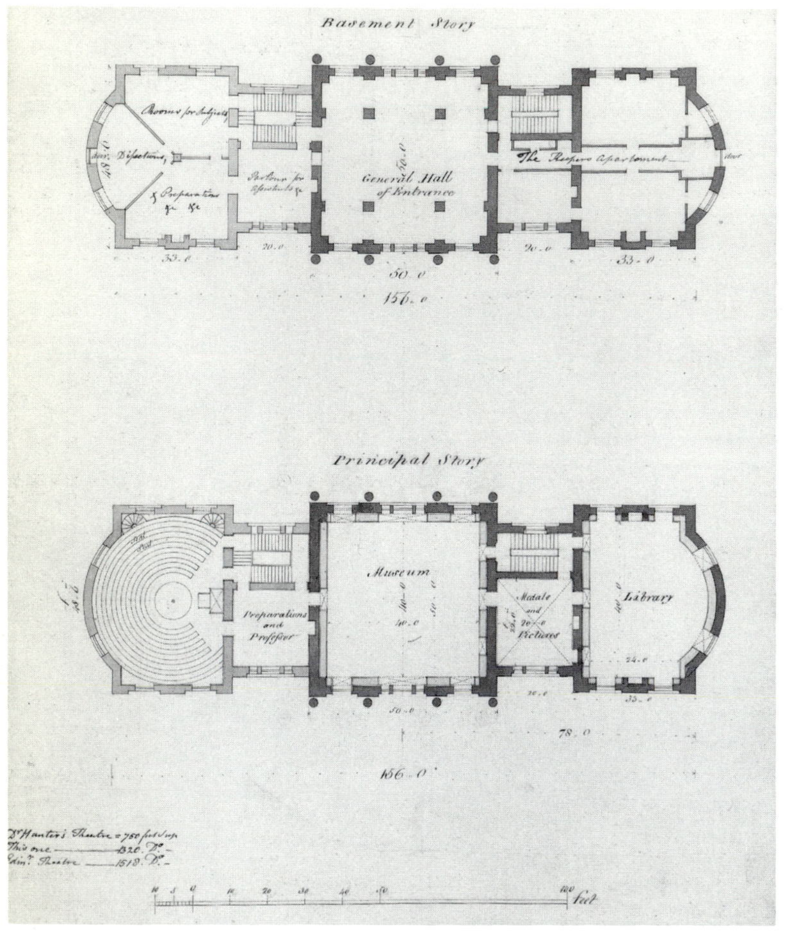

Figure 7.23

Robert Mylne's design for the Hunterian museum, Glasgow (n.d., 1799?)

Source: Original drawing by Robert Mylne, by permission of the Librarian, Glasgow University Library

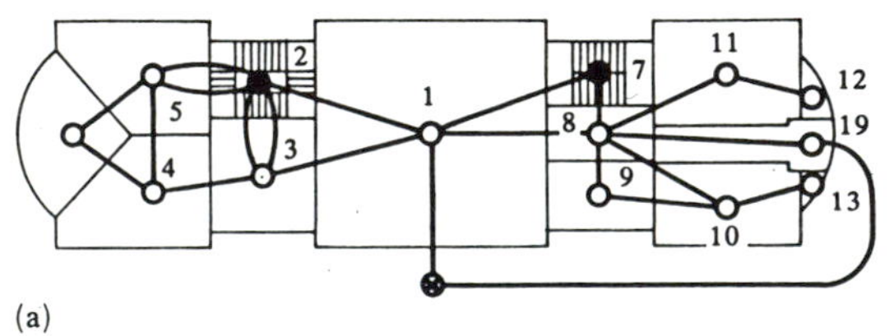

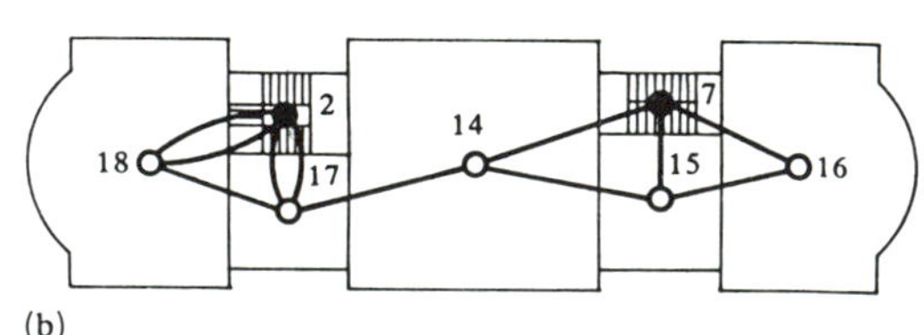

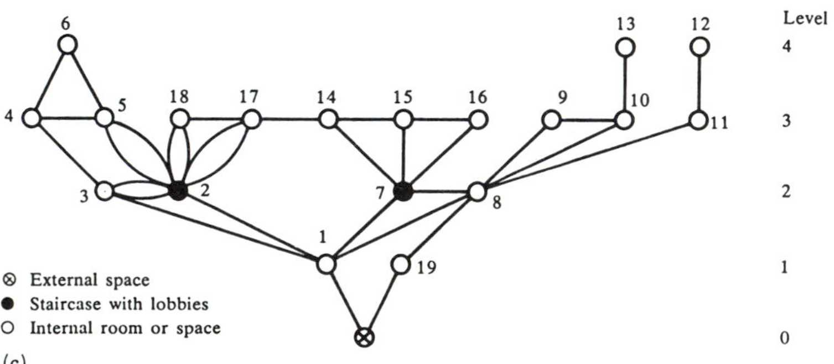

Figure 7.24

Schematic plans, ground floor (a), first floor (b), and spatial map (c), of Mylne's Hunterian museum

Source: Author's drawing, redrawn by *Environment and Planning B: Planning and Design* (1987) vol. 14, Pion, London

1 General entrance
2 Stairs
3 Parlour for assistants
4 Preparation
5 Room(s) for subjects
6 Dissection
7 Stairs
8 Keeper's apartment
14 Museum
15 Medals and pictures
16 Library
17 Preparation and professor
18 Anatomy theatre
19 Lobby

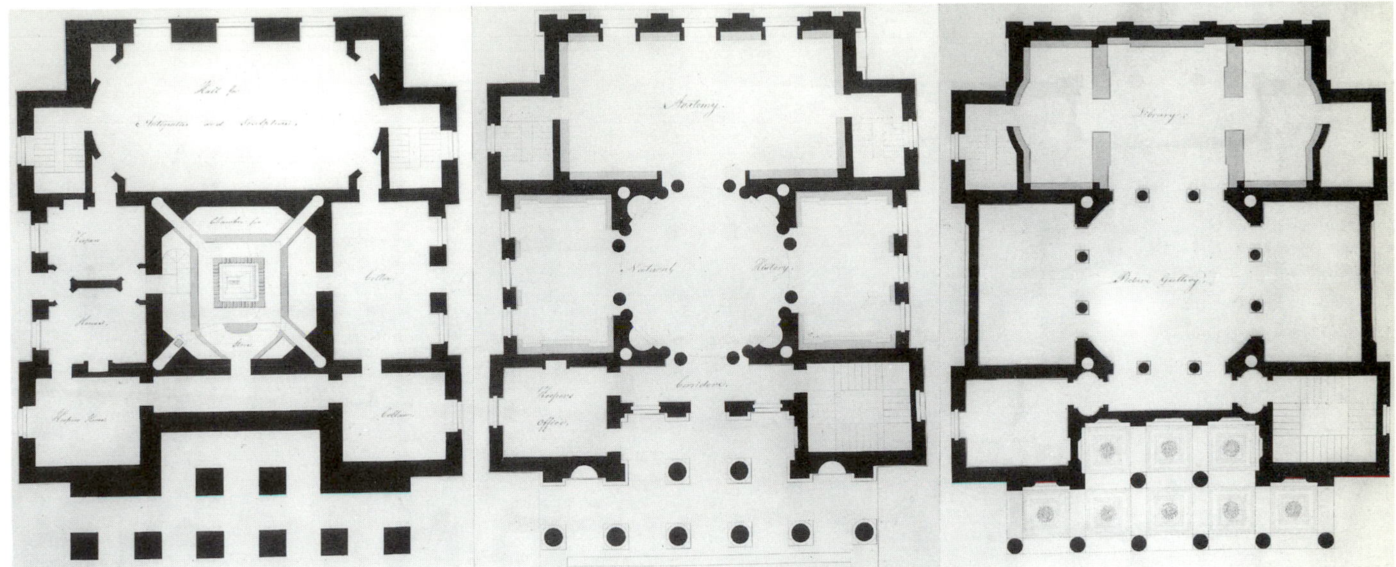

Figure 7.25
William Stark's design for the Hunterian museum, Glasgow (1803): basement plan, ground floor plan, first floor plan, front elevation
Source: From original drawings in Scottish Record Office (RHP 1997), reproduced with the approval of the Keeper of the Records of Scotland

with the King's library in the east wing, the natural history collection above, the Middle Eastern antiquities and the Elgin marbles in the west wing, and a huge collection of vases above. Although there are a few local rings, in general movement was in either direction through the galleries, that is round one very large ring.

The collection was soon divided, with sections transferred to other museums or forming the nuclei of new ones. In 1809 the medical and anatomical collection was transferred to the Hunterian Museum in Lincoln's Inn Fields (in what was later to become the Royal College of Surgeons), which had started life in John Hunter's house in Leicester Square, was purchased for the nation in 1799 six years after his death and finally transferred to the Hunterian in 1806. The Zoological Society transferred their collection to the British Museum in 1855 which simply made the conditions of the natural history department even worse. After prolonged battles in Parliament and with the scientific community this section was finally moved into Alfred Waterhouse's splendid new Natural History Museum in South Kensington but not till 1880.

Its first Director, Richard Owen, previously the disgruntled Superintendent of natural history at Bloomsbury, is a key figure in any analysis of classification and space. He sketched his basic idea as early as 1859 (Figure 7.29). The central rotunda houses the 'Index gallery' – 'an epitome of natural history (to show) the characters of the Provinces, Classes and Orders and Genera of the Animal Kingdom'. Behind it was to be a lecture theatre, so that the two basic ways for producing knowledge are juxtaposed. Two long transverse galleries at the front, for two branches of the evolutionary tree – mammals to one side, birds to the other – are permeable to the rotunda from which they derive their taxonomic validity. They, in turn, validate the comb-like spaces for individual collections along their entire length. Although Darwin's *On the Origin of Species* was exactly contemporary, Owen remained sceptical and chose the static system originating with Linneaus and culminating with Cuvier. The rear,, deepest spaces were linking galleries of the most ancient strata of nature – mineralogy, geology and paleontology. His basic ideas survived the numerous

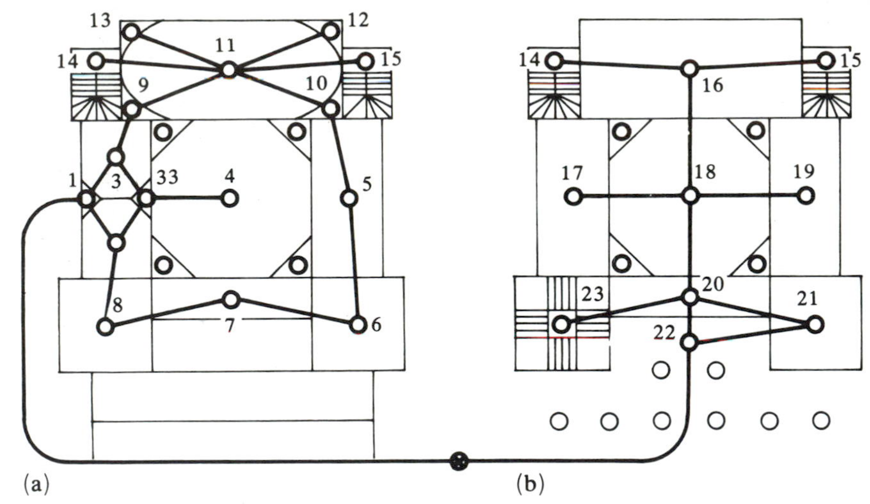

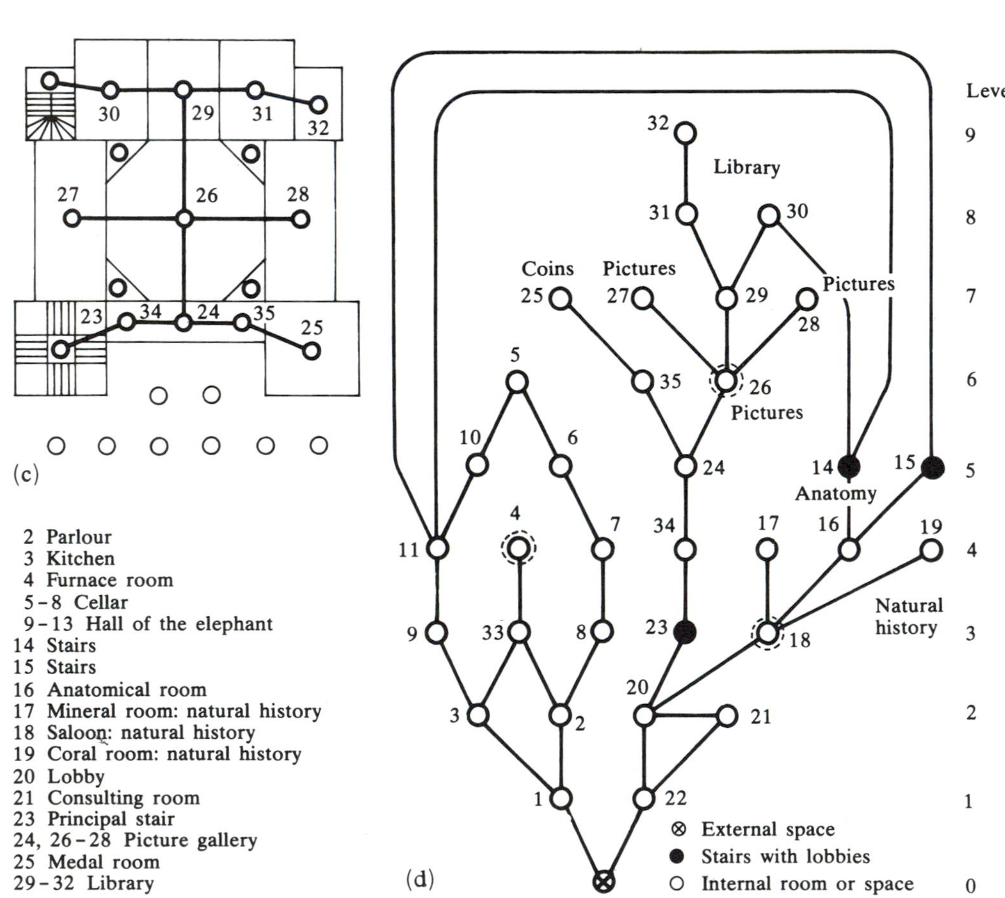

Figure 7.26

Schematic plans, basement (a), ground floor (b), first floor (c), and spatial map (d) of Stark's design for the Hunterian museum (NB plans slightly at variance with that in Figure 7.25, and based on notebook sketches by Peter Nicholson. Chief difference – basement 'antiquities and sculpture' of Figure 7.25 here replaced by 'hall of the elephant'.)

Source: Author's drawing, redrawn by *Environment and Planning B: Planning and Design* (1987) vol. 14, Pion London

Figure 7.27
Breakdown of collection syntax at the British Museum in Montagu House
Source: Department of Prints and Drawings, British Museum

changes between his first sketch and Waterhouse's final plans of the 1860s and 1870s.

I have referred to Peponis and Hedin's (1982) study. They contrast the simple axial unity of the original Birds' Gallery, based on the central promenade aisle off which open a series of identical lateral cubicles, with the fragmented and tortuous patterns of the redesigned Human Biology Hall behind it (Figure 7.30). The first represents Owen's static view of classes of which he was one of the last adherents. The visitor and the scientist share the ability to learn by looking; 'what the expert knew was the same classification system that was made visible to the visitor'. Central space both unifies and controls, and emphasises through the density of people shared learning. The second represents the shift from natural history to biology. Evolutionary theory, modern genetics, statistics and biochemistry are now needed to explain the inner, invisible laws. The expert can transmit this knowledge in charts, videos, diagrams and models, but specimens no longer explain anything. The expert's and the visitor's worlds of knowledge are now widely separated. Moreover the spaces created are deeper and smaller – as individual rather than social learning is the rule – and full of rings. There is no critical sequence, there being no reason for instance why a genetic explanation should precede a biochemical one.

The removal of natural science from the British Museum is symptomatic of the final fracture between arts and science. Another separation – between 'fine' and 'useful' art – eventually had its material outcome in the Victoria and Albert and the Science Museums in South Kensington described by Physick (1982). Their origins are in the School of Design set up in 1836, housed first in Somerset house and transferred to Marlborough House in 1841. By then the Government had set up 17 such schools mainly in the growing industrial towns and the London school concen-

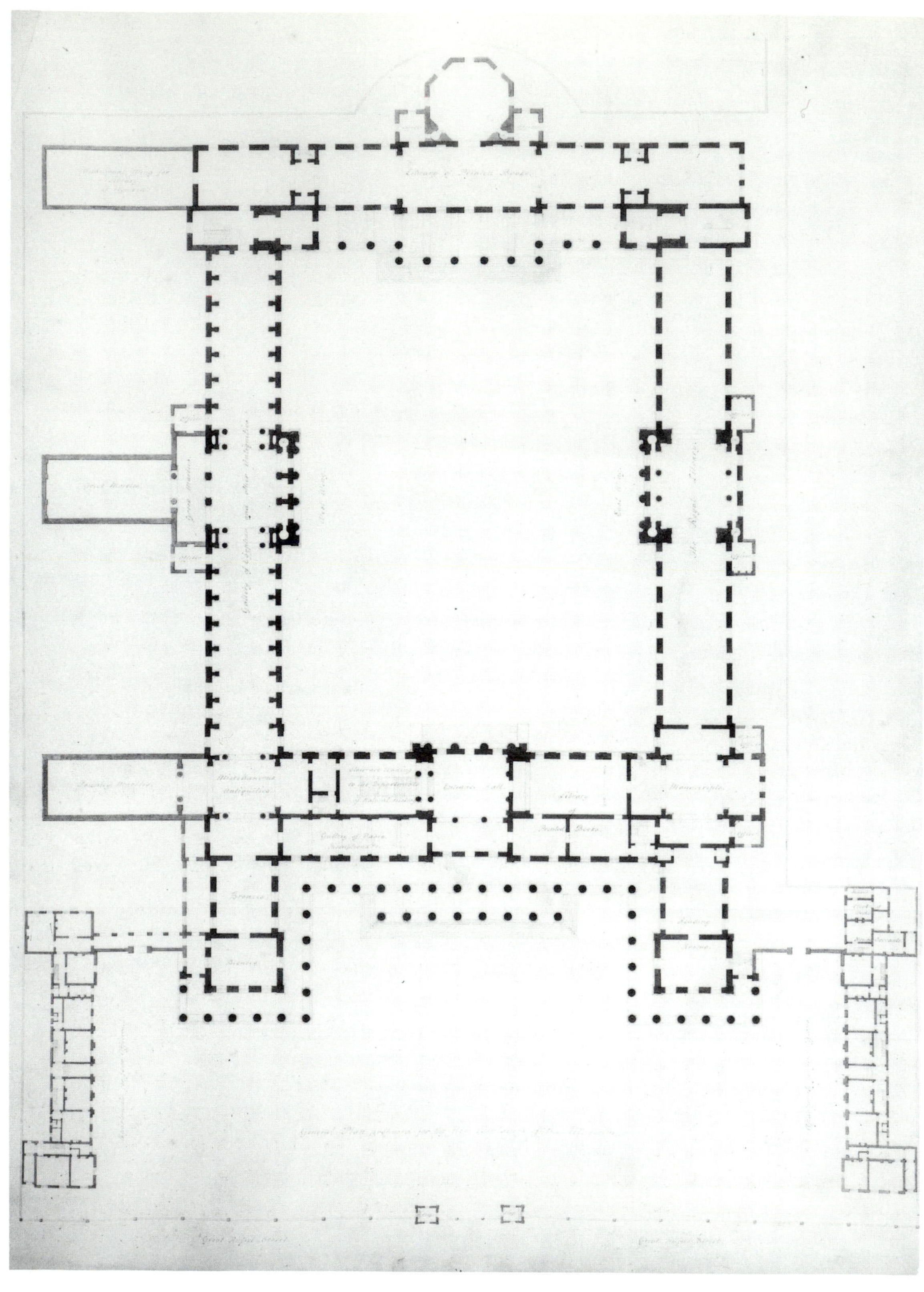

Figure 7.28

Robert Smirke's plan for the British Museum (1827)

Source: Department of Prints and Drawings, British Museum

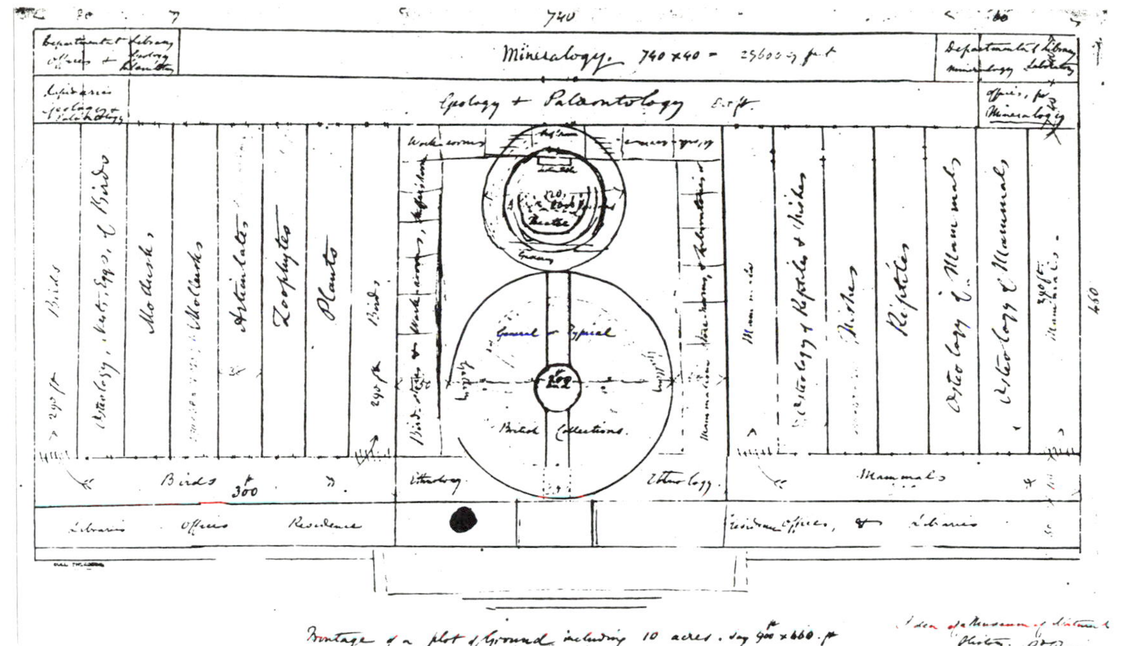

Figure 7.29

Richard Owen's sketch layout for the Natural History Museum (1859)

Source: Natural History Museum Collection, London

trated on teacher training and also housed a museum of industrial design. The Department of Practical Art, governed by the Board of Trade, became the Department of Science and Art in 1856, in the wake of the Crystal Palace. The Great Exhibition made painfully obvious the lack of proper training in industrial design. Henry Cole, one of its promoters, was appointed Superintendent of the central school in 1852 and transferred to its museum a number of the exhibits. Shortage of space eventually forced it in 1856 into temporary buildings on a new site in South Kensington..

The complex grew. At first it was envisaged that the National Gallery would find a home here, and overspill paintings from Trafalgar Square were accommodated. This temporarily diluted – by addition – the intentions which sprang from the Crystal Palace: to raise to museum status applied art and design combined with science and technology for production. In a final dilution – this time by subtraction – the Science Museum acquired its own site in Exhibition Road whilst what became the Victoria and Albert on the other side of the road kept the art and design collections.

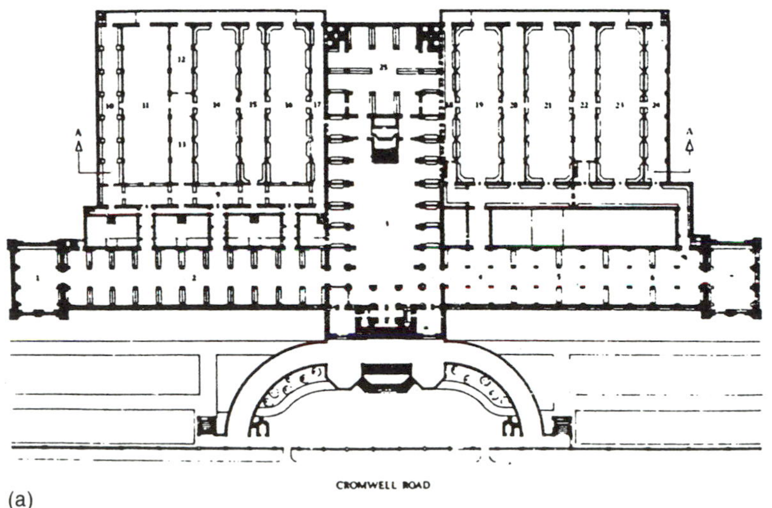

(a)

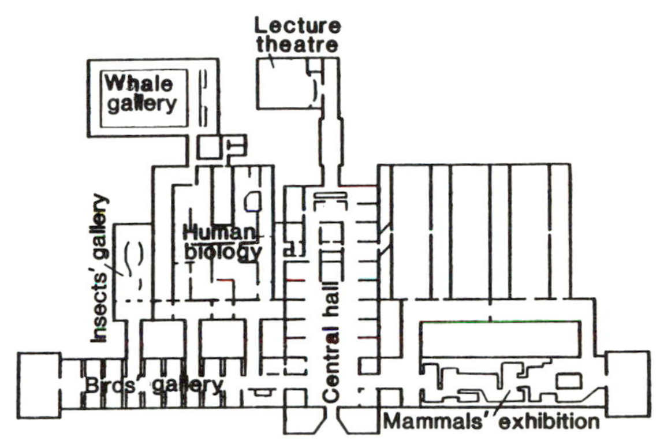

(b)

Figure 7.30

Natural History Museum, plan on completion (a), and Peponis and Hedin's spatial analysis (b)

Source: Peponis and Hedin (1982) (b)

Figure 7.31

Leeds Philosophical Hall (1819–21), first floor plan (a), and exterior view (1821) (b); Yorkshire Philosophical Society's museum (1827–9), ground floor plan (c), and exterior view (d); The Rotunda, Scarborough (1828), ground floor plan (e), and exterior view (f)

Source: Author's drawings based on Brears (1984) (a, c and e); William Boyne *History of Leeds* 5(75), Leeds City Library, (b); Allen (c. 1830) *History of the County of York* vol. i (d), and engraving by C.J. Smith and John Cole (f), by courtesy of York Reference Library, North Yorkshire County Library Service

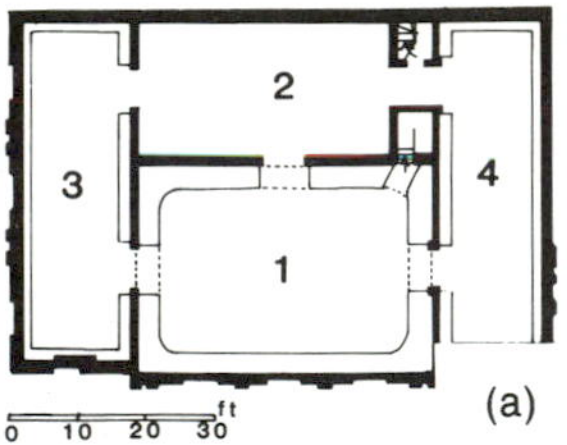

(a)

Key

1 Museum with gallery
2 Library
3 Museum
4 Museum

(b)

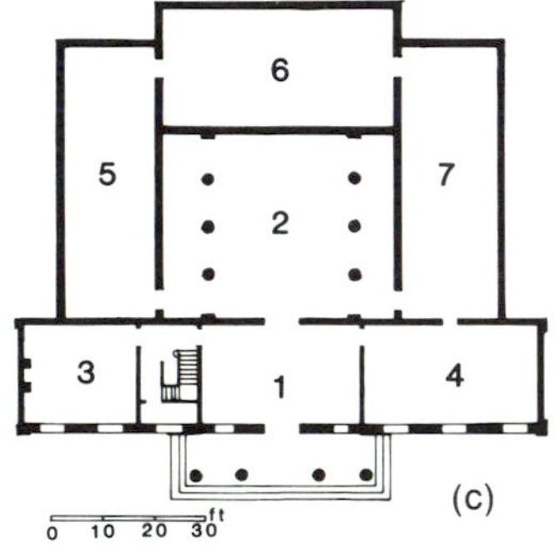

(c)

Key

1 Vestibule
2 Lecture room
3 Council room
4 Library
5 Museum
6 Library
7 Museum

(d)

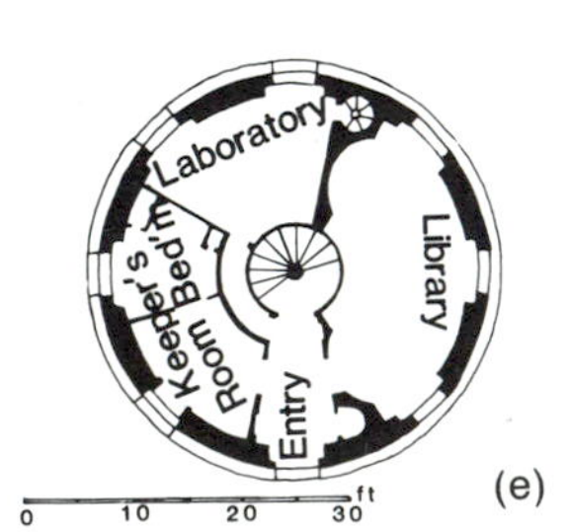

(e)

(f)

The Athenaeums, Literary and Philosophical Societies and bourgeois scientific institutions whose libraries I have looked at always had a museum; sometimes only that. Brears (1984) describes the English scene to 1850. Of the twenty he traces no less than nine were in Yorkshire where the combination of liberal and radical politics with the huge wealth generated by the textile industry diverted some of the surplus into the purchase of time for scholarly leisure.

The Leeds Philosophical Hall (1819–21) designed by Soane's pupil Richard Chantrell had the lecture hall and laboratory on the ground floor (Figure 7.31(a) and (b)) below the library and museum. This was the model for the Yorkshire Philosophical Society's Museum (1827–9) plannned by R.H. Sharp and given a Classical elevation by Wilkins (Figure 7.31(c) and (d)). As at Leeds the lecture hall was surrounded by a ring of museum spaces. But here a front shallow block contained the council room, vestibule, and, in the fashion of mechanics' institutes, the library. The Society also had an adjacent observatory and botanic garden. One of the smallest but symbolically most telling museums was The Rotunda at Scarborough (1828) built, again, according to designs by Sharp (Figure 7.31(e) and (f)). The miniature domed Pantheon had an oculus and a Roman coffered ceiling. The circular plan enabled the specimens of the fossil collection to be displayed in their correct stratigraphical position, an idea apparently borrowed from the Leverian Museum in the Rotunda at Blackfriars Bridge.

The small eclectic collection of curiosities, unlike the Prince's *kunstkammer* which opened this narrative, was now a place of commercial, popular entertainment which makes a good point to close it. From 1795 to 1809 William Bullock housed his extraordinary collection of items from Cook's South Seas expedition, arms and armour, models, works of art, and a mass of botanical and zoological specimens in Lord Street, Liverpool. On transferring it to London he employed Peter Robinson to design the Egyptian Hall in Piccadilly (1810–11). A pharmacy and a bookshop at the front sandwiched the 'great room' from which another hall – the 'Pantherion', projected deep into the building. It was 'intended to display the whole of the known Quadrupeds, in a manner that will convey a more perfect idea of their haunts and mode of life' (Figure 7.32). Entrance was through a basaltic cavern modelled on the Giant's Causeway or Fingall's Cave on the Isle of Staffa. The animals were set in an 'Indian hut, situated in a Tropical Forest', each against suitable botanical specimens. It not only presages Disneyland but, with the armour on the first floor in a mock medieval hall, Glasgow's Burrell Gallery too.

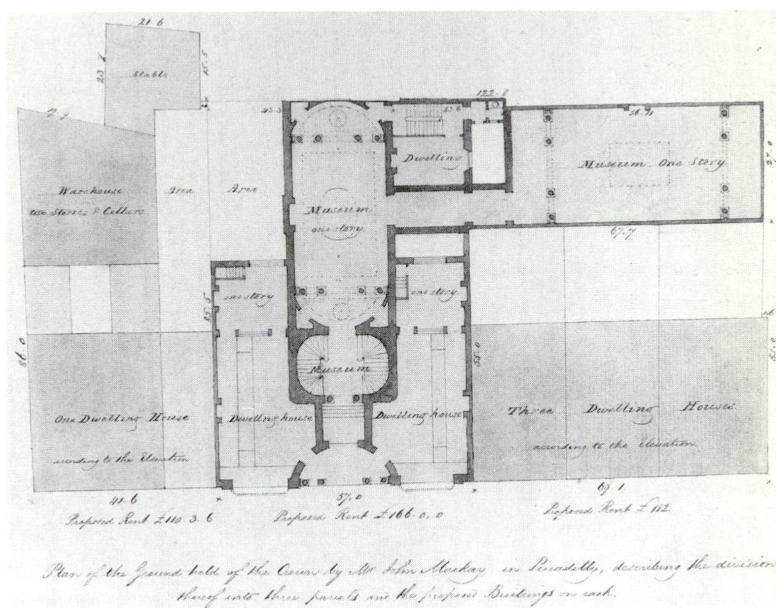

Figure 7.32

Egyptian Hall, Piccadilly (1810–11), plan

Source: Public Record Office (drawing CREST 6/115)

Nature reordered

William Hunter's brother John personifies the link between collections of dead and living specimens for he had his own museums, first at Earl's Court and later in Leicester Square, and at the former also a menagerie and experimental garden and orchard. The link arose from their common roots in science and hermetic mysteries. However zoos and gardens also had roots in display and amusement.

Gustave Loisel's still unmatched three volume history of zoos (1912) traces, from Roman times, the transformation of menageries and aviaries from small groups of cages to the splendid monuments of the Renaissance kings and princes. Joseph Furttenbach (1628: 30 and Plate 13) imagined a fortification which enclosed a magical world of arbours, bridges, temples and streams 'where wild animals can be allowed to run free' in a miniature wilderness. But in reality animals were in enclosures or cages, sometimes surrounding a central observation point as in Varro's aviary which Weinbrenner intended to reconstruct in the neo-Classical manner (Valdenaire 1926: 39), and Girard and Anton Zinner's 1716 radial menagerie for Prince Eugene of Savoie's Belvedere palace (Loisel 1912 vol. 2: Plate IV). Versailles, with its eight trapezoid enclosures and central observation pavilion has already been mentioned. As always this kind of space stands for the power of the viewer by an inversion of the theatre – observer on the central stage, observed in the peripheral auditorium.

During the popular fury at Versailles in October 1789 many animals were destroyed. The few survivors with others collected from all over Paris were placed into the *Jardin des Plantes* in 1793 by decree of the Convention's committee of public instruction. Buffon, when he became director of the *Jardin* (1739) had already used it as a place for a total *exposé* of natural history. But in 1790 a group of scientists proposed to add a museum, a library, and a course of lectures to make it, in combination with the garden and residual zoo, France's leading research centre for natural history.

Its young secretary, Geoffroy-Saint-Hilaire, speculated that:

> a collection of living animals would be an advantage for the instruction of the public and for the progress of natural history, and that it would be the means of acquiring and multiplying, within the territory of the republic, many useful species that now exist only in foreign countries.
>
> (Geoffroy-Saint-Hilaire 1818–22)

Instruction, scholarly study, conservation and breeding – here are the foundations of modern zoology. His *Philosophical Anatomy* (1818–22) embodies the results. There is an unbroken link from Buffon, the greatest natural scientist of the century, through Daubenton who worked with Buffon on his descriptive and anatomical material, to Geoffroy-Saint-Hilaire and finally his young assistant Cuvier who produced his massive taxonomy of living and fossil animals (1817–30). Darwin drew on Buffon's and Cuvier's work, adding his explanation of how, through natural selection, the species they had already classified had evolved. In a process that could have occurred nowhere except France, the 1793 *Mémoire sur la Ménagerie* placed before the Convention detailed arguments for linking a garden with a zoo and opened the first modern political debate about science.

British gardens also originated in the scientific, exotic and herbal tradition – of Oxford and Cambridge colleges, the medical societies and collections for botanical and medical scholarship. But by the early nineteenth century the agricultural revolution was well advanced, and the Board of Agriculture was working, under its first president Sir John Sinclair the great Scottish 'improver'. A distinction was being made between science and utility in gardens, analogous to that between 'fine' and 'useful' art (or design). In Curtis's London Botanic Gardens (Salisbury 1810: 113– 14 and Plate), set up in the 1780s in Lambeth and then moved to Brompton, medicinal and agricultural plants were in separate beds; but science (as in Owen's 'Index gallery') had the upper hand for one bed demonstrated the *entire* vegetable taxonomy in the Linnaean mode. There was a library and a course of lectures. This modest garden not only promoted medicine, pharmacy, botany and agriculture, but was also intended to help artists in an attempt to recover a unity of knowledge in the vegetable kingdom no less visionary than William Hunter's had been for the human body. But it was not to be. Agricultural science and economics not only separated from botany but, today, botanists lead the resistance against the ecological destruction wrought by farming.

There was an analogous divergence for animals. London's Zoological Society (1825, Royal Charter 1829), an offshoot of the Linnean Society founded in 1788, was an attempt to hold utility and science together. It was to serve for zoological experiment and to study such 'living subjects of the Animal Kingdom as may be introduced and domesticated with advantage in this country'. Zoology was 'a most important part of Natural Theology' in that it displays the Creator's 'wisdom and power', but, at the same time, it has economic aims – for animals are 'employed in social life, for labour, clothing, food etc.' and they are important in 'various departments of industry and commerce' (Chalmers Mitchell 1929: 8–10). The Charter's objectives were to be achieved by setting up for members and the public a zoo and a library, providing materials for museums and anatomists, publication of zoological research and maintaining and assisting research in anatomy and taxonomy. The model of the *Jardin* cannot have been far away. But the museum component had precedents nearer home.

One was the immense collection of animals, birds, fossils and shells assembled by Ashton Lever in his Leicester Square home, Leicester House, from 1773 onwards. In 1786 it was sold in

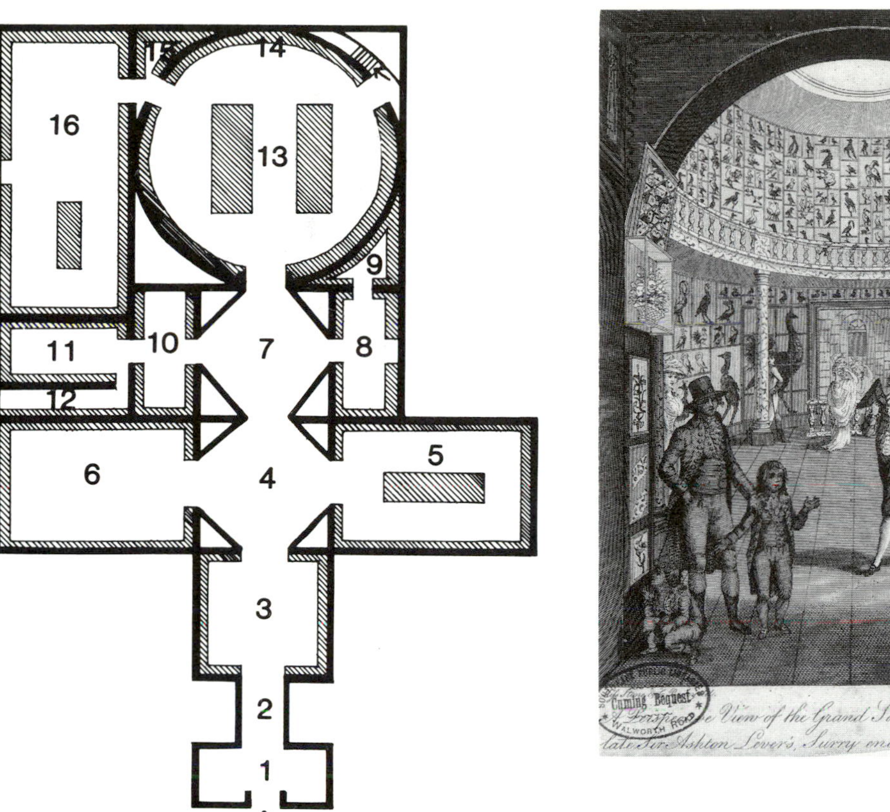

(a)

(b)

Figure 7.33

Leverian museum in Blackfriar's rotunda (1788), plan (a), and interior of rotunda (b)

Source: Author's drawing based on sketch bound into *A Companion to the Museum etc.* (1790), London, Southwark Council Local Studies Library, with thanks to Thomas deWit (a); frontispiece of above (b)

Key

1 Arms
2 War clubs
3 Oceanic curiosities
4 Wasps nests, wood polished, minerals
5 Minerals
6 Shells, marbles, organic remains of the insect world
7 Dress of a Chinese man of status
8 Dresses, old shoes, Montague
9 Miscellaneous
10 Monkeys
11 Amphibious animals
12 Anatomical?
13 Butterflies and moths, insects
14 Birds
15 Fish, miscellaneous
16 Elk, quadrupeds, old china – Roman urns, bone and skulls, etc., antiquities

a lottery won by Joseph Parkinson who transferred it to the Rotunda, at the south end of Blackfriars Bridge, designed by James Burton (1788). The cylyndrical space displaying the huge bird collection (Figure 7.33) is the deepest, at the end of a series of cabinet-lined galleries. After Parkinson sold the collection and the building in 1809 the domed space was converted into a lecture theatre for the Surrey Institution not unlike John Anderson's earlier conversion for his Glasgow Institution.

The Society's site in Regent's Park created problems in Nash's élite estate. There were fears of unwelcome sights, sounds and smells. The Society had to promise the Commissioners of Woods and Forests that the buildings would 'for the most part be low and in no way offensive', moreover there was to be a high surrounding wall. At the start both zoological and botanical gardens were envisaged, as well as an 'attached' museum. The zoo went ahead rapidly from 1826 with the appointment of Decimus Burton as architect but provision for the Society's offices, library and museum was slower and altogether more fraught. Though Burton's plans incorporated them in Regent's Park, lack of funds kept the Society in its rented accommodation in Bruton Street till 1836 when it moved into John Hunter's old house in Leicester Square. In 1841 a competition was held for a new building inside the zoo, won by E.W. Elmslie with a nostalgic revival of the Renaissance 'cabinet'.[2] But once more funds were lacking and two years later the rooms moved into a house in Hanover Square, the collections having been

Figure 7.34

Burton's original design for the layout of London zoo

Source: Richard Taylor (1830) *List of all the Animals in the Gardens of the Zoological Society etc.* 9th edn, London

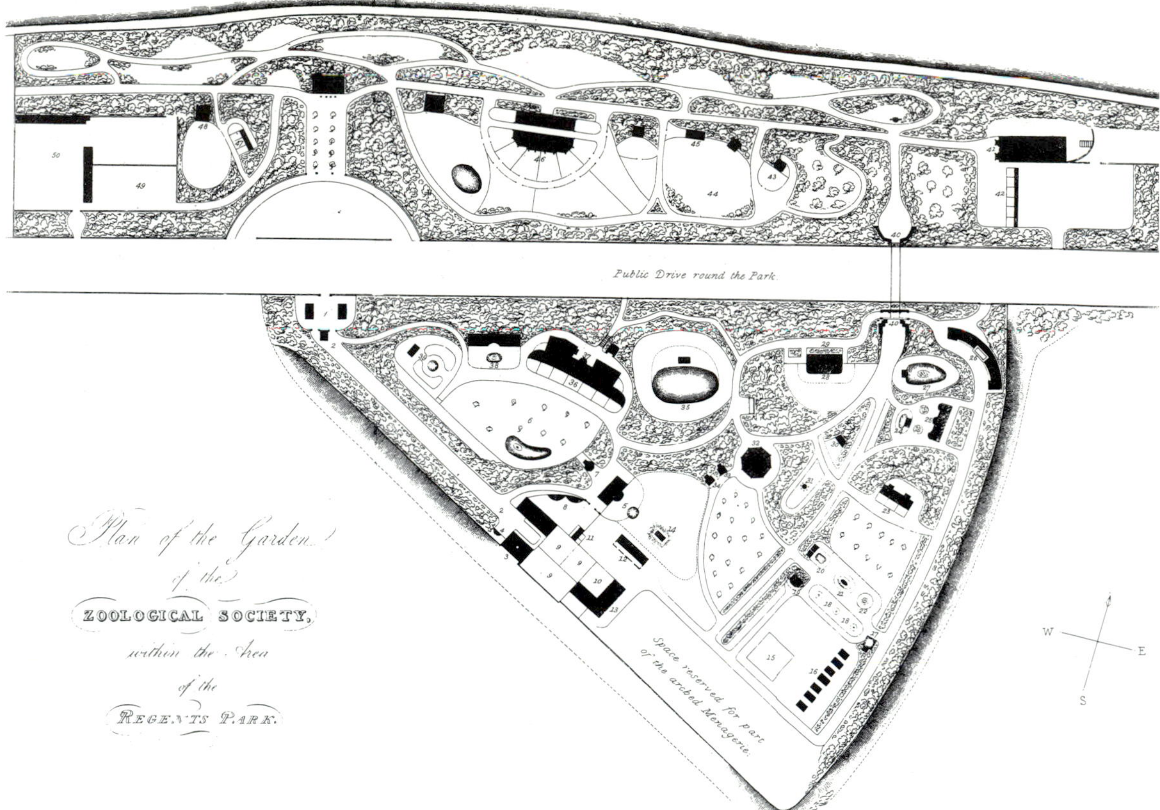

Key

1 Entrance lodges
2 Terrace
3 Bear pit
4 Rustic seat
5 Llama house
6 Lawn and pond
7 House and cage for maccaws
8 Courtyard
9 Yards for deer, etc.
10 Yard and shed for deer, etc.
11 Sloth bear's den
12 Dens for large quadrupeds
13 Winter repository
14 Shed and enclosures for goats
15 Square enclosure for antelopes
16 Movable aviaries
17 Polar bear's den and bath
18 Monkey poles
19 Harpy eagle cage
20 Seals' house
21 Otter cage and pond
22 Enclosure for tortoises
23 Monkey house
24 Beaver pond
25 Falcon aviary
26 Aviary for small birds
27 Pond for small ducks
28 Cattle-sheds and yards
29 Owl cages
30 Turtle dove cage
31 Enclosure for rabbits
32 Eagle aviary
33 Guinea pig enclosure
34 Wolf's den
35 Pond for geese
36 Large aviaries
37 Keepers' apartments
38 Enclosure for pelicans
39 Emu house and yard
40 Tunnel
41 Repository
42 Dog kennels
43 Ostrich shed
44 Ostrich paddock
45 Kangaroo shed
46 House and yards for wapiti deer, etc.
47 Pecary sties
48 Tapir's house
49 Gardeners' yard, etc.
50 Carpenters' yards and sheds, etc.

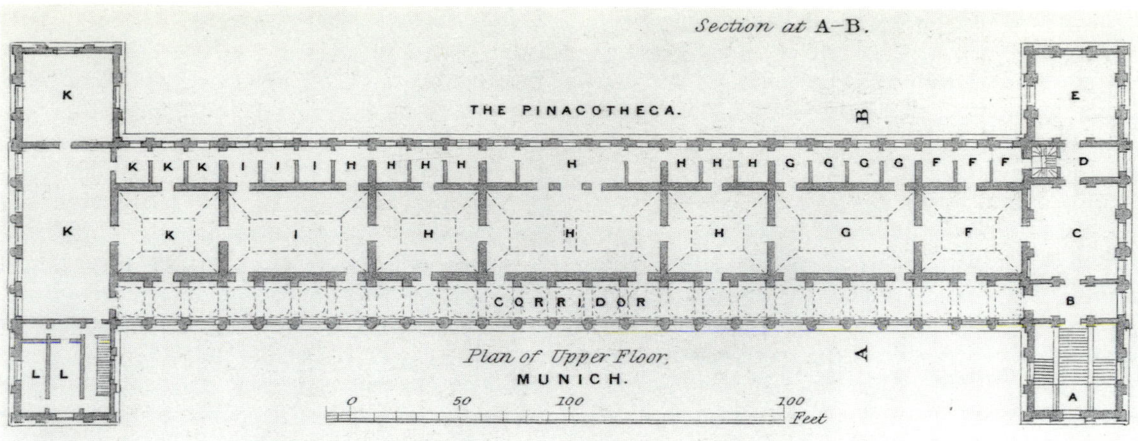

Figure 7.35
Upper floor plans of von Klenze's Alte Pinakothek, *Münich (1826–36)*
Source: Papworth and Papworth (1853), British Architecture Library

transferred into a converted building in the zoo finally to land up in the British Museum in 1855.

Burton's first sketch (1827) shows cages and enclosures dotted about in free-flowing *parterres* on both sides of the (public) Drive (Figure 7.34). The entrance is on the axis of the keeper's lodge on the other side of the Drive, and the two largest structures are aviaries on the north side. He already intended to create a topological unity by tunnelling under the Drive. From the entrance a straight terrace ran to animal enclosures. Until 1834 only the south was developed though an 1830 plan shows both sides. The first animals to be encountered were the most fierce – in the absence of large cats, these were the bears. Their place was taken by the new carnivores in 1851. Though Vigors, the last President of the Linnean Society and the first Secretary of the new one, intended to produce a taxonomy 'in a series more strictly consonant with their natural affinities than any that has hitherto been proposed' (Bennett 1830 and 1831) by 1830 he still did not feel ready to publish and instead relied on a version of Cuvier. On the ground there is little sign of any 'affinities'. There is a pell-mell sequence of mammals and birds, water and land animals, wild and domestic. Rabbits and armadillos shared an enclosure. The spatial principle is of a peripheral walk with *sorties* into rings which penetrate deep into the site.

The growth of the gardens is serially illustrated and described by Scherren (1905). Despite much expansion and moving around of specimens, the idea of a serial walk remained.

No botanical gardens were created in Regent's Park, but Burton did design those of the Royal Botanic Society in 1838 with separate scientific, agricultural and commercial collections.

Politics and pictures

As enmeshed in politics as the *Jardin* was France's, in fact Europe's, largest art gallery, the Louvre. Duncan and Wallach (1980) call it a 'universal survey museum' – a presentation of art history in its totality, covering all times, places and types. This Enlightenment idea was guiding the transformation of princely and royal galleries in the palaces where the visitor had been dazzled by the paintings in a dense arrangement in what they call 'a tapestry-like effect' whose 'iconographic programmes ... glorified the ruler and his realm'.

Now schools of painting and stylistic development were to determine organisation. The *philosophes* had demanded the creation on these new lines of a Royal gallery in the Louvre, with public access – though in reality of a very restricted kind. Louis XVI planned such a project in the 1770s, but the Revolution intervened and demanded the creation of a 'national monument ...(as) one of the most powerful ways of proclaiming the illustriousness of the French Republic'. The Convention designated the Louvre as The Museum of the French Republic in 1793 and set about its re-organisation.

Everything – grouping, hanging, spatial experience and surface ornamentation – was aimed to make concrete the abstract concept of the people's nation state, a Republic which would be a reincarnation of the Classical culture of Greece, Rome and the Renaissance. Axes were used in Classical ways, first as tree-like routes, the trunks compulsory, the branches offering a choice of destinations but no choice of routes to a given destination. The incidents placed along these trees were new. The foot of the grand staircase at the end of Daru Gallery, leading to the Victory of

Samothrace – representing 'the everlasting triumph of the nation and the state, presented in the guise of the triumph of culture' – is the 'first major moment in the ritual walk' (Duncan and Wallach 1980: 458). Secondly, other axes are on rings to give grandeur.

Huge funds were released for the glorification of the nation and for satisfying municipal ambition. Ludwig I of Bavaria, whilst still Crown prince, intended to make Münich Germany's greatest city. Leo von Klenze's design for the Glyptothek (1815–30) set the pattern for severe Classicism. All rooms were in a continuous ring around the four sides of the courtyard. Schinkel's Berlin *Altes Museum*, in the Durandesque grand manner, had a huge central rotunda which he described as a 'sanctuary', flanked by two courtyards and enclosed on three sides by long galleries. Von Klenze, in the Münich *Alte Pinakothek* (1826–36) made an important spatial departure. The large, interconnected galleries were conventional enough. The upper floor was arranged in chronological sequence of 'schools' – Flemish, German, French, Spanish and Italian – and the lower floor in types – drawings, paintings, mosaics, terra cotta vases, porcelain, glass and enamels. The innovation lay in the system of circulation. On one side the main galleries opened into a series of small ones; on the other into a 420 feet long corridor ('loggia') which creates many rings and enables the visitor to construct any sequence (Figure 7.35).

Britain was less ambitious. Though the National Gallery collection was started in 1824, its construction to Wilkins's design only started in 1833. Till 1869 it also accommodated the Royal Academy and substantial additions were made, the latest Venturi and Scott's Sainsbury Wing (1991). Each addition made the spatial structure deeper and added to the original two-branched tree (dividing from the centre) a number of rings. The site limited the length of the first plan (Figure 7.36) whose *en filade* symmetrical sequences forced the Trustees to adopt a fixed model of 'schools'.

The only precedent was John Soane's extraordinary Dulwich Gallery (1814). Its five end-to-end galleries crossed, at the centre, the axis of a mausoleum to his patron and friend Noel Desenfans and his wife, and to Francis Bourgeois through whom the Desenfans collection of paintings had been left to Dulwich College (Figure 7.37).

Classification and power

By the mid-nineteenth century the production of knowledge had come a long way from the chamber of curiosities. With the ever-finer subdivision of knowledge and space went the subdivision of labour into new disciplines and professions: teachers, librarians, curators, conservators and researchers with new professional bodies, journals, educational systems and scholarly activities. Collections still attracted their specialist clienteles but the political pressure for public access won the day. To do that three problems had to be solved. First objects had to be not only visible and orderly, but safe. Surveillance and security became dominant. Second, the public had to be entertained. No all-consuming obsession could be assumed. Owen had already tried to combine scholarship and entertainment with his alternating research and public galleries at the Natural History Museum. Third, the overt ideological framework which underpinned the old collections – glorification of King, Church or State – had to become covert by appealing to such universals as religion, art, science, reason and nature which were beyond debate.

In the Ashmolean's 1836 catalogue the 'natural objects' are said to be arranged according to principles drawn from Paley's *Natural Theology* 'to induce a mental habit of associating the view of natural phenomena with the conviction that they are the media of Divine manifestation and by such association to give proper dignity to every branch of natural science'. Though the relation between science and conservative theology had not yet reached the crisis precipitated by Darwin, it was already thorny; the critical and analytical potential of science had to be defused by using descriptive science to emphasise the richness of nature.

Ideological positions shaped the content, classification and explanation of collections, and the design of their buildings. Architects, curators and exhibition designers formed alliances to respond to these positions. When von Klenze assembles Classical fragments into a painterly composition he shares with the curators of the *Alte Pinakothek* their vision of the grandeur of Classical art.

To the old subjects another was added after 1848 – politics. Museums commemorated independence and liberation movements; soon a whole range of war and naval museums filled with booty from colonial ventures were founded. In Leningrad October 1917 was celebrated in

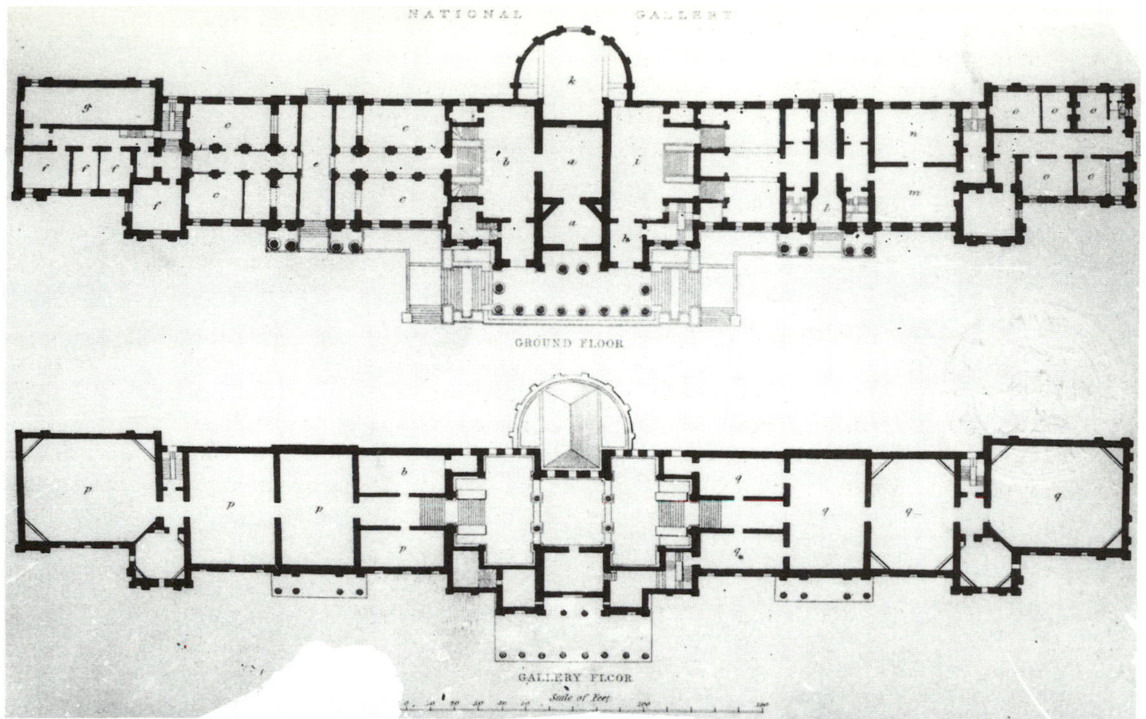

Figure 7.36
Wilkins' National Gallery (1831–8), ground and first floor plans

splendid palaces. After World War II concentration camps became museums. Recently many new subjects have emerged: work, social and everyday history, the post, design, travel, tobacco, wine, machines, industrial archeology and film, to name but a few. And there has been a revolution in display. Museums always had the edge over the written text through the power of concrete reality. But, largely influenced by television, another kind of reality has become even more powerful – that of the simulation. The traditional make-believe of wax statues, models and reconstructions has been largely superseded by computers, lasers, audio effects, synthetised smells (though not yet Aldous Huxley's 'feelies'), video and holography which can simulate reality in unprecedented ways. Eco (1987) describes the imitation castles, cathedrals and excavations which are more real than reality as 'hyper-reality' – the ultimate fake. But the contradiction he exposes was at the heart of the museum from the start, even when real objects were used: by framing and disconnecting them from historical space and time, they were already unreal. In focusing on the new techniques Eco fails to notice that the oldest one of all, the formation of space, is harnessed to the same contradiction.

The contradictions often serve to create assymetrical social relations by obliteration. In museums of industrial archeology of workers in their work environment and the associated ill health, danger, poverty and housing. In mercantile museums the slaves disappear; in those of everyday life women are either invisible or spotlit in 'womanly' activity of housework, child-rearing and comforting the male breadwinner.

Gombrich's art shrine has expanded today to the whole building as a sacred place. The polemics of architectural debate are as fixed on museums and galleries as they were on churches in the nineteenth century. These commissions carry the greatest international prestige. Because they are now sacred objects in their own right there are now museums of museums and of architecture.

Figure 7.37
Soane's Dulwich Gallery (1814), ground floor plan
Source: Based on drawings in Dorothy Stroud (1961) *The Architecture of John Soane*, Studio, London

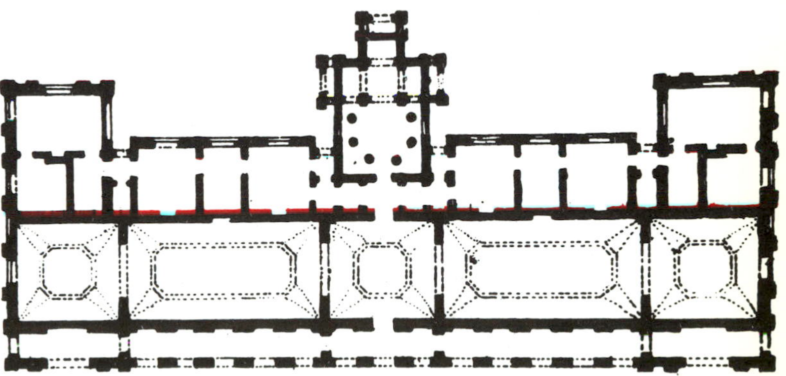

What is the way out of these contradictions if there is no collection without selection, no history without position, if the objects are not only precious as commodities but beautiful and fascinating, and if the buildings are exciting? Authentic answers will share the view that history is being made today, by and for each individual, and that it is memory which gives this process meaning. Neither the past nor the present make sense by themselves. A museum which does not enable visitors to find meaning in the present has failed.

Though every individual's experience of the present is unique, there is a shared web of ideas which have always been around: about art, technology and nature. These spring from human relations. If objects of the past can be presented without tearing this web (without 'framing' them) not only are they contextually enriched, but they serve as models of what relations are like. The object connected to its past relations connects visitors to their present ones.

In written history no single view remains unchallenged. In the absence of censorship many histories exist side by side. But such pluralism is not open to creators of museums. Resources are scarce and many objects unique; it is impossible to 'write' alternative museums. The openness has to be within each institution.

Several practical consequences follow, for both the collections and the buildings.

For the collections, first, location inevitably places an item in a class, within a sequence. It is said that in Glasgow's Kelvingrove Museum the simple rule applied to pottery was that if a pot was complete it went into Decorative Arts, if broken into Archeology! Curators are however guided by more sophisticated systems, such as the Social History and Industrial Classification System which, according to one museum worker, cuts 'vertically into activities' so that a needle is both an article of production and of consumption. Moreover it has multiple uses – making decorative needlework, clothes and furnishings, or for paid sewing in the home. It has social and economic ramifications. She could have added that its twin, the pin, is the very object Adam Smith used to illustrate the division of labour; this, far more than any of its uses, earns it an exalted place in history. So she recommends that:

> the slant of classification may be offset by operating it (the system) differently to develop a dynamic model … with multiple references which prompt the user to connect to the spheres of working life, community life, and personal life, and which suggest the comparison and interdependence of activities and interests in different spheres. More thorough recording and collecting, with emphasis on the provenance – the detailed history and context – of every object would itself extend or override the boundaries of the classification.
>
> (Porter 1988: 114).

The example is one tiny object, the argument is general. And today, for the first time, communication technology can easily satisfy these aims, and in stunning ways.

Second, it goes almost without saying that camouflaging or keeping silent over painful, unpopular or uncomfortable evidence is eschewed.

Third, the theoretical position within which the entire collection is presented, is made as explicit as possible.

Fourth, every opportunity is taken to link past, present and future societies – of makers, users, museum builders and visitors. If the museum stretches beyond recording history to making it, it will need frequent re-arrangement. Theoretical crises (like the arrival of Darwin) or practical crises (like ecological pressures) both changed natural history collections. The world art market changes the presentation of paintings. Computer databases change the use of books.

For the buildings, first, alternatives to siting these buildings within a 'cultural centre' are available: subject grouping as in the *Jardin*, making links with work or dwelling space, or making location mobile.

Second, Von Klenze's Münich corridor marked a radical departure from determined spatial sequences. But if briefs demanded that users be able to construct alternative sequences, many plans other than a string of rooms alongside a corridor can be imagined. Modern design can exploit visibility, movement and use of the vertical dimension in ways which alter the experience of space. Though Disneyland appears to do this, it has merely substituted novel for traditional forms of constraint. But there can be an opposite failure, of limitless choice. The building, and back-up information systems such as the data base installed in the new Sainsbury wing of the National Gallery, can give vast spatial freedom. If this is not to degenerate into chaos, the visitor also needs the freedom to choose alternative

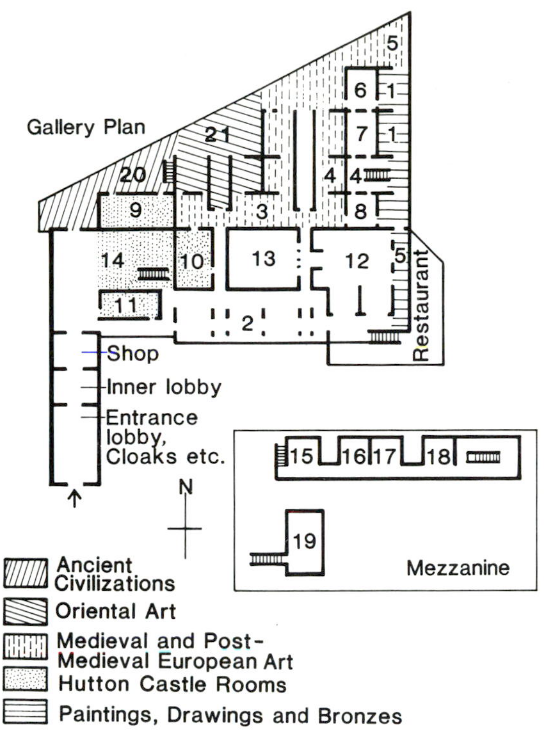

Key

1 Carpets and near eastern ceramics
2 Stained glass and furniture
3 Tapestries
4 Needlework and lace
5 Sculpture
6 Elizabethan room
7 Seventeenth- and eighteenth-century room
8 Gothic domestic room
9 Drawing room
10 Hall
11 Dining room
12 Temporary exhibition area
13 Lecture theatre
14 Courtyard
15 Old masters
16 Nineteenth-century French paintings
17 Pastels: Degas and Manet
18 Special displays from the collection

Figure 7.38
Burrell Gallery, Glasgow, ground floor plan
Source: Author's drawing

theoretical positions. A clear presentation would show the consequences of choice on the selection of exhibits and the spatial sequence in which they are viewed.

Third, the tradition of an overall integrating space – such as Owen's Index Gallery or a central spine – should not be easily abandoned.

Fourth, a fixed formal language creates problems. The somnolence-inducing forms of the Louvre were shattered by the intervention of Pei's glass pyramid. A language like 'high-tech', though it appears to be neutral at the Sainsbury Centre or Beaubourg, in fact carries such a burden of metaphorical meanings – of supermarkets and machines – that there is a halo effect on exhibits. The Stuttgart *Staatsgalerie*, where the powerful forms are outside the exhibition space, suggests one solution. Another is museum-as-theatre where a completely neutral infrastructure of technical support and services can be clad temporarily in a variety of 'stage settings'.

For authoritarian régimes the museum is an essential prop. For free market capitalism it is equally essential, and the market uses similar opportunities to validate itself in culture. I have mentioned Glasgow's Burrell Gallery; it will serve as an illustration of this point.

On a publicity leaflet a sixteenth century doorway with the armorial bearings of the Hornby family is seen built into smooth modern sandstone. Through it are visible two pieces of ancient sculpture – one on a pedestal, the other in a glass case. In the background, seen through the glazed wall, is the woodland pushing right up to the building. Everything of importance is said by this image.

William Burrell, a wealthy Glasgow shipowner, died in 1958 and left a spectacular art collection to the city together with capital for a gallery. The Deed specified a minimum distance from the city centre, on grounds of pollution. Eventually the 1970 competition specified a site in Pollok Park, part of the Stirling Maxwell family's estate for seven centuries, for which William Adam had designed Pollok House. It attracted 242 entries and the winners were Barry Gasson, John Meunier and Brit Andresen the first of whom saw the building through to execution.

We have seen that the brief required competitors to reproduce the three main rooms of Burrell's residence, Hutton Castle.

The entrance, through another Hornby doorway in a projecting wing, leads through foyers, cloakrooms, information desks and shops to the great courtyard formed by the Hutton rooms. Then to a gallery of ancient sculpture and pottery that terminates in the glass screen which continues along the full north edge of the building. The tapestries and medieval galleries occupy the central north section; the Gothic, Elizabethan, seventeenth and eighteenth century galleries, as well as modern paintings the east flank; and stained glass the south front (Figure 7.38).

Texts in the foyer introduce Burrell and the collection. Then the sequence, following the most natural flow, is: Hutton Castle rooms, ancient art; medieval art and tapestries; post-medieval and modern art and stained glass. The invisible text of the brief which in many ways 'designed' the building, the visible text in the foyer, the site, space and the classification say the following:

1. Art collecting is the business of the wealthy. As in the past, their generosity then transfers the valuable investment to state or city.
2. The adjacency of another, established collection, in a historic country house (Pollok) gives the site a head start as a hallowed spot.
3. The removal from the city centre, and the placing in the corner of a meadow in abrupt juxtaposition to woodland, constantly present through the north glass screen, associates nature with art. The innocence of one rubs off on the other.
4. The hacking off from churches and castles of large pieces of decorated masonry and their incorporation into a modern fabric is an architectural analogue of framing – isolating works of art torn out of material and social contexts. Embedding revered objects makes the building revered.
5. The compulsory foyer text – whatever else can be passed by, that cannot – establishes the primacy of the three Hutton rooms and makes Burrell the collector the real subject. The gallery becomes a modern reproduction of his 'house'.
6. Any semblance of a chronological sequence can easily be circumvented, so that the collection asserts that artistic value transcends history (so one of Burrell's ancient Chinese pots is as 'great' as an Impressionist painting a few metres away). The traditional curator is left with the problem of how to reassert the importance of period – historical time.

The Burrell is as much about entertainment as was the Egyptian Hall for its plebeian audience, not just by virtue of the quality of its collection, but by the fascinating testimony of how taste is generated by wealth. There are two other types which entertain. One makes spectacular topographical and historical presentations. The other, by associating art with trade and industry celebrates them directly. The first is the panorama or diorama, the second the exhibition building. Both housed ephemeral material in ephemeral containers.

CHAPTER 8

Ephemeral knowledge

An attack on the senses

The rational, encylopaedic museum abandoned hermetic mystery and alchemy. Although Enlightenment – illuminating the dark, making visible the hidden, finding natural laws where there had only been the random caprice of supernatural agents – had brought an astonishing change, the popular appeal of the new museums was limited by their immense size and their staid, static displays. A revisit was an exact repeat. Something altogether more striking and dynamic was needed to satisfy curiosity.

The old design skills for seeing and hearing acquired in theatres were to be stretched in unimaginable ways. And this could be done with least inhibition when the objects of display were temporary, and the way they were seen and heard could become an end itself. Such ephemeral worlds of sight and sound are the precursors of Disneyland and Eco's 'hyper-reality'. They originate in two quite different contexts – entertainment and trade.

Panoramas and dioramas[1]

The techniques are foreshadowed in the paintings of Joseph Wright of Derby's (Paulson 1975). He was patronised by Josiah Wedgewood and, through him, tied into the Birmingham Lunar Society and its wide circle of Radicals, scientists and industrialists. His metaphors contain the elements of a new synthesis betwen science and art, a convergence of the laboratory and the studio. Wright's interest in light sources led him to create dramatic contrasts between illuminated and dark areas; the light on the experiment destroys the mystique of science. By showing science in the home it is seen as both satisfying curiosity and arousing emotion. It is both entertaining and familiar.

The panoramas and dioramas also fused science with art, and amusement with instruction. They too exploited advanced optics and lighting techniques to create dramatic spectacle. Of course the idea of vast maps which gradually grew into perspective aerial views was not new. Hyde (1988) traces it to Berberi's Venetian bird's eye prospects, Dürer's battle scenes and Baroque ceiling paintings. These, with their carefully contrived *trompe l'oeil* devices, were developed to astonishing limits by the Jesuit Andrea Pozzo in his late seventeenth century ceiling paintings in the Roman church of St Ignazio. Pirenne (1970) described Pozzo's 'net' – a rectangular grid of thin cords fastened horizontally just below the springing of the vault – through which he projected his perspective onto the curved surface of the vault. From the fixed viewpoint the effect is staggering – the architecture of the painting seeming to continue seamlessly that of the building. Knowledge of perspective enabled planned distortion to be used as Holbein demonstrated in his *Ambassadors.* It eventually led to a whole science of anamorphism – distorted painting on curved surfaces which, from prescribed viewpoints, would lead to ultra-realism, sometimes with the assistance of cylindrical or conical mirrors.

Stafford (1984) sees in Enlightenment travel accounts 'the scientific gaze (in a) quest for transparency'. The texts and illustrations are ever-more elaborate devices for reaching reality in all its detail. 'The interest in duplicating the human body in wax or in manufacturing a seamless identity was, like the contemporaneous mania for panoramas, dioramas or daguerrotypes, predicated on the desire for totally accurate representation'. The aim was nothing less than to deceive observers into believing that they were in the presence of the authentic.

Optical devices such as pinhole boxes and the *camera obscura* were as old as the hills. Leonardo da Vinci knew them. But the renewed interest in light and the microscope and telescope for seeing deeper into nature caused these old techniques to re-surface. Above all the position of the observing subject at the centre of the universe, who now expected to see and hear everything, to have the inner secrets of the object revealed, required new display techniques in which the boundaries between science and art were demolished. And not only nature, but human nature was the subject for such a gaze as we have already seen in Bentham's Panopticon.

Amongst the domestic devices was the Zograscope for *vues d'optiques*. A double convex lens was supported in a frame on a pillar. Hinged to the top edge of the frame was a mirror whose angle could be adjusted. Prints viewed through the lens by reflection in the mirror, and hence reversed, had the appearance of great depth and were specially striking when perspective was used. From the mid-eighteenth century to the early nineteenth their production was an industry carried out notably in London, Paris, Augsburg and Basano.

An early public device was the Eidophusikon or 'Various Imitations of Natural phenomena represented by Moving Pictures' devised by a French painter – Philippe de Loutherbourg who was employed as a scene painter by Garrick at Drury Lane as soon as he arrived in England in 1771. His scenery for the 1773 production of the *Christmas Tale* inaugurated a new era in its spectacular use of light, modelling and realistic detail. In 1781 he set up the Eidophusikon in his Lisle Street house. A ten foot wide box had mechanically operated moving scenes of storms at sea, dawn over London and moonlight over the Mediterranean. He used gauze and other translucent materials behind painted opaque silhouettes, slides and reflectors, illuminated by 'artificial' (gas?) lighting. There was music, and sound effects such as thunderclaps accompanied by simulated lightning.

The forward leap was made by Robert Barker, an Edinburgh portrait and miniature painter, in the mid-1780s. He was already teaching a 'mechanical system of perspective' to art students and now produced a 360° view of the city seen from the top of Calton Hill – at first assembled as a part circle in six segments, 25 feet in diameter. Initially there were defects: only straight lines at eye level appeared horizontal, others appeared curved. Distortions were introduced on the cylinder by making straight lines curved and curved ones straight. The top and bottom edges of the picture had to be hidden by shades and a barrier was needed to prevent too close an approach. The interior was in semi-darkness, the lighting falling onto the painting from a central, overhead source. The viewing platform was approached by an opening in the floor. After patenting it Barker exhibited this panorama at Holyrood, the Assembly Rooms, Glasgow and in 1789 at the Haymarket in London.

There was popular and expert acclaim – Reynolds is reputed to have made the astonishing admission that it was 'capable of representing nature in a manner far superior to the limited scale of pictures in general' and David was equally complimentary in Paris (*Art Journal* 1857: 46). Barker's first purpose-built building, the Rotunda (1793) designed by Robert Mitchell, opened in Leicester Square with two cylinders, the Large Circle of 90 feet diameter and 40 feet height giving a surface of 10,000 square feet, and the Upper Circle with 2700 square feet (Figure 8.1). An inverted cone skylight lit the top panorama, and a glazed annular ring the lower one.

With his assistant John Burford and his son Henry Aston he now embarked on a massive production programme: the Battle of Trafalgar, Napoleonic war scenes, topographical views of Constantinople, Paris, Lisbon, Copenhagen, Cairo, St Petersburg were just a few (*Art Journal* 1857: 47). His first London panorama of 1792 was based on sketches from the roof of the Albion Mills. After exhibiting it in a temporary building behind his house in Castle Street, a full 360° version, with a surface of 2700 square feet, was transferred to Leicester Square three years later. He soon had competitors.

At Spring Gardens the London 'Eidometropolis' panorama (1802–3) was painted by one of England's most eminent artists, Thomas Girtin. Barker's as well as the other artists' paintings travelled widely in Britain, Europe and America. The Albion Mills view was in New York by 1795,

Section of the Rotunda, Leicester Square, in which is exhibited the PANORAMA.
Coupe de la Rotonde, dans laquelle, est l'exhibition du PANORAMA, Leicester Square.
Robt. Mitchell, Architect

Figure 8.1

Mitchell's Panorama, Leicester Square (1793), section

Source: Robert Mitchell (1801) *Plans etc. of Buildings Erected in England and Scotland etc.*, London, plate 14, British Architecture Library

and versions toured Paris, Leipzig, Hamburg, Vienna and Amsterdam. Large fortunes were amassed through multiple and engraved versions.

James Barlow and an American, Robert Fulton, imported the idea to Paris through a 1799 *brevet d'importation* which they ceded to M. and Mme Thayer who constructed the first two Parisian panoramas in the Boulevard Montmartre, each with a diameter of 17 metres and a height of 7 (d'Helft and Verliefden 1978). They acted as sentinels to a new urban passage and as nuclei to a manifestation of 'an industrial consumer society oriented towards fashion, luxury tastes and profit' (1978: 55) consisting of shops, theatres, cafes, baths, bazaars and hotels. In 1800 the architect-painter Dufourney recommended panoramas to the Assembly as 'objects both instructive and useful'. In 1807 Thayer constructed a 32 metre panorama in the Boulevard des Capucins; on visiting this Napoleon ordered the architect Cellerier to design *eight* rotundas for the Champs-Élysées – however the events of 1812 intervened.

Berlin's rotunda was designed by a panorama painter, Breysig (1800). A second building (1808) exhibited a view of Palermo based on sketches by Schinkel. The fashion spread all over Europe and across the Atlantic.

In Britain it advanced with equal rapidity. One of Barker's sons, Thomas Edward branched out with Richard Reinagle in the Strand (1803). But undoubtedly the major project was the Colosseum in Regent's Park.

Its developer, the surveyor Thomas Hornor, had already produced splendid estate surveys in the form of bird's-eye views based on detailed maps by a technique he called 'panoramic chorometry'. For the Colosseum he painted a 360° view of London from sketches laboriously produced from the top of St Paul's Cathedral over a period of three years. By 1823 the 24,000 square feet canvas was ready to be painted inside Decimus Burton's building – a 16-sided polygonal, 130 feet diameter Grecian version of Rome's Pantheon with a dome and oculus (Figure 8.2). In the central shaft twin helical staircases twisted round the hydraulic passenger lift ('the ascending room') – London's first. At the top were Wren's original ball and cross from the dome of St Paul's. The lift opened onto three viewing levels. From the third a separate flight led to the open air roof gallery around the oculus from which the visitor ejoyed the view of the '*real*' panorama. 'Thus to invite comparison of the portraiture with its original, seems an act not only

Figure 8.2

Colosseum, Regent's Park, London (1823–8), panoramic view with Colosseum, and central tower in rotunda with passenger lift

Source: Ackermann (1831) *Panoramic View Round the Regent's Park* (view); Ackermann (1829) *Repository etc.* (central tower), both in the Guildhall Library

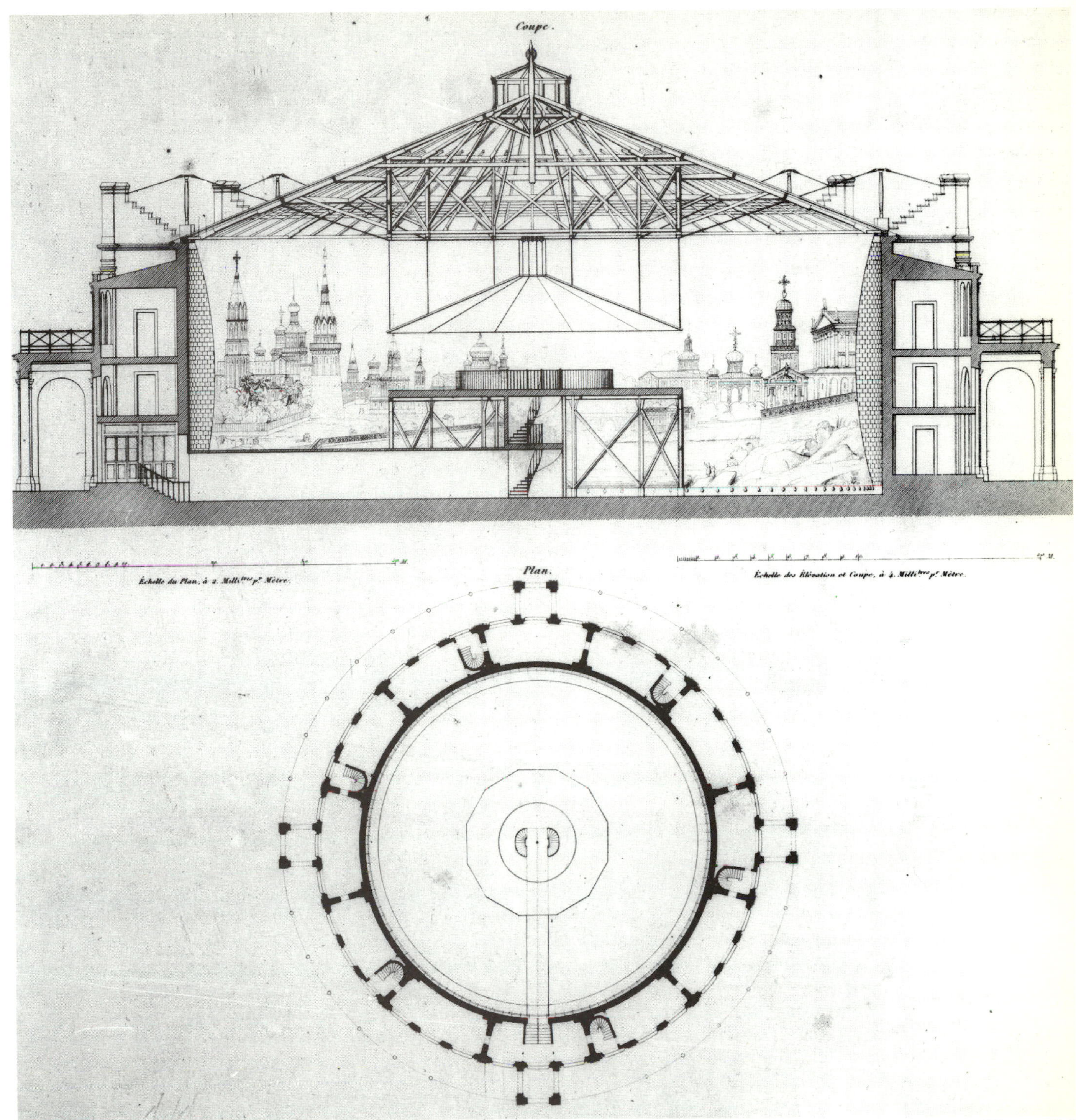

Figure 8.3

Hittorff's Paris panorama (1838), section and plan

Source: Quatremère de Qunicy (1832), British Library

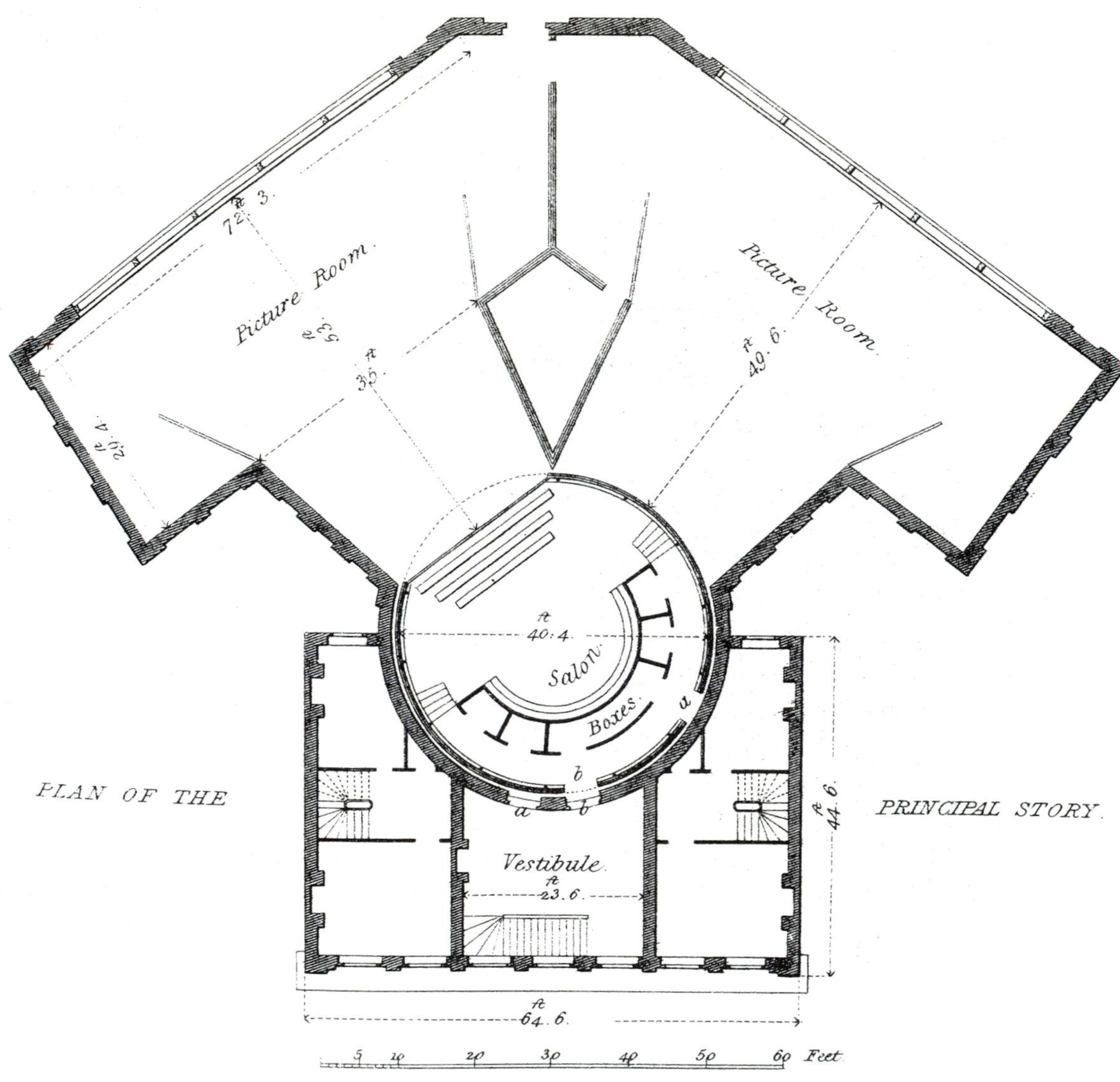

Figure 8.4
Pugin's Diorama, Regent's Park, London (1823), plan
Source: Britton and Pugin (1828)

of candour but of boldness, approaching to temerity'. So unscathed does Hornor emerge from this test that '... on returning to the picture, (the visitor finds) that he has a strong incentive for re-viewing it' (Britton and Pugin 1828: 273–4).

Cantilevered from the central shaft at the top were music and ball rooms, one level down an annular refreshment room and at the base, covered in a kind of tent, a 'Saloon of Arts' with seats and statuary. Other elements were added. Outside a covered gallery led to a landscape:

> which seems to belong to another region. There art combining with nature, has realised some of the ideal compositions which imaginative theorists have formed of the romantic and the picturesque; for the artist has created a scene, which cannot fail of exciting both surprise and wonder. Valley and hill, rock and cataract, pine-forest, glaciers, and snow-capt Alps, constitute a sort of solitude presenting no sign of social or civilised life: a vista, where depth, and height, and expanse, seem to beguile the eye and deceive the senses. From the gloom of this wilderness a subterranean passage leads, by gentle gradations, to a scene of refined culture – a Conservatory.
>
> (Britton and Pugin 1828: 273)

Its exotic plants and birds, 'grottos encrusted with shells, madrepores, corals, spas of every hue, stalactites', enhanced by paintings and sculpture were intended for 'elegant recreation (and) philosophic research'. On emerging the visitor 'finds the idea of time and space confounded' – a feeling of having encountered infinity, a foreshadowing of 'hyper-reality'.

The Colosseum fell on hard times – attendances dropped and it became shabby. It was substantially altered and improved by William Bradwell who re-opened it in 1855. The London view was repainted to eliminate the smoke haze which was apparently present in earlier versions. A night view was added, and on top of the building a moving panorama in a *camera obscura*.

In Charles Langlois's 35 metre Paris panorama (1830–1) in the rue des Marais three-dimensional scenery could be placed in front of the canvas since ground glass in the skylights did away with the troublesome shadows. J.-J. Hittorff's 40 metre version for Langlois in the Champs-Élysées (1838) was, in a sense, a critique of London's Colosseum which he had visited. Its viewing platform was supported by twelve tension cables fixed to exterior buttresses instead of a central column (Figure 8.3). For both the first (1855) and the second (1889) universal exhibitions it was replaced by ever larger versions.

Fawcett (1974: 153–8) discusses the role of panoramas in the diffusion of artistic fashion to the provinces. If purpose-built rotundas were not available, as at Birmingham (1802) and Liverpool, ballrooms, assembly rooms or theatres were pressed into service.

Near the Colosseum another attraction took form – the diorama – which crossed the Channel in the opposite direction. It was actually a hugely magnified Eidophusikon, invented by Daguerre (of photography fame) and Bouton, both pupils of Prevost, one of the painters in the Thayers' Montmartre rotundas. Their 1822 Parisian diorama in the rue Sanson was such a runaway success that they immediately expanded to London where Augustus Welby Pugin's 200-seater opened in Regent's Park in 1823.

Dioramas were far more elaborate. Two different paintings on translucent material, one in front of the other, were illuminated by an overhead skylight from the front and through a diffuse glass window from the rear. The manipulation of a series of screens and blinds, some opaque some translucent, by cords and pulleys enabled either picture to be displayed or gradually merged into the other simulating the passage of day to night, sunlight to moonlight and summer to winter. Two alternative scenes, seen through a dark tunnel of opaque screens, were displayed at a distance of some 15 metres from the observer. The change from one to the other was achieved by rotating the circular auditorium on a central pivot (Figure 8.4).

Dioramas, like the panoramas, quickly spread in Britain, Continental Europe and America; Schinkel produced one for C.W. Gropius in Berlin (1827), and they appeared in America in the mid-1830s.

Other spectacular representations were 'mobile' panoramas, which were in fact enormous paintings on rollers which could be spooled to move past a viewing aperture, toy panoramas, transportable, horse-drawn ones, and Cosmoramas which were improved peepshows viewed through a convex lens. One of the most remarkable was by James Wyld, producer and seller of maps, whose Monster Globe was erected in the centre of Leicester Square in 1851 (he originally intended it to be inside the Crystal Palace). On the inside surface of a 60-foot diameter globe the entire surface of the earth was represented at a horizontal scale of 10 miles to one inch and a vertical one of one mile to one inch (Figure 8.5). It could be viewed from four levels. Seas, deserts, vegetation and snowy mountains were all in colour; volcanoes were all erupting, each with a plume of cotton wool attached to its peak. In the peripheral spaces were exhibitions of maps, curiosities and astronomical representations.

An 1842 photographic panorama was based on Daguerre's work. It made the connection between the ancient theatre, the art of scene painting, culminating in the spectacular techniques we have been looking at, on the one hand, and the cinema, television and holography on the other. These make-believe worlds all needed purpose-built spaces. Extragavant popular spectacles were no less a means of producing knowledge than the scholarly, staid museums and galleries. They added the experience of simultaneity and grandeur. The bird's-eye views momentarily transported observers into a position of privileged potency where urban chaos no longer dominated. They were allowed a share in victorious battles, royal splendour or exotic and remote nature and urban topographies which were still the province of the explorer or wealthy traveller.

Exhibitions

The idea of exhibiting processes as well as products had a precedent in the Elector

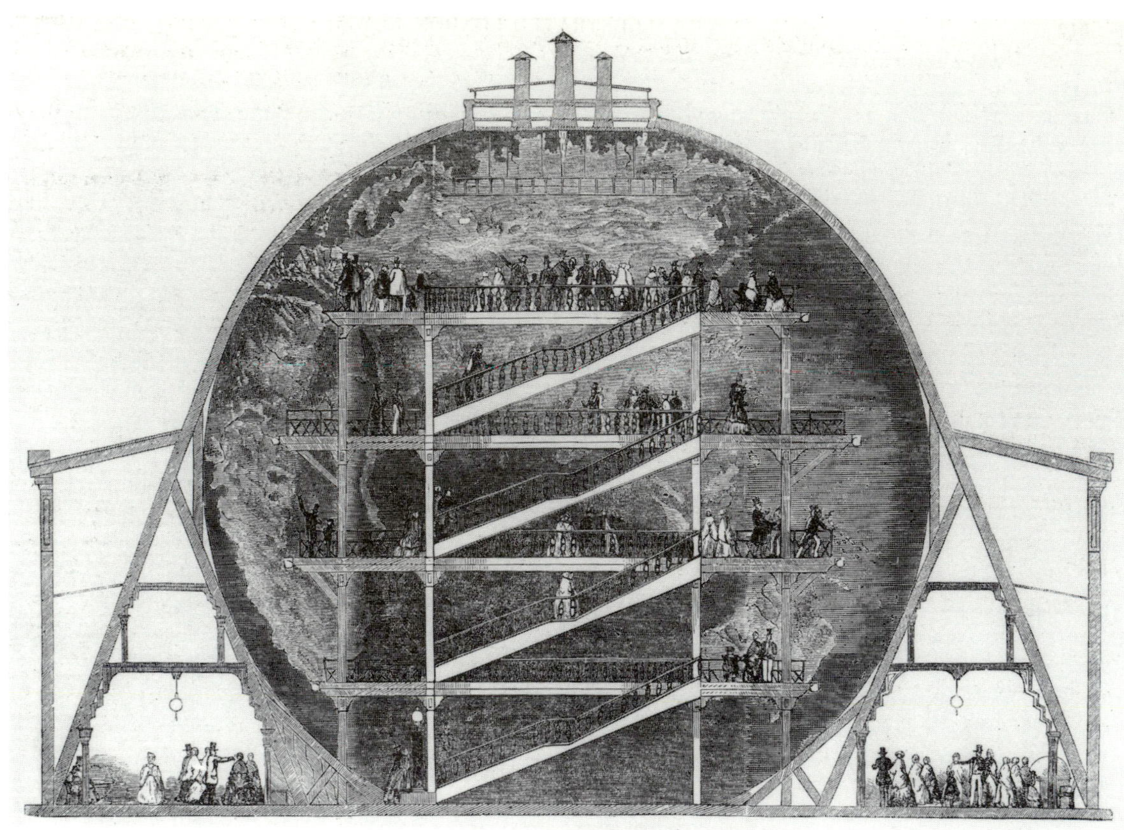

Figure 8.5

Wyld's Monster Globe, Leicester Square, London (1851), section and exterior view

Source: *Illustrated London News* (1857) June (section), and *The Builder* (1851) April (exterior)

Augustus's sixteenth century Dresden museum where three quarters of the collection consisted of tools, and the rest of their products. And long before the Industrial Revolution there were industrial exhibitions. Carpenter (1972: 465–86) traces them to a late seventeenth century Paris show of inventions followed by sporadic exhibitions in the latter half of the eighteenth century. In 1797, again in Paris, a regular series was established (*The Illustrated Exhibitor* 1851: 23–4), the first in the disused Chateau St Cloud. The Marquis d'Avèze, Commissioner of the three Royal Manufactories – Gobelins (tapestries), Sèvres (china) and Savonnerie (carpets), in an attempt to resuscitate them from their desperate, near-derelict state, organised this splendid show of 'all the objects of industry of the national manufactures'. Though approved by the Ministry of the Interior's section of Arts and Manufactures, and successful, it was brought to a sudden close by the Revolutionary upheavals of that year. However the following year saw the setting up of a *Temple of Industry* in the Champs-de-Mars which lasted three days, with juries, prizes and a published catalogue. The third was in 1801, followed by others in 1802 and 1806. After 1821 there was one every five years.

The 1844 exhibition was held in a vast wooden structure measuring 206 by 100 metres, enlarged for 1849 by an enormous cattle shed. In the central courtyard, open to the sky, was a fountain surrounded by gardens. Access was through the textile section flanked by Parisian industrial products and deep in the rear were chemicals and machinery. Nature was the unifying motif, textiles – familiar in their immediacy to the body and in terms of everyday usage – formed the lead-in, small products of common usage the framework, and the normally invisible chemicals and machines were the culmination.

Other early exhibitions were in Ghent (1803), Bern (1804), Trieste (1808), Kassel (1817), Münich (1818), Berlin (1822), Dresden (1824), Dublin (1824), Milan (1826), Prague (1828), St Petersburg (1829) and Stockholm (1834). Little is known of their settings. Sometimes they were in prestigious buildings: in Moscow the Kremlin, and several of the early Parisian ones in the courtyard and pavilions of the Louvre, thus confirming the link already made between industry, State prestige (Royal or Republican), and art. St Cloud, with its splendid wooded park, added the fourth ingredient – nature.

So by the time the Royal Society of Arts in

Figure 8.6
1849 Birmingham Exhibition
Source: *The Illustrated London Exhibitor* (1851) 2: 25, 14 June, in author's possession

London began to organise exibitions in the 1840s there was a European tradition of using them to encourage national manufacture and competitive export, with substantial support by national and regional governments. Besides the benefit to firms, they were a popular success. Technology came to be a matter of national pride and machines, raw materials and mass-produced products symbols of Progress. This was a lesson which the world's leading industrial nation was slow to learn.

The roles of Prince Albert and Henry Cole are well known. The former obtained the Royal Charter for the Society in 1847 having become its President four years earlier, the latter became one of the most dynamic members of its Council in 1846. From its foundation in 1754 the Society had awarded prizes for useful inventions in agriculture and textiles. In 1756–7 the Society put on formal displays of manufactured goods, awarded prizes for products such as tapestries and porcelain, and, by 1759 it had a repository for models and samples designed by William Chambers. The Society held the first ever public exhibition of works by contemporary British artists in 1760 which led to the foundation of the Royal Academy of Arts in 1768 and to a corresponding shift in the Society's work from 'fine' to 'useful'. At the end of the century the Society turned its interest to colonial products. Following some 1829 papers on national industries the collection of raw materials, manufactures and inventions was extended. As yet there was little public interest. In its 1846 summer show mass-produced pottery was shown – an example of what Cole came to call *Art Manufactures* in which the fine arts and design crafts were allied with production.

By 1847 Prince Albert and Cole had initiated the first industrial exhibition in the Society's rooms; it was an immediate success with attendance of 20,000 visitors. The second in 1848 attracted 70,000 and the third in 1849 100,000. By this time there were also provincial exhibitions, one in Birmingham in a basilical wooden structure (Figure 8.6).

That same year Cole accompanied Matthew Digby Wyatt on a visit to the Quinquennial in Paris on behalf of the Society. On their return, with Thomas Cubitt the builder, they obtained the Prince's enthusiastic support and plans moved fast towards an 1851 date for an *international* exhibition of the 'industry of all nations'. Its subject would be 'Machinery, Science and Taste' which crossed national boundaries and belonged to the 'Civilized World'.

Amongst the members, and executive and building committees of the Royal Commission, appointed in 1850 under the Prince's presidency, were Cobden, Cole, Owen Jones, William Cubbitt, Charles Barry, C.R. Cockerell, Charles Eastlake, John Gott, Wyatt, Brunel and Robert Stephenson – key figures in politics, engineering, architecture, painting and ornamental design. Despite the dominance of Classicism in the architectural membership, Gothic was eventually given a voice through the commission to Pugin for a medieval court.

Hyde Park was the chosen site and a brief was drawn up. But the Commission's chief pre-occupation was a working classification system. The Prince had his own:

1 The raw materials of industry
2 The manufactures made from them
3 The art used to adorn them.

The Commissioners saw its illogic; for instance it made impossible unambiguous distinction between iron ore (1) and cast iron (1 *or* 2). Where should the machinery for making cast iron be placed? They procured the services of a brilliant Scottish chemist and educator, Lyon Playfair. He devised his own Pliny-esque classification behind which the mind of a chemist was evident:

A Metallurgy
B Chemical manufactures
C Vitreous-ceramic manufactures
D Textiles
E Organic manufactures
F Engineering and machinery
G Architecture, fine art, music
H Agriculture, horticulture.

In the event the system adopted had six main Divisions, not dissimilar to Playfair's, and 30 classes, of which one was art and 29 were industrial.

Division			*Class*
A	Raw materials	I	Mining, quarrying, metallurgical operations and products
		II	Chemical and pharmaceutical processes and products generally
		III	Substances used for food
		IV	Vegetable and animal substances, chiefly used in manufactures, as implements, or for ornaments
B	Machinery	V	Machines for direct use, including carriages and railway and naval mechanisms
		VI	Manufacturing machines and tools, or systems of machinery, tools and implements
		VII	Civil engineering, architectural, and building contrivances
		VIII	Naval architecture, military engineering, ordnance, armour and accoutrements
		IX	Agricultural and horticultural machines and implements
		X	Philosophical (i.e. scientific) instruments and processes depending upon their use, and musical, horological and surgical instruments
C	Manufactures: textile fabrics	XI	Cotton manufactures
		XII	Woollen and worsted manufactures
		XIII	Silk and velvet manufacturers
		XIV	Manufactures from flax and hemp
		XV	Mixed fabrics, including shawls, but exclusive of worsted goods
		XVI	Leather, including saddling and harness, skins, fur, feathers and hair
		XVII	Paper and stationery, printing, and bookbinding
		XVIII	Woven, spun, felted and laid fabrics when shown as specimens of printing or dyeing
		XIX	Tapestry, including carpets and floorcloths, lace and embroidery, fancy and industrial work
		XX	Articles of clothing for immediate personal or domestic use
D	Manufactures: metallic, vitreous and ceramic	XXI	Cutlery and edge-tools
		XXII	Iron and general hardware
		XXIII	Works in precious metals and in their imitations, jewellery and all other of virtu and luxury not included in all other classes
		XXIV	Glass, including stained and painted glass,optical glass, etc.
		XXV	Ceramic manufactures – china, porcelain, earthenware etc.
E	Miscellaneous	XXVI	Decoration, furniture and upholstery, including paperhangings, papier-maché and Japanned goods
		XXVII	Manufactures of mineral substances, used for building or decoration, as in marble, slate, porphyries, cements, artificial stones etc.
		XXVIII	Manufactures from animal and vegetable substances, not being woven or felted or included in other sections
		XXIX	Miscellaneous manufactures and small wares
F	Fine arts	XXX	Sculpture, models (in architecture, topography and anatomy) and plastic art (All other fine arts were excluded).

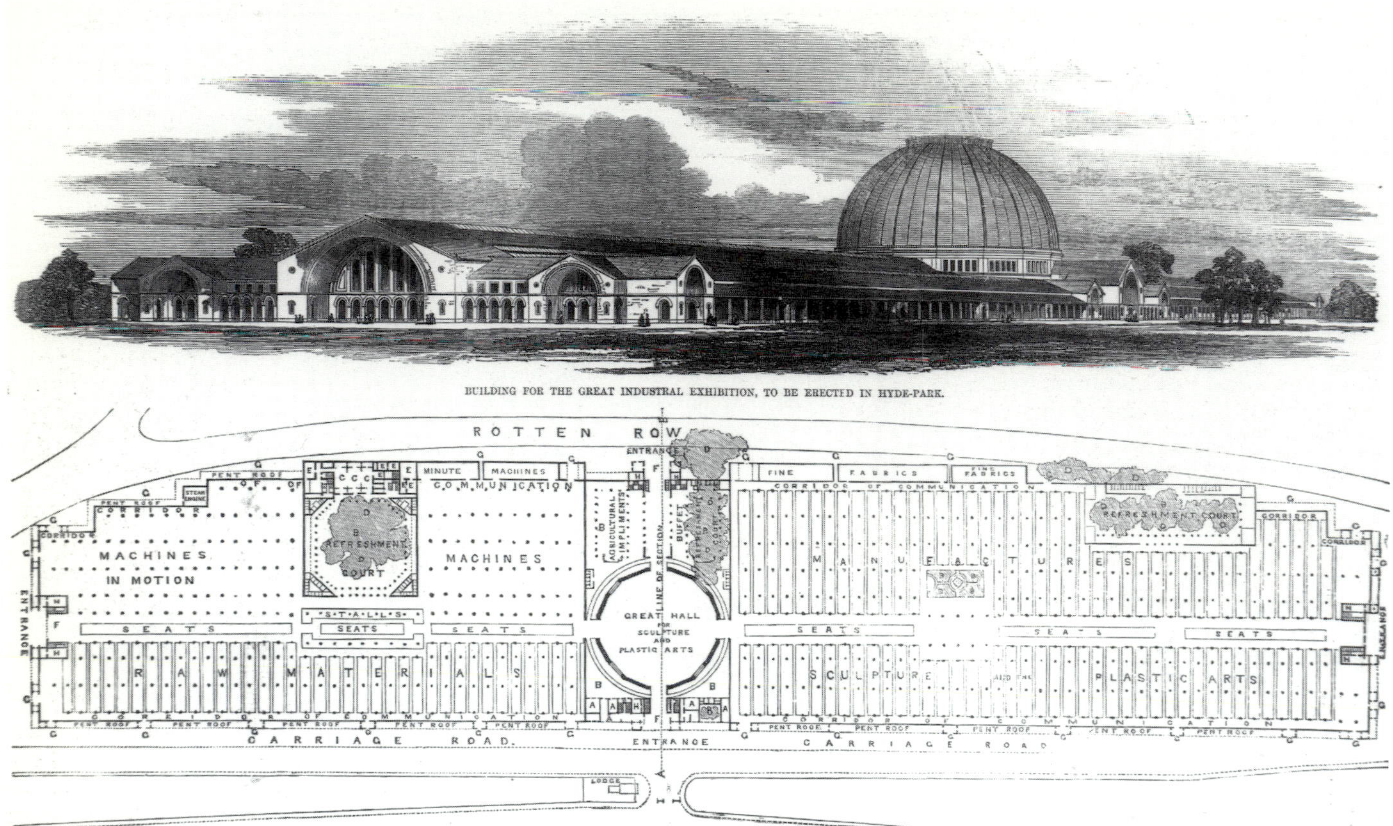

Figure 8.7

The Commissioners' design for the 1851 exhibition building (1850)

Source: *Illustrated London News* (1850) 22 June, British Library

Despite first appearance, there *is* a structure, an elaboration of the Prince's and Playfair's crude systems. The former separated raw materials, the products made from them, and the artistry which made them more than merely utilitarian. It left out the means of production which Playfair's did include, and added a separate category for all the fine arts, which included architecture and music.

Tools or machines convert the raw materials (A), some inorganic (I and II), some organic (III and IV). In the former some are used as found (I) some need sophisticated processing (II). In the latter, the materials are obtained from the animal or vegetable kingdoms. Some of these are consumed as food (III) the rest are turned into products (IV).

The conversion results in five groups of products. One (F) has the pure purpose of beauty with a single class (XXX). Significantly music and architecture have disappeared. Despite the realities of an art market, these are things which according to the ruling ideology are literally price-*less*, of no economic value. Another has only economic and utilitarian value – (B) the tools and machines for making things. These are capital goods. In between pure beauty and pure utility lie three groups of products which are both useful and beautiful.

Of the three groups of consumer products, one (C) consists of organic materials: textiles, the covering of animals – fur, hide (leather), feathers and hair – and paper-based products. They are divided into those defined by substance (XI–XVII), those by production processes (XVIII) and those by end-use (XXIX and XX). A second group (D) consists of inorganic materials, and they have two of these classes – substance (XXIV and XXV) and end-use (XXI, XXII and XXIII). The same is the case for the third, miscellaneous group (E) – substance (XXVII and XXVIII) and end-use (XXVI and XXIX).

There are some oddities. Non-productive machinery (X) classes scientific and medical with musical instruments. These are all 'machines' for producing something abstract, some kind of knowledge. Machines for material production are divided into civil (V, VI, VII and IX) and military (VIII), in line with the French distinction between military engineering and everything else, which was 'civil'. As always, especially interesting are

Figure 8.8

The Crystal Palace (1851)

Source: Victoria and Albert Museum, courtesy of the Board of Trustees of the V&A

excluded categories – they simply do not fit. These misfits, needing a 'miscellaneous' group (E), say more about the system than those which it includes. It contains things which have markedly ornamental qualities, but not enough to make them into (useless) pure art, in the class of 'miscellaneous manufactures and small wares' (XXIX) such as soap, perfumery, preserved fruits, candles, amber for pipes, artificial flowers, chocolate, taxidermy, snuff and fishing tackle. These are luxury, leisure and gourmet items – things which the stern manufacturing morality squeezed out of production.

What dimensions run through this thinking? One is technology-craft. Machines were celebrated alongside a nostalgia for traditional handcrafts so that cheek by jowl with the mass-produced cotton from the latest looms were elaborate hand made lace and brocades. A second is beauty-use, which removes works of art from material or productive reality. Arising from this is the third, stages in utility. It runs from direct use (foodstuffs), to products usable after transformation (iron ore or metal tools) and finally material objects which can neither be consumed nor used for any production purpose (medical and musical instruments). A fourth is organic-inorganic which appears to represent nature-technology.

In March 1850 the Building Committee issued the competition brief which yielded 245 entries. As none satisfied the Commissioners, they produced their own (Figure 8.7). It was met with universal derision. Using a mixture of traditional and new technology, it had a huge central dome covering the 'great hall for sculpture and plastic arts'. The axis of the front and rear entrances divided the length of the front into raw materials on one side and further sculpture and plastic arts on the other, the end points of a production dimension from unformed substance to totally 'useless' product. Along the centre and rear were the machines to one side – static and in motion – and finished products on the other. The Commissioners' faithfully reproduced their classification in space, and kept to the Prince's wish that national boundaries be obliterated for there were no spatial indicators of geography or nationhood.

The genesis of Paxton's revolutionary design (Figure 8.8), using mass production factory and site processes to put together a huge glazed shed constructed of three materials – iron, timber and glass – has often been described. From the famous blotting paper sketch, through two versions, the second of which incorporated the huge elms under the raised transept, the project was completed in less than nine months.

The classification system no longer appeared in space. The primary articulation became national, the central transept dividing the entire building into a western, British and colonial, and an eastern, foreign half. Within each the group and class boundaries were only loosely evident.

The building can either be read as a single huge bounded space or as one articulated by the grid of structural members, staircases, partitions and exhibits. In the latter case what emerges is a shallow spatial structure with innumerable rings. That is, there is a vast number of routes that can be chosen – a very weak programme – which maximises the probability of chance encounters between visitors and exhibits. The transparency of the envelope makes almost everything visible at once. This, with the free movement, brought experience as close to simultaneity as the limitations of space allow, closer than any large building had ever done. It was nearer to the bird's-eye experience of a panorama than to the sequential programme of a museum.

Just as the printed library catalogue is a book like all the books it contains, so the Crystal Palace had an odd inside-outness – both a container and a sample of the contained. This was recognised by the Jury in awarding the Civil Engineering, Architectural and Building Contrivances medals. It headed the list with the Council's medals to those who created the *building* – Prince Albert for its 'conception and prosecution', Paxton for its design, and Fox and Henderson, the contactors, for its execution, and only then descended to items one would have expected – for instance Bunnett and Company's 'patent shutter and water closet'.

That Paxton was a fish out of water in the company of the wealthy Royal, industrial and banking promoters, was erased by constant reference to his work for the Duke of Devonshire at Chatsworth, and his botanical expertise evidenced by membership of the prestigious Linnaean and Horticultural Societies. His expertise as a landscape designer coupled to the choice of the park site emphasised the first underlying theme: nature. This was a machine-in-nature. The second was art, which civilised technology. A contemporary guide recommended a tour to include steam machinery, statues and models, and furniture; the first represented 'a type of power', the second 'imaginative beauty' and the third the 'idea of use (since) symbols of power, and beauty, and usefulness (are) the elements of civilisation' (*The Illustrated Exhibitor* 1851: 108). Its transparency was an essential artistic metaphor for industrial production not as something opaque or threatening but visible and accessible.

The third theme is world conquest and the establishment of peace through trade. The transept which bisected the building was 'as it were, the equator of the world in Hyde-park' (1851: 9). The world consisted of Britain in one

Figure 8.9

Exhibit of moving machinery in the Crystal Palace

Source: Dickinson Brothers (1854) *Comprehensive Picture of the Great Exhibition of 1851*, London, Guildhall Library

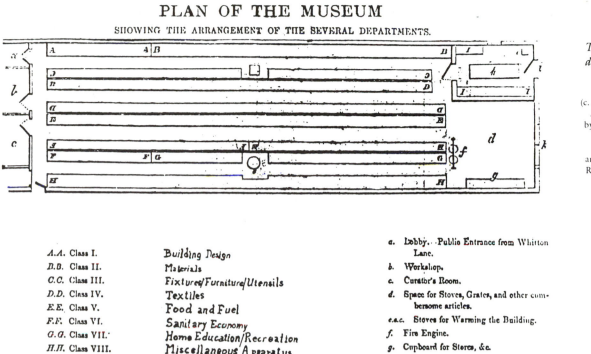

PLAN OF THE MUSEUM

SHOWING THE ARRANGEMENT OF THE SEVERAL DEPARTMENTS.

A.A.	Class I.	Building Design
B.B.	Class II.	Materials
C.C.	Class III.	Fixtures/Furniture/Utensils
D.D.	Class IV.	Textiles
E.E.	Class V.	Food and Fuel
F.F.	Class VI.	Sanitary Economy
G.G.	Class VII.	Home Education/Recreation
H.H.	Class VIII.	Miscellaneous Apparatus
I.I.	Class IX.	Library

The position of these letters on the Plan shows the direction in which the classes are to be consecutively inspected.

a. Lobby.—Public Entrance from Whitton Lane.
b. Workshop.
c. Curator's Room.
d. Space for Stoves, Grates, and other cumbersome articles.
e.e.e. Stoves for Warming the Building.
f. Fire Engine.
g. Cupboard for Stores, &c.
h. Library Table.
i. Private Entrance.
k. Goods Entrance.

The length of each full row of stands is 60 feet, the width of the Hall 29 feet.

Figure 8.10 *Plan of Thomas Twining's museum of domestic and sanitary economy*

Source: T. Twining (c. 1866–71) *The Economic Museum . . . Twickenham,* by permission of Mr B.L. Pearce, Twickenham Local History Society and London Borough of Richmond Libraries and Arts Services

half and all the rest in the other. At the opening the Archbishop of Canterbury gave thanks for 'the peace that is within our walls and plenteousness within the gates'. And the Crystal Palace was held to be 'a veritable peace Congress, manufactured by the many-coloured hands of the human family'.

Religion was a fourth theme; '(it) resembles, in some respects, the form commonly adopted in cathedrals' (1851: 9). Like its Parisian predecessor, it is a 'temple' of industry.

A fifth is Royalty. The Prince's was deeply involved; the opening and closing ceremonies were great Court occasions. This was hammered home by two equestrian statues of the Royal couple, one on each side of the crystal fountain at the entrance.

Engels was graphically describing the slums of industrial cities; only two years had elapsed since the second great cholera epidemic; Chadwick's and his Commissioners' unprecedented and terrifying Report on public health was only nine years old; and Dickens' was starting to address the conflict between human nature and the industrial city. Clearly the machine was in urgent need of defence for too much was at stake. It could be cleaned up, polished and presented as a shining piece of sculpture so that the gentry in crinolines, velvet cloaks, frock coats and silk top hats, and the workers lounging in immaculate white trousers, could be perfectly at home (Figure 8.9). By surrounding it with art, nature, shining light, royalty and religious sentiment, not only could its innocence and nobility be asserted, but it could be disssociated from dirt, danger, noise, disease, poverty and squalor.

The movement set in train in Paris reached its climax here and rippled through the world well into this century. For the 1862 London exhibition a popular print shows 'Albert the Good' in a central medallion. The flowing base ribbon proclaims 'The Earth is the Lord's and the Fulness thereof', whilst at the top the flags of the nations radiate from a beehive. A young Britannia extends a 'Welcome to all nations', while from a lower medallion of 'Art, Science, Manufacture and Trade' flow 'Peace and Plenty'.

The sweeping consequences of 1851 for the development of design education and museums have already been mentioned. The South

Kensington complex could not have occurred without it. Nor were the consequences only metropolitan. Thomas Twining's 1869 Museum of Domestic and Sanitary Economy in Twickenham (Pearce 1987) had nine sections: building design, materials, fixtures/furniture/utensils, textiles, food and fuel, sanitary economy, home education/recreation, miscellaneous apparatus, and a library. The most surprising class is the 'home', for all the rest are the objects which the visitor knows *about*, but this one, like the more traditional library, is about what the visitor knows *with*. And, as in the spatial sequence of the Hunterian Museum, the entrance lobby leads the visitor first to encounter the concrete – the seven material classes. Next in depth is the home, which deals with a higher level of abstraction ('education/recreation'). Deepest is the library – where invisible knowledge is stored in texts (Figure 8.10).

But in another type for the production of knowledge the relation between metropolis and province is different. Chalklin (1980) has examined English capital expenditure on culture in the provinces between 1760 and 1830. Not only is it substantial, but innovatory. In particular one type of space – the lecture theatre of the learned institutions – became formative.

CHAPTER 9
Invisible knowledge

Dramatic fragments

The essence of teaching space is that the audience catches a small fragment of a *corpus* of knowledge at a time, a *corpus* to which the performer has access. And the fragment is presented as a dramatic spectacle.

Though the places for political assembly, law-making or the administration of justice – council chambers, parliamentary assemblies and lawcourts – share some features with teaching spaces, because what is being produced is not knowledge but legal and political structures, the likeness is superficial. Equally superficial is the likeness to liturgical space. In both cases the participants, both performers and audience, share the invisible knowledge, belief system or practice.

The teaching space is closer to the theatre, where the full story is not revealed to the audience till the end. The ancient actor–audience relation indeed gave its name to the first teaching space – the anatomy *theatre.*

The lecture theatre

Charles Stephanus (1545) makes this very connection in his prescription for a wooden, temporary, semicircular anatomy theatre covered by a waxed canvas awning: at the front 'where the men of antiquity had their proscenium (stage) there should be set up an anatomy table'. The three classes of audience were separated in public space prior to entry by external staircases leading to steps and semicircular gangways at each level of the two- or three-storey structure. Nearest to the table were the medical professors; in the second row the candidates; behind them 'without distinction medical students, surgeons and members of the public who like to behold the wonders of nature' (quoted by Stollenwerk 1971: 354), could stand or sit, come and go at will, and watch comfortably. On the title page out of the grim reaper's mouth flows a cartouche inscribed 'Virtue alone blunts this blade'; dissection involves facing morality and death.

Perhaps Stephanus was drawing on a permanent building of this form built a year earlier in Basel by Vesalius. By the time the theatre at Leyden (1593) was built the form had evolved to a near-full circle or horse-shoe of tiered seats in a square space (Figure 9.1). The artist has located animal and bird skeletons in unlikely places all over the theatre, and equally unlikely human ones – including one helmeted equestrian one – carrying flags with mottoes to remind the viewer of mortality. In a central cupboard the dissecting instruments are displayed. Padua followed Leyden a year later. Others like the *Domus Anatomica* in Copenhagen University (1645) were oval or square. The third London home of the Royal College of Physicians (1674–89) in Warwick Lane, designed by Wren and Hooke, had its 40 foot diameter, domed, circular anatomy theatre over a similarly shaped entrance lobby. Even by the standards of the time the 45° rake of the five concentric rings of seats was steep.

The seventeenth century octagonal, domed theatre of the Royal Academy of Surgery in the rue des Cordeliers, Paris (Figure 9.2) was in the same tradition. But it had a feature which its successor raised to an astonishing formal statement. The main entrance to the theatre led

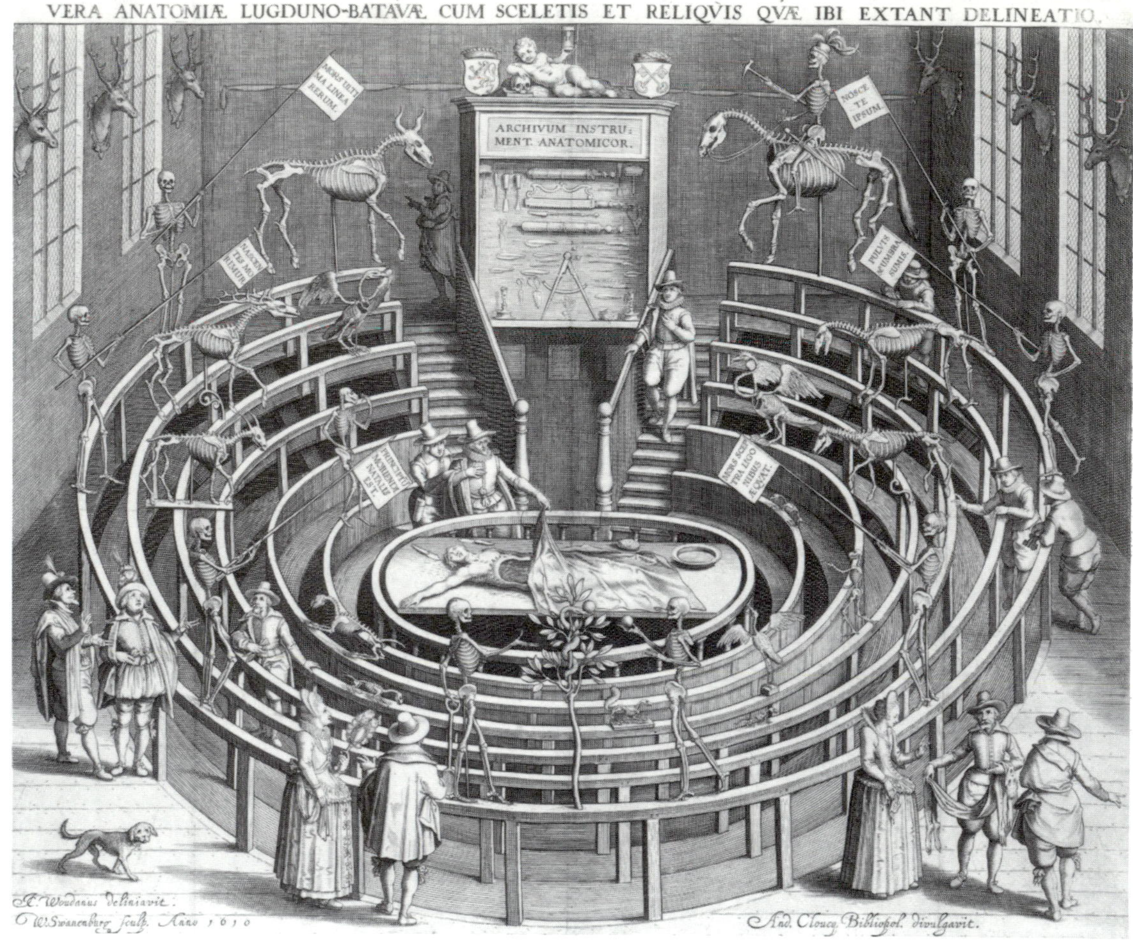

Figure 9.1

University of Leyden anatomy theatre (1593)

Source: From a print (1610) by Jan Cornelisz Wondt ('Woudanus'), engraved by W. Swanenburg, Rijksmuseum, Amsterdam

directly, through a narrow wedge-shaped gap between the tiered seats, to the dissecting table, the audience entering by two small side entrances and stairs to their seats. The lecturer thus made a ceremonial entrance.

The successor was Gondoin's nearby *École de Chirurgie* (1769), regarded as the most innovative building of the time (Figure 9.3). Gondoin reverted to the classical semicircular theatre, covered in a Pantheon-like coffered half dome with half-oculus. Though the theatre was on the far side of a colonnaded courtyard, spatially it was but a few steps from the square outside. One simply passed through a triumphal arch set into an open colonnade to be faced, across the open space, by a massive six-columned temple portico. Behind that was another arch, set into the lower colonnade which ran behind the portico and round the entire courtyard, opening to the theatre interior. A short distance away was the dissecting table placed like an altar on this axis. Behind it was visible the tiered seating at the deepest point in space. The audience gained access by two lateral entrances, an annular passage and rear stairs. Though all this was visually shallow so that the demonstration was a public spectacle from the courtyard, permeability was only shallow for the lecturer who could make his ceremonial entry.

The street front 'showed the king (Louis XV), followed by Minerva and surrounded by the sick, ordering the construction of the building, while the Genius of Architecture presents the plan, and Surgery, accompanied by Vigilance and Providence, guide the actions of the king' (Braham 1980:140). The pediment of the portico showed 'Theory and Practice swearing upon an altar of Eternal Union'. Inside spectators were faced with images of the king 'encouraging (the surgeons') progress and rewarding their zeal, while the gods were engaged in transmitting the principles of anatomy and staunching the blood spilt in defence of the country' (1980: 141).

The complex also included a rectangular theatre for midwives, a chemistry laboratory, a

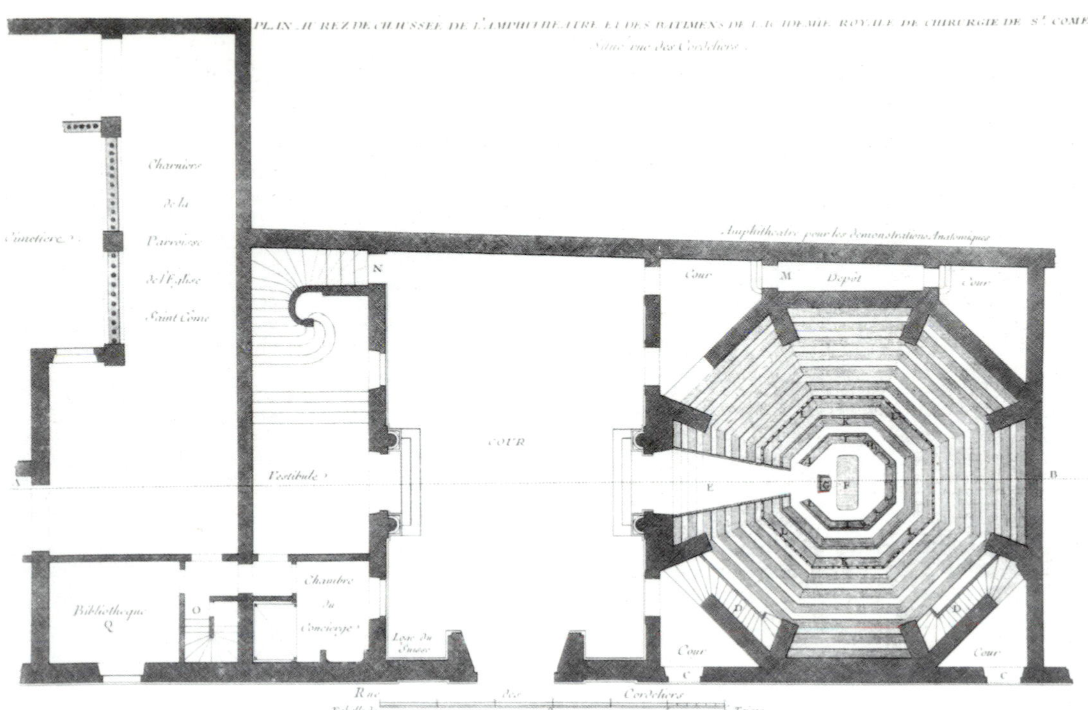

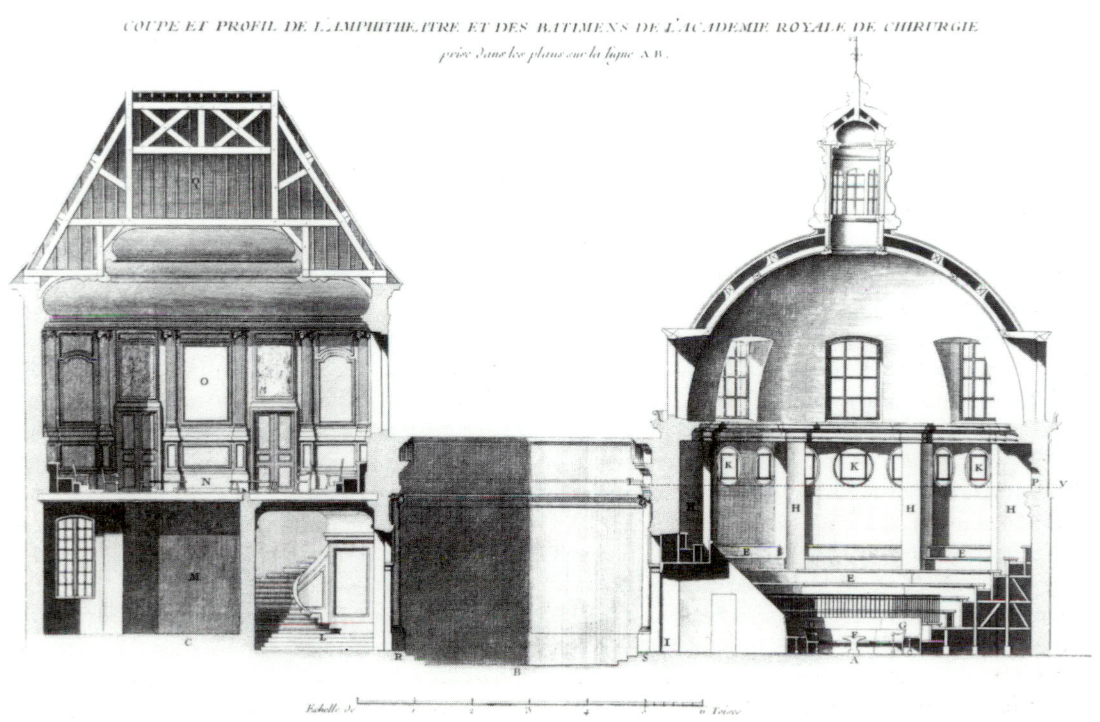

Figure 9.2

Anatomy theatre in the Royal Academy of Surgery, rue des Cordeliers, Paris (late seventeenth century), plan and sections

Source: J.-F. Blondel (1752–6) *L'Architecture Françoise etc.*, British Architecture Library

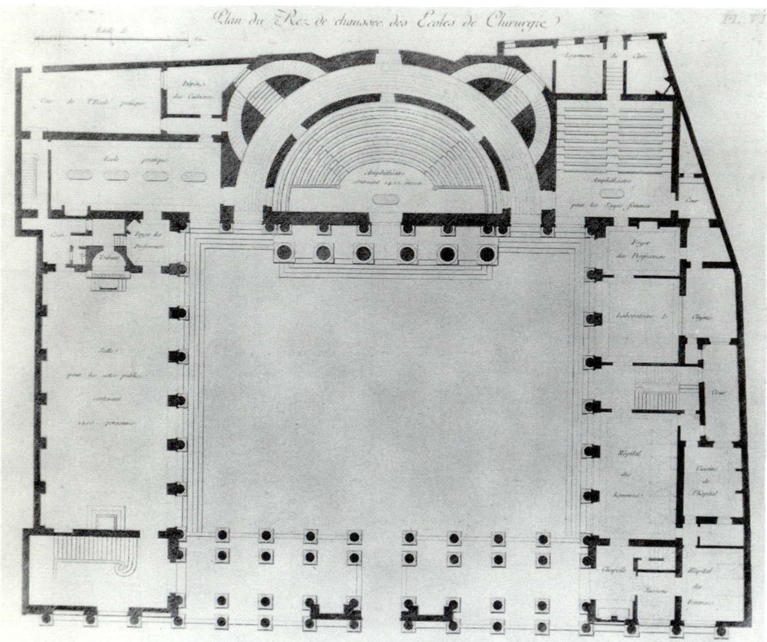

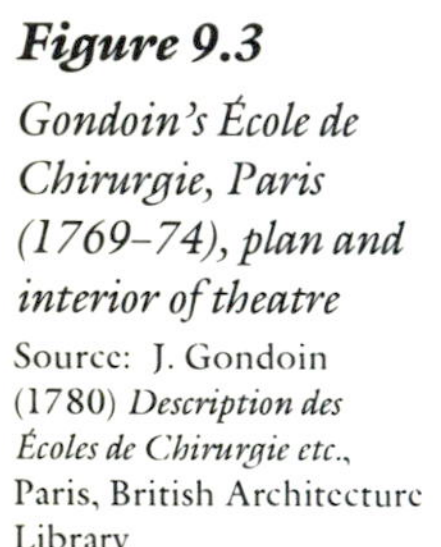

Figure 9.3

Gondoin's École de Chirurgie, Paris (1769–74), plan and interior of theatre

Source: J. Gondoin (1780) *Description des Écoles de Chirurgie etc.*, Paris, British Architecture Library

small hospital ward, a large public hall, and a smaller four-tabled dissecting room for the best pupils training for the army. At the upper level was a library, a museum of instruments, a top-lit lecture room and offices. It has been suggested that the influence of the theatre spread far beyond medical, and indeed other academic, fields into the political space of the Chambre des Cinq-Cents, the Salle de Sénat in the Palais de Luxembourg and the Salle du Tribunat in the Palais-Royal.

The steep rake ensured freedom from obstruction and gave the audience almost a plan view. The shallower slope of the teaching galleries in the schools I discussed earlier was designed for maximum eye contact between teacher and pupil; here the slope was designed for maximum visibility of the cadaver. The professor's eyes at this angle remain almost hidden, especially if he was bent over his task. The movement from full circle, to horseshoe and semicircle represents increasing asymmetry of power.

That the full circle fully embeds the teacher is also experienced by the audience – for each member sits not only next to, but facing, across the teaching arena, other members participating in the same activity. Once the plan is reversed, with the lecturer's entrance connected to a deep, private laboratory or preparation room, which is screened from the audience and to which there is direct private access from outside, the asymmetry between lecturer and audience is complete whatever segment of circle is adopted for the auditorium. In the liturgical setting the analogous device is the chancel screen between nave and choir-chancel-altar, or the Orthodox iconostasis which totally screens the sanctuary.

The anatomy tradition was long-lasting. We have seen in William Hunter's model anatomy school of 1763 a completely circular theatre. That eventually built in Great Windmill Street was square – its seating arrangements are unknown. His brother John's house and school in Leicester Square had a semicircular theatre. A number of the designs for the Glasgow successor had horseshoes or semicircles. In Robert Adam's 1789

Edinburgh University plan only anatomy kept to the centric (octagonal) form; other subjects ('classes') had rectangular theatres with parallel rows of tiered seats (Fraser 1989).

But there are examples from the early eighteenth century with centric forms used for non-medical teaching. Goldman (1720) editing earlier designs by Sturm, published a 'trivium' school in which circle segments are awkwardly squeezed into each of the three wings. In his university college (Figure 9.4) it is the great central 'solemn' auditorium which is circular, surrounded by an annular library space, while the theatres for anatomy, theology, law, medicine and surgery, mathematics, philosophy and experimental physics are rectangular. In the 1750s Matthew Brettingham was one of a number of architects proposing grandiose schemes for various academies. His 'Academy of Arts' had a circular theatre not only for 'Anatomical Dissections and Dissertations' but also for 'Design after Nature' (BAL Drawings Collection).

In Latrobe's military academy (1800) the lecture room was semicircular but the lecturer, unlike those in Gondoin's theatre, could make no ceremonial entry (Turner 1984: 62 and Figure 59), nor in Wilkins' University College London (1827–9). In the unexecuted proposal for a college in Newcastle (c. 1831) a whole family of part-circles were squeezed into rectangular spaces (Forgan 1989).

This degree of acceptance by major institutions made it inevitable that when learned societies, both amateur and professional, needed a lecture space it was, as Forgan (1986) has shown, this form which became the model. These institutions varied enormously in the size and nature of their membership. The audience in some was specialised and élite, often with the same status as that of the lecturer through common membership or equivalent scholarship. In these cases the seating arrangements and auditorium plans embody this relation. In other cases there are non-members – of a single class or of a mixture of classes – requiring spatial segregation to express their social distance.

John Anderson's Institution was founded in 1796 under the Will of the great and disgruntled Professor of Natural Philosophy in Glasgow University (previously Professor of Oriental Languages). Its initial name – the New School of Arts and Manufactures – accorded with Anderson's intention to offer popular courses in arts, manufactures, natural philosophy and chemistry. Working men and women were targeted from the start. After two years in the recently disused grammar school in George Street the Institution moved to a newly-built flesh-market on the corner of John and Ingram Streets in 1798 (Markus 1985). The building, never used for its original purpose, had a 45 foot diameter domed, top lit, circular space at its centre. This space was fitted out by the architect Robert Smith, who was the original feuholder of the plot, as a 500-seater lecture theatre. There was an upper level gallery (originally intended for poultry) with an annular passage. A contemporary guide book comments that, even before this it was more like an 'amphitheatre' than a 'public market' (Denholm 1798: 131–2). Smith also provided a museum, library, apparatus room and offices. When the Institution moved back into the George Street grammar school in 1828 the dome was transported and re-erected at the rear of this existing building, lock stock and barrel, where it became the museum and, on its upper gallery, the library.

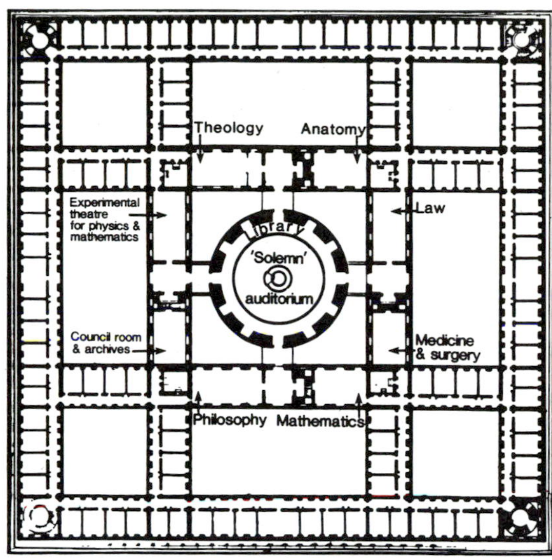

Figure 9.4
Plan for a university college by Goldman (after Sturm), 1720
Source: Goldman (1720)

Anderson's colleagues and theatre were formative in London's new Royal Institution, chiefly the brainchild of Rumford who had returned to England in 1798 from his Bavarian exploits for the enforced control of beggars. Especially close to his heart were the practicalities of Poor Law reform – workhouses, soup kitchens, diet reform, improved stoves, hearths, chimneys and institutional ovens and cookers. He proposed a private subscription:

establishment for feeding the Poor, and giving them useful Employment; And also for furnishing Food at a cheap Rate to others who may stand in need of such assistance. Connected with an Institution for introducing, and bringing forward into general Use, new Inventions and Improvements, particularly such as relate to the Management of *Heat* and the saving of *Fuel*; and to various other mechanical Contrivances by which *Domestic Comfort and Economy* may be promoted.

(Rumford 1796–1812 Vol. I: 113–88)

In 1797 he became a life-member of *The Society for Bettering the Condition of the Poor* (SBCP) whose *Reports* were edited by Sir Thomas Bernard. The connection between the Society and the Board of Agriculture set up in 1793 under Sir John Sinclair of Thurso as its first President, has been well studied (Berman 1978), especially the large overlap of 'improving' (that is 'enclosing') landed gentry membership. The SBCP emphasised cottage industry, allotments, domestic economy and reduction of Poor Relief. Rumford proposed to add a 'House of Industry' – a marvellous *double entendre* for he meant not a workhouse but a public display of inventions. In 1798 he wrote to Bernard from Münich to promote this elaboration of his 1796 idea. By 1799 the SBCP had approved it. Its aims were: diffusion of knowledge on useful mechanical inventions, teaching courses of 'philosophical' lectures, and a repository of fireplaces, utensils, models of steam engines, ventilators, farm implements and spinning wheels. It was to have a London lecture room and laboratory, and a list of suitable lectures which combined agricultural and industrial topics was proposed. In the same year and with the King's patronage the Royal Institution came into being and installed in a house at 21 Albemarle Street. Bernard, Sinclair and other members of the Board of Agriculture and the SBCP were amongst the first Proprietors.

The growth in the presentation of science as 'public spectacle' or 'theatre of the upper class' was drawing to a close (Schaffer 1983). Spectacular demonstrations of electrical, optical and atmospheric phenomena had a political role in establishing, within a rational and Deist universe, an equally 'natural' economic and social world. Inkster (1980) examines the function of the public lecture in the flux of social class in the early Industrial Revolution. Porter (1980) challenges the view that provincial science emerged as a response to industrialisation and sees it much more as an alternative to art, music, and cultivation of literary taste – 'an attempt by provincial élites ... to bring Enlightenment to their own doorsteps'. The Royal Institution (RI) is important because in it so many of these strands converge and so many future developments are anticipated.

The first Proprietors included landed gentry, scientists, Whig politicians, a bishop, a Duke and an Earl, with a strong Evangelical presence. No fewer than 18 of the 58 were MPs, including Palmerston, Pitt and Wilberforce. The scientific programme was pitched at the professional, the bourgeois layperson and, quarter of a century before Mechanics' Institutes, the artisan. Women were members from the start.

The premises were immediately converted and the spatial arrangement embodied Rumford's and his collaborators' ideas. Thomas Webster, a young Scot, was in charge of the project as Clerk of Works and was probably responsible for much of the design. He had been admitted to the Royal Academy schools as an architecture student in 1793. Later he described himself as a 'Teacher of Architecture, Perspective etc.'. Although help and opinions were sought from other architects – notably George Saunders whose *A Treatise on Theatres* (1790) was the most scientific treatment of auditorium acoustics and optics at the time – and James Spiller, a pupil of James Wyatt's, the 1800 design was basically Rumford's and Webster's.

Until it was complete a first floor rectangular space at the south end of the block was used for lectures. Webster and his colleagues produced several studies for tiered seats to surround the demonstration table (Figure 9.5). In some the lecturer stands on a raised podium which, together with the steep rake of the seats, provides maximum visibility. The cramming of up to 380 people into a room 47 feet long and less than 24 wide resulted in a proximity between lecturer and audience which negated the normal 'distancing'.

The permanent two-floor semicircular lecture theatre was at the north end entered at the first floor, by means of an annular passage which ran under the seats. The lecturer entered through a doorway at the back and to one side of the desk from a preparation room. There was a unique feature: a direct entrance from the street, through a vestibule and the repository of models, by a three-flight staircase to a four-row gallery at the rear of the theatre. Several versions of the design have to be analysed to reconstruct exactly what happened.[1]

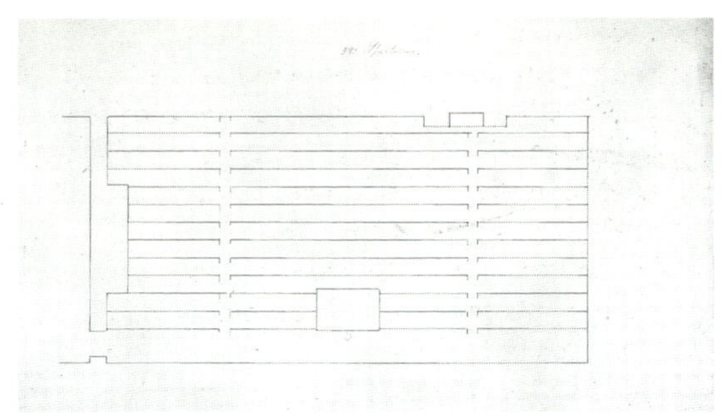

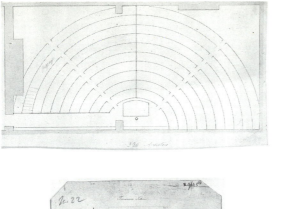

Figure 9.5

Studies by Webster and colleagues for seating in the Royal Institution's first lecture theatre (1798)

Source: BAL/RIBA Drawings Collection

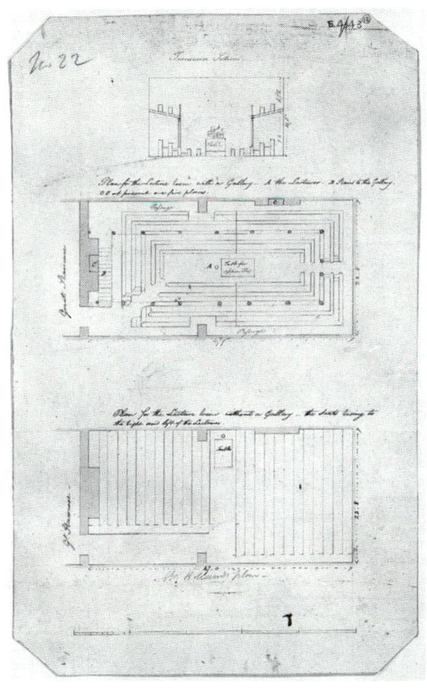

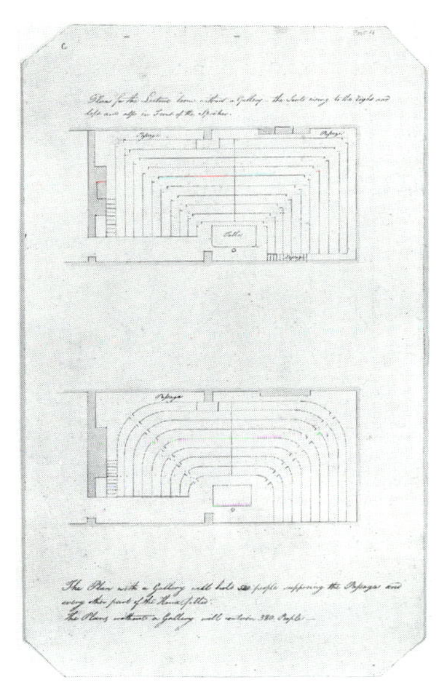

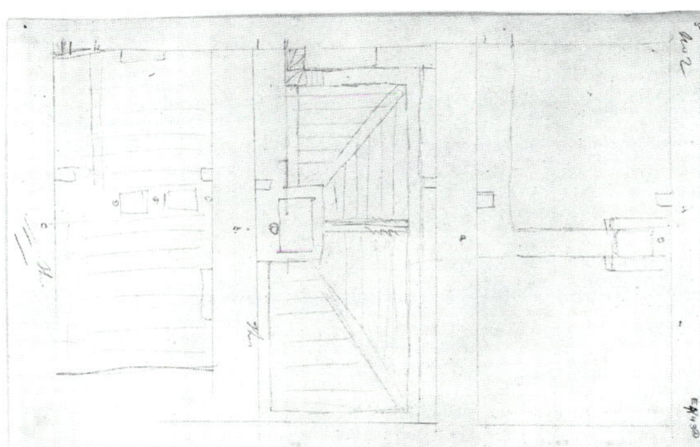

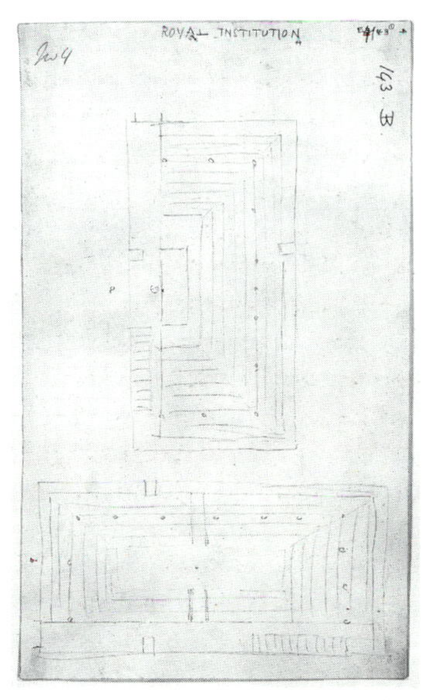

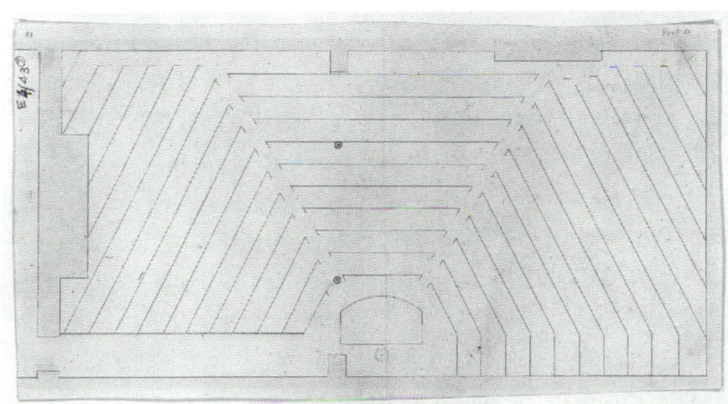

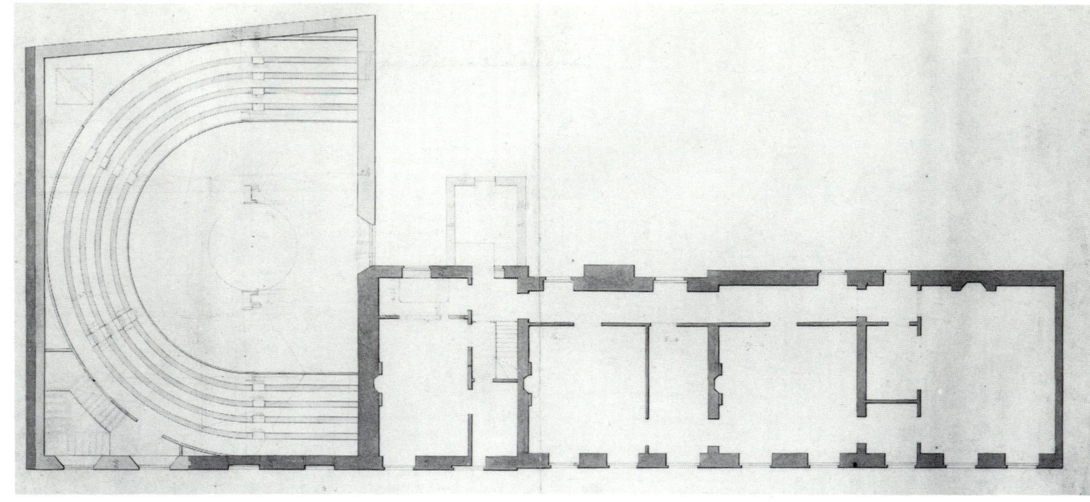

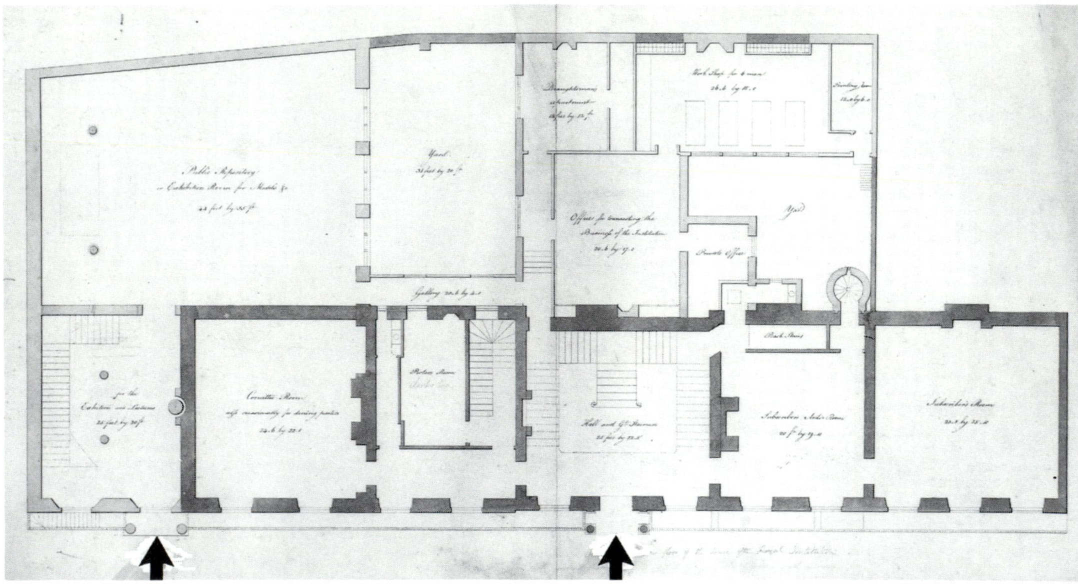

Figure 9.6
Royal Institution, London, second floor plan, showing mechanics' gallery and ground floor plan, showing main and mechanics' entrances
Source: BAL/RIBA Drawings Collection

In his autobiography Webster (c. 1837) says that:

> In designing the Lecture Room of an institution so peculiar, my object was to adopt it for different ranks in society, for any attempt to destroy any distinction must be absurd. I constructed a gallery intended for those who either wished not to be observed or who, for obvious reasons, would not wish to sit down by their employers, it was also to receive such enquiring mechanics as had gained a title to be there. To this gallery a separate stone stair led from the street....
>
> (Webster c. 1837: 13–14)

On one drawing he noted that the separate access would keep the subscribers' quarters 'clean and quiet' (BAL/RIBA Drawings Collection). Another, close to the actual conversion, shows the separate mechanics' entrance with its own two-columned portico (Figure 9.6), leading to the repository and the stairs which ascend directly to the mechanics' second floor gallery. On Figure 9.7 the first floor access to the theatre from the main staircase by the annular passage is seen.

Late in 1799 Thomas Garnett was appointed as Professor of Philosophy, Mechanics and Chemistry, and also as Scientific Secretary and editor of the Journals. He was completing his third year as Professor in Anderson's Insitution at Glasgow and had been in correspondence with Rumford. His first courses at the RI were in the temporary

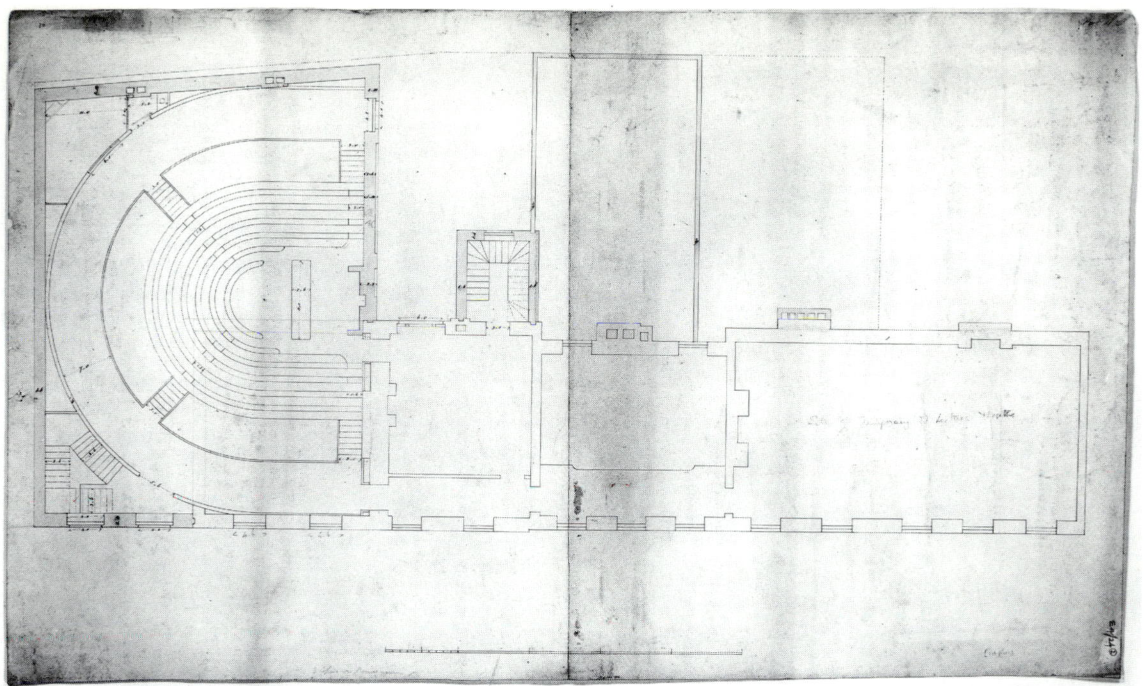

Figure 9.7
Royal Institution, London, first floor plan showing gallery from main staircase for 'polite' access to lecture theatre
Source: BAL/RIBA Drawings Collection

lecture theatre; the permanent one was under construction but it is probable that either his ideas, even at this stage, caused Webster to insert the mechanics' entrance and staircase or that his influence had been exerted earlier, through Rumford. It is almost certain that the circular lecture theatre in Glasgow had separate external access to its gallery which was probably reserved for mechanics. So by 1800 the idea of a 'segregated mix' of artisans and polite society was not new (and it was certainly very old in theatres). It is intriguing to trace the RI lecture theatre back through Webster and Rumford, Anderson, Garnett's teachers at Edinburgh – Alexander Munro II and Joseph Black, through William Cullen, and then Alexander Munro I and William Plummer both of whom were students of Boerhaave at Leyden and must have sat in that famous anatomy theatre.

Rumford and Webster also proposed to serve mechanics in other ways. Webster's intention was:

> to instruct bricklayers, joiners, trimmers, ironplate workers, as these were the trades most connected with our improvements at that time. In a large room on the ground floor, we built up for practising men chimneys and types of fireplaces of all kinds in a slight manner and pulled them down again and built up others. We fitted up improved models of fireplaces in old-fashioned cottages, also boilers of various kinds and showed how smoky chimneys might be cured; models of various culinary vessels were made and put in the model rooms.
>
> (Webster c. 1837: 10–13)

This workshop and repository appear in the basement of some plans and on the ground floor (Figure 9.6) – where it was actually placed – of others. Webster did start a small mechanics' school and on one basement plan a 'school room' is shown accessed directly from the mechanics' stairway, as well as drying, ironing and wash rooms, and a 'great kitchen' (BAL Drawings Collection). The same scheme on the ground floor had a draughtsman's apartment.

Garnett resigned after a personal row with the Managers in 1801; there was a reaction against the working class elements in the RI and they were soon eliminated. Both Webster and Rumford left in 1802. But not before Webster was 'rudely asked what (he) meant by instructing the lower classes in science' (Webster c. 1837: 14), and the staircase was demolished in what he calls 'very erroneous reasoning'. Russell (1983: 151–4) uses 'The Demolished Staircase' as a symbol for the ensuing period of conflict over working class scientific education.

Other early changes included conversion of the temporary lecture room into the library, and the

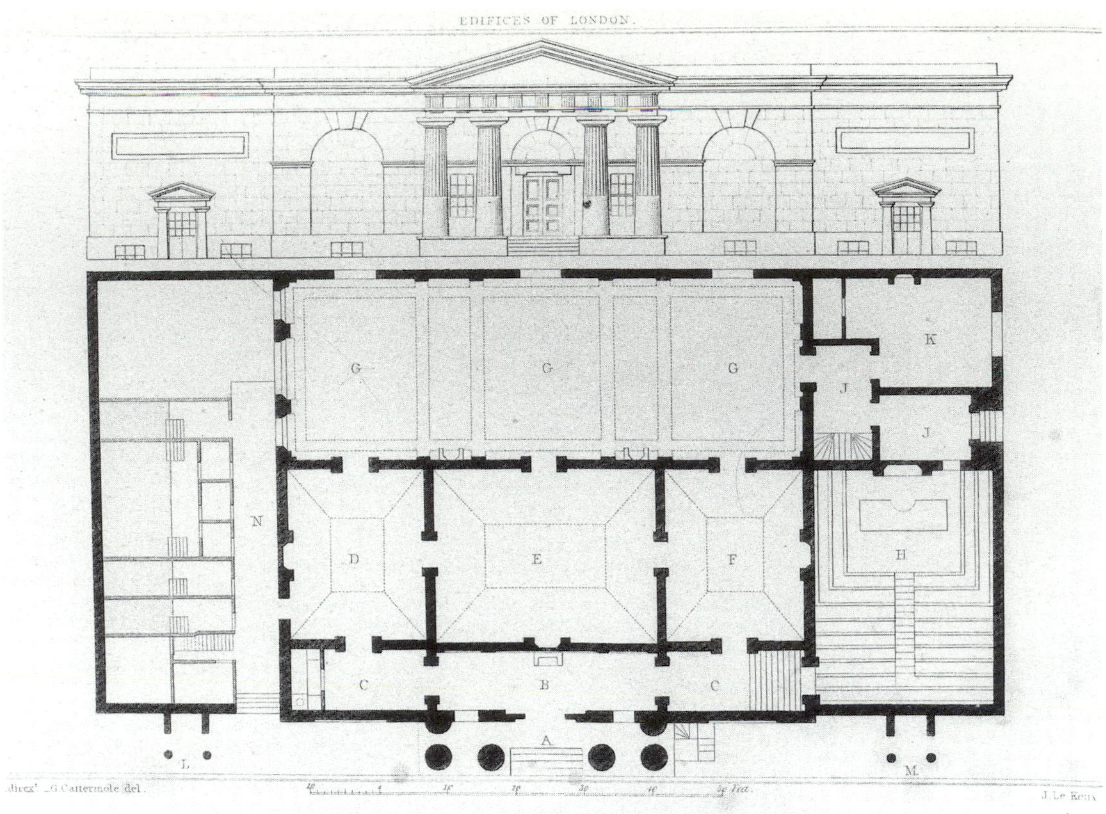

Figure 9.8
Russell Institution, London (1808), elevation and plan
Source: Britton and Pugin (1828)

removal of the experimental kitchen in the basement for a small lecture room to be attached directly to the chemistry laboratory (which itself had taken the place of Rumford's intended blacksmith's shop) for potentially dangerous, or at least smelly, demonstrations following the precedent of the Ashmolean. It was here that Humphry Davy who became lecture assistant in 1801 performed his renowned work, to be followed by Thomas Young, Michael Faraday and a long line of distinguished scientists.

During the brief moment that the RI crossed class boundaries the mechanics' spaces were segregated and shallow. Deep access was for Subscribers, Proprietors and serious scientists. The presence of the mechanics had not been camouflaged; in fact their entrance was clearly articulated.

Hays (1983) has described the subseqent growth. of London's lecturing empire. The performances were centred on science, and theatre plans followed the RI quite closely. The Russell Institution was built in 1800 as a card and assembly room to designs by James Burton. In 1808 it was altered for its new use. Its lecture theatre was, as at the RI, embedded at one end (Figure 9.8). But at William Brooks' London Institution (1815–19) whilst it followed the RI in form, with tiered semicircular seating and even the same 'wrap-around' lecturer's desk, it was articulated as a separate block, linked by an umbilical cord through an octagonal antechamber to the front building which, with its two great pamphlet and newsrooms and grand central staircase, was in the developing club pattern.

But such lecturing and its spaces were not, of course, limited, to the capital. Shapin (1974) has analysed the audience for Scottish science in the eighteenth century. He has also (1983) shown how early in the next the triple interest of the petty bourgeoisie, the scientific lecturers and the phrenologists combined into a social structure of great complexity. In Ireland the Royal Dublin Society, founded in 1731, promoted agricultural and manufacturing innovation and eventually built its lecture rooms at Poolbeg Street in which not only the RI but English provincial institutions were influential (Byrne 1986).

One of the earliest provincial theatres was in the Leeds Philosophical and Literary Society whose Hall, which I have already mentioned, had parallel raked seats and a wrap-around lecturer's

Figure 9.9
'The Great Room' in the Royal Society of Arts, London
Source: From Isaac Taylor's print (1804), RSA Library, London

table on the RI model. The theatre was replaced by a 400-seat semicircular one in 1862 (Brears 1984 and Thoresby Society 1969: 72–3). Bristol's lecture room of 1823 fitted the RI type tiers awkwardly into a square (Fawcett 1974: 115 and Figures 10 and 11). Newcastle-upon-Tyne's 'Lit. and Phil.' acquired a new building, designed by John Green (1822–5) which included a 300-seat theatre with its apparatus room (Watson 1897). I have referred to the Yorkshire Philosophical Society (1827–9) where the square lecture theatre with parallel, raked seats between two rows of Ionic columns was embedded in the museum galleries.

In the anatomy theatres and university lecture rooms there was a lecturer–audience relationship which required a segregation based on temporary status and not class – for in due course the taught would become the teachers' equals. In the institutions for amusement or instruction of the public, difference in status was fixed and accentuated by difference of class. And there were other participants; we have seen provision for the amusement of the public in the anatomy theatres and in the public lecture room colleagues would often be located near, or behind the lecturer's desk, sometimes in clearly distinguished seating.

There was a third type of lecturer–audience relationship, where scientific and social space was shared because ideas, theories and experiments were discusssed amongst equals. In the most prestigious societites, academies and institutes Fellows or *Membres* presented their ideas to equally eminent colleagues in a space which was both a meeting and a lecture room, of a kind which the Royal Society, in its wanderings from Oxford (1648) to Somerset House (1780) never really acquired. The Royal Society of Arts, though having its own élite membership, was designed to attract a wider public from the start so the layout of its meeting room is a hybrid. On the central axis were two long parallel tables across which Fellows faced each other, enclosed by a horseshoe-shaped low barrier headed by a throne-like President's chair. The rest of the audience were in parallel horseshoe-shaped rows of seats – all on a level floor (Figure 9.9).

Chambers' grandiose plan for the RSA (c. 1758) preceded Adam's Adelphi. Its meeting room was oval with a level floor, and two of the four circular corner pavilions were devoted 'to sculpture and models (BAL Drawings Collection). Architects had a field-day uniting the proliferating learned societies. Amongst John Goldicutt's

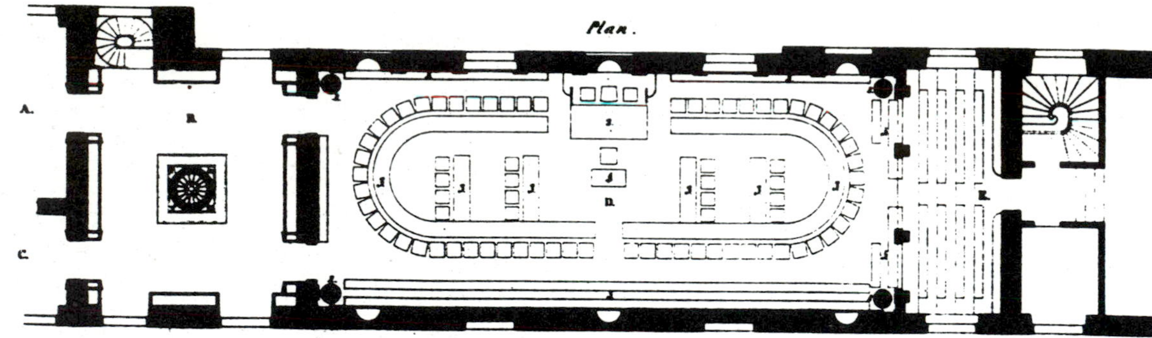

Figure 9.10
Lebas' design for the meeting room of the French Academy of Sciences in the Palais de l'Institut (1831–2)
Source: Quatremère de Qunicy (1832), British Library

several dreams one, 'The London Amphitheatre' (1832), was a vast four-armed scheme to house the Royal Academy, The Royal Society of Literature, and the Asiatic, Geographical, Astronomical, Medical and Chirurgical, Horticultural, Zoological, Architectural, Commercial and Linnaean Societies with a whole variety of lecture spaces. Its centrepiece was a vast circular lecture room and 'occasional theatre' (BAL Drawings Collection).

Such institutions mushroomed all over Europe and America. Some fitted neatly into existing structures; Vaudoyer's great circular meeting room of the French *Institut* (1806) was under the dome of the former *Église des Quatre Nations*. In Hyppolite Lebas's meeting room for the French Academy of Sciences' (1831–2) in the *Palais de l'Institut* the public and the members enter the oblong space from opposite ends (Figure 9.10). The speaker is on the centre of the short axis. Behind is a baize-covered table raised on a step with three officers' seats. The members are seated on the level floor at four tables and in an elongated double horseshoe ring which completely encircles the speaker. The officers and a number of members therefore face the speaker's back. Along the four walls are the seats for 'assistants' (candidates, junior members or demonstrators). At one end is a two-storey visitors' gallery, accessed from a separate staircase and entrance, with transverse seats on a shallow rake.

The speaker and members are equals, close to each other on one level. The slight elevation of the officers and a discontinuity in the ring resulting from the setback of their seats, are sufficient to suggest a supervisory role rather than one of authority; one that does not disrupt the inward looking unity of shared knowledge. The assistants, like stage hands, are squashed on narrow seats against the walls with inset niches, and have become almost part of the furniture. The public is distanced but its lack of knowledge requires it to be given every aid – such as raked seats for good visibility.

The meaning of lecture spaces is carried by three features:

1 Their location in relationship to other spaces and to the outside.
2 The distinctions in access not only between different classes of the 'legitimate' audience, but between the general public and the lecturer. The last is especially important in enabling the audience to read relationships. The lecturer may appear (a) from a public ceremonial place, as in Gondoin's theatre, bringing the aura of Royal or State authority, (b) from an inner laboratory *sanctum* in which the secrets of science remain locked, or (c) through an entrance and space shared with the audience, thus displaying a solidarity.
3 The seating plan and the sectional details of barriers, rakes, steps and levels together establish the working relations between lecturer, persons of status (such as Fellows or Council members), the audience and the public.

Rude mechanicals

Even in the completely changed social context of lecture theatres for working class mechanics' institutes it is these features which remain significant. Rumford's and Webster's quickly-scotched plans for the education of mechanics were not the first. The Spitalfields Mathematical Society was set up in 1717 by silk weavers for lectures, experiments and a library. A similar one followed in Manchester a year later. Anderson was issuing free tickets to his experimental philosophy lectures at Glasgow University in 1780. In Birmingham the

Sunday Society, set up in 1789 to give practical and technical instruction to young men who had completed the Sunday school, spawned the Brotherly Society in 1796 to train Sunday school teachers in these same useful subjects, besides sacred history and morals. By 1814 the equivalents of the Literary and Philosophical Societies, from which mechanics were barred, were being proposed in Scotland for the 'middling and lower ranks of the community' (Kelly 1957: 68). Three years later a Mechanical Institution was formed in London. In 1821 the Edinburgh School of Arts was set up – perhaps the first proper mechanics' institute – with courses in chemistry, mechanics and drawing.

In Anderson's Institution Garnett had attracted lay men and women from the start. When he departed for London in 1799 his successor George Birkbeck established the free class whose members had to be working mechanics. Gradually the class acquired its own apparatus and library. When Andrew Ure took Birckbeck's place in 1804 the class grew vigorously until, in 1823, sparked off by a diagreement about the apparatus and books, the mechanics took off to form their independent insitution, with the support of Birkbeck and Brougham, at first in a disused chapel but by 1826 it had a purpose-built building in North Hanover Street.

1823 was decisive. In Scotland both Kilmarnock and Greenock, inspired by Glasgow, followed suit; Liverpool and Sheffield Mechanics' and Apprentices' Libraries were founded; and London's MI was established, Birkbeck and Brougham active amongst its founders and supported by Place, Bentham and Cobbett. Its radical manifesto quoted Bacon – 'Knowledge is Power' (the motto also adopted by the London *Mechanics' Magazine* in the same year). Its 'objects' included the setting up of a library (both reference and ciculating), a museum of models, minerals and natural history, and an experimental workshop and laboratory; the holding of lectures in natural and experimental philosophy, practical mechanics, astronomy, chemistry, literature and the arts; and the running of adult classes ('schools') in arithmetic, algebra, geometry and trigonometry and their applications to perspective, architecture, mensuration and navigation. Of course Birkbeck drew on his experience of Glasgow and the RI (of which he was a Governor) and the formative role of Scotland was much in evidence.

Its first home was a Presbyterian chapel in

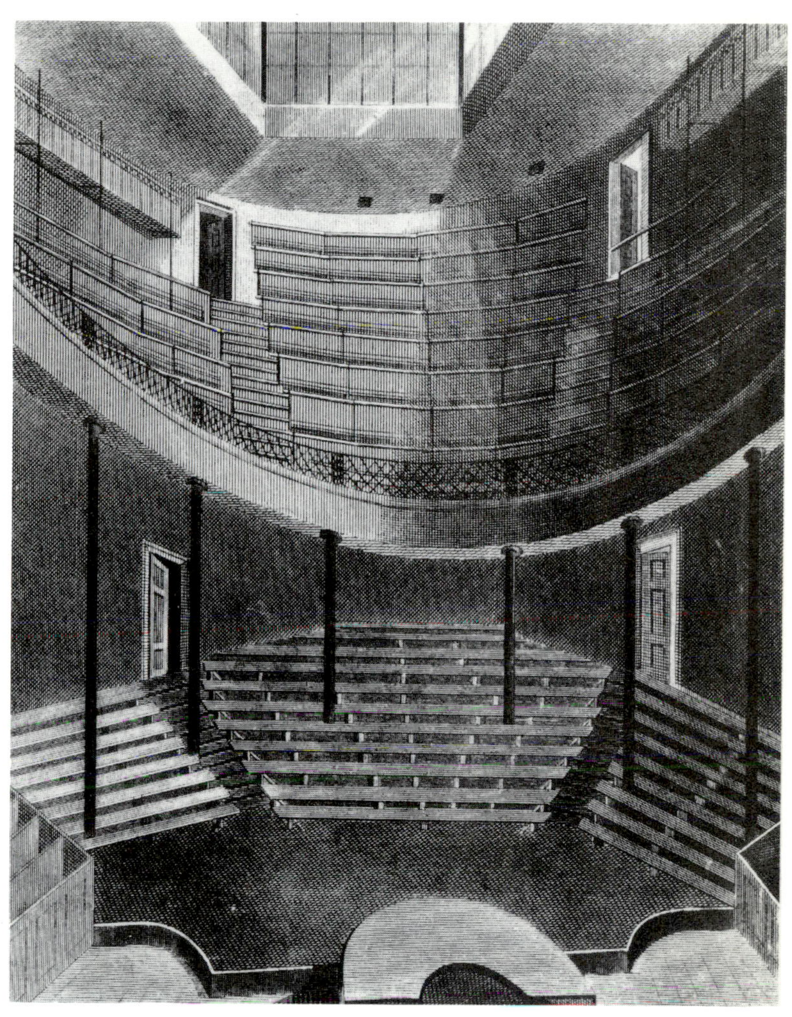

Figure 9.11

Lecture theatre of the London Mechanics' Institute (1824–5)

Source: *London Mechanics' Register* (1825), University of London, Birkbeck College Library

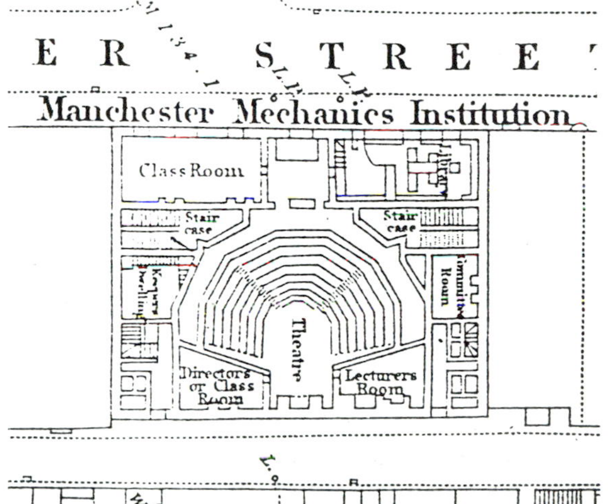

Figure 9.12

Manchester Mechanics' Institution, Cooper Street (1827), plan

Source: 1850 O.S. map, Manchester Public Library

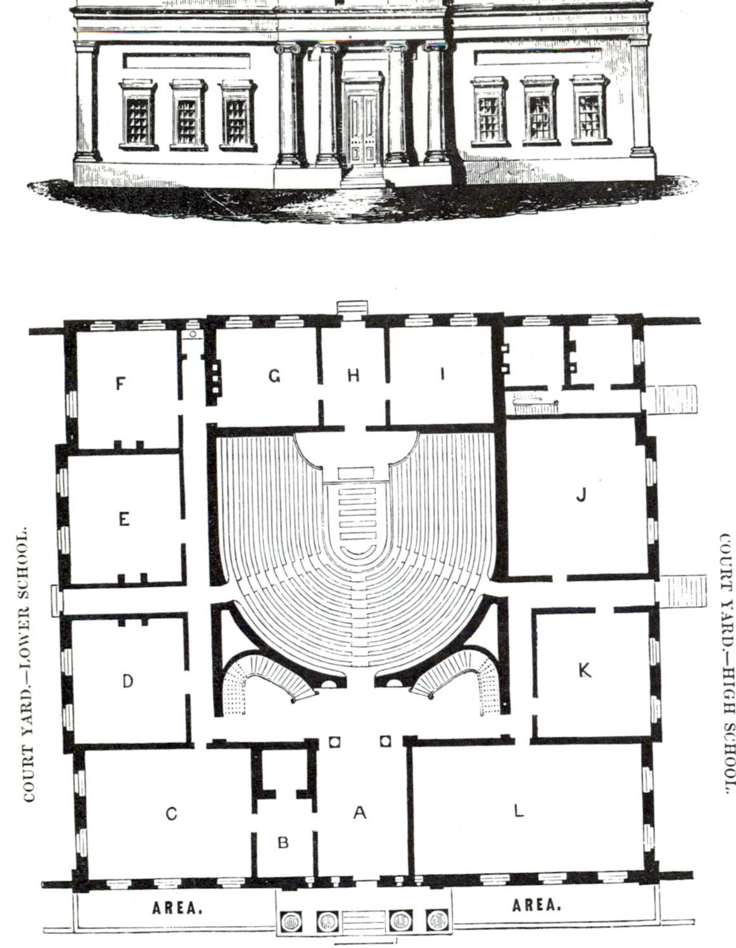

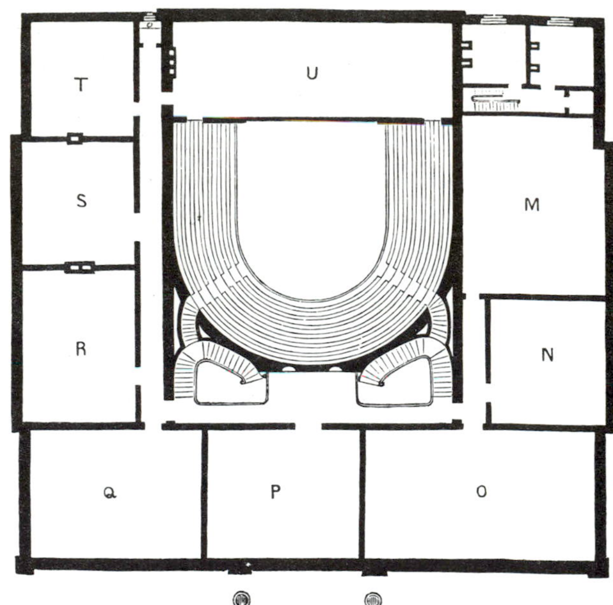

REFERENCE TO PLAN.

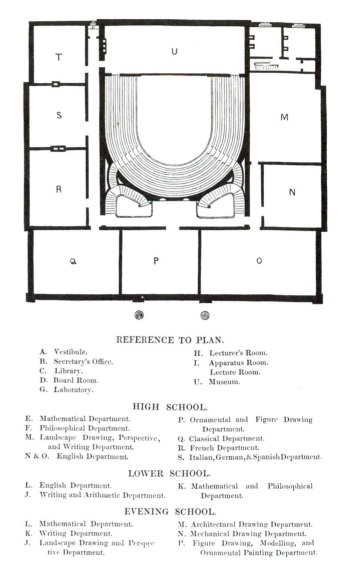

A. Vestibule.
B. Secretary's Office.
C. Library.
D. Board Room.
G. Laboratory.
H. Lecturer's Room.
I. Apparatus Room. Lecture Room.
U. Museum.

HIGH SCHOOL.

E. Mathematical Department.
F. Philosophical Department.
M. Landscape Drawing, Perspective, and Writing Department.
N & O. English Department.
P. Ornamental and Figure Drawing Department.
Q. Classical Department.
R. French Department.
S. Italian, German, & Spanish Department.

LOWER SCHOOL.

L. English Department.
J. Writing and Arithmetic Department.
K. Mathematical and Philosophical Department.

EVENING SCHOOL.

L. Mathematical Department.
K. Writing Department.
J. Landscape Drawing and Perspective Department.
M. Architectural Drawing Department.
N. Mechanical Drawing Department.
P. Figure Drawing, Modelling, and Ornamental Painting Department.

Figure 9.13

Liverpool Mechanics' Institution (1835–7), elevation, ground floor plan and first floor plans and key

Source: *Liverpool Mechanics' Institution Leaflets* (1837) vol. I (*Prospectus*), British Library

Monkwell Street but by 1824 a building in Chancery Lane was leased and a new lecture theatre built on an adjoining site (Figure 9.11). Its architect was Robert McWilliam, a vice president. There were two levels of steeply raked seats, a wrap-around lecturer's desk and what appear to be box seats closest to the lecturer – possibly for officers.

Manchester's MI was founded in 1824 – a year in which more than twenty were set up in Lancashire and Yorkshire – at first in rented rooms in Cross Street. A new building opened in Cooper Street in 1827 (Figure 9.12) with a two-storey lecture theatre for 1000 on a steep rake within a seven-sided horsehoe. There were several classrooms, a library and a newsroom. Subsequently a chemical laboratory, extra classrooms and a new theatre dome were added. John Dalton of the 'Lit. and Phil.' and the Royal Manchester Institution which was exactly contemporary, strongly supported the mechanics.

Manchester saw a short-lived radical experiment which tried to break the link with industrialists and the predominantly lower-middle class membership which was perceived as having hijacked the movement. It aimed to give workers real control and defined itself as a movement of liberation through education rather than one for making workers contented with their lot (Tylecote 1974). The New MI (1829) planned a splendid building to include a lecture theatre, classroooms for adult education, a library and reading room, an infants' school, meeting rooms for trade unions and temperance and benefit societies, and an exhibition hall. Political and religious debate would not be banned (a request for history classes in the MI was turned down because it might 'lead to the introduction of political debates'). The building project was abandoned in 1833 but revived and executed by the Owenites in 1839 as the Hall of Science. The New MI finally folded in 1835.

Liverpool MI was founded in 1825. The buildings designed by Arthur Hill Holme (1835–7) are the fully fledged, second generation plan dominated by the two-storey, galleried lecture theatre (Figure 9.13). The lecturer's room behind the desk has a direct outside entrance. Adjacent on either side are the laboratory and the apparatus room. The library is by the main entrance and there are fourteen classrooms. The published timetable and the plan key show the great range of the subjects in the 'lower', 'high' and 'evening' schools; the classrooms thus have triple functions. Besides the basic curriculum in writing, reading and various branches of mathematics (including a separate class in conic sections), Greek and Roman history, classics, political economy, moral philosophy, figure drawing, modelling and ornamental painting appear.

Surprisingly by 1839 *The Society for the Diffusion of Useful Knowledge* (founded in 1825 under Brougham's *aegis*) was promoting Keighley MI as a model (Figure 9.14), though it was widely known as one of the few which, like the New MI in Manchester, was a genuinely working men's creation (Duppa 1838). By the time official guidance was offered to architects the heyday of MIs was over. By 1851 about 700 had been set up, concentrated in the large towns and in the industrial hinterlands, but it was not until 1860 that the Yorkshire Union of MIs published a set of design precedents in the expectation of another spate of building in response to recent enabling legislation. The first was an 1843 Act giving exemption from rates to societies established for purposes of science, literature or the fine arts. The second was the 1854 Literary and Scientific Institutions Act which allowed sites up to an acre in area to be gifted to such bodies. MIs evidently expected to benefit from both, but the growth of public elementary education, the foundation of numerous technical and art colleges and eventually the 1870 Education Act, made them redundant.

As in the case of Sunday schools, recent analysis of MIs has construed them in several ways. Shapin and Barnes (1977) argue that the kind of science taught was 'designed precisely to constrain its recipients and stultify their imagination' – in other words to achieve control over workers. The connection frequently made by promoters between science and religion, especially Paley's natural theology, lends force to this argument since the orderliness of nature was not only a revelation of divine nature but of the orderliness of society. On the other hand Russell (1983) argues that the evidence is less clear:

> the role of science in the Mechanics' Institutes was chiefly to minister to local patriotism, frequently to provide useful practical knowledge, but only occasionally to serve as an instrument for controlling the turbulent society of England in the early nineteenth century.
>
> (Russell 1983: 173)

The radical Methodist and Dissenting streak in many of the MIs lends support to Russell.

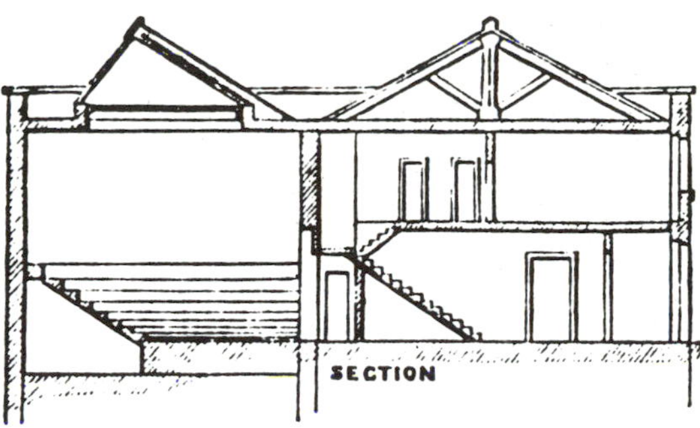

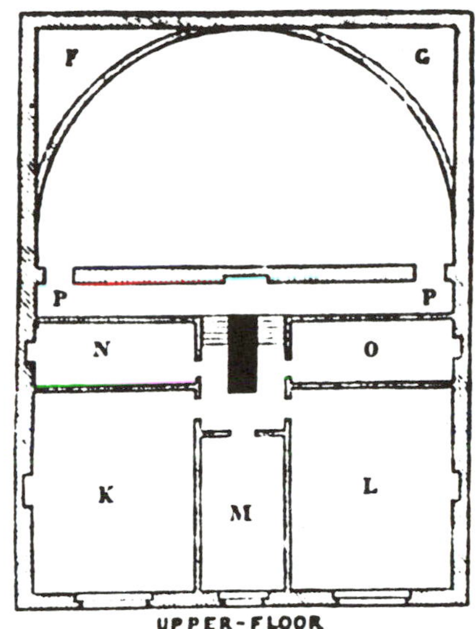

Figure 9.14
Keighley Mechanics' Institute (c. 1837), upper floor plan and section
Source: Unknown

Analysis of the buildings does not help to resolve these opposed assessments. Undoubtedly they were modelled on the genteel 'Lit. and Phil.' and élite academic models. They contained the same range of functional spaces and used the same formal language – even though cost restrictions caused their Classicism to be shorn down. The lecture theatres also followed these models, the main differences lying in their freedom from the segregatory forces evident at the RI, and from the complex internal formal hierarchies of the Paris *Académie des Sciences.* So they can be read as material gestures of a compliant workforce creating for itself, or accepting, forms which reproduced existing social structures and would ease harmonious upward mobility. Equally they can be read as the appropriation of familiar forms as a radical challenge to the very power sources which invented them. The long journey from Leyden to Keighley shows that their meaning cannot be discovered only in the archeology of the building; its programme, financing, management, the rhetoric of its foundation and use, and its membership rules are essential evidence.

PART IV

BUILDINGS AND THINGS

Introduction

A late sixteenth century woodcut represents an allegory of trade (Figure IV.1). The usual reproductions of less than half the image conceal that it is about much more than trade: it is the entire narrative of material production, exchange and legal control.

Under the arms of leading merchant cities is a view of Antwerp, the fortified harbour full of ships. A huge fountain holds a pillar from which hang scales of justice, with creditors and debtors balanced in its pans. The ribbed bowl, on which is inscribed every kind of manufactured and natural product, is flanked by scenes of production – saw mills, smelters, smithies, fields – and enormous activity of packing, crating, and carrying in caravan formation. Below it are destructive images of war, death and price fluctuations. Under the fountain the throned merchant is surmounted by a tabernacle containing 'the secret book' – an inventory. In four raised, Classical porches, which remind Pevsner (1979: 197–98) of the *mansiones* of Renaissance theatres, are scenes of weighing, a group of negotiators discussing mining matters, a large writing office and some men counting money and jewels. Amongst a profusion of barrels, treasure chests, boxes, bales and bundles are figures of integrity, taciturnity and languages; cashiers, clerks, men counting coins and filling them into bags; and a central figure of fortune on a globe. Money, documents, books and contracts are prominent. The artist would know the mercantile skill of families such as the Fuggers in Augsburg (where the woodcut was produced) and his text celebrates the 'laudable, beautiful, very ancient art of book-keeping'. The rich architecture is perhaps intended to recall not a theatre but a temple-with-court, possibly a synagogue with the central torah and a raised priest's or judge's seat.

The splendour of mercantile buildings is not the sole reason for architecture's prominence in the allegory. Buildings both materialise and symbolise manufacture and trade. To produce them material is won from the land by mining, quarrying or harvesting, formed into components and assembled. Along the line various parties exchange the land, materials, components and the tools of production, and add value by labour. The final purchaser also owns or has rights over the land on which the entire assembly is placed. The capital invested comes to rest on land; the product returns to its origins. No wonder the building is a powerful symbol.

It has value in its use, or as an exchange commodity. This grossly simplified description could apply to any capital product. Buildings are different however. In them other goods are produced, including those – for instance windows – needed for making further buildings, as well as the tools for production including the outdoor processes of fishing, farming and forestry. Innovations in technology such as the production of cast iron result not only in steam engines, but in new kinds of buildings for making steam engines.

Figure IV.1

The Allegory of Trade, late sixteenth-century woodcut (Jost Amman?)

Source: *Germanisches National Museum*, Nürnberg, reproduced by courtesy of the Trustees of the British Museum

And as the allegory implies, the buildings in which exchange takes place may themselves become subjects of exchange. So they are both the containers and the contained. What they contain are things and people.

The categorical difference – their unique property of containing people in space – has a special aspect here. Whilst products like the chests and boxes in the woodcut are containers for other products, only buildings are containers which interface products with people.

Production or exchange is the purpose of the types in this Part. In a textile mill mechanical power is distributed in space so that it finishes up at machines which interface with raw materials, workers and supervisors to produce cloth. In a market the cloth, those who own it (or their agents) and potential customers are interfaced to maximise the probability of an exchange.

Making and exchanging things is so basic to civic order that judicial powers control what can be made and sold, by whom, and where. They also set out contractual obligations. These controls are enforced in special judicial places.

The Industrial Revolution changed demand as radically as supply. An analysis of consumption is essential alongside the traditional one of production and, as Campbell (1987) shows, entails issues which are irrelevant in the latter: the Puritan ethic, fashion, imitation of superior social classes, romanticism and the rise of modern consumer hedonism based on imagination. Places of exchange are as important to a typology of the Industrial Revolution as those of production.

As always the origin of these production, exchange and judicial spaces are in non-specialised aggregations: factories containing offices and apprentice dormitories; merchant houses integral with workshops, warehouses, counting houses and shops; and markets with guildhalls, courts and council chambers. The specialised types which emerge eventually converge again, in visions of the perfect city, new utopias with production instead of justice at their heart.

CHAPTER 10
Production

Living space as workspace

The Crystal Palace modelled the processes of material production and exchange by removing them from their *habitat* and enclosing them in a vast glass showcase. The spaces they occupied in the real world were invisible.

Even more strikingly, the people involved in production were invisible. In the real world they had three roles: as sources of motive power using their bodies, chiefly hands and arms; as controllers; and as providers of resources. This approximates to labour, management and capital. Feudal pre-industrial economies prefigured these labour-capital relations. In non-feudal ones all these roles are combined in one kin group whose members own the capital, make and own the tools, grow or win the raw material from land they own, use their own bodies for motive power - or obtain help from wind, water or animals – and consume or exchange their products. Living and working space are either undifferentiated, or contiguous. The farmhouse dairy, the weaving loom in the living space or in a loft over the house, or the jeweller's bench by the living room window are familiar survivals; a few were even exhibited in the Crystal Palace.

The early production complex

Monks, emperors, time and space

The manufactory (to differentiate it from the factory of the Industrial Revolution) needed major capital investment and employment of paid labour. Increased scale, though the most obvious, is not the most significant change. There is a new economic base and with it a new social structure for production, far beyond my scope to analyse. But the buildings prefigure the factory and it is relevant to ask where such capital came from.

The public funding of the punitive workplaces we have already examined in Chapter 4 was one source.

The other was Royalty, aristocracy, the great merchant families and their mercantile associations, owners of landed estates, Popes and princes of the church. Their disposable capital, much of it invested in manufactories, was one definition of their power. The production-orientated military and naval arsenals, and colonial industrial settlements, drew on the same capital and on the same 'top down' design models.

For all these to be controllable for profit, space and time had to be regularised, as they were in the later factory system. Madge (1982) sees the origins for modern production in the medieval monastery's discipline, communal order, work ethic and time regulation. A machine, the clock, made possible the systematic time-keeping of the Benedictine Rule. He follows Mumford (1934: 12–18) who places this somewhere in the thirteenth century. Cippola (1967: 39) is more specific: it was the invention of the verge escapement with foliot in the middle of that century which was the breakthrough. Thompson (1974: 39–77) - in the context of the seventeenth century - rejects determinist explanations for changes in the pre-industrial apprehension of time. The mechanical inventions, rather than causes, were symptoms 'of

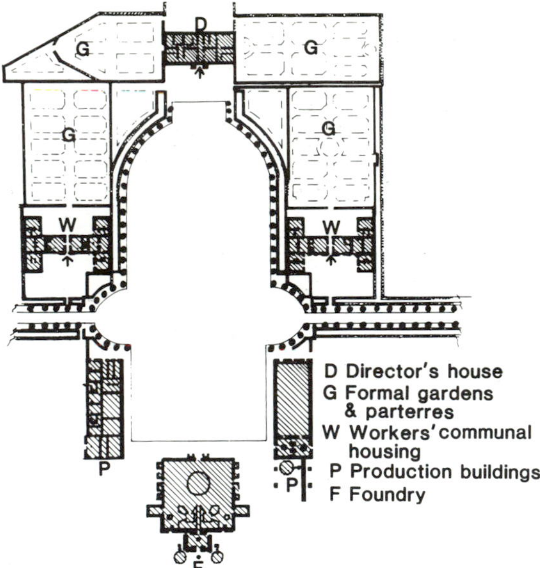

Figure 10.1
Toufaire's plan for Le Creusot (1781)
Source: Author's drawing based on original plan in the Côte d'Or Archives, Dijon

a new Puritan discipline and bourgeois exactitude'. Braudel (1982: 431) speaking of Huygens' seventeenth century revolutionary inventions of the pendulum and the adjusting spiral also denies their causative role. 'No innovation has any value except in relation to the social pressure which maintains and imposes it'. He goes further: 'there is (no) such thing as technology itself', which, though it rules out causative explanations, leaves room for those which reveal assocations.

Clocks enabled regular intervals to be sounded by the monastic, and then secular, church bells, soon to be translated into the continuous visual analogue of fingers moving over the clock face. Through the senses of sound and sight they achieved a structuring of time which had long been anticipated in the organisation of monastic space. The ninth century plan of St Gall (Horn and Born 1979) uses a standard module. It both looks backward to the land grids of the Roman *agrimensores* and forward to the graph paper planning of Durand in 1800. Its grid enabled corridors, passages and stairs designed for quick and easy circulation to penetrate the plan. Economy of time was gained through regularity of space.

The time-discipline of the factory system also had its spatial correlates. To get from a house to a factory for the start of a shift required them to be close. To ensure that no time was wasted on the job required constant visual surveillance which depended on long visual axes and spatially shallow production spaces.

These same spatial devices and symmetrical, axial forms were hallmarks of the 'grand' manufactories – precursors of the factory – where three kinds of products were made. First, precious, rare or luxury goods for consumption by a class that owned the plant. The profits came directly to the Royal or élite coffers, or indirectly through licensing and the payment of *royalties*. Typically it was salt, silk, glass, porcelain, tapestries and carpets and fine metal casting. Second, products needed directly for Royal and government policy; mints and paper mills for coinage and notes, and arsenals for fabricating ships, ordnance, and naval and military supplies. Third, the products of coerced workforces: either in the colonies, where slaves or transported convict labour produced sugar, tobacco, cotton and timber, or the miscellaneous things made by prisoners nearer home.

Workers in Royal manufactories were scarce and possessed craft secrets. With their families they were housed in relative comfort, with provision for their daily needs within the confines of an enclosed site with strictly controlled access. Colbert's Royal tapestry, carpet and textile manufactories of Gobelins set up in the 1660s for Louis XIV were like this. In its school of design sixty apprentices underwent a rigorous six-year apprencticeship. The workshops, school, chapel, houses, courts, gardens and offices filled the enormous site, entered through a grand axial gateway. The model for this inward looking, protected, secretive and hierarchical set-up was the *château enclos*.

There was a whole family of such industries: plate glass and mirrors at St Gobain in Aisne, wrought iron at Buffon's forges on the Armançon in Burgundy (the Royal monopoly having been ceded in 1560); and cast iron the 1781 Royal Foundry at Le Creusot, also in Burgundy (Devillers and Huet 1981), designed by Pierre Toufaire, chief engineer in the Royal port of Rochefort.

He placed at one end of the long axis the 'agent's' – that is the director's – house, at the other the production block containing the two furnaces (Figure 10.1). On either side of the former are H-shaped blocks of workers' houses and of the latter, workshops. A tree-lined avenue crosses the courtyard on the short axis and gives access through two gates set back in apsidal recesses. The courtyard is open for unimpeded surveillance. But the entrance to the workers' houses is from the avenue outside the gates, making them spatially shallower than the agent's house and the furnaces. Depth represents the power of control, as it does in traditional public space. But here there is a specific meaning – it also represents the power of capital. Formal devices underline the spatial strategy: the long axis unites control and investment, and the houses of those with least power become lateral sentinels.

Royal production space was often of spectacular scale. In Spain Royal textile factories were established for wool, silk and cotton during the eighteenth century (Clayburn La Force 1964: 337–63). One wool and serge enterprise employed over 1000 workers and by the end of the century, over several sites, 24,000, in architect-designed mills. The 'palace' as a model worked even in heavy industry, with its strong forms of kilns, smelting cones and blast furnaces. In the 1799 Polish Royal ironworks at Chorzow the architect was Count Wedding and the engineering technology was based on Scottish precedent (Bukowski 1973). On the main axis of the symmetrical plan lies the blowing machine, flanked by two workshop wings and, further back, by two conical blast furnaces. There is not a trace of residential space.

The model worked equally well at settlement level. Polish Royal industry goes back to the Thirty Years' War, when refugee artisans had new towns (*nowe miasto*) built for them often adjacent to medieval centres (Gutkind 1972: 86–7). In the late eighteenth century Stanislaus Augustus developed sites for the production of luxury goods such as glassware, faience, playing cards and silk girdles. He also invested in heavy industry – textiles, forges, blast furnaces and gunsmithies – mostly through his Royal Treasurer of Lithuania. The 1780 industrial town of Kunsztow (Figure 10.2) on the river Lososna is typical. The water-powered wool, linen, silk, metalware, paper and fancy goods factories were dotted along the river which meandered through the town. An octagonal architectural 'circus' was bounded by workers' houses, as were most of the streets radiating from it. One led to a formal public space; another to an oval circus and, through it, to a public market. Anyone familiar with Bath would have felt at home in this Baroque layout despite differences between an élite, decadent social travelling circus and a busy factory town.

To pursue these issues in detail I have chosen Joseph II's late eighteenth century silk project in Budapest. To understand it, and the English silk mill we shall examine later, we need to understand a bit about the process. The cocoons are first placed in hot water to release the filament thread and soften the gum. The threads from several cocoons are clustered, usually by a woman seated by the pans, and a standing child winds the handle of a reel to form a skein of the compound thread. The skein is then wound onto bobbins. For some products a single such thread is twisted ('thrown') to give it strength, for others such as the warp for weaving ('organzine') two or more are wound together and then thrown again, this time in the opposite direction. For warp it is then again wound onto bobbins from which it is 'warped' onto a large drum ('creel') and then transferred to the 'beam' which is placed in the loom. For other uses the thrown thread is wound onto reels to form skeins which are then cut to length, formed into balls ('bier warping') and transferred to the loom shops. For the weft ('tram') threads from the bobbins are loosely twisted together, and wound onto 'quills' or 'pirns' which are then placed in the shuttle. Short staple fibres left over as waste from reeling and throwing can be spun together to make spun silk.

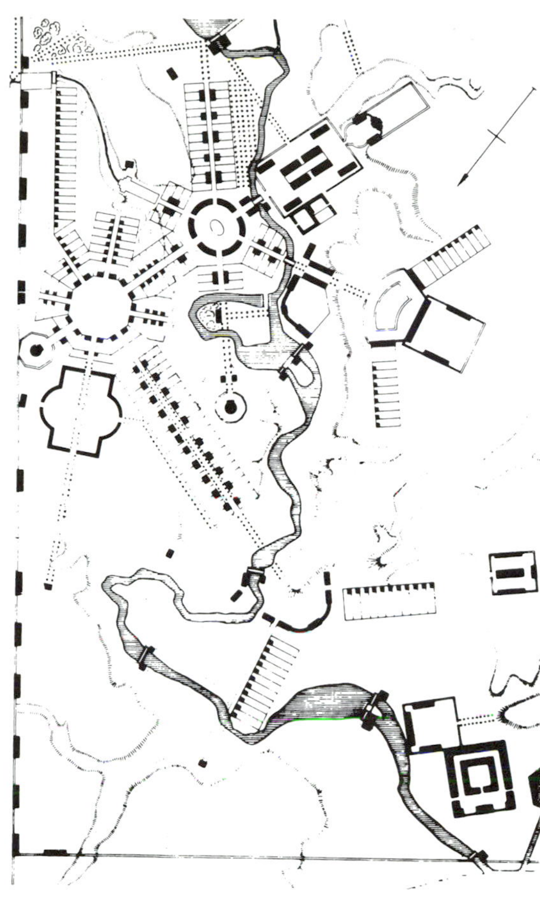

Figure 10.2
Plan of Kunsztow (1780)
Source: Gutkind (1972)

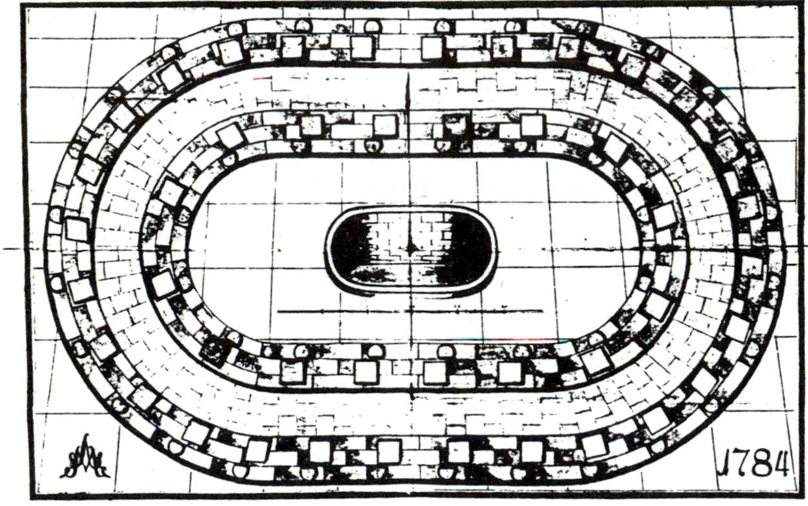

Figure 10.3

Mazzocato's silk cocoon unwinding factory, Óbuda, Budapest (1784), plan

Source: Hungarian National Archives, Budapest

During the centuries of hand power Sicily and Calabria became the most advanced centres. What makes silk of special interest is that the early application of water power made factory production feasible long before it appeared in other textiles. Undershot waterwheels were used for throwing in thirteenth century Italy (Derry and Williams 1960: 100) and a fifteenth century sketch shows a system basically like that which we shall find in the Lombe brothers' 1719 Derby mill. Bologna became the centre for such mills in the sixteenth century (Poni 1972) when the technology was still a carefully-guarded secret. When in 1607 Zonca published his treatise in Padua a water wheel is shown driving a tall cylindrical warping machine and a similar, vertical-axle throwing machine. Poni (1972) traces the spread of the 'Bolognese' silk mills in the Venetian Republic and Henderson (1958–9) in Germany. By Joseph II's time the technology was widely used in Europe.

He was immersed in 'Enlightened' projects – advances in medicine and science, educational and prison reforms, and re-organising the army and the civil service. Investment in new technology was a key strategy. He had already built in Ó-Buda (literally 'Old Buda'), a six-storey silk spinning mill in 1780, designed by Lander Lörinc. A single water wheel drove, on each of five floors, three huge vertical axle twisting and throwing cylinders which, according to Horváth (1840: 216) held a total 4240 spindles.

Unwinding the cocoons was still a primitive process, and much of the raw silk was imported. Joseph wanted to domesticate its manufacture and in 1781 invited the Treviso expert Mazzocato to Vienna to advise him.[1] In 1785 Mazzocato and his family arrived in Ó-Buda to take charge of an existing unwinding workshop. A year earlier he had already prepared a plan for an oval single-floor plant (Figure 10.3), though a part-perspective shows a two-floor structure. There are two concentric rows of pillars which are also chimneys, 28 in the outer ring and 16 in the inner, around an open central court with a well. A woman-and-child pair is located by the boiling pan at each pillar and the two rings are 'mis-aligned', the inner not obscuring the outer so that a supervisor could see every worker from the court.

Lander's successor the architect Joseph Tallher executed the project in 1785–6 (Figure 10.4) on a site to the west of the old unwinding workshop. His two-storey oval had a sweeping Baroque staircase to its upper floor and a central doorway under it to the lower. Tallher 'regularised' the alignment of the pillars according to the best principles of academic architecture, thus at a stroke rendering impossible continuous surveillance. Mazzocato protested, in a complaint uncannily like that of Jeremy Bentham six years later when he discovered that the Adam brothers had undermined the principle of central surveillance in the panoptical Edinburgh Bridewell by placing the prisoners' day rooms between the cells and the central observation tower. He was no more sucessful than Bentham: a special commission ruled that there was no significant difference between the two plans, and between either of them and the executed building. Nemes (1984) remarks on the 'logic' of maintaining that a building is like *both* of two quite different designs.

The manufactory entrance was not aligned with that to the courtyard. This chicane ensured that the former was hidden from the street by a technique not unlike that used in Islam to shield house interiors. The street block housed the master's and the children's sleeping quarters, the long south wing the women's dormitory and the north wing store rooms. The spatial structure brought the master and the workers to the surface to share control over access to the deep production space.

Similar plants were built elsewhere and Nemes (1984) sees in them forerunners of Bentham's Panopticon invented for the same reason – production surveillance. She also sees a kinship with other projects of Joseph's, notably the Vienna *Narrenturm* asylum of 1783, designed by Canevale, also invited to Vienna by the Emperor;

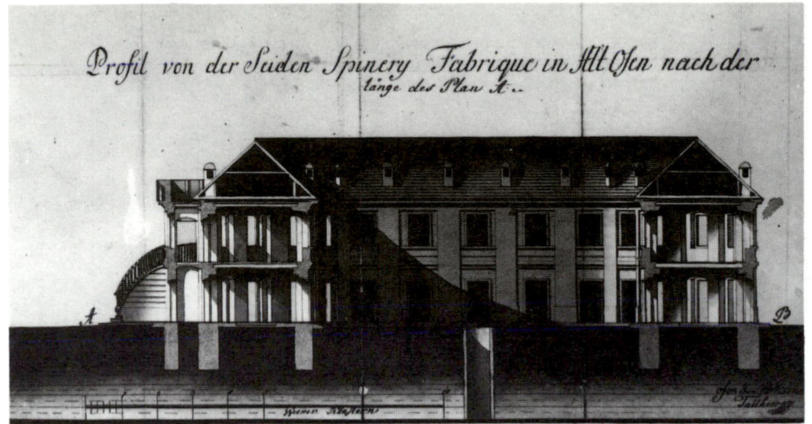

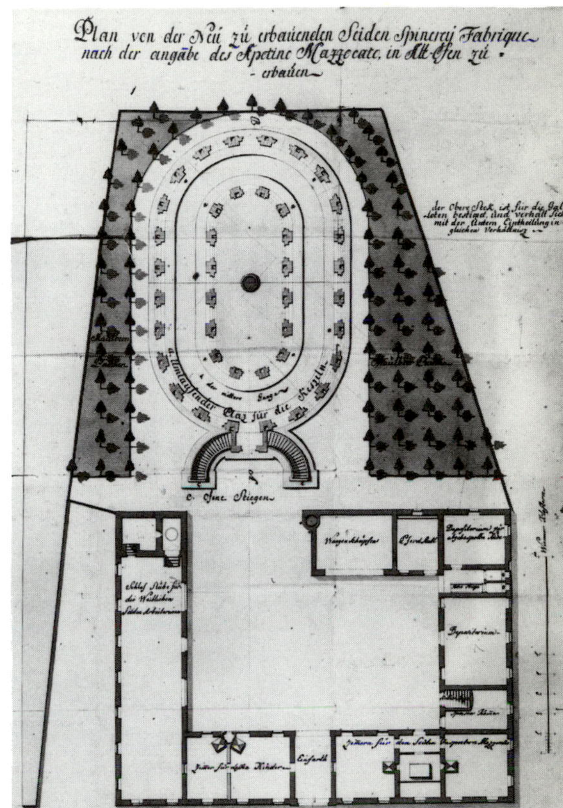

Figure 10.4

Tallher's silk cocoon unwinding factory, Óbuda, Budapest (1785–6), section and plan

Source: Hungarian National Archives, Budapest

she considers the possibility that the two designers met.

In contrast to Joseph's concern with technical detail, Louis XV, through Ledoux, worked at the most spectacular scale in the 1770s Royal salt works at Chaux in the Franche Comté. Not surpisingly Chaux has been the subject of much speculative writing; Vidler (1990) provides an illuminating interpretation, and Pawłowski (1961: 255–92) and Gallet (1980) good analytical histories. Of course there is Ledoux's own baffling *l'Architecture* (1804) whose text and images of Chaux explore Encyclopaedic reason, 'architecture parlante', Rousseauist concepts of nature, a new social doctrine of planning, and a vernacular expressive style.

As assistant to the *Inspecteur des Salines* for eastern France Ledoux knew the centuries-old disorderly *salines.* His first design (1773) was a typological exercise, for no specified site – a square enclosure still pervaded by the Colbertian *enclos* in the tradition of the great seventeenth century courtyard hospitals and, ulimately, the châteaux. For complex reasons this scheme was rejected and Ledoux's second, almost semicircular scheme, one half of a scheme designed to replace the first plan, was actually built (Figure 10.5) but a number of features survived from the square design.

The entrance with its extraordinary rusticated hexastyle portico is flanked by the house of the guards and the prison, as well as the bakehouse and lawcourt. On either side are two blocks of workers' communal dwellings to complete the semicircle, with rear produce gardens. Across the diameter lie the two salt production buildings and centrally between them the director's house with the chapel. It was always Ledoux's intention to complete the other half. In the imaginary exercises which occupied him for the rest of his life he developed designs both for the town and for its individual buildings.

The famous aerial view (Figure 10.6) shows all the key ideas. The main axis runs from the entrance gate through the central chapel and director's house to the rear gate and then into the distant forests. It controls both symbolically and in pratice the woodcutters and charcoal burners upon whose regular work and delivery schedules the continuous process depended. This axis, with communal houses and other buildings at forest intersections, was for surveillance over that notoriously unruly workforce, and acted as a constant reminder of the power which lay at the centre.

The interior court was to be lit at night by four huge torches to make visible all movement between dwellings and factory. The complex was surrounded by a low wall, moat, peripheral road and trees, outside which, on individual pastoral plots, were the public buildings – school, hotel, public baths, markets – and the houses of officers, artists and master craftsmen.

Vidler (1981–2: 54–63) notes that the central surveillance united production control with reli-

Figure 10.5

Ledoux's final scheme for Chaux (almost as built), plan and director's house and chapel

Source: Ledoux (1804)

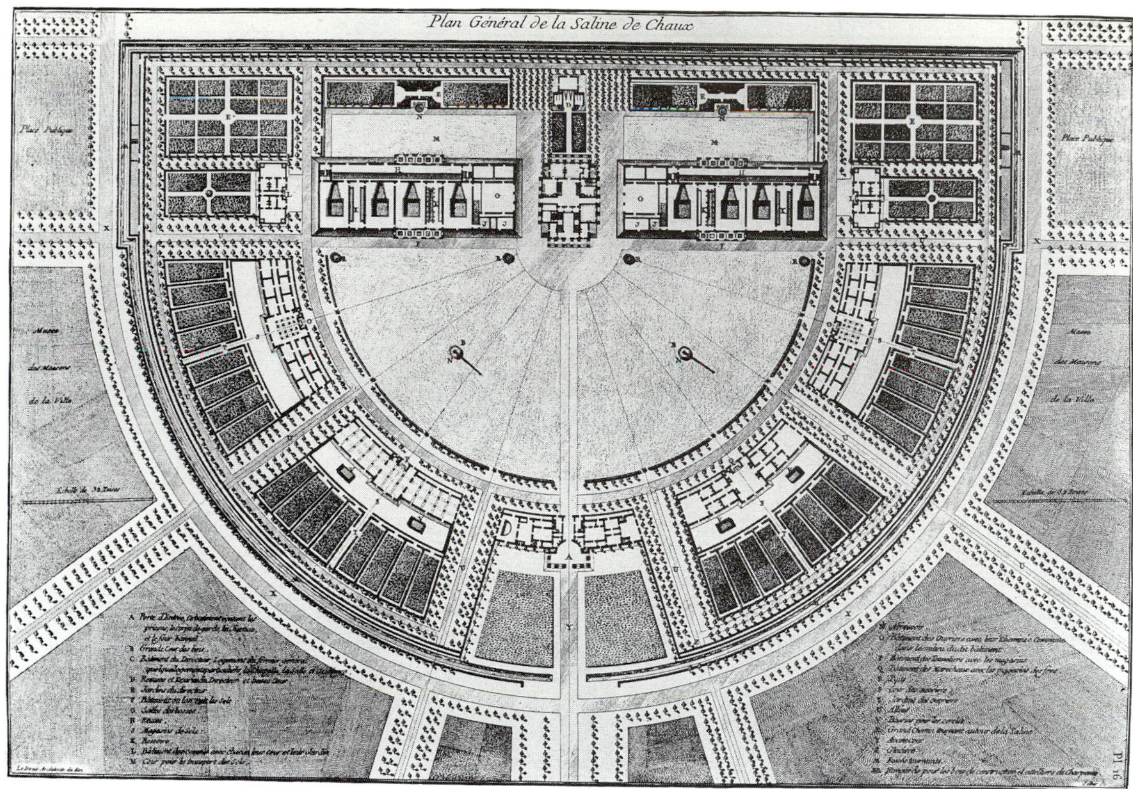

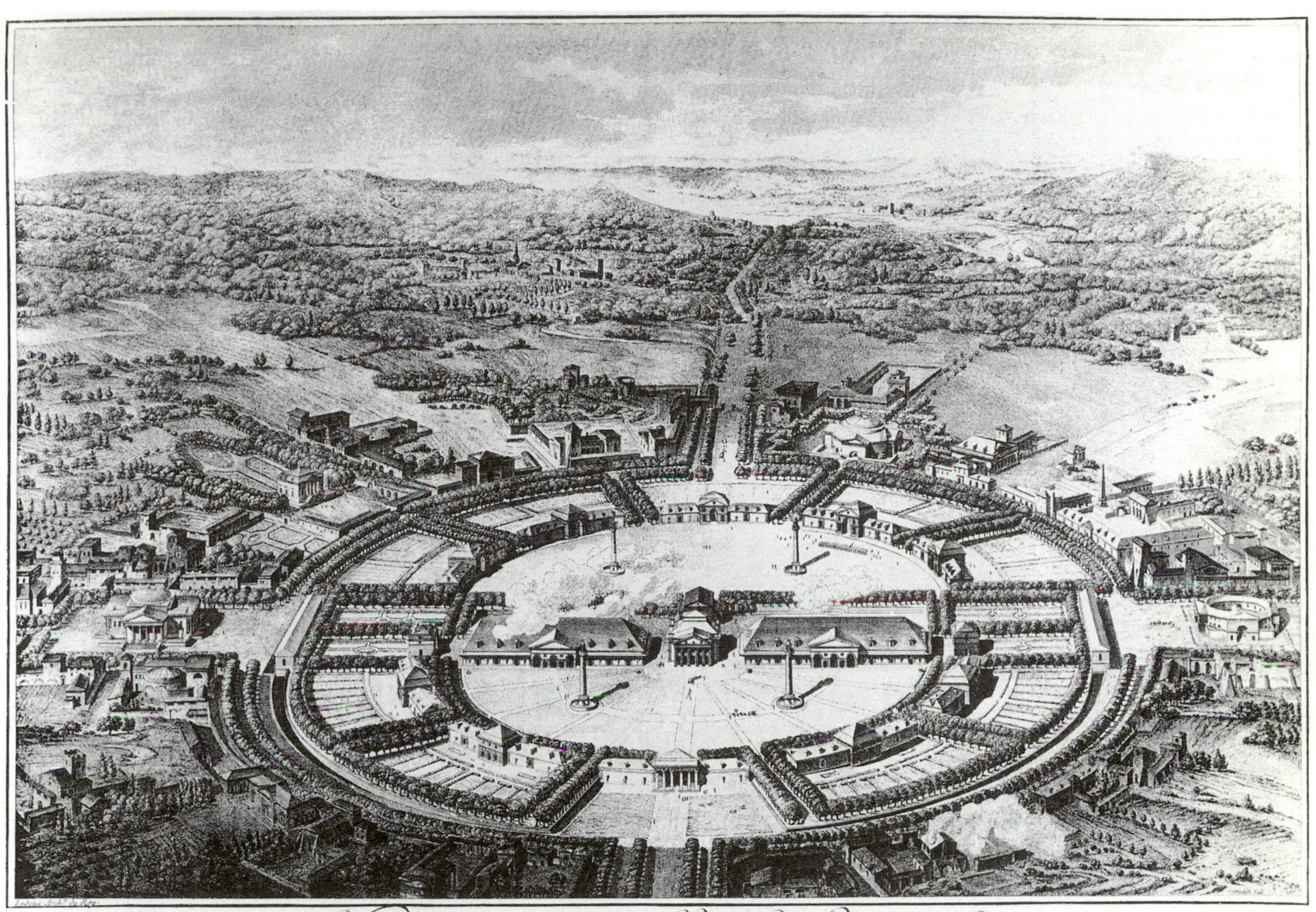

Figure 10.6

Aerial view of Ledoux's near-circular scheme for Chaux in its entirety

Source: Ledoux (1804)

gious authority and, with the circular guardhouses in the forest, prefigured Bentham's Panopticon. Less obvious is that spatially, from the gatehouse, all entrances are at the same depth – to the workers' communal dwellings, the director's house and the production spaces. The gate, with its guard house, was shallower. It had to fulfil the two traditional functions: filtering out moral and physical impurities at the peripheral town wall, and protecting an inner, secret world which was totally transparent to its inhabitants, irrespective of rank.

There are other ambivalent features. The public buildings, totally at variance with any traditional town, are *outside* the 'wall' and the gate. They are for a range of functions which conflate the controller/controlled ('inhabitant/visitor') categories – agents of the Director, middle managers, craftsmen, workers and strangers. They are the shallowest buildings on the site so that with respect to them the workers are deep, in the zone where the controlled would indeed be in a conventional institution. But also at that depth are the Director, the sacred centre and the productive unit. Quite unlike the governor of Bentham's Panopticon who was on the shallow surface – as controllers always are in institutions – the Director here is in the deep space which represents power in *non*-institutional buildings. In other words he, his workers and the validating sacred centre are forced into a spatial solidarity by the overriding production goal.

Whilst formal devices – rings of public buildings, walls and workers' houses, axes, and a focal centre – clarify category distinctions, they obscure the important relations revealed by spatial structure.

Investors on lower rungs of power followed

Figure 10.7
Thomas Sandby's design for the Fitzmaurice bleachworks in Wales (c. 1785)
Source: BAL/RIBA Drawings Collection

the same models but by more modest means. The *Archives Nationales* in Paris contain a wealth of projects by the landed aristocracy for their estates; at first groups of water wheels on the estate's river for sawmills, potteries, iron forges or paper making. As the projects expanded into complete production complexes they adopted the model of the Royal manufactories and of their own *châteaux*.

But even these classes occasionally had vast pretensions. When Thomas Sandby designed a bleach works for the Fitzmaurice family in Wales (c. 1785) he started off with a huge curved palace with a high central block and flanking projecting domed porticos (Figure 10.7) and even the final design was only slightly pruned.

More surprising than the use of the 'palace' for Royal and aristocratic investments is its survival in the 'bottom up' projects of self-made entrepreneurs. When Boulton and Watt employed Benjamin Wyatt II to design their manufactory at Soho, Birmingham (1765–6) – the largest of its kind in Europe – they were given a Palladian country house facade: slightly projecting centre pavilion, with a lunette over the entrance and a shallow dome, and two equally slightly projecting end pavilions (Figure 10.8). But the side wings projected deeply *backwards* forming a great rear court, instead of receiving its visitors with open arms. The hidden court presages a period of secrecy and industrial spying. The symmetrical facade was a front for apprentice dormitories, offices, workshops and stores. The complex grew by accretion and by 1788 consisted of a hotchpotch of courtyards, dwellings, counting and engine houses, rolling mills, furnaces and a mint. What had started off as camouflage, finished up with the burgeoning and revolutionary plant bursting its polite envelope.

Military production

The grandest schemes continued to be the Royal investments in military or naval projects on the scale of town development. Colbert was behind the largest such as the naval arsenal at Rochefort. The instructions were to build it 'quickly (and to make it) beautiful and grand'. Building started in 1666; by 1670 cannon foundries, forges, naval barracks, wet and dry docks, officers' lodgings, a huge, thin ropery and drying room designed by Blondel – Director of the Royal Academy of Architecture – mastshops, offices and warehouses were complete. The plan (Figure 10.9) has the morphology of normal public space: in the deep area is the 'King's House' built on the foundations of the original castle, the residence of the superintendent and his staff ('inhabitants'). The gridded civilian part of the town for 'visitors' – workers and ratings (housed in civilian lodgings) – is in the outer, shallow zone. But something else has happened – the docks and production units are also deep, so, once again, the power that resides in both capital and its control is represented by depth.

Another system of arsenals was developing – the galleys filled with chained slaves, mostly Muslims captured in war or purchased from non-Christian sources in north Africa and the near-east (Bamford 1973). They also received domestic convicts (*forçats*) – vagabonds, beggars and criminals. Those too weak to manage the oars

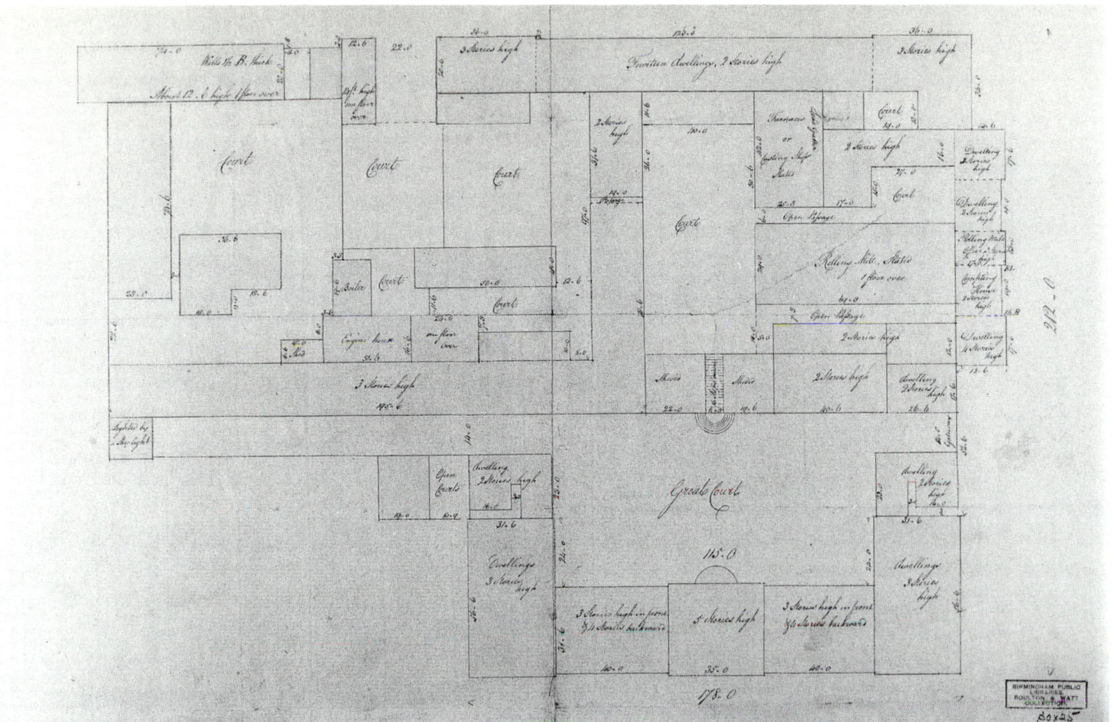

Figure 10.8
1788 plan and exterior view of Wyatt's Soho manufactory, Birmingham (1765–6)
Source: Boulton and Watt Collection, Birmingham Public Library, reproduced by permission of Birmingham Central Library, Archives Division

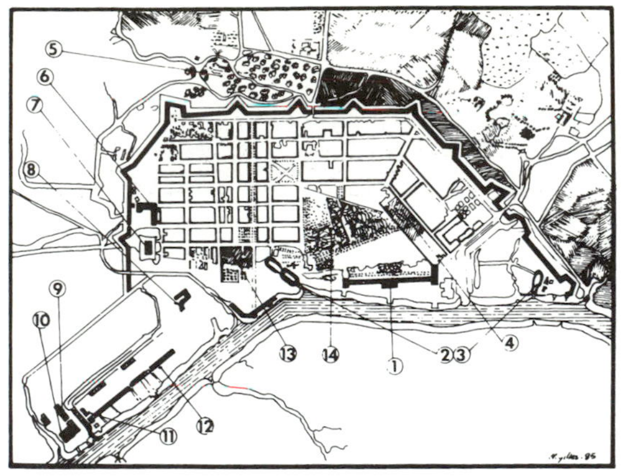

Figure 10.9

Rochefort naval arsenal

Source: Admiral Dupont and Marc Fardet (1986) *L'Arsenal de Colbert, Rochefort*, Centre International de la Mer, Rochefort

were permanently incarcerated in disused ships – the hulks. The main depot at Marseille was vastly expanded for Louis XIV by Colbert and his son from 1665 to include a magnificent new arsenal where the slaves not on campaign worked with the old and maimed. The arsenal's output was equally essential for the naval and military as well as the civilian economy.

In the galley arsenal three traditions of discipline converged – the penal, the military and the productive. The élite Galley Corps was trained to achieve all three by means which included the organisation of space.

Galleys at Toulon, Brest and Rochefort shared the intake with Marseille, but their condition and status deteriorated continuously after about 1700. The life of the galley slave had become a curious mixture of small liberties, self-supporting labour and squalor. The galley system and its Corps were wound up in 1748 (though they struggled on for three decades) to be replaced by the *bagnes*, factory workhouses which fed, housed and kept under surveillance their inmates in total insitutions located at the harbours. The disciplinary codes and staff were largely taken over from the galleys and hulks. Though Colbert had proposed a *bagne* for Marseille as early as 1669 organised on the lines of those in Malta, Tangier and Leghorn, it was well into the next century before France took this step.

Brest was one of the sites dismissed by Colbert and his commissioners when Rochefort was chosen. It was not fully developed for another century. In Chapter One I have mentioned its largest building, the *bagne* designed for 20,000 prisoners by Choquet de Lindu in 1757 and published by Diderot. Rosenau (1970: 78–9) includes it in her survey of prisons; but it is more important as a factory.

A block (Figure 10.10) housed 2000 chained men on two floors. They slept in two huge halls, the canvas mattresses (*tolats*) for twenty prisoners arranged on either side of a central, pierced, spine wall. The halls were separated from the central administration by open iron grilles and, at night, by locked heavy wooden doors. The entrance and communicating staircase, spaces for watchmen, the officer in charge, surgeon, chaplain and a chain gang office were at the centre, together with a mobile altar in a cupboard which was wheeled to the foot of the staircase for celebration of Mass. Each hall had a tavern divided into two halves; one for the free wine provided by the King, the other for its purchase by the *forcats*.

All had to work, some in workshops in the great courtyard. Products were sold from small shops to which the public had direct access by a corner entrance into the courtyard.

The basement plan and section show a highly sophisticated sanitary system of canals, pipes, shafts, reservoirs, privies, laundries and kitchens which ensured clean water supply, drainage and sewage, fresh air, clothes and body washing, and cooking, without which the entire system would degenerate into squalid and dangerous chaos.

The spatial structure has the almost fully-developed institutional inversion: inhabitants in shallow, outer zone, visitors (*forçats*) and their work space in the depth, though the direct entrance for trading with the public diminishes its full rigour.

The export of *bagnes* to France's overseas territories, starting with Guyana in 1790, adds colonial order to the traditional penal, military and productive ones, a convergence which encapsulates several features of the factory system.

Demangeon and Fortier (1978) see the naval arsenals as antecedents of modern town planning. In the name of production all systems were expanded to a hitherto unmatched urban scale. Space became precisely defined by function and fragmented. Technology was exploited. And buildings were 'dematerialised' – by which they mean the abandonment of style, formal models or vocabularies – to become 'screens' in a regular grid. Effectively these created 'a pefect negative of what classical towns had been' (1978: 30). These insights are valuable but the over-emphasis on formal transformations inhibits analysis, as is evident in their interpretation of Cherbourg.

The design of the English Royal docks and their arsenals was strikingly similar, even without sponsorship by an Absolute monarch, Revolu-

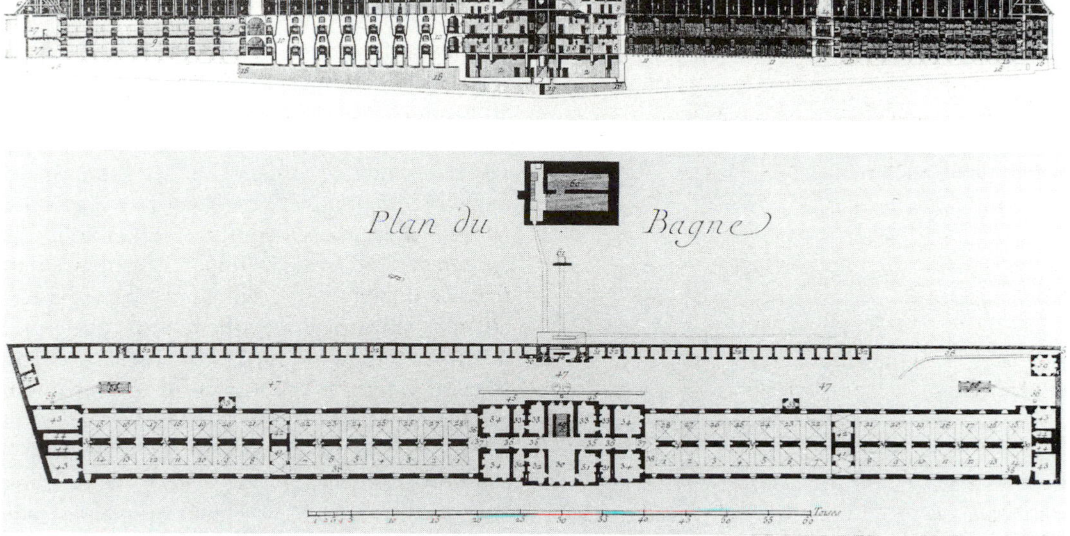

Figure 10.10
Choquet de Lindu's design for the bagna *at Brest (c. 1757), longitudinal section and plan*
Source: Diderot

tionary Assembly, Emperor, encylopaedic Enlightenment or physiocratic rigour. Plymouth (Devonport), started in 1692, makes a good case study (Figure 10.11).

Amongst its first buildings was the palatial terrace of officers' houses probably designed by Robert Hook; the central pavilion is the Commissioner's, and the two end pavilions were offices. At right angles was the long ropery and, at its tip, the great storehouse. During the following 150 years' expansion the workers' housing moved outside the enclosed area altogether (Coad 1983). In the shallow zone inside the gate all the functional and ideological control spaces were located – the chapel, pay office, master warden's house, the officers' terrace and guardhouse. Deeper in were warehouses and the workshops, including the ropery which was turned at right angles to its original line along the eastern boundary. By the waterside were the production docks.

Whilst this structure at first seems ambivalent, neither institution nor normal public space, it becomes firmed up as the characteristic space of production. At the start is Le Creusot where valuable plant shares depth with controllers, but the controlled are at the shallow surface. The *bagne* at Brest is its reverse, almost a pure institution. At Chaux controllers and controlled share space with each other, and with the plant, deep within; at Budapest and Plymouth they do so on the shallow surface, but the plant stays at depth. This is the feature common to all the models and a natural

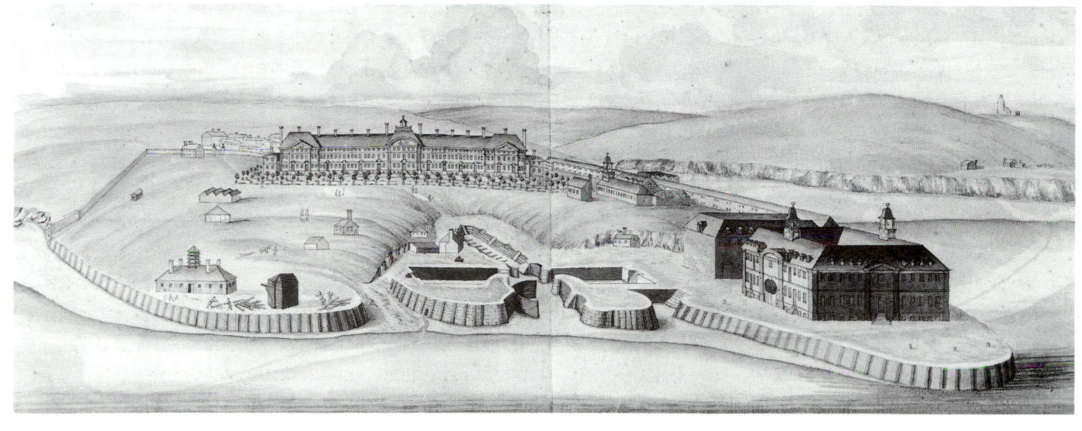

Figure 10.11
Devonport dockyard in 1698
Source: View by Dummer, British Library Lansdowne Collection

Figure 10.12
Eighteenth-century military camp layout
Source: Lochée (1778)

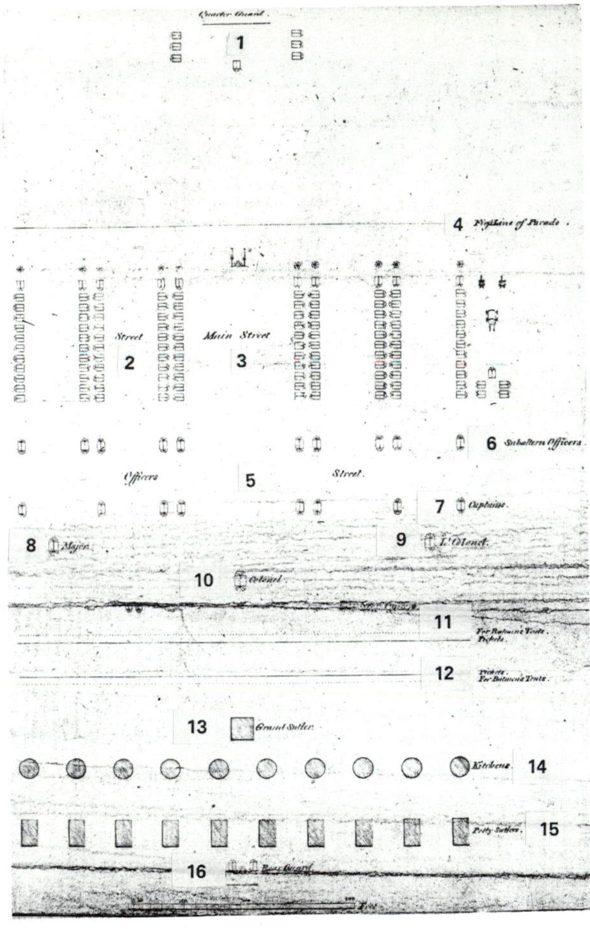

Key

1	Quarter guard	9	Lieutenant colonel
2	Street	10	Colonel
3	Main street	11	Ratings' tent pickets
4	First line of parade	12	Batmen's tent pickets
5	Officers' street	13	Grand sutler
6	Subaltern oficers	14	Kitchens
7	Captains	15	Petty sutlers
8	Major	16	Rear guard

consequence of the redefinition of power in terms of capital investment instead of social rank.

The sanitary innovations in the naval arsenals made them even more like 'laboratories', the English dockyards ahead even of the hospital at Rochefort and the *bagnes.* The architect of the first English naval hospital, Haslar (1746–61) used several overseas precedents but the clinical work of its first physician James Lind was innovatory and had significance far beyond the navy. We have seen how Stonehouse became a model for the French Academy of Sciences in their search for a hygienic replacement for the old Hôtel Dieu.

I have several times linked production and military discipline. Is it borne out in their spaces?

In battlefield and naval formations the need for movement makes it difficult to grasp the underlying spatial organisation. Military space is clearer in the camp. Its origins are in Roman land surveying and town planning.

Dilke (1971) says that the accuracy of Roman land surveyors – the *agrimensores* – remained unmatched until the late eighteenth century. The system was based on a division of land into the *iugerum* – quarter acre plots which a man with two oxen could plough in one day; two of these, a *heredium,* considered sufficient for a smallholding; and a hundred of those which gave the *centuria,* a tribal and later colonial agricultural unit. 'Centuriation' was the division of the land into a grid by lines which were both tracks and limits (*limites*), the *decumanus* in one direction, the *cardo* in the other. When widened into the two principal streets they were the *decumanus maximus* and the *cardo maximus.* That land division links military and colonial activity is obvious. Less so but well established by Rykwert (1976) is its extension into city planning.

The grid is ubiquitous – used throughout Rome, sixteenth century Latin American colonies, North American settlements, nineteenth century cities of Europe, and the new town of Milton Keynes. Without boundary, centre or hierarchy, it is completely open. It is the most basic, and also the most 'democratic' spatial structure. To form civil urban space, the grid is *de*formed to accommodate social structure, that is asymmetries of power. At key crossings large holes, such as the *forum,* are made. Variations of street width and of plot size are introduced, and axes are created. The enclosing boundary wall is pierced by gates aligned with key grid lines. All these appear in military planning. The Roman origins of 'castrametation' – the laying out of camps – are still visible in the eighteenth century army (Lochée 1778) when a model layout (Figure 10.12) has a central axis on which is located the colonel's tent at the rear, flanked symmetrically by his lieutenant colonel and major on a line one step shallower and at right angles to the axis. Next are three lines of tents on large plots, for descending ranks of officers, separated by wide officers' streets, and finally blocks of densely spaced tents with narrow streets for the men at the shallowest layer. There are peripheral guards. At the deepest point on the axis, behind the colonel, is the grand sutler heading another, inner pyramid – that of the kitchens and the line of petty sutlers. This looks like a good analogue for some of the towns and factories with their walls, gates and towers, shallow workers' housing, increasing depth representing increasing power and control. The spaces of maximum productive value lie deep within.

The most obvious building successors are barracks, but they take us too far from production. Nearer are the Irish 'plantation' towns and the Dutch and British colonial-industrial settlements of the India Companies where the merchants, soldiers and civil servants experimented with the most advanced urban design ideas. King (1971) has described the triple, segregated structure: colonial administration, military cantonment and the traditional city of the indigenous population, producing clearly defined civil, military and residential space. This clarity disappears as industrialisation drives development. It was not a one-way traffic between home and colony. James Peacock dreamt of a *Magnificent and Interesting Establishment* (1790), refined into *A Plan for Establishing a United Company of British Manufactures* (1798) which was a transplantation to London of a colonial settlement, complete with factories, warehouses, 'sale-shops' and communal housing. Analysis of colonies from the production perspective would be rewarding; but this too has to be shelved.

Such 'top-down' industrial development was fading into insignificance beside the factory system, the 'bottom-up' process of the Industrial Revolution, and 'grand' design only reappeared with production utopias. At the opposite pole were tiny, ramshackle machines no less significant in their social implicatioms.

In the Scottish Highlands at a time of great exploitation crofters were required under pain of expulsion from house and land to bring their corn to the landlord's water mill for grinding and sale, naturally at punitively depressed prices to give the latter maximum profit under the system of 'thirlage'. Crofters resisted by building small water mills, which were traditional in parts of Scotland (Shaw 1984), with a *horizontal* wheel on a vertical axle which could be submerged in even a mountain stream and used to drive a modest pair of stones. They could easily be hidden, though naturally if the landlord's factor discovered them on his searching rides they were destroyed. This resistance throws into relief several aspects of motive power. First that its possessor has the economic power to enforce a social order. In other words political power, in this case in its most naked form involving physical force. Secondly that a competitor, here a subversive one, cannot survive without an alternative source. And thirdly that both are likely to use the same technology – in this case water wheels – though in a grossly asymmetrical fashion.

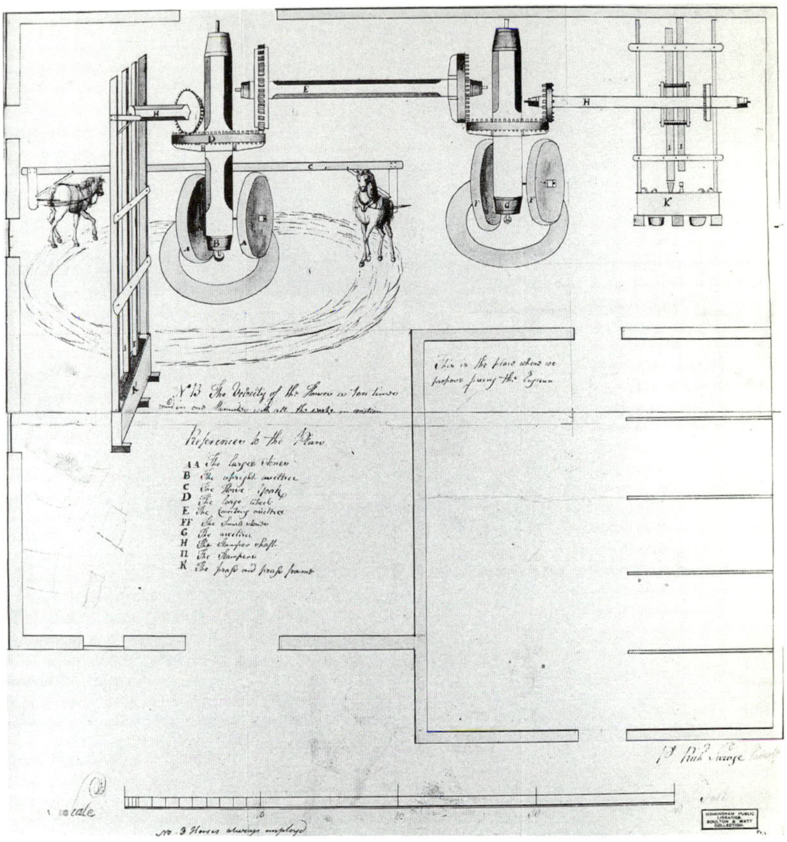

Figure 10.13

Horse-driven oil seed crushing mill at Hull (c. 1784)

Source: Boulton and Watt Collection, Birmingham Public Library, reproduced by permission of Birmingham Central Library, Archives Division

This germinal case points to an association which we have started to explore already. The power of land, capital and the law were all involved in running country estates, colonial settlements, arsenals with galley slaves and 'grand' manufactories. And in all of them aspects of military discipline were present, as they were in the coercive institutions. What is surprising is that when the 'bottom up' factory system gets going, camps, barracks and prisons are not far below the surface.

The factory system

The factory and mill are the most revealing industrial forms in their organisation and space. In older economic histories it was common to trace their development through technological changes of machinery and power sources. The social dimensions of production were missing. The story of the Highlands mills bears out Braudel's (1982) comment that without these technology makes no sense. Berg (1985) shows how rich was the mixture of production modes, social relations, power sources and technology, often in the same settlements. Cheek by jowl were domestic hand loomshops, both independent and organised through the 'putting-out' system operated by a merchant; co-operative and communal workshops; and large water-powered mills. The 'putting-out' system, so closely linked to seasonal agricultural employment, she calls 'proto industry'. Chapman's (1974) evidence for this is quite specific. Industrial and agricultural production spaces were integrated; many of the early textile workshops were in the traditional 'long' or 'laithe' house farm, where house, dairy and shippon had been under one long roof. The workshop was added, as an extra unit, or even replaced a farm space.

Freudenberger and Redlich (1964: 394 *et seq.*) argue that the factory is defined by concentrations of fixed capital and supervised, organised labour (such as do not occur in domestic workshops), and not by motive power sources. Chapman develops a triple classification for factory evolution. If the domestic system is added as a fourth, and recalling Berg's warning that power sources cross boundaries, this allows four types of social and economic relations to be distinguished:

1. One or more domestic processes carried out by households. When apprentices and journeymen are taken on, the producer becomes a 'master' or 'first hand', who either remained independent, buying raw material and marketing his own finished goods, or taking in the 'put out' work of a merchant middleman and receiving a piece-rate.
2. The centralisation of a single process requiring some capital – for instance the fulling mill, or small workshops of stocking frames, looms, silk throwing or reeling machines or dyeing vats. In some cases limited water power was used. The owner, who might have started as master of a domestic unit which sometimes continued alongside, employed labour on a time or piece-rate.
3. The 'proto-factory' in which several batch processes are centralised into a large unit with a systematic grouping of machines, with or without water power, without linked semi-automatic processes. Workers earn time or piece-rate wages and are under a paid overseer. Chapman (1974: 471) reckons that before 1780 in the textile industry such units produced the greatest concentrations of capital. Organisationally, though not at all architecturally, these are the British equivalents of the Royal manufactories in Continental Europe.
4. The factory proper, in which the technologies of motive power and automatic machinery are organised for flow production in 24-hour operation. Water or steam power is a necessary but not sufficient defining feature. The earliest cases are all in textiles, such as the 1717 Derby silk mill and Arkwright's cotton mills.

Workers' housing is examined later, and with it the type 1 and 2 workspaces. The factory proper is my present focus. Its huge literature is full of case studies which bear out the primacy of organisation and capital as argued by Freudenberger and Redlich (1964). Without capital technical inventions withered; with capital even traditional methods flourish. But one technology – of motive power – despite the warnings, *is* crucial in explaining location and spatial development.

Animal power – of the horse or ox used on a treadwheel or circular path – is as ancient as hand power. The hardware was part of the fixed capital. Both horizontal and vertical horse-driven shafts were in use by the sixteenth century, the horse walking on a circular path (Clark, 1927–8). Smeaton used such wheels to drive pumps. The Hull horse-driven oil seed crushing mill of the 1780s (Figure 10.13) transmits power for several functions by its shafts and gears. The building follows and encloses the shapes produced by the machinery.

Capital purchases mechanical and social power. The latter has two forms – over the workforce and over competitors – and explains space much better than the former. In type 1 the master exercised limited power over his family, apprentices and journeymen. In types 2 and 3 the machinery is no longer domestic, and the paid labour needs space designed for discipline and surveillance. This comes to maturity, socially and spatially, in type 4.

The mill

Silk is of special interest since, as we have seen, the earliest application of water power to a proper factory was in silk production. The arrival of mechanised silk spinning in England is one of the landmarks of factory history.

The first was Thomas Cotchett's three-storey 1702 mill on an island in the Derwent at Derby. According to Hutton (1791: 195) it failed through being underpowered, having one wheel ('engine') when it needed three. Its engineer George Sorocold was again employed in 1717 by the brothers John and Thomas Lombe to build the much larger, five storey silk mill next to Cotchett's, still driven by a single (23 foot diameter) waterwheel. John had, apparently stolen the secrets of the twisting and throwing machines from Leghorn.

There are no extant plans; Nixon's famous 1794 exterior view, with some descriptions, are the only guides (Figure 10.14). It shows the oblong box 110 feet long and 39 feet wide, five floors high above a basement which was probably transversely vaulted in brick. The vaults were externally expressed in the large arches springing at water level.

The view is idyllic and pastoral. The mill forms part of a composition of older buildings dominated by the Perpendicular tower of All Saints' church. In the foreground a punter's pole pushes one small boat whilst in another the oarsman is resting. Two boys, one naked on the bank of the calm Derwent, are swimming whilst a third companion cheerily waves to two figures crossing the weir. A few rooks circle in a lightly clouded sky; the trees are in full summer foliage. The deserted mill is peacefully integrated with nature, town and church.

The town plan (Figure 10.15) tells a different story. The mill dominates the town by its bulk, though located at its edge on an island. It is directly linked to the church by Mill Lane and only a few spatial steps from the market place, the county hall and the assembly room. Just as the engraving fits industry harmoniously into nature, so its location integrates it harmoniously into society - commerce, civic government and leisure.

The construction was timber, almost certainly with two rows of columns forming three longitudinal bays. The upper three floors had winding machines and the two lower ones huge, vertical cylindrical twisting and throwing machines, four of each. Defoe (1742: 67) speaks of an 'engine' with 22,586 wheels and 97,746 movements which produce 73,726 yards of silk for every rotation of the waterwheel. Barlow (1836: 709) says that 'the whole of this elaborate machine, though distributed through so many apparte-

Figure 10.14
The Lombes' silk mill at Derby (1717–19)
Source: Nixon (1774)

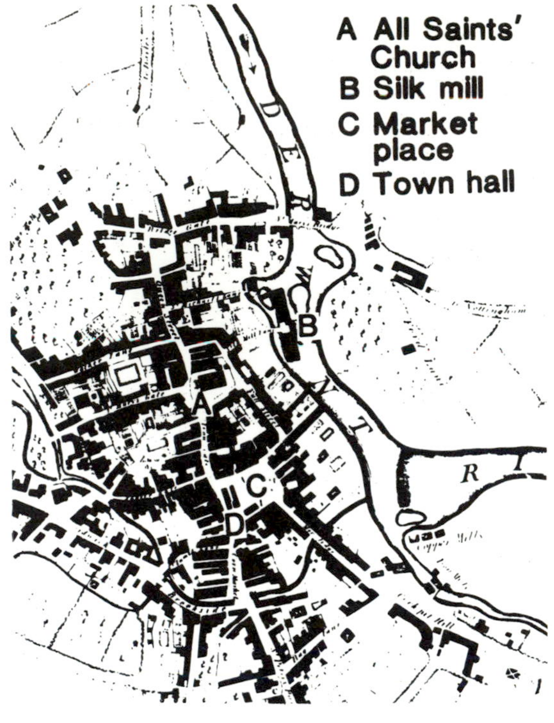

Figure 10.15
Town plan of Derby
Source: British Library

ments (sic), is put in motion by a single water-wheel'. There were three hundred workers.

Historians have long recognised the prophetic nature of the Derby mill. How an apparently fully developed factory appeared more than half a century before the great cotton mills remains a mystery. It is less frequently recognised that nearly all the essentials of the mature mill building are already present.

The semi-automatic machinery was driven by a single source whose power was distributed first by a horizontal shaft at basement level whose length was limited by its torsional resistance. It drove vertical shafts penetrating the floors and each machine. These, stacked vertically on top of each other, could be regarded as one gigantic machine. Height was limited both by structural considerations and the resistance of the more slender vertical shafts. The overall cubic capacity was given by the maximum number of machines that could be packed in and which, in combination, did not overload the water-wheel and the shafts.

All factories have three structures – social, spatial and power transmission. Here they are not yet homologous. The mill is owned and controlled by the investor, each floor supervised by one of his agents, and a worker at each machine. This social structure can be exactly mapped onto space: the entire mill containing all its processes and entered at one point is one bounded space, the space on each floor is dedicated to a single process, and each machine articulates a fragment of floor space for itself and its attendant worker. But the distribution of motive power has another structure. The water wheel and its low-level *horizontal* shaft drive a number of vertical shafts (probably four) each of which drives some machines on *all* floors. Thus the supervisor on one floor has charge of machines driven by several vertical shafts. Each worker shares space with others attending machines driven by other vertical shafts; other workers attending machines driven by the same shaft are invisible. The structure of power transmission crosses those of social control and space (Figure 10.16).

Shortly we will see that in the fully developed cotton mill the water wheel (and later the steam engine) at one end or in the centre drives a single *vertical* shaft which drives, on each floor, a horizontal shaft connected by belts to individual machines. Figure 10.16 shows that an inevitable technical logic then makes the homology of the three structures perfect. The new cotton machinery was smaller, rotated on a horizontal axis and there were many more units on a floor, whilst the great cylindrical silk machines had to rotate on a vertical axis. But there was also a commercial logic. Social control, power transmission and space had to be united by a single hierarchy so that the owner could sell off, or rent one floor. He could even charge a rent for the power he supplied.

Though Lombes' Patent expired in 1732 the next was probably Roe's 1743 mill in Macclesfield, soon to be followed all over the north of England.

Little has changed since Mantoux (1928) asked why such an 'important event (as the Lombes' silk mill) should have been so neglected' (1928: 196). It is still considered marginal because it was premature and the silk industry never exerted an effect on the factory and urban system as whole. But there can be no doubt about its momentous significance for building design. Though there were changes to come in the arrangement of drive shafts its form became the quintessential type of the Industrial Revolution and survived for two centuries.

The silk hand loom, only overtaken by the power loom in the early nineteenth century, was often within the house though the Huguenots constructed substantial attic loomshops in Spitalfields. It is new machines for cotton and wool which were decisive in the textile mill.

The spectacular inventions were in spinning but the first was in weaving – Kay's Flying Shuttle (1733), designed for wool but widely used for cotton by the 1760s. The shuttle was now projected mechanically at speed; it released cloth width and hence loom design from the limits of the weaver's armspan, and increased output. The weaver now consumed the output of ten instead of four spinners. Clearly their productivity had to increase and inventors rose to the challenge. The story is familiar, even from school textbooks: Wyatt and Paul's roller spinning machine (1738); Arkwright's 96-spindle 'Water Frame' (1769), with later patents for carding and roving machines; Hargreaves' 'Spinning Jennny' with 8, 16 and then up to 100 spindles (not patented till 1770); and finally Crompton's 'Spinning Mule' (1779) – a combination of the Frame and Jenny (sometimes called the 'Mule Jenny'). Not only did production increase but the yarn was finer and stronger and so finished articles became both cheaper and better.

As the number of spindles increased, so did the size of the Frame. But it was the Mule which most affected mill design. At first it was a wooden, domestic machine with 48 spindles and a discontinuous movement driven by a handle. Soon water power was applied to driving the spindles, but to drive the carriage also by rotary power and thus make the entire process continuous and fully automatic awaited the invention of the self-actor. Until then the Mule spinner moved the carriage by turning a handle on a driving wheel and employed female and child assistants as 'piecers' – to twist together broken threads – and to clear out waste. Though William Kelly in New Lanark had developed a form of automatic machine by 1790 driven by water power it was not yet commercially successful. Nevertheless there were continuous improvements both in the number of spindles – commonly 240 by 1790 – and their speed. As the operative was only required for one operation which could be done on two Mules alternately, the machines were placed back to back in pairs and hence needed a wider clear floor space (Figure 10.17).

Experiments on a self-acting Mule were successfully concluded in the 1820s when the number of spindles handled by one operative again increased, from 400–600 to 1660. The movement of the carriage now took up as much as 2 metres – double that when the machines were back to back. Fairbairn (1863: 172) maintains that this, above all, caused mill widths to be doubled or tripled.

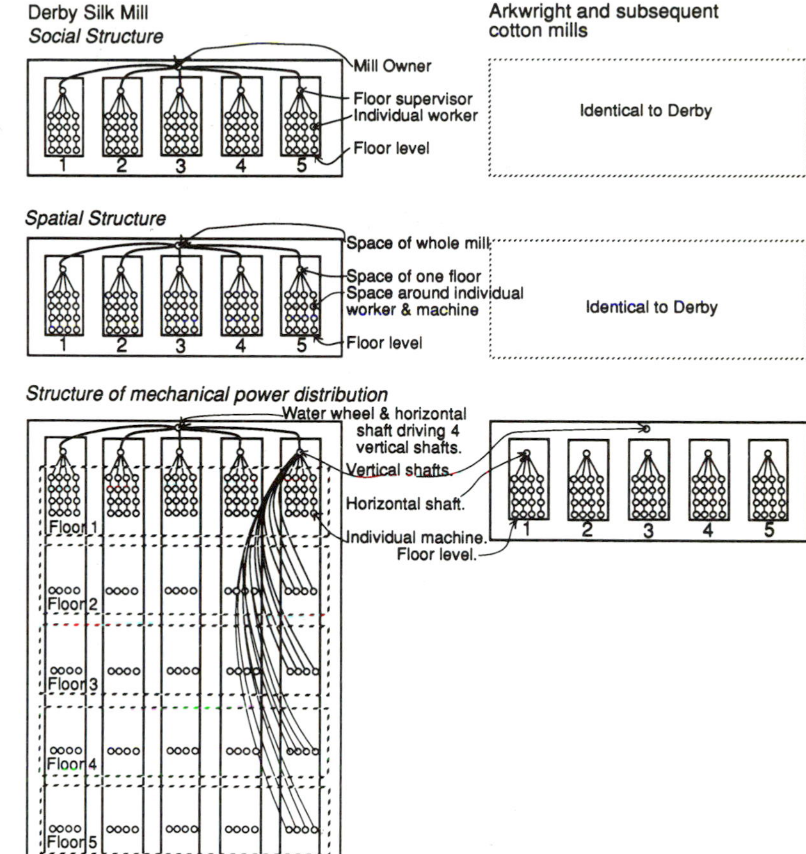

Figure 10.16
Homology of mechanical power distribution, social structure and spatial structure in textile mills
Source: Author's drawing

The Jenny could be used as a domestic hand-powered machine or grouped in workshops. The other machines were water driven until Boulton and Watt's new rotative steam engines were harnessed, first for the Frame in 1785, and then for Mules in the early 1790s. By then the new steam technology was widespread. These engines incorporated Watt's earlier patents: the separate condenser (1769 and 1773); the double acting engine (1782) in which steam was applied on *each* face of the piston alternately; the valve to use the steam expansively (1782); and the conversion of the reciprocal movement of the beam to rotation by the 'sun-and-planet' gear. The rotary movement was further improved with the parallel motion triple-rod drive, a kind of a pantograph (1784), and the steam governor (1787) which steadied it under variable loads.

Steam greatly increased capacity but did not alter the power distribution except for the location of the source. This was now in an attached engine house, whereas previously it had

Figure 10.17
An early nineteenth-century mule shop. The mules are back-to-back, the spinner activates the driving wheel, two 'piecers' attend the machines, and a child clears waste from underneath the frame
Source: E. Baines (1835) *History of the Cotton Manufacture in Great Britain*, London

been directly under the mill, at the centre or at one end. It was not till the 1860s that vertical shafts began to be abandoned altogether in favour of direct rope drives from the fly wheel to each horizontal shaft by a cluster of ropes passing through a rope race.

The effect of rotative steam engines reached beyond the design of the mill itself to its location. Industry was liberated from the remote sites with water power. Briefly the two technologies were uneasily juxtaposed by the reciprocating engine which was only usable to raise water into reservoirs for driving water wheels – a task traditionally performed by windmills. Arkwright's first use of steam, at his Wirksworth mill, was for raising water onto the wheel.

Once the mills moved into Manchester, Stockport and Glasgow, into new labour pools, the need to build workers' settlements disappeared. Their role as precursors of industrial utopias will become evident later.

The mill form responded to changes in machinery, power sources and structural technology. Arkwright's first mill at Cromford, like the Lombes' half a century earlier, had five storeys. With more powerful wheels able to drive more Frames this increased to seven in the second (1775–6). Though both height and length were still limited by the torsional resistance of timber shafts, by placing the water wheels in the centre instead of the end, overall length increased. The power distribution was now fully developed, as described before – vertical drive shaft from the wheel, and a horizontal one for each floor. Width was limited by the need for daylight in the middle which depended on window area. With the loads and vibrations to be resisted by the walls the maximum window area was at first about fifteen per cent of the wall which gave about ten metres as the maximum practicable width. By the 1820s window areas had increased to about thirty per cent.

The form of the shell of the archetypal mill grew logically from internal forces like a soap bubble.

In style the mills were simple, relatively short vernacular boxes, with elaboration limited to entrances, bell cupolas and central pediments. At the Masson Mill (Figure 10.18) Arkwright adopted pared-down Palladian motifs and a mixture of brick with stone dressings. Though in general he followed the trend to unadorned plainness the bones of a Classical tradition survived. His 1779 red brick Haarlem mill at Wirksworth in Debyshire has a lightly rusticated stone base with a heavy string course and an attic storey with reduced window sizes (Figure 10.19).

The first change happened late in the century when, as at the Albion Mill, cast iron replaced wood for shafts and gears. Shaft and mill lengths increased to one hundred metres, without a change in width. An interesting transition occurs in David Dale's mill at Catrine in Ayrshire. At first each of four water wheels drove the 50 metres long horizontal iron shaft on *one* of the four floors, till, in 1824, inspired by the new steam engines, an enormous single water wheel was substituted to drive the four horizontal shafts by one vertical one. There was an auxiliary steam engine located in a separate engine house. By the 1820s the substitution of wrought for cast iron shafts permitted even further increases in length and height.

The second change was to accommodate the automatic Mules of the 1820s by widening the mills. The long, oblong box gave way to a squarish block, achieved by increasing the number of bays and through larger spans of cast iron beams of new sectional form. Oil and gas light compensated for the consequent diminution of daylight. Much more self-conscious attempts were made to give these mills 'architectural' and especially Classical qualities. William Fairbairn was the great proponent of giving mills 'considerable architectural pretensions ... (as compared with) ... the uncouth buildings' which preceded them (1863: 172) and he put this into practice in his six-storey 1827 mill (Figure 10.20) with projecting corner pilasters which ran the full height of the building, segmental-headed windows and a heavy crowning cornice. Grander still was Orrell's Stockport seven storey H-plan mill (c. 1832) where even the free-standing chimney took the form of a classical column on a pedestal (Figure 10.21).

Strutt's Derwent sites at Derby, Milford and Belper formed a great enterprise. At Milford the first mill was operational by 1778, at Derby, a silk mill, by 1771 and soon a framework knitting and cotton mill, and at Belper by 1776. The panoptical 'round' building has been discussed. A 1784–6 Belper mill destroyed by fire in 1803 was immediately replaced by the T-shaped North Mill (Figure 10.22) and became influential after its

Figure 10.18
Arkwright's use of Palladian motifs at the Masson mill, Cromford, Derbyshire (1783)
Source: Author's transparency

Figure 10.19
Arkwright's reference to basic Classical elements in his Wirksworth Mill, Derbyshire (1779)
Source: Author's transparency

Figure 10.20

Fairbairn's 'uncouth' (a), and 'improved' (b) mills

Source: Fairbairn (1863), author's copy

(a)

(b)

Figure 10.21

Orrell's Stockport Mill (1832)

Source: Ure (1835)

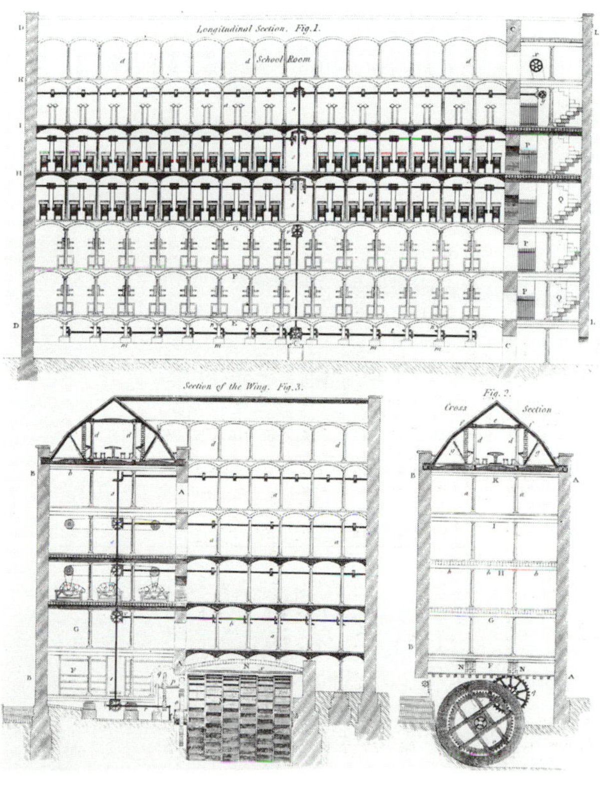

Figure 10.22

Strutt's North mill, Belper (1803–4), contemporary drawing and interior today

Source: From Farey's plate in Rees's *Cyclopaedia etc.* (1802–19), vol. 10, sec. I, part 19, plate XIV, 1808; author's transparencies (interior)

Figure 10.23

Albion mill, London (1783–6)

Source: *New London Magazine* (1790) July

Figure 10.24

Details of beam and column at Strutt's Milford warehouse (1792–3)

Source: Johnson and Skempton (1955–6), reproduced from the *Transactions of the Newcomen Society* by permission of the Society's Council. The Newcomen Society promotes, encourages and co-ordinates the study of the history of all types of engineering and technology from the earliest times to the present day. Details from Executive Secretary, Newcomen Society, Science Museum, London SW7 2DD. Artwork courtesy of Professor A.W. Skempton

detailed description in Rees's *Cyclopaedia* (1802–20). There was an oddity here. The enormous water wheel drove a vertical shaft which, in the by-now-conventional way, drove horizontal ones on each floor of the leg of the 'T', but only on the three upper floors of its cross bar. Rising through the two lower floors were 14 small vertical shafts driven by a low level horizontal shaft turned directly by the wheel. This arrangement was tailored for the Frames on these floors above which were all the other processes. The power distribution was a hybrid between the two forms analysed above.

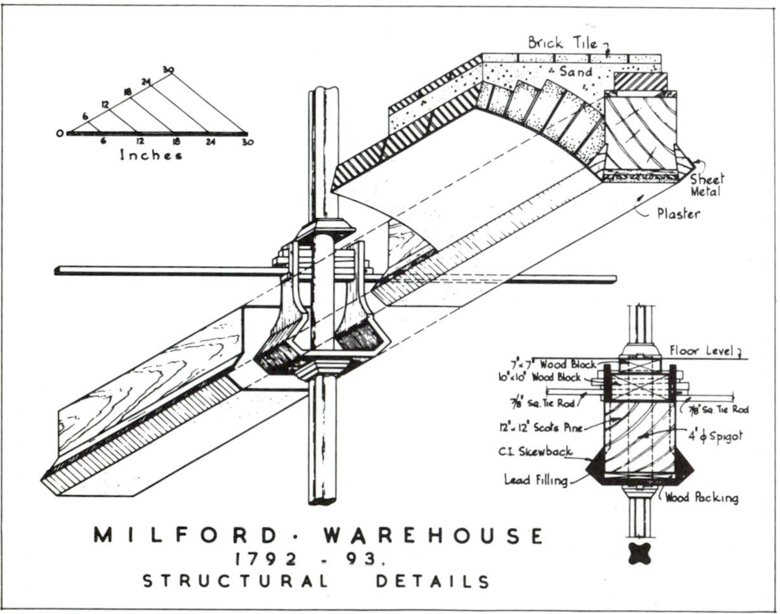

The iron skeleton

Artists were inspired and the public amazed by a spectacular fire in March 1791 which destroyed the five-year-old Albion Mill on the Thames in London. Through its technology it had become Europe's most renowned industrial building. Only two of its three Boulton and Watt double acting steam engines had been installed. They drove twenty pairs of millstones capable of grinding corn to produce a prodigious 150 bushels of flour an hour. They also drove hoists and cranes, and all the sifting, dressing and fanning machinery. John Rennie, newly graduated from Edinburgh University, was Watt's assistant engineer and was instrumental in making the machinery, including its drive shafts and gears, in iron, leaving only a few cogs in wood for quietness. Though iron had appeared in other plants, it was never before on this scale.

Samuel Wyatt's building, much squarer than the contemporary textile mill, was also more sophisticated with fashionable proportions, neo-Palladian windows, lunettes and rustication for the base on the six-storey river front but ashlar on the rear where the ground level was two floors higher (Figure 10.23). Columns and beams were of timber and the foundations were deep strip footings linked by inverted barrel vaults to create a massive floating raft.

The destruction dramatically represented the gap between building and mechanical technology. More than any other single incident it was a turning point for the development of structural iron and 'fireproof' construction.

Skempton and Johnson (1962) have carried out the classic studies on the structural innovations which had immense consequences. Hamilton (1952) and Skempton (1956) have analysed their theoretical basis. New spans allowed mill space to be articulated in new ways, and they were the root of the technology which shaped exhibition buildings, markets, railways stations and offices.

Step one, the substitution of cast iron for timber columns, the use of shallow brick arches for the floor and the protection of timber beams by plaster, was taken by Strutt in his 1792–3 six-storey cotton mill in Derby (Johnson and Skempton 1955–6 and 1956–7). The two rows of cruciform section columns gave three 9-foot bays spanned by timber cross beams. Between these, brick arches – hollow clay pot ones on the top floor – spanned and supported a floor of sand and tiles. There were also wrought iron tie rods running longitudinally between the columns. The details of how one column supported the next and of the transverse beams are known from his contemporary warehouse at Milford (Figure 10.24). The same construction was used in the Belper West Mill (1793-95), a 200-foot-long, six storey mill with a single central row of columns.

The skewback of Strutt's cast iron shoe had four functions. It connected the columns and allowed a spigot spacer to be inserted between them; it anchored the wrought iron tie rods; it formed a base for the floor arches; and it held the timber beams. The beams had timber fillets attached to their sides to continue the skew along their full length, and they were covered in sheet iron. The gap between the shoe and the ends of the beams was filled with wood and lead.

Step two followed at once: the timber for beams was replaced by cast iron in the 1796–7 Shrewsbury flax mill built by the Benyon, Bage and Marshall partnership (Figure 10.25). Bage was the engineer and received subtsantial advice from Strutt which in most ways he followed, even giving his cast iron beams a built-in thicker bottom section which recognised the need for extra material in this brittle substance so strong in compression and so weak in tension, and also providing built-in skews for the brick arches. Three rows of columns divide the plan into four 9-foot bays. The beams spanned continuously from the side walls to where they met at the centre. They were 'turtle backed' – that is deeper at mid-span, thus showing a response to the maximum bending moment, but lacking in similar intuition where they cross the outer rows of columns where the bending moment is negative and the section should have reversed itself. Of course the negative moment could have been avoided by making the beams simply supported. The columns have an entasis, with maximum thickness at about the point of maximum buckling stress.

There is a fascinating resolution to the conflict between the alignment of the central column and the horizontal drive shaft. The column head was split to allow the shaft to pass *through* it (Figure 10.26).

Progess was now rapid. In Boulton and Watt's seven storey cotton mill at Salford for Philips, Wood and Lee (1799–1801), the Bage section became an inverted 'T', with only a vestigial skew. Spans increased and the continuous beams met at the centre (Figure 10.27), with a depth of 13 inches in mid-span and over the outer rows of columns, but only 11 at the central joint, the walls and the points of contraflexure. Skempton and Johnson (1962) point out that this would be logical for a rectangular section beam and they therefore believe that the lower flange was conceived not structurally but as a support for the arches.

The hollow, cylindrical columns were also

Figure 10.25
Interior view of cast iron columns and beams in Benyon, Bage and Marshall mill, Shrewsbury (1796–7)
Source: Author's transparency

Figure 10.26
Split-head column capital at Benyon, Bage and Marshall mill, to allow alignment of drive shaft with column centre
Source: Author's transparency

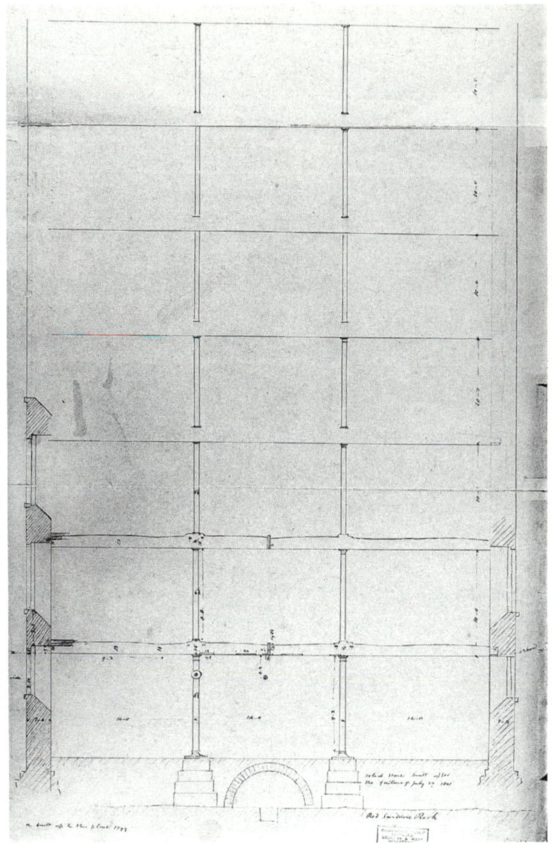

Figure 10.27

Philips, Wood and Lee mill, Salford (1799–1801), cross-section

Source: Boulton and Watt Collection, Birmingham Public Library, reproduced by permission of Birmingham Central Library, Archives Division

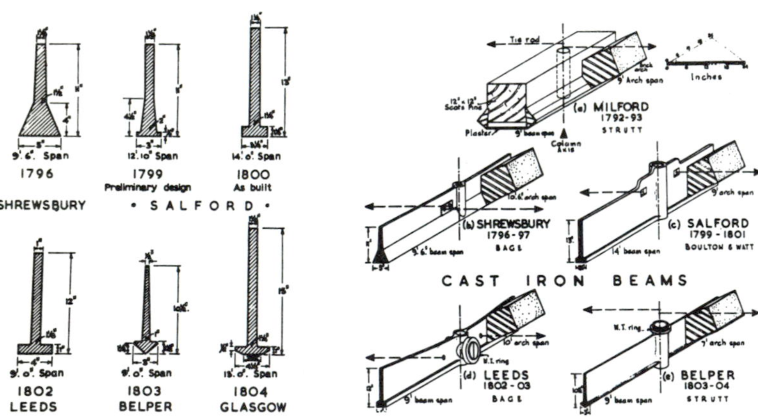

Figure 10.28

Evolution of the cast-iron beam

Source: Skempton and Johnson (1962)

steam heating pipes. The mill was the first to be gas-lit, after 1805, and there was a powerful steam engine at one end.

The third and fourth all-iron mills were both designed by Bage for the Benyons; at Leeds in 1802–3 and at Shrewsbury in 1803–4. In the former, for the first time, the beams were in simple bending with increased mid-span depth of the web, and a statement by Bage proves that he was now using the flange in a truly structural way to resist tension.

By the time Strutt came to build his Belper North Mill Bage had convinced him of the advantage of all-iron construction over his own hybrid system. He tapered the bottom flange to an edge, thus giving the brick arches a smooth continuity with the flange finishing in a fine arris. The roof was entirely cast-iron. The beams at the Houldsworth mill in Glasgow (1804) brought to completion a structural revolution which took little more than a decade; its entire sequence is plotted in Figure 10.28. The inverted 'T' beam became the standard until well into the 1840s.

Very quickly cast iron flowered well beyond these basic, utilitarian forms. At the Stanley woollen mill at Stonehouse in Gloucestershire the main mill (1813) is a veritable cathedral of iron (Figure 10.29). Its Tuscan columns, painted to look like marble, support an elaborate iron tracery which, like the Shrewsbury mill built a mere seventeen years earlier, has the split head to allow drive shafts to be located on the structural grid. But what a long way this is from Bage's crude device.

The age-old rectangular timber beam had already been turned into a truss in the eighteenth century with wrought iron tension rods fastened to the walls and stretched over a pivot projecting down from its centre. In one case the pivot was adjustable by means of a huge wing nut. More usually the rods simply passed over grooved iron shoes. Fairbairn applied the same principle to cast iron beams in a series of later experiments (Figure 10.30).

The step from timber to cast iron was so rapid that the theory lagged behind. Design of sections was empirical and intuitive. Hamilton (1952) traces the story from Galileo's *Two New Sciences* (1638), one of which was the strength of materials, and shows that he envisaged a rectangular beam which was in uniform tensile stress at all its layers. The French scientist Mariotte (1686) improved on this – by representing the tensile stress as zero at the top of the beam and reaching its maximum at the bottom. Robert Hooke by 1678 had enunciated his law *ut tensio sic vis* – extension is proportional to load – but its significance remained unrecognised till Young (1807) presented a full theory of elasticity nearly one hundred and thirty years later. The stress distribu-

Figure 10.29
Cast iron structure of Stanley mill, Stonehouse, Gloucestershire (1813)
Source: Author's transparencies

tions which these three theories gave are shown in Figure 10.31.

Bage gave a theoretical explanation for the design of the inverted 'T' beam which still assumed a uniform ditribution of tensile stress, but only in the flange, and he tested beams to failure. Since Young's modulus was not yet used, the idea of measuring deflection and developing a bending moment theory had not occurred. Fairbairn improved the design of 'T' beams following his Leeds tests in 1824. At the same time both Tredgold and Hodgkinson experimented on cast iron and Tredgold's equal flange beam was one outcome. Both Hodgkinson and Fairbairn demonstrated that this was weaker than the 'T' section but Hodgkinson promoted the *un*equal flange beam (Figure 10.28). Fairbairn accepted that as the ideal, but pushed it to an extreme form to bring empirical results into line with formulae based on breaking strength. The increased strength required at mid-span was obtained not by deepening the web – as in the turtle-back beam with all its inconvenience for floor thickness – but by increasing the *width* of the bottom flange in a form which on plan was parabolic (Figure 10.32).

Column theory lagged far behind. Only in 1840 did Hodgkinson develop one – still based on Euler's original 1757 formulation – and not till 1857 did Rankine publish the first general column equation of practical value.

By the 1840s Fairbairn and others had moved on to wrought ('malleable') iron, just as its mass production was becoming feasible. Riveted wrought iron box and tubular beams for the Conway and Menai bridges had shown their excellent strength to weight ratio. An early building application was at Wolverhampton in about 1850 using built-up 'I' sections. Fairbairn claimed that possibly spans of 60 feet and certainly of 30 were feasible on either side of a central row of columns, thus making space for machinery much less restricted. Though still toying with unequal flanges in 1857 (Fairburn 1857–8: 86) he correctly predicted that the rolling of homogenous wrought iron beams would become a commercial proposition if they had equal *width*, though he now favoured an increased top *thickness*, reflecting his conviction that wrought iron, in opposition to cast, was so much weaker in compression than in tension that only this could ensure simultaneous failure under a given load. Once he abandoned it the step to the

(a)

(b)

(c)

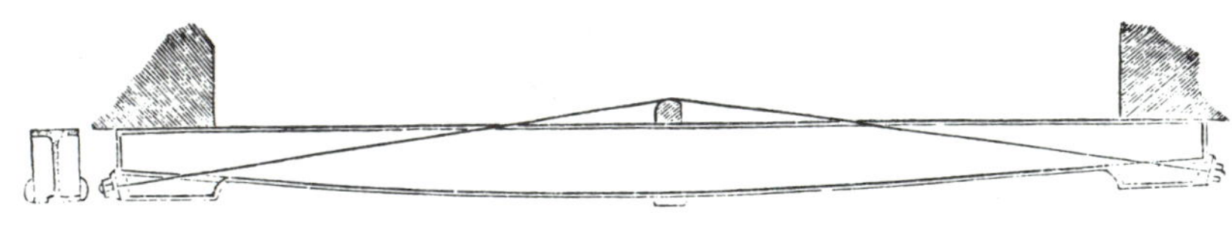

(d)

Figure 10.30

Trussed joists: timber with tension rod at St Mary's mill, Nailsworth, Gloucestershire (late eighteenth century) (a); fastening of tension rod through external wall at Nailsworth (b); Haarlem mill, Wirksworth, Derbyshire (1799), tension rod distanced from timber joist by huge wing nut (c); Fairbairn's trussed cast iron beam (d)

Source: Author's transparencies (a, b and c); Fairbairn (1857–8) (d)

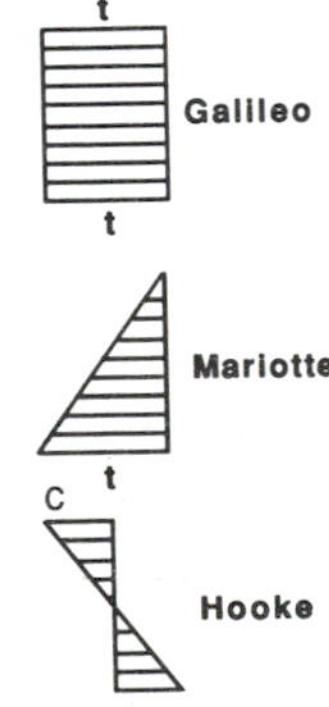

Figure 10.31

Stress distributions in beams according to different theories

Source: Author's drawing

completely symmetrical wrought iron beam was small. And this of course was the origin of the modern rolled steel section.

Weaving in a 'studio'

One further invention entailed an equally radical building innovation – the power loom. Edmund Cartwright, a clergyman of wide interests but no mechanical training, invented a working power loom where the motion of the warp threads and shuttle were mechanically synchronised. Two years after his 1785 patent he set up a small factory at Doncaster with 20 looms driven by animals; four years later he had a steam engine. But he was beset with business troubles and despite various improvements made by Horrocks of Stockport, by 1813 there were still only 2400 looms, a few abroad. Then followed an explosive increase: 12,159 in 1820, 45,000 in 1829 and 85,000 by 1835, all steam driven.

These heavy looms created such vibrations that they were only safe on ground floors. But much larger spaces were needed and the single storey weaving shed was the answer. Economy ruled out high, large-span roofs so the problem was solved by a series of small pitched roofs glazed on one or both sides. The next step was logical – to make the pitch *un*equal, glazing only the steeper, north-facing slope to avoid direct sunlight and give a steady light as in artists' studios. This was Fairbairn's brainchild in about 1830 (1863: 172).

The sheds were fine-tuned to their machinery, the structural grid determined by the loom width, and the looms oriented and located so that the maximum light intensity was on the cloth (Figure 10.33). The increased land required now set off a reverse migration *out* of the large towns. All new mills had a weaving shed and it was added to many old ones.

Fairbairn's firm established a flourishing 'turnkey' export trade – buildings, water wheels or steam engines, machinery and expertise – such as the woollen works for the Sultan of Turkey near Izmet (1843). His grandest scheme was for the Oriental Spinning and Weaving Company in Bombay (c. 1858). The entire process from raw materials at one end to cloth dispatch at the other was enclosed in a vast 350 foot by 300 north light shed, with a two storey office and warehouse near the entrance (Figure 10.34).

These huge open spaces generated new relations. Diverse processes had to be accommodated, differentiated and controlled by elaborate management techniques rather than physical barriers. Surveillance became easier; this both increased control and discipline but also gave new opportunities for worker solidarity. The weaving shed was a new type, in embryo the open production space of the Ford motor plant had arrived.

Such comprehensive approaches were not matched in Europe until the new generation of visionary production settlements such as Saltaire where Fairbairn used his colonial experience. The six storey mill was 550 feet long – Fairbairn claims that a typical floor is longer than the Louvre's

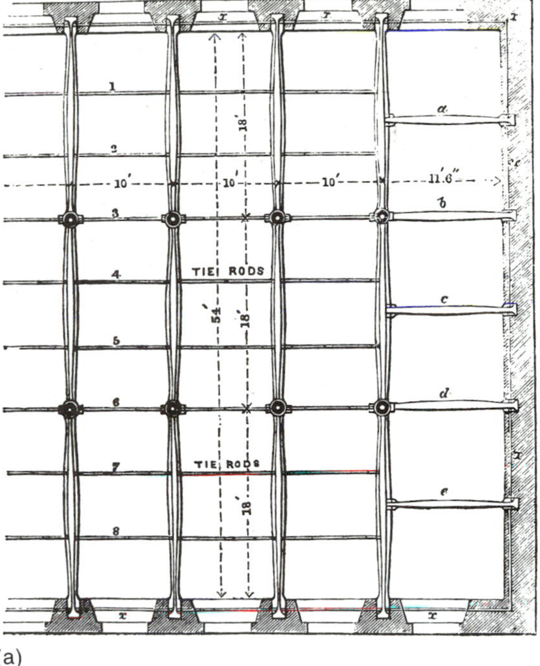

(a)

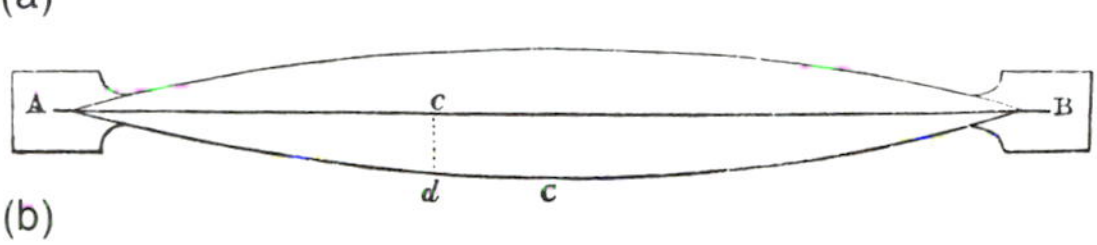

(b)

Figure 10.32

Fairbairn and Hodgkinson's parabolic flange beam, used in end bay of mill at right angles to main span (a), and theoretical form of beam (b)

Source: Fairbairn (1857–8)

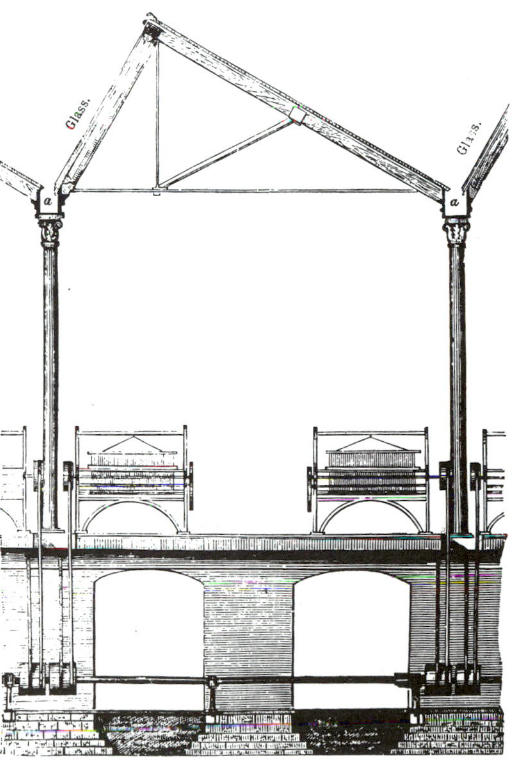

Figure 10.33

Typical Fairbairn north-light roof, weaving shed at Saltaire

Source: Fairbairn (1857–8)

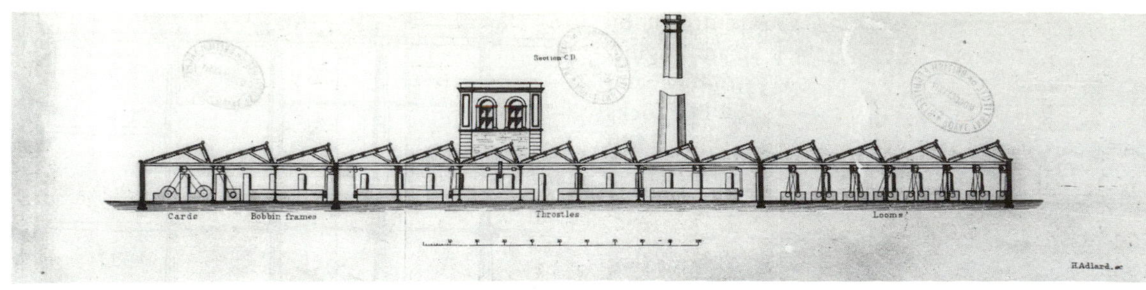

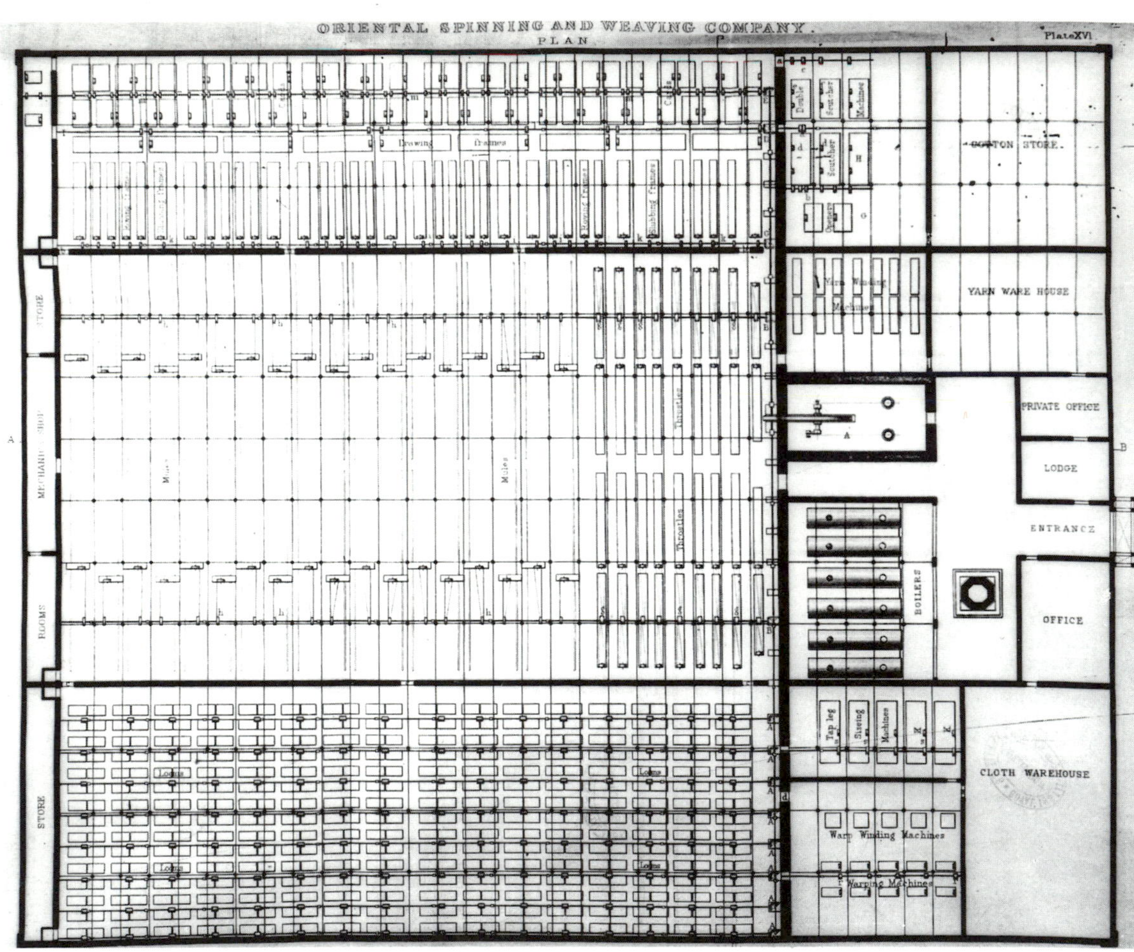

Figure 10.34
Fairbairn's design for the Oriental Spinning and Weaving Company, Bombay (c. 1858), cross-section and plan
Source: Fairbairn (1871) *Mills and Millwork* 3rd edn

Long Gallery. The unequal flange, turtle-back cast iron beams span a single row of off-centre columns (Figure 10.35) to allow machinery to be laid out symmetrically on either side of a clear passage and route for the drive shaft. The huge north light combing shed had 18-foot square modules, whilst those for the weaving shed were 18 feet by 36 with the horizontal power drive *under* the floor and the apertures for the drive belts clustered at the column bases. The roof uses wrought and cast iron, timber and glass; the cast iron gutters rest directly on the columns and are moulded to give their Corinthian capitals a classical entablature.

A 'fireproof machine'

The brick arch floors were concrete-filled and stone-paved. 'Fireproof' construction was developing fast. The initial hopes for cast iron were soon dashed. Fires became more disastrous when there was a collapse; the weight of the new struc-

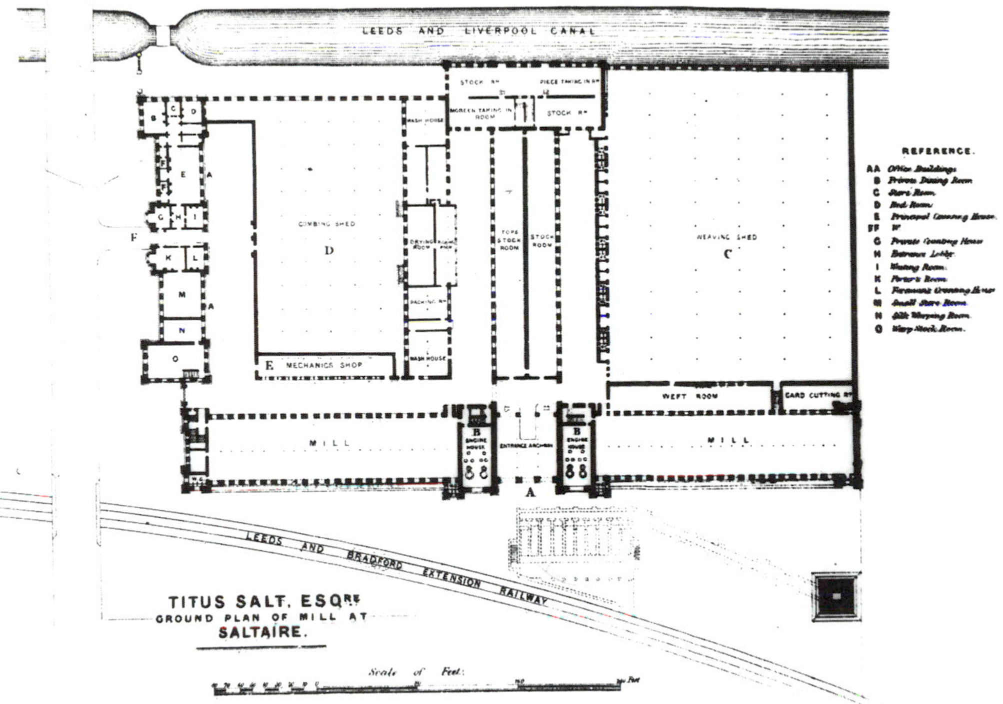

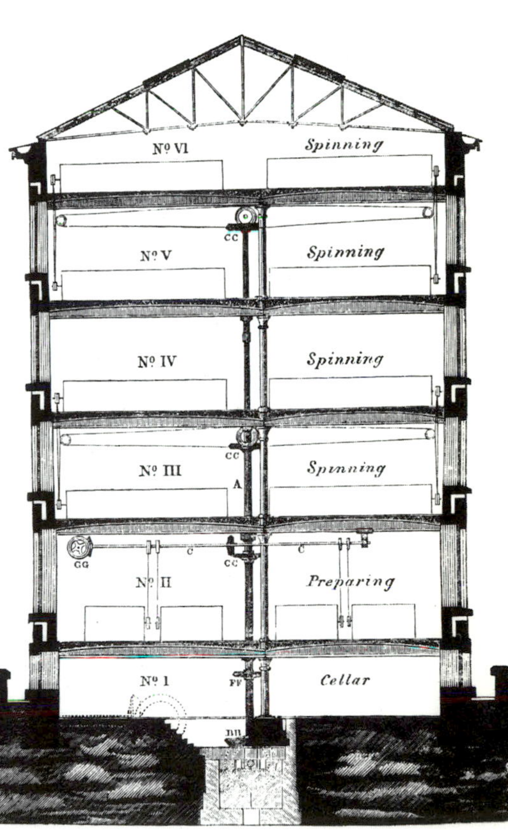

Figure 10.35

Saltaire mills: plan, exterior view and section of six-storey block

Source: Fairbairn (1857–8)

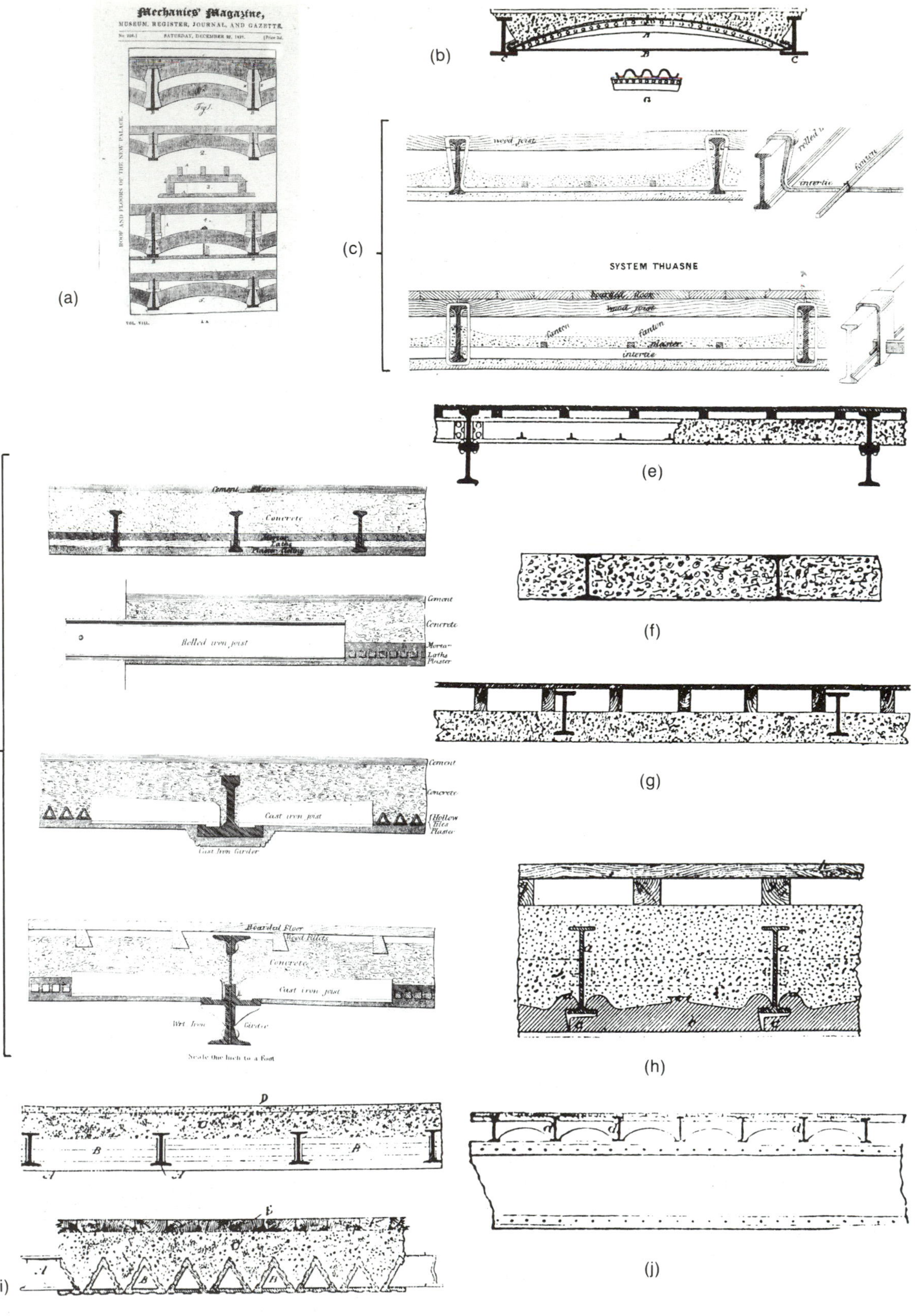

Figure 10.36

Nine fireproof floors: Davy's at New St James's Palace (c. 1827) (a), Naysmith's (1848) (b), French systems (1850s) (c), Fox and Barrett's (1850s) (d), Phillips' (1870s) (e), concrete and iron floor (1870s) (f), timber, concrete and iron floor (1870s) (g), Swarbrick's (1875) (h), Homan's (1887) (i), Fairbairn's (j)

Source: S.B. Hamilton (1958) *A Short History of the Structural Fire Protection of Buildings*, National Building Studies Special Report No. 27, HMSO, London; H.B. Burnett (1854) 'Description of the French Method of Constructing Iron Floors' *Notices of Meetings at the RIBA* 1st series, vol. 5, 1854–5; Fairbairn (1857–8); and *Mechanics' Magazine* (1827) 22 December ture, once a fire started on an upper floor, virtually knocked a hole through the mill. Moreover the cast iron, unlike heavy timber members, when suddenly cooled by water cracked and failed abruptly. The arched floors, despite tension rods and stiffening arches or beams in the end bays, exerted such lateral thrust that if one bay went there was progressive collapse of the entire precarious structure. Even without a fire this happened in the 1844 Oldham mill where more then twenty people were killed following the failure of a single beam (Fairbairn 1857–58: App. II 274–9).

In early attempts to lighten floors, stepped bricks or hollow pots were substituted for brick, and exposed iron was protected. Davy's hollow pots for the floor of the New St James's Palace (1827) abutted against carved padstones which completely enveloped the cast iron joists apart from the surface of the bottom flange. In St George's Model Lodging House (1846–7) as in Prince Albert's 1851 model workers' houses, Herstlet's patent hollow tiles in arches supported the floor. In an 1848 patent, hollow pipes were embedded in Portland Cement to form a lightweight slab.

Figure 10.36 shows a number of British and French systems. Notable was Fox's, first used in the Gloucester lunatic asylum in 1833–4, in which two layers of wooden laths spanned between the small cast iron joists, with a top coat of mortar and a bottom one of hard cement covered by plaster which protected the main beams too. In Barrett's Patent, triangular terra cotta tiles replaced the laths. In Wilkinson's 1854 system a precast concrete floor had wire ropes embedded 'to act as tension rods'. This, with those that relied on wrought iron joists in the lower half, was on the threshold of reinforced concrete.

Mill technology went beyond static systems; two dynamic ones brought buildings even closer to machines.

The first resulted from the engineer's intuition that a building was a moving, adjustable object, with a need for empirical controls analogous to those on machines. One example was the tuning of a trussed timber beam by an adjustable wing nut to alter its structural resistance. In Strutt's North Mill each stack of cast iron columns supporting the five floors could be independently and precisely levelled to suit its loading and soil conditions by a basement cast iron wedge in a shoe (Figure 10.37). In Arkwright's Masson Mill the cast iron gutters were given dual adjustability to cope with two common failures: an inadequate or negative slope impedes the flow of water; and the wrong spacing from the roof which causes the run off to shoot right over or trickle behind the gutter. A vertical slip joint allowed adjustment to the level of the gutter, and a horizontal to its distance from the roof (Figure 10.38).

Figure 10.37
Adjustable column bases at Belper North mill (1803–4)
Source: Author's transparency

Figure 10.38
Adjustable gutter at Masson Mill, Cromford, Derbyshire (1783)
Source: Author's transparency

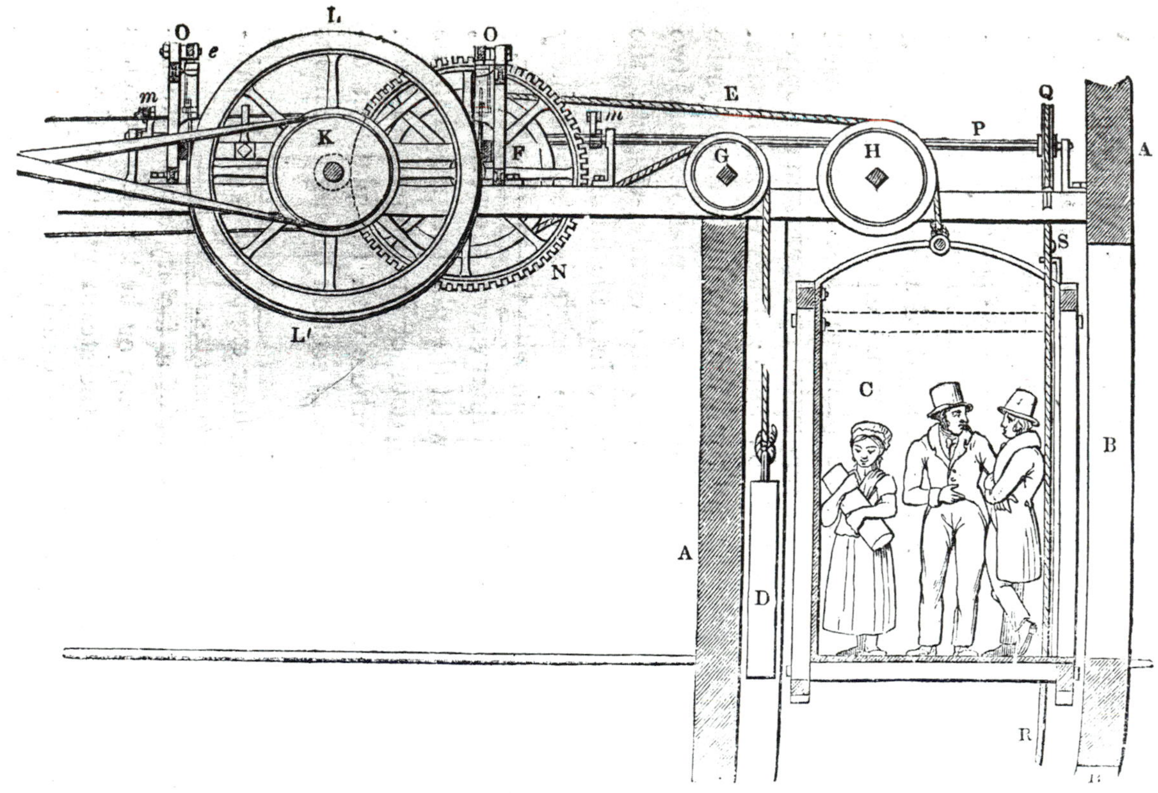

Figure 10.39
Ure's 'teagle' hoist (late eighteenth century)
Source: Ure (1835)

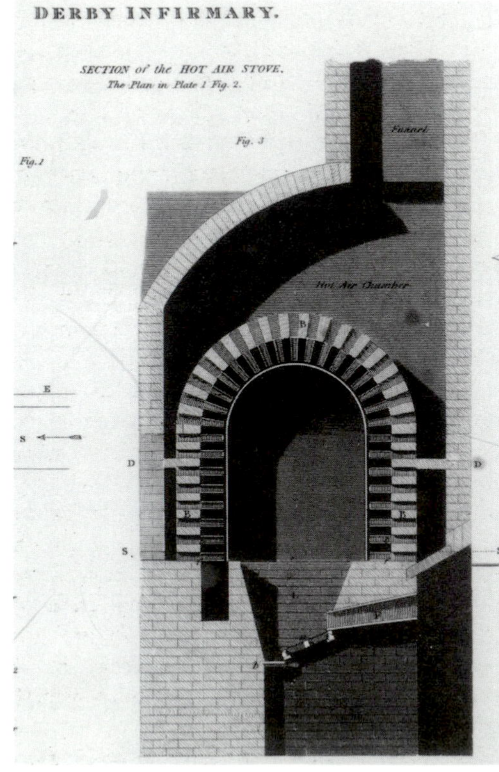

Figure 10.40
Strutt's 'cockle' stove at Derby Infirmary (1806–10)
Source: Sylvester (1819)

The second dynamic system was for movement – of people, material substances and energy. Lifts and hoists, pipes for water and waste; pipes and ducts for steam, water or air heating; air ducts for ventilation; gas pipes and electricity cables; drive shafts and belts; and bell cables, speaking tubes and pipes for air-pressure-operated message capsules all made the building, in César Daly's words, 'a living body, with its own circulatory and nervous system' (Daly 1857: 346–8).

The traditional means for movement were cloisters, corridors and staircases – static spatial systems through which people and objects moved. Lifts and hoists reversed this; there was now a dynamic system where a piece of moving space contained static people or objects. Of course hoists and winches powered by animals or human treadwheels for building sites, mines and theatres had a long history (Gavois 1983). It is again in textile mills that the first powered passenger hoist, the 'teagle', appeared (Figure 10.39). In 1835 Ure (45) said that such 'moveable platforms' had been introduced by mill masters 'long ago'. Certainly in Strutt's 1793–5 Belper West Mill there is a hoist by the side of the stair-

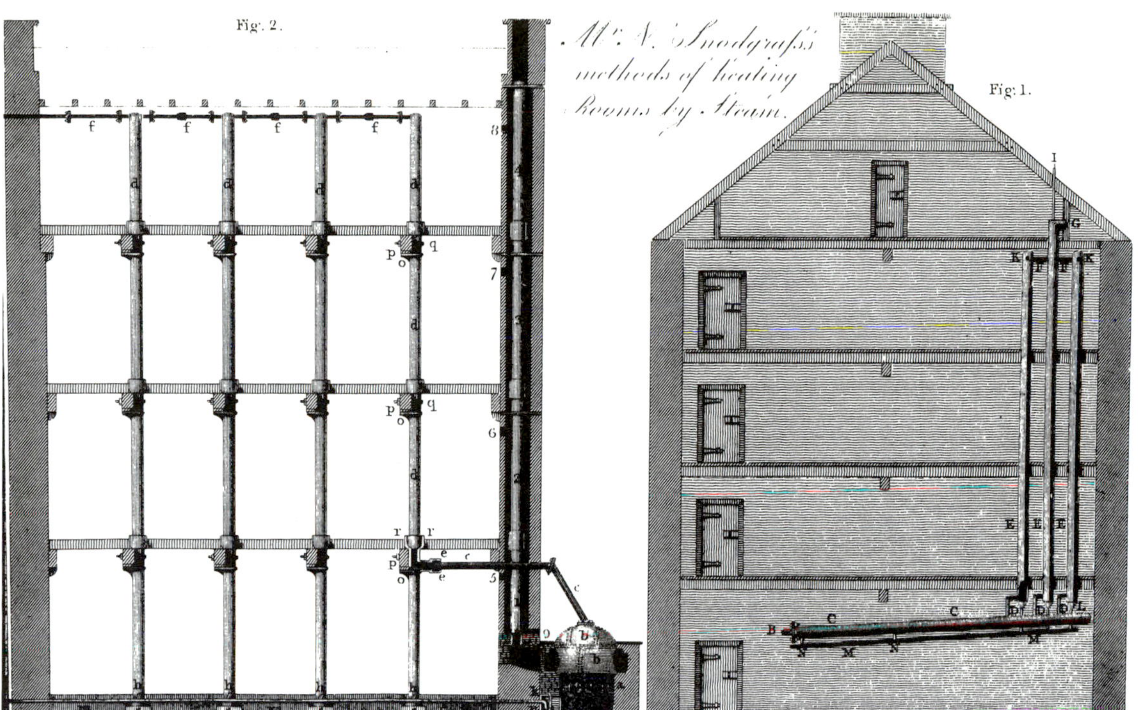

Figure 10.41

Snodgrass's proposal for using columns as steam heating pipes (1806)

Source: *Transactions of the Royal Society of Arts* (1806) XXIV: 118–28, also reprinted in *Philosophical Magazine* (1807) XXVII: 172–81, March

case and in his 1803–5 North Mill at one end. Both were worked by the main water wheel and, at least in the latter, were attended by a boy who rode on a seat on top of the cradle and pulled guide ropes. The motion was smooth, there were safety doors on each level, a counterbalance weight, differential pulleys and a safety device attached to the engine. In other words all the makings of a modern lift system. But since most non-industrial buildings had no steam engine this form of lift did not find its way into them. And there was a major technical snag – the hemp ropes quickly wore out. After the invention of wire rope by Smith and Newall in the early 1830s a Captain Huddart in the Deptford Dockyard found a way of forming 'stranded' rope twenty years later which made available safe cables for steam lifts. And the lift was now on the threshold of the next step – hydraulic power.

Joseph Bramah had patented the hydraulic press in 1795 and it found wide industrial application using hand or steam pumps to provide the water pressure. In 1846 William Armstrong used hydraulic power for lifting huge weights with the quayside cranes in Newcastle-upon-Tyne docks; earlier uses were in the mines. By the late 1840s they were widespread on construction sites and appeared in a building at the New York Crystal Palace Exhbition in 1853. In Britain we have seen them in the Westminster Palace Hotel (1858) and the Grosvenor and others followed quickly.

The movement of fresh air and energy for heating in the early mills was equally pace-setting. For his 1792–3 Derby mill Strutt built a 'cockle' warm air stove. Fresh air was drawn into a domed hot air chamber of wrought or rolled iron plates over the coke furnace (Figure 10.40). The chamber was connected by ducts to all parts of the building. The system soon found its way from mills to public buildings such as Derby Infirmary (1806–10) of which the engineer Sylvester published the technical details in 1819. By that date he had used it in the North Staffordshire infirmary, the Wakefield and Nottingham lunatic asylums and in Leek Parish church.

The other widespread system used steam. Though William Cook had designed a multi-storey steam heating system in 1745 (*Philosophical Transactions* 1745: 370) and Watt had experimented with it at Soho in the 1780s, its first large-scale application was in a mill at Dornoch in Scotland in 1799. We have seen the columns used as steam pipes in the Salford mill. Snodgrass published a similar design in 1806 (Figure 10.41). The first technical work by Buchanon in 1807 remained the standard reference till replaced by Tredgold's in 1824.

The whole set of related technologies of

Figure 10.42

Eight types of 'domestic' manufacture: plans and spatial maps

Source: Author's drawings (from sources quoted in the text)

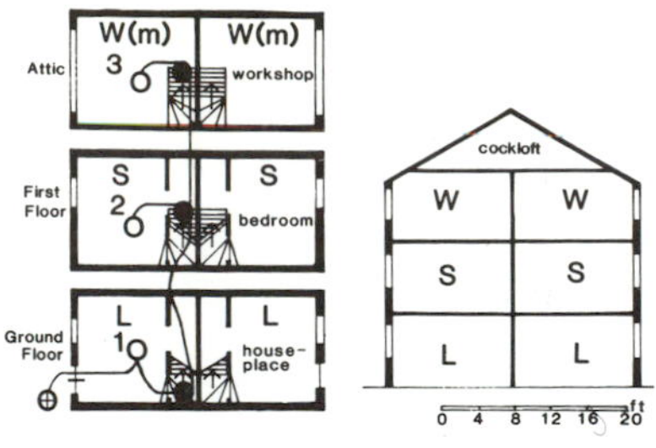

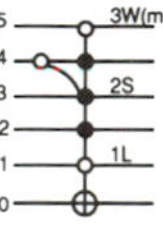

(i)

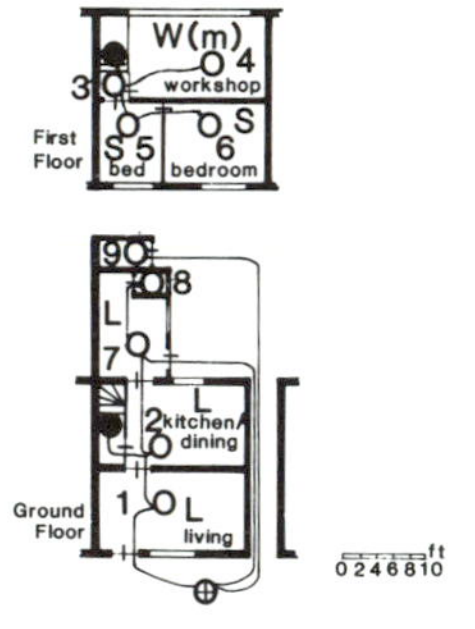

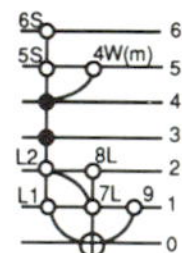

(ii)

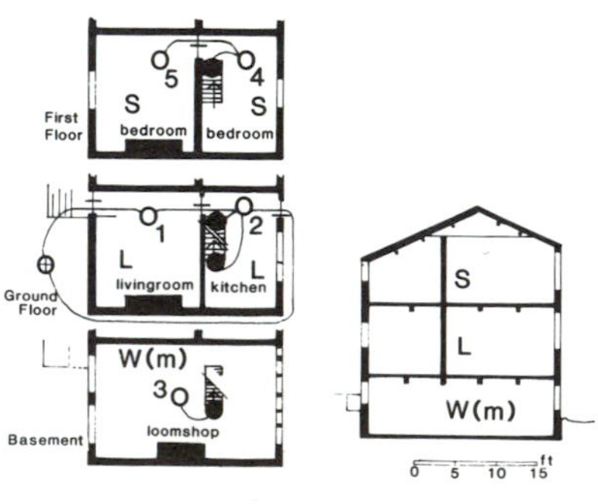

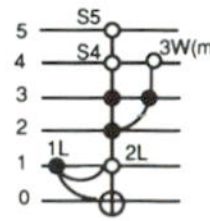

(iii)

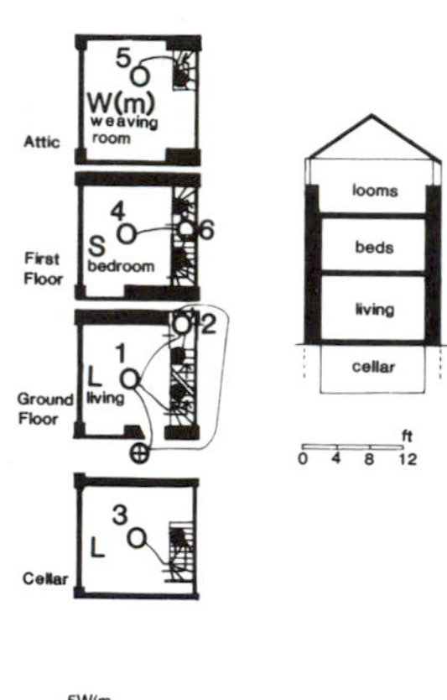

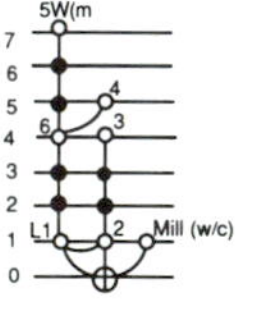

(iv)

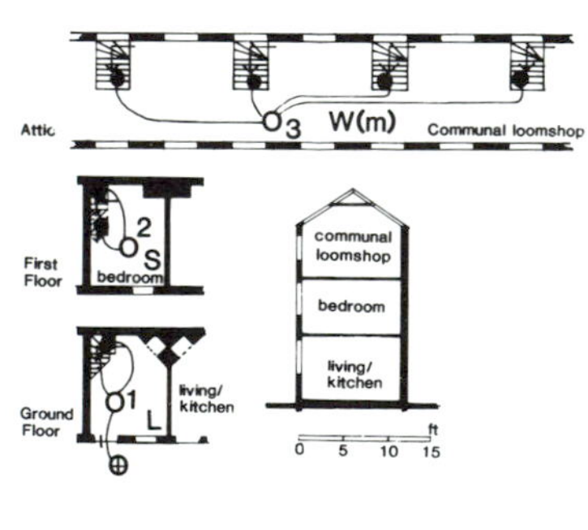

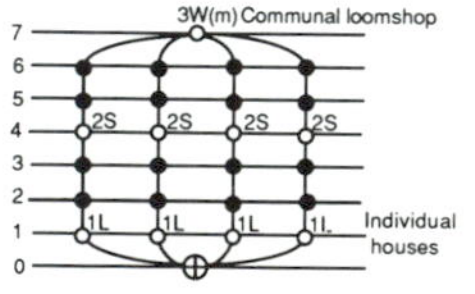

(v)

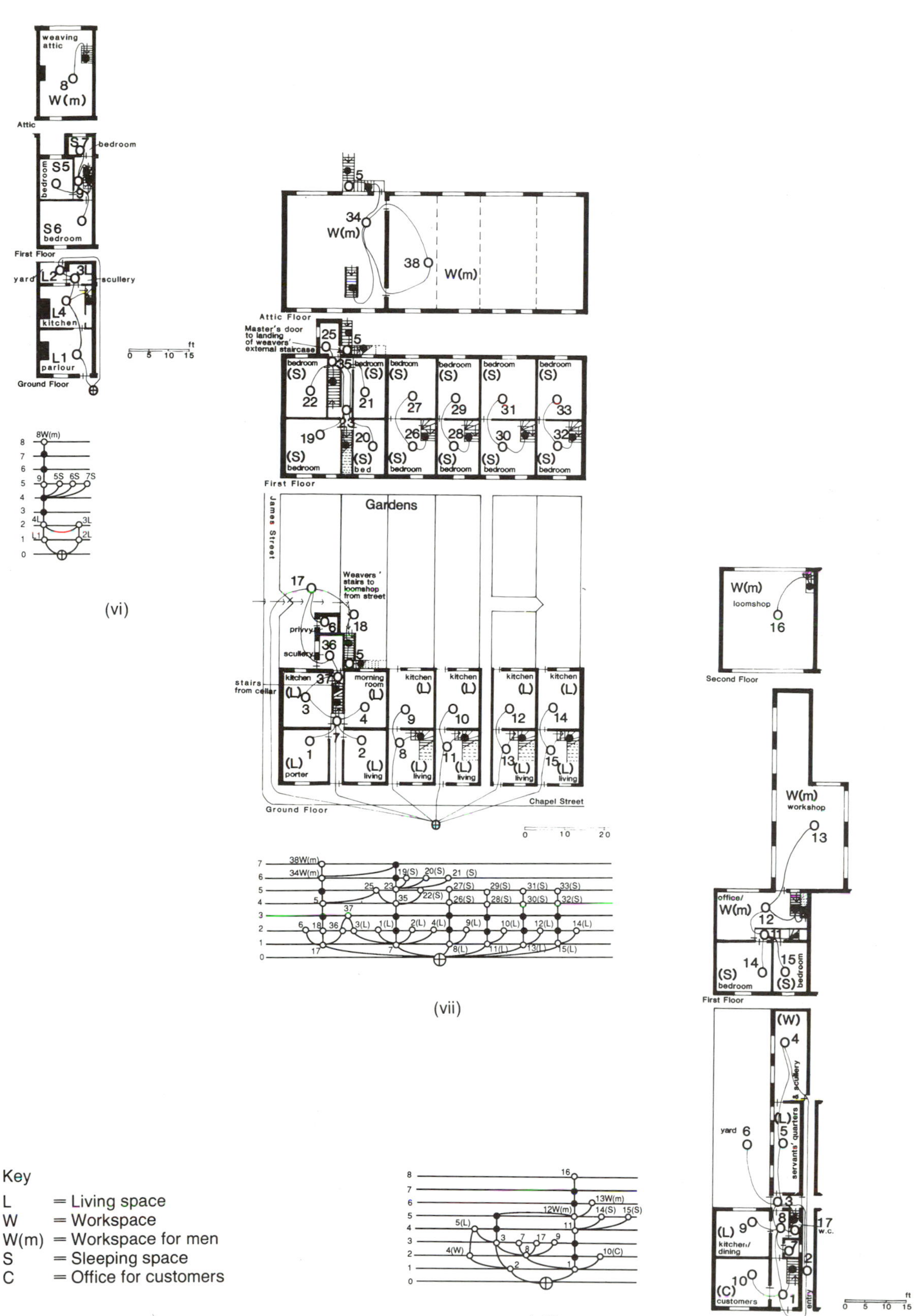

(vi)

(vii)

Key

L = Living space
W = Workspace
W(m) = Workspace for men
S = Sleeping space
C = Office for customers

(viii)

structures, materials, services and lifts sprang up in the mill. High building would have been impossible without it. The consequences for land values, urban density, morphology and social structure were immense. But there is an even stronger reason to focus on the mill. In it we can see the most striking feature of the factory system: the reorganisation of space to exploit machinery and power sources in a new social system. Of course there were radical shifts in other industries; for instance in Samuel Bentham's and Isambard Brunel's 1801 naval blockmaking factory at Portsmouth – integrated, automated and steam-power-driven (Gilbert 1965). But ultimately it is the mill which changed both the social and material fabric of the nineteenth century town.

Working and living

Production brings together the worker, the machine, any power source, the raw materials and built space. Culture shapes this workspace, as indeed the space for reformation, recreation and the production of knowledge. The Introduction explains the exclusion of ordinary living space, the dwelling, from the analysis. But housing is so inextricably linked to production – work and living space often being hard to distinguish – and in the new 'top down' utopian projects of total order housing became such a crucial element, that it cannot be excluded entirely.

The most universal type is the farm – where living space is combined with that for animals, hay, feedstuffs, corn, tools, and dairy. Accommodating a spinning wheel or loom often needed only the easy transformations described by Smith (1971) such as the 'hall' of the Pennine hallhouse into a loomshop in the seventeenth century, or the addition of first floor spinning galleries at right angles to the main building in farms near Kendal. In others the kitchen was converted. As long as seasonal agriculture and a textile process were run by the same household from and in the same buildings it was the older farming culture which remained dominant in shaping space.

With the separation of non-farming work new types emerge. At first a machine such as a loom or spinning wheel was in the main living space. In large towns with land shortages and high rents often there *was* only this one space. George (1951: 56) describes the eighteenth century London artisan dwelling of a silk-weaver as a single room used for sleeping, living and working, in a house shared with other similar households.

Once the machine has a dedicated space, the variations are almost endless. Figure 10.42 sets out a few of the workspace types I am about to discuss. The simplified spatial maps omit some trivial spaces and combine all floor levels.

A step up in status were the Macclesfield silk weavers with living accommodation on the ground floor, sleeping on the first and loomshops on the second with characteristic wide windows. The spacious lofts over the Spitalfields Huguenot houses accommodated apprentices too. The smallest version was the hosiery framework knitters' back-to-back terrace house in Nottingham, with a single room on each of three floors – living room-kitchen, bedroom and workshop (i). More elaborate was the Coventry ribbon loom weaver's house with a wide-windowed workshop and two bedrooms on the first floor (ii); or the Middleton loomhouse next to the ground floor living room, or in a basement (iii).

All these have a main (front) door with, in some cases, a rear (yard) door. The work, living and sleeping spaces are linked internally by a staircase, or a door, or through a private yard. Those who work in the space also live in the dwelling. In every case the workspace and the sleeping space(s) are at the deepest point. Whilst this self-contained spatial structure suggests economic independence, it in fact supported three different types of capital and labour relations.

The first is indeed that of the independent domestic unit of, say, the Yorkshire worsted 'master' weaver who buys his wool from a spinner, weaves or knits it, and sells the cloth to a merchant of his choice.

Second, it could be the place which takes in a merchant's 'put out' work, with strictly controlled supply of raw material and an equally strict price 'list' for a finished product often made on a machine rented from him. This widespread system was characteristic for silk framework knitters and lace makers. The contract gave the employer control over the labour market and effectively created a dispersed 'factory' in which the social and material conditions could be every bit as exploitative as those which a factory hand was forced to accept.

Third, it could be a company house, built by the mill owner for rent to his workers, as in Arkwright's 1770s North Street terrace at Cromford (iv). In the top floor weaving shop, over a bedroom, a living room and a cellar, the men wove the yarn which the women and children produced in the huge spinning mills. The production relations which appear to be internalised within the household and its space, are in reality totally dependent on and controlled by an external relation which has its own workspace.

Company-built workers' houses without any workspace, such as the brick terraces at Styal in Cheshire and the housing Strutt built for his workers at Belper, were commonplace but are better thought of as components of the planned production settlement.

One development is the grouped plan where some houses have larger work spaces which stretch over others where work is confined to living space. Smith (1971: 254–6) illustrates a block of four loomhouses; two, on the higher part of the site, have two-storey dwellings with attic loomshops which stretch over the adjacent three-storey dwellings. Such spacious loomshops probably housed more than the family members; employed journeymen might live in the basement, forming part of an extended household.

A derivative is a type which belongs to co-operative labour. Each household still has its own loom or other machine, and its own access to a workspace, usually in the attic, but these are inter-connected. Lowe (1977) reports that flannel weavers in mid-Wales shared a loomshop over the row of their tiny two-floor cottages (v). Caffyn (1986: 13) has an example in Linthwaite, Yorkshire, where in a row of six houses each has its top floor loomshop connected to adjacent ones by doorways through the party walls instead of being completely open; the spatial structure is however identical to that in mid-Wales. She also describes early workers' Friendly Societies for mutual help in dealing with sickness, old age and unemployment and, by the late eighteenth century, building houses for members. A case is the Loyal Georgian Society founded in Halifax in 1779. Many Yorkshire towns and villages to this day have have 'Club Row'.and 'Club House' terraces. Further work might establish a link between such clubs and the co-operative labour in shared loomshops.

If the householder rented his attic loomshop to an outsider a separate external entrance was provided. Or, as in the three storey silk weavers' houses in Hope Street, Macclesfield (vi), the internal staircase was located immediately by a rear door so that the outworkers would not have to pass through the house.

Once the master is able to invest in more machinery and needs the employed labour of journeymen, apprentices or labourers a new type emerges. The workspace becomes a large, open shop either attached to the rear or side of his house or running over the top of a number of other houses, in both cases with its own direct entrance or staircase from outside. In the late eighteenth century James Arnold built a three storey double fronted master's house in Chapel Street Macclesfield at the end of a terrace of two storey weavers' houses which had no workspaces (vii). The attic of the master's house (34) opens into an open loomshop (38) which is continuous over the small houses but to which access is only by an internal staircase in his house and an external one from the back. His first floor landing also opens onto the half-landing (5) of the external stair. The weavers – whether they lived in the rented terrace houses below or elsewhere – gained access and worked under surveillance.

In West Yorkshire houses at Addingham, Caffyn distinguishes between the 'shared workshops' (our co-operative type, with access into a common space from each house) and industrial accommodation above such houses which was 'cut off entirely from the living accommodation' (Caffyn 1986: 18–19).

Such open workshops over terraced houses are found in the Nottingham hosiery and lace industries (Chapman 1971), in Coffin Row in Linthwaite (Bodey 1971), and in the flannel loomshop at Newtown in Wales (Lowe 1977: 24–5) all with independent external access and all examples of Ashmore's 'Pennine' type (Ashmore 1969).

The Coventry ribbon weavers' house (viii) looks conventional enough, but something new was happening. A ground floor front room (10) was reserved for receiving customers (c) and a workshop-office (12) appears on the floor above opening onto workshops in a 'tail' at the rear (13), and, by a narrow staircase, to the top floor loomshop to which workers have independent access. The workshop-office becomes the integrating space on several rings of the spatial map.

The spatial structures for capital and labour relations in some of these types put them on the threshold of the mill. Long after that arrived a brief throwback appeared in Coventry between 1847 and 1859.

The first-hand journeymen ribbon weavers were competing with the steam powered mills (Prest 1960). Rather than leave home, they decided to import steam power by attaching an engine house at one end of existing rows of three storey terrace houses, or putting it in the centre of new triangular layouts. The capital was the master's – the Quaker Cash brothers' – and the tenant paid a combined house and 'steam' rent for the shaft which, running along the entire top floor through the party walls, rotated continuously. Behind an amalgam of Owenite socialism, Quaker benevolence and self-help was the dream of peaceful domestic industry set in agricultural smallholdings. Had this been authentic co-operation rather than paternalistic dependency it could have harnessed modern technology to traditional social structures in a solution which William Morris, despite his rooted opposition to machines, might have welcomed. As it turned out it was doomed to extinction.

The alternative to all these combined work and dwelling spaces was communal housing. Chaux and the Soho Manufactory had early examples in palatial settings. Pollard (1964) describes a whole range: Orr's singe building for 35 families in Paisley; Sir James Morris's 'castellated lofty mansion, of a collegiate appearance, with an interior quadrangle, containing dwellings for forty families, all colliers, excepting one tailor and one shoemaker who are considered as useful appendages to the fraternity'; and Houldsworth's communal block at Anderston in Glasgow.

Perfect cities of production

The ill-fated Owenite community at Orbiston (1825–8) was the outcome of sweeping proposals made to Lanark County by Robert Owen. A central residential block for 800 people included two huge communal dining rooms, a lecture hall on the axis where traditionally the chapel would have been, and two school rooms. The bed-sitting rooms for men and women were on either side of the axis. It was to be a co-operative of industry, craftwork and agriculture drawing on the experience of nearby New Lanark and of the American New Harmony project which had fully engaged Owen since 1824 – hence his spirit hovered over Orbiston *in absentia*. It broke down within three years (with only the north wing of the central block and the five storey 'Jericho' workshop complete) in a welter of mismanagement and back-sliding into the ways of the 'Old Society' (Donnachie 1971).

There is a graduated *continuum* from Arkwright's settlements to Orbiston. But all, as also later utopian schemes, have 'top down' imposed order, uniformity, control and cohesion. They are complete. The experiments in remote hills and valleys deeply influenced them and then nineteenth century housing and planning whose sanitary, public health, zoning, legislative and social policies they prefigure. Three very different utopian projects show this and bring the narrative of production space to a natural end.

New Lanark is significant in itself; but even more so when seen as part of a chain at one end of which is the founder David Dale who links it directly to Arkwright and hence the birth of the Industrial Revolution, in the middle Robert Owen with all his other schemes, and at the other end his visionary disciples on both sides of the Atlantic. If one includes the beginnings of the Trade Union and Co-operative movements, and Owen's influence on education, the ramifications are immense.

Dale moved from Ayrshire to Paisley in the 1750s to become an apprentice and then a journeyman weaver. There followed a period as a shopkeeper in Glasgow. Marrying into the family of a Director of the Royal Bank he became its Glasgow agent in 1783. That year Arkwright arrived in Glasgow, in deep trouble with the Lancashire mill owners who were trying to prevent his acquiring a monopoly over the Water Frame – in which they succeeded two years later. His mills were subject to rioting mobs. On seeing the Clyde Falls he immediately entered into partnership with Dale to build the first mill at New Lanark. It was completed in 1785, but by the time spinning started in 1786 Arkwright had severed his connection with Dale and become involved with a mill at Stanley in Perthshire. By 1791 Dale had three more mills (including one to replace the first, which burnt down in 1788). The basic layout was fixed in five years.

From the start Dale provided meeting rooms for four sects; one was his own – the Old Scots Independents. His religion is relevant. The eighteenth century splits from the Church of Scotland are well documented.[2] The Secession Church was founded by John Glas in 1733 in opposition to the Patronage Acts and the various scandals around the forcing of ministers upon unwilling Parishes. From it branched the Relief Church in 1752 to weaken further the power of church courts, give ministers greater freedom and lead a return to primitive disestablishment. When Glasgow Town Council obtained the legal right to appoint a minister to the Wynd Church in the

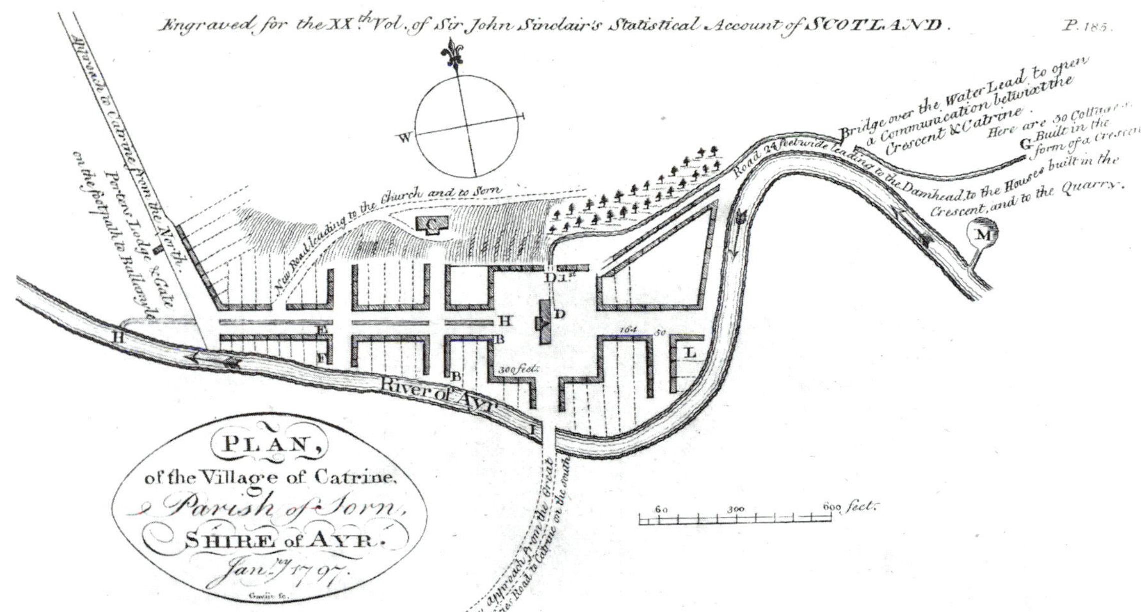

Figure 10.43
David Dale's mill village at Catrine in Ayrshire (1796)
Source: Sir John Sinclair (1798) *Statistical Account of Scotland etc.* 20: 185, Creech, Edinburgh

1760s a section of its congregation which included Dale seceded to form a Relief group. Dale led a further splinter group to put up its own church in Greyfrairs Wynd and then amalgamate with some existing congregations in Fife to form the Old Scots Independents sometimes known in Glasgow as the 'Daleites'. They soon had congregations in Paisley, Hamilton, Dundee and Dale's in New Lanark.

All this would be unremarkable in the complex web of Scottish Presbyterianism were it not for Dale's Moravian connections. They link him, enigmatically, to the narrative of industrial space. Moravians, founded by John Huss in late fifteenth century Bohemia, Moravia and parts of Poland, were the first Reformed group in northern Europe. They almost disappeared during the Thirty Years' War. A remnant was re-established in 1722 when Count Zinzendorf gave them shelter on his Saxony estate of Herrnhut. Soon this Church of the United Brethren had missions in America and all over Europe. By 1735 Moravians had set up their London community in Fetter Lane whose membership included the brothers Wesley, Whitefield, Ingham and others who were to become founders of Methodism.

The Brethren's model of community was independence and economic self-sufficiency with democratic control of worship, education, work and leisure. The church building was central often symmetrically flanked by the (unmarried) brothers' and sisters' dwellings, communal housing for families ('Elders'), workshops, farm buildings, shops and inns. Continental precedents had established a vocabulary of avenues, axial symmetries, central church, and spacious formal gardens, all set in agricultural estates and rural parkland. This model shaped the first English communities at Fulneck in Yorkshire (1746), Ockbrook in Derbyshire (1750) and Fairfield near Manchester (1784). Dale's birthplace, Ayrshire, had a community in 1765 and by 1780 a church and ancillary buildings in Ayr (*Kilmarnock Standard* 1903).

The Wesleys' erstwhile companion Benjamin Ingham became a leading Moravian and founder of Fulneck which he left in 1753 to set up his own, Calvinist, 'Inghamite' sect which soon had eighty Lancashire and Yorkshire communities. Soon he was making links with Scottish Secessionists, though formally 'Daleites' and Inghamites were not united till 1814. Dale knew the Moravians – from Ayr or through Ingham, and he may have visited Fulneck and other communities. When he set up his 1786 mill village at Catrine in Ayrshire in partnership with Claud Alexander he used the Moravian model. The five storey mill was in the centre of a 300-foot square of workers' houses (Figure 10.43), the position often occupied in Moravian setlements by the church. On the main street lie more houses, a fulling mill, Jenny factory, brewery, and shops, and down its centre ran the mill race. There was a school, possibly in the mill, and on a cross axis a 1500-

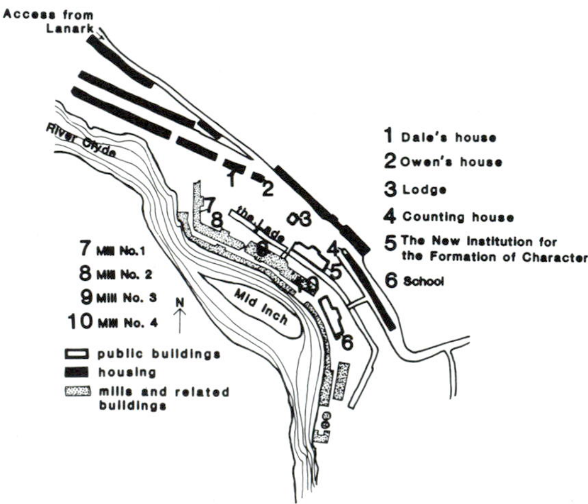

Figure 10.44

New Lanark, John Winning's drawing (c. 1818), and plan

Source: New Lanark Conservation Trust (drawing), and Author's drawing based on 1863 O.S. maps (plan)

seat chapel. Some cotton picking and all weaving was carried out in the houses; there was also a farm on which millworkers were encouraged to work in their spare time, partly to ensure their good health.

Although New Lanark was larger, Catrine represents a purer version of Dale's vision. And it would certainly be familiar to Owen whose later projects amalgamate its physical form with the social objectives of New Lanark.

When Owen married Dale's daughter in 1799 he had behind him Manchester business experience as a partner and mill manager of Peter Drinkwater's, and a partner in the Chorlton Twist Company which acquired New Lanark from Dale and put Owen in charge in 1800. Despite complex changes in capitalisation, partnerships and control Owen remained the moving power until 1825 and retained his financial interest until 1828 (Butt 1971). Jeremy Bentham and William Allen became new propietors in 1813 and Owen hoped that at last he would be free to conduct his social and educational experiments. But as ideology rather than capital was now the basis of partnership, so too it became a cause of conflict. Allen, alarmed at Owen's agnosticism, insisted on regressive changes which included the sacking of the teachers trained in Owen's methods and their replacement with conventional Lancasterian ones. From now on the image of Owen as a respectable businessman and social reformer began to be superceded by that of an atheist and dangerous radical.

His material interventions were modest in relation to his political and social claims. They consisted of some additional housing – Nursery Buildings (c. 1810), the New Institution for the Formation of Character in 1809–13, the interior completed in 1816, and the School completed by 1819.

Entrance to the village was at a sharp bend in the road which descended steeply into the valley. This shallow point acted as a gate, with the Dale family residence Braxfield House on one side in a dominant position. The shallowest buildings are

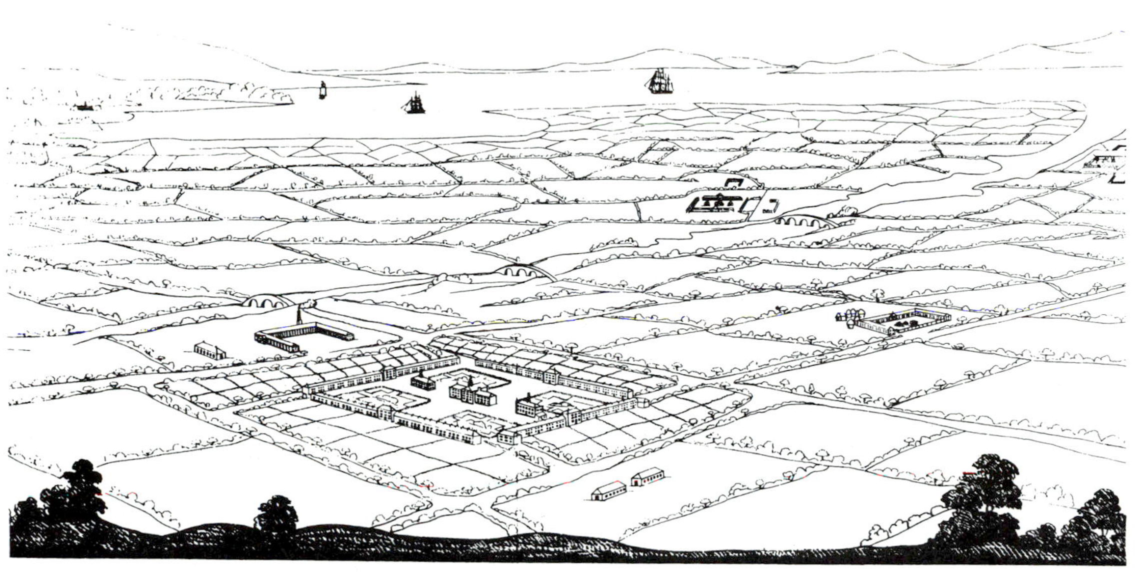

Figure 10.45
Owen's 'village of unity and mutual co-operation' (1817)
Source: Owen (1817)

houses – Braxfield Row, with its individual terraced garden plots on the other side of the road, and Broad and Long Rows behind. Dale's and Owen's houses were in the centre of the site, as was, formally, the Institution. The bow-fronted Counting House at the tip of Caithness Row had a controlling view of all vehicular and pedestrian traffic. The School was aligned with number 4 mill (Figure 10.44).

The mills by the river and the two educational buildings shared the greatest depth. Intermediate were managers' houses, administrative centre (Counting House) and some housing. Shallowest was the outer 'wall' of workers' houses. It was this spatial structure and the form of Dale's Catrine that Owen developed with obsessional zeal in his radical utopianism. Work, education, social interaction and leisure were organised according to principles of reason and justice spelled out in the *New View of Society* (1813). But because Owen's ideas are so dramatic it is easy to overlook Dale's more pragmatic originality. He had already developed advanced education in the school of Glasgow Town's Hospital where he was a Director and which, together with Edinburgh's Charity Workhouse, later supplied New Lanark with pauper children. Beyond feeding, clothing and lodging them he provided about ten school teachers to teach an advanced curriculum in both evening and day classes in mill Number 4. Their hygienic and nutritional régimes were controlled and their working hours regulated according to age.

The Institution's strange amalgam of production and social reform is described in Owen's 1812 pamphlet written, with a certain naiveté, to attract new London partners. 'Any characters, from the savage to the sage or intelligent man, might be formed by applying the proper means'. The crude, poor, indolent, drunken and thieving mob he had collected at New Lanark became 'conspicuously honest, industrious, sober and orderly . . . they become almost a new people, and quite ready to receive any fixed character which may be deemed the most advantageous for them to possess'. Power was the key for Owen saw himself as exercising a rational, just and benevolent omnipotence to choose both the means and the ends. The pamphlet spells out how the Institution would accommodate education from infancy to adulthood, communal entertainment, cooking and eating, and religious worship.

His 1817 *Report to the Committee for the Relief of the Manufacturing Poor* was also presented to the House of Commons Committee on the Poor Laws. It proposes communities of about 1200 persons living in rural and manufacturing self-sufficiency. After a critique of unemployment, poverty and ignorance the text launches straight into the physical settlement whose form is a powerful symbol.

The housing encloses three aligned buildings (Figure 10.45) – a communal central kitchen and dining room, flanked by an infant school with a lecture room over it on one side and a school for older children, with committee rooms and a library for adults on the other. Three sides of the square are tenements of four-roomed houses for families with no more than two children. The fourth is the dormitory for excess children and those over three years old, with the superintendent's house at the centre and the infirmary and guest house at its two ends. Two of the other sides also have central blocks – for superintendents, a clergyman, a surgeon, teachers and other staff. The third has a central store room. Manufactories, slaughter houses, stabling, wash and bleach houses, farms, breweries and corn mills are dotted about outside the perimeter in a pastoral landscape of arable land and orchards. Several such 'squares' are scattered over a landscape which also has an estuary harbour with sailing ships. More's *Utopia* has become fused to a tidied up New Lanark. This was the earliest version of Owen's famous 'parallelograms', soon to be ridiculed in the Commons and elsewhere as 'quadrangular paradises'.

His friend Francis Place discovered John Bellers' 1696 Quaker tract *Proposals for Raising a Colledge of Industry of All Useful Trades.* Owen was as prolific in the creation as in the absorption of ideas; this, most liberal, seventeenth century idealism was as much grist to his mill as the rigours of the Shakers. No wonder Bellers, with his mixture of agriculture, craftwork and manufacture to provide a balance between capital and labour, and to whom education was the key to social change, appealed to Owen. In a Bellers community of 300, 200 would do everything necessary for self-sufficiency – 'a plentiful living for the poor' – whilst 100 would produce 'a profit for the rich'. Even the word 'colledge' was based on principles of unforced co-operation:

> work-house bespeaks too much of servitude for people of estates to send their children for education; and too much of Bridewel (sic), for honest tradesmen to like it; and the name community implies a greater unity in spirit, than colledge doth ... (which) relates more to an outward fellowship than an inward communion.
>
> (Bellers 1696)

The title of Owen's 1821 work in which the parallelograms next appear is worth quoting in full: *Report to the County of Lanark of a Plan for Relieving Public Distress, and Removing Discontent, by giving Permanent, Productive Employment, to the Poor and Working Classes; under arrangements which will essentially improve their character, and ameliorate their condition; diminish the expenses of production and consumption, and create markets co-extensive with production.* It encapsulates the entire unlikely scheme for mopping up post-war unemployment and poverty. The community has now grown to 2000. The Council listened politely to a presentation which must have taken hours, and reported favourably, but saw it merely as a means of obviating the need for expenditure on a County Bridewell. Owen reacted by pointing out that confining delinquents would require specific provision and that in any case the plan was sufficiently general to be 'applicable to the middling and higher classes of society'.

A thinly veiled reference to Adam Smith attacks the division of labour for producing 'mere animal machines' and instances 'the unhealthy pointer of a pin'. All will work at a range of occupations and all are formed in the schools to have 'giant powers' which enable them to leapfrog the social structures – the 'lowest in the scale (is placed) many degrees above the best of any class'.

The plan (Figure 10.46) is essentially that of 1817. But Owen is moving away from realities of production – the U-shaped manufactory and the farms are merely sketched in – and concentrates all effort on housing and education. The houses are kitchen-less, on the earlier principle of communality. The bedrooms face outwards, the living rooms inwards; nature is the inspiration for inner life, the community for social life. Strutt's most modern valve-controlled heating and ventilation system is proposed.

Owen had been attracted to France during a prolonged visit in 1817 but increasingly he turned to the cradle of revolution and host to every kind of visionary community – America – where Owenite societies had already sprung up. On hearing in 1824 that a community of Rappites was about to move from its Indiana settlement 'Harmony' he immediately left to inspect it and negotiate its purchase. He began to give public lectures on his vision for a 'New Harmony', the first to the House of Representatives in the presence of the President in February 1825, even before the purchase was complete. The long text must have taken hours to deliver. A visual aid showed an ideal village now grown to a population of 5000 in a square with 1000-foot sides. But the scheme was universal – for the 'present buildings in villages, towns and cities will as rapidly disappear as the new combinations before you can be introduced into practice'.

The design was by Thomas Stedman Whitwell,

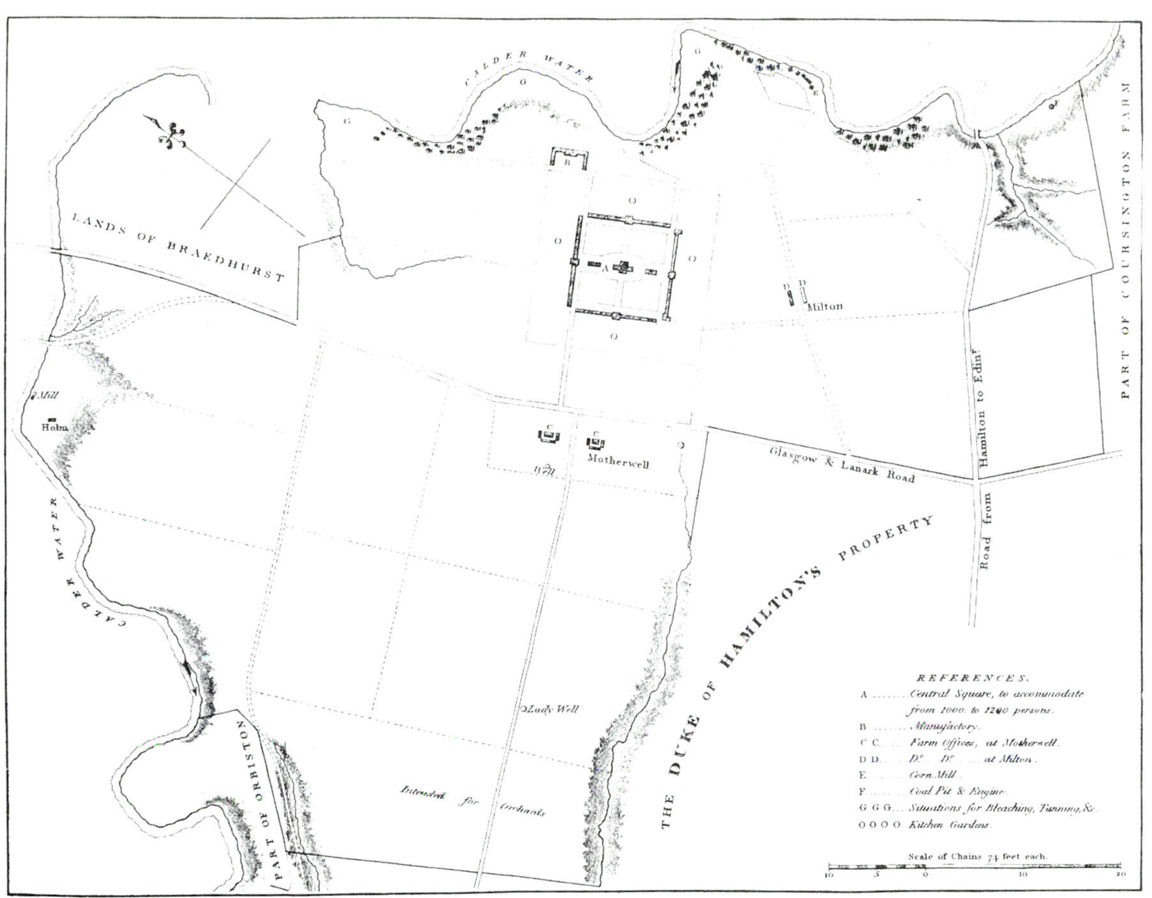

Figure 10.46
Owen's proposed villages for the County of Lanark (1821)
Source: Owen (1821)

an English architect who joined Owen at the start but left by 1826, according to Maclure (one of Owen's Scottish companions) 'excited by disappointed pride, ambition & revenge, aided by his electioneering habits of intrigue, cunning & declamation ... a thorn in all your sides' (Maclure 1826). Later that year Owen returned from a visit to Scotland with a six-foot square wooden model which he presented to the President for his Government's use.

Owen's vision was becoming unreal. A vast raised platform with an 'esplanade' emphasises its shrine-like isolation. The central circular conservatory is of course 'botanically arranged'. Somewhere is a school, academy and university. An arcaded cloister runs round the inner face of the three-storey housing. The central and corner pavilions contain laboratories, the infirmary, library, museum and chapels; and lecture, ball, concert, conversation, committee and public rooms. Four vast inward-projecting blocks are kitchens, dining 'departments', stores, and washing, drying, brewing and other domestic facilities. Their huge Doric column chimneys also act as the 'illuminators of the establishment' (shades of Chaux), clock towers and observatories.

Alongside Whitwell's drawing (Figure 10.47) on the cover of the first issue of his journal *Crisis* in 1832. Owen associated himself with Plato, Bacon and More through what has, now, become an obsessional image.

New Harmony soon suffered the characteristic dissensions, fragmented experiments and financial crises (Wilson 1964) that saw its demise in 1828. Returning home the following year Owen found trade unions and co-operative societies which had become markedly more radical in his absence. He became re-engaged and for a while brought Owenism and socialist trade unionism together. Local and national unions flourished, the grandest of Owen's own 1833 creation – the Grand National Consolidated Trades Union. But the competitive Reform Bill agitation, the 1834 'Tolpuddle Martyrs' and a series of unsuccessful strikes and successful lock-outs set the movement back by decades and the flag passed to the Chart-

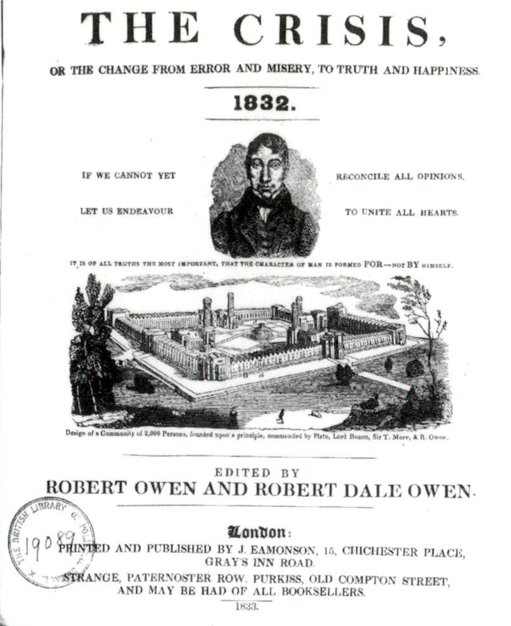

THE CRISIS,

OR THE CHANGE FROM ERROR AND MISERY, TO TRUTH AND HAPPINESS.

1832.

IF WE CANNOT YET RECONCILE ALL OPINIONS,
LET US ENDEAVOUR TO UNITE ALL HEARTS.

IT IS OF ALL TRUTHS THE MOST IMPORTANT, THAT THE CHARACTER OF MAN IS FORMED FOR—NOT BY HIMSELF.

Design of a Community of 2,000 Persons, founded upon a principle, commended by Plato, Lord Bacon, Sir T. More, & R. Owen.

EDITED BY
ROBERT OWEN AND ROBERT DALE OWEN.

London:
PRINTED AND PUBLISHED BY J. EAMONSON, 15, CHICHESTER PLACE, GRAY'S INN ROAD.
STRANGE, PATERNOSTER ROW. PURKISS, OLD COMPTON STREET, AND MAY BE HAD OF ALL BOOKSELLERS.
1833.

Figure 10.47

Whitwell's design for Owen's New Harmony (1825)

Source: Owens' journal *Crisis* (1832), British Library of Political and Economic Science

ists. Owen now concentrated on setting up Halls of Science which were secular temples and preaching houses.

The 1839 Harmony Hall, or Queenswood, in Hampshire was short-lived. It was financed by Owen's Home Colonisation Society which propagated ethical secularism. Under its auspices he published a plan for 'Self-Supporting Home Colonies' (1841), Owen's last direct involvement, at the age of seventy, in visionary design. In a rehash of New Harmony the four corners were now schools, the central conservatory was ringed by concentric paths and planting, there were baths on either side of the four huge service buildings and four play-grounds and gymnasia (Figure 10.48).

A group of disciples now took over. Some carried Owen's ideas into more or less orthodox Christianity. John Minter Morgan's 'Church of England Agricultural Self-Supporting Institution' developed into the Christian Commonwealth (1845). Though barely distinguishable from an Owen parallelogram, its central building was of course a church (Figure 10.49).

More Owenite were the trio of Atkins, Pemberton and Buckingham who each presented their ideal town to a meeting addressed by Owen, now 84, in St Martin's Hall, London (Owen *et al.* 1855).

Atkins had a central, 60-foot diameter, domed circular school covering a mechanically driven globe. From here radiate four 150-foot long museums giving access to dwellings, lecture halls, libraries, and 'industrial work rooms'. There are farms, gardens, laboratories, factories and workshops.

Pemberton's one mile diameter circular town, *The Happy Colony* (1854), was for British workmen in New Zealand. Everything was on concentric rings: outermost a pleasure park; next houses and orchards; then botanical and horticultural gardens, arboretum, fountains and four churches; followed by two rings of more dwellings and one of factories and warehouses set amongst ornamental trees and orchards. At the centre is a university of four colleges, each with adjoining conservatories, workshops, swimming baths and riding schools (Figure 10.50). Between the Classical buildings are terrestrial and celestial maps, and circular groves 'embodying history, the Muses, mythology, the miniature farm etc.'. Pemberton followed Locke, the Associationists, Owen and the phrenologists (though rejecting their 'philosophy of the mind') in viewing the child as 'a perfect *carte blanche* to any system' (his emphasis). In his explanatory dialogue the Renaissance Fool and Wise Man are replaced by a 'philosopher' and the 'delegates of the workmen of Great Britain'.

Buckingham's (1849) model town of 'Victoria' was a 'concentric' square (Figure 10.51) with 100-foot wide, glass-covered streets. The meeting judged that it might be 'unsuitable to our present habits and manners'.

Owen's son Robert Dale was a true chip off the old block. Though equally opposed to organised religion, and author of the first American birth control manual in 1830, he nevertheless acquired more conventional influence as Congressman for New Harmony and then for the First District of Indiana until 1846. His 1824 history is an important source on the New Lanark schools. In heading the select committee to set up the Smithsonian in 1845 he entered architectural debate with a detailed cost analysis to prove that Neo-classical, with its wasted space of useless peristyles and costly detached columns, was much more expensive than Gothic Revival. His father must have been proud of him.

For Owen and his followers a radical social vision was the end, profitable business the means. It was an ambivalent partnership. But a new mid-century confidence inverted this. Profits could actually be increased by stabilising workers in a total institution. The two remaining cases embody this audacious assumption in entirely different contexts.

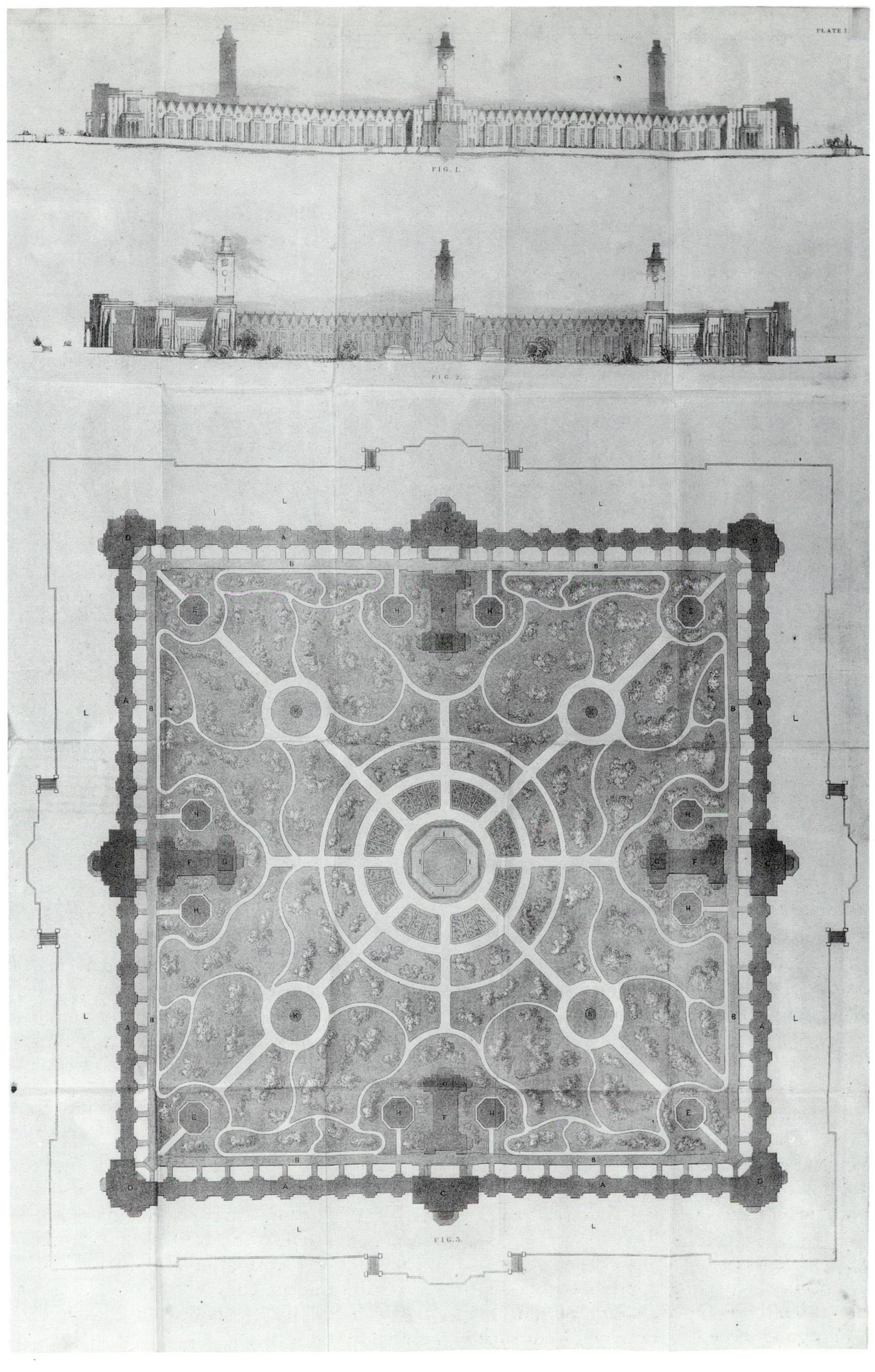

Figure 10.48

Owen's 'self-supporting home colony' (1841)

Source: Owen (1841), Glasgow University Library Special Collections

Figure 10.49
Minter Morgan's Christian Commonwealth (1845)
Source: Minter Morgan (1845)

By the 1840s Titus Salt had acquired wealth through the use of alpaca and other unusual fibres in worsted textiles, and civic recognition as a prominent Whig, Congregationalist, Reform supporter and philanthropist (Reynolds 1983). Bradford was not only proud of its Mechanics' Institute but embodied all the brash arrogance and cultural timidity of the new merchant class. The 1848 Revolutions, the alarming vigour of Chartism and the disorderly and polluted condition of the expanding town propelled Salt into adjacent open country on the River Aire to create a harmonious new order at Saltaire (1851–71). Almost certainly he had heard both Minter Morgan and Buckingham lecture in Bradford. We have seen that Fairbairn became his mill engineer; the architects were the best known local firm – Mawson and Lockwood.

Bradford was debating civic architecture. Ruskin was to complain that churches and schools were always Gothic, mills and mansions never, thus severing religion from life (Hardman 1986). The mill owners and the landed gentry could not win, even once they opted for Gothic, since, within the capitalist system it could never be the fruit of justice and freedom, and hence was a mockery. They were merely building a Babylon to the 'Goddess of Getting-on'. At Saltaire, ten years before the Bradford Exchange debate, the architects were gingerly edging their way to Babylon with a few Venetian Gothic windows in otherwise heavy Italianate facades.

It is plan rather than style which distinguishes Saltaire from the Owenite precedents. The grid was controlled not at its boundary but by allowing the crossing of two governing axes to mark its centre, as in Classical times (Figure 10.52). At the ends of one were the entrance to the mill offices and the Congregational church. Along the axis at right angles were strung out the social functions – mill dining room, shops, Sunday and day schools, Institute, almshouses and hospital (initially baths and wash-houses, hotels, a covered market, an abattoir and a music room were also envisaged). The first should be read as the heavenly axis – of God and bounteous production – the second as the earthly one – of daily life and shelter against all its hazards.

The housing, on a grid to the southwest of the crossing, was of three types – two-storey cottages for workers, larger houses for overlookers and spacious three-storey terraced houses for executives and professionals. Some large boarding houses for single operatives were converted to family dwellings. The types were distiguished by size, number of rooms, plot dimensions, formal composition and ornamentation, and location. The first parallel rows between Caroline Street

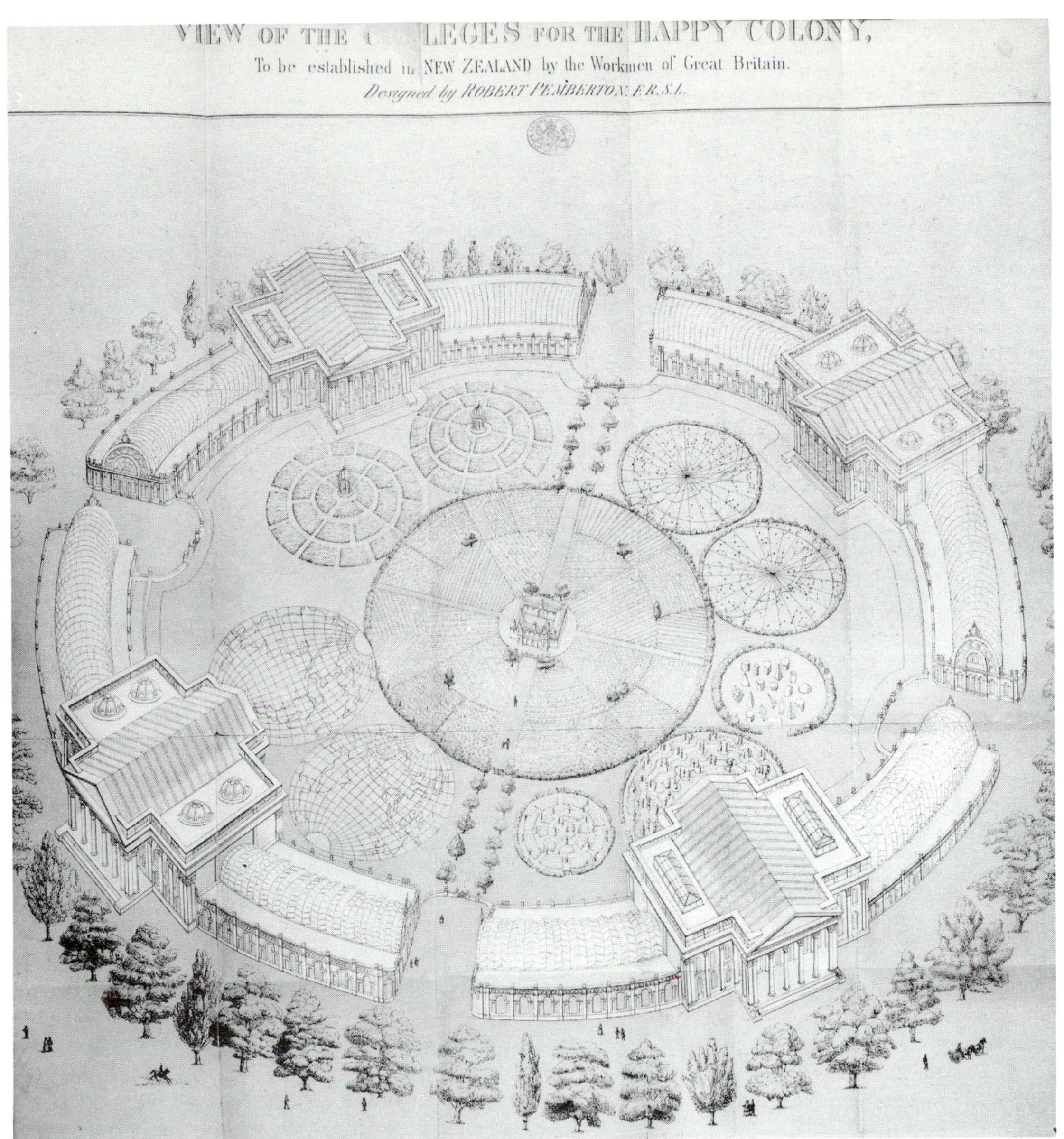
VIEW OF THE C LEGES FOR THE HAPPY COLONY,
To be established in NEW ZEALAND by the Workmen of Great Britain.
Designed by ROBERT PEMBERTON, F.R.S.L.

Figure 10.50
Centre of Pemberton's 'Happy Colony' (1854)
Source: Pemberton (1854)

and Albert Terrace had 110 workers' cottages, 53 overlookers' and some boarding houses. The higher status houses were at corners and terrace ends, nearer the crossing. The next block of workers' cottages was bounded by Caroline, Titus and George Streets, followed by those to the south of Titus Street, now parallel to it and aligned with the contours. Further terraces were built to the south and east, with a few of the larger types where the main road passing through the village demanded a more imposing frontage. The executive houses on the western boundary, Albert Road, had a superb valley view and were leeward of the mill. From the crossing houses diminished in radial 'ripples'.

As in the modern town, status is signified by forms, rent books and by command of the key points of public space – crossings, wide and important streets and urban-rural edges ('suburbs'). Status also gave freedom from pollution, in the local version of the 'west end' which always develops when there are prevailing westerlies. Buildings with primary ideological purpose, those with public utilitarian functions and housing are in three distinct zones.

Owen's theories grew alongside and within his projects. Salt's pragmatic ideas were formed before he started. In contrast, prior to the founding in 1846 of Andre Godin's metalware and stove factory at Guise in Picardy there was an

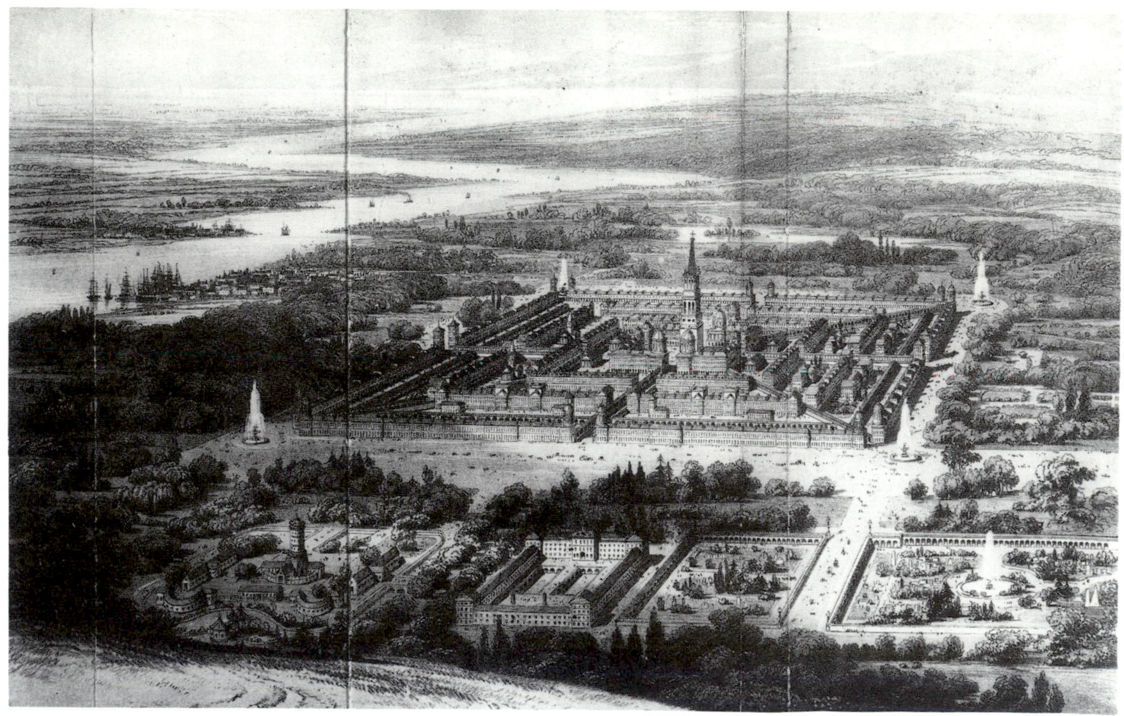

Figure 10.51
Buckingham's 'Victoria' (1849)
Source: Buckingham (1849)

abstract, highly developed theory – Charles Fourier's.

Godin became Fourier's disciple in 1843. Fourier's utopian philosophy, even amongst other extraordinary ones of the century, was uniquely bizarre. Its basis was the law of 'passionate attraction', through which natural instincts, if followed without constraint, bring the universe into harmony. But law, exploitative and competitive industrial production, fixed marriage partnerships, poverty, inequality and monotonous work discipline all militated against their satisfaction. The theory demanded the minute hierarchical organisation of social life. The lowest level was the Group, with seven as its minimum size – three in the centre for equilibrium and two in each wing, in friendly rivalry, competition and co-operation. A minimum of five Groups constitute a Series, again with a centre and two wings. Each Group or Series is dedicated to a specific activity – a branch of agriculture, mechanical production, office management or creative arts. A number of Series combine into a Phalanx of 1620 to 1800 people which makes up the self-sufficient, harmonious Phalanstery.

The building grew out of this underlying structure – a centre and two wings – and was to be set in fields, orchards and gardens with every conceivable amenity besides apartments: hotel, communal cooking and dining facilities, council rooms, library, nurseries, schools, recreation rooms, sanatoria and workshops. Detached granaries and stables complete the complex. Seven eighths of members could be farmers or mechanics and one eighth capitalist investors, artists or scientists. Profits would be divided, five twelfths to labour, four to capital and three to skill or talent. The completely interchangeable roles allowed all to take turns according to desire.

Fourier's most ardent disciple was the École Polytechnique-educated architect Victor Considérant. Besides developing the theory through the *École Societaire* set up in 1825, he was of course uniquely qualified to translate it into material form. Indeed of his nearly thirty publications after becoming associated with Fourier the very first was an architectural treatise on the Phalanstery (1834). Considérant was a simple determinist. 'Architectonic characteristics vary with the nature and form of societies' (1834: 36); 'architecture is the written text of history' (p. 39); 'the correlation is so intimate that one can reconstitute the social history of a period even if all its traditions are extingusihed, all its text have perished, if there but remain a sufficient remnant of its munuments, public architecture, painting' (p. 50). Primitive huts, nomads' tents, Gothic cathedrals, the slums of Paris, mills, prisons and barracks prove this.

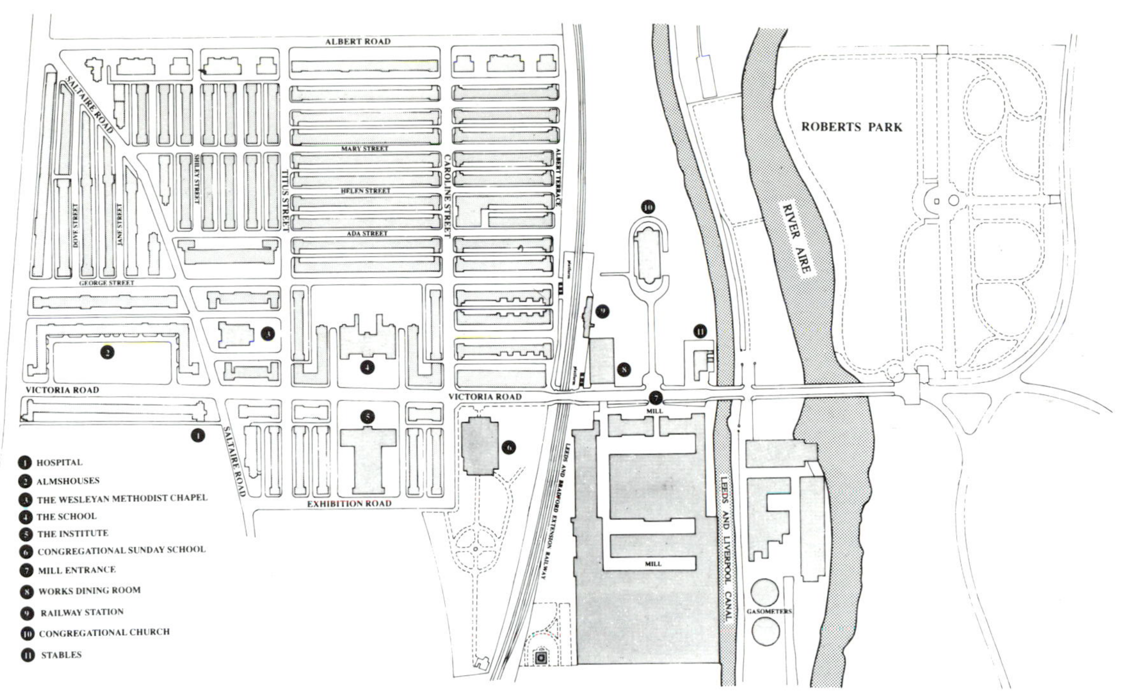

Figure 10.52

Saltaire plan

Source: Drawn by Bradford City Art Gallery, Bradford Art Galleries and Museums

His Phalanstery is a social palace (Figure 10.53); under its central 'Tower of Order' are council chambers, treasury, and reception, banquet, concert and ball rooms, workshops, factories, farms, schools and hotel. Detached at each end are the church and theatre. The upper levels are dwellings, in a range from modest two-room flats to sumptuous mansions. Choice is free and is not irrevocable. Crucial is the ground floor arcade above which glass galleries run round the entire complex and connect every wing. It is 'the channel, the magisterial artery' through which the life of the Phalanstery circulates, symbolising social harmony, the supreme law of Association, and the satisfaction of the Passions (Considérant 1834: 66).

Employee numbers at Guise grew from thirty in 1846 to 330 by 1857. In 1853 he had built a small factory with its own Familistère near Brussels, not so much for political reasons but to penetrate foreign markets. He participated in the February 1848 Revolution in Paris and though regarded as a dangerous socialist by Napoleon III it was Fourierism that dominated his life. He invested a substantial sum in a Fourierist colony in Texas but withdrew it in 1857 and started to plan for a community at Guise. Building started the following year.

The four membership categories and their voting, legal and profit-sharing rights were based on Fourier's prescriptions but Godin parted ways on several important issues. First, on the question of the Passions and the laws of Association. Second, the family remained the basic unit. Third, as housing was the focus for a community the main design effort went into a palace of houses rather than a comprehensive miniature town; hence the change from 'Phalanstère' to 'Familistère'. The site did however include alongside his factories and housing, a theatre, shops, baths, communal dining rooms and a gymnasium. Significantly, no matter how he tried to distance himself from Owen, the most striking elements were the nursery, attached to and on the central axis of the Familistère and facing it, on the same axis, a detached infant and primary school, and theatre.

Figure 10.53

Considérant's Phalanstery (1834 and 1848)

Source: Considérant (1848)

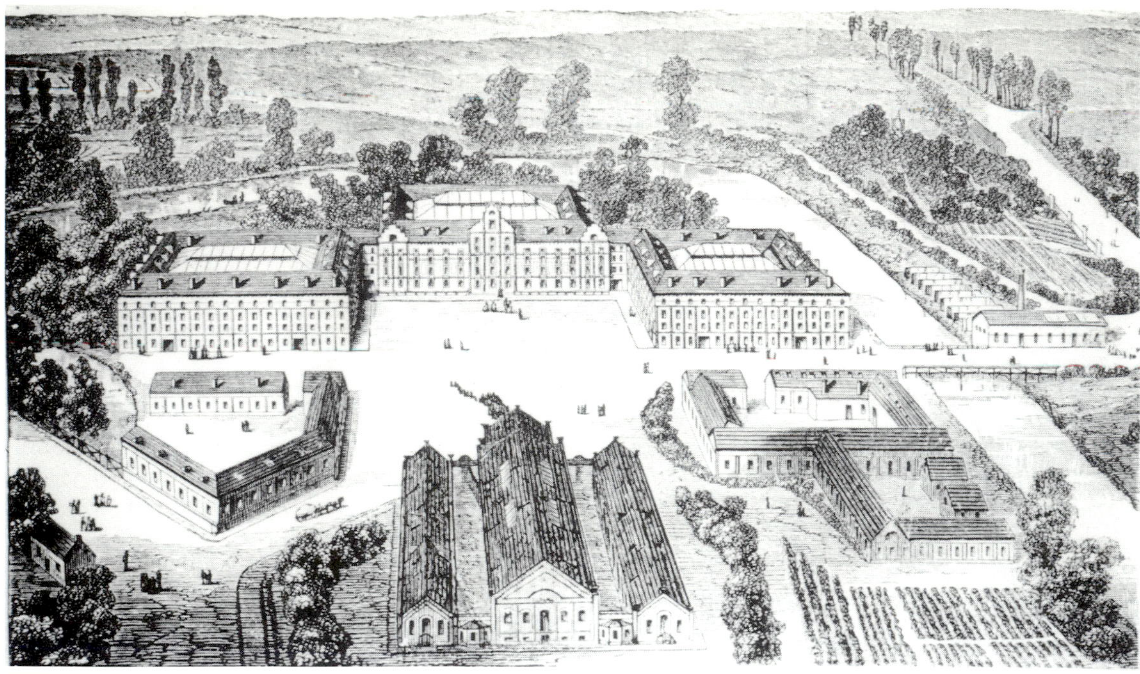

Figure 10.54
'Familistères' at Guise, aerial view and interior of one court
Source: Godin (1871), (view), and author's transparency (interior)

Three glazed and one detached unglazed four storey courts were built between 1859 and 1883 (Figure 10.54). All houses are entered from internal galleries which are linked by diagonal passages where courts meet at corners. Two- and four-roomed dwellings face both outwards and inwards. In every detail of planning, services and form, Godin loaded the two- and four-roomed houses with the entire philosophical apparatus of his version of Fourierism.

The galleries were the visible symbols of continuous social interaction:

> 1500 persons can see and visit each other, rest from domestic chores, meet in the the public space (the court) without worrying about the weather and never having to travel more than 160 metres.... This ease of relationships contributes to making the Social Palace the best fitted for raising the moral and intellectual standards of the population.
>
> (Godin 1871: IV ch. 20 para. VI)

The courts were for children's play, public meetings and Festivals of Work and of Childhood. As the workers would not become overnight 'little saints ... the principal means for attaining order in the Familistères is that each person's life is exposed' (para. XLII).

The courts stood for unity, order and harmony. Above all they represented the power of

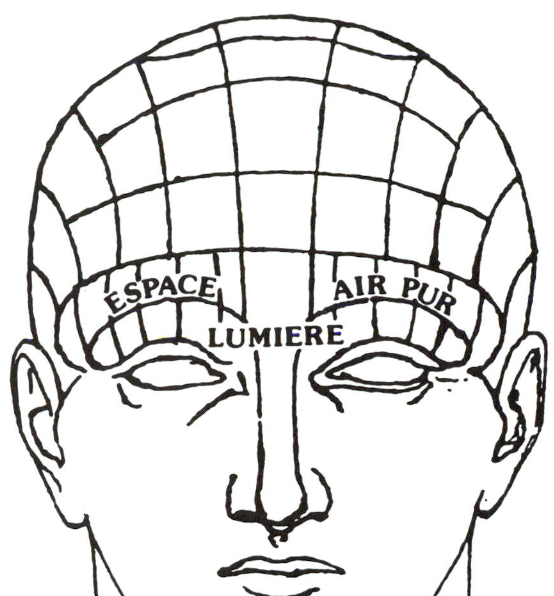

Figure 10.55

Godin's phrenological head, showing zones of space, light and fresh air

Source: Godin (1871)

light – the illumination of the mind and spirit, the symbol of progress, the obliteration of secrecy and darkness and, with it, the limitation of private life to a narrowly confined zone of space and time. Fresh air through inlet and extract ducts, running water and male and female water closets in each corner of every floor provided unprecedented hygienic standards.

Godin's phrenology ascribed to the three frontal zones of the brain the qualities of Light, Space and Fresh Air (Figure 10.55). In the Familistère he sought a consonance between brain and environment.

The production utopia is the end point of the familiar sequence: generalised aggregations, divergence and specialisation, followed by integration.

CHAPTER 11
Exchange

A wheelwright may make a wheel for his own cart. But once it is exchanged as a commodity a relation with the buyer is created. The wheel crosses a threshold between the boundaries of two separate social and economic worlds. And the space for this transaction becomes symbolically highly charged.

When the bartering of one good for another (G–G) develops into commodity exchange through money, either goods are sold and the money used to buy more goods (G–M–G), or money is used to buy goods which are sold at a profit to generate more money (M–G–M). The producer operates in the first mode, the merchant in the second. In commodity exchange a whole class of middlemen connect the producer with the consumer. And at each point these exchanges need their own space – abbatoirs, warehouses, corn and coal exchanges, offices, banks, stalls, fairs, markets and shops. All exchange is in space.

G–M–G space may be attached to production space – say the street shop fronting the workshop. But more usually it is a dedicated place – a stall in a market, a shop, or a booth in a cloth hall shared with other vendors. Much of M–G–M exchange is in symbolic goods such as contracts, bills of exchange, stocks or shares which have their own spaces such as exchanges and banks. Commodity may be labour – people instead of goods. Leaving aside the classic case of slave labour, as Marx, Braudel and others have done, the hiring of labour for wages long pre-dates the industrial system. Braudel (1982) describes medieval hiring fairs and labour markets in Auxerre, Hamburg and elsewhere whose spatiality was well established. In sixteenth century Paris workers with specialised skills were locatable at specific bridges, squares and streets.

And of coourse the movement of goods by water or land needs space at every point for loading, unloading, storage and inspection – quays, warehouses, offices, toll booths and custom houses. And laws control all this – enacted and administered in law courts, guildhalls and council chambers.

The Poznan merchant's house has dwelling, production, storage and exchange within the boundary of a single owner's household. The shop is separated from the street by an intermediate entrance hall. In the Schmalkalden house it is alongside the hall, with an open window direct to the street for display and sale (Figure 11.1). The combination of making and selling for centuries dominated the wealthier quarters of the Hanseatic towns. The urban space maximised the probability of encounter between merchants, and made access for bulky goods arriving by land or sea easy. These streets were in what Hillier and Hanson (1984) describe as 'integrating' positions – with direct access from the town or harbour edges and easy passage to the market and squares. The importance of these streets is signified by their richly embellished gabled facades.

The house-shops were subservient to and competitive with the town market which, in all cultures, has been a major urban structuring device. Agnew (1979) has made a connection between the market as urban space and as a linguistic form. But the *un*market starts outside town limits. Brown (1947) and van Gennep (1960) describe trading in ancient Greece in the no-man's-land between settlements. The produce was left for barter exchange at such a boundary, sometimes in 'silent trade' when the traders never actually met. The spot was marked by a heap of stones – the 'herms' of the god Hermes. Gradually the neutral zone shrank to a boundary and Hermes became not only the messenger, but the threshold god, the thief, the trickster, the god of trade; hence the duplicity and cunning ascribed to him which are so necessary for the merchant who becomes the professional threshold-crosser.

When the market entered the town agora, Hermes' shrines came in with it, to protect its liminal character. This was not only a consequence of its extra-urban tradition. The act of transferring property from one owner to another entails the crossing of social and spatial thresholds. We should recall Mary Douglas's (1966) explanation for the protective function of the ritual taboo which surrounds body orifices where the boundary between inside and outside breaks down and creates a dangerous ambiguity. The transfer of goods across boundaries of land, buildings and social units of production, even when it becomes very sophisticated in the mercantile and capitalist systems, requires its own ritual elaboration.

Sometimes sacred drama validated the threshold: one short side of Ostia's agora abutted the theatre. And even as thresholds became increasingly protected by secular prescriptive rights based on custom, Royal grants, guild law, town councils and the civil courts, the association with religion remained strong. London's mid-fifteenth century Leadenhall market was founded with an endowment for a group of priests, clerks and schoolmasters at Holy Trinity chapel who had a specific brief to care for the market people. Market crosses on top of buildings or as detached monuments survived into the eighteenth century as permanent reminders that honesty and fair dealing were the mercantile messages of the Cross. Some trading spaces, especially the annual fairs, remained liminal, outside the town altogether.

Medieval markets were in integrating and central, shallow urban space, on the main routes from the town gate. London's pre-Fire markets described in Hugh Alley's 1598 *Caveat* were strung along the east–west axis of the City from Aldgate to Newgate. There were exceptions: first Smithfield, for live animals, outside the city wall altogether next to the open site for the annual St Bartholomew's Fair; secondly Queenhithe and Billingsgate, the corn and fish markets located on the banks of the Thames; and thirdly the incorporation of Southwark into the City in 1556 and its linking by the ancient Southwark Bridge as the main entry from the south, created a north–south

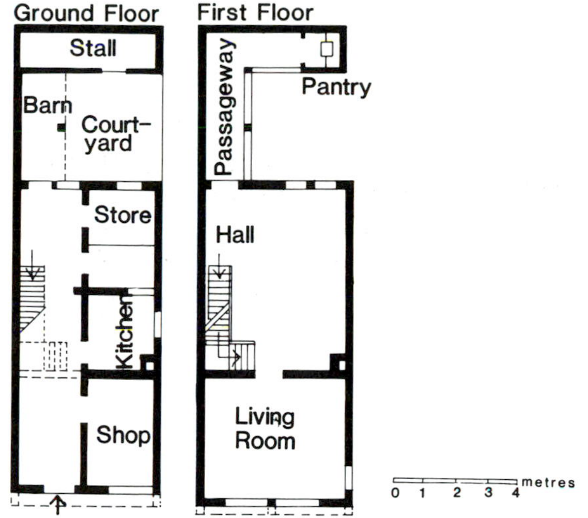

Figure 11.1
Merchant's house at Schmalkalden (c. 1500)
Source: Author's drawing adapted from Buttner and Meissner (1982) *Town Houses of Europe*, New York, St Martin's Press, p. 130

line of markets along the Fish, Gracechurch and Bishopsgate Street axis.

The spatial type was a square or street widening, with open or covered grouped central stalls and others attached to houses at the periphery. Some of the colonnaded free-standing buildings were combined as early as the thirteenth century with upper level halls for civic government in what Tittler (1991) calls the *domus civicus*. Others remained simply as 'crosses' or covered colonnaded spaces. All these became so much part of the European urban tradition that many are in use today.

The law forced exchange into places where it could be controlled. There were three offences – engrossing, forestalling and regrating. The first was buying up the whole or large part of the total stock of a commodity with the intention of reselling at enhanced prices and now with a monopoly. The second was intercepting suppliers before their products arrived in the market – say at the quayside or outside the gate. The third was buying products in one market and re-selling in another. All were strategies for circumventing the rules intended to maintain a symmetrical balance of power between seller and buyer; all carried stiff penalties imposed on the basis of information provided by an army of paid informers. And each involved spatial transgression.

Leyburn gives an equally good description of the markets that survived or were rebuilt after the Fire (Masters 1974). The main locations remained but they were moved from the thoroughfares into adjacent squares so resolving the long-standing conflict with traffic. Individual spaces were greatly enlarged, regularised and specialised so that each

Figure 11.2
St John's market, Liverpool (1822), plan, exterior view and interior view
Source: From prints in the Liverpool Public Libraries

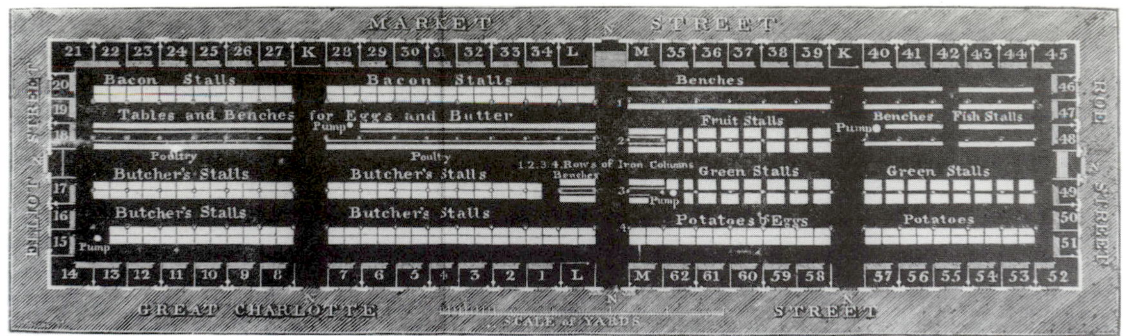

CORRECT PERSPECTIVE

VIEW OF THE NEW MARKET,

Liverpool.

OPENED ON THURSDAY, MARCH 7, 1822.

site became associated with a limited range of goods. A number of open, colonnaded buildings appeared in the centres of the squares.

The Parisian markets grew quite differently. A nucleus was established north of the Seine on a site which was also a cemetery. Expanded and enclosed behind a wall in the twelfth century the *Marché des Innocents* grew by gradually nibbling away at the streets, squares and open spaces around it. By the eighteenth century an entire *quartier* was taken over.

But the industrial city with its population explosion after 1800 created a massive new demand for food supply. It was met either by centrifugal dispersion or centripetal concentration. Either a number of specialised market squares and halls were scattered over different locations, or all activity was concentrated into huge covered markets.

A centrifugal case is described by Blackman in her study of food supply in Sheffield between 1780 and 1900 (1962–3). The markets for fruit, live cattle, fish, corn and other products had been clustered around the town hall until 1784 when each was moved and rebuilt both to a much larger scale and at a greater distance from the centre.

Leeds is an even clearer case. Up to the 1820s the town's traditional markets were strung out along the Briggate, with some activity also near its northern and southern extremitites in Vicar and Headrow Lanes (Grady 1980). Moving from south to north the commodities were cloth, general goods, fish, meat, corn, pigs and horses. The meat stalls were in the Old Shambles under the town hall which was part of a chain of island structures at the northern and wider end of the Briggate. In addition five dispersed cloth halls for white, coloured and other fabrics were built between 1710 and 1793. We shall return to these. In the seven years from 1823 to 1830 all this was replaced or added to by substantial dispersion and specialisation.

St John's market in Liverpool (1820–2), designed by John Foster Senior and Junior was an early centripetal project. Over a rectangular grid measuring 183 yards by 45, four rows of 23-feet-high cast iron columns supported a timber roof (Figure 11.2). Six entrances articulate the main avenues; four smaller longitudinal and two lateral ones divide the area into sixteen islands, of which the eight larger ones to one side are devoted to meat (4), bacon, butter and eggs (2) and poultry (2). The other side has green vegetables, fruit, eggs, potatoes and fish. The peripheral stalls are for the same range of produce, and cheese and bread in addition.

The food classification is revealing. First, retail strategy overcame the principles of Classical composition, for with the unequal division between the two sets of produce, entrances on the long sides had to be eccentric. Second, eggs are the only produce to cross the boundary between this lateral division. They are also ambiguous in the town outside for they appear in butchers' shops, dairies, fishmongers and greengrocers. Moreover they are equally ambiguous in the cuisine: they can be eaten as an *hors d'oeuvre*, as main or side dishes, they are ingredients for pastry, desserts and dressings, and they are preserved. Their preparation involves use in their raw state, boiling, frying, baking and pickling. Third, one side had the high unit price products, the other the cheap ones which, in a port town, included fish. In the market as a whole the ratio of space occupied by meat to that occupied by vegetables (including potatoes) was the same as the ratio of their consumption in the contemporary diet. Burnett (1989: 53) reports that in 1824 a typical family with three children consumed seven pounds of the former and thirty-five of the latter per week, in contrast to thirty pounds of *all* other foods combined, including twenty-four pounds of bread and flour.

Charles Edge's 1832 Birmingham market was almost identical. In the 1825 Salford market the dominance of meat and vegetables excluded all other produce. The grandest provincial scheme of this kind was Dobson's 1834 New Market for meat and greens inside Grainger's Newcastle complex. Though much larger than Liverpool, the spatial order of the enclosed grid and the gates was the same.

These markets are different from the conventional trading street or square; they create permeabilities during shopping hours, and vast, impermeable blocks at other times. The individual shops are spatially deeper from public space. Through the standardisation of units, control of rents and opening hours, and hygienic provisions, though the stall-holders are all competitors, they also have a new solidarity in being tenants of the same interventionist landlord. Consumers are used to being confronted by individual traders; their power is more or less balanced. But in this new situation the relation becomes asymmetrical. Some of the consumers' conventional choice and bargaining power is removed as they face a more powerful alliance and their spatial and temporal choices are limited. In some respects such a controlled market is the predecessor to the modern integrated shopping complex.

The centrifugal and centripetal patterns developed on a vast scale in the Metropolis. In London it was the former, which makes it impossible to discover the relationship between space and wholesale or retail consumption without extending the analysis to the urban scale. That is beyond my present scope. Of course individual units in this pattern, such markets as Hungerford and Covent Garden designed by Britain's greatest market architect Charles Fowler, are full of formal, spatial and technical interest (Stamp 1986 and Taylor 1968).

Paris continued its ancient centripetal tradition right up to the grand final act – Baltard and Callet's 1853 *Halles Centrales.* Lemoine (1980) recites the entire narrative: Boffrand's 1748 grandiose fish, vegetable and corn markets on either side of a central royal square; and projects by Barbie (1765), Maille Dussaussoy (1767), Jaillot (1778) and Loret (1780) in which vast squares, shop-lined avenues and grids appeared, often with ornamental fountains in the centre of the *places* sporting allegorical figures of abundance, health and purity. Louis XVI's 1786 cloth hall was condemned by Baltard and Callet (1862: 8–9) as 'heavy and cold ... (like) a funeral monument'. At that time the cemetery, 'a source of infection', was finally closed. Even the soil was removed. By Imperial Decrees of 1811 the entire area was to be rebuilt, but little was done for decades.

Markets became favourite student topics, and when it became the subject for the 1792 *Grands Prix* competition a radical marriage of grandeur with public utility was inaugurated which became the Revolutionary ideal. Competitors were asked to include law courts, a police station, a house for guards, and a principal fountain. They responded with immense agora-like layouts, colonnaded courts and pavilions, and apsidal basilicas. It was how Ledoux planned his huge greek cross market for Chaux.

In Durand's *Parallèle* one page showed markets, public squares and shopping arcades drawn to one scale, as was his wont, with the result that the page was dominated by the huge Isfahan open market square, in stark contrast with a tiny fish market at Marseille. Central, at the top, is a familiar Paris landmark, the one monumental structure of the market *quartier* which went beyond dream to execution: le Camus de Mezières' 1763–72 *halle au blé.* A circular 40 metre diameter court was surrounded by the open trading arcade vaulted for fire resistance. The carrying of heavy sacks of corn to the upper granaries presented a special problem which de Mezières overcame by two intertwining helical staircases, one each for upward and downward traffic. In 1782–3 Legrand and Molinos covered the court with a timber dome, replaced by Belanger and Brunet in 1811 in cast iron, after its destruction by fire in 1802. The immense formal power of the rotunda, together with that of the sixteenth century church of St Eustache, has dominated all later replanning proposals.

Durand's graph-paper lent itself naturally to market planning. It perfectly represented the order of trading governed by strict rules about opening times, rentable space and hygiene. The grid achieved the internal openness which maximised the interface between buyers and sellers, and also distinguished the market from the disordered surrounding space. The expansionist mood of the First Empire encouraged proposals of this type initiated by Fontaine's 1811–14 drawn catalogue of Parisian markets.

Bruyère, director of public works, prepared an 1813 plan with six gridded structures centred on the axis of the *halle au blé.* These grouped the merchandise into tripe, poultry food, fish, fruit, vegetables, dairy produce (butter, cheese and eggs), and a butchers' market to balance the existing cloth market in the *rue de la Poterie.* Nothing took place till the 1840s. Baltard and Callet prepared several schemes in competition with others. Work did start on one but was halted by Napoleon in 1853; when Haussmann appeared on the scene as the new Prefect of the Seine in that year Baltard and Callet's design was finally adopted.

Half a century's drive to order, modern technology, sanitation, classification and the conquest of urban chaos came to fruition. The architects transformed the fragmented provision into twelve glass and iron, modularly gridded, pavilions arranged laterally on an axis aligned with the *halle au blé* (Figure 11.3). The rotunda had two pavilions wrapped round it, and two others for the administration and public services. On the long axis was a huge, glazed alley, and crossing it were one open and four glazed alleys.
The pavilions were:

1 Pork and tripe, wholesale.
2 Poultry and game, wholesale.

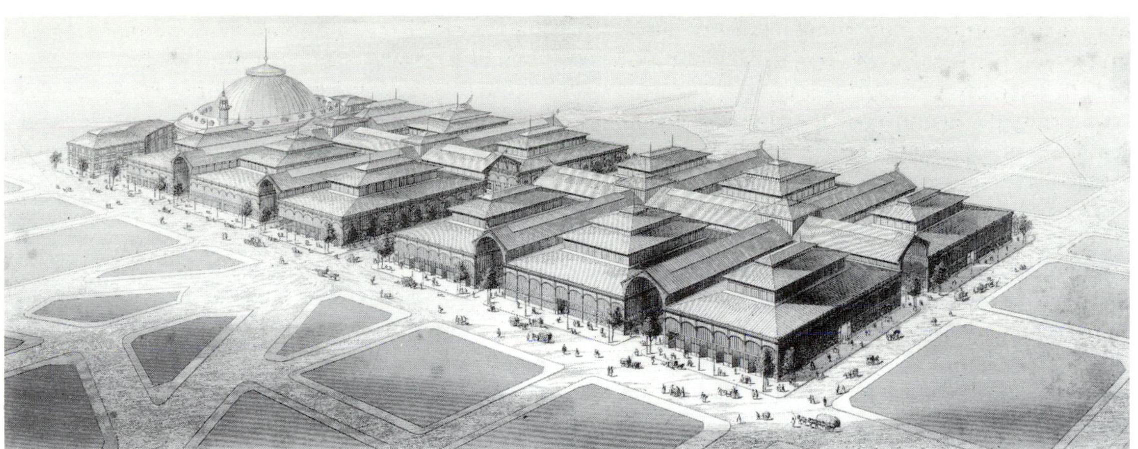

Figure 11.3
Aerial view of Baltard and Callet's Les Halles, Paris (1835)
Source: Baltard and Callet (1862), British Library

3 Meat (non-pork), wholesale.
4 Poultry and game, wholesale.
5 } Fruit vegetables and medicinal herbs,
6 } wholesale in the morning, retail in the afternoon.
7 Fruit and flowers, semi-wholesale and retail.
8 Vegetables and greens, retail, with 330 separate stalls.
9 Seafood, fresh and salt water fish, wholesale and retail.
10 Butter, eggs and cheese, wholesale.
11 Poultry, game and greens, wholesale and semi-wholesale, for later conversion to oysters.
12 Butter, eggs, cheese, cooked meats, potatoes, onions, mushrooms, bread and kitchen utensils, retail.

The pattern of meat products at one end, fish and dairy products at the other, with a large intervening vegetable and flower section, reproduces the sequence of the old market.

At basement level were enormous stores, a poultry abattoir, butter mixing rooms, bread warehouses, running water tanks for fresh and salt water fish, and a room where 600,000 eggs a day were examined by candlelight. There was also an intricate drainage system which the designers claimed was a reproduction of that of the city. Most Parisians, they state, know that under their city are canals, drains, gas and water pipes and electric wires 'in a marvellous complexity ... the veritable arteries of the great city' which pursue, in darkness and silence their philanthropic and hygienic work (Baltard and Callet 1862: 24).

The public health problems of markets were now to the fore and dominated design. Live animals, dung, newly slaughtered animals and birds, freshly caught fish, vegetables and potatoes covered in earth, together with their rustic owners, were not only nuisances, but metaphors for contamination, chaos, decay and crudity in opposition to order, hygiene and urbanity. Nowhere was this more acutely felt than in live animal markets.

In London, in the year of the Crystal Palace, Dr Bushman, senior physician to the Metropolitan Free Hospital, published a defence on 'moral and sanitary' grounds of the new market for live animals and carcasses to replace Smithfield (1851). He foresaw baths and wash-houses to cleanse the area and:

> exterminate incalculable evils arising from the practice of loathsome and poisonous trades (which have) become the very focus of fetor and malaria, depravity and crime. Courtyards overflowing with blood and putridity; sheds in ruins, black with slimy deposits of many years, and the laboratories of pestilence for two millions and a half of human beings; hives of unblessed industry; the schools of petty theft and prostitution; and the secret dens where the malefactor flies the arm of the law and laughs at justice ... the race proceeding from the close and confined districts, and which supply a large number of thieves in the metropolis, is short and stunted in growth; the intellectual faculties of low order; physically weak; such persons are prone to crime, with a pertinacity which can be explained only by imperfect development of the mind.
>
> (Bushman 1851: 44)

This was also a nest of 'cretinism ... and insanity and its attendant evils. They (the City authorites) desire all this physical and moral foulness shall be for ever swept away' (1851: 29).

The market had now become more than a dangerous threshold between city and no man's land, or between the worlds of different owners. Its ambiguity spanned between life, health, nourishment and virtue, and physical and moral disease; between order and chaos, or urban gentility and rustic coarseness. But its very chaos could be turned into an instrument for social progress. A promoter of a vast Lancasterian monitorial school for Glasgow's Gorbals proposed that it be funded by profits from public markets (Fox 1814) which would support 'a mighty machine, put into our hands by Supreme Intelligence, which may be applied to the amelioration of the condition of society at large'.

The shop did not carry this symbolic burden. Combined with the shopkeeper's house, and sometimes with a workshop, it extended the social relations on one side of the counter to the domestic economy rather than to Royal, municipal and guild power. Access to the shop on the public side is directly from uncontrolled public space – the street or square – rather from the controlled concourse of the market.

Of course there were all kinds of hybrids. Even before shops gained the ascendancy in the seventeenth century, they already appeared at the edges of markets as shuttered booths which were either extensions of the peripheral houses or independent, rented stalls.

Shops and market share some features but there is a clear difference between the shopping street and the market hall which corresponds to differences in the goods, the vendors and the purchasers. The relations of exchange are different.

Though some shops dealt in the same perishable foods found in the market, they developed a range of specialities, especially in delicate or expensive goods. An entire street or quarter could be dominated by, say, jewellery, leather or spice.

The vendors were different. The shopkeeper was likely to be a bourgeois property owner, resident near or above the shop, urban, skilled in a craft or with specialist mercantile knowledge. The market stallholder was from the rural hinterland, a temporary visitor, rustic, either unskilled or with farming or horticultural skills. The difference in social class would be evident in clothing, manners, speech and familiarity with such urban institutions as banks and coffee houses.

The shop purchaser was wealthier and better dressed. Whilst masters and mistresses used these clean, private spaces, their servants were in the crowded markets, exposed to robust language and the activities of thieves and pickpockets.

The spatial structures (Figure 11.4) make the difference clear. But it goes further than that; there is a variation in individual shops and their hybrids.

Type (i) is spatially independent from, and internally unconnected to any adjacent dwelling (whose owner may however also own the shop and rent it out). Vendor and purchaser share an entrance, though the former penetrates deeper, behind the counter which keeps the latter in the shallow space. When goods are handled through a shop 'window' open to the street the immediate pavement area becomes the outer part of the shop, and the door serves only the vendor. Market stalls or booths are also like this but lack the rear service entrance from a more segregated space.

The Type (ii) shop is attached to and internally connected with the vendor's house, whose separate entrance, also used by the household's apprentices, servants and assistants, may be from the front or from a side or rear passage. The shop is a shallow tree, the house a deep one. The interface at the counter makes a ring if the exchange transaction is taken as a form of permeability.

Type (iii) is an independent rented shop unit in a space shared with similar units. Seventeenth century 'bazaars', such as the Exeter Change in London's Strand, were of this type. Early nineteenth century cities abounded in them. Purchasers shared an entrance and from a common mall had access to the counters of individual, often competitive, vendors. The latter had their own shared entrance which gave access to their

Figure 11.4

Spatial structure of exchange spaces

Source: Author's drawing

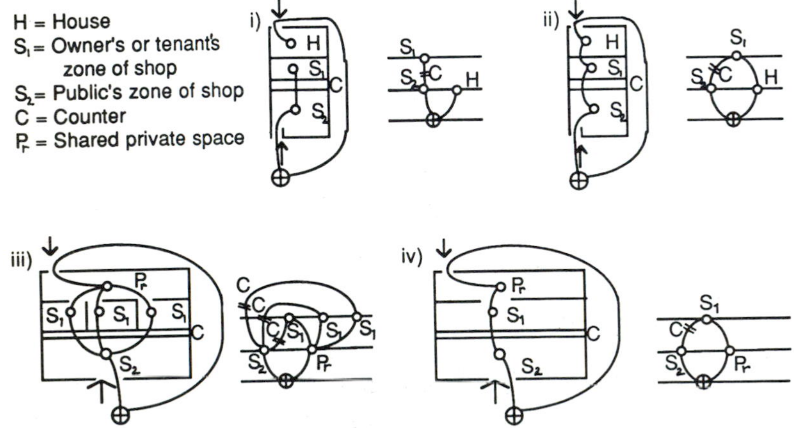

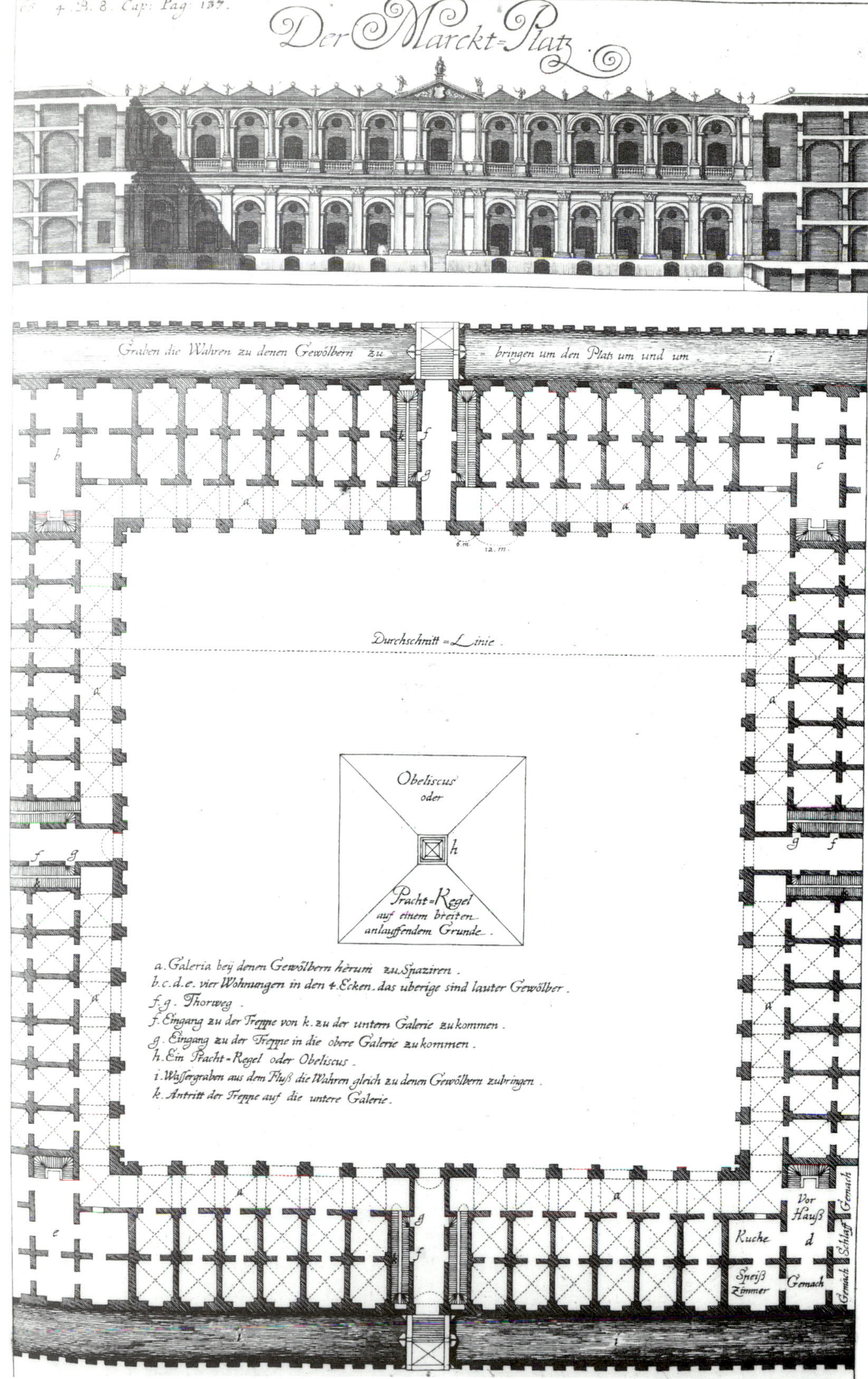

Figure 11.5

Sturm's model market (1696)

Source: Nicolai Goldman (1708) *Vollstandige Answeisung zu der Civil-Baukunst etc.* Leipzig, British Library individual spaces. The owner-manager imposed strict rules about opening times, decorum, categories of goods, prevention of haggling or bargaining and tenants' dress and speech. In Manchester men and women vendors were confined to separate floors. Other functions might be incorporated – at Exeter a menagerie, in Manchester an art exhibition, diorama and physiorama, and in Liverpool a grand promenading saloon (Adburgham 1964: 18–24). There is a dual tree structure; again this is transformed into a series of rings if the transactions across the counter are read as permeabilities.

It is but a small step to type (iv) – the partitions disappear and the entire shop becomes the trading area of one vendor, with the long continuous or island counters found in late eighteenth century shops for fashionable clothes, furnishing fabrics, books and china. Two or more such open spaces on top of, or alongside each other make a proto-department store. Adburgham (1964: 80–4) describes Harding, Howell and Company's five 'shops' (departments) in the 1796 conversion of the Schomberg House in Pall Mall. Although huge in comparison to Type (i), and spatially more complex, in principle it differs in only one respect – its separate vendors' entrance with staff and service space has replaced the house. The Parisian *magasin de nouveautés* of the 1840s – an emporium of silks, woollens, cloths, shawls, lingerie, hosiery, gloves, ready-to-wear, umbrellas, furs and sewing goods – was an expansion of the principle. Several such emporia under a single owner with a specialist department on each floor, wrapped round a central open and integrating covered atrium, as in the 1869 Bon Marché, was the true department store.

One ancient form, where a number of identical cells on one or more levels face into a courtyard, found new uses. At upper levels covered walkways run in front of the cells. This is the Classical market reconstructed by both Alberti and Palladio and idealised by Filarete. The great German building typologist Sturm used it for his model in the late seventeenth century (Figure 11.5). From the thirteenth century it appears in Italian, German, Low Countries and Baltic (Hanseatic) cities in adaptations where the ground floor space of cellular shop units is enclosed and has council chambers, treasuries, courts, chapels and warehouses at upper levels. Examples abound: Torun, with general and specialised shops, Minden with shops facing both outwards into public space and inwards into a courtyard; Bruges; Ghent and Ypres. Permeability from the urban space varied. At Bruges there was another version for cloth dealing which prefigured a type which appeared just before the Industrial Revolution.

In the Yorkshire woollen or worsted cloth halls the vendors produce only one specialised product, and the purchasing merchants or their agents deal only in that. There was no retail function, therefore no need to attract the public. In fact both through location, and by limiting permeability and controlling entrance, everything was done to keep the public out.

The cloth was produced by cottage spinners, weavers and fullers in the surrounding Dales. One or two pieces were taken to a nearby town weekly to what was, in effect, a wholesale market. The open air trestle tables soon moved into the new cloth halls erected by one town after another (Smithies 1988). The merchants appeared on the appointed day and at the fixed hour to buy cloth for direct re-sale to domestic clothiers or for export. Trade started and finished precisely at the peal of a bell and any infrigement of this rule resulted in severe fines. This system assured both competition and equality of opportunity. In the early decades of the nineteenth century such wholesale exchange diminished as the merchants found it simpler to deal directly with the mill owner at the factory which took over from domestic production. Unprogrammed competition was replaced by long term contracts.

The enclosed space was often windowless, the gate was controlled, and the internal walk gave the merchants free and sheltered movement. Each producer had a fixed location – either behind a trestle table or at a counter in front of closed, lockable cell-like units (Figure 11.6).

In the earliest halls 'stalls' were back-to-back on either side of a spine wall. The 1712 Wakefield hall was of this form, as were Bradford's 1773 Piece Hall and the 1778 Wakefield hall, both two storeys high above a storage level. In Huddersfield's 1766 Cloth Hall, originally on one floor, two halves of an ellipse were joined by a central spine hall. The 'shops" windows faced into the court, and on the outer side each had a table in the walkway. Leeds had a series of halls. That of 1711 was a small two-storey building with trestle tables laid out on two arcaded floors round a court. It was followed by the 1756–8 Coloured or Mixed Cloth Hall. A single gate led into the court off which opened long thin halls with an alley between two rows of open stalls. The two sides of

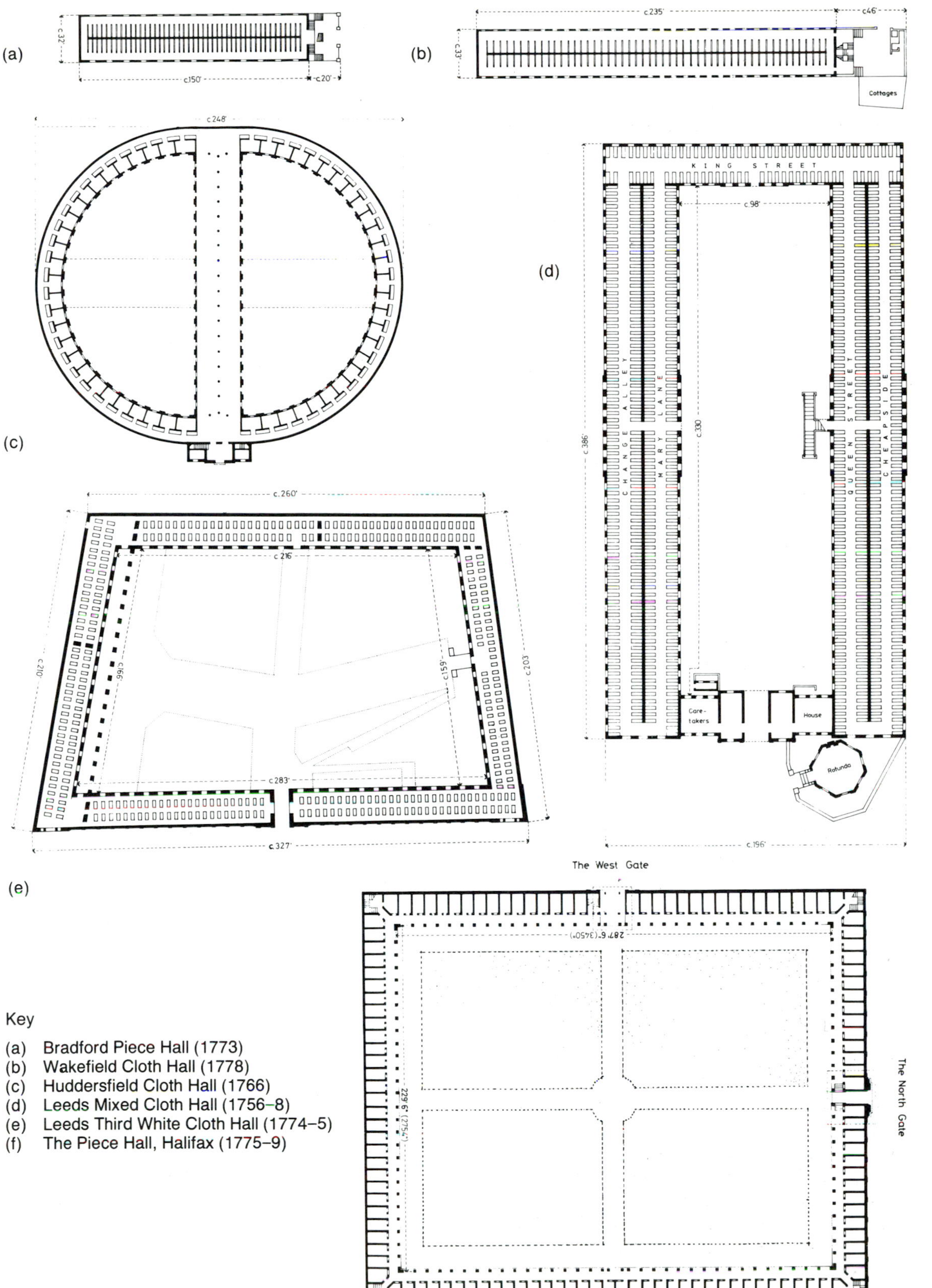

Figure 11.6 *Six eighteenth-century Yorkshire cloth or 'piece' halls*

Source: Smithies (1988), by permission of Philip Smithies who also generously provided copies of his drawings the halls were twinned, separated by a spine wall on the Wakefield and Bradford plan. The alleys were named, as was common, after the original streets where the outdoor piece markets had been held. An upper floor was added, served by a monumental staircase, together with an octagonal 'rotunda' for money dealing and exchange outside the gate. The plan of the 1775 Second White Cloth Hall is not known. The 1774–5 Third White Cloth Hall, a single storey building, had double rows of stalls in open halls.

The grandest was the 1775–9 Halifax Piece Hall; due to the sloping site it was part two- and part three-storey, the upper level colonnaded with Tuscan columns, the lower with square rusticated pillars. Originally there was a single gate. The plan combined the Leeds courtyard form with the Huddersfield 'shops'.

Despite the type sharing formal features with the classical market, its meaning is quite different. Its location ensures minimum public access by making it deep and segregated with regard to the urban space. A single point access was strictly controlled. Its units, whether cellular or tables, were for one product only, often just one item. It was open for only a few hours a week, was at a distance from the dwellings of both producers and merchants, and yet the volume of business transacted was both assured and enormous. Its individual shops or tables are spatially deep even from the segregated urban space of the block. All this combines to signify an élite, confraternity-like solidarity of purchasers and vendors. One brought unique selling skills, the other unique craft production skills.

A similar space had long been used by mercantile élites for wholesale dealing on the basis of samples of sugar, corn, coal, minerals, wool and cotton, or for the exchange of symbolic goods such as money, contracts, forward options (for instance corn not yet grown or fish not yet caught), bills of exchange, stocks and shares. Braudel (1982: 82 *et seq.*) traces one origin of this symbolic market to the great fairs, 'ancient instruments for ever being re-tuned'. Towns like Leipzig became dominated by their fairs and continuously rebuilt open spaces for them. These enormous retail markets drew the entire urban and rural hinterland population and became the *locus* for carnivals, music, travelling players and circuses. But they were also wholesale markets for international merchant houses. Though there were piles of goods, those trading on the largest scale brought no merchandise, and very little money; they dealt in bills of exchange which represented 'the entire wealth of Europe' (1982: 91). The goods being transacted were in docks and harbours, huge warehouses, depots and cellars. Inside the fairs, or in surrounding inns, the space where merchants traded was one origin of exchanges.

When these became a mercantile type they fulfilled four requirements:

1 An exclusive space, securely cut off from the plebeian population.
2 Maximum internal openness, so that through the free and easy movement of merchants the probability of chance encounters is maximised.
3 Rich visual and auditory information on opportunities, bargains and news.
4 The imposition of sufficent order and spatial classification to allow participants to identify readily those dealing in specific categories of goods, or specialising in specified geographical markets.

Corn was traded on the basis of samples weighed on special scales which showed the estimated weight of the sacks. Amsterdam's seventeenth century corn exchange, London's in Mark Lane designed by George Dance the Elder in 1749–50 and the much grander *Halle au Blé* in Paris had the same form: a strictly controlled entry into a court open to the sky, surrounded by sheltered colonnaded or arcaded space for the merchants and their samples. Its durability is witnessed by the huge, elliptical two-floor 1860 Leeds Corn Exchange designed by Brodrick to replace that of 1826 on an island site in the Briggate. The centre was covered and part glazed and so could accommodate the dealing, and since the elaborate system now needed bureaucracy, the periphery became office space. The 1755 London Coal Exchange had the same form.

Exchanges for symbolic goods had the same requirements: external closure, controlled access, internal open but sheltered space for transactions, and private offices. Besides the tradition of the fairs, Braudel (1982) points to the fourteenth century exchanges of Italy and even further back to the regular meeting places for merchants and money changers in twelfth century church porches. Even in a second century AD Roman square in Ostia the mosaic pavement marked places reserved for merchants and owners of foreign ships. But the great growth took place in the fifteenth and sixteenth centuries for which Braudel provides an extensive list.

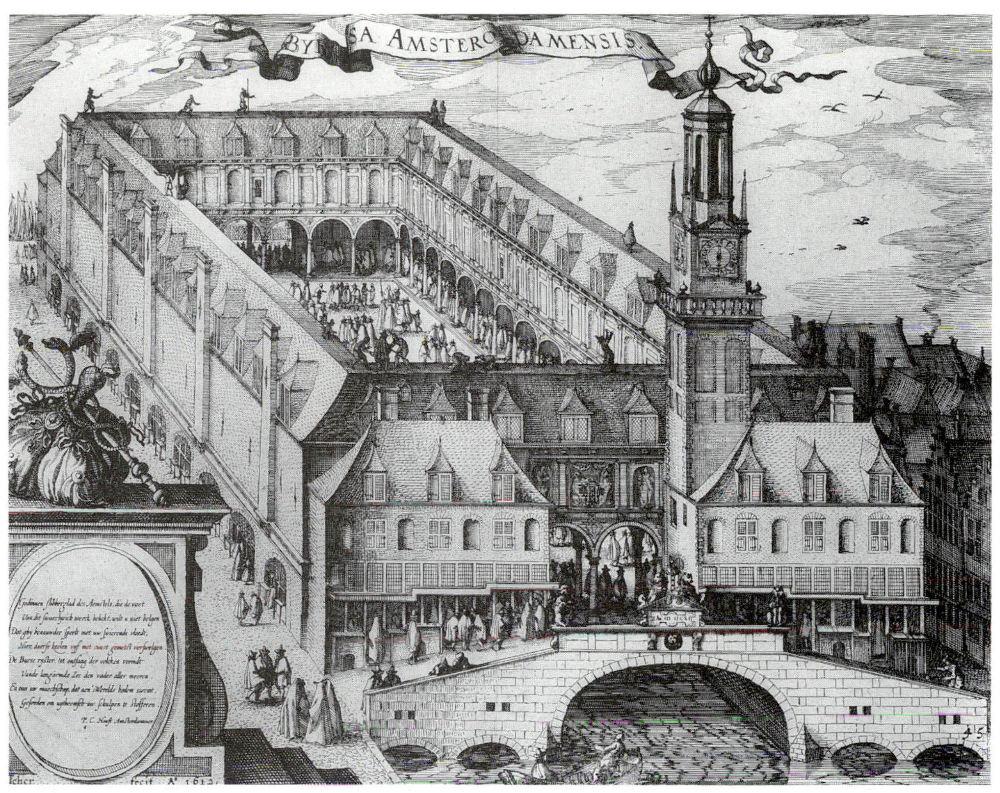

Figure 11.7

Amsterdam Exchange (1608–11), aerial view and courtyard

Source: Visscher's 1612 engraving in the Rijkdienst voor de Monumentenzorg, Zeist (view); Berckheyde's painting in the Amsterdam's Historisch Museum (courtyard)

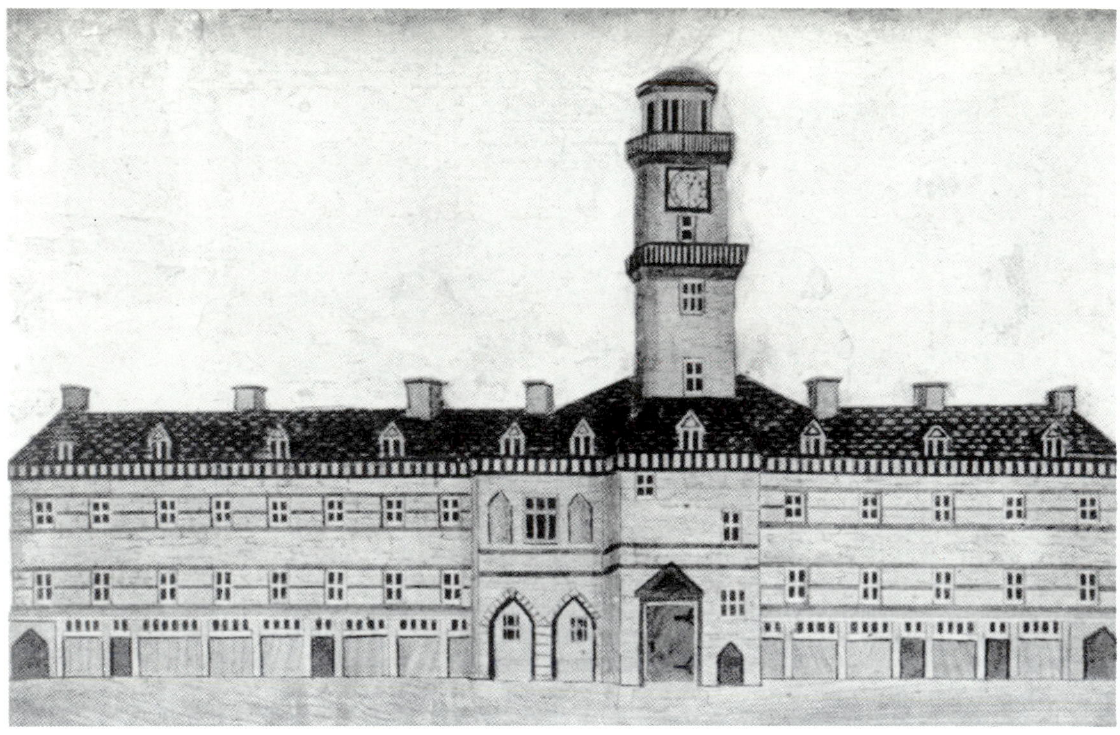

Figure 11.8

London's first Royal Exchange: exterior, from a wood inlay, and Hollar's view of the courtyard

Source: Guardian Royal Exchange (UK) Limited (exterior); Guildhall Library, Corporation of London (courtyard)

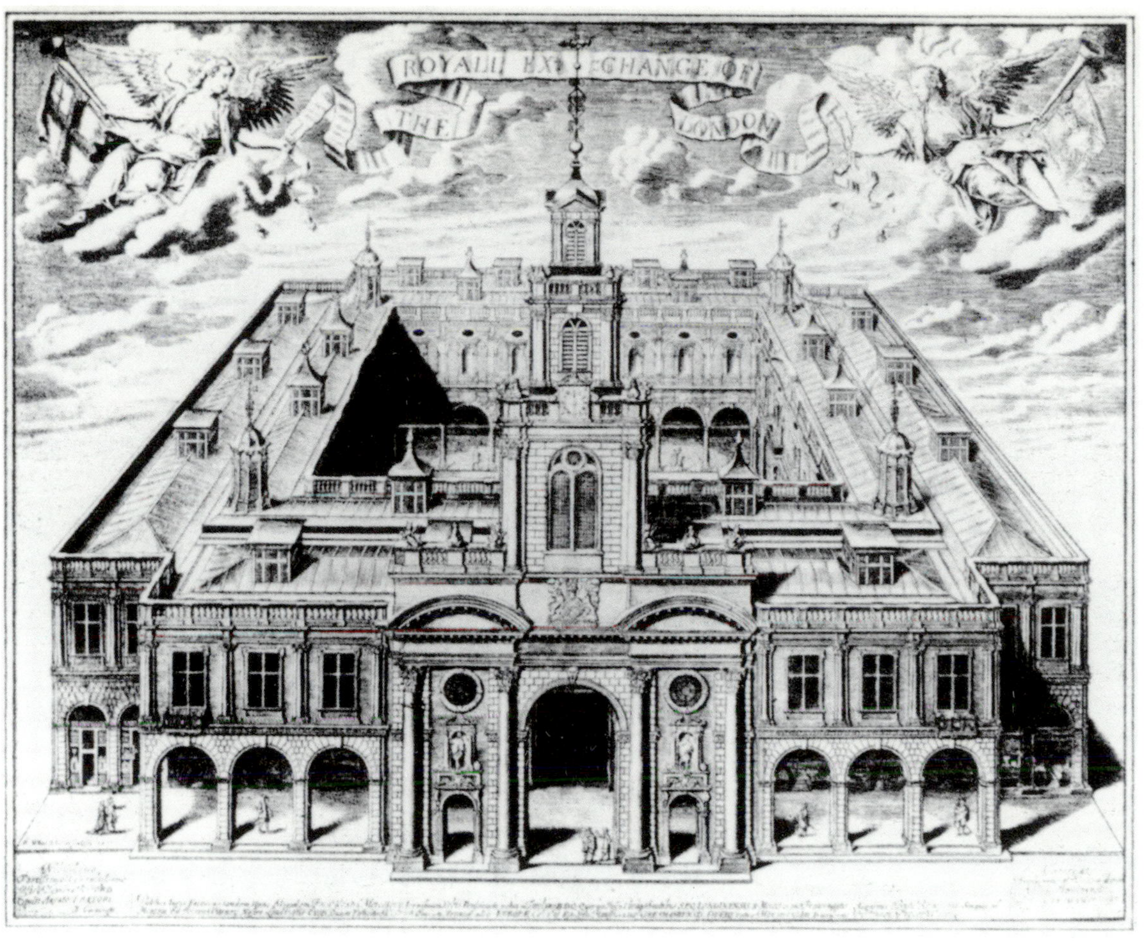

Figure 11.9
Jerman's second Royal Exchange, London (1667–71)
Source: Guardian Royal Exchange (UK) Limited

Amsterdam's exchange of 1608–11 initiated both a new architectural model (already foreshadowed at Antwerp and Seville) and a mercantile one. There was an open interior court with its arcaded walks opening onto offices. Entrance was through a double gateway on one short side (Figure 11.7). In the two hours after noon as many as 4500 crowded into this space. Amsterdam dominated European finance well into the eighteenth century.

London's Royal Exchange built in 1566–7 on a Cornhill site was set up to challenge the dominance of Antwerp and as a way for the Queen and the merchants to undermine the surviving privileges of the Hanseatic Steelyard merchants. The promoter, Sir Thomas Gresham, Royal representative at Antwerp and in effect Ambassador to Europe, financed it and obtained the Royal title in 1570.

Many of the materials and design ideas for the modest four-storey brick structure came from Holland (Figure 11.8). Its entrance under a clock tower led to an arcaded inner court for trading, on familiar lines, though the presence of shuttered shops or booths round its exterior, and shops for milliners, armourers, apothecaries, booksellers and goldsmiths on its upper floors, gave it an ambiguity. On Gresham's death his own livery company, the Mercers, and the City, inherited it. It was totally destroyed by the Fire.

Of the plans for rebuilding London, two are of special interest in their proposals for the new Royal Exchange. In John Evelyn's it was in one of five river front piazzas, each devoted to trade. Wren treated it as the centre of a splendid financial configuration. The first represents old-style utilitarian mercantilism, the second heralds modern capitalism.

In the event Jerman's 1667–71 building followed closely the original plan, clothed in a more elaborate exterior (Figure 11.9). Invisible boundaries divided both the court and peripheral arcades into 'walks', each the domain of merchants specialising either in a trade, a geo-

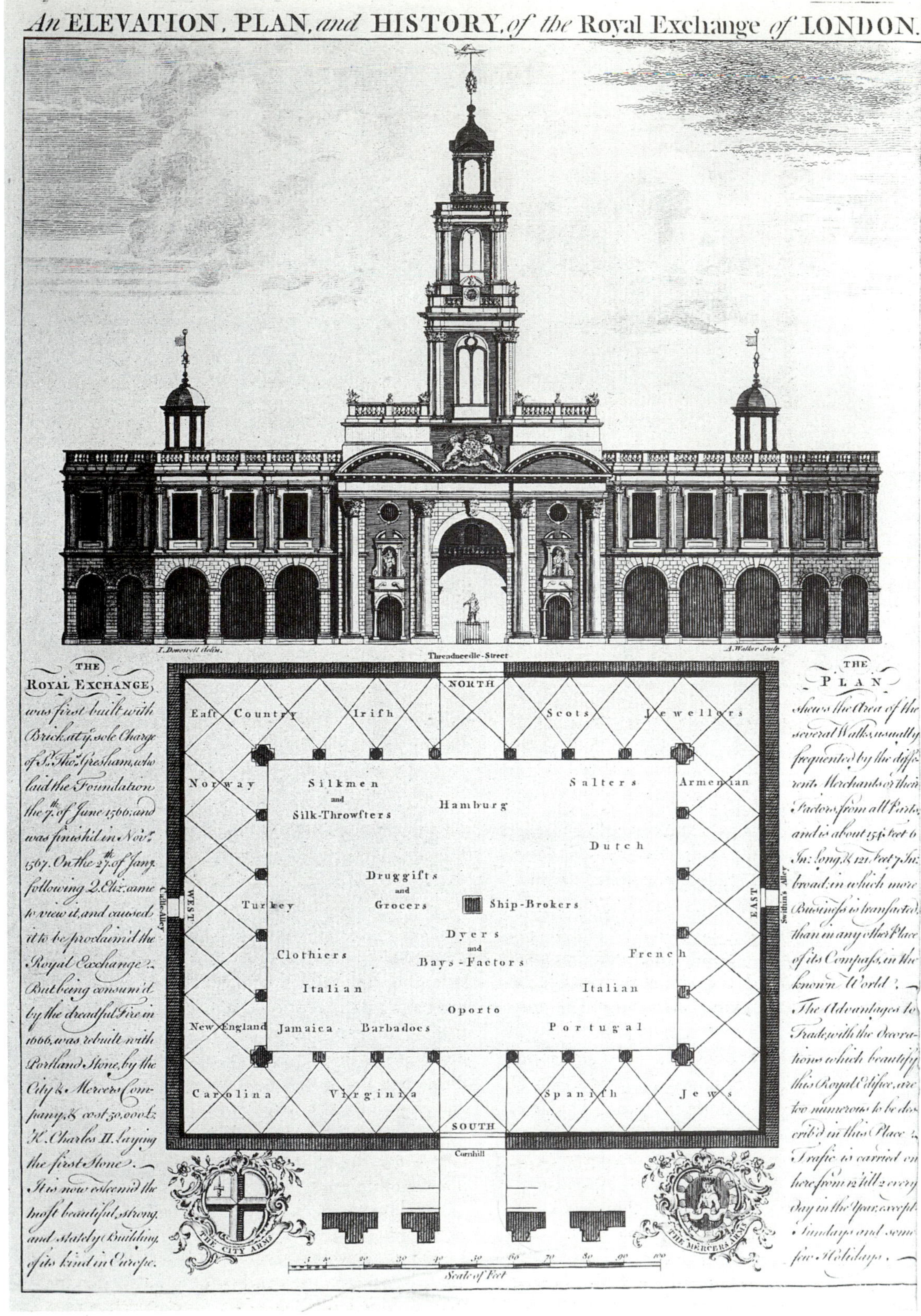

Figure 11.10
Merchants' 'walks' in the second Royal Exchange, London
Source: Eighteenth-century engraving

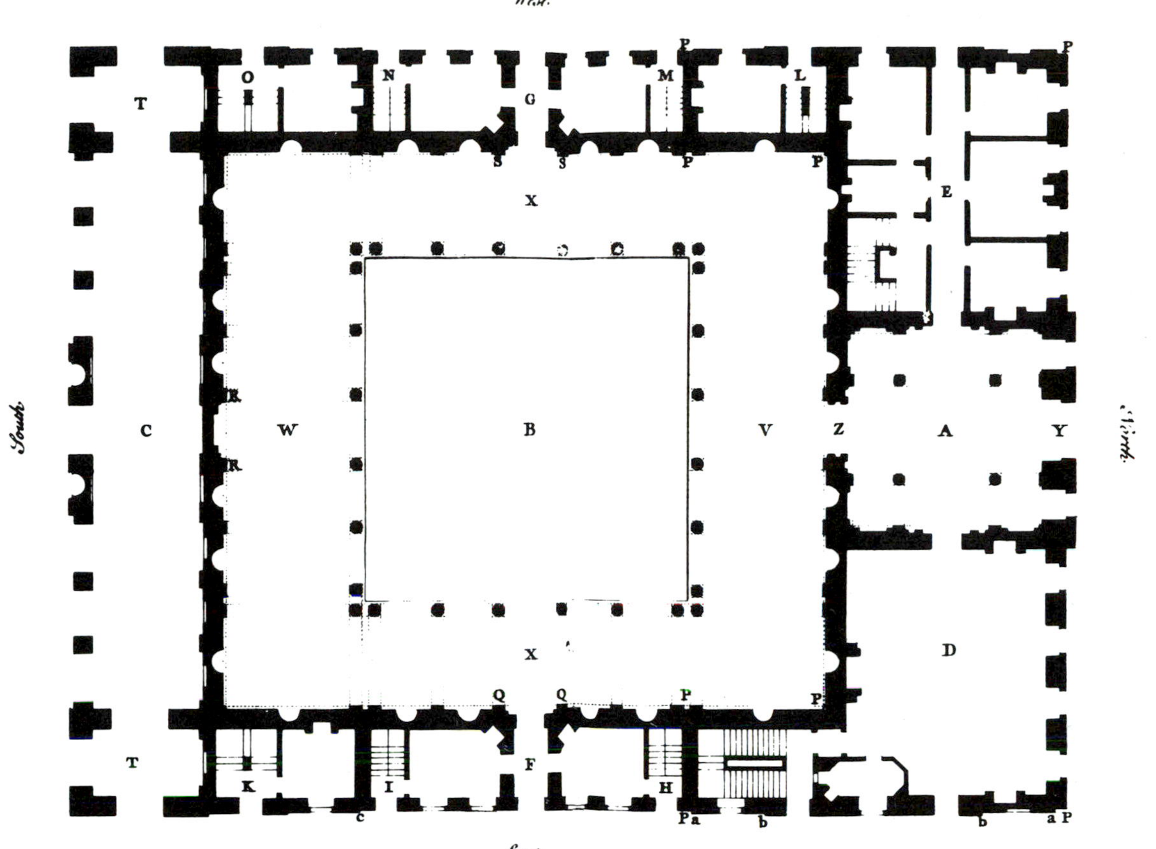

Figure 11.11 *Wood's Bristol Exchange, plan (1745)*
Source: J. Wood (1745) *A Description of the Exchange, Bristol*, British Library

graphical area or a class of goods such as silk, cloth, groceries and drugs, salt, and jewellery. In addition insurance (or 'ship') brokers and dyers and bays-factors had their own spots (Figure 11.10). The upper level shops gradually fell into disuse to be replaced by the offices of the Royal Exchange Assurance and other companies. Densely packed round the site were dozens of coffee houses and clubs to cater for the merchants.

The provincial exchanges had to raise capital by attaching other facilities. In Bristol John Wood the Elder prepared two designs; in the executed version (1740–5) a two storey Palladian structure was placed on a heavily rusticated base. The merchants entered through an axially placed hall, or two smaller lateral entrances (Figure 11.11). Facing outwards, and impermeable from the exchange, was a covered market; the building also contained coffee houses, a tavern and commercial offices.

Edinburgh's exchange designed by John Adam in 1753 included many shops, houses, two printing houses, three coffee houses and a custom house. The trading court was never popular, and even in Edinburgh's climate the merchants continued their business largely in the street. Manchester's of 1729, adjacent to the market, had a colonnaded court at ground level topped by a splendid assembly room which not only served for balls and receptions, but lectures and exhibitions of textile machinery. The much larger one of 1809 also had a coffee house and newsroom. By then cotton was the main commodity. The 1749–54 Liverpool Exchange was commissioned from John Wood the Elder on the strength and following the precedent of Bristol. The upper floor was the town hall.

Dealing in stocks and shares started off in the Royal Exchange in the brokers' 'walk'. But by the 1690s they were transferring their activities to nearby coffee houses and taverns, an arrangement that survived till Peacock's Stock Exchange was built in Capel Court in 1801–2 with a central arcaded nave-like apartment with clerestory windows.

Whether transaction is of real or symbolic goods, we have already seen examples of the association between its spaces – the markets and exchanges – and those where the laws which controlled the exchange were administered. The colonnaded or arcaded market, permeable to the public space round it and covered by an upper level guildhall, council chamber or court, became omnipresent in Europe and European colonies. What were the origins of this link?

The most convincing answer, tested on English data, has been provided by Tittler (1991). His point of departure is a critique of Rigold's survey (1968) which claimed to establish two types. The earlier was the 'hall' either on a single storey or above an undercroft of store rooms, cellars and vaults, with ecclesiastical, civic and legal functions for moots, guilds, manorial courts and town councils. Often it housed associated records, archives, treasure, maces, armoury and ceremonial robes. The ground level and later upper level manorial hall was the precedent. Rigold says that the next stage, which develops from the first, is the hall above an open public market with either an external or internal staircase. Tittler produces evidence that this is not how it happened.

Between about 1500 and 1640 the two types existed and developed in parallel. The former was enclosed, and was often tightly inserted into blocks with only its street face exposed. The latter was usually open on all, or at least three, sides and Tittler provides evidence from Dorset and other counties. As the power of the manors and guilds waned after the Reformation and town government became more autonomous and increasingly tied to the mercantile economy – often the mayor and leading town officials also being the most prominent merchants – the second type began to dominate the first. This, rather than evolution, explains its greater survival rate.

Both types accommodated other functions – lock-ups and gaols, houses of correction, school rooms, kitchens for both banquets and feeding the poor, granaries, almshouses, hospitals and blind asylums, and common ovens. In both, the 'hall' element underwent an evolution from a simple, unitary space to one subdivided for several functions. Town government and court were combined by the manorial court or moot, and one space and furniture layout served for both. The first elaboration was their separation – the former into a council system with two tiers, usually of 12 and 24 or 24 and 48, with clerks, recorders and serjeants at arms – the latter into a court room with a jury room. The mayor often needed a 'parlour' adjacent to the council chamber, and something like an accounting office ('chequer', 'guild' or 'booth' hall, or 'tolsey'). The court function was also elaborated by dividing the Mayor's court, and later the magistrates', from the Assizes.

The increasing power represented by these buildings is clear not only in their functional and spatial articulation but also in formal features of clocks, bell cupolas, balconies – both for public ceremony and for surveying the open market square – and ceremonial staircases, heraldic emblems, flags and iconography relating to the town's history. Stylistically the plain vernacular gradually gave way to self-conscious early Renaissance, then Palladian and eventually neo-Classical forms.

During the three centuries it took to reach Gothic forms, a powerful civic icon had developed. In Chapter 2 we have seen the 'memory' of the open ground floor in the form of a blind arcade or colonnade which formed the base of so many nineteenth century town halls. Sometimes this resulted from the actual filling-in of the earlier space to convert it to civic use.

PART V
CONCLUDING REMARKS

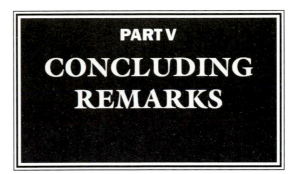

The two library classification systems in worldwide use place 'architecture' in class 700, the 'fine arts'. In Dewey's it is at 720, between 'landscape gardening' and 'sculpture'. Much of what I have explored here is encapsulated by this 720, architecture-as-art. The alternative, architecture-as-technology, never became sufficiently strong to cause 'architecture' to shift to class 600, 'useful arts', where 'building' (690) does appear. Nevertheless these two definitions of architecture did become concrete in the institutions of architectural education in late eighteenth century France, the first in the *École des Beaux Arts* and the second in the *École Polytechnique*. The two systems, in various mixtures, are still the basis of architects' education throughout the world. We have seen how both theory and practice were able, through them, to avoid treating buildings as social objects. In whose interest was this?

During our period new types of building, of unprecedented size and complexity, were needed. At the same time new methods of financing them arose and the social context of architectural practice changed. All this disturbed traditional ways of commissioning buildings. Sponsors, whether public or private, could no longer take it for granted that alongside overt functional purposes, the covert programme of all buildings – to reproduce the sponsors' position of power which gave them access to the resources to invest in the first place – would be achieved. Control over the design outcomes now had to be exercised by so defining the task that certain questions went unasked and therefore by default certain outcomes were assured.

It worked something like this. An unwritten pact between investors and architects defined architects either as artists or as engineers. The former was, and remains, dominant. These definitions were embedded in the map of knowledge in libraries, in educational establishments, books and journals, the media, historical research and even in the workplaces ('studio'). The pact appeared to give architects unlimited freedom over questions of form, though in reality Royal Fine Arts Commissions, planning law, and restrictive clauses in briefs clawed back much of that. Vigorous critical debate on form, in which architects' critical energies were totally absorbed to the extent that they could (metaphorically) kill each other if they wished, was the order of the day. Alternatively technological performance was defined as their distinguishing skill.

In return the sponsors took charge of the brief as an explicit expression of their functional demands. But to put it beyond debate, it was given the appearance of a neutral text (as if language could ever be innocent) prescribing 'objective' technical and programmatic requirements. An appropriately neutered language was developed.

Over spatial relations there was silence, on both sides. They were achieved by implicit reproduction of those structures which had, in the past, worked well for the covert programme. The formal and technical inventions were radical enough to hide the deep conservatism of these spatial solutions.

The pact ensured that asymmetries of power in society, and impediments to the bonds which are so subversive of such relations, were kept intact in buildings. And that is pretty well the situation today. There is a real difficulty in challenging it because this accepted discourse has taken on the power of a myth. It is classless, stretching from Royalty to community tenants' groups.

I have tried to provide some pointers towards the kind of analytical tools which may penetrate the myth. I have developed them in the context of that period when society and its buildings were shaken to their roots. If the tools have helped to illuminate anything about those buildings, they may be robust enough to use today. What might they be useful for?

Most obviously they might sharpen criticism and scholarship and, therefore, teaching. But how they might affect the practice of design is less clear. Over the years of teaching these ideas I have regularly come across a few students, often the most gifted, who at the end of a course expressed doubts about wishing to continue as architects. In part they had experienced a kind of awakening, which gave rise to contradictions which their youthful enthusiasm found difficult to accept. In part it was a feeling that analytical skill would somehow be at loggerheads with creative design, or even destroy it. I then presented them with the real options which they would face in practice.

First, they might be lucky enough to find clients with whom they share values; for those clients the analytical skills of the designers they employ simply help to elucidate the roots of their shared values.

Second, if they are in possession of skills which put them a step ahead, or rather a step deeper, than their clients, architects can initiate a mutual learning process during design which will generate solutions satisfying to both.

Third, in the absence of either of the first two, architects may have to design by 'subversion'. That is, use their unique professional skills at a level which only they can fully grasp. This involves interpretations of the brief, finding forms and creating spatial structures which either now, or in the future, will open as many doors as possible toward shared power relations and freedom for bonds to develop. Such properties will be beyond the apparent demands of the brief. In fact many architects do have a self-image as servants of the public who add to society greater value than that which the specific client seeks. But really to achieve this requires the designer to possess analytical skills which put – and keep – her or him well ahead of the layperson in understanding meaning.

It may consist of a richer, perhaps even ambiguous, interpretation of the brief; of finding a technology which allows spatial structures to be cheaply altered; of providing an information system which allows for effective day-to-day control by users; or of using a formal language which does not create overpowering meanings *for* people but is capable of receiving meanings *from* them. To negotiate such results requires skills of a high order.

Finally a fourth situation confronts all architects from time to time. The sponsor may demand services for a task in which they cannot participate. Most of us would claim that under no circumstances would we have worked on the design for Auschwitz; or, today, in the design of a South African apartheid-based housing scheme. Everyone draws a line somewhere, although where is a complex personal decision, especially when commissions are hard to get and economic survival may be at stake. But even line-drawing needs skills which go beyond 'gut feelings'.

The fact that architects have it in their power to create objects of staggering beauty, which respond to people's deepest desires, makes the choice of practice agonising. A pointer towards 'heavenly mansions' – buildings which have structure but at the same time leave freedom for just relations and strong bonds – was given by Piranesi in the mid-eigheenth century. I have described before (Markus 1982, 1989) how his *Carceri* etchings – which have nothing to do with real prisons – represent two worlds. One is subterranean – dark, massive, full of ambiguous machines which could be intruments of torture or machines for construction, and paradoxical spaces – 'staircases leading to nowhere, impossible perspectives and unfinished vaults'. Through an opening there is often visible an upper world where normal Classical buildings sit in the light of day. He seems to suggest that it is *their* order and reason which sits on, truly imprisons, a hidden world of dangerous freedom. He may be saying more than this – that the creation of order which is the point of all architecture has a paradox at its core. The rules, classifications and systems needed are alienating and imprisoning. To cope with the paradox without despair may require architects to adopt the creative resignation of the poet. I quoted T. S. Eliot (1944) at the start of this book. A line from that same poem is as good a way to finish as I can imagine: 'For us, there is only the trying. The rest is not our business'.

Notes

1 The shape of the argument

1 It may be surprising, considering how much I have been influenced by the theories, practices and ideas of Saussure, Barthes, Lévi-Strauss, Eco and structuralism and semiotics in general – especially in my analysis of meaning in social relations and my making 'meaning' approximately equivalent to 'the signified' – that I should start my discussion of language with a source in the field of material culture. The reason is that Kouwenhoven and others in that field have used concepts of meaning and communication in studies of material objects in ways which make it but a small step to apply them to buildings.

2 A typical case is the conversion of the Deux-Nèthes Carmelite Church into a law court, with the judge's seat placed into the apse (National Archives, Paris Series N. III no. 4839).

3 The bibliography lists a key work by each of these prolific authors.

3 Formation

1 Helen Clayton (undated) has given a brief history. The manuscript minutes from 9 February 1798 are in the archives of the Church of Ireland College, Dublin. Susan Parkes (1984: 21) suggests that the day schools may have opened earlier.

2 Some drawings and photographs survive in the archives of the Primary Building Branch, Department of Education, Dublin.

3 *A Plan for the Formation and Establishment of Sunday Schools; To which is prefixed An Address on the Importance and Utility of those Institutions*, (1806) quotes Friars' Mount as a model. (The *Plan* is anonymous but the author *may* be Hartwell Horne, whose handwritten inscription in the British Library copy [c. 20. 8307(2)] claims this.)

4 The school is shown in an outline on Horwood's 1819 26 inch to 1 mile map and its dimensions correspond to the 1806 description referred to in note 3 above.

5 An undated leaflet in Stockport public library refers to writing classes in 'one open room which will be fitted up' on 'the third storey'. This suggests that before writing rooms in the attic were constructed, use of the 'Large Room' was envisaged. The leaflet probably dates from 1804–5.

6 Two Manchester examples are St Matthew's, Liverpool Road (1827) and St John's, Gartside Street (1827) Sunday schools whose plans appear on the 1850 ordnance survey map.

7 Lancaster (1809a) argues that Chevalier Paulet's school founded at Paris in 1777 used 'mutual' instruction and invalidates Bell's claim as its 'inventor'. Pictet de Rochemont in the *Journal de Genève*, 29 December 1787 and 5 and 12 January 1788 describes Paulet's school in detail. It was organised in a military hierarchy to educate military orphans in geography, history, literature, mathematics, art and design, music, dancing and military skills. 'Officers' and 'sub-officers' were children who, in turn, instructed their fellows. Practical skills in tailoring, rope-making, joinery and sculpture were also taught. Ramon de la Sagra in *Voyage en Hollande et en Belgique etc.* (1839: 58) traces the beginnings to America; he claims it crossed the Atlantic to Germany in 1788, and then to Holland in 1792 where it was perfected by Schimmelpennink. In *L'Enseignement Mutuel etc.* (1818: 11) Hamel describes M. Herbault's 'mutual' school at the Hôspice de la Pitié in Paris set up in 1747.

8 The third edition of *Infant Education* (1825) became internationally known, in part because it was so detailed, including a model plan. For instance, Wortheimer translated it into German and published it in Vienna in 1826. It was this translation which was used by Terez Brunszvik as a model for central Europe's first infant school opened in Buda (Budapest) in 1828. Its detailed history is given by Ottó Vág (1980).

9 The Rev. H. Yarnitzky (ed.) *St Patrick's, Manchester:*

Centenary Souvenir, 1832–1932 (1932: 17) refers to the 'school on the housetops'. Adshead's map of Manchester (1850) shows *half* the terrace as a 'school' but this is likely to be a graphic convention for showing the upper level, for on the O.S. map of the same date the entire block is shown as a row of terrace houses.

10 Seaborne (1971) gives the cost per place for seven of Kendall's schools and eleven of Clarke's, taken from H. E. Kendall's *Designs for schools and school houses etc.* (1847) and J. Clarke's *Schools and school houses etc.* (1852) respectively.

4 *Re-formation*

1 These included Edinburgh (1738), York (1740), Bristol (1742), Exeter (1744), Liverpool (1749), Shrewsbury (1740s), Newcastle (1751), Gloucester (1775), Manchester (1769), Dumfries (1778), Hull (1782), Northampton (1793) and Dundee (1794).

2 Arnold Zuckermann (1976–7: 222–34) describes both Triewald's and Sutton's work but does not refer to Sutton's *An historical account of a new method for extracting foul air etc.* the second edition of which was published in 1749.

3 A comprehensive summary of ventilation and hygiene in military, naval and penal institutions was given in two unpublished papers at the International Colloquium on penal history (eighteenth and nineteenth centuries) held at Fontevraud, France in September 1982. These were 'Purifier l'air des Prisons' by Alain Corbin, University of Tours and 'Les Médecins des prisons en France au XIXe siècle' by Jacques Léonard, University of Rennes II.

4 The entire plan is given in Ochsner and Sturm's *The Organisation, Construction and Management of Hospitals* (1907: 467). Details of a ward block appear in Isambard Brunel's *The Life of Isambard Kingdom Brunel: Civil Engineer* (1870: 470). Both are reproduced in Thompson and Goldin (1975: figures 157 and 158).

5 Louis S. Greenbaum (1975: 43–56) gives a detailed account.

6 I made an early review in 'Pattern of the Law', *Architectural Review*, 1954 vol. 116 no. 694 pp. 251–6. Other useful surveys of examples and literature are in Pevsner (1979: 159–68); Rosenau (1970: 77–96); Tomlinson (1980: 94–119); and, the most complete recent monograph, Evans (1982). Of course one of the most illuminating but, at the same time controversial, interpretations – partly on account of its somewhat ahistorical base – is Foucault's (1977). A more discursive account of Foucault's approach is reported in a dialogue 'Jeremy Bentham: le panoptique' under the title 'L'oeil de pouvoir'. The French version was printed for the National Assembly in 1791 and it, together with a translation of the English version and followed by a postface by Michelle Perrot, was reprinted in 1977. Melossi and Pavarini (1981) argue that the prison embodies a special version of the production relations of the modern factory, and use Italy and America for their main evidence. For pre-industrial revolution development (but not of buildings) Weisser (1982) gives a coherent account. One of the most insightful accounts is given in Ignatieff (1978).

7 The best account of the complex and of Carlo Fontana's involvement is Braham and Hager (1977: 137–50 and figures 332–72). The prison was made famous partly through Howard's description and illustration of it from 1770 onwards.

8 Manuscript and typescript notes supplied by Mrs M. E. Robson, Belper (1983) explain the operation of the revolving chamber. Fitton and Wadsworth (1958: 219–21) describe the Round Mill and also refer to Simon Goodrich's Journals which for August 1804 describe the building.

5 *Cleanliness is next to godliness*

1 The design is shown in an engraving at the Musée Carnavalet, Paris 'Perruquier, baigneur, étuviste, bain de Poitevin établis sur la Seine 1761' (item Topo. 9c). The history of the Seine and other Paris baths is described in the exhibition catalogue 'Deux Siècles d'Architecture Sportive à Paris: piscines, gymnase …', Délégation à l'action artistique de la ville de Paris and Direction de la Jeunesse et des Sports, Paris, 1984.

2 The swimming pool built in the 1770s with its rows of seventeen changing rooms is already shown on Bickley's 1780 map (Birmingham Public Library, Archives Department, item 383069). On Sherriff's 1808 map it is labelled 'pleasure bath' (item MS 919). Various authors quote late eighteenth century editions of William Hutton's *An History of Birmingham*, at which time there were seven baths. William West in *The History, Topography and Directory of Warwickshire etc*, (1830) describes ten baths.

7 *Visible knowledge*

1 The plates are in *Palaty Sanktpeterburgskoi Imperatorskoi Akademii nauk Biblioteki i Kunstkemerg*, (1741). A good commentary appears in N. V. Guberti (1891: 147–51); and a more modern one by Oleg Neverov in Impey and McGregor (1985).

2 Elmslie's drawings for a three-floor museum are in the Public Records Office, Chancery Lane, London (M.P.E. 915, no. 237 in printed catalogue).

8 *Ephemeral knowledge*

1 I am indebted to Hyde (1988) for the following summary of panoramas and their precursors.

9 *Invisible knowledge*

1 Versions of the design are in Caroe (1963); a set of framed drawings at the Institution; and a number of designs in the BAL/RIBA Drawings Collection, London, catalogued under 'Webster'. The drawings I have illustrated are not necessarily part of a consistent set but have been chosen to highlight specific features in the development of the design.

10 *Production*

1 Nemes Márta 'Magyarország első panoptikonja: a budapesti-óbudai selyemgombolyitó manufaktura' (Hungary's first panopticon: the silk cocoon unwinding factory at Óbuda, Budapest' *Művészettörténeti Értesitő* (1984; no. 4, 261–70). I am indebted to Nemes Márta and Szirmai János for the sources of illustrations and for the information on the cocoon unwinding factory.

2 For example: *Dictionary of National Biography*; 'The Old Scottish Independents', *Transactions of the Congregational Historical Society*, (1920–23: 181–9; Ross (1900: ch.X); and an anonymous pamphlet (undated: 162–77) in Glasgow University library entitled *David Dale*.

Bibliography

Achilles, R. (1976) 'Baroque Monastic Library Archtecture', *The Journal of Library History*, XI: 249–55.

Adburgham, A. (1964) *Shops and Shopping, 1800–1914*, London: Allen & Unwin.

—— (1979) *Shopping in Style: London from the Restoration to Edwardian Elegance*, London: Thames and Hudson.

Agnew, J.-C. (1979) 'The Thresholds of Exchange: Speculation on the Market', *Radical History Review* 21: 99–118.

Alberti, L. B. (1485, 1980) *The Art of Building in Ten Books*, trans. J. Rykwert and R. Taverner, Cambridge, Mass.: MIT. Press.

Alcott, W. A. (1832) *Essay on the Construction of School-houses etc.*, Boston: Hilliard, Gray, Little and Wilkins.

Alley, H. (1598) 'Caveat' in I. Archer, C. Barron and V. Harding (eds) 1988, *Hugh Alley's Caveat: the Markets of London in 1598*, London: London Topographical Society Publication no. 137.

Anderson, P. (1980) 'The Leeds Workhouse under the Old Poor Law: 1726–1834', *Transactions of the Thoresby Society* 17 (2): 75–113.

Anonymous, (1741) *Palaty Sanktpeterburgskoi Imperatorskoi Akademii nauk Biblioteki i Kunstkemery*, St Petersburg: Imperial Academy of Sciences.

—— (1786) *An Account of the Work-Houses in Great Britain in the Year MDCCXXXII etc.*, 3rd edn, London.

—— (1802) 'An Account of the Establishment and Support of Sunday Schools etc.', *The Wesleyan Magazine*: 389–90.

—— (1806) *A Plan for the Formation and Establishment of Sunday Schools: to which is prefixed An Address on the Importance and Utility of those Institutions*, London.

—— (undated) *David Dale*, pamphlet in Glasgow University Library, no publication details.

Architects' Journal (1989) 8 February: 6.

Architectural Magazine (1835) II: 511–2.

Art Journal (1857): 46.

Artz, F. B. (1946) 'L'enseignement technique en France pendant l'époque révolutionaire 1789–1815', *Revue Historique* 196: 256–86 and 385–407.

Ashmore, O. (1969) *The Industrial Archeology of Lancashire*, Newton Abbot: David & Charles.

Ashpitel, A. and Whichcord, J. (1851) *Observation on Baths and Washhouses*, London.

—— (1853) *Baths and Wash-houses: an Account etc.*, London.

Audin-Rouvière, J. M. (1793) *Essai sur la Topographie Physique et Médicale de Paris etc.*, Paris.

Bacon, F. (1594) *Gesta Grayorum*, London.

Bahmueller, C. F. (1981) *The National Charity Company: Jeremy Bentham's Silent Revolution*, Berkeley: University of California Press.

Baker, D. (undated) *Workhouses in the Potteries, City of Stoke on Trent historic buildings survey*, Stoke on Trent. (1984 is the date suggested by the Guildhall Library, London).

Ball, M. (1983) *Housing Policy and Economic Power*, London: Methuen.

Baltard, V. and Callet, F. (1862) *Monographie des Halles Centrales de Paris etc.*, Paris.

Baly, P. P. (1852) *A Statement of the Proceedings . . . Baths and Washhouses for the Labouring Classes etc.*, London.

Bamford, P. W. (1973) *Fighting Ships and Prisons: the Mediterranean Galleys of France in the Age of Louis XIV*, Minneapolis: University of Minnesota Press.

Barlow, P. (1836) *Treatise on the Manufactures and Machinery of Great Britain*, London.

Barnard, H. (1848) *School Architecture etc.*, New York: Barnes.

—— (1850) *School Architecture etc.*, 4th edn., New York: Barnes.

Battie, W. (1758) *A Treatise on Madness*, London.

Beccaria, C. B. (1764) *Dei Delitti e delle Pene*, Livorno.

Bell, A. (1797) *An Experiment in Education*, London.
——— (1808a) *The Madras School, or Elements of Tuition etc.*, London.
——— (1808b) *Sketch of a National Institution for Training up the Children of the Poor etc.*, London.
——— (1827) *A Manual of Public and Private Education etc*, London.
Bellers, J. (1696) *Proposals for Raising a Colledge of Industry*, rpt in G. Clarke (ed.) (1987) *John Bellers his Life, Times and Writings*, London: Routledge & Kegan Paul.
Bender, J. (1987) *Imagining the Penitentiary: Fiction and the Architecture of Mind in Eighteenth Century England*, Chicago: University of Chicago Press.
Bennett, E. T. (1830 and 1831) *The Gardens and Menagerie of the Zoological Society Delineated*, London.
Bentham, J. (1791a) *Panopticon; or the Inspection House*, London.
——— (1791b) *Panopticon; Postscript*, London.
——— (1816) *Proposals for Establishing in the Metropolis a Day School etc.*, London.
Bentmann, R. and Mueller, M. (1975) *La Villa, Architecture de Domination*, Bruxelles: Architecture et Recherches/P. Mardaga.
Berg, M. (1985) *The Age of Manufactures, 1700–1820*, London: Fontana.
Bergdoll, B. (1987) 'The Architecture of Isolation: M-R. Penchaud's Quarantine Hospital in the Mediterranean', *Architectural Association Files* 14: 3–13.
Berman, M. (1978) *Social Change and Scientific Organisation: the Royal Institution, 1799–1844*, Ithaca, NY: Cornell University Press.
Bernard, T. (1809) *Of the Education of the Poor etc.*, London: Society for Bettering the Condition of the Poor.
Bilby, T. and Ridgeway, R. B. (1834) *The Infant Teacher's Assistant*, 3rd edn, London.
Blackman, J. (1962–3) 'The food supply of an industrial town: a study of Sheffield's public markets 1780–1900', *Business History* V, 1 and 2: 83–97.
Blomfield, J. (1933) *St George's, 1733–1933*, London: The Medici Society.
Blondel, J.-F. (1771–7) *Cours d'architecture . . . donnée en 1750 et les années suivantes*, Paris.
Bodey, H. A. (1971) 'Coffin Row, Linthwaite', *Industrial Archeology* 8 (4): 381–91.
Bodleian Library (1982) *James Gibbs, 1682–1754 and the Radcliffe Camera*, Oxford: The Bodleian Library.
Bolzoni, L. (1980) 'L'"invenzione" dello Stanzino di Francesco I', *Le Arti del Principato Mediceo*, Florence: SPES.
Boog Watson, W. N. (1979) 'Early baths in Edinburgh', *The Book of the Old Edinburgh Club* XXXIV (2).
Boullée, E.-L. (c. 1781–97) *Architecture, Essay on Art*, trans. by H. Rosenau (ed.) (1974), London: Academy Editions.
Bourdieu, P. (1971) 'The Berber House' in M. Douglas (ed.) (1973) *Rules and Meanings: an Anthropology of Everyday Knowledge*, Harmondsworth: Penguin.
Braham, A. (1980) *The Architecture of the French Enlightenment*, London: Thames and Hudson.
Braham, A. and Hager, H. (1977) *Carlo Fontana: the Drawings at Windsor Castle*, London: Zwemmer.
Braudel, F. (1982) *Civilization and Capitalism, 15th–18th Century* vol. 1 *The Structures of Everyday Life: the Limits of the Possible*, trans. M. Kochan, revised S. Reynolds, London: Fontana.
Brears, P. C. D. (1984) 'Temples of the Muses: the Yorkshire Philosophical Museums, 1820–50', *Museums Journal* 84 (1): 3–19.
British and Foreign Schools Society (1831) *Manual of the System of Primary Instruction etc.*, London: The Society.
British Parliamentary Papers (BPP) (1835) *First Annual Report of the Poor Law Commissioners*, 35.
——— (1857–8) *Return of Cost of Building Workhouses in England and Wales 1840–1858*, (337), 49, I.
——— (1870) *Report of the Commissioners of the Inquiry into Primary Education in Ireland*, XXVIII.i, vol. I, part I.
Britton, J. and Pugin, A. (1828) *Illustrations of the Public Buildings of London etc.*, vol. 2, London.
Brougham, H. (1825) *Practical Observations upon the Education of the People etc.*, 15th edn, London.
Brown, N. O. (1947) *Hermes the Thief*, Madison: University of Wisconsin Press.
Browne, O'D. T. D., (1947) *The Rotunda Hospital, 1745–1945*, Edinburgh: E. and S. Livingstone.
Browne, W. A. F. (1837) *What Asylums Were, Are and Ought To Be*, Edinburgh.
Brunel, I. (1870) *The Life of Isambard Kingdom Brunel: Civil Engineer*, London: Longmans Green.
Buckingham, J. S. (1849) *National Evils and Practical Remedies*, London.
Builder (1851) IX, 418: 834.
Builder (1852) X, 502: 597.
Building Design (1989) 17 March: 60.
Bukowski, M. (1973) 'Industrial Buildings in Upper Silesia', *Industrial Archeology* 10, 4: 357–66 and 449–55.
Burgoyne, M. (1829) *An Address to the Governors and Directors of the Public Charity Schools etc.*, London.
Burnett, J. (1989) *Plenty and Want: a Social History of Food in England 1815–Today*, 3rd edn, London: Routledge.
Burton, J. (1830) *List of the Animals in the Gardens of the Zoological Society*, London.
Bushman, J. S. (1851) *The Moral and Sanitary Aspects of the New Cattle Market etc.*, London.
Butt, J. (ed.) (1971) *Robert Owen, Prince of Cotton Spinners: A Symposium*, Newton Abbot: David & Charles.
Byrne, K. R. (1986) 'The Royal Dublin Society and the Advancement of popular Science in Ireland, 1731–1860', *History of Education* 15 (2): 81–8.
Caffyn, L. (1986) *Workers' Housing in Yorkshire, 1750–1920*, London: HMSO.

Campbell, C. (1987) *The Romantic Ethic and the Spirit of Modern Consumerism*, Oxford: Blackwell.

Caroe, A. D. R. (1963) *The House of the Royal Institution*, London: The Royal Institution.

Carpenter, K. E. (1972) 'European Industrial Exhibitions before 1851 and their Publications', *Technology and Culture* 13 (3): 465–86.

Catarsi E. and Genovesi, G. (1985) *L'infanzia a scuola etc.*, Bergamo: Juvenalia.

Chadwick, E. (1842) *Report . . . on an Inquiry into the Sanitary Condition of the Labouring Population of Great Britain*, London: HMSO.

Chalklin, C. W. (1980) 'Capital Expenditure on Building for Cultural Purposes in Provincial England, 1730–1830', *Business History* XXII, 1: 51–70.

—— (ed.) (1984) *New Maidstone Gaol Order Book, 1805–23*, Maidstone: Kent Archaeological Society.

Chalmers Mitchell, P. (1929) *Centenary History of the Zoological Society of London*, London: The Society.

Chambers, R. (1850) *Chambers' Papers for the People*, vol. III, Edinburgh.

Chapman, S. D. (1971) 'The History of Working-Class Housing in Nottingham during the Industrial Revolution' in S. D. Chapman (ed.) *The History of Working-class Housing: a Symposium*, Newton Abbot: David & Charles.

—— (1974) 'The Textile Factory before Arkwright: a Typology of Factory Development', *Business History Review*, XLVIII(4): 451–78.

Church of Ireland Training College (undated) *The Centenary Book*, Dublin: Falconer (possibly 1911).

Cipolla, C. M. (1967) *Clocks and Culture, 1300–1700*, London: Collins.

Clark, H. O. (1927–8) 'Notes on horse-mills', *Transactions of the Newcomen Society* VIII: 31–9.

Clark, J. W. (1901) *The Care of Books etc.*, Cambridge: Cambridge University Press.

Clarke, J. (1852) *Schools and School Houses*, London.

Clark-Kennedy, A. E. (1962) *The London: a Study in the Voluntary Hospital System*, 2 vols, London: Pitman Medical.

Clayburn La Force, J. (1964) 'Royal Textile Factories in Spain, 1700–1800', *The Journal of Economic History* XXIV, 3: 337–63.

Clayton, H. (undated) *To School Without Shoes: A Brief History of the Sunday School Society for Ireland 1809 to 1979* (no publication details).

Cleland, J. (1816) *Annals of Glasgow etc.*, 2 vols, Glasgow.

Cliff, P. B. (1986) *The Rise and Development of the Sunday School Movement in England 1780–1980*, Redhill: National Christian Education Council.

Coad, J. G. (1983) *Historic Architecture of the Royal Navy: an Introduction*, London: Gollancz.

Cochin, J.-D.-M. (1845) *Manuel des Salles d'Asile*, 3rd edn, Paris: Hachette.

Coleridge, S. T. (1817) 'Lay Sermons' in R. J. White (ed.) *Collected Works of S. T. Coleridge*, London: Routledge & Kegan Paul.

Colquhoun, P. (1800) *A Treatise on the Police of the Metropolis*, London.

—— (1806) *A New and Appropriate System of Education for the Labouring People*, rpt 1971, Shannon: Irish University Press.

Colvin, H. M. (1954) *A Biographical Dictionary of English Architects*, Cambridge, Mass.: Harvard University Press.

—— (1978) *A Biographical Dictionary of British Architects 1600–1840*, 2nd edn, London: Murray.

Colvin, H. M., Ransome, D. R. and Summerson, J. (1975) *The History of the King's Works*, vol. III, London: HMSO.

Connolly, J. (1847) *The Construction and Government of Lunatic Asylums etc.*, rpt with introduction by R. Hunter and I. Macalpine 1968, London: Dawson.

Considérant, V. (1834) *Considération Sociales sur l'Architectonique*, Paris.

Cooter, R. (1984) *The Cultural Meaning of Popular Science: Phrenology and the Organisation of Consent in Nineteenth Century Britain*, Cambridge: Cambridge University Press.

Corbin, A. (1982) 'Purifier l'Air des Prisons', paper given at the International Colloquium on Penal History (18th and 19th Centuries), Fontevraud, France, September.

Corry, J. (1817) *The History of Macclesfield*, London.

Council on Education (1845) *Minutes of the Committee of Council on Education, 1844*, I, London: HMSO.

Cousin, V. (1833) *Rapport sur l'État de l'Instruction Publique dans quelque pays d'Allemagne et particulièrement en Prusse*, Paris.

Couturat, L. (1901) *La Logique de Leibniz*, Paris.

Crabbe, G. (1810) Letter XVIII of 'The Borough', 'The Poor and their Dwellings' *The Life and Poems of the Rev. George Crabbe*, vol. 3, (1834), London.

Cruttwell, R. (1789) *Plans of the Sunday Schools and Schools of Industry established in the City of Bath*, Bath.

Curnock, N. (ed.) (1909) The Journal of the Rev. John Wesley, A.M., Vol. II, London: Charles H. Kelly.

Curtis, S. J. (1967) *History of Education in Great Britain*, 7th edn, London: University Tutorial Press.

Daly, C. (ed.) (1857) Revue de l'Architecture et des Travaux Publics: 15.

Damisch, H. (1982) 'The Museum Device: Note on Institutional Change', *Lotus International* 35 (II): 9.

Davis, J. C. (1981) *Utopia and the Ideal Society: A Study of English Utopian Writing 1516–1700*, Cambridge: Cambridge University Press.

Defoe, D. (1742) *A Tour thro' the Whole Island of Great Britain etc.*, rev. edn, S. Richardson (1842), London.

Demangeon, A. and Fortier, B. (1978) *Les Vaisseaux et les Villes*, Bruxelles: Mardaga.

Denholm, J. (1798) *The History of Glasgow*, Glasgow.

Derrida, J. (1986) 'Pointe de Folie – Maintenant l'Architecture; Bernard Tschumi:La Case Vide –

La Villette, 1985', *Architectural Association Files* 12: 65–75.

Derry, T. K. and Williams, T. I. (1960) *Short History of Technology*, Oxford: Oxford University Press.

Deux Siècles . . . Paris (1984) *Deux Siècles d'Architecture Sportive à Paris: Piscines, Gymnase etc.*, Exhibition Catalogue, Paris: Délégation à l'action artistique de la ville de Paris et Direction de la Jeunesse et des Sports.

Devillers, C. and Huet, B. (1981) *Le Creusot: Naissance et Développement d'une Ville Industrielle 1782–1914*, Champ Vallon: Seyssel.

Dickson, M. (1986) *Teacher Extraordinary: Joseph Lancaster 1778–1838*, Lewes: The Book Guild Ltd.

Digby, A. (1978) *Pauper Palaces*, London: Routledge & Kegan Paul.

—— (1985) *Madness, Morality and Medicine: a Study of the York Retreat 1794–1914*, Cambridge: Cambridge University Press.

Dilke, O. A. W. (1971) *The Roman Land Surveyors; an Introduction to the Agrimensores*, Newton Abbot: David & Charles.

Dolbey, G. W. (1964) *The Architectural Expression of Methodism – the First Hundred Years*, London: The Epworth Press.

Donnachie, I. (1971) 'Orbiston: a Scottish Owenite community 1825–28' in J. Butt (ed.) *Robert Owen, Prince of Cotton Spinners: a Symposium*, Newton Abbot: David & Charles.

Donnelly, M. (1983) *Managing the Mind*, London: Tavistock Publications.

Douglas, M. (1966) *Purity and Danger: an Analysis of the Concepts of Pollution and Taboo*, London: Routledge & Kegan Paul.

Duncan, C. and Wallach, A. (1980) 'The Universal Survey Museum', *Art History* 3(4): 442–69.

Duppa, B. F. (1838) *A Manual for Mechanics' Institutions*, London: Society for the Diffusion of Useful Knowledge.

Durand, J.-N.-L. (1801) *Recueil et Parallèle des Édifices de tous Genres, Anciens et Modernes*, Paris.

—— (1802–9) *Précis de Leçons d'Architecture Données à l'École Polytechnique*, Paris.

Dwellings for the Working Classes (1918) *Report on Dwellings for the Working Classes*, Cd 9191, London: HMSO.

Eagleton, T. (1976) *Marxist Literary Criticism*, London: Methuen.

Eco, U. (1986) 'Function and Sign: Semiotics of Architecure' in M. Gottdiener and A. Ph. Lagopoulos (eds) *The City and the Sign: an Introduction to Urban Semiotics*, New York: Columbia University Press. First published 1969.

—— (1987) *Travels in Hyper-reality*, London: Picador.

Edinburgh Review (1807–8) 'Lancaster's Improvements in Education', XI: 61–73.

Eliot, T. S. (1944) *Four Quartets*, London: Faber & Faber.

Ellis, A. (1956) *The Penny Universities: a History of the Coffee-houses*, London: Secker & Warburg.

Evans, R. (1971) 'Bentham's Panopticon: an Incident in the Social History of Architecture', *Architectural Association Quarterly* 3(2): 21–37.

—— (1982) *The Fabrication of Virtue; English Prison Architecture 1750–1840*, Cambridge: Cambridge University Press.

Fairbairn, W. (1857–8) *On the Application of Cast and Wrought Iron to Building Purposes*, 2nd edn, London.

—— (1863) *Treatise on Mills and Mill Work*, vol. II, London.

Fawcett, T. (1974) *The Rise of English Provincial Art etc.*, Oxford: Oxford University Press.

Fitton, R. S. and Wadsworth A. P. (1958) *The Strutts and the Arkwrights 1758–1830*, Manchester: Manchester University Press.

Fleming, J. (1962), *Robert Adam and his Circle*, rpt 1978, London: Murray.

Floyer, J. (1697) *An Enquiry into the Right Use and Abuse of the Hot, Cold and Temperate Baths in England*, London.

Floyer, J. and Baynard, E. (1722) *The History of Cold Bathing, Both Ancient and Modern*, London.

Flynn, B. (1989) 'Cooking up a Brave New World – Edinburgh', *The Independent*, 30 January: 22.

Forgan, S. (1986) 'Context, Image and Function: a Preliminary Enquiry into the Architecture of Scientific Societies', *British Journal for the History of Science* 19: 89–113.

—— (1989) 'The Architecture of Science and the Idea of a University', *Studies in the History and Philosophy of Science* 20(4): 405–34.

Forrest, A. (1981) *The French Revolution and the Poor*, Oxford: Blackwell.

Forsyth, J. A. S. (1969) 'The County Lunatic Asylums 1808–1845 etc.', unpublished B.Arch. dissertation, University of Newcastle upon Tyne.

Foucault, M. (1967) *Madness and Civilisation: a History of Insanity in the Age of Reason*, trans. R. Howard, London: Tavistock Publications.

—— (1977) *Jeremy Bentham: Le Panoptique, Précédé de l'Oeil du Pouvoir*, Paris: Belford.

—— (1982) *Discipline and Punish: the Birth of the Prison*, trans. A. Sheridan, Harmondsworth: Penguin.

Foulston, J. (1838) *The Public Buildings Erected in the West of England*, London.

Fox, J. (1814) *Proceedings of the Glasgow Lancastrian (sic) Society etc.*, Edinburgh.

Frampton, K. (1980) *Modern Architecture: A Critical History*, London: Thames and Hudson.

Franck, A. H. (1705) *Pietas Hallensis etc.*, London.

Frankl, P. (1914) *Die Entwicklungsphasen der Neueren Baukunst*, trans. J. F. O'Gorman, 1969, *Principles of Architectural History: the Four Phases of Architectural Style, 1420–1900*, Cambridge, Mass.: MIT Press.

Francoeur, L. B. (1824) *Lineal Drawing . . . as taught in the*

Lancastrian (sic) Schools in France etc., London.
—— (1827) *L'Enseignement de Dessin Linéaire etc.*, Paris.
Fraser, A. G. (1989) *The Building of Old College: Adam, Playfair and the University of Edinburgh*, Edinburgh: Edinburgh University Press.
Free-School Society (1820) *Manual of the Lancasterian System etc.*, New York: The Society.
French, P. J. (1972) *John Dee: the World of an Elizabethan Magus*, London: Routledge & Kegan Paul.
Freundenberger, H. and Redlich, F. (1964) 'The Industrial Development of Europe: Reality, Symbols, Images', *Kyklos* XVII: 372–403.
Furttenbach, J. (1628) *Architectura Civilis etc.*, Ulm.
Galileo Galilei (1638) *Discorsi e Dimostrazioni Matematiche Intorno a Due Nuove Scienze*, Leyden: Elzevir.
Gallet, M. (1980) *Claud-Nicolas Ledoux, 1736–1806*, Paris: Picard.
Gastellier, M. (1791) *Instructions sur les Moyens d'Entretenir la Salubrité, et de Purifier l'Air des Salles dans les Hôpitaux Militaires etc.*, Paris.
Gavois, J. (1983) *Going Up: an Informal History of the Elevator from the Pyramids to the Present*, London: Otis Elevator Company, Birdsall.
Genet, J. (1967) *The Thief's Journal*, trans. B. Frechtman, Harmondsworth: Penguin.
van Gennep, A. (1960) *The Rites of Passage*, trans. M. B. Vizedom and G.L. Caffee, London: Routledge & Kegan Paul.
Gentleman's Magazine (1818), LXXXVIII, January–June: 113–6.
Géoffroy-Saint-Hilaire, E. (1818–22) *Philosophie Anatomique*, Paris.
George, M. D. (1951) *London Life in the Eighteenth Century*, 3rd edn, London: London School of Economics.
Giedion, S. (1944) *Space, Time and Architecture: The Growth of a New Tradition*, Cambridge, Mass.: Harvard University Press.
—— (1952) 'Sixtus V and the Planning of Baroque Rome', *Architectural Review* 111(664): 217–26.
Gilbert, K. R. (1965) *The Portsmouth Blockmaking Machinery*, London: HMSO.
Girouard, M. (1978) *Life in the English Country House*, Yale, Conn.: Yale University Press.
—— (1981) *Alfred Waterhouse and the Natural History Museum*, London: British Museum (Natural History).
—— (1986) 'Moonlit Matchmaking: Assembly Rooms of the Eighteenth Century', *Country Life* CLXXX(4644): 540–4 and 4645: 764–6.
Glasgow (1814) *First Report of General Committee . . . (of) a Lunatic Asylum*, Glasgow.
Godfrey, W.H. (1955) *The English Almshouse*, London: Faber & Faber.
Godin, J-B. A. (1871) *Solutions Sociales*, Paris: Le Chevalier.
Goffman, E. (1970) *Asylums*, Harmondsworth: Penguin.
Goldman, J. (ed.) (1720) *L. C. Sturm Anweisung allerhand Öffentliche Zucht und Liebes Gebäude etc.*, Augsburg.
Gombrich, E. H. (1977) 'The Museum: Past, Present and Future', *Critical Enquiry* 3: 449–70.
Goodman, J. (1982) 'Towards a Social History of Baths and Wash-houses', *Issues* 3: 12–14.
Gorz, A. (1989) *Critique of Economic Reason*, trans. G. Handiside and C. Turner, London: Verso.
Goyder, D. G. (1824) *A Manual of the System of Instruction Pursued at the Infant School, Meadow Street, Bristol etc.*, 3rd edn, London.
—— (1825) *A Manual of the System of Instruction Pursued at the Infant School, Meadow Street, Bristol etc.*, 4th edn, London.
Grahame, K. (1950) *The Wind in the Willows*, London: Methuen.
Grady, K. (1980) 'Commercial, Marketing and Retailing Amenities, 1700–1914' in D. Fraser (ed.) *A History of Modern Leeds*, Manchester: Manchester University Press.
Granville, A. B. (1841) *The Spas of England and Principal Sea-Bathing Places*, vol. 2, London.
Greenbaum, L. S. (1974) 'Tempest in the Academy: Jean Baptiste Le Roy, the Paris Academy of Sciences and the project of the new Hôtel-Dieu', *Archives Internationales d'Histoire des Sciences* 24: 122–140.
—— (1975) '"Measure of Civilization"; the Hospital Thought of Jacques Tenon on the Eve of the French Revolution', *Bulletin of the History of Medicine* 49(1): 43–56.
Grew, N. (1694) *Musaeum Regalis Societatis etc.*, London: Newman.
Grosvenor, S. (1856) *History of the City Road Chapel, Sunday, Day and Infant Schools*, London.
Guberti, N. V. (1891) *Material dlja Russkoi Bibliografii . . . 1725–1800*, Moscow.
Guide de l'Enseignement (1819) *Guide de l'Enseignement Mutuel*, Paris.
Gutkind, E. A. (1972) *Urban Development in East-Central Europe: Poland, Czechoslovakia and Hungary*, vol. III of *International History of City Development*, New York: The Free Press.
Hadfield, B. and Gosling, J. G. (1984) *Stockport Sunday School Bi-Centenary*, Stockport.
Hales, S. (1743) *A Description of Ventilators etc.*, London.
Hamel, J. (1818) *L'Enseignement Mutuel etc.*, Paris.
Hamilton, D. (1980) 'Adam Smith and the Moral Economy of the Classroom System', *Journal of Curriculum Studies* 12(4): 281–98.
—— (1983) 'Robert Owen and Education: A Re-assessment', in W. M. Humes and H. M. Paterson (eds) *Scottish Culture and Scottish Education, 1800–1980*, Edinburgh: John Donald.
Hamilton, S. B. (1952) 'The historical development of structural theory', *Proceedings of the Institute of Civil Engineers* III: 374–419.
Hammond, J. L. and B. (1947) *The Bleak Age*, rev. edn, Harmondsworth: Penguin.
Hardman, M. (1986) *Ruskin and Bradford an Experiment*

in Victorian Cultural History, Manchester: Manchester University Press.

Harris, J. J. H. and Tearle, F. (1848) *The School-Room: Part I Its Arrangement and Organisation etc.*, London.

Hays, J. N. (1983) 'The London Lecturing Empire, 1800–50' in I. Inkster and J. Morrell (eds) *Metropolis and Province: Science in British Culture, 1780–1850*, London: Hutchinson.

Heath, S. H.(1910) *Old English Houses of Alms: a Pictorial Record with Architectural and Historical Notes*, London: Francis Griffiths.

d'Helft, B. and Verliefden, M. (1978) 'Les Rotondes de l'Illusion', *Monuments Historiques* 4, 'Architecture et Spectacle': 54–60.

Henderson, W. O. (1958–59) 'The Rise of the Berlin Silk and Porcelain Industries', *Business History* I(1 and 2): 84–98.

Higgins, P. L. H. (1826) *An Exposition of... the Infant System of Education in Ireland*, London: Goyder.

Hildesheimer, F. (1981) 'Les Lazarets sous l'Ancien Régime', *Monuments Historiques* 114: 20–4.

Hillier, B. and Hanson J. (1984) *The Social Logic of Space*, Cambridge: Cambridge University Press.

Himmelfarb, G. (1968) 'The Haunted House of Jeremy Bentham' in *Victorian Minds*, London: Weidenfeld & Nicolson.

Hobsbawm, E. J. (1971) *The Age of Revolution*, London: Weidenfeld & Nicolson.

Home Office (1989) *The Prison Design Briefing System*, revised 1990 and 1991, London: HMSO.

Hooke, R. (1678) *De Potentia Restitutiva; or of Springs, Explaining the Power of Springing Bodies*, London.

Horn, W. and Born, E. (1979) *Plan of St Gall*, Berkeley, Ca.: University of California Press.

Horváth, M. (1840) *Az ipar és Kereskedés Története Magyarországban etc.*, (*The History of Industry and Commerce in Hungary etc.*), Buda: Royal Hungarian University Press.

Howard, J. (1777) *The State of the Prisons in England and Wales*, Warrington.

—— (1784) *The State of the Prisons in England and Wales*, 3rd edn, Warrington.

—— (1789) *An Account of the Principal Lazarettos etc.*, Warrington.

—— (1791) *An Account of the Principal Lazarettos etc.*, 2nd edn, London.

Hunter, W. (1784) *Two Introductory Lectures*, London.

Husserl, E. (1970) *The Crisis of European Sciences and Transcendental Phenomenology: an Introduction to Phenomenological Philosophy*, trans. D. Carr, Evanston, Illinois: Northwestern University Press.

Hutton, W. (1791) *The History of Derby etc.*, London.

Hyde, R. (1988) *'Panoramania' The Art and Entertainment of the 'all-embracing' View*, London: Trefoil in association with the Barbican Art Gallery.

Hyland, A. (1987) 'National Education' reprints *Annual Report of the Commissioners of National Education, 1835* in A. Hyland and K. Milne (eds) *Irish Educational Documents*, vol. I, Dublin: Church of Ireland College of Education.

Hyland, A. and Milne, K. (eds) (1987) *Irish Educational Documents*, Dublin: Church of Ireland College of Education.

Ignatieff, M. (1978) *A Just Measure of Pain: the Penitentiary in the Industrial Revolution 1750–1850*, London: Macmillan.

Illich, I. (1986) *H_2O and the Waters of Forgetfulness*, London and New York: Marion Boyars.

Illustrated Exhibitor, The (1851) *The Illustrated Exhibitor* 2, 14 June.

Impey, O. and MacGregor, A. (1985) *The Origin of Museums*, Oxford: Oxford University Press.

Inkster, I. (1980) 'The Public Lecture an Instrument of Science Education for Adults – the Case of Great Britain c. 1750–1850', *Paedagogica Historica* XX, 1: 80–107.

Inkster, I. and Morrell, J. (eds) (1983) *Metropolis and Province: Science in British Culture, 1780–1850*, London: Hutchison.

Ison, W. (1952) *The Georgian Buildings of Bristol*, London: Faber & Faber.

Ives, A. G. (1970) *Kingswood School in Wesley's Day and Since*, London: Epworth Press.

Jameson, F. (1990) *Post-Modernism the Cultural Logic of Late Capitalism*, London: Verso.

Jetter, D. (1966) *Geschichte des Hospitals* vol. I *Westdeutschland von den Anfängen bis 1850*, Wiesbaden: Franz Steiner.

—— (1971) vol. II *Zur Typologie des Irrenhauses in Frankreich und Deutschland, 1780–1840*, Wiesbaden: Franz Steiner.

—— (1972) vol. III *Nordamerika 1600–1776 (Kolonialzeit)*, Wiesbaden: Franz Steiner.

Jobson, F. J. (1850) *Chapel and School Architecture*, London.

Johnson, H. R. and Skempton, A. W. (1955–6 and 1956–7) 'William Strutt's Cotton Mills, 1793–1812', *Transactions of the Newcomen Society* XXX: 179–205.

Josten, C. H. (1985) *Elias Ashmole, F.R.S. (1617–1692)*, Oxford: Ashmolean Museum and Museum of the History of Science.

Just, D. J. (1983) *Times Higher Education Supplement*, 18 November: 21.

Kaufmann, E. (1955) *Architecture in the Age of Reason: Baroque and Post-Baroque in England, Italy and France*, rpt 1968, New York: Dover Publications.

Kay J. P. (1832) *The Moral and Physical Condition of the Working Classes etc.*, London.

—— (1839) *The Training of Pauper Children etc.*, rpt 1970, Manchester: E. J. Morten.

Kelly, G. A. (1955) *The Psychology of Personal Constructs* New York: Norton.

Kelly, T. (1957) *George Birkbeck: Pioneer of Adult Education*, Liverpool: Liverpool University Press.

—— (1966) *Early Public Libraries etc.*, London: the Library Association.

Kendall, H. E. (1847) *Designs for Schools and School Houses etc.*, London.

Kilmarnock Standard (1903) 'The Moravian Church in Ayrshire', *The Kilmarnock Standard* 27 June.

King, A. D. (ed.) (1971) *Colonial Urban Development: Culture, Social Power and Environment*, London: Routledge & Kegan Paul.

—— (1980) *Buildings and Society: Essays on the Social Development of the Built Environment*, London: Routledge & Kegan Paul.

Kirkman Gray, B. (1905) *A History of English Philanthropy*, rpt 1967, London: Frank Cass.

Kloosterhuis, Ir. C. A. (1981) *De Bevolking van de Vrije Koloniën der Maatschappij van Weldadigheid*, Zutphen: De Walburg Pers.

Kouwenhoven, J. A. K. (1982) 'American Studies: Words and Things' in T. J. Schlereth (ed.) *Material Culture in America*, Nashville, Tenn.: American Association for State and Local History.

Lancaster, J. (1803) *Improvements in Education etc.*, London.

—— (1805) *Improvements in Education as it respects the Industrious Classes of the Community*, 3rd edn with additions; rpt. F. Cordasco (ed.) 1973, Clifton, NJ.: Augustus M. Kelley.

—— (1806) *Outline of a Plan for Educating Ten Thousand Poor Children etc.*, London.

—— (1809a) *An Account of a Remarkable Establishment of Education at Paris*, London.

—— (1809b) *An Address to Friends and Superintendents of Sunday Schools etc.*, London.

—— (1809c) *Hints and Directions for . . . School Rooms etc.*, London.

—— (1810) *The British System of Education etc.*, London.

—— (1812) *The British System of Education etc.*, Washington.

—— (1816) *Manual of the System etc.*, London: British and Foreign School Society.

—— (1821) *Lancasterian System of Education etc.*, Baltimore.

Laqueur, T. W. (1979) *Religion and Respectability: Sunday Schools and Working Class Culture 1780–1850*, New Haven and London: Yale University Press.

Laurencich-Minelli, L. (1984), 'L'Indice del Museo Giganti Interressi Etnografici e Ordinamento di un Museo Cinquecentesco', *Museol. Scient.*, I (3–4): 191–242.

—— (1985) 'Museography and Ethnographical Collections in Bologna during the Sixteenth and Seventeenth Centuries' in O. Impey and A. MacGregor (eds) *The Origin of Museums etc.*, Oxford: Oxford University Press.

Lecointe, J. (1790) *La Santé de Mars etc.*, Paris.

Le Corbusier (1925) *City of Tomorrow*, rpt 1947, London: Architectural Press.

Ledoux, C. N. (1804) *L'Architecture Considerée sous le Rapport de l'Art, des Moeurs et de la Législation*, Paris; facsimile edn 1981, Nordlingen: Dr Alfons Uhl.

Lefebvre, H. (1974) *The Production of Space*, trans. D. Nicholson-Smith, 1991, Oxford: Blackwell.

Leibniz, G W. (1896) *New Essays Concerning Human Understanding*, trans. A. G. Langley, New York: Macmillan.

Lemoine, B. (1980) *Les Halles de Paris*, Paris: L'Eguerre.

Léonard, J. (1982) 'Les Médecins des Prisons en France au XIXe Siècle', paper given at the International Colloquium on Penal History (18th and 19th Century), Fontevraud, France, September.

Levi, P. (1962) *If This is a Man*, trans. S. Woolf, London: New English Library.

Lincoln, G. (ed.) (1896) 'The Witch-Persecution at Bamberg', translations and reprints from *Original Sources of European History*, vol. 3, Philadelphia: University of Pennsylvania.

Lochée, L. (1778) *An Essay on Castrametation*, London.

Locke, J. (1689–90) *Essay Concerning Human Understanding*, A. D. Woozley (ed.) 1964, London: Collins.

Loisel, G. (1912) *Histoire des Ménageries de l'Antiquité à Nos Jours*, 3 vols, Paris: Doin.

Longmate, N. (1974) *The Workhouse*, London: Temple Smith.

Lowe, J. B. (1977) *Welsh Industrial Workers' Housing*, Cardiff: Museum of Wales.

McCann, P. (ed.) (1977) *Popular Education and Socialization in the Nineteenth Century*, London: Methuen.

McCann, P. and Young, F. A. (1982) *Samuel Wilderspin and the Infant School Movement*, London: Croom Helm.

McClure, R. K. (1981) *Coram's Children, The London Foundling Hospital in the Eighteenth Century*, New Haven and London: Yale University Press.

McIntosh, P. C., Dixon, J. G., Munrow, A. D. and Willetts, R. F. (1957) *Landmarks in the History of Physical Education*, London: Routledge & Kegan Paul.

Maclure, W. (1826) Letter to Madame Fretageot, Ohio, 2nd August reprinted in A. E. Bestor (ed.) 1973, *Educational Reform at New Harmony*, Clifton, NJ.: Kelley.

McRae, R. (1961) *The Problem of the Unity of the Sciences: Bacon to Kant*, Toronto: University of Toronto Press.

Madge, J. (1982) 'Monasticism and the Culture of Production', *Issues* 3: 1–4.

Mantoux, P. (1928) *The Industrial Revolution in the Eighteenth Century*, revised T. S. Ashton (ed.) 1970, London: Methuen.

Mariotte, E. (1686) *Traité des Mouvements des Eaux*, Paris.

Markus, T. A. (1954) 'Pattern of the Law', Architectural Review CXVI: 251–6.

—— (1982) *Order in Space and Society, Architectural*

Form and its Context in the Scotland Enlightenment, Edinburgh: Mainstream.
—— (1985) 'Two Domes of Enlightenment: Two Scottish University Museums', *Art History* 8(2): 158–77.
—— (1989) 'Class and Classification in the Buildings of the late Scottish Enlightenment' in T. M. Devine (ed.) *Improvement and Enlightenment*, Edinburgh: John Donald.
Masson, A. (1981) *The Pictorial Catalogue; Mural Decoration in Libraries*, trans. D. Gerard, Oxford: Oxford University Press.
Masters, B. R. (1974) *The Public Markets of the City of London Surveyed by William Leybourn*, Publication No. 117, London: The London Topographical Society.
Melossi, D. and Pavarini, M. (1981) *The Prison and the Factory: Origins of the Penitentiary System*, trans. G. Cousin, London: Macmillan.
Milner, G. (ed.) (1880) *Bennett Street Memorials etc.*, Manchester.
Minter Morgan, J. (1845) *The Christian Commonwealth*, London.
Mordaunt Crook, J. (1972) *The British Museum: a Case-study in Architectural Politics*, Harmondsworth: Penguin.
Morris, W. (1891) *News from Nowhere*, London: Reeves and Turner.
Morrish, P. S. (1973–5) 'John Clark Revisited: Aspects of Early Modern Library Design', *Library History* 3: 87–107.
Mumford, L. (1934) *Technics and Civilization*, London: Routledge.
Muthesius, S. (1982) *The English Terraced House*, New Haven and London: Yale University Press.
National Society (1814) *Second Annual Report of the National Society*, London: The National Society for Promoting the Education of the Poor in the Principles of the Established Church.
Neale, R. S. (1981) *Bath: a Social History 1680–1800, or a Valley of Pleasures yet a Sink of Iniquity*, London: Routledge & Kegan Paul.
Neickelio, C. F. (1727) *Museorum . . . Raritaeten-Kammern etc.*, Leipzig and Breslau.
Nemes, M. (1984) 'Magyarország első panoptikonja: a budapesti-óbudai selyemgombolyitó manufaktura' (Hungary's first panopticon: the silk cocoon unwinding factory at Óbuda, Budapest', *Művészettörténeti Értesitő* 4: 261–70.
Neverov, O. (1985) '"His Majesty's Cabinet" and Peter I's *Kunstkammer*' in O. Impey and A. MacGregor (eds) *Origin of Museums*, Oxford: Oxford University Press.
Newman, L. M. (1966) *Leibniz 1646–1716 and the German Library Scene*, Library Association Pamphlet no. 28, London: the Library Association.
Nightingale, F. (1859) *Notes on Hospitals*, London.
Ochsner, A. J. and Sturm, M. J. (1907) *The Organisation, Construction and Management of Hospitals*, Chicago: Cleveland Press.
O'Gorman J. F. (1972) *The Architecture of the Monastic Library of Italy 1300–1600*, New York: New York University Press.
Ohlander, J. (1923) *Göteborgs Folkskolevasen I Gamla Dagar Och I Vara*, Göteborg: Wettergren and Kerbens.
Ormerod, H. A. (1953) *The Liverpool Institution etc.*, Liverpool: Liverpool University Press.
Ovenell, R. F. (1986) *The Ashmolean Museum, 1683–1894*, Oxford: Oxford University Press.
Owen, R. (1812) *A Statement Regarding the New Lanark Establishment*, Edinburgh.
—— (1813) *A New View of Society etc.*, rpt 1970, Harmondsworth: Penguin.
—— (1817) *Report to the Committee of the Manufacturing and Labouring Poor*, reprinted in 1858, *The Life of Robert Owen etc.* Supplementary Appendix, vol. 1A, London.
—— (1821) *Report to the County of Lanark of a Plan for Relieving Public Distress etc.*, Glasgow.
—— (1841) *A Development of . . . Self Supporting Home Colonies; etc.*, London: Home Colonization Society.
Owen, R., Atkins, J., Pemberton, R. and Buckingham, J. S. (1855) *Robert Owen's Address delivered at the Meeting in St Martin's Hall etc.*, London.
Owen, R. Dale (1824) *An Outline of the System of Education at New Lanark*, Glasgow.
—— (1874) *Threading My Way*, rpt 1967, Clifton, NJ.: Augustus Kelley.
Oxley, G. W. (1974) *Poor Relief in England and Wales, 1601–1834*, Newton Abbot: David & Charles.
Pallister, R. (1973) 'Educational Capital in the Elementary School of the Mid-nineteenth Century' in M. Seaborne (ed.) 1973, *History of Education*, 2(2), Newton Abbot: David & Charles.
Panofsky, E. (1957) *Gothic Architecture and Scholasticism*, London: Thames and Hudson.
Papworth, J. W. and Papworth, W. (1853) *Museums, Libraries and Picture Galleries etc.*, London.
Parkes, S. M. (1984) *Kildare Place: The History of the Church of Ireland Training College 1811–1969*, Dublin: Church of Ireland College of Education.
Parry-Jones, W. Ll. (1972) *The Trade in Lunacy: A Study of Private Madhouses in England in the Eighteenth and Nineteenth Centuries*, London: Routledge & Kegan Paul.
Paulson, R. (1975) *Wright of Derby: Nature Demythologised; Emblem and Expression*, London: Thames and Hudson.
Pawłowski, K. K. (1961) 'Town planning problems in the works of Claude-Nicolas Ledoux', *Kwartalnik Architectury I Urbanistyki* VI(4): 255–92.
Peacock, J. (1790) *Proposals for a Magnificent Establishment etc.*, London.
—— (1798) *The Outline of a Plan for establishing a United Company of British Manufactures*, London.

Pearce, P. L. (1987) 'Thomas Twining (1806–95); the determined improver', part 1 *Journal of the Royal Society of Arts* CXXXV(5375): 845–7.

—— part 2 *Journal of the Royal Society of Arts* CXXXV(5376): 942–4.

—— part 3 *Journal of the Royal Society of Arts* CXXXV(5377): 62–4.

Pemberton, R. (1854) *The Happy Colony*, London.

Peponis, J. and Hedin, J. (1982) 'The Layout of Theories in the Natural History Museum', *9H* 3: 21–5.

Pevsner, N. (1979) *A History of Building Types*, London: Thames and Hudson.

Petit, A. (1774) *Mémoire sur la Meilleure Manière de Construire un Hôpital de Malades*, Paris.

Philosophical Transactions (1745): 370.

Physick, J. (1982) *The Victoria and Albert Museum: the History of its Building*, Oxford: Phaidon, Christie's.

Pinel, P. (1800) *Traité Médico-Philosophique sur l'Aliénation Mentale ou la Manie*, Paris.

Pirenne, M. H. (1970) *Optics, Painting and Photography*, Cambridge: Cambridge University Press.

Pollard, S. (1964) 'The Factory Village in the Industrial Revolution', *English Historical Review* 79(312): 513–31.

Poni, C. (1972) 'Archéologie de la Fabrique: la Diffusion des Moulins à Soie "alla Bolognese" dans les États Vénitiens du XVIe au XVIIIe siècle', *Annales* 27: 1475–96.

Ponteil, F. (1966) *Histoire de l'Enseignement 1789–1964*, Paris: Sirey.

Porter, G. (1988) 'Putting your House in Order: Representation of Women and Domestic Life', in R. Lumley (ed.) *The Museum Time Machine*, London: Routledge.

Porter, R. S. (1980) 'Science, Provincial Culture and Public Opinion in Enlightenment England', *The British Journal for Eighteenth-Century Studies* 3: 20–46.

Prest, J. (1960) *The Industrial Revolution in Coventry*, Oxford: Oxford University Press.

Privy Council (1844) *Minutes of the Committee of Council on Education . . . 1842–3*, London: HMSO.

Proceedings of the Wesley Historical Society (1912) 8: 55–6 and 77–8.

Pugin, A. W. (1843) *An Apology for Christian Architecture in England*, rpt 1969, Oxford: St Barnabas Press.

Quatremère de Quincy, A-C. (1832) *Dictionaire Historique d'Architecture*, Paris.

Quiccheberg, S. (1565) *Inscriptiones vel Tituli Theatri Amplissimi, Complectentis etc.*, Münich.

Rayman, R. (1981) 'Joseph Lancaster's Monitorial System of Instruction and American Indian Education, 1815–38', *History of Education Quarterly* 21(4): 395–409.

Reed, P. A. (1982) 'Form and Context: a Study of Georgian Edinburgh' in T. A. Markus (ed.) *Order in Space and Society*, Edinburgh: Mainstream.

Report . . . Wash-house (1925) *Report on the 'Kitty Wilkinson' Public Baths and Wash-House*, Liverpool: City of Liverpool.

Reynolds, J. (1983) *The Great Paternalist: Titus Salt and the Growth of Nineteenth-century Bradford*, London: Temple Smith.

Richardson, E. C. (1935) *Classification – Theoretical and Practical*, New York: Wilson.

Rigold, S. E. (1968) 'Two Types of Court Hall', *Archeologia Cantina* 83(1)–22.

Robinson, J. M. (1979) *The Wyatts: an Architectural Dynasty*, Oxford: Oxford University Press.

Robson, E. R. (1874) *School Architecture etc.*, London.

Robson, M. E. (1983) 'Notes on the Revolving Chamber, Belper', unpublished manuscript.

Roche, D. (1979) 'Urban Reading Habits during the French Enlightenment', *The British Journal for Eighteenth Century Studies* 2: 138–49 and 220–30.

Rolfe, W. D. I. (1985) 'William and John Hunter: Breaking the Great Chain of Being', in W. F. Bynum and R. S. Porter (eds) *William Hunter and His World*, Cambridge: Cambridge University Press.

Rosenau, H. (1970) *Social Purpose in Architecture, Paris and London Compared 1760–1800*, London: November Books, Studio Vista.

—— (1976) *Boullée and Visionary Architecture*, London: Academy Editions.

Ross, J. (1900) *A History of Congregational Independency in Scotland*, Glasgow: Maclehose & Sons.

Rothman, D. (1971) *The Discovery of the Asylum*, Boston: Little Brown.

Rowe, G. (1845) *Illustrated Cheltenham Guide*, Cheltenham.

Royal Sea Bathing Infirmary (1791–3) *Minutes of the Founding Committee, Court of Directors and Governors and their Sub-committees, Royal Sea Bathing Infirmary. Margate*, vol. 1791–1856, Kent Archives, North East Area, Ramsgate.

Rumford, Count B. (1797) *Essays, Political, Economical and Philosophical*, 3rd edn, vol.I, London.

Russell, C. (1983) *Science and Social Change 1700–1900*, London: Macmillan.

Russell, J. B. (1980) *A History of Witchcraft: Sorcerers, Heretics and Pagans*, London: Thames and Hudson.

Rykwert, J. (1976) *The Idea of a Town*, London: Faber & Faber.

Salisbury, W. (1810) 'Plan of Mr Salisbury's Botanic Gardens Explained', *Gentleman's Magazine* LXXX: 113–14.

de la Sagra, R. (1839) *Voyage en Hollande et en Belgique etc.* Paris.

della Santa, L. (1816) *Della Costruzione e del Regolamento di una Pubblica Universale Biblioteca etc*, Florence.

Saunders, G. (1790) *A Treatise on Theatres*, London.

Savignat, J-M. (1980) *Dessin et Architecture du Moyen-Age au XVIIIe Siècle*, Paris: École Nationale Supérieure des Beaux-Arts.

Schaffer, S. (1983) 'Natural Philosophy and Public

Spectacle in the Eighteenth Century', *History of Science* 21(1): 1–43.

Scherren, H. (1905) *The Zoological Society of London etc.*, London: Cassell.

von Schlosser, J. (1978) *Die Kunst-und Wunderkammern der Spätrenaissance*, Braunschweig: Klinkhardt & Biermann.

Schneekloth, L. H. and Bruce, E M. (undated) 'Building Typologies: an Enquiry', unpublished paper, Department of Architecture, State University of New York and the Caucus Partnership, Buffalo, New York.

Schofield, R. E. (1963) *The Lunar Society of Birmingham*, Oxford: Oxford University Press.

Schulte-Albert, H. G. (1971) 'Gottfried Wilhelm Leibniz and Library Classification', *The Journal of Library History, Philosophy and Comparative Librarianship* VI: 133–52.

Scotland, J. (1969) *The History of Scottish Education*, vol. I, London: University of London Press.

Scottish Home and Health Department (1973) *Design Guide: Health Centres in Scotland*, Edinburgh: HMSO.

Scruton, R. (1979) *The Aesthetics of Architecture*, London: Methuen.

Scull, A. T. (ed.) (1981) *Madhouses, Mad-doctors and Madmem: the Social History of Psychiatry in the Victorian Era*, London: The Athlone Press.

—— (1982) *Museums of Madness*, Harmondsworth: Penguin.

Seaborne, M. (1971) *The English School Its Architecture and Organisation 1370–1870*, London: Routledge & Kegan Paul.

Semper, G. (1860–3) *Der Stil in den technischen und tektonischen Künsten oder praktische Äesthetik*, Frankfurt-am-Maine.

Sennett, R. (1971) *The Uses of Disorder: Personal Identity and City Life*, Harmondsworth: Allen Lane, the Penguin Press.

Shapin, S. (1974) 'The Audience for Science in Eighteenth Century Edinburgh', *History of Science* 12: 95–121.

—— (1983) '"Nibbling at the Teats of Science": Edinburgh and the Diffusion of Science in the 1830s' in Inkster and Morrell (eds) *Metropolis and Province: Science in British Culture, 1780–1850*, London: Hutchinson.

Shapin, S. and Barnes, B. (1977) 'Science, Nature and Control: Interpretating Mechanics' Institutes', *Social Studies of Science* 7(1): 31–74.

Shaw, J. (1984) *Water Power in Scotland, 1550–1870*, Edinburgh: John Donald.

Short, J. R. (1991) *Imagined Country: Society Culture and Environment*, London: Routledge.

Silver, P. and Silver, H. (1974) 'The Kennington National Schools', *The Education of the Poor: the History of a National School 1824–1974*, London: Routledge & Kegan Paul.

Simon, J. (1988) 'From Charity School to Workhouse in the 1720s: the SPCK and Mr Marriott's Solution', *History of Education* 17(2): 113–129.

Skempton, A. W. (1956) 'The Origin of Iron Beams', *Actes du VIIIe Congrès International d'Histoire des Sciences*, 1029–39, Florence.

Skempton, A. W. and Johnson, H. R. (1962) 'The first iron frames', *Architectural Review* 131(781): 175–86.

Smith, A. (1776) *The Wealth of Nations* from extracts in S. Eliot and B. Stern (eds) 1979 *The Age of Enlightenment*, London: Ward Lock Educational with the Open University Press.

Smith, W. D. (1974) *Stretching Their Bodies: the History of Physical Education*, Newton Abbot: David & Charles.

Smith, W. J. (1971) 'The Architecture of the Domestic System in South-east Lancashire and the Adjoining Pennines' in S. D. Chapman (ed.) *The History of Working-class Housing: A Symposium*, Newton Abbot: David & Charles.

Smithies, P. (1988) *The Architecture of the Halifax Piece Hall, 1775–1779*, Halifax: privately published.

Society for Promoting the Education of the Poor of Ireland (1813) *Hints and Directions for the Building, and Fitting-up, and Arranging School-rooms*, Dublin: The Society.

—— (1825) *The Schoolmaster's Manual etc.*, Dublin: The Society.

Spark, A. (1792) *Rules, Orders and Regulations to be duly Observed and Kept in the Parish School of Industry in King Street, Golden Square*, London.

Stafford, B. M. (1984) *Voyage into Substance*, Cambridge, Mass.: MIT Press.

Stamp, G. (1986) 'The Hungerford Market', *Architectural Association Files* 11: 59–70.

Stark, W. (1807) *Remarks on Public Hospitals for the Cure of Mental Derangement, etc.*, Edinburgh.

State of the Schools of Industry (1801) *State of the Schools of Industry Kendal July 1, 1800 to July 1, 1801*, Kendal.

Stephanus, C. (1545) *De Dissectione Partium Corporis etc.*, Paris.

Steuart, D. and Cockburn, A. (1782) *General Heads of a Plan for Erecting a New Prison and Bridewell in the City of Edinburgh etc.*, Edinburgh.

Stoat, J. (1826) *A Description of the System of Enquiry; . . . Circulating Classes etc.*, London.

Stockport (1796) 'Stockport Sunday School Committee Book from 18th May 1794 to 2 October 1796', Manuscript in Stockport Public Library.

—— (undated) 'Scheme for Building a Large Commodious Chapel, Sunday School, Preachers' Houses and 5 Large Schools in Stockport and its Vicinity', unpublished manuscript in Stockport Public Library (watermark is 1797).

Stollenwerk, M. (1971) 'Krankenhausentwürfe die Nicht Verwirklicht Würden', doctoral thesis, Technical University of Aachen.

Stow, D. (1834) *Moral Training etc.*, 2nd ed., Glasgow.

(No first edition has been found although Stow insisted that the edition referred to here was the second edition.)
—— (1836) *The Training System etc.*, 1st edn, Glasgow.
—— (1839) *National Education . . . Moral Training and the Training System etc.*, Glasgow.
—— (1850) *The Training System etc.*, 8th edn enl., London.
Sturm, L. C. (1720) *Vollständige Anweisung . . . Spitäler vor Alte und Kranke etc.*, Augsburg.
Summerson, J. (1980) *The Classical Language of Architecture*, rev. and enl. edn, London: Thames and Hudson.
Sunday School Union (1816) *Directions for Carrying into Effect the Plan of Monitors*, London.
Sutton, S. (1749) *An Historical Account of a New Method for Extracting Foul Air etc.*, 2nd edn, London.
Sylvester, C. (1819) *The Philosophy of Domestic Economy*, London.
Szasz, T. (1971) *The Manufacture of Madness*, London: Routledge & Kegan Paul.
Taylor, J. (1968) 'Charles Fowler, 1792–1867: a centenary memoir', *Architectural History* 11: 57–94.
Taylor, J. S. (1979) 'Philanthropy and the Empire: Jonas Hanway and the Infant Poor of London', *Eighteenth Century Studies* 12(3): 285–305.
Teyssot, G. (1977) 'Citta-Servizi: La Produzione dei *bâtiments civils* in Francia 1775–1848', *Casabella* 424: 56–65.
Thompson, E. P. (1968) *The Making of the English Working Class*, Harmondsworth: Penguin.
—— (1974) 'Time, Work-discipline and Industrial Capitalism' in M.W. Flinn and T. C. Smout (eds) *Essays in Social History*, Oxford: Oxford University Press.
Thompson, J. D. and Goldin, G. (1975) *The Hospital: A Social and Architectural History*, London: Yale University Press.
Thoresby Society (1969) *The Publications of the Thoresby Society* LII.
Timms, E. and Collier, P., (1988) *Visions and Blueprints, Avant-garde Culture and Radical Politics in Early Twentieth Century Europe*, Manchester: Manchester University Press.
Tittler, R. (1991) *Architecture and Power, the Town Hall and the English Urban Community, c. 1500–1640*, Oxford: Clarendon/Oxford University Press.
Tod, T. (1783) *Observations on Dr McFarlan's Inquiries Concerning the State of the Poor*, Edinburgh.
Tomlinson, H. (1980) 'Design and Reform: the "Separate" System in the Nineteenth-century English Prison' in A. D. King (ed.) *Buildings and Society: Essays on the Social Development of the Built Environment*, London: Routledge & Kegan Paul.
Tovey, C. (1859) *The British Library*, London: Longman.
Town Council of Dundee (1827) *Report on Sessional Schools*, Dundee: a Committee of the Town Council.
Transactions of the Congregational Historical Society (1920–3) 'The old Scottish Independents', 18: 181–9.
Tronchet, R. R. (1972?) *L'Enseignement Mutuel en France de 1815 à 1833*, 2 volumes in 3, unpublished manuscript, possibly dissertation for the University of Lille, in Bibliothèque de l'Institut de Recherche Pédagogique, Paris.
Tuke, S. (1813) *Description of the Retreat etc.*, York.
—— (1819) 'Practical Hints on the Construction and Economy of Pauper Lunatic Asylums' in W. Watson and J. P. Pritchett *Plans, Elevations and Description of the Pauper Lunatic Asylum lately Erected at Wakefield for the West Riding of Yorkshire etc.*, York.
Turner, J. M. (1988) 'Victorian Values – or Whatever Happened to John Wesley's Scriptural Holiness?', *Proceedings of the Wesley Historical Society* XLVI, 6.
Turner, P. V. (1984) *Campus: an American Planning Tradition*, Cambridge, Mass.: MIT Press.
Turner, W. (1562) *A Booke of the Natures and Properties of the Bathes in England . . . Germany and Italy*, Collen.
Tylecote, M. (1974) 'The Manchester Mechanics' Institution, 1824–35' in D. S. L. Cardwell (ed.) *Artisan to Graduate*, Manchester: Manchester University Press.
Tzonis, A. and Lefaivre, L. (1986) *Classical Architecture: the Poetics of Order*, Cambridge, Mass.: MIT Press.
Ure, A. (1835) *The Philosophy of Manufacture*, 2nd edn, London.
Valdenaire, A. (1926) *Friedrich Weinbrenner; sein Leben und Seine Bauten*, Karlesruhe.
Varey, S. (1990) *Space and the Eighteenth Century English Novel*, Cambridge: Cambridge University Press.
Venturi, R. (1966) *Complexity and Contradiction in Architecture*, New York: Museum of Modern Art.
Vicq d'Azyr, F. (1805) 'Éloge Historique: Hunter' vol. II, *Oeuvres*, Paris.
Vidler, A. (1981–2) 'The Theatre of Production', *Architectural Association Files*, 1(1): 54–63.
—— (1990) *Claude-Nicolas Ledoux: Architecture and Social Reform at the End of the Ancien Régime*, Cambridge, Mass.: MIT Press.
Voldman, D. (1981) 'Laboratoires Précurseurs: les Hôpitaux Militaires au Siècle de Lumières' in 'Architecture des Hôpitaux', *Monuments Historiques* 14: 25–33.
Wadsworth, A. P. (1951) 'The First Manchester Sunday Schools' rpt in M. W. Flinn and T. C. Smout (eds) 1979 *Essays in Social History*, Oxford: Oxford University Press.
Watkin, D. (1980) *The Rise of Architectural History*, London: The Architectural Press.
Watson, R. S. (1869) *Industrial Schools*, Newcastle-upon-Tyne.
—— (1897) *The History of the Literary and Philosophical Society of Newcastle-upon-Tyne (1793–1896)*, London.

Webb, I. (1976) 'The Bradford Wool Exchange: Industrial Capitalism and the Popularity of Gothic', *Victorian Studies* XX(1): 45–68.

Webb, S. and Webb, B. (1963) *English Local Government* vol. 7 *English Poor Law History*, London: Frank Cass.

Webster, T. (c. 1837) *Autobiography of Thomas Webster F. G. S. etc.*, manuscript in the Library of the Royal Institution, London.

Weinreb, B. and Hibbert, C. (eds) (1983) *The London Encyclopaedia*, London: Book Club Associates.

Weisser, M. R. (1982) *Crime and Punishment in Early Modern Europe*, Brighton: Harvester Press.

Wentworth, E. (1813) *Instructions for the Monitors of Friars' Mount Sunday School*, London.

West, E. G. (1981) *Where did we go Wrong? Industrial Performance, Education and the Economy in Victorian Britain*, Lewes: The Falmer Press.

West, W. (1830) *The History, Topography and Directory of Warwickshire etc.*, Birmingham.

Wilderspin, S. (1823) *On the Importance of educating Infant Children etc.*, London: Goyder.

—— (1824) *Infant Education etc.*, 2nd edn, London.

—— (1825) *Infant Education etc.*, 3rd edn, London.

—— (1829) *Infant Education etc.*, 4th edn, London.

—— (1832) *Early Discipline Illustrated etc.*, London.

—— (1840) *A System for the Education of the Young etc.*, London.

Wilkinson, R. (1819) *Londina Illustrata*, vol. 1.1, London.

Williams, A. (1979) *The Police of Paris, 1718–1789*, Baton Rouge and London: Louisiana State University.

Wilson, W. (1825) *The System of Infants' Schools etc.*, 2nd edn, London.

—— (1829) *A Manual of Instruction for Infants' Schools etc.*, London.

Wilson, W. E. (1964) *The Angel and the Serpent: the Story of New Harmony*, Bloomington, Indiana: Indiana University Press.

Wood, S. (1839) *An Account of the Common Schools in the States of Massachussetts, New York and Pennsylvania*, rpt 1968, London: The Woburn Press.

Wolff, J. (1981) *The Social Production of Art*, London: Macmillan.

Wright, T. G. (1850) *Cholera in the Asylum etc.*, London.

Yarnitzky, H. (1932) *St Patrick's, Manchester: Centenary Souvenir, 1832–1932*, Manchester.

Yarranton, A. (1677) *England's Improvement etc.*, London.

Yates, F. (1984) *The Art of Memory*, rpt, London: ARK Paperbacks.

Yorkshire Union of Mechanics' Institutes (1860) *Buildings for Mechanics' Institutes etc.*, London.

Young, T. (1807) *A Course of Lectures on Natural Philosophy and the Mechanical Arts*, London.

Zink, R. (1982) 'Hexenverfolgungen in Bamberg: Willkür oder Wahn?' ('Witch Persecution in Bamberg: aberration or delusion?'), *Bamberg Heute* 1: 9–12.

Zonca, V. (1607) *Nuovo Teatro di Machine et Edificii*, Padua.

Zuckerman, A. (1976/7) 'Scurvy and the Ventilation of Ships in the Royal Navy: Samuel Sutton's Contribution', *Eighteenth Century Studies* 10(2): 222–34.

Index

NB 'architecture' and 'architectural' are concepts so basic to the entire text, and so woven into every part of it, that it was thought cumbersome and confusing to index them.